Choosing Equality

Choosing Equality

Essays and Narratives on the Desegregation Experience

Edited by Robert L. Hayman Jr. and Leland Ware
Foreword by Vice President Joe Biden

The Pennsylvania State University Press
University Park, Pennsylvania

Library of Congress Cataloging-in-Publication Data

Choosing equality : essays and narratives on the desegregation experience /
Robert L. Hayman Jr. and Leland Ware, eds.

p. cm.

Includes bibliographical references and index.

Summary: "Examines the desegregation experience, with a focus on the impact of the Supreme Court's decisions from Brown v. Board of Education in 1954 through Parents Involved v. Seattle School District in 2007. Assesses desegregation in Delaware, one of the states involved in the original Brown litigation"—Provided by publisher.

ISBN 978-0-271-03433-1 (cloth : alk. paper)

1. Discrimination in education—Law and legislation—United States—History.
2. School integration—United States—History.
3. Brown, Oliver, 1918–1961—Trials, litigation, etc.
4. Topeka (Kan.). Board of Education—Trials, litigation, etc.

I. Hayman, Robert L. II. Ware, Leland, 1948– .

KF4155.C46 2009

344.73'0798—dc22 2008047841

Printed in the United States of America

Published by The Pennsylvania State University Press,
University Park, PA 16802-1003

It is the policy of The Pennsylvania State University Press to use acid-free paper. Publications on uncoated stock satisfy the minimum requirements of American National Standard for Information Sciences—Permanence of Paper for Printed Library Material, ANSI Z39.48–1992.

To my loving wife, Melva Ware, PhD, for her continuing patience and support
— LW

For Alice and Caleb
— BH

Contents

Foreword by the Honorable Joseph R. Biden Jr.

Our nation is far different today than it was fifty years ago, when the Supreme Court announced its decision in *Brown v. Board of Education*. Racial discrimination—then buttressed by our legal system—is no longer sanctioned by law. Segregated lunch counters and water fountains—commonplace then—are now relics of the past. Barriers like poll taxes and other shams—once tolerated—are no longer permitted to bar African Americans from voting.

America is indeed a far better and much richer country today because of the enlightenment delivered, in no small part, by the decision in *Brown*, by the brave attorneys who fought for it, and by the leaders and foot soldiers of the movement for civil rights. They awakened a nation to the cause of equality and justice for all, and because of their courage and foresight, America is stronger.

Yet it is that sense of accomplishment that is today, perhaps, the greatest enemy to equality. Having survived the civil rights movement and then reaped the benefits that struggle produced, we are inclined to believe that our work is done, that racial disparities no longer exist. But that simply is not true.

Although we may no longer tolerate legal discrimination and segregation, we live, more than ever before, segregated lives in segregated neighborhoods. We worship in segregated churches, synagogues, and mosques. And a half-century after *Brown*, our children—still and yet again—attend largely segregated schools.

Now is no time to rest on the accomplishments of yesteryear. We must remain vigilant in our efforts and true to the vision of legends like Dr. Martin Luther King Jr. and Shirley Chisholm and Thurgood Marshall and Barbara Jordan, all of whom knew what we all now know—namely, that America can only be great when all its citizens are afforded an equal opportunity to grow and learn and themselves be great.

I was called to the U.S. Senate more than thirty years ago, inspired largely by this promise of equal opportunity and by the legions of brave Americans who risked life and limb to ensure that America kept that promise. When I began my service in 1972, we were living in tumultuous times. Only a few years before, this country had witnessed the assassination of its bravest sons. We had survived a war abroad, and our security at home—threatened by unfriendly foreign powers and a deeply divided public—was uncertain. I thought then, as I do now, that vigilance and strong, outspoken leadership could usher in the healing and transformation we so desperately needed.

Some of that leadership comes from extraordinary individuals. I knew some of them in Delaware. As a kid from Claymont, Delaware, I knew about the Seitz family. I knew that the Seitz family had contributed to the well-being of my state in every single aspect of their lives, and for more than a single generation. I knew that Judge Seitz was a genuine hero. One of the proudest moments in Delaware history, and one of the proudest in American history, occurred when, led by Judge Seitz, we finally acknowledged that separate was not equal.

And I knew about Louis L. Redding. When I was a young lawyer, he scared the living heck out of me. He was an intimidating force, but I knew that force had been used to great good. And perhaps the highest compliment I received when I first ran for the Senate came one day when I was with Louis Redding. We were together on one of those little corner elevators, going up, and he looked at me and he said in that distinctive and distinguished voice, "I think you should run." That was the totality of it—the beginning and the middle and the end of it. And I walked out of that elevator, thinking I was walking on a cloud, for Louis L. Redding thought I should run.

And I knew the incredible contributions so many Delawareans had made to our struggle for racial equality. Perhaps no one demonstrated more personal courage in that struggle than Littleton Mitchell. Lit Mitchell was an extraordinary crusader—he still is—and I was and remain inspired by his example. In the face of seemingly insurmountable obstacles, he led the charge to secure fair housing, equal access to public accommodations, and equal educational and employment opportunities in our state. And so when I had an opportunity to appoint someone to the national *Brown v. Board of Education* Fiftieth Anniversary Commission, I wanted Lit. I suppose I could have appointed someone who was more decorous or a bit more diplomatic. I didn't want that; we don't need that. I wanted someone who would tell the truth; I wanted someone who would wear his heart on his sleeve. Lit will do that. And he will kick and scream, because it is time to kick and scream. There are times, after all, to be angry about what is happening. We need to be angry.

The fact of the matter is that, just a few years after we commemorated the fiftieth anniversary of *Brown v. Board of Education*, I feel a great deal of pride in my state. I am so proud of all that Delaware did to confront the wrong of segregation and to advance the cause of equality. But I also feel a great deal of frustration too, and even a little bit of shame.

Our state has a shameful history. That is not an easy thing to write. But it is the truth. Ours is a shameful past.

We fought on the side of the North in the Civil War. However, Delaware was one of the border states; we were a slave state. And we held on to slavery until the bitter end, long after the northern states had abolished it, long after it filled any economic need. We clung to slavery even when there were hardly any slaves in the state, even when most black Delawareans were already free. Even after the Emancipation Proclamation, even after the Civil War, we would not give up slavery. It took the Thirteenth Amendment to abolish slavery in Delaware, and Delaware, the First State, where most black citizens had already been free for a generation, refused to ratify that amendment. Delaware—a border state, a slave state that fought on the side of the North. That schizophrenia has persisted for a long time in this state, and there are vestiges of it still.

Delaware has, per capita, the tenth-largest black population in America. And in many respects, when it comes to race, Delaware *is* America, both North and South. As in the North, we had large black migrations into our cities, primarily Wilmington, and with it the ghettoization of our black communities. But as in the South, in southern Delaware, many black farmers became sharecroppers, and they lived next to white folks, and they still do. And so in Delaware we have a curious mix of living patterns, and of customs, and of attitudes. Part North, part South. Part slave, part free. A segregated state, struggling for equality.

It is so much a part of us. Each one of us in our youth can mark those moments that animate our passion. For many of us, it was the civil rights movement. I don't pretend to have understood it at the time. I don't pretend to have fully known about inequality. But it was one of those things that hits you hard in the gut—and it makes you want to scream, and it makes you want to cry, and it makes you want to fight.

In 1954, I was attending an all-white Catholic grade school in Claymont, Delaware. But I could sense the coming changes. Dr. King was in "the South," trying to change things. I came to see what he was trying to change, and I came to see that "the South" was not a distant land. This was an awakening for white boys who didn't know many black folks. It was really kind of an epiphany.

And I came to understand. It *was* America. And it was also Delaware. I have to admit, to my embarrassment, that when I was a kid I knew more about what was going on in Selma than I did about Milford, Delaware. But I learned.

And we learned. As a state and as a nation, we learned. And we've come a long way.

Brown v. Board of Education was a large part of that learning curve. *Brown* was the product of great individual acts of courage—by Louis Redding, and Thurgood Marshall, and Chancellor Seitz, and Chief Justice Warren. Yet *Brown* also produced great acts of courage; *Brown* was emboldening. *Brown* helped reconstruct our public institutions, and it revived our public faith. It reminded us what we could be; it reminded us what we *should* be.

In America, our schools do more than teach; our courts do more than decide cases; our legislatures do more than make laws. In America, our public institutions reflect the distinctive virtues of American life: they offer hope for achievement, for transformation, for redemption.

Let me share with you a personal lesson that comes from a page in American political history that is until now unwritten. It has long resonated in my heart. It is a lesson of redemption.

When I first arrived in the Senate, I met with John Stennis of Mississippi. He was in his seventies at the time and was chair of the Armed Services committee. He had long been a segregationist, a senator from the Old South. And yet he would become my friend.

We sat at the end of this gigantic, grand mahogany table he used as his desk. It was, I was told, the table on which the Southern Manifesto had been signed.

Senator Stennis patted the leather chair next to him when I walked in to pay my respects as a new young senator, which was the order of the day. He said, "Sit down, sit down; sit down here, son." And he looked at me and he said, "Son, what made you run for the Senate?" Before I could think better of it, I told him the exact truth: "Civil rights, sir." As soon as I did, I could feel the beads of perspiration on my head, and I got a very uneasy feeling. Yet John Stennis looked at me and said, "Good, good, good." And that was the end of the conversation.

Eighteen years later, after we shared a hospital suite for three months at Walter Reed Hospital, we became friends. I met with him again at that same table. This time he sat behind it, in a wheelchair. John Stennis was leaving the Senate, and I was likely to occupy his office.

I went in to see him, and he looked at me and said, "Sit down, Joe, sit down," and he tapped that chair. And he said something that startled me. "Remember," he asked, "the first time you came to see me, Joe?" I shook my head; I didn't remember. He leaned forward, and he recited the story. And I laughed, and said to him, "I was a pretty smart young fellow, wasn't I, Mr. Chairman?"

He said, "Joe, I wanted to tell you something then that I'm going to tell you now. You are going to take my office, aren't you?" And I said, "Yes, sir, Mr. Chairman." And he ran his hand back and forth across that mahogany table in a loving way, and he said, "You see this table, Joe?" I replied, "Yes, sir, Mr. Chairman." He said, "This table was the flagship of the Confederacy from 1954 to 1968. We sat here, most of us from the Deep South, the old Confederacy, and we planned the demise of the civil rights movement."

Then he looked at me. "And now it's time," he said, "it's time that this table go from the possession of a man against civil rights to a man who is for civil rights."

I was speechless. And he said, "One more thing, Joe." He said, "The civil rights movement did more to free the white man than the black man."

I looked at him. I didn't know what he meant. And then he said, in that distinctive, old, Southern voice, "It freed my soul, it freed my soul."

Strom Thurmond was another man who, in the end, made his choice and moved to the good side. When I arrived in the Senate, I disagreed deeply with Strom on the issue of civil rights and on many other issues, but I watched him change. Making that change took great courage, and it was in part a reflection of his individual bravery. But it reflected something else too.

The place in which I work is a majestic place. If you are there long enough, it has an impact on you. If you respect the institution and those in it with whom you serve, you come to understand how strongly people feel about things, and you learn to appreciate their perspectives and their passions, and to honor their deeply held views, even when their views are very different from your own, even when you know—as surely as you can ever know anything—that they are wrong. That respect is contagious—and it is transformative. You can find in it the possibility of redemption.

That, in my mind, is why *Brown* matters the most. *Brown* was the renewal of a promise; it was a demand for respect. It was a reminder of what our laws could do, of what our schools *should* do, of what our nation must be. It redeemed a generation and pointed the way to redemption for those that followed.

But that is a hard path. Our sins have been many, and their roots run deep. Real equality—our full redemption—remains elusive. It was a lot easier to get Rosa Parks a seat on the front of the bus than it has been to get Rosa Parks's children a genuine opportunity to own the bus company. It gets more complicated. It gets more difficult. And in some respects, it gets more difficult every day.

The view of the Constitution that prevailed in *Brown v. Board of Education* is still the majority view—but maybe not for long. The view of the Constitution that upheld the Civil Rights Act of 1964 and the Voting Rights Act of 1965 is still the majority view—but it may be in peril.

I cannot help but worry that we are seeing today the gradual ascendancy of a new generation of legal thinkers—a new generation with some very old ideas. Read what the Federalist Society is writing. Listen to what Judge Bork said at his hearing: "The wave is coming." Learn about the Chicago School of Law and Economics. And understand that these people mean what they write. They are serious about states' rights; they are serious about economic liberty. They think that we have gone too far in promoting social equality. They want to honor "private choices"—of those who have the means to choose; they want to vindicate "merit"—for those who have been trained in "merit's" ways. They are conservative in their nostalgia for some of the old ways, but they are downright radical in their willingness to change the law—and transform society—to fit their vision. They are bright people. They are honorable. And they are wrong.

And so at this time in our history, as we make our new destiny, it is very important that we commemorate our achievements. They define who we are. They remind us where we came from and help us understand how we got here. They help us see the choices and see what we still can become.

If we had had more families like the Seitzes, then we might be better off than we are today. And if we had more Louis Reddings, and more Lit Mitchells, then there would be less to fear in our future. But it is our job now. We must forge our own path to redemption.

As my grandfather would say, at the end of our good-byes, "Keep the faith." And as my grandmother would say, as I walked out the door, "Spread it."

Acknowledgments

The editors would like to express their appreciation to the organizers of the Redding Symposium on the 50th Anniversary of *Brown v. Board of Education*: Celebrating the Past, Considering the Present, and Contemplating the Future, for the generous support they provided for this project. The supporters include the American Civil Liberties Union–Delaware, the Delaware State Bar Association, the University of Delaware's School of Urban Affairs and Public Policy, Widener University School of Law, and the Metropolitan Wilmington Urban League. Thanks also to the Young Family Foundation, source of the H. Albert Young Fellowship in Constitutional Law, which Professor Hayman was honored to hold from 2003 to 2005.

Introduction

Robert L. Hayman Jr. and Leland Ware

In 1958, the distinguished jurist Learned Hand appeared at Harvard Law School to give the prestigious Holmes Lecture in Law. Judge Hand, then eighty-seven years old, used the occasion to voice his disapproval of the Supreme Court's decision in *Brown v. Board of Education*. He complained that the decision was typical of the Warren Court's activism: *Brown*, he insisted, undermined the political process by substituting the Court's judgments for the will of the people.

A year later, it was Columbia professor of law Herbert Wechsler who was called on to deliver the Holmes Lecture. In Wechsler's speech, and in the article that memorialized it in the pages of the *Harvard Law Review*, he too found fault with *Brown*. Wechsler declared his sympathy with the effort of the Court, but professed his inability to discern in the opinion a "neutral principle" that would legitimate the decision.

Though Wechsler counseled against defiance of the decision, his critique, like Hand's before it, had the inevitable effect of bolstering resistance, both "massive" and passive. The critique lent academic support to the view that the justices of the *Brown* Court had, in the words of the infamous "Southern Manifesto," exercised "naked judicial power and substituted their personal political and social ideals for the established law of the land."[1]

In time, *Brown*'s defenders would outnumber its critics, and the decision would ultimately be enshrined in, and perhaps at the top of, the constitutional canon. The challenge to *Brown*'s legitimacy could still claim a nominally impressive pedigree—dating at least to the Hand and Wechsler lectures—but for the most, part, it was relegated to the fringes of academic discourse, where it has lurked harmlessly for the past few decades.

Brown, to be sure, retained some doubters, and their rumblings of disapproval occasionally invaded the mainstream, as when Justice Scalia suggested that he, for one, likely would have voted the other way had he sat on the *Brown* Court. But for the most part, *Brown*'s place in the constitutional canon and in our cultural ethos was secure, so much so that that in recent years, nearly all mainstream jurists and theorists—including, and perhaps especially, political conservatives—were obliged to concede that the case was correctly decided after all.

But perhaps no longer. The fiftieth anniversary of the *Brown* decision in 2004 presented an occasion to revisit the case, and the verdict was decidedly mixed. *Brown*'s supporters celebrated the promise inhering in the decision, but that promise, they conceded, seemed unfulfilled and perhaps broken. A new wave of critics, meanwhile, professed sympathy with *Brown*'s goals, but confessed grave doubts about the decision's role in advancing them.

And thus a new critique of *Brown* was crystallized, poised now to accept the role of conventional wisdom. The decision was *not* correctly decided at all, it holds, but the error was largely pragmatic. The difficulty now is not so much that *Brown* is illegitimate, that it cannot be justified as a matter of constitutional doctrine or political theory. That criticism serves largely as context or subtext. The dominant criticism now is that *Brown* has been either ineffectual or counterproductive; that it represents a broken promise, a "tragic failure," a "hollow dream"; or, still worse, that it discouraged or preempted more effective forms of relief and encouraged a backlash that actually harmed the struggle for racial equality.

We have been surprised by the momentum that has built behind this critique. More is happening here than simple contrarianism, more than the relentless aspiration to perverseness that sometimes characterizes our academy. We believe, in fact, that these criticisms have been offered in good faith generally—perhaps uniformly—by people who share *Brown*'s explicit commitment to racial equality. We believe that these criticisms warrant serious consideration, as part of a constructive dialogue on the surest way to achieve that equality. But for the reasons that follow—presented in the balance of this introduction and the remainder of this book—we believe that this new critique is mistaken and that the mistakes it manifests are serious enough to warrant rebuttal.

And they are serious mistakes, in part, because the issues are not merely academic ones—in any sense of that term. Two recent events make this clear.

In April 2006, the Nebraska governor was signing legislation dividing Omaha's public schools into three racially identifiable school districts: one black, one Hispanic, and one white. Among the bill's sponsors was Nebraska's only African American state legislator: his intent, Ernie Chambers insisted, was to create a district that "we, meaning black people, whose children make up the vast majority of the student population, would control." The explicitly segregative legislation was unique principally in its frankness: it joined a large number of recent laws that have implicitly mandated a return to racially segregated schools. The underlying message of all these laws is clear: *Brown* was wrong; *Brown* has failed.

But that message is wrong, and many people—in fact, we believe, most people—know that the message is wrong. Ben Gray is a television news producer in Omaha and the co-chairman of the African-American Achievement Council. He describes the segregative plan as "a disaster." "Throughout our time in America," Gray says, "we've had people who continuously fought for equality, and from *Brown v. Board of Education*, we know that separate is not equal. We cannot go back to segregating our schools."[2]

Other school districts refused to go back. Believing that the dream of *Brown* was not a hollow one and determined not to break its promise, these districts continue to do all that they can to maintain—or establish—desegregated schools. This book tells the story of one such district—the Brandywine School District in Delaware—in some detail. And in the summer of 2007, the U.S. Supreme Court wrote a chapter in the evolving story of two other school districts.

The school boards in Louisville, Kentucky, and Seattle, Washington, attempted to prevent the segregation of their public schools by considering race in the process of making student assignments. As the dispute over their student assignment plans played out before the Supreme Court, it inevitably evolved into a battle for the heart of *Brown.*

A majority of the Supreme Court rejected the school boards' plans. In the opinion of the Court—or, at least, in the plurality opinion written by Chief Justice Roberts—*Brown* was not about segregation at all. What *Brown* disapproved of was not racial apartheid, was not the racial caste system of which racial segregation was such a necessary part. Rather, what *Brown* disapproved of was the consideration of "race"—toward any ends. Thus, the Court concluded, *Brown* requires school districts to "stop discriminating on the basis of race."

That decision—about which we say much more in the concluding chapter of this book—is part and parcel of the new critique of *Brown*, a bitter vindication of the view that a real end to segregation cannot be achieved through the courts and perhaps not through "the law" at all. Indeed, the very idea of *de*segregation seems alien and unattractive to this Court: Justice Thomas, channeling the defenders of Jim Crow in his concurring opinion, derides the efforts of the school boards as "forced race mixing."

But this is not the *Brown* Court, far from it. Justice Stevens, writing in dissent, found "cruel irony" in the Court's reliance on *Brown*. "It is my firm conviction," he concluded, "that no member of the Court that I joined in 1975 would have agreed with today's decision." Justice Breyer, in the principal dissent, maintained that the rejections of these anti-segregation plans "threaten the promise of *Brown*"; worse, the "plurality's opinion, I fear, would break that promise."

We agree. We agree because we believe that the promise of *Brown* was real, and because we believe that the promise of *Brown* was—and remains—realizable. We cannot go back. We must not. And that, ultimately, is the lesson of this book.

Did *Brown* Fail?

We did not set out to defend *Brown* when we initiated this project in 2003. Our goal, in fact, was quite neutral—to fairly assess the legacy of the decision on its fiftieth anniversary—and we approached the task with a skepticism born of decades of frustration with the slow pace of progress in eliminating American apartheid.

Although much of the planned project would be national in scope, we resolved to develop a more particularized inquiry into the Delaware desegregation experience. Partly this was for historical reasons. Delaware played a very significant role in the original *Brown* litigation. Two of the five consolidated cases in *Brown—Bulah v. Gebhart* and *Belton v. Gebhart*—arose in Delaware school districts, and a Delaware civil rights lawyer, the late Louis L. Redding, represented the plaintiffs in those cases.

However, Delaware seemed an appropriate case study for broader reasons. The state presents, in fact, a near-perfect microcosm of the tensions and paradoxes that characterize our national experience with race. Delaware is both North and South in its sensibilities. It was a slave state, but one whose black citizens were, on the eve of the Civil War, nearly all free. It was a Jim Crow state, with an overt politics of race, but one with very little evidence of racial hostility among its populace. It was the site not only of massive resistance to desegregation but also of one of the largest and most peaceful metropolitan desegregation efforts. And today, it is the locus not only of a statewide Neighborhood Schools Act, designed to end busing and a return to "local control," but also of local school districts—predominantly white—that have defied that act in their determination to avoid resegregation.

The contributors to this project generally shared our attitude toward *Brown*. They recognized what it had done; perceived clearly what remained undone; were deeply ambivalent about its role in shaping the current state of affairs; and, on *Brown*'s ultimate legacy, were largely agnostic. Yet the insights they shared, the evidence they offered, and the testimony they gave increasingly pointed to the conclusion that ultimately animated this book: the decision in *Brown* was, above all else, vitally necessary to the struggle for racial equality, in Delaware and in the nation.

As the project began, then, we honestly did not know what tenor the commemoration of *Brown* would assume: it might turn out to be a birthday celebration, or it might be a eulogy. There was already plenty of reason to suspect the latter possibility. The new critique of *Brown* was emerging. Tom Wicker had titled his 1996 survey of desegregation *Tragic Failure*. The subtitle of Derrick Bell's 2004 book was *Brown v. Board of Education and the Unfulfilled Hopes for Racial Reform*. Charles Ogletree had recently lamented the "failed promise of integration," and both Gerald Rosenberg and Michael Klarman had drawn attention with books that were lustily skeptical of *Brown*'s achievements.[3]

Indeed, even our symposium participants had voiced doubts. Jack Balkin had assembled nine scholars to revisit the *Brown* opinion, and the shortcomings they perceived were addressed in opinions that told us "What *Brown v. Board of Education* Should Have Said." The subtitle of James Patterson's exegesis of *Brown* accurately conveyed his ambivalence: "A Civil Rights Milestone and Its Troubled Legacy." And far less ambivalent was the essay that Robert Lipkin contributed to our project, which concluded, "Integrating public schools "has been a de facto disaster."

The negative appraisals of the desegregation effort may not be demonstrably wrong, but we believe that they do run counter to an impressive body of evidence. Any assessment of *Brown*'s success must begin with one undeniable fact: public schools are less segregated today than they were before *Brown*. There were roughly 4,000 school districts in the South when *Brown* was decided; all were segregated. By the end of 1957, 712 of those districts were desegregating, and, as a result 300,000 black students were, for the first time, attending integrated schools.

The progress, of course, would be neither steady nor permanent: the pace of desegregation slowed, and schools in many districts have gradually resegregated. We are not, as a result, where we should be—but, then again, we are well beyond where we once were.

And the ultimate goals of desegregation have been advanced significantly by the effort. The black-white achievement gap narrowed substantially in the second half of the twentieth century, and it is likely no accident that the gap narrowed most dramatically in the South. Racial attitudes improved by nearly every measure in the same time frame; the percentage of white Americans who favored separate schools, for example, declined from 68 percent in 1942 to 50 percent in 1956, 35 percent in 1963, and 4 percent in 1995.[4]

Skeptics are quick to point out that these results followed developments quite beyond *Brown,* most notably, the Civil Rights Act of 1964 and Voting Rights Act of 1965, which, Professor Lipkin contends, "are a greater foundation to integration than the *Brown* decision" (see Chapter 15). The historical record suggests an alternative conclusion.

Brown was the result of a carefully planned and executed legal strategy. In the early 1930s, Charles Houston, the NAACP's first legal counsel, proposed a series of lawsuits demanding that southern states comply with *Plessy* by providing equal allocations of financial and other resources for black students in segregated schools. Underlying this strategy was the belief that the segregation system would eventually implode: the financial burden of having duplicate educational systems for blacks and whites would become so great that the states would be forced to abandon segregation at the graduate and professional school level.

Houston also predicted that the litigation campaign would stimulate public interest and encourage the affected communities to continue the fight after the NAACP led the way with test cases. Houston wrote that one of his principal goals was "to arouse and strengthen the will of the local communities to demand and fight for their rights."[5]

This goal was finally achieved with *Brown*, which sparked an era of civil rights activism on an unprecedented scale. In the 1950s and 1960s, African Americans united in a broad-based effort to demand a full measure of constitutional freedoms. Boycotts, sit-ins, and other forms of protest spread rapidly across the South. As Houston predicted in the 1930s, the NAACP's litigation campaign encouraged local communities to demand and fight for their rights. After a decade of struggle, often in the face of violent resistance, a series of congressional enactments in the 1960s ended de jure segregation.

However, the critics are not so sure that the grassroots civil rights movement—and its subsequent legislative successes—are to any great degree the product of *Brown*'s intervention. On this score, for example, Michael Klarman's sophisticated analysis of *Brown* devolves uncharacteristically into a rather reductionist search for *Brown*'s "causal influence" on the Montgomery bus boycott. But there seems little point in engaging a debate about which specific event is the more proximate cause of integration. The point is that the events in question are very much intertwined.

Consider that the decision in *Brown* preceded the Montgomery bus boycott by more than a year. The decision was known to Rosa Parks, to Dr. King, and to the rest of the boycott's leaders, and it hardly seems a stretch to say that it was an inspiration. Dr. King mobilized the boycott at a December 5, 1955, rally this way:

> My friends, I want it to be known—that we're going to work with grim and bold determination—to gain justice on the buses in this city. And we are not wrong. We are not wrong in what we are doing. If we are wrong—the Supreme Court of this nation is wrong. If we are wrong—God Almighty is wrong. If we are wrong—Jesus of Nazareth was merely a utopian dreamer and never came down to earth. If we are wrong—justice is a lie. And we are determined here in Montgomery—to work and fight until justice runs down like water, and righteousness like a mighty stream.

"This decision," King wrote of *Brown* in 1958, "brought hope to millions of disinherited Negroes who had formerly dared only to dream of freedom."[6] Significantly, it was the Supreme Court itself that ended the boycott by declaring bus segregation unconstitutional—on the strength of its decision in *Brown*. The Court—and the lower federal courts that universally (and somewhat surprisingly) followed its lead—would remain a source of hope for the grassroots civil rights movement. For nearly a decade, in fact, it was the sole (secular) institutional source of hope. And, of course, there would have been no civil rights acts without the grassroots civil rights movements. The connection, for example, between the events at Pettus Bridge and the Voting Rights Act of 1965 is clear and immediate.

Those who argue that *Brown* was ineffective give insufficient recognition to the significance of the case and its continuing influence. *Brown* was not merely a case about schools. It was the culmination of a decades-long attack against an elaborate system of racial subordination that prevailed in America during the first half of the twentieth century. It was the end of Jim Crow itself, not merely separation in public schools, that was the objective of the NAACP's efforts to secure the constitutional rights of African Americans. That is the legacy of *Brown*, and its significance should not be underestimated. That it was achieved by a small group of civil rights lawyers makes it all the more amazing.

Was *Brown* Counterproductive?

A second criticism of *Brown* takes the critique one step further: it holds that *Brown* not only failed to achieve much good, but it actually precipitated considerable harm. This criticism has two strands, each focusing on a distinct harm. In the first, the principal harm is the inherent paternalism of *Brown*, which views black separateness as inherently inferior, and assimilation into white America as the only cure. In the second version, the principal harm of *Brown* is that it stimulated a white backlash, thereby negating the prospects for peaceful progress in matters of race.

The first harm identified by critics of *Brown* is almost of moral magnitude: it is the contention that a certain racial paternalism is manifest both in the desegregation project and in the specific rationale of the *Brown* opinion (i.e., that the inequality in segregated schools was found in the sense of inferiority generated among black students). Derrick Bell has long warned against the dangers that inhere in conflating integration with equality—"the priority for black parents," he writes, "has always been better schools, not desegregated schools"—and he has made the case for separate black schools.[7] Writing in this volume, Professor Lipkin contends that *Brown* "contains an invidious paternalism that is morally undesirable, indeed to put it bluntly, morally offensive" (see Chapter 15). And a similar argument—perhaps the same one—has been pressed by Justice Thomas: "It never ceases to amaze me that the courts are so willing to assume that anything that is predominantly black must be inferior."[8]

Yet the argument, which likely is rooted in a justifiable criticism, seems overstated. Judicially mandated desegregation is not invidiously paternalistic, at least not in its attitudes toward black Americans. The same goes for the *Brown decision*, which, at the risk of pressing too fine a point, is distinct from the *Brown opinion*. The amicus brief of the social scientists submitted to the Court in *Brown* described a vicious cycle of racial hierarchy in which racial segregation was but one link. Breaking the link by ending segregation, it was argued, would ultimately end racial hierarchy, because the distinctions of race would gradually fade to oblivion: all students would attend the same schools, learn the same formal and informal lessons, and learn with each other, from each other, and about each other. There is nothing invidiously paternalistic about this contention, at least not toward black students. It might be paternalistic (or at least vaguely insulting) in suggesting that white Americans would only provide the same educational opportunities to black Americans if they were forced to share a classroom or that white Americans needed to unlearn the faulty lessons of racialist thinking and could only do this by sharing a classroom with black Americans. But none of this is insulting to black Americans.

Nor, for that matter, is the "stigma of inferiority" relied on in Chief Justice Warren's opinion in *Brown*. The first Justice Harlan clearly had it right in his *Plessy* dissent: compulsory segregation was intended to—and did in fact—stamp black Americans with a badge of inferiority. The social scientists' brief made much of this contention and documented it with modern studies. Chief Justice Warren was right to recognize it, and it was—and is—sufficient to establish the inequality prohibited by the Fourteenth Amendment.

The difficulty with the *Brown* opinion, however, is that it looks at only one part of this stigma: its impact on black students. In focusing on the ways in which the stigma may have been internalized, the opinion itself is indeed a bit patronizing—but even at that, its characterization as "invidiously paternalistic" seems a bit strong. It may well be that the greater harm of segregation, the real impact of the stigma, was its distortion of the thought processes of *white* Americans—the social, economic, and political decision makers, who, through segregation, were continually encouraged to believe that black Americans were inferior (i.e., less qualified or unqualified). Chief Justice Warren did not say that. He probably could not have, and still commanded the Court (he certainly would not have secured unanimity). Should he have said it anyway? *Fiat justitia pereat mundus.*

The second harm said to be attributable to *Brown* inheres in the white backlash that followed the decision, which, the critics suggest, made political progress less likely. "By demanding change first on an issue on which whites were most recalcitrant," Klarman writes, "*Brown* encouraged massive resistance."[9] That resistance, the theory goes, in turn stifled legislative action, and legislative action, as Professor Lipkin contends in Chapter 15, would have been more efficacious because it would have been perceived as more legitimate.

These are not implausible claims, and they warrant the extensive examination that the critics have initiated. The case in support of the claims, however, is not a strong one. Indeed, the evidence seems to weigh heavily against each of its two critical premises: first, that *Brown* has stifled legislative action, and second, that *Brown* has been relatively ineffectual, at least in part because it has been perceived as relatively illegitimate.

Did **Brown** *Stifle Legislative Action?*

There is very little evidence to suggest that either desegregated schools or a scheme of segregated but genuinely equal schools was on the legislative horizon in 1954. *Brown*'s critics sometimes seem to assume that democratic processes of government prevailed in the South of the 1950s and 1960s. But those of us who grew up in the South during the post-*Brown* era have an entirely different perspective. We saw and experienced, firsthand, the conditions that existed at that time. There was simply no hope of securing any change through the legislative process. In reality, the region was ruled by a Bourbon aristocracy that presided over a region filled with rotten boroughs. All African Americans, and many poor whites, were completely disenfranchised by poll taxes, understanding clauses, and other devices. As William Hastie explained, "Throughout the first third of this century, the effective institutionalization of racism was the common experience of most Negroes. 'Settled' American law required and sanctioned such rigid and comprehensive segregation and subordination of blacks that, to most people, even talk of any significant movement toward an equalitarian legal order seemed visionary, or even foolish."[10]

In the South, white supremacy was enforced by brute force, violence, and intimidation. Lynching and other forms of racial violence inflicted on African Americans occurred regularly, before and after *Brown*. This makes the premise that *Brown* prompted a negative reaction that might otherwise have not occurred completely unfounded. The "reaction," the era of massive resistance, was merely a continuation of tactics that were developed in the post-Reconstruction era and used after that time to enforce racial subordination.

Under such circumstances, it is highly improbable that the state legislatures would have been moved either to desegregate the public schools or to equalize the segregated public schools—not, at least, without the threat of judicial intervention. To the extent that some schools were being upgraded prior to *Brown*, it was occurring only as a response to the NAACP's "equalization" strategy that was brought to bear on graduate and professional schools in the pre-*Brown* cases as the first phase of the NAACP's long-term attack against segregated schools.

Otherwise, segregation was entrenched, and so too were material inequalities. The bare fact of segregation undoubtedly had its own inherent virtues for white supremacy, but the scheme of subordination was ultimately dependent on the segregation of black Americans into inferior facilities. And white America was not about to give this up.

W. E. B. Du Bois's frustrations—which *Brown*'s critics frequently cite in support of a "separate but equal" alternative—were rooted in this very recognition. By the fourth year of the Great Depression, Du Bois had tired of the futile struggle against segregation. "The net result," he wrote in 1934, "has been a little less than nothing." If anything, he imagined that things were getting worse: "Segregation may be just as evil today as it was in 1910, but it is more insistent, more prevalent, and more unassailable by appeal or argument." More broadly, Du Bois had concluded that white America was not about to give up the object of segregation, which was "to so isolate the Negro that he will be spiritually bankrupt, physically degenerate, and economically dependent." The educational advancement of black Americans had no impact on this scheme: "white people on the whole are just as much as opposed to Negroes of education and culture, as to any other kind."[11]

What, then, could black Americans do? "We cannot use the power of a State because we are not a State," Du Bois observed. "We cannot dictate as a proletariat, because we are a minority." The only recourse was to "run and support our own institutions," to educate black children "in decent Negro schools and to arrange and conduct and oversee such schools."[12] White legislatures had no role in this vision, because Du Bois was certain that they wanted no role—or, at least, no positive role. And nothing in the historical record, at least until *Brown*, suggests that he was overly pessimistic.[13]

Would the *federal* government have intervened? Would Congress or the executive have done as much, or more, to promote equality without *Brown*? One can imagine such scenarios, but they all seem somewhat divorced from the political realties of 1954.

It appears highly unlikely that Congress would have acted affirmatively to outlaw segregation. Consider the tepid reaction of the two political parties to the *Brown* decision. The draft Republican platform for the 1956 election originally contained a plank declaring, "The Eisenhower administration supports the decision in *Brown v. Board of Education.*" That was changed—on the president's insistence—to read, "The Republican party accepts the decision in *Brown v. Board of Education.*" Meanwhile, the Democrats, with Strom Thurmond and the Dixiecrats back in the fold, nominated Adlai Stevenson as their presidential candidate. Regarding desegregation, Stevenson insisted, "We must proceed gradually, not upsetting habits or traditions that are older than the Republic." The congressional delegations from the eleven states of the old Confederacy were recruited as signatories to the Southern Manifesto of 1956; nineteen of twenty-two senators complied, and so too did eighty-one representatives. Congress itself would refuse to lend any support to the desegregation effort, until it required compliance with standing desegregation decrees as a condition to the receipt of federal educational funds in the Civil Rights Act of 1964. In theory, Congress might have acted more boldly if it were exercising its own initiative, and not following the lead either of the Supreme Court or the grassroots movement, but there is little in logic or experience to suggest that this would be so.

Was Brown *Perceived as Relatively Illegitimate?*

At the theoretical heart of the comparative critique of *Brown* is the argument that legislative alternatives would have been more efficacious because they would have been perceived as more legitimate. Thus, as Professor Lipkin puts it, "desegregation might have come about legislatively without dragging along the countermajoritarian charge associated with judicial review." But the argument is based on two unproven assumptions: first, that *Brown* and the desegregation project were significantly impaired by the "countermajoritarian charge," and second, that comparable legislative initiatives would not have faced their own daunting challenges.

Regarding the first assumption, *Brown* is sometimes said to be vulnerable to charges of overreaching because it lacks a consensus "interpretive rationale." In truth, that may be the greatest testament to the soundness of the decision. The fact that the decision can be justified on intentionalist grounds, or on naturalist grounds, or on pragmatic grounds, or, as the late Charles Black suggested, simply by reference to common sense, seems a strength, not a weakness.[14] Moreover, to whatever extent this plurality of justifications is perceived as a weakness, the situation is hardly unique to *Brown.* Indeed, it is hard to recall a Supreme Court opinion—let alone one of such notoriety—that is supported by a consensus of theorists and jurists, united behind a single interpretive rationale. This deficiency, then, if it is one, seems to rest less in *Brown* than in the modern state of interpretive theory.

Moreover, it simply is not clear that the "countermajoritarian difficulty" is a difficulty for anyone other than constitutional theorists. In fact, the available evidence suggests that the American people like their constitutional rights, and they like the fact that the courts—including the Supreme Court—stand ready to protect those rights from the actions of the political branches. Indeed, Americans seem relatively pleased with the work of the Supreme Court; a recent review of the literature concludes that "aggregate levels of support for the Court are consistently higher than levels of support for Congress and the executive, and they appear relatively more stable as well."[15]

It also is not clear that *Brown* presents any unique "countermajoritarian" problem, even for the constitutional theorist. *Brown* was not, after all, a sudden and shocking outlier. Deliberately or not, the Court had been laying the foundations for desegregation in the decade prior to *Brown*. *Shelley v. Kraemer* rejected the fatuous symmetry argument in 1948, and two years later, in *McLaurin v. Oklahoma* and *Sweatt v. Painter*, the Court found segregated institutions of higher learning unequal in part because of the obvious intangible inequalities. The Court declined to revisit *Plessy* in those latter two cases, but it eviscerated most of *Plessy*'s logic. The subsequent leap to *Brown* was really not a great one—not, at least, as a formal legal matter. Just where on the progression to *Brown*, then, did the Court cross the lines of legitimacy?

Legislative initiatives, meanwhile, are hardly immune from criticism. Their legitimacy simply is challenged on different bases and using different rhetoric. The acts of the First Reconstruction were said to be "radical" and "revolutionary," destined to "destroy the foundations of the government" and to install a "central despotism." Many of these claims were revived in the long, tortuous debate over the Civil Rights Bill of 1964, and they remained unsettled after the bill's enactment. On signing the Civil Rights Act into law, President Johnson famously remarked to Bill Moyers that he feared he had just given the South to the Republicans for their lifetimes. He was very nearly right. One suspects that a congressional initiative to desegregate the schools would have been at least as controversial as the Civil Rights Act and would have generated similar resistance. The schools provision, after all, was so controversial during the First Reconstruction that it was dropped from the bill that eventually became the Civil Rights Act of 1875. It might have faced less resistance in Congress—and among the populace—during the Second Reconstruction, but that Second Reconstruction would have been initiated without the ten years (at least) of capital that Congress received from the *Brown* decision.

Choosing Equality: Desegregating Delaware, Desegregating the Nation

Professor Klarman, following Justice Stanley Reed's prediction, suggests that desegregation would have come to Delaware and the other border states within a generation, even without *Brown*. At the time of the decision, he contends, Wilmington already "was in a state of acceptance and readiness."[16]

But the historical record does not support this claim. The Delaware experience, we believe, demonstrates exactly why *Brown* was necessary. It also demonstrates why *Brown*'s legacy remains very much a work in progress and why the ultimate success or failure of *Brown* will be a product of our choices.

The materials in Part I of this book attempt to place *Brown* in an appropriate historical context. We believe that many of the criticisms of *Brown* fail to fully account for the entrenched nature of segregation, a circumstance that made legislative correction highly unlikely and concerted white resistance nearly inevitable. The essays included in Part I all offer accounts of the relentless scheme of oppression inhering in Jim Crow segregation, a scheme, the authors note, that was carefully sustained by political action.

Bob Hayman's extended review of the history of "race" in Delaware documents the deep roots of racial hierarchy in the state. Delaware's color line emerged in a tentative, ad hoc fashion, typical of its development in the other American colonies. Yet the state's nineteenth-century experience still provides a unique subject for study. Over the course of the century, Delaware became a slave state without slaves (on the eve of the Civil War, more than 92 percent of Delaware's black population was free), and the resultant paradox appears to have been resolved by a distinctive politics of race. Race thus acquired a unique political salience in Delaware—it was not simply a proxy for bondage—that would set the pattern for the postbellum South and that would endure in the state for many generations beyond the demise of the peculiar institution. In Delaware, that is to say, race mattered—at least among the state's ruling class—and it was made to matter intensely.

This account is bolstered by a remarkable interview (conducted by the late A. Leon Higginbotham) with then-federal judge Collins J. Seitz, who, as Delaware Chancellor, was the presiding judge in Delaware's Courts of Equity; for more see Chapter 2. First ordered the desegregation of Delaware's schools. Reminiscences about Judge Seitz (by his son) and attorney Louis Redding (by his biographer) help round out the Delaware story.

The remaining essays in Part I offer assessments of *Brown* with an eye toward the context that generated it. Juan Williams's essay recalls an interview with Thurgood Marshall conducted some forty years after the *Brown* decision. Justice Marshall, it is clear, was frustrated by the slow pace of progress, but it is equally clear that he was gratified by the "tremendous amount of positive change" initiated by *Brown*. The journey that Marshall took to and from *Brown* also makes clear why Williams believes that the decision can still inspire us and that, indeed, "it must serve as an inspiration for the challenges we confront today."

Robert Cottrol warns against viewing *Brown* in isolation. The decision in that case, he notes, was part of the synergy of anti-discrimination forces; the opinion "amplified the voices that were saying that discrimination was wrong" and may have inspired that same realization in many others.

Finally, Jack Greenberg, Louis Redding's co-counsel during the Supreme Court's review of the Delaware case, suggests that the "massive resistance" summoned against *Brown* may well have been an unavoidable part of our evolution. An abiding acceptance of the decision could come only with the transformation of the American political system. The singular achievement of *Brown*, he suggests, may well be that it made this transformation possible.

Which is not to say that the transformation is complete; it is only to say that the remaining obstacles to transformation were not created by *Brown*. Part II makes this clear in its review of the efforts to enforce—and to resist—the desegregation mandate.

Leland Ware's essay charts the progress of desegregation in Delaware, making it clear why judicial action, including the action in *Brown*, was the only viable course. The essay details the history of resistance to the implementation of desegregation plans in Delaware, a resistance that was typically supported and perhaps generated by state officials.

Professor Ware's essay is followed by a series of firsthand accounts of the desegregation effort. The first is an original interview with senior federal judge Murray M. Schwartz, who, over the course of three decades, supervised the metropolitan desegregation effort in Delaware. Orlando Camp and Ed Kee then describe what it was like for a black high school student to experience "massive resistance" in 1954 Delaware, and local activists Littleton Mitchell and Jea Street chart the course of community advocacy in the two generations of Delaware desegregation disputes.

Finally, Roger Goldman reminds us that some of the barriers to racial equality have been constructed by the Supreme Court: a few, perhaps by the Warren Court, as it struggled with the task of working alone, but many more by later iterations of the Court, many of whose members would display a remarkable lack of enthusiasm for the desegregation project.

Yet most of the obstacles are rooted in segregation itself, not in the Court's effort to eliminate it. That, we think, is the overriding message of the essays in Part III of the book.

These essays attempt to assess the legacy of the desegregation project. James Patterson remains uncertain of *Brown*'s legacy: how much did it influence the grassroots civil rights movement, equalize educational opportunities, and improve American race relations? Patterson sees a mixed record, with some undeniable progress, yet also much stasis. But the difficulty, it seems, does not inhere in *Brown*. The Court's effort, he believes, was hampered at the outset by a lack of political support and in the decades since by the white public at large, whose backing for desegregation has been "scattered and weak."

Bob Lipkin's essay, as we have noted, is typical of the new critiques, and we include it here as serious food for thought. But for reasons made clear in this Introduction, and throughout the text, we find his critique unpersuasive.

Paul Finkelman is also unpersuaded by it and offers a detailed rebuttal to the new critiques, with a particular focus on the work of Michael Klarman. Finkelman believes that the *Brown* decision was, for all its limitations, a revolutionary moment and a cultural watershed: the opinion shattered the air of inevitability that surrounded the scheme of segregation, a scheme that was far more entrenched and much more pervasive than many of the blithe criticisms of *Brown* would suggest.

Jack Balkin situates *Brown* in the broader history of social movements. For him, the desegregation decisions, and the litigation strategy that produced them, were necessary but not sufficient parts of the movement toward racial equality. *Brown* was a monumental achievement, but the same forces that necessitated judicial action also limited its effectiveness. The Court, in effect, did what only it could do, and likely all that it could do, to advance the cause of racial desegregation.

Two additional essays in this volume afford unique insights into the insidious power of segregation. Nancy Levit notes the ways in which the racial resegregation of our schools parallels the renewed interest in gender-segregated education. She finds a broad imbalance in the public discourse on both forms of segregation: the perceived benefits of separation attract great attention and are afforded much weight, whereas the costs of (re)segregation—costs that can be and have been empirically established—are slighted into oblivion. Patricia Williams, meanwhile, notes that the hierarchy sustained by racially segregated schools is also defined by class—in both economic and aesthetic terms. Segregation thus maintains a pervasive cultural divide, "a kind of invisible emotional aesthetic—a set of unspoken taboos that reinforce the free-floating overlap of race and economics into something like a caste system."

The book concludes with a return to the desegregation effort in Delaware. That Delaware has come a long way, but still has far to go, is evident from Jeffrey Raffel's analysis of the state's charter schools and from the analysis of race and education in contemporary Delaware by Michele Fuetsch and Leland Ware.

This latter essay notes the persistence of resistance to desegregation by official Delaware. When the federal courts terminated the desegregation decree for New Castle County, the most populous of Delaware's counties, the resistance found full expression in a Neighborhood Schools Act, state legislation that directed local school boards to develop student assignment plans that would place students in schools nearest their residence. The high degree of residential segregation meant that the act would ensure a return to segregated schools, but in perhaps the most eloquent tribute to the legacy of *Brown*, the local school districts—once the havens for pro-segregation resistance—refused to realize the act's obvious intent. Community leaders in one district denounced the "Re-segregation bill"; formed a multiracial alliance of students, parents, and interested residents called "Kids in Diverse Schools"; and formulated their own student assignment plan explicitly designed to maintain diverse student bodies in each school. The sponsor of the Neighborhood Schools Act was left fuming when the State Board of Education unanimously approved the district's plan.

Thus, one community, at least, chose equality.

The final essay of the book confronts the new challenges presented by the Supreme Court's decision in the 2007 desegregation cases, *Parents Involved in Community Schools v. Seattle School District No. 1.* Here again, for better or worse, Delaware points the way. The Neighborhood Schools Act adopts precisely the approach championed by the Court. An analysis of the impact of the act (based on data from the 2006–7 school year) reveals what the Court's approach would portend for the nation.

As the essay notes, however, the decision in *Parents Involved* is not bad simply because of its likely consequences. Rather, the decision is bad because it is an utter betrayal of *Brown*, perpetrated, shamelessly, in *Brown*'s name. But the Court's homage to *Brown*, however disingenuous or misguided it may be, is nonetheless a remarkable testament to the continuing vitality of the original desegregation decision. And the Court's subversion of the desegregation project—bitterly contested by four dissenters and achieved only through the capitulation of a wary and ambivalent concurrence—demonstrates why the battle for the legacy of *Brown v. Board of Education* remains vitally important.

The dialogue that we join here with the critics of the *Brown* decision is partly about the case's legacy. The critics look at the historical record in the half-century since and see a very mixed record in the struggle for equality. Desegregation started, but it was not completed. Civil rights laws—and affirmative action laws—were passed, but met with mixed success, both in the courts and in transforming American social life. We are more equal than we were in 1954, but we still have a very long way to go. The critics wonder whether there might have been a better way. Might we have been better off without *Brown*? Their tentative conclusion is that we might be, that *Brown* deserves no special credit for the good that has transpired (it would have happened anyway), but must shoulder the blame for the bad (which stems mostly from the abuse or misuse of judicial power).

We see the same world that these critics see, but we cannot blame the *Brown* decision for our many failures. *Brown*, to our minds, announced the beginning of a Second Reconstruction, and for fourteen years, we struggled anew to realize the promise of equality. We failed to achieve full equality, but we do not think that the seeds of failure were planted by *Brown*. The roots of racial inequality were very deep—they still are—and the Court's time was short. By 1968, it was over. We cannot blame *Brown* for the events of that year: the assassinations of Dr. King and Senator Robert Kennedy, the turmoil at the Democratic Convention, the election of Richard Nixon, or for the scandal that plagued Abe Fortas and signaled the demise of the Warren Court. In that same year, after all, the Court affirmed its commitment to *Brown* and insisted, in a case argued the day before Dr. King's murder, that segregation must be eliminated "root and branch."

But race has been nurtured in the soil of American apartheid for centuries. It likely will take many generations to clear our path. *Brown* pointed the way, but as Senator Biden instructs in his foreword, "we must forge our own path to redemption."

And *Brown* gave us a choice of paths. In the years that followed, we sometimes chose well. Too often, we did not. But none of it was predetermined; none of it was inevitable. The choices—good and bad—were ours. And they remain ours, and for that reason, the dialogue we join here is about not only *Brown* and its legacy but also the future of the struggle for equality; it is about *our* future.

There should be no uncertainty about the legacy of *Brown* or about the generations of advocates and activists who generated its vision. They had a dream. And they did the most dangerous work, in the fifties, sixties, and seventies. They left to our generation a different sort of task: to do the tedious work of implementing the dream. This task required a different kind of creativity—the farther we progressed, the more complex was the resistance—but mostly it required resolve: that we would do the hard work and make our own minor sacrifices.

In too many ways, it is true that we failed. We heard the voices of the civil rights generations, but too often, we ignored their messages. Our generation was seduced by those other voices. Just as many of our ancestors succumbed to the call of "states' rights" and "superior races," so we fell for the allure of "neighborhood schools" and "bell curves." It is a shame what we have done.

We seem, today, very unequal. Our schools are plagued by "savage inequalities." There are, we suppose, many causes. These are, we are sure, complex problems. But we were obliged to figure them out. And someday we will.

Consider, finally, several unrenowned voices in the struggle for equality. They are heard in the true story of a young boy in Delaware. Caleb is his name.

Shortly after he was born, Caleb's grandmother began to assemble a scrapbook for him. She did not finish it; she ran out of time. But she did complete a section on her parents and her childhood. His grandmother had a tough childhood, but not, she insisted, an unhappy one. And she wanted Caleb to know what her mother taught her: "that even though you are poor in money," she wrote, "you can still be rich in love."

When the grandmother was gone, her son, Caleb's father, was the first to read the scrapbook. He was disappointed by the legacy that she left; he wished his mother had left something less sentimental, something more profound. And almost immediately, he felt ashamed. What had happened to him? How cynical had he become, how lost was he that he could no longer grasp that elegant truth—that what mattered above all was love. The man, a law teacher, blamed law school for this reaction; he blames it for most everything, but this time it was deserved. Because in law school we are taught—and we teach—that love *is* trite, that it is *not* relevant, that it can neither sustain nor withstand rigorous analysis; we divorce comprehension from compassion, justice from mercy, law from love. And that is wrong; and the ghosts of Jim Crow that still haunt our schools are part of the price that we pay.

In her last weeks, Caleb's grandmother had relived some memories with her son. They found her high school yearbook from Henry C. Conrad High School, Wilmington, Delaware, Class of 1954. Among the pictures in that yearbook, among a sea of white faces like his mother's, were scattered those of a few black kids. His mom, he learned, was in the first desegregated classes. Somehow, they had made that happen. His mom was the most loving person the man had known. Desegregation, he knew, had not caused that, but it did, he thought, let her be loving.

A few summers after the death of his grandmother, Caleb was at a birthday party for one of his friends. One of the parents asked the kids what they wanted to be when they grew up. They took turns answering, and the answers were mostly predictable: animal doctor, firefighter, astronaut. One little boy in a Scooby-Doo T-shirt said he wanted to be Shaggy; a week before, according to his mom, he had wanted to be Velma. And then it was the grandson's turn—"Caleb, what do you want to be when you grow up?"—and the law teacher's son, still just four years old, said, "I want to be the person who gives food to people who don't have any."

His answer is subject to interpretation. Maybe he was saying that he wants to be a waiter. Yet we prefer a different construction. We prefer to see, in his response, hope.

Hope that his grandmother's vision lives in his heart.

Hope that the work of her generation will be continued by his, unencumbered by our generations' neglect.

Hope that the voices of hate that have soiled our history will always be matched, and someday silenced, by the resilient voices of love.

And above all we see hope, inherent in the faith that sustains our struggle, that the sweetest of our voices are those still to be heard.

Notes

1. For an excellent overview of the early debate on *Brown*, see Barry Friedman, *Neutral Principles: A Retrospective*, 50 Vand. L. Rev. 503, 507–14 (1997).

2. Sam Dillon, *Law to Segregate Omaha Schools Divides Nebraska*, N.Y. Times, April 15, 2006.

3. Michael J. Klarman, *From Jim Crow to Civil Rights: The Supreme Court and the Struggle for Racial Equality* (Oxford University Press, 2004); Gerald Rosenberg, *The Hollow Hope: Can Courts Bring About Social Change?* (University of Chicago Press, 2008).

4. Howard Schuman et al., *Racial Attitudes in America: Trends and Interpretations* 103–110 (Harvard University Press, 1997).

5. Houston Memorandum from Charles H. Houston for the Joint Committee of the NAACP and the American Fund for Public Service, Inc. 1–2 (Oct. 26, 1934) (NAACP Records,

Collections of the Manuscript Division, Library of Congress, Group I, Series C, Box 196, Subject File: American Fund for Public Service), quoted in Michael J. Klarman, *Civil Rights Law: Who Made It, and How Much Did It Matter?* 83 Geo. L. J. 433, 453 (1994).

6. *The Rising Tide of Racial Consciousness*, in *A Testament of Hope: The Essential Writings and Speeches of Martin Luther King Jr.* 145, 146, ed. James M. Washington (Harper, 1986); Taylor Branch, *Parting the Waters: America in the King Years, 1954–63* 140–41 (Simon and Schuster, 1988).

7. Derrick Bell, *Law, Litigation, and the Search for the Promised Land*, 76 Geo. L. J. 229, 235 (1987) (reviewing Mark V. Tushnet, *The NAACP: Legal Strategy Against Segregated Education*, 1925–1950 (1987)).

8. Clarence Thomas, *Missouri v. Jenkins*, 515 U.S. 70, 114 (1995) (Thomas, J., concurring).

9. Michael J. Klarman, *From Jim Crow to Civil Rights: The Supreme Court and the Struggle for Racial Equality* 465 (Oxford University Press, 2004).

10. William Hastie Richard Kluger, *Simple Justice* 204 (Alfred A. Knopf, 1976).

11. W. E. B. Du Bois. Quotes are from articles in *The Crisis* from 1933–34, reprinted in W. E. B. Du Bois, *Writings* 1235–63 (Library of America ed., 1986).

12. *Id.*

13. On Du Bois's frustration with the struggle against segregation and his eventual split with the NAACP because of it, see Arnold Rampersad, *The Art and Imagination of W. E. B. Du Bois* 162–69 (Schocken, 1990).

14. For a brief survey of these defenses of *Brown*, see Robert L. Hayman Jr., *Neutral Principles and the Resegregation Decisions*, 9 Widener L. Symp. J. 129 (2002). Charles Black wrote, "[T]he basic scheme of reasoning on which these cases can be justified is awkwardly simple. First, the equal protection clause of the Fourteenth Amendment should be read as saying that the Negro race, as such, is not to be significantly disadvantaged by the laws of the states. Secondly, segregation is a massive intentional disadvantaging of the Negro race, as such, by state law. No subtlety at all. Yet I cannot disabuse myself of the idea that that is really all there is to the segregation cases. If both the propositions can be supported by the preponderance of argument, the cases were rightly decided." Charles L. Black Jr., *The Lawfulness of the Segregation Decisions*, 69 Yale L. J. 421, 421 (1960).

15. Valerie J. Hoekstra, *Public Reaction to Supreme Court Decisions* 13 (Cambridge University Press, 2003).

16. Michael J. Klarman, *From Jim Crow to Civil Rights: The Supreme Court and the Struggle for Racial Equality* 345–46 (Oxford University Press, 2004) (quoting August Meir, *The Successful Sit-Ins in a Border City: A Study in Social Causation*, 2 J. Intergroup Relations 230, 231 (1961)).

PART I

The Context: Race and Segregation

CHAPTER ONE

A History of Race in Delaware: 1639–1950

Robert L. Hayman Jr.

Prologue

Twenty years after the decision in *Brown v. Board of Education*, the public schools in New Castle County, Delaware, were still racially segregated. I attended one of them, a high school of some three hundred students—three of whom, I think, were black.

In the fall of my senior year, our football team played against Wilmington High School, a school that was virtually all black. It was an important game; our team had played for, but lost, the state championship the year before, and the Wilmington team this year was supposed to be very good.

The pregame ritual was fairly typical. The head coach gave his usual speech and then left the locker room to the three team captains. Their short speeches were loud, profane, and really pretty ordinary. Except that on this day, the last of the speeches climaxed with a summons to "kick these niggers' asses."

One of the three black kids at our school was a sophomore on the football team. Stuart was his name—we called him "Stu." At the sound of "nigger," my eyes went instinctively in his direction. I think lots of others did too. At some point in the short, odd silence that followed, the team captain must have been reminded of Stu. He glanced in Stu's direction and said, "That's not you, Stu. You know what I mean." Stu nodded, the speech concluded, and the locker room emptied.

I'm not sure why Stu nodded. I figured he had no choice. But then again, maybe he really did understand what was being said; maybe he really did "know what I mean." I didn't, not at all. I still don't. But I knew less about these things than Stu did.

I never talked to Stu about it. Nobody did, as far as I know. But we won the game that day and eventually made it to the state finals again, where we lost to an all-white Catholic school team. Nobody said anything about Catholics in the pregame speeches; maybe they should have. Two of our three captains were Catholics, so I guess the task would have fallen to the third. The other two, I suppose, would have known what he meant.

Introduction

Delaware has been among the most racist states in the nation, and the vestiges of that racism haunt it today. That, at least, is one of the three hypotheses that emerged from this investigation. It is a difficult hypothesis to test, not least because it relies on a very slippery concept, "racism," that has vastly different meanings to different people. But according to most conventional understandings of racism—as an ideology of natural racial supremacy, as a description of overt race-based oppression, or as an internalized or institutionalized scheme of unfair racial advantages—Delaware's history and its current reality reflect a disturbingly high level of American racism. And as a native Delawarean, I find that shocking.

Delaware's legacy of racism begs the question that leads to the second hypothesis. Why? Why would Delaware be plagued by such racism? The easy answer is that Delaware was a slave state, and racism was essential to slavery, and slavery in turn was essential to the state's economic life. But the easy answer does not work, because slavery in Delaware was not essential. In fact, over the course of the nineteenth century, slavery in Delaware steadily faded to the margins of economic life, so much so that, on the eve of the Civil War, fully 92 percent of Delaware's black population was free. Hypothesis two, then, is that racism endured in Delaware partly in spite of the fact that it was disconnected from slavery, but mostly *because* of that fact. Delaware's unique paradox—the slave state whose black citizens were free—was resolved by a distinctive politics of race. Race thus acquired a distinctive political salience in Delaware—it was not simply a proxy for bondage—that would endure, and that has endured, for many generations beyond the demise of the peculiar institution. In Delaware, that is to say, race mattered, just as it did in the other slave states, only more so.

But it did not matter to everybody, and that is hypothesis three. Race mattered, this essay suggests, only to some people and only in some contexts, and these were defined almost entirely by reference to politics—simple, partisan politics. Delaware's politics has long been infested with an ugly, venomous racism, but its people—black, white, of all races and colors—have consistently risen above it.

This essay divides the history of race in Delaware into four eras. The first, the colonial era, covers the history up until the Declaration of Independence in 1776. The second, the era of abolitionism and of the black codes, covers the period from Independence until the Civil War. The third era is very short, but it is eventful: it is the period of Civil War and Reconstruction, an era covering the years 1861–77. The essay concludes with an overview of the Jim Crow era, covering the period from the end of Reconstruction in 1877 to 1950, the year that Chancellor Collins J. Seitz ordered the desegregation of the University of Delaware.

The Colonial Experience to 1776

The story of race in Delaware might begin in 1639, with the arrival of the first African, "a negro named Anthony." In one sense, the story might have an earlier beginning: Europeans first arrived in Delaware in 1631, and of course, the indigenous peoples—the Lenape and Nanticoke tribes of Indians—were in Delaware for many centuries before their arrival. In another sense, the story of race might have a much later beginning: the color line appears in Delaware, as in the rest of the colonies, only gradually during the seventeenth century, and the modern conventional understanding of race—the conception of "race" as a biological entity—does not emerge until the nineteenth century. Anthony's arrival is of critical importance—it marks the first interaction on Delaware soil between peoples of African and European descent—but race in Delaware both predates his arrival and comes into being many years later.

The Europeans and the Indians

The first Europeans arrived in what is now Delaware in 1631, when the Dutch established a settlement they called Swanendael, in a place now called Lewes. The settlement was destroyed by local Indians after a rather odd dispute, the only case, according to historian John Munroe, "of a serious Indian onslaught upon Europeans in the history of Delaware." Members of a second Dutch expedition briefly resided in Delaware from 1632–33.

The second European settlement—and the first permanent one—was established in 1638, when the Swedes settled at Christina on the banks of the Delaware River, so named by an English sailor in 1610 on behalf of the royal governor of Virginia, Lord de la Warr. Roughly 1,000 settlers would reside in Christina at its peak. In 1651, Petr Stuyvesant of the Netherlands established Fort Casimir in what is now New Castle, principally to secure Dutch access to the Delaware, but also perhaps to provoke the Swedes. If it was a trick, it worked: the Swedes attacked and captured the fort in 1654, but it was quickly retaken by Stuyvesant, who continued his assault southward to take Christina. All of New Sweden was then surrendered to the Dutch.

It was next England's turn to play conqueror. As part of the Anglo-Dutch wars after the Thirty Years War, England attacked New Netherlands, conquering it in 1664. Delaware was then held by the English for a decade, was reconquered by the Dutch in 1673, and taken again by the English the following year. Thereafter, it would be ruled by England until Independence, initially as a part of the New York colony and subsequently under the grant to William Penn.

Penn received the northernmost portions of Delaware in 1681, as part of the grant to establish a refuge for the Society of Friends. A year later, the Duke of York conveyed to Penn the area around New Castle and south of it. The boundaries of the unnamed colony were challenged by Lord Baltimore in the late seventeenth century and were not formally drawn until the middle of the eighteenth century.

In 1704, the Lower Counties of the Pennsylvania colony established their own representative assembly. That assembly governed Delaware under the supervision of the proprietary governor of Pennsylvania and the English Crown until the summer of 1776, when, as part of the broader movement toward independence, it suspended operations of the royal government and called for a state constitutional convention. A constitution was drafted and ratified in a matter of months; it proclaimed a new "State of Delaware."[1]

The Europeans encountered two predominant tribes of Indians in Delaware: the Lenape in the north, and the Nanticoke in the south. The Lenape were "friendly and hospitable" in their first dealings with the Dutch and Swedes, but over time the relationship soured. The Indians did not fully comprehend the meaning of the land deals they struck with the European settlers, and the Europeans exploited their confusion. Moreover, once the settlers took control of the Indian lands, they found the Lenape of increasingly little use. Unlike the hunters of the Minquas tribe (also known as the "Susquahannock") from Pennsylvania, the Lenape, who were mostly farmers and fishers, had no pelts and little else to offer the settlers in trade. By 1647, Governor Printz was suggesting that a force from Sweden might be sent to exterminate the tribe:

> Nothing would be better than to send over here a couple of hundred soldiers to keep here until we broke the necks of all them in this river, especially since we have no beaver trade whatsoever with them but only the maize trade. They are a lot of poor rogues. Then each one could be secure here at his work, and feed and nourish himself unmolested without their maize and also we could take possession of the places which are most fruitful, that the savages now possess.[2]

Printz made his attitude well known to the tribe, warning the chiefs "that in case they hereafter practice the smallest hostilities against our people then we would not let a soul of them live."

Relationships continued to worsen as the English took control, and the tribe suffered the worst of it. The Lenape lost their lands to swindling and confiscation, their freedom to kidnapping, their health to liquor and new diseases, and their lives in intermittent battles. C. A. Weslager, in the seminal modern history of Delaware, concludes of the Lenape, "They welcomed the settlers to the land, provided them with food and befriended them in every way. As time passed, the whites consolidated their position in the Delaware Valley, and in their quest for power and profits, they neglected to return the kindness that had been shown them."[3] The end result was a mutual hostility, interrupted by an occasional treaty of little lasting import. In the end, the Lenape—dubbed the Delaware Indians by the English—left their native lands to escape the Europeans.

The Nanticoke in Sussex County fared little better. They were systematically driven from their lands, first by English squatters, then by the encroachment of English livestock, and eventually "at the point of a gun." The English conceded a reservation to the Nanticoke in 1698, but the settlers did not respect it; a second reservation was created in 1711, but again aggressive settlers continued to harass the tribe. In 1742, the Nanticoke conspired with other peninsula tribes to drive out the English, but the effort was foiled before it started. After the leaders of the plot were arrested, tribal members began to abandon their homes and head north to Pennsylvania. In 1768, the tribe was paid $666.66 for the rights to its two reservations, and the Nanticoke lands were gone.[4]

Bound Labor

Bound labor was a part of the Delaware colonial experience almost from the beginning. At least a few of the colonists in New Sweden were unfree European laborers; the African bondsman Anthony joined their number in 1639. The precise legal nature of "Black Anthony's" servitude is unknown. "It seems likely," reports historian Carol Hoffecker, "that, since the Swedes had had no previous experience with chattel slavery, he was treated much the same as those Finns and Swedes who, as employees of the New Sweden Company, were servants rather than freemen."[5]

The presence of the Swedes presented a clear challenge to Dutch primacy in the region. In response, the Dutch West India Company determined that a permanent, well-populated, and well-defended settlement was critical to the protection of its interests. But Dutch citizens were not eager to migrate to New Netherlands: they suffered little oppression in the Old World and could perceive few incentives in the New. The Company found a solution in bound labor. The combination of Dutch dominion over the African slave trade in the mid-seventeenth century and Stuyvesant's success in persuading the Company to open the slave trade to private citizens ensured the steady presence of bondsmen in New Netherlands throughout its existence.[6]

Servitude remained a prominent feature of the European settlements after the English conquest in 1664. Both the duke of York, who initially controlled the land, and his successor, William Penn, pursued colonization of the region through a mix of immigrants, some free, some not. When the assembly of the Lower Counties passed a bill in 1775 prohibiting the importation of slaves, Williams Penn's grandson, Governor John Penn, vetoed it. The English colonists in Delaware would continue to import unfree labor until 1776, when the first state constitution declared, "No Person hereafter imported into this State from Africa ought to be held in Slavery under any Pretence whatever, and no Negro, Indian or Mulatto Slave ought to be brought into this State for Sale from any Part of the World." The constitution did not prohibit the importation of indentured servants from Europe. That system, however, had virtually disappeared by the end of the eighteenth century, even though state legislation permitting bound apprentices or servants would remain on the books until 1921.[7]

This brief history should not be read to imply that the European colonists—Swedish, Dutch, and English—embraced the elegant distinction manifest in the 1776 constitution: that between African slave, on the one hand, and European servant, on the other. Such was certainly not the case. Throughout the seventeenth century and well into the eighteenth, the colonists employed bound laborers indiscriminately, under a wide variety of terms of servitude and without much regard to their bondsmen's point of origin.

The demographics of the servile class were in fact quite fluid and dependent largely on the exigencies of the day. Both the Swedes and the Dutch attempted to meet the labor needs of their colonies with European labor—free and unfree—but failed to secure sufficient numbers. In the short-lived Swedish colony, which had limited access to the slave trade, and especially in the colony of the Dutch, who for a time dominated that trade, the inexpensive alternative was African labor. By 1664, on the eve of the English conquest, African laborers probably accounted for about one-fifth of the Delaware population.[8]

Under English rule, the demographics of the unfree population would remain very much in flux for several generations. Some English planters attempted to use Indian laborers. The practice was not widespread and was doomed to fail in

Delaware just as in the other colonies; nonetheless, it was sufficiently common to warrant express prohibition in the 1776 constitution. The English had much better success with European bondsmen. Unlike the Swedes and Dutch, the English had a fairly large pool of countrymen eager to leave the Old World, even if it meant arriving in the New World in some form of servitude. In addition, English courts were not unwilling to sentence convicts to terms of labor in the various English colonies. As a result, a significant number of European servants came to Delaware under English rule. In the early years, these servants were mostly English; in the later years—in the mid-eighteenth century—they were mostly Scotch-Irish (with some Irish, English, Scotch, and German laborers as well). The English bondsmen seem to have received more favorable treatment than their Celtic counterparts, and as the years progressed, European servitude in Delaware assumed an increasingly ethnic cast. The result was an undeniable social hierarchy among white Delawareans and an English preoccupation with "the troublesome Celts" that belie the simple black-white distinction imagined in some histories of the era.[9]

The increased supply of European labor meant that African labor was concomitantly less important in the early generations of English rule. The result was a dramatic decline in the African proportion of the colony's population; by 1700, it likely was lower than 5 percent. But this was soon to change. The British victory in the War of the Spanish Succession (Queen Anne's War) yielded the Treaty of Utrecht of 1713, in which France conceded to the British the right to participate in the *absentia*, the slave trade with Spanish America. This concession guaranteed British domination of the global slave trade and consequently ensured an ample supply of African slaves for all the American colonies. Philadelphia soon emerged as a hub of the burgeoning slave trade, and the revival of tobacco markets meant that Delaware growers had a need for this cheap labor. The substantial decline in the immigration of European servants during the French and Indian War (1754–63) completed a dramatic shift in the demographics of bound labor and of the colony as a whole. By 1790, the date of the first national census, 21.6 percent of the state's population was of African descent.[10]

The distinction between slave and servant, meanwhile, was for many generations more theoretical than real. In the early years, the Delaware colony had little formal law governing its unfree labor; the status of its bondsmen, as a consequence, was largely ambiguous. No law, then, upheld the theoretical distinction between the slave, held in perpetual bondage, and the indentured servant, bound for a term of years, and neither did the distinction necessarily prevail in practice: "servants" were sometimes held for practically indefinite terms, and "slaves" were commonly freed after a prescribed term of service.

"Racism" in Delaware

The racial attitudes that the Europeans brought to America and the way they took root in American soil have been the subject of considerable historical debate. In the end, however, the last half-century of historical scholarship seems to have generated more substantial agreement than the debates might suggest. The details remain controversial, but it probably does not strain the historical consensus to suggest that racism in America evolved in four stages.

1. *Color Consciousness: 1619 to c. 1662.* The early European colonists were undoubtedly aware of the color of the Africans' skin, and it assumed at some level a certain importance as a defining characteristic. But the fluidity of the servile and free classes, the integration of free blacks into the social and political communities, and the as-yet impoverished conception of "race" all suggest that whatever racism may have characterized the early colonies was vague, incomplete, and far from universal.
2. *The Formalization of Race: c. 1662 to c. 1776.* The restrictions of servitude hardened in the late seventeenth century, culminating in the adoption of the first major slave codes in 1680–82. Servitude became both perpetual and inheritable, typically transferred from the mother. Race emerged in this time period as a determinant of legal status: the law gradually embraced the presumption that the "negro" was a slave and the "white" person was free. Interestingly, in this time frame there was no concerted effort to define either "negro" or "white": only the Virginia legislature made the effort, as it struggled to give meaning to the term "mulatto." At the same time, restrictions on "free" blacks surface in this period, though the inconsistencies in and among the "black codes" reflect continuing ambiguity and ambivalence.
3. *The Explication of Race: c. 1776 to c. 1835.* There were three ways to resolve the contradiction between the ideology of the revolutionary generation and the fact of chattel slavery. One way was to cure it through the abolition of slavery; this indeed was the response of those states in which slavery was not an economic imperative. A second way was to concede the philosophical inconsistency, but tolerate the contradiction on practical grounds; this was the initial response, at least, in the Upper South, where slavery was assumed to be but a passing phase. A third way was to modify the ideology to incorporate what was by then a racial slavery—to carve out, in effect, a racial exception to the rules of liberty and equality. This, of course, would be the response wherever slavery needed more than an embarrassed defense—and that would be, eventually, throughout much of the American South. It is only in this limited sense that "racism" was born with the new nation.
4. *The Scientization of Race: c. 1835–?* The nascent "science" of "race" found a receptive audience in the antebellum South, where a besieged practice was in desperate need of some ideological foundations. Science, of course, furnished the very best kind of post-Enlightenment foundations: "truths" that were not merely "self-evident," but "proved." Samuel Morton's *Crania Americana*, an 1839 exercise in racial craniometry, helped launch a tradition that would persist through emancipation, two Reconstructions, and beyond. Throughout, whenever "race" has been really needed to rationalize or justify inequality, some "science" has been at hand to support it.

The Delaware experience with "race" largely tracked this model. Indeed, Delaware presents a useful microcosm of the nation, even, remarkably, when the racial experiences of the northern and southern states diverged.

In Delaware, as in the rest of the American colonies, the slave-servant distinction was not a racial one—at least not until well into the eighteenth century. The conditions of passage, to begin with, were roughly the same for European and African bondsmen: mortality rates on the voyages of European bondsmen, many of whom were unwilling voyagers, may have rivaled the 5 to 15 percent mortality rates of the African slave ships. Once in the colony, no laws dictated the distinctive treatment of African and European bondsmen. "There is no special legislation in Delaware regarding Negroes until the end of the seventeenth century," reports Reed's history; "Until then, Negro servants and slaves were subject to the same regulations which applied to white servants."[11]

Eventually, a color line was drawn in Delaware, just as it was in the rest of the colonies. But as elsewhere, it emerged gradually, was drawn incompletely, and responded largely to the exigencies of the day.[12]

Early race-specific measures likely reflected an effort to assert control over the rapidly increasing population of unfree African labor. In 1700, the Pennsylvania legislature established separate "negro" courts for serious crimes by black residents, slave and free; these courts disappeared in Delaware when the Lower Colonies established their own legislature in 1704. They were revived, however, in 1726, but only for "negro or mulatto" slaves, not for free black colonists. The legislative code of 1726 that revived the tribunals—and that was itself based on the Pennsylvania code of 1706—also contained some race-specific punishments, or some "curious provisions," according to Scharf's 1888 history of the state. "Some of the punishments," Scharf reports, "were exceedingly barbarous":

> Attempted rape of a white woman by a negro, was to be punished by standing the criminal four hours in the pillory at the Court House on some court day, with both of his ears nailed to the pillory, and before he was taken from the same, both ears were to be cut off close to his head. In case of theft by a slave his master was compelled to make restitution, and the negro was to be whipped. Negroes carrying arms without the master's special license were to receive twenty-one lashes on the bare back, and if any negroes above the number of six not belonging to one master, should assemble, not on lawful business of their owners, each one was to be whipped at the discretion of the court with any number of lashes not exceeding twenty-one.[13]

The trend continued with a 1752 law that provided that slaves who assaulted whites must stand in the public pillory for two hours and then receive thirty-nine lashes; free blacks and mulattoes were fined a specified amount (between £5 and £10) for the same offense, whereas free whites were fined "according to the heinousness of the offense."[14]

The desire to attach an inheritable marker to servitude, meanwhile, seems the motive for a 1723 law that provided that the illegitimate mulatto children of white mothers would be indentured until the age of thirty-one, ten years longer than the indenture for illegitimate white children.[15]

By the time of Independence, the laws of the Delaware colony clearly identified African labor as a distinct concern. The extent to which the color of the bondsmen's skin was a factor in this process is impossible to know. What can be said for certain is that, as the eighteenth century progressed, the demographics of the unfree population shifted dramatically, from white to black. At the same time, the terms of servitude changed: indentures virtually disappeared, and bondage—following the customs that prevailed in neighboring Maryland—became perpetual. "Racism" might have been a factor in these developments, but it is important to note that it could not have been the racism of "white supremacy," which insisted on a natural order of white over black and which compelled, or rationalized, such laws as those banning interracial marriages. As Independence approached, that vision of "race" was still a half-century away.

Independence and Abolitionism: 1776–1861

The political ideology of the American Revolution was difficult to square with the fact of perpetual servitude. Few leaders of the revolutionary effort even bothered to seek a reconciliation between the two. There was, as a consequence, little intellectual defense of slavery among the founding generation. Many of the leaders of the independence effort—and many of the framers of the national Constitution—were unequivocally opposed to the institution and favored its abolition. Most of the rest barely tolerated slavery, were embarrassed by their affiliation with it, and anticipated its eventual demise.

In spite of this apparent consensus, the events of the late eighteenth century clearly foreshadowed the ideological divide that would eventually split the nation. Within three decades of Independence, the states in the North proceeded to abolish slavery; New Jersey would be the last, initiating its abolition process in 1804. But in the South, philosophical discontent was tempered by economic need. Slavery, as a consequence, was spared destruction and was to be permitted to run its natural course. At the turn of the century, it appeared as if the natural course might be nearing its end, and that slavery would be gone within a generation or so. But of course, that did not happen. The invention of the cotton gin and the emergence of new markets for agricultural exports gave new life to the peculiar institution. Slavery's resurgent importance and the intensity of nineteenth-century abolitionism thus necessitated an altered disposition in the South, and the result was a new, vigorous defense of slavery, one rooted in the laws of nature and in the color of the bondsmen's skin.

Delaware managed to reflect many of these conflicting national trends and, in the process, became a perfect metaphor for the contradictions and paradoxes that characterize America's experience with race. Like its northern neighbors, Delaware began the march toward abolition when it declared its independence: the state constitution of 1776 prohibited the importation of slaves. Before the end of the century, Delaware effectively banned the out-of-state sales of slaves and adopted laws to expedite their manumission. But like its southern neighbors, Delaware would never abolish slavery. Delaware defended the institution with an increasing intensity as disunion approached, and the overtly racist ideology it embraced would inform its public stance for many generations to come. And yet, slavery was not important to Delaware; on the eve of the Civil War, more than 90 percent of the state's black population was already free. Thus emerges the curious portrait of antebellum Delaware: an anti-slavery state that would not abolish slavery, a slave state in which the black population was free.

Slavery and Abolition

Slavery's decline in Delaware was likely attributable to two phenomena: a decreasing need for bound labor and an increasing commitment—partly political, partly religious—to an ideology of equality.

Regarding the first, bound labor grew inefficient in mid-eighteenth-century Delaware when grain replaced tobacco as the state's leading staple crop. The shift likely reflected a combination of factors: the demands of European markets, the inherent inability of Delaware growers to expand their holdings (political borders to the west and south, and water to the north and east, precluded the development of large tobacco plantations), and the exhaustion of the soil due to the tobacco planters' failure or inability to rotate their crops. It was so complete that tobacco, an important crop in 1700, was "practically unknown" in Delaware by 1775. The shift in crops had substantial implications for the labor force: harvesting grain was much less labor intensive than tobacco, and the work of cultivation was more seasonal. As a consequence, it was probably cheaper for Delaware planters to hire extra wage laborers during the growing season than it was to pay the costs of maintaining a surplus of bound laborers—"slaves" or "servants"—year round.[16]

Concurrent with this shift in labor needs, and perhaps partly as a result of it, the ideological opposition to slavery in Delaware began to find its voice. The most vocal early opponents were explicitly motivated by religion: the Quakers in New Castle and Kent counties and the Methodists, principally in rural Kent, embraced abolitionism as a part of their spiritual mission. Their efforts had two objectives: first, to encourage the manumission of slaves by individual slaveholders, and second, to secure legislation ameliorating the pains of slavery and, ultimately, mandating its abolition.

The manumission efforts of the early Delaware abolitionists were extraordinarily successful. In 1776, the Philadelphia Yearly Meeting of the Society of Friends took the final step in proscribing slaveholding among its members by mandating disownment for the offense. In doing so, it at last arrived at the position advocated for decades by the two Monthly Meetings (the Quaker congregations) in Delaware. Under the leadership of David Ferris, the Wilmington Monthly Meeting in 1758 prescribed disownment for any member who bought or sold slaves; the Duck Creek Monthly Meeting, led by Warner Mifflin, enforced a similar edict. Records of the Duck Creek society indicate that between 1774 and 1792, Duck Creek Friends manumitted approximately 460 Delaware slaves; in a single decade, 1770 to 1780, Delaware Quakers manumitted more than 600 slaves, perhaps as much as 10 percent of the state's slave population.

In lower Delaware, meanwhile, the Methodists were the principal force behind manumissions. Introduced to Delaware in the 1770s as part of the broader Methodist revival, the religion spread rapidly through rural Delaware. As with the Quakers, pacifism and abolitionism were vital tenets; although they kept no official records, it appears that most Delaware Methodists freed their slaves between 1775 and 1810.[17]

Quakers and Methodists were the driving force behind the abolitionist societies formed in Delaware in the late eighteenth century. The first of these, the Delaware Society for Promoting the Abolition of Slavery, for Superintending the Cultivation of Young Free Negroes, and for Relief of Those Who May Be Unlawfully Held in Bondage, was formed in 1788. Its constitution declared slavery "universally disgraceful and pernicious [and adverse] to good morals, to the rights of mankind, the feelings of humanity and the sacred obligations of the Christian Religion." The Society disbanded, probably in 1800, and regrouped later that year as the Delaware Society for Promoting the Abolition of Slavery and for the Relief and Protection of Free Blacks and People of Colour, Unlawfully Held in Bondage or Otherwise Oppressed. The reorganized Delaware Society survived into the 1830s. Organized anti-slavery efforts after that time were principally the work of the Quaker Meetings, and especially—in the antebellum era—of the Progressive Meeting at Longwood (Pennsylvania).[18]

The legislative advocacy of these groups yielded decidedly mixed results. Their efforts did, on the one hand, produce two vital changes in Delaware law: the state eased the requirements for manumission and prohibited the out-of-state sales of slaves. On the other hand, the groups failed to achieve a goal that seemed, throughout the nineteenth century, eminently achievable: the state never did abolish slavery.

In 1782, Delaware's chief executive (known then as the president) addressed the opening of the 1782–83 term of Delaware's House of Assembly. John Dickinson, a convert to the Friends, concluded his address with an appeal that largely defined the moderate form of the abolitionist agenda:

> Another Amendment Humanity compels me to propose—that Persons manumitting healthy Slaves not advanced in Years, should not be obliged to give Security for their Maintenance, and that Slaves should not be sent upon Sale or otherwise to Places distant from their usual Residence, by which means affectionate and near Relations are cruelly separated from one another, and the remainder of their Lives extremely embittered. The Legislatures of several neighbouring States, moved by a deep Sense of the divine Favors to them in this Contest for their own Freedom, and by an enlightened Commiseration, have lately passed Laws for alleviating the Afflictions of this helpless and too often abused Part of their Fellow-Creatures. I entertain the warmest Hopes, that the Legislature of this State will emulate the most generous and wise Examples of this Kind.[19]

Dickinson's plea was unsuccessful, but the setback was only temporary. In January 1786, the House of Assembly admitted "a Deputation of seven Persons from the Monthly Meetings of the Society of People Quakers, residing in this State" and accepted from them "a Petition from 204 Persons of that Society, setting forth the distressed situation of the Negro Slaves in this State; and praying, that such Relief be afforded them as the Natural Rights of Mankind, and the Injunctions of the Christian religion, require." The petition, the first of many filed by the Society of Friends with the Delaware legislature, reiterated Dickinson's call to ease the manumission process by eliminating manumission bonds, posted in theory to provide support to the freed slave, but that had the predictable effect of discouraging voluntary emancipations. It requested as well a ban on the out-of-state sales of slaves, a practice that resulted, as Dickinson noted, in the destruction of personal relationships, but that also sustained slavery by ensuring a market—at times quite lucrative—for surplus laborers. Finally, the petition called on the Delaware legislature to enact laws providing for the gradual abolition of slavery.[20]

In 1787, the Delaware legislature responded, though just in part. It adopted a bill, introduced in the Assembly by prominent Methodist abolitionist, Richard Bassett, that eliminated the manumission bond in all cases of healthy slaves aged eighteen to thirty-five. The act also declared out-of-state sales of black slaves and servants "contrary to the principles of humanity and justice, and derogatory to the honor of the state" and banned such sales except on the approval of three justices of the peace. In 1789, in response to petitions from the Friends and the newly formed abolition society, the legislature modified the ban on out-of-state sales by requiring the approval of five justices of the peace. In 1793, it adopted an additional deterrent to unlawful sales by granting immediate and unconditional freedom to any slave sold in violation of the law.

The laws appear to have had the desired effects. The pace of manumissions escalated. Manumission documents—which, by a law of 1797, had to be recorded with the state—continued to recite religious or other altruistic reasons for the act. One Mary Schee, for example, manumitted a slave named Joseph in 1806, holding that "slavery is inconsistent with the will of God," and Hester Catalina Wynkoop emancipated a slave named Isaac in 1805, due to the "utter abhorrence with which I view all kinds of bondage and especially that which dooms a fellow creature to vassalage for life." But "[b]y far the most important reason for manumission," notes historian Harold B. Hancock, "was economic." Delaware slaveholders had an overabundance of bound laborers, and it was grossly inefficient to continue to hold them. The acts of the Delaware legislature had eliminated the primary disincentive to manumission—the manumission bond—and, in effectively banning out-of-state sales, had eliminated the only viable economic option.[21]

And so the slaves were freed. In 1790, 30.4 percent of Delaware's black population was free; by 1800, that proportion had grown to 57.3 percent, and by 1810, to 75.8 percent. By the time of the 1860 census, the last to include slaves, 91.6 percent of Delaware's black population was free. Delaware was home to only 1,798 slaves in 1860, compared to a free black population of 19,829. It was only sensible, then, that Delaware, alone among the slave states, embraced the legal presumption that its black residents were free, and not slaves. This partly explains why Delaware (joined on this score only by Maryland, Louisiana, and South Carolina among the slave states) never endeavored to contrive legal definitions for the various "races."

Conditions for what remained of Delaware's slave population, meanwhile, were on the whole neither better nor worse in Delaware than in the other slave states of the Upper South. In spite of repeated entreaties from abolitionist groups, Delaware took no measures to stop the physical abuse of slaves. In Delaware, as elsewhere, slaves were subjected to physical discipline, and it is likely that very few escaped the lash. State records document beatings so brutal and barbaric that the victims died. In some cases, the perpetrators faced criminal charges, but these either resulted in mild sanctions or were dismissed entirely. The state itself administered whippings to slaves: the criminal codes of 1829 and 1852 prescribed up to sixty lashes as partial punishment for most felonies, and even "unlawful assembly" was punishable by ten to forty lashes under the earlier code and by twenty lashes under the later one.[22]

Delaware's abolitionists failed as well to attain their ultimate goal: they could not secure the legislative abolition of slavery. They petitioned the legislature repeatedly and, on a few occasions, nearly won the day. In 1803, it took the vote of the Speaker of the House to break a tie in the Assembly and defeat a bill for gradual abolition. In 1823, an emancipation plan won the support of Governor Caleb Rodney, whose message to the legislature insisted that "slavery in every shape and form, and under any circumstances, is a blemish upon the fair fabric which we have erected in this country, to liberty." But the legislature failed to act. In 1847, a bill to end slavery for all persons born after 1850 was forwarded from committee to the full House. Slavery, the committee reported, was inconsistent with the "modern" view that labor needed incentives to be productive. The House approved the bill by a vote of 12-8, but the Senate attempt to take up the measure failed on a 5-4 vote, and the bill was "indefinitely postponed."[23] A Senate motion to reconsider failed on a tie vote. It was to be the last chance to secure abolition. "It is discreditable to Delaware," *The National Era* editorialized in 1854, "that the owners of two thousand slaves are permitted to control ninety thousand freemen, fetter their consciences, degrade their nationality, and impede the general prosperity by continuing a system as barbarous as it is impolitic."[24] Such protests would continue, but Delaware would remain a slave state.[25]

Slavery and Freedom in Delaware

Freedom, of course, did not always come legally, and neither was it always lost through legal means. In the age of slavery, Delaware was an important way station on the extralegal routes in and out of freedom. It is impossible to know how many free black Delawareans were kidnapped and sold into slavery in the Deep South. It is clear, however, that the practice was common. A kidnapping law enacted in 1793 seems to have done little to discourage the crime, for "the business of kidnapping free Negroes, especially young children, continued to flourish in Delaware." As a consequence, notes William H. Williams, "most free African Americans in the state lived in constant fear that they or members of their families would be seized by white kidnappers and sold to slave masters in the deep South."[26]

The most notorious of the kidnappers was Patty Cannon, operator of a tavern in Reliance, Delaware, strategically located on the Maryland state line. With her son-in-law Joe Johnson, Cannon led a gang of thugs that terrorized free black Delawareans for decades. Hers, reports Scharf,

> was the most celebrated kidnapper's tavern along the whole border and contained a prison whose miseries rivaled those of the Black Hole in Calcutta. In the centre of

> the attic a dungeon about twelve feet square was constructed, the walls being made of plank firmly spiked together and containing staples to which the kidnapped negroes were sometimes shackled. Often as many as ten persons, of either sex, were crowded into this small space, where they were kept days at a time without a sufficient allowance of food and barely enough air to sustain life. Then they would be taken, usually, to Galestown, Maryland, and placed in the hold of a small vessel to be borne to a plantation in the South. So artfully was this dungeon concealed from the uninitiated that its existence, although suspected, was not revealed for many years, and not until almost every species of crime had been committed by this gang.[27]

A body was discovered buried on the tavern grounds in 1829; subsequent digging revealed more remains, including the skeletons of several children. The number of her victims—kidnapped or murdered—is unlikely ever to be known, but the viciousness of her deeds was of such epic proportions that a 1938 survey of Delaware by the Federal Writers Project reported that black parents were still warning their children to beware of Patty Cannon.[28]

At the same time, Wilmington, Delaware, was a critical stop—the last before freedom—on the Underground Railroad, and Delawareans played a vital role in the railroad's success. Thomas Garrett was Wilmington's "Station Master" for perhaps thirty years. Garrett's house, at 221 Shipley, was the closest station to the Pennsylvania border. The house of Isaac and Dinah Mendenhall, members with Garrett of the Progressive Friends, was the first Pennsylvania station across the Delaware border. Among the other "conductors" Garrett befriended was Harriet Tubman, with whom he collaborated on at least eight occasions.

Garrett made no secret of his efforts, and at one point, it cost him. In 1846, Garrett and John Hunn were sued in federal court by two slave owners for assisting fugitive slaves. They were tried in the New Castle County Courthouse in 1848; the defendants were represented by U.S. Senator John Wales, and the slaveholders by James A. Bayard, who in 1851 would defeat Wales in his reelection bid for the Senate. Presiding over the trial were District Judge Willard Hall, the "Father of Public Education" in Delaware, and the Chief Justice of the U.S. Supreme Court, Roger B. Taney, before long the author of the Court's opinion in *Scott v. Sandford*. The case against the defendants was not an open-and-shut one—they plausibly maintained that the alleged fugitives either were, or appeared to be, free—but the plaintiffs appear to have benefited from a favorable charge to the jury and were awarded judgments totaling $7,900. The personal judgment against Garrett exceeded $5,000, but the Station Master was unrepentant. In an address to the court after the delivery of judgment, Garrett said the following:

> I am called an Abolitionist, once a name of reproach, but one I have ever been proud to be considered worthy of being called. For the last twenty-five years I have been engaged in the cause of this despised and injured race, and consider their cause worth suffering for; but owing to the multiplicity of other engagements, I could not devote so much of my time and mind to their cause as I otherwise should have done. The impositions and persecutions practiced on those unoffending and innocent brethren, are extreme beyond endurance. I am now placed in a situation in which I have not so much to claim my attention as formerly, and I now pledge myself, in

> the presence of this assembly, to use all lawful and honorable means to lessen the burdens of this oppressed people, and endeavor according to ability furnished to burst their chains asunder, and set them free.

"Thomas," the Sheriff is reported to have said later to Garrett, "I hope that you will never be caught at this business again." "Friend," came Garrett's reply, "I haven't a dollar in the world, but if thee knows a fugitive who needs a breakfast, send him to me."

Garrett seems, if anything, to have intensified his efforts in the succeeding years. In the end, he may have assisted nearly three thousand slaves on their flight to freedom.[29]

Free Black Delawareans

The paradox that characterized Delaware's experience with slavery was reflected as well in the experience of free black Delawareans. In significant respects, they were integrated into and indeed were a vital part of the state's social and economic life. At the same time, they were never fully part of the public life of nineteenth-century Delaware, and official discrimination against them grew much worse as the century progressed.

Most free blacks Delawareans lived in the countryside. In 1800, 84 percent lived in rural areas; in 1860, 75 percent still lived in rural Delaware, whereas 14 percent lived in towns and villages and 11 percent in the city of Wilmington. On their manumission, black Delawareans quickly established households, typically with nuclear families. A study of 272 black households in nineteenth-century Appoquinimink and St. Georges revealed that 242 (89 percent) included adult males and 235 (86 percent) included children. The data tend to belie the thesis that slavery was fatal to the social structure of the enslaved people. Indeed the author of the study concludes as follows:

> The strength and durability of the free black families after the years in slavery and the transition to freedom proved that blacks had established a cultural heritage of their own. . . . Although black people had to accommodate their cultural values to the exigencies imposed by slavery, they never abandoned those values. Blacks emerged from bondage with values and institutions that enabled them to build a solid and lasting social structure.[30]

Black and white Delawareans enjoyed at least modest integration in their religious life. Absalom Jones, born a Sussex County slave, became the first black priest in the Protestant Episcopal Church (and founded the Free African Society in 1787), and Methodist preachers generally welcomed both black and white parishioners. Even here, though, integration was not complete; black churchgoers, for example, were typically assigned to the gallery. Over time, black Methodists established their own churches, and black Delawareans played a prominent role in the formation of new Methodist sects. Peter Spencer organized the United American Methodist Episcopal Church and African Union Methodist Protestant Church; Richard Allen, a former Kent County slave, organized the African Methodist Episcopal Church, the largest black denomination.[31]

"Statistics prove," reports Munroe, "that free blacks found a place for themselves in the economic life of this state."[32] That undoubtedly was true, though for most free black Delawareans, their place seems to have been at the bottom.

In rural Delaware in 1860, most free blacks worked as farmhands. No more than 10 percent were tenant farmers, and just a few owned their farms in fee simple. Of those who worked in towns and villages, more than half, mostly women, worked as domestics or servants, one-third worked as laborers, and the balance worked in a variety of positions for unskilled labor.

Those who migrated to the city found that few decent jobs were made available to them. In 1860 Wilmington, the vast majority of free working blacks were employed as servants or laborers. 26 percent of the free men were in semi-skilled or skilled positions, and 6 percent were employed as skilled artisans. These numbers, interestingly, represent a decline from 1814, when the figures stood at 30 percent and 14 percent, respectively, likely reflecting an increased effort to systematically exclude free blacks from the skilled trades.

Statewide, less than 2 percent of Delaware's working free blacks were in skilled trades or professions. However, some form of land ownership was not uncommon: perhaps 20 percent of Delaware's free blacks owned real property. And some black Delawareans enjoyed considerable prosperity. These, however, were the exceptions; poverty was the rule.

Significantly, free black Delawareans had very little access to formal education. In the early part of the nineteenth century, some black students likely attended the state-assisted "pauper schools," but in 1821, the legislature prohibited state aid to black students. The 1829 law that created the state's public school system was an extraordinarily unambitious one, dependent completely on self-funding by the school districts it created. Yet even this modest opportunity was explicitly limited to white students. In spite of the fact that the law's principal author, Judge Willard Hall,[33] was said to be an outspoken critic of slavery, there is no evidence that any thought was ever given to including Delaware's free black children among the new law's beneficiaries.

Black students were thus entirely dependent on private education, either in Quaker schools or in schools established by free blacks. An 1837 visitor to Delaware could find just one such school. "The free people of color in Delaware," Williams Yates thus reported, "are in a most dreadful state of destitution in regard to schools."[34] An 1839 study by the Delaware Bible Society determined that, although more than five of every seven white adults in the state could read, the same was true for just two of every seven black adults.[35] A decade later, Martin R. Delany would report the following to Frederick Douglass:

> There are some two thousand of a colored population in Wilmington, all of whom appear to be quite an industrious and laboring people, but seem not to have been instilled with the higher incentives of life. Education, as heretofore, has been greatly neglected and probably but little cared for by the colored people; hence, the characteristics of the slave stand prominently, and a stranger passing through the place, might well mistake four-fifths of the colored persons whom he would see in the streets to be slaves.[36]

Of the 14,403 Delaware schoolchildren reported in the 1850 census, just 187—1.3 percent—were black. Ten years later, the proportion was still the same.[37]

Which is not to say that the Delaware legislature was ignoring its free black citizens. It was not. Indeed, as the nineteenth century progressed, it paid them increasing attention: the restrictions in Delaware's version of the notorious "black codes" grew more severe with time, just as they did in the other slave states.

In the year that the Quakers filed their first abolition petitions with the Delaware legislature (1786), some white inhabitants of Sussex County filed a petition of their own, "praying that a law may be enacted for the better regulation of free negroes and mulattoes; and that those manumitted in other states may be prohibited from residing in this state." The request was referred to committee, but in due time, the petitioners would get their way.[38]

The so-called political rights—rights thought to be enjoyed by those worthy of a place in the body politic—were the first ones lost by black Delawareans. The Declaration of Rights in the 1776 constitution insisted that "every Freeman . . . hath a Right of Suffrage." The constitution went on to limit the franchise to existing voters, which excluded most black Delawareans, but perhaps not all. But the 1792 constitution explicitly limited the franchise to "every white freeman," and whatever voting rights might have been enjoyed by black Delawareans were thus extinguished for the next eighty years.[39]

The legislature then undertook to ensure the availability of cheap black labor by creating a sort of quasi-slavery. In 1807, it decreed fines for free blacks who returned to the state after being gone for more than two years. In 1811, the permitted period of absence was reduced to six months; in 1849, to sixty days; and in 1863, to five days. The point of the laws was made clear in the preamble to the 1849 revision, which lamented the "habit" among free blacks "of leaving the State during the most important working seasons, when their labor is most necessary to the white population, and of returning within the term of six months allowed . . . destitute, diseased, with bad habits and bad morals to spend the winter among us in idleness and disorder, to the great inconvenience of the citizens of this State." The 1849 law also made it a crime for free blacks to be unemployed and without means of support. The penalty was sale into servitude for the balance of the calendar year, after which time the convicted had thirty days to find work or else be resold. The result was a glut of cheap labor every January.

And then there were the apprenticeships and indentures. The leading study of Delaware's peonage practices concluded that Delaware, "perhaps to an extent unmatched by any other American state, utilized servitude both as a device to control the labor market and as a part of its penology program." "First and foremost to feel the impact of these labor controls," the study noted, "was the free Negro."[40]

The state recognized the "right" of free black Delawareans—like free white Delawareans—to secure apprenticeships for their children. However, an examination of the cases involving the apprenticeship of white children "raises a suspicion" that apprenticeship "was merely a device for cheap labor exploitation."

That suspicion rises to the level of near certainty in the cases involving black children, "which lacked the proper educational safeguards generally observed in binding out white children."[41]

At the same time, a complex scheme of indentures consigned many otherwise free adults to bondage. Delaware's debtors were permitted to "consent" to indenture as an alternative to imprisonment until 1827, when that alternative was eliminated for women and white men. For black men, such indentures remained an option. The racial disparity was heightened in 1841, when the legislature eliminated bondage for the satisfaction of civil judgments against white defendants. For black debtors, however, this particular form of "debt bondage" persisted until the Civil War.

Involuntary indenture, meanwhile, was a part of Delaware's penal system throughout the nineteenth century, and over time, it too would acquire a distinctive racial cast. The first race-specific measure of note was the Servitude Act of 1807, which required fourfold restitution from black defendants convicted of larceny and authorized their sale into servitude for up to eleven years to secure satisfaction. The following year, the penalty for free blacks was changed to corporal punishment, but the indenture penalty was restored in 1811, and the penalties increased in a series of measures in the 1820s. White convicts, it must be noted, continued to be sentenced to indentures under race-neutral laws, and in fact a review of the records from 1822 to 1840 concluded that "there seemed to be no more inequity or caprice in the sentencing of Negroes than in that of white offenders."[42]

An 1828 law authorized indenture for free blacks "likely to be chargeable to the County"; among those victimized by the law was a twenty-four-year-old pregnant woman named Rachel Blackiston. An 1837 law authorized sales into servitude for defendants unable to pay the fines and costs associated with a conviction for assault, but the law provided that indigent white defendants might be discharged from the obligation. In 1839, the racial exemption was extended to all offenses. The last white convict sentenced to servitude received that sentence in 1840. Indentured servitude as a penal sanction was thereafter limited to black defendants and persisted until after the Civil War. The list of offenses punishable by servitude would in fact continue to grow through the antebellum era, perhaps reaching its apex—or nadir—in an 1852 law that authorized compulsory servitude for "idle and vagabond free Negroes and free mulattoes."

The fine line between "voluntary" and "involuntary" indenture is illustrated by an 1861 statute, adopted on the eve of war, which permitted black debtors to contract with their creditors to work off their indebtedness. Debtors who failed to satisfy the terms of such contracts could be sold into servitude by the county sheriff for a period of up to seven years. Variations on these "voluntary" debt indenture laws—all applicable only to black debtors—were reenacted and revised throughout the nineteenth century. The final law was not repealed until 1915.[43]

Other laws regulated family life in a fashion that both ensured a supply of labor and clarified the racial hierarchy. An 1810 half-free law provided that persons with contracts of manumission would be considered slaves during any period of indenture. Any children born to such persons would also be slaves, until the age of twenty-one if female, and twenty-five if male. A law enacted the following year permitted the indenture of free black children whenever their parents could not prove their self-sufficiency. Under the law, girls could be bound to labor until the age of eighteen and boys until the age of twenty-one. And in 1829, the legislature prohibited marriage between "a white person and a negro or mulatto." An anti-miscegenation law enacted in 1807 had been repealed a year later, but this time the ban would remain on the books, in varying forms, until such laws were rejected by the Supreme Court in 1967.

The Virginia slave insurrection led by Nat Turner in 1831 had repercussions throughout the slave states, and Delaware was no exception. Indeed, the fears of Delaware's slaveholders were exacerbated by rumors of a local insurrection. The rumors, it evolved, were based on an elaborate bit of trickery; "[i]n truth," Carol Hoffecker notes, "the only troublemakers were a group of whites who dressed up to look like blacks and staged a 'shoot-out' along the Nanticoke River near Sanford at election time."[44] But "confusion and dismay," records Scharf,

> took possession of every mind. The business of the election stood still, and one of the clerks in his fright ran off with the ballot-box, and could not be found until the alarm had partially subsided the next day. It was soon, however, discovered that all the reports were wholly without foundation, and yet the people throughout the two lower counties acted exactly as if they had been strictly true.[45]

The legislature certainly behaved as if the rumors were true, for it immediately enacted a set of repressive measures aimed exclusively at the free black community. The act of 1832 made it illegal for black Delawareans to possess firearms, subject to individual exceptions for those dependent on hunting for their subsistence. The act also prohibited assemblies of more than twelve free blacks or mulattoes past 10 P.M. in the winter unless they were attended by at least three "respectable white men"; mindful that Nat Turner was a preacher, it prohibited preaching by new black residents unless they first received a judge-issued license.[46]

Delaware's free black citizens responded in 1833 with a petition requesting that the new law be repealed. The petition noted the act's "demoralizing effect upon the People of Colour, for by placing them under suspicion . . . [it] takes from them one of the strongest inducements to virtuous action." The petition was ignored. It was essentially the same state of affairs four years later, when William Yates visited the state. "I had hoped to find slavery in Delaware merely nominal," Yates wrote; he continued as follows:

> How far my expectations were realized will be seen hereafter. An error into which a distant observer is liable to fall on such a view of the subject as has been just given, arises from the fact that the so called free people of color are only nominally free. . . . [U]nder the wretched and mongrel system of laws which have been enacted in regard to them, they enjoy but a mongrel liberty, a mere mock freedom; being subject to many of the disabilities and disadvantages of both conditions; and enjoying few of the benefits of either.[47]

Things only got worse. In 1845, the legislature prohibited black Delawareans from buying or selling alcohol. In 1851, it tightened the restrictions on black gatherings.

The *Revised Statutes* of 1852 summarized the various restrictions on Delawareans of color this way:

> No free negro, or free mulatto, shall be entitled to the privilege of voting at elections, or of being elected, or appointed, to any office of trust, or profit, or to give evidence against any white person except as is provided in chapter 107, or to enjoy any other rights of a freeman, other than to hold property, or to obtain redress in law and in equity for any injury to his or her person or property.[48]

Delaware's Slavery Paradox

In 1852, Delaware's elite met for the purpose of drafting a new state constitution. Senator James A. Bayard, leader of Delaware's Democrats, proposed two measures. The first was a constitutional provision prohibiting the abolition of slavery. The second prohibited the immigration of free blacks to Delaware.

Restrictions of the latter sort had a curious history in Delaware, one that fairly reflected the state's intense ambivalence on matters of color. Immigration was prohibited in 1807, but that act was repealed in 1808. Immigration was prohibited again in 1811, and that act was repealed in 1831. Immigration was prohibited for a third time in 1851, and that ban was in effect when Bayard proposed that it be accorded constitutional status.

Two Sussex Whigs—Daniel Corbit, a Quaker from Odessa, and Truston P. McColley, a Methodist lay preacher from Milford—led the opposition to Bayard's proposals, and in the end, both were rejected, a circumstance rendered less important when the proposed constitution, the first submitted to popular referendum, was soundly defeated.[49] But the rejection of Bayard's proposals speaks volumes about Delaware. The state with an active ban on black immigration—its third such ban—would not put that same ban in its constitution. Yet the state that would not abolish slavery would not prohibit its abolition either.

Accounting for this paradox is not easy. Nor is it easy to explain precisely why the Delaware legislature never did abolish the institution of slavery. James Munroe attributes this inaction to a certain conservative disposition: "the devotion of the state to a policy of gradualism, to perpetuation of what could be salvaged of the old order, prolonged the legal existence of slavery."[50] Carol Hoffecker perceives the same, at least in the antebellum era:

> The key to Delaware's politics amid the swirl of conflicting emotions and events that brought on the Civil War and Reconstruction was stubborn conservatism. The majority of the state's voters could be swayed by fears of secessionism and abolitionism alike. Their futile hope was for a restoration of the lost world of the past.[51]

William H. Williams concurs; although Delaware's political leaders "were troubled about the morality of slavery," they were also "strongly influenced by their own and their constituent's growing racism, and the reluctance, implicit in government officials in a very conservative state, to abandon the old order."[52]

But a contemporary commentator thought it was simply partisan politics:

> The great obstacle to emancipation in Delaware is not the power of the oligarchy within the State, but its power in the Union. It is the absolute control of the miscalled

> Democratic party, by the slave interest of the South, which prevents the Legislature of Delaware from abolishing Slavery. It is the interest of that party to uphold Slavery. It has no hold upon the affections of the people, and therefore allies itself with the great and powerful institution of Slavery. This institution gives it the control in nearly all the Southern States, and by means of Federal patronage it has heretofore managed to control enough of the Northern States to keep it in power. But its shams and devices, its frauds and corruptions, are at length understand by the Northern people, and its sands have nearly run out. When it ceases to have Federal patronage to dispense, it will lose the last link that binds Northern demagogues to its fortunes. By the same corrupt appliances, this slave Democracy, has kept up a Pro-Slavery feeling in Delaware, and prevented the States from commencing the work of emancipation.[53]

The partisan political account seems particularly compelling. Delaware was, after all, a closely divided state; as with the nation, its southern and northern interests lay in uneasy balance. The bulk of its population lived in its northernmost county, New Castle County, which was home to the state's largest city, Wilmington, a bare twenty-five miles from Philadelphia. But the idiosyncracies of Delaware's constitution placed effective control of the legislature in the hands of the two lower counties, Kent and Sussex, home to the dwindling population of slaves and of slaveholders. It was the fear that free black voters would tip the scales against them—in favor of the Whigs in the earlier part of the nineteenth century and the Republicans later—that, historian Patience Essah explains, motivated southern Democrats, in Delaware and in the nation: "Fear of partisan political demise . . . explains why from the American Revolution to the Civil War and beyond, Delaware Democrats resisted all attempts to legislate the abolition of slavery. . . . No matter how weak a financial institution," Essah concludes, "slavery buttressed perceptions of white and Democratic superiority."[54]

Whatever the explanation, Delaware would retain the peculiar institution. And although slavery in Delaware declined over the course of the nineteenth century, its chief vestiges—race and racism—would only grow more important in the state, just as they did elsewhere. Delaware's political leaders were indeed determined to defend slavery, and its vestiges, "to the Civil War and beyond."

Civil War and Reconstruction: 1861–1877

During the Civil War, Delaware was among those anomalous border states: slave states that did not leave the Union. Yet Delaware's loyalty was not a foregone conclusion. In June 1861, the Delaware legislature entertained a secessionist appeal from a Mississippi envoy. Although the appeal failed—the vote against secession was unanimous in the House, but just 5-3 in the Senate—the envoy's report was sufficiently encouraging that Alabama and Georgia subsequently sent delegations. Most of Delaware's political leadership—including Governor William Burton and the entire congressional delegation—openly sympathized with the South, though historian James Munroe suggests that the response of the Delaware assembly was "probably more truly representative of the feelings of the average Delawarean."[55]

That average Wilmingtonian, certainly, was the source of great distress for the powerful Bayard family. On the eve of secession, Thomas Bayard warned his father,

Senator James Bayard, then traveling in the South, of the prevailing spirit in the Wilmington community:

> You will now realize the strange, wild, savage spirit of war that has arisen in the North and cowed men into compliance or silence. Here it has run completely over us, and I have felt the bitterest contempt for the public tone. The Abolitionists are rampant, waving American flags, subscribing money freely and urging mob spirit wherever they can. We seem to be a mere servile dependency of Pennsylvania, and her word is law to Delaware. I await your coming as calmly as I may, but my heart is full of abhorrence for the Northern sentiment, and contempt for the community.[56]

In the end, Delaware's place in the Union probably was secured only when Governor Burton appointed Henry du Pont, West Point graduate and strong unionist, to command the Delaware regiments in the war between the states.

The complex thread of Delaware's racial thought—and its frequently schizophrenic nature—was clearly evident in the politics of the Civil War era. In late 1861, President Lincoln endeavored to experiment with compensated emancipation as a solution to the vexing problem of slavery. He chose Delaware as the experimental site. At Lincoln's request, Congressman George P. Fisher, the first and only Republican in Delaware's congressional delegation, presented a bill to the Delaware General Assembly that would have gradually freed Delaware's slaves over a ten-year period, with an average of $500 being paid to each slave owner for each emancipation. But the legislature balked. The Democrats were no fans of Lincoln and claimed to resent federal interference in the state's internal affairs. Even Republicans professed concern about the costs of the scheme and its inequitable treatment of those who had voluntarily manumitted their slaves. In the end, the bill was withdrawn in the face of a narrow but certain defeat.

Fisher paid for Lincoln's gambit in his 1862 bid for reelection, when Democrats branded him an abolitionist and a champion of "negro equality." The campaign was incendiary, and on election day, Lincoln sent federal troops to the Delaware polls. Democrat William Temple won the 1862 election amid allegations of electoral fraud and then died before he could assume office. Democrats boycotted the special election of 1863, ostensibly to protest the appearance of federal troops the previous fall. The result was a victory for Republican Nathaniel B. Smithers, who prevailed by a count of 7,286 votes to 13.

Democrats reentered the field the following year, running explicitly now as the "White Man's Party." "No more drafts," their slogan promised, "no more taxes, no negro equality." Their congressional candidate, John A. Nicholson, carried the lower two counties to narrowly defeat Smithers in his reelection bid. It was the beginning of a quarter-century of near-total domination by Democrats. Republicans would send just one person to Washington in the next twenty-five years, a one-term Congressman elected in 1872.[57]

The oppression of black Delawareans continued throughout the civil war. Slavery remained the law, and for roughly 1,800 Delawareans, it remained their life. Slaves continued to be bought and sold, right up to the time of the ratification of the Thirteenth Amendment in 1865. As late as 1864, the state was still enforcing its ban on the immigration of free blacks. In that year, Rev. Thomas M. Kinnard, of the BME Church of Canada, visited his birthplace in Delaware. He was promptly arrested for violating the ban, fined $50 and costs, and, lacking the funds to pay the fine, was offered for sale into servitude. He was bought by the family that manumitted him years earlier, who then arranged his emigration.[58]

After the war, the national government was faced with the task of rebuilding the nation, this time with a stronger commitment to the union of the whole and to the equality of the whole of the people. The federal Reconstruction effort in the slave states—those in the late rebellion, as well as those that remained loyal—sought and achieved a measure of equality for black Americans that had not been seen in generations.

Except in Delaware. Reconstruction Delaware is nothing less than an oxymoron. Although black freedmen throughout the South experienced some semblance of "a new birth of freedom," black Delawareans in the Reconstruction era remained trapped in a mythologized past of white dominance. For Delaware's black citizens, the period after the Civil War was a time of little progress. As historian Harold C. Livesay wrote in 1968, "While most former slave states are currently going through . . . a 'Second Reconstruction,' Delaware is in the midst of its first."[59]

At the national level, official Delaware—its congressional delegations, its governors, its legislatures, and most of its public leaders—opposed every part of the Reconstruction effort. When the fugitive slave laws were repealed in 1864, Delaware's delegation voted against the bill—even Republican Congressman Smithers, who would in fact be the only Republican in either House to oppose the measure. When the Thirteenth Amendment, abolishing slavery, was debated in Congress, Delaware's delegation—now all Democratic—argued against it. When it was approved by Congress and submitted to the states for ratification, Delaware voted against it (6-3 in the Senate, 12-7 in the House).

When the first civil rights bill in the nation's history—the bill of 1866—was before the 39th Congress, Delaware's delegation was unanimously opposed. So too was the Delaware Assembly, which passed a "Joint Resolution on Federal Relations" expressing its disapproval:

> Eighth. That in the opinion of this General Assembly the passage of such a law by Congress will be but the commencement of a system of legislation designed hereafter to be extended to the States, which, if persevered in by Congress and tolerated by the people, will ultimately degrade the free white men of this country to the level of the negro, so far as Congressional action can affect this result.

The congressional delegation—Congressman John A. Nicholson of Dover and Senators Willard Saulsbury and George R. Riddle—all voted against the bill. It passed by a substantial margin, was vetoed by Andrew Johnson, and then was passed again, overriding the veto; this was the first override of a presidential veto in U.S. history. The Delawareans voted against the override as well. The same Congress proposed the Fourteenth Amendment. The Delaware delegation, of course, unanimously opposed it. So too did the Delaware Assembly, which refused to ratify it (the decisive House vote was 15-6). And when the 40th Congress took up the Fifteenth Amendment—giving to the freedmen the franchise—the delegation was again unanimous in its opposition, and when it passed, yes, Delaware refused to ratify it: the vote against ratification was 7-2 in the Senate and 19-0 in the House.[60]

Compounding the sin of opposition was the mode of expressing it. The objections were voiced in the most inflammatory terms. The racism, by any definition, was patent. Consider the record of congressional debates.

In 1860, Congress considered a measure to allow black students to attend the District of Columbia's free schools. In the course of the debate, Delaware's senior senator, James A. Bayard Jr., made clear his views on the prospects for racial equality. Senator James Harlan of Iowa inquired of Bayard, "If the negro population were all as well educated as the white people, would they then be our equals?" The question, Bayard replied, was "as to the unity or diversity of the races." "Without entering into the question," he offered (before entering into the question),

> which I leave to philologists and ethnologists . . . I have no shadow of a doubt, from my own observation of the negro race, of its inferiority. I am no slaveholder; I never expect to be one. I am perfectly willing to admit that in my own State slavery is of very little value and of little moment; yet I could give the reasons why I think the law of slavery must be maintained there while the relative number of negroes remains in the State so large in proportion to the white population; but it unnecessary to trouble the Senate with that now. My answer to the honorable Senator is, that, from my reading of the history of the past, from my own personal observation of the character of the race, I believe it would be impossible to carry the civilization of the negro race as a race—I do not speak of individual cases—to equality with the white man with any benefit either to them or the white race. . . . Sometimes the black man—and generally he is a cross where he does so—has exhibited powers beyond his race; and gentlemen draw from that the deduction that the race is capable of elevation. I have looked at this question of races, I have examined history, and I can find no instance where the black race has ever advanced to anything like ordinary civilization.

"I do not look to individualities," Bayard continued,

> I deal with men as races. . . . In the providence of God, why He made the distinction, and when He made it, is one of those matters which it is not for me to enter into. The color alone does not make the difference. The difference in the organic structure of the race, as affecting their capacity, is far greater and more prominent, though it may not be as obvious to the eye, as the mere distinction of color. . . . It is enough for me to know that, in my judgment, the difference exists; that one race is more animal and less intellectual than the other; that one race is incapable of civilization; and if you attempted to carry it to the same extent as the other it would result only in insanity, and I cannot agree to put them on an equality.[61]

Sometimes Delaware's political leaders blended the new myth of racial inferiority with a nostalgic yearning for a mostly imagined past. In 1864, Senator Willard Saulsbury—who maintained a personal scrapbook titled "Negroes," filled with reports of supposed atrocities by black Americans—felt compelled to record a rare disagreement with his Maryland colleague, fellow Democrat Reverdy Johnson. Slavery, Johnson had suggested, was virtually dead. "I do not believe with the Senator from Maryland in the conclusion that slavery is dead," Saulsbury said. He continued as follows:

> I never wish to see it die even in the little State where I live, though we have no slaves there to make it any consideration to us in a pecuniary point of view. Born in a slave State, seeing none of the great injuries arising from that institution which seem to be so patent to the vision of men now, I desire to close my eyes under the same influences and institutions under which they were opened. If there were not a slave within our State, I still should want a slave code to keep out your intermeddling negroes who wish to associate on terms of equality and to ride in railroad cars and other public conveyances with white people. Sir, the finger of God Almighty has drawn the distinction between the races, and abolitionism is infidelity; it is a war upon the ordinances of God's providence, and it emanates and exists among a people less orthodox in religious creed than any other portion of the United States. There is no "ism" of the modern days which has ever sprung up in a slaveholding State. Woman's rightsism, spiritualism, and every other ism, together with abolitionism, have their origin in a locality where slavery is more distasteful than it is in other localities, but not among a people who are more kindly disposed to the negro race or who treat them more kindly when among them. Sir, for slavery itself I care not. It is only the influences and the spirit of abolitionism that I dread, and that I wish to be free from.[62]

Three years later, it was apparently nostalgia of a constitutional sort that moved Saulsbury to raise a point of order during deliberations on the proposed Fifteenth Amendment. The president of the Senate inquired as to the point of order. "It is that it is not in order now to attempt to amend the Constitution," Saulsbury replied, "that instrument having been blotted out of existence long ago."[63] The president overruled the objection.

Sometimes, what Delaware's leaders expressed can only be described as race hate. In 1864, Congress considered a bill to prohibit discrimination in the District of Columbia's rail cars. Saulsbury mocked the perceived preoccupation with the welfare of black Americans:

> Poor, helpless, and despised inferior race of white men, you have very little interest in this Government; you are not worth consideration in the legislation of the country; but let your superior, Sambo's interests come in question, and you will find the most tender solicitude in his behalf. . . . What a pity it is that there is not somebody to lampblack white men so that their rights could be secured.[64]

In 1866, Congressman Nicholson explained his opposition to the proposed Fourteenth Amendment. The Constitution, Nicholson said, was once in "the most perfect equilibrium," but "[t]hat nicely adjusted balance is now, by this amendment, to be permanently overthrown. The line of demarcation between State and Federal power, which has been already too much obscured by the great latitude of construction given of late to the several grants of power, is now to be entirely obliterated." As Nicholson went on, a different basis for opposition emerged. "I certainly think that the negro should be protected in his life, liberty, and proper," Nicholson insisted, "and believe that he has always enjoyed this protection, and that at this very moment he stands in no need whatever of those who have constituted themselves his especial friends, and clamor now so loudly for his rights." He was now warming to the task:

> Now, the negro race in this country constitute such a class which is easily and well defined. . . . [t]he radical difference between them and the white race should be recognized by legislation. . . . For the negro is not actuated by the same motives as the white man, nor is he deterred from crime except by punishments adapted to the brutal, sensual nature which characterizes him. The negro's idea of freedom is to do nothing but bask in the sunshine. The negro woman now disdains to pick cotton, and her present ambition is to "send her daughter to boarding school, and keep a piano." And they are assisted very much in these mischievous notions by such legislation as the Freedman's Bureau and civil rights bill.[65]

In 1869, James Bayard explained his opposition to the Fifteenth Amendment by noting that there were three widely recognized exceptions to the rule of universal suffrage: age, sex, and race. Regarding the second of these, Bayard said,

> I will not argue this question either with communists or socialists, nor with the woman's right party, because the folly of this species of fanaticism, though it has made great progress lately, is not sufficiently widespread to need an elaborate refutation. . . . But there is a difference in the physical, mental, and moral structure of the sexes which fits them for different duties, and the pursuit of different avocations. . . . In my belief, if the [woman's] sex is dragged down into the political arena, the coarse and selfish, and too often brutal struggle for place and power and spoils, will impair its influence and demoralize woman's nature, and that deference which now exists, and her real influence over man will gradually but certainly fade and be lost, and with that loss we shall be, as a people, retrograde in civilization.

An even worse fate, Bayard warned, would attend removal of the racial restriction: "equality of political power can only end in the conflict of races."[66]

Willard Saulsbury joined the debate a few days later. It was not, he insisted, a partisan fear that motivated his opposition to black suffrage: "Although it be true that nearly one fifth of her population are free negroes," he observed, invoking a somewhat anachronistic phrase fully four years after emancipation, "yet every negro vote that you get only adds two white votes to the Democratic party." Of white Delawareans, Saulsbury said,

> When God Almighty made the mold that made that people, and when He cast that people in the mold which he made, he molded them of that material and made the mold of that material that it is impossible that they and their descendants can ever be so degenerate as to feel pride and honor in association, politically or socially, with an inferior race. Let those who feel that such is their nature and that such is their want of mental and moral illumination that they have to invoke the superior wisdom and the superior morality of the negro race take them to *their* bosoms and welcome them into the political council of *their* States. The people of my State are not placed in any such situation, and they do not need the additional enlightenment which they are to get from Africa.

And how profound were the differences between the races, according to Saulsbury. God created man, he noted, and "this creation of His has different hues of skin, different mental and moral organizations; we find them inhabiting different societies, with different orders of intellect; and I would say different orders of beings."[67]

In 1870, the Delaware legislature chose not to return Willard Saulsbury to the Senate (the likely explanation, Munroe reports, was to be found in his excessive fondness for drink).[68] He was replaced by his older brother Eli, but their racial politics were indistinguishable. In early 1872, Eli Saulsbury assailed Charles Sumner's proposed civil rights bill, which included a provision prohibiting discrimination in public schools: "I especially object to the measure proposed by the Senator from Massachusetts, to its general object and purpose, because it proposes the degradation of the white men and women of the country, and seeks to place them upon an equality socially and in every other respect with a race their inferiors by nature as well as by instinct and civilization." The bill, Eli Saulsbury insisted, would foment widespread racial discord:

> Men will not send their children to schools where they must associate and grow up with negroes, and the white men who are now dependent upon common schools for the education of their children, are the very last men who would consent to do so. For one, I should regard it as far less evil to see the common schools in my State abandoned than to see them converted into mixed schools for white and colored children.

In his conclusion, Saulsbury's dire predictions for the future yielded to a fantastic description of the past:

> All the measures which have been incepted and carried out by Congress, looking to an equalization of the races, have tended in no small degree to disturb the harmony which heretofore existed between the white and colored people of the country. You witness it in the South and in every other State where there are large numbers of negroes. Your legislation has engendered distrust, and in many instances hatred on the part of the negro toward the white race, and lessened the regard which the latter have heretofore felt for the former.[69]

Two years later, with the bill still pending, Saulsbury would issue an explicit threat:

> I warn Senators, those who live in States that are not affected by this legislation, that a very different state of feeling does exist and will exist in reference to mixed schools in those States having large negro populations, and it may be that when this hostile legislation is forced upon them a feeling of dislike will be kindled which will not inure to the benefit of the colored race.[70]

Finally, consider the remarks of Thomas F. Bayard Sr.—successor to his father James in the Senate—objecting to the Enforcement Act of 1870, the implementing legislation for the Fifteenth Amendment. Congressional actions, the younger Bayard complained, were designed only to benefit black voters, not white: "It has been only for the ignorant, semi-barbarous race unfit for voting, manufactured into voters and allies of the Republican party to sustain themselves a little longer in power."[71] Later, objecting to the schools provision of the civil rights bill, Bayard elaborated on the incapacities of black Americans. Whites and blacks, he insisted, served different economic functions. Education was needed to prepare skilled labor, and "the skilled labor of the country means the white labor of the country." Black Americans needed to be prepared for other uses:

> The black labor, useful, excellent, valuable as it is, is not skilled labor. Neither manufactures nor commerce in its minor grades, nor mechanics in any of their forms, are materially aided by the contribution of what I may term the negro labor of the United States. They fill, as we all know, a most important and an essential grade in society. As menial servants there are none so available, none, in my opinion, who are their equals. The ready, kindly sympathy which they from their natures are so calculated and enabled to express makes them the most agreeable and useful menial servants. It is a class essential to the community. A community without the menial class is utterly defective. It is a grade quite as essential to the welfare and happiness of the community as the higher grades of intellect.[72]

Delaware's congressional delegation was consistent in its use of racist rhetoric, and it was quite typical of Delaware's leadership. In 1866, the Delaware General Assembly voiced its opposition to the first proposed civil rights bill with a resolution that included this declaration:

> The immutable laws of the creator have affixed upon the brow of the white race the ineffaceable stamps of superiority and that all attempts to elevate the negro to the social or political equality of the white man is the result either of an unwise and wicked fanaticism or a blind and perverse infidelity, subversive of the ends for which this government was established, and contrary to the doctrines and teachings of our fathers.

Throughout Reconstruction and beyond, the rhetoric would be repeated—in legislative halls, in the governor's mansion—predictably, persistently, ad nauseam.

It does not seem, however, that this hate-filled rhetoric either caused or reflected a more broad-based backlash against the freedmen. The region embracing lower Delaware, it is true, was not completely spared the racial violence that marked much of the South in the Reconstruction era. An 1866 report of the Freedmen's Bureau found that conditions for the freedmen in West Virginia, Virginia, and much of Maryland were "generally satisfactory," a situation "in marked contrast to portions of the State of Maryland, especially the seven lower counties on the eastern shore, where much bad feeling exists against both freedmen and bureau, and complaints are daily received of outrages and acts of injustice."[73] An army colonel investigating conditions in the region reported as follows:

> I am convinced that the colored people of this District need the strong arm of the Federal Authority for their protection. The civil authorities of the lower part of Delaware and the Eastern Shore of Maryland accord them no rights; their churches are burned, their schools broken up, and their persons and property abused and destroyed by vicious white men with impunity; and their appeals to the civil authorities are utterly disregarded.

In 1869, a new schoolhouse for black students in Slaughter Neck was burned; Sarah Owens, the black teacher at the school, was not saved from violence by boarding with a local minister in Georgetown. His house was stoned, and Owens spent a long night hiding in a barn. She fled to her family home in Philadelphia, where her mother insisted she remain. Between 1867 and 1869, the State witnessed a dozen or more instances of race-motivated school burnings; the teachers in each instance were driven from town. Little was done to prevent or punish the acts. In 1867, a Freedman's Bureau investigator reported,

> So far as the *reading* of the laws is concerned, the colored man in Delaware has fair justice secured to him; in the *working* and *executing* of the laws the popular prejudice against the race ever works to his disadvantage, and a jury will have no hesitation in convicting a black man upon evidence that would be deemed insufficient for a white man's conviction.[74]

Still, it is by no means clear that even in the immediate postbellum era, white Delawareans were, on the whole, noticeably hostile toward black Delawareans. "The general feeling of the whites toward the blacks," the Bureau investigator reported, "is total indifference—their presence in the community being simply endured for their usefulness—and the colored people must in a great measure—unless their political condition is improved—depend for such elevation above their present condition upon the success of such efforts as are now being made for their moral and educational improvement."[75]

As this report suggests, the prospects for improving the plight of black Delawareans would ultimately turn on the success of efforts in two areas: securing the franchise and securing more and better schools. But in the Reconstruction era, the government of Delaware ensured that voting rights would be largely a fiction, and educational rights a distant hope.

The Freedmen and the Franchise

After the Fifteenth Amendment had been ratified, an assembly of Delaware's leading black citizens gathered to celebrate the achievement and to demonstrate their gratitude. The assembly adopted a series of resolutions on April 14, 1870. They read, in part, as follows:

> Whereas, The nation has restored political rights to the colored citizens deprived of these rights heretofore simply on the ground of the color of their skin, and Whereas, The Nation has thus planted itself anew upon the imperishable doctrines of the Declaration of American Independence.
>
> Resolved, that our grateful thanks are first due to that God who is Lord of lords and King of kings . . .
>
> Resolved, That the President, Cabinet, Congresses, Legislatures, and loyal people, who proposed and sustained this restoration to us of political rights and privileges, have won our lasting gratitude,

> Resolved, That we hereby pledge to them to prove the fitness of the trust by the worthiness of our conduct. That realizing the responsibilities resting on us, we mean to use the ballot for no merely narrow or selfish ends, but for the best good of the State and nation, thereby aiding to perpetuate a Union which our fathers and their fathers, their brothers and our brothers, together helped to save.

But it would be a long time before black Delawareans could prove their fitness for the franchise, because official Delaware turned the Fifteenth Amendment into a cruel hoax. Before the adoption of the amendment, the disenfranchisement of black Delawareans had been complete. So total was their exclusion from political life—and so difficult were the political obstacles confronting their supporters—that in 1867, the U.S. House of Representatives was moved to order hearings on conditions in Delaware. The purpose of the inquiry, conducted by the House Judiciary Committee, was to determine whether action was needed to bring Delaware into compliance with Article 4, Section 4 of the federal Constitution; that is, whether Congress needed to act to ensure that Delawareans enjoyed a "republican form of government." Among those who testified at the hearings was Caleb S. Layton of Sussex County, who had served in each house of the Delaware legislature, as Delaware's secretary of state, and, for eight years, as an associate justice of the Superior Court. Layton was asked about the prospects for reform in Delaware.

> Q. From your knowledge of the prevailing opinion and prejudice in the counties of Kent and Sussex, do you think it probable that these disabilities to which the blacks are subjected will be removed by your legislature?
>
> A. I do not think they will.
>
> Q. From the prevailing opinion of those two counties, do you think there is any hope that they would authorize a convention of the people of the State, with delegates apportioned according to the population of the State?
>
> A. That has been tried so frequently that I do not think any relief can be expected from that source. We had a convention about 1852 or '53. That question then came up, but Kent and Sussex combined against New Castle and overruled her. Then in the legislature there have been several efforts since that time made, but in every instance Kent and Sussex combined against New Castle, and the present system of representation has been continued.
>
> Q. If the better informed portion of the population of those counties were disposed to do justice in that particular, would they not, in your opinion, be sustained by the prevailed opinion amongst other clauses?
>
> A. If the intelligent portion of the population, and those who are active politicians, were to unite for the purpose of doing justice in this matter, it is very likely the masses would go with them.
>
> Q. Is such a union probable?
>
> A. I do not think it is.

Four days of similar testimony painted a bleak picture of Delaware politics, but Congress was soon distracted by the impeachment of Andrew Johnson, and nothing came of the hearings.[76]

The Fifteenth Amendment produced shockingly little change in the composition of Delaware's electorate. After it was ratified, it was expected that some 4,500 black voters would be added to the rolls. But only taxpaying residents could vote, and in their return to the Levy Court (the tax collector's report filed with the states' tax agency), Democratic tax collectors routinely listed prospective black voters as "delinquent" or "dead" or as having "left the state." Partly as a consequence, the Republican supporters of black Delawareans were routed in the 1870 elections. Afterward, the *Delaware Gazette* rejoiced that "Negroism is dead and buried forever. So far as practical effect is concerned, the XVth Amendment is a nullity in Delaware." Newly elected Governor James Ponder told the General Assembly in his inaugural message, "It is a source of gratification to me that I owe my election exclusively to the votes of the white citizens of the State."

In the wake of the elections, U.S. District Attorney Anthony Higgins secured grand jury indictments against the entire Levy Court and several tax collectors; they had conspired, Higgins alleged, to keep black citizens off the voting rolls by misrepresenting their tax status. By wrongly claiming that black voters either had paid no taxes, were delinquent in their taxes, or were not on the assessment list at all, the conspirators succeeded, by Higgins's "low estimate," in unlawfully disqualifying one thousand to fifteen hundred black voters. The 1872 trial of one of the tax collectors, Archibald Given of Wilmington, became something of a *cause célèbre*. The case was certified to circuit court because of the constitutional issues and, according to the order, "the unusual importance of the cases." Presiding at the trial was Supreme Court Justice William Strong. Among the attorneys representing the defendant Given was Senator Thomas F. Bayard, who had secured his seat in the very election at issue. The jury found Given guilty of submitting false returns, and Justice Strong fined him $2,000 plus costs. The Democrats in the Delaware senate immediately passed a bill to pay Given's fine, but on its third reading in the House, the bill was indefinitely postponed.[77]

The Assembly, it evolved, had larger aspirations. Repeating the scene of a decade earlier, federal troops were once again at the Delaware polls in the election of 1872. Their presence, coupled with a weak showing by Democratic presidential candidate Horace Greeley, produced a rare Republican victory, as James R. Lofland of Milford won the congressional race with 52 percent of the vote.

But no state officers were up for election, and the General Assembly remained under control of the Democrats—by a margin of fourteen to seven in the House and by eight to one in the Senate. In 1873, this legislature enacted the Assessment and Collections Laws, a series of measures—perhaps written in part by Bayard—that would secure Democratic control of the state. After the Given conviction, noted the editors of the *North American Review*, in a scathing 1885 essay on the state of political affairs in Delaware, race-specific disenfranchisement was risky: "In order . . . to disqualify the blacks, it was necessary now to disqualify Republicans in general, without distinction of race or color." The *Review* may well have confused the means and motives—it seems at least equally plausible that black voters were targets because they were Republicans—but there was no mistaking the ultimate effect: "there seems no doubt," the *Review* concluded, "that the old Commonwealth of Delaware is substantially in possession of a thoroughly organized band of political conspirators, who have taken it out of the hands of the people, and hold it under their absolute dictation."[78]

The mechanisms were devious. Under the laws, only taxpayers—those with sufficient taxable property to be on the assessment list—were permitted to vote. Tax collectors were obliged to be available at some "public place" to collect taxes from those on the official roll. Prospective voters not otherwise on the tax rolls were required to pay a poll tax and to make a personal application to an assessor, also obliged to be available at some "public place," for enrollment on the assessment list. As a part of this process, each applicant was required to present one affidavit from a freeholder to support the claim of residence. If the applicant received no satisfaction, he could petition the Levy Court.

Under these laws, no outright fraud was needed to disenfranchise black Delawareans. Collectors and assessors selected public places far from black neighborhoods; black applicants found it difficult to find freeholders willing to attest to their residence; and record-keeping "mistakes"—misspelled names, names entered in the wrong records, names that assessors or collectors somehow failed to enter at all—were strictly fatal to voting rights. Little satisfaction, meanwhile, was available from the Levy Court, which was not obligated to actually hear the petitions and which could adjourn at any time without ruling on their merits.

Perhaps the most devious part of the law was its sanction. Once a collector declared a taxpayer delinquent, the taxpayer was to be removed from the assessment list for one year. But that determination was to be made in March, and taxes were collected in February. As a consequence, removal from the list (in March) precluded the taxpayer from paying the coming year's taxes (the next February). The soonest the taxpayer could be restored to the list was in the second February following disqualification. The sanction for alleged delinquency, in effect, was disenfranchisement for twenty-three months.[79]

It was an ingenious scheme, and it worked. After the 1876 election, the *New York Times* reprinted the report of the *Wilmington Commercial*, claiming that more than thirteen thousand persons were disenfranchised by application of the 1873 law. "The Democratic Majority in this State," the front page of the *Times* declared, "is the result and product of fraud."[80] Henry Conrad would write of the law that it, "was clearly designed to make it difficult to get colored men qualified as voters, and those who framed it builded it even better than they knew, as by it the Democratic party was enabled to continue in almost uninterrupted control in the State for twenty-five years after its passage."[81]

The election of 1874 was, in may ways, typical of the Reconstruction era. On August 11 of that year, the Wilmington *Daily Gazette* summarized the upcoming elections this way: "the issue that is pending in Delaware and that is to be settled in November next, by the ballot, comes down to the question . . . Shall the Negroes Govern Delaware?"

The sixth plank of the 1874 Democratic platform was devoted to an assault on the pending civil rights bill, the ill-fated Civil Rights Act of 1875, which would prohibit racial discrimination in public accommodations. It insisted that

> We denounce this wild, cruel, and reckless measure, called the Civil Rights Bill, as grossly violative of the letter and spirit of Federal and State constitutions, and only calculated to sow new seed of discord between the states and the people, and to encourage, if not compel, an intermingling of these races whose essential differences have been marbled and established by Almighty God.

On the eve of the election, the *Delawarean* editorialized, "The American citizen who will not maintain his own race against the Radical party and its negroes and the Civil Rights Bill is utterly unworthy of the glorious heritage which the Revolutionary patriots of the white race staked 'their lives, fortunes, and sacred honor' to obtain for him."

Not one Republican was elected to statewide office in the 1874 elections; Democrats won the congressional, gubernatorial, and every state legislative contest. As a result, the only Republican in the entire state legislature would be a single holdover in the state senate, Leander Riddle. The *Delawarean* celebrated the results:

> Almost alone, we stood up against the cohorts of Radicalism for several years, and when negro suffrage was forced upon us, we hesitated not for a moment, but spurning affiliation politically with the colored race, declared our determination to appeal only to white men for support. No new departure stains our creed or shames our record, and despising the *social equality* proposed by our opponents, we hurled the "Civil Rights Bill" back upon them in this campaign with terrible effect. . . . All hail the Democracy of Delaware. Your state is safe.[82]

Congress passed its civil rights bill, and it went into effect as the Civil Rights Act of 1875. A conservative Supreme Court would strike down the law eight years later, but Delaware recanted far more quickly. Less than two weeks after passage of the act, a bill was introduced in the General Assembly that was designed to effectively nullify the federal ban on discrimination. The law—drafted, debated, and passed by the assembly in a single session—authorized keepers of inns, restaurants, theaters, or places of public amusement to refuse service to persons whose reception or presence "would be offensive to the major part of his customers" or patrons. Public carriers were authorized to assign separate places to such persons, provided, of course, that "the quality of the accommodation shall be equal for all." The law nowhere mentioned race, but it did not need to; the intent and effect were clear. The law would remain on the books until 1963.

The Education of the Freedmen

At the end of the Civil War, educational opportunities were nearly nonexistent for Delaware's black citizens. It was not for lack of effort within the community. In a letter dated October 20, 1865, William H. Turner of Milton advised the *Christian*

Recorder—the official newspaper of the AME Church, and one of the leading voices of black America in the late nineteenth century—as follows:

> You may learn by this that God has not forgotten the poor and despised African race, though we are in Delaware under the frowns of that class of people who hate the colored man. But God has blessed us so much as to enable us to get up a thriving day-school at Milton, which numbers thirty scholars.[83]

The federal Reconstruction effort was focused on the rebel states; originally, for example, the Freedmen's Bureau was to operate only in the states of the vanquished Confederacy. But in 1866, reports of "the Delaware situation" moved Gen. Oliver O. Howard, superintendent of the Bureau, to establish a Bureau-supervised educational district comprised of Delaware, Maryland, and the District of Columbia, and the following year, the Bureau opened an office in Wilmington.

The Freedmen's Bureau contributed several thousand dollars to black education between 1866 and 1870, as much as $6,300 in a single year. It also supervised the efforts of the Delaware Association for the Moral Improvement and Education of the Colored People, a private philanthropic society established in 1867. With support from the Bureau, and a number of white benefactors in Delaware and around the world, the Delaware Association established thirty-two schools for black children during the Reconstruction era: only seven such schools—three in Wilmington, two in Camden, and one each in Newport and Odessa—predated its efforts. Enrollment in the schools swelled to 1,200. Black residents, meanwhile, formed the Howard Fund to raise money for the tuition of poor students; the Fund had 400 members by 1870. As a result of the effort, it appears that no child ever was denied instruction because of an inability to pay.

Most white Delawareans, it seems, were not opposed to such efforts. Caleb S. Layton testified during the congressional hearings of 1867 that "as far as I know, . . . to a man, all who are called Republicans are in favor of the education of the colored people, and a very large number of those in the other party." "I have heard many Democrats very frankly say," he continued, "that they could see no reason why the colored people should not be educated, because as citizens education would make them more intelligent, and better citizens."[84]

But the state did nothing to assist black education, though it did not hesitate to collect taxes from the community. In 1867, the *Christian Recorder* editorialized as follows:

> The State's authorities have made no provision for the education of the colored population, but they are careful to tax them to the fullest extent to educate poor white children, and to support other Institutions of the State.
>
> The true friends of our race are, however, doing an excellent work in this State, by building school houses and establishing schools with funds contributed by the benevolent, and assisted by the efforts of men of color.
>
> The colored children are thus being educated. This is good; but then it is to be hoped that the people of the Diamond State will soon learn that the diffusion of knowledge is the only true basis for the perpetuity of the State and the development of her resources. Ignorance will never build up an enlightened State, nor will it make strong the ties binding the different members of the

> compact together; but let education and enlightenment be placed within the reach of all, and the result will be that an aristocracy will not govern the mass, but every man will be a ruler and take a deep and abiding interest in the success of every department of the State. There is no greater mistake than that "policy" which does not provide for the education of the masses.[85]

But the situation did not much improve. The Freedman's Bureau awarded its last grant to Delaware in 1870. Philanthropic grants, meanwhile, diminished as Reconstruction wore on. By 1872, the *Christian Recorder* was describing the Delaware Association as "a feeble society." It "does a little for the for the education and moral improvement of the people," the *Recorder* observed, "and but a little. It runs a few schools but the people are obliged to pay a goodly share in their expense and one must pauperize himself and pay in order to share their benefit."[86]

In December 1872, the pastor of the Bethel A.M.E. Church in Wilmington, T. G. Steward, called on black Delawareans to convene in Dover. He identified three concerns in need of immediate address:

> 1st. In that we are excluded from the school provisions made by the State. *Our children do not go to public schools.*
>
> 2nd. In that we are uniformly excluded from the juries of the State and Federal Courts within the State.
>
> 3rd. An unholy prejudice festered by this unfair conduct of the legal authorities excludes us from professions and the mechanic arts, and dooms us inevitably to the hardest work and the lowest wages.[87]

White Republicans objected to Steward's call for a black convention; it should not be "one-sided," they insisted, and should have "no sectorian or selfish object in view." But the convention was held in 1873, and Rev. Steward issued a report for public release. It included the following prayer for relief:

> We specially ask now that equal school rights be afforded us. This we do not ask *merely* as a matter of right, but as a crying necessity-a necessity without which the future of our race appears almost utterly hopeless. . . .
>
> [For] our population of over twenty-thousand souls, or nearly one-fifth of the entire population of the State, the legislature does not provide a solitary school, nor appropriate a single dollar of State money. We hold this discrimination as against the genius of our government; insulting to the laws of Congress; detrimental to the best interests of the State, and outrageous to the colored tax payers.
>
> We say against the spirit of the age, because nonprogressive in its character and in the interests of ignorance; because tending to perpetuate poverty, multiple crime, and aid in human degradation.[88]

Later that year, a bill to provide state support for black schools, supported by a tax on black citizens, failed to advance in the General assembly. Black schools still received no state support, although black taxpayers continued to support white schools. At the end of the legislative session, the *Recorder* editorialized thusly:

> The legislature has adjourned without passing any School Law or passing any general Law of public interest, benefit or importance. It has been engaged during

> the entire session principally upon Divorce Acts and local Cattle Laws; making a specific Cow Law for each school district in the state, it would appear from the immense number of Acts of this sort passed.[89]

In 1875, the threat of federal intervention prompted funding measures for black schools in other states. In Delaware, black citizens—supported by the Delaware Association and energized by a series of sympathetic reports in the *Daily Commercial*, a Republican newspaper—petitioned the Assembly to support black education. The consequent bill provided funding for black schools through the imposition of taxes on black citizens, at a rate of 30 cents per 100 dollars of assessed property. The monies collected would go to the county treasurers, who would in turn give them to the Delaware Association. The law was passed, and Delaware became the only state in the nation to fund its segregated school with segregated revenues.

The Delaware School Act of 1875 was not a monumental success for black education—a result that should not have been surprising and that may well have been intended. The Delaware Association was already struggling to raise funds from the white community; the fact of public funding—even *de minimis* public funding—seemed to sap the remaining enthusiasm for the effort. By the end of 1875, the Association was in debt. Tax monies from the counties were inexplicably delayed, and when the money finally arrived in 1876, it proved sufficient to cover just a third of the schools' operating expenses. The rest of the funding had to be supplied by the black community, in the form of private donations. "The colored schools in the State of Delaware are said to be in a demoralized condition," reported the *Christian Recorder*. "Having appropriated to its own use, the labor of its colored people, it now proceeds to curse their children, with ignorance, because they are poor."[90] The dominant view among white Delawareans, reported Henry C. Conrad, actuary for the Association in the late Reconstruction era, was "that colored people were ignorant and should remain so; that States were not in duty bound to educate them; that if they desired education and advancement they must get them through their own exertions and at their own expense."[91]

The End of Reconstruction

As Reconstruction came to a close—the Hayes-Tilden Compromise of 1877 is typically seen as marking its end—the black citizens of Delaware still waited for it to begin. While the rest of the nation had struggled to overcome its past, official Delaware had seemed content mostly to reimagine it. In Delaware, partisanship had conspired with an overt racism to restore a lost order that never really was. And precisely because this lost order was a myth—elegant, ethereal, unblemished by the complexities and real struggles of Delaware's experience with race—it gained a strong grip on the imagination of too many white Delawareans. Contemporary observers could see it happening. In 1873, the *Recorder* said this of Delaware's ruling party:

> The democracy of this state are the simple old fashioned sort. The rum loving, Negro hating sort who have kept themselves entirely uncontaminated from all

> the modern notions of rights and wrongs, and who hold to the doctrines of the fathers and abhor progressions and improvements. A simple plain and honorable people are they whose principles being few in number are easily learned and easier remembered. In fact, it is the easiest thing in the world to be a Delaware democrat. It is just simply to live "the other and foremost" and think you are going the other way. Put your face on the back of your head and you become a Delaware democrat of most approved pattern.[92]

Three years later, the *Recorder* surveyed the national Reconstruction effort and concluded that "Kentucky and Delaware are yoke fellows in the common work of trying to keep the irrepressible negro down." "[B]ut," the paper promised, "he will come up despite of them."[93]

Jim Crow Delaware: 1877–1950

Since declaring its independence in 1776, the State of Delaware had incrementally but steadily imposed a series of disadvantages on its black citizens. Beginning in the middle part of the nineteenth century, official Delaware—and Delaware's officials—had incrementally and steadily escalated the level of the racist rhetoric used to justify these disadvantages. As the nineteenth century drew to a close, the scheme of disadvantage was so intricate and so pervasive that it had become almost entirely self-perpetuating. The racist rhetoric, meanwhile, was so common and so constant that it must have seemed, to many white Delawareans, both normal and natural. The racial hierarchy, then, was deeply entrenched. The Jim Crow era—for present purposes, from 1877 to 1950—was as a consequence largely a period of stasis, and for black Delawareans, that meant three more generations of oppression.

Jim Crow Law and Politics

As a matter of law, the period from 1877 to 1950 was fairly uneventful. On the one hand, that meant that the legal oppression did not much worsen—an unremarkable fact perhaps, inasmuch as the oppression was already so pervasive that it would have been difficult to make things worse. And yet Delaware tried.

The state's singular legal achievement of the era—the adoption of a new state constitution in 1897—at least altered, if it did not greatly enhance, the disadvantages experienced by black Delawareans. It did so principally in two areas: in its treatment of the franchise and in its treatment of the schools.[94]

Regarding the first, the constitution abandoned the tax prerequisite to voting. On the surface, this may appear to be a welcome reform. In fact, however, the state had simply learned that its tax scheme could no longer ensure the disenfranchisement of unwanted voters. In 1894, John Edward "Gas" Addicks reportedly contributed enough money to keep two thousand Republican voters on the assessment lists, securing an unprecedented Republican victory in that year's statewide elections. And so to reform its election laws, Delaware replaced the tax prerequisite with a literacy test: prospective voters needed to demonstrate an ability to write their name and to read the Delaware constitution. Even a good faith application of this standard—which, of course, was neither anticipated nor effected—would have had a dramatic impact on black voters. Heroic efforts from within the black community had radically reduced illiteracy, which was nearly universal in the community in mid-century, but at century's end, roughly half the black population still remained illiterate.

As for the schools, Article X of the constitution mandated that "separate schools for white and colored children shall be maintained." That provision did not much alter the standing practices, but the movement to constitutionally mandated de jure segregation had the effect both of stifling prospective reform efforts and of eliminating any local options. The constitution also provided that, in apportioning funds, "no distinction shall be made on account of race or color," but that language did no more than bring the document into compliance with the empty rule of *Plessy v. Ferguson*, and its substance was never honored.

But if it is true, on the one hand, that legal oppression did not greatly increase in the Jim Crow era, it is equally true, on the other hand, that the era saw—with one notable exception—no improvement in the legal status of black Delawareans. Partly this was a reflection of their political status. Through the latter half of the nineteenth century, the Democratic leadership of the state—the Bayards, the Saulsburys, and others—acted, in the words of John Munroe, "like feudal lords of this little principality, resolved to keep the peasants—if they were black—in their place and to prevent them from being made use of by the nouveau riche Republican merchants and manufacturers of the cities."[95]

North American Review magazine sent an investigator to Delaware in 1885, who reported that "there is no doubt whatever that a very large part of the citizens of Delaware, belonging to one of its great political parties, are as thoroughly disenfranchised, by legal chicanery, as any community of negroes in Mississippi were ever disenfranchised by political intimidation." "There seems to be no doubt," the report continued, "that the Commonwealth of Delaware is substantially in possession of a thoroughly organized band of political conspirators, who have taken it out of the hands of the people, and hold it under their own absolute dictation." The *American* magazine published its own survey of American political life the following year: only Delaware, it concluded, "maintains so composedly and so contentedly the usages and ideas of the mediaeval period of American politics."[96]

Black Delawareans had a particularly difficult time acquiring and exercising power in this political scheme. For much of the era, the Democratic party would have nothing to do with them—nothing positive, at least. The Republican party was thus the only game in town. But black political leaders, to a much larger extent than the leaders of other ethnic groups, were generally excluded from the Republican party machinery. Other ethnic leaders—in the Irish and German communities, for example—could be relied upon to deliver substantial blocs of votes from discrete wards. But black leaders, whose constituents were widely scattered and widely disenfranchised, had no such leverage. Even the most menial patronage jobs were thus denied them. In 1891, Carol Hoffecker reports, "The Republican-dominated county government rejected two black political leaders for janitorial positions on the grounds that blacks became 'stuck-up' when they held government jobs."[97]

The turn of the century brought some modest change. In 1901, Thomas E. Postles, a black businessman, was elected to Wilmington's City Council. That same year, Delaware for the first time appointed one of its black citizens to a state position, when Governor John Hunn hired John Barclay to work in the State House, as a janitor. The NAACP opened a chapter in Wilmington in 1912, which, in time, would make possible a consolidation and coordination of efforts on behalf of black Delawareans.

The most significant change, perhaps, occurred in national politics, when the national Democratic Party began to compete for black votes. Black Delawareans—like poor and working-class people around the nation—responded favorably to Franklin Roosevelt's New Deal. The state Democratic party had remained hostile to the black electorate through the 1920s, but in 1932, the Delaware Democrats deleted all racial references from their party rules. Black Delawareans, to be sure, remained justifiably suspicious of local Democrats, but the absolute monopoly on their loyalty once claimed by the Republican Party was at last clearly broken.

Still, change in Delaware was almost immeasurably slow. As late as 1947, black Delawareans were almost invisible at the legislative hall: of fifty-three appointed positions, they held just one, as a messenger (they also held a number of janitorial positions). Of the twenty-three positions in the Department of Education in 1947, none were held by black Delawareans. One member of the seven-member Board of Health was black. There were about forty other official state boards, with more than 250 members, but none were black. Delaware employed one hundred state highway policemen in 1947; none were black. Of the thirty-six county officers in 1947, none were black. And no black Delawarean served in the legislature until 1948, when William J. Winchester, a Wilmington businessman, was elected to the House as a Republican.[98]

The legislative processes were effectively closed to black Delawareans for most of the Jim Crow era. The courts, meanwhile, afforded little relief. There were no black lawyers in Delaware until 1928, when Louis Redding was admitted to the bar. He was Delaware's only black member of the bar until 1956.[99] No civil laws afforded protection against private discrimination; indeed, the 1875 nuisance law continued to sanction it. The criminal justice system, meanwhile, offered punishments to black citizens, but little protection. In 1880, the U.S. Supreme Court ruled in *Neal v. Delaware* that the failure to include black citizens in the jury pool violated the Fourteenth Amendment. The following year, a black man—Moses America—was summoned for jury duty, but for the most part, the mandate of *Neal* would be ignored. The de jure discrimination against black criminal defendants was a part of the past, but de facto discrimination remained a very real part of the present. Delaware, alone in the nation, retained a whipping post for punishment, and employed it through 1952. Between 1900 and 1942, 1,320 individuals received whippings; of these, at least 66.2 percent were black.[100]

Private racial violence, by remarkable contrast, seems to have been much less pervasive in Delaware than it was elsewhere. The Klan was present—at times noisily so—but there is no record of Klan violence against black Delawareans. Jim Crow Delaware, in fact, seems to have suffered just one racially motivated lynching. In 1903, a black man named George White was accused of the rape and murder of a white girl and detained in the New Castle County Workhouse. On the evening of June 21, Rev. Robert A. Elwood of the Olivet Presbyterian Church—preaching from a pulpit "festooned with bloodtstained weeds purportedly" from the scene of the crime—"urged his flock to take the law into its own hands." They did. The next day, a mob overwhelmed the workhouse, dragged White to a nearby field, and burned him at the stake. No one was prosecuted; Elwood received a mild censure from the New Castle Presbytery.[101]

Jim Crow Schools and Jobs

The one significant bit of progress in the Jim Crow era occurred in education. The situation was bleak in the late nineteenth century. On May 26, 1881, a fifteen-year-old black girl named Clara V. Davis, who had recently moved to Kent County from Philadelphia, wrote a letter to the *Christian Recorder.* "I like Delaware," she wrote, "all but the schools, for there is only a very little chance to learn any thing at school here."[102] The year of her letter, ironically, was the year of the state's first direct appropriation for the education of its black students in the grand sum of $2,400.

The following year, the Reverend T. G. Steward, pastor of Bethel A.M.E. Church in Wilmington, published an indictment of the state's segregated schools in the *Recorder*. What does it mean to call these schools "mixed schools," he asked; what precisely is mixed, all of us "being children of one common Father, God—all possessed of the same qualities and powers of emotion and expression and of intelligent capabilities found nowhere else except among men. When the lip of prejudice refers to mixing the schools, he asks, not 'what do you mean?' knowing that there is nothing can be meant; but 'what do you think you mean?'" "What can our lawmakers mean," he continued, "by the term 'public schools,' since the colored citizens are debarred their use? Common humanity is one. There can be no severing of the interests of a portion without injury to all."[103]

The Delaware legislature responded modestly to this and other entreaties. In 1883 the appropriation to black schools doubled to $5,000; in 1887 it increased to $6,000; in 1891, to $9,000. Put in perspective, the state's contribution to the education of 5,542 black children in eighty-five different schools in 1890 was just over one dollar per child per year. There was no college for black students and only one such high school in the entire state. Many of the schools were one-room shanties. Perhaps the clearest evidence of the disparity between black and white education in the era is to be found in the length of the school term: in 1887, the average term for white students was 8.4 months; for black students, it was 4.7 months.

As the twentieth century progressed, the education of black Delawareans remained largely stagnant. In 1917, black families were paying school tax rates that were three times as high as those for white families, but they were getting little for their sacrifice. The schools—there were now 108 of them—were "dilapidated and poorly heated," overcrowded, and had no or very poor sanitary facilities. Their teachers were still woefully underpaid, earning just $315 a year. A second high school had opened in Dover, in conjunction with opening of the black college, but high school remained a rare privilege: the combined enrollment in the two black high schools was 135, and of these just 82 were Delaware citizens.[104]

But 1917 brought the promise of change. The state's leading industrialist, Pierre S. du Pont, was also the leading Progressive. Believing that public education was the key to progress, and believing, with very good reason, that Delaware's system of education was, for all students, among the most backward in the nation, du Pont organized an effort to reform the schools. He donated massive sums to improvement through his philanthropic organization, Delaware Service Citizens, and invested massive political capital in generating public support for a fully funded, state-supported system. In an effort to preempt at least one set of objections, du Pont offered to donate all the sums needed to build new schools for black students, with no attendant taxpayer expense.

Yet objections could not be preempted. As Alice Dunbar Nelson wrote,

> When Pierre S. du Pont came forward in 1917 with a proposition to raise Delaware's educational standard and bring her up from the thirty-seventh place in the educational roster of the states he was bitterly opposed by the farmers, who saw in his scheme an infringement of their ancient and honorable rights of working children on their farms; by the canning factories, of which there are legion, who foresaw in compulsory education a curtailment of the cheap child labor, which has made the canning of tomatoes, peas, and crab meat profitable; by the illiterates, who foresaw a raise in taxes that would not benefit them directly, and by the demagogues, who raised the howl of white people being taxed to "educate niggers."[105]

But the demagogues lost this battle. Delaware's 1921 education law created a genuine public school system, and it required an equivalent education for the state's black and white students. True to his word, du Pont contributed more than $2.6 million to the construction of new black schools; his total contribution to the education project was estimated at $10 million.

It was a start. But providing a genuinely equal education for black and white students would require an ongoing commitment, and there was none. The segregated schools, in fact, were never equal, and neither, as a result, were the educational opportunities. The large majority of black students still attended one-teacher schools scattered about the state; high school opportunities were still remote. A 1923 study of "negro school attendance" determined that the number of high school students was "so small and high school opportunities so far removed from the homes of pupils that the attendance and absence records of school pupils have been omitted from the tables of this book."[106]

In 1940, more than a third of black Delawareans over the age of twenty-five had less than five years of formal schooling. Howard High School, Wilmington's only high school for black students, was built to accommodate 750 students; 1,039 were enrolled there in 1946. Between 1938 and 1942, the school graduated 416 students; of that number, 37 went to college out of state, and in a statistic that speaks volumes, of that 37, just 5 returned to Delaware. In 1946, thirty-four of the black schools still had just one teacher; fifteen of these one-teacher schools were home to the first through eighth grades. Inequities continued to abound—in teacher salaries, curricula, facilities, materials. The state of education was, undeniably, better than it once was. But it was a long, long way from equal.[107]

The story of higher education is similar. The 1890 federal legislation for land-grant colleges required some apportionment of funds for black students. In response, in 1891, the state chartered the State College for Colored Students, to be located in Dover. The college, struggling to overcome the same obstacles that confronted other black schools in Delaware, received a boost from Pierre S. du Pont, who funded the construction of new buildings on the campus; by 1932, a half-century after it opened, the school was able to offer for the first time a four-year bachelor's degree program. The first baccalaureates graduated in 1934; there were five of them. But the du Pont money did not last. In 1948, the school—which had changed its name the preceding year to Delaware State College—was so underfunded that it lost its accreditation.[108]

Such was the progress for black Delawareans, in the age of Jim Crow.

In all other respects, the Jim Crow era was largely a continuation of the past. In 1890, 9,639 black Delawareans worked as unskilled laborers. By contrast, just 393 held jobs as skilled or semi-skilled workers, and just 53 worked as professionals, 43 as teachers. Put in other terms, black Delawareans comprised 16.8 percent of the state's population, but 42.5 percent of its unskilled laborers, just 3.1 percent of its skilled and semi-skilled workers, and only 2.5 percent of its professionals.[109]

Black workers, of course, were not the only ones to face prejudice. An 1888 article in the *Wilmington Every Evening* noted of Delaware's Italians, "As labor they are cheap and easily controlled and that is the reason they are here." Two months later, the Wilmington City Council unanimously adopted a resolution condemning the employment of Italians and Hungarians on public work projects. But over time, European ethnic groups would gain access to power—to political power as a distinct voting bloc and to economic power through unions. But union membership—the key to industrial employment in the late nineteenth and early twentieth century—was not available to black workers; many national unions restricted their participation, and many locals barred them altogether. Black workers were forced to accept unskilled low-wage jobs, were viewed by unions as unskilled competitors undermining their bargaining power, and were thus locked in a vicious cycle of underemployment.

In 1956, Jerome Holland, president of Delaware State College, reported his study of more than a half-century's worth of economic data. For black Delawareans, he concluded, the employment patterns of 1890 would remain essentially unchanged for the next sixty years. In 1940, black workers comprised 43.2 percent of the state's unskilled laborers, but 5.3 percent of its semi-skilled and skilled workers, and just 2.2 percent of its professionals, proportions nearly identical to those in 1890. The single notable change in the period was in the role of organized labor, which by mid-century had become, according to Pauline Young, "the most recognizable force working toward integration in private employment."[110]

Jim Crow Delawareans

In some respects, Jim Crow Delaware combined the worst of the northern and southern racial experience. As historian Jacqueline Jones puts it, "The state's peculiar power structure, based on an unholy alliance between upstate corporate money (centered in Wilmington) and downstate rural interests (dispersed through Kent and Sussex counties) had produced an intriguing hybrid, blending the worst of the Deep South's de jure discrimination with the worst of the North's de facto hypocrisy."[111]

But the segregation that ruled Delaware's politics, its law, its schools, and its economy was much less complete in the realm of the social, in the daily life of Delaware's people. The 1875 nuisance law that countenanced segregation allowed for significant variation, and by 1950 there was plenty. Part of this was regional: segregation was more prevalent in the lower two counties. Part of it seems quite haphazard: the libraries were no longer segregated in 1950, and neither were the trains and buses; restaurants were still largely segregated; some movie theaters were segregated, some were not; and most churches were segregated, but some were not.

In 1943, Wilmington Friends school scheduled a basketball game against the city's black high school, Howard High. The city's leading Catholic school, Salesianum, followed shortly, and then so did the white public schools. That progression, perhaps, offers a powerful metaphor.[112]

The people of Delaware—not the capital "P" abstraction of political rhetoric, but the small "p" people, the real folks who have lived here—tell a different story about race, different from the one told by the state's political leaders, different from the one memorialized in the state's laws. Consider these Delaware voices—recorded by historian Jeanne D. Nutter—of African Americans who grew up in Jim Crow Delaware.[113]

Listen to Marjorie Wright Scott, of Wilmington:

> We got along very well with [white people]. I used to play with—there was an apartment house across the street from where I lived. And I remember I had a girlfriend named Audrey Murray, who was white. And we were very friendly, and we didn't have any arguments, and there were white people down French Street. . . . There were Jewish stores, one at Thirteenth and Walnut and one at Kennebeck Street. The owners were very nice to black people. We never had any problems with them. They were very friendly at that time. . . . [We] never really had any big fusses about race that I can remember. I didn't really become aware of that until I was much older.

Here is how Howard K. Toliver, of Wilmington, remembers his childhood:

> We lived on Eighth Street and we lived in an Italian neighborhood. The people there were really good to us. . . . Most of the time I lived out on the "Hill." We played with them—played football with the Italians—but couldn't go to school with them.

Robert J. Fleming Jr., of Wilmington, shares these memories:

> We had a lot of fun together and although we were being segregated, we really didn't let it bother us that much. We were raised with the Italians and we got along fine. They would always say, "How come you all go to a different school?" And I said, "Well, this is just the way it is." But we'd come home from school. We would go out on the playgrounds and play together . . . we had a very close association of not only the black children but the blacks and whites at that time on the West Side.

Gladys Green Clark, of New Castle, recalls her childhood this way:

Well, as a child, the neighborhood I lived in has always been a mixed neighborhood. We had Irish, Italians, and of course we were called "colored" at that time. And we all played together, and we didn't have any problems at that time, racially, because as I said, the neighborhood we lived in has always been mixed.

Listen to Doris Lydia Camper Crommarte, of Newport:

[In 1954] Representatives from all the high schools in the state . . . gathered for one week for a music camp [in Dover]. . . . I believe there was like 104, something like that, of the white children there. There were only six black Americans, and then about three of them dropped out. So there were only about three of us I think by the time it was all over. . . . But by being raised in an all-white community, we used to live down in Newport before we moved up to Cedar Heights, and of course there were only just a handful of black children that lived down there in Newport and we were raised down there until we went to high school. So there was no problem as far as me mingling. To me it was just wonderful. I had no problems at all mingling. . . . [One] thing I do remember. We had recreational time when we weren't practicing. So a group of us decided to walk to town. We were within walking distance, to go to the movies. There were our white friends along with us. When we got there to pay for our tickets, the lady was ushering me to go around the side. I didn't quite understand what she meant. What it was, the black people were supposed to go around the side and up the steps up to a balcony. Black people had to sit up in the balcony, and the white people could go inside the regular door. It shocked me because I had never experienced anything like that. And of course, all my little white friends . . . they said "Hey we'll all go." And they went . . . we all went together. And we all went up to the balcony. . . . They were going to separate our friends from us. And we had to go up, and they had to go down, but they chose to go up with us.

Clifton Alvin Lewis, of Newark, shares these memories:

I came to be the first black to play American Legion Baseball. I was about thirteen or fourteen. With the guys in Newark, it was no problem, 'cause many of them I knew. There was a white boy from New Castle, a boy named Sutton, who became a good friend of mine, so I didn't have any problems with them. I had problems when I went out to Conrad and played. I had trouble with some of the teams from downstate, when I played against them. . . . But I didn't have to say anything. I didn't have to fight for myself. The Gregg boys (who lived not far from me), [their] mother, a short Irish woman, she follows every game. I remember we were playing Conrad and I came up to bat. I got, "Nigger this and nigger that." All this you know while I'm trying to get my composure. And she came down out of the stands and grabbed two bats. She went up in the stands to this guy and said, "If you say anything else to him, I'm gonna hit you in the head with these bats. If I wanted to, I could turn him loose on you and he'd whip you but he's tryin' to do the right thing. But I'm gonna take up for him." . . . It was a strange town. Newark was a strange town. The blacks lived here, the white lived there, but there was more harmony than it was anything else. I guess it might have been more harmony than in any small town in Delaware.

Here is what Robert George Harding, of Delaware City, remembers:

> Delaware City was very friendly. At a time when I was a youngster, if boys would come from New Castle and things like that, and if they started something with us, the white boys would run them out of town, you know. You basically had this kind of relationship. Kennard and I played ball with all the white boys whenever they had a game or something. They'd call Kennard and I to play ball with them. It was just a nice town. Everybody knew everyone. All the adults would correct the children, white or black it didn't matter, you know. So basically, it was a good town to grow up in.

And, finally, William Pell Wallace, of Wilmington, recalls the following:

> We had Italians, Irish, Polish people. Generally, you got along with them. As youngsters, we played in the street, it was just that you knew you couldn't go to their schools. You couldn't go to their theaters. But when you were in the streets, you played and you knew their families and they knew yours and usually the families got along very well. It was just that segregation which was the law at that time didn't allow you to get to know them any better or any differently.

Conclusion

In 1950, the final year of this survey, Chancellor Seitz ordered the desegregation of the University of Delaware. The university did not appeal his order; it had seen it coming, and it was prepared. In that same year, Sallesianum High School admitted five black students.

The story of race in Delaware does not, of course, end in 1950. In 1951, the Wilmington YMCA opened its cafeteria to all races, and the Delaware National Guard admitted its first black members. In 1952, the rest of the Catholic parochial schools desegregated; in 1953, the Hotel du Pont opened to all races.

But desegregation did not follow in a rapid or steady progression. In 1968, eighteen years after Chancellor Seitz ordered the desegregation of the University of Delaware, black students were still assigned to segregated dorms. Incredibly, they comprised barely 1 percent of the school's student body. Black students staged a protest. A faculty commission acknowledged the inequalities and called for remedy. Yet still in 2006, the College Board reported that only 5 percent of the university's entering class was black, despite black Delawareans comprising 20 percent of the state's population.

Chancellor Seitz ordered the desegregation of two of Delaware's public schools in 1952, an order eventually affirmed by the Supreme Court as part of *Brown v. Board of Education*. The schools immediately affected by the order did in fact desegregate and did so largely without incident. For the rest of the public schools, the desegregation effort was frustrated by what might be termed the "passive resistance" of the Delaware legislature. Less overt and hysterical than the resistance in the old Confederacy, it was effective all the same, preserving segregation in the schools through reliance on residential segregation and the artificial boundaries of the preexisting school districts. Finally, in 1976, the federal courts ordered the consolidation of New Castle County's school districts to effectuate real desegregation. Two years later, Judge Murray M. Schwartz fashioned a remedy that included inter-neighborhood busing. Much violence was predicted, and official Delaware seemed surprised when the schools desegregated peacefully.

Yet that official resistance never ended. In 1995, the State Board of Education secured an order from the local federal judge terminating the desegregation decree. The school districts remained plagued by racial inequalities within and between schools, but the judge—following the mild standard set forth by an increasingly conservative Supreme Court—ruled that the vestiges of segregation had been eliminated "to the extent practicable."

The local school districts were free to revise their attendance zones, to stop busing, and, in effect, to resegregate their schools. But they did not. They chose to keep their schools desegregated.

And so the Delaware legislature intervened. A proposed Neighborhood Schools Bill targeted the four New Castle County school districts that had operated under the desegregation decree. Those districts were required to develop "neighborhood schools plans" that assigned students to the school nearest their home. The law would end busing and prohibit the consideration of race in student assignments. The bill, according to a local newspaper columnist, "came about because some parents and lawmakers were frustrated that school busing didn't disappear after the federal court lifted its desegregation order."[114]

There was in fact little pressure for such a bill, and when it was pending, it generated no widespread popular support. As the *Delaware News Journal* noted, "Despite the contentions of state Rep. Wayne Smith, the principal advocate of neighborhood schools, that they are heavily favored, the evidence says otherwise."[115] Indeed, most parents, black and white, seemed quite supportive of their local school boards and quite content with the status quo. "It's the same old story," said State Senate Majority Whip Harris B. McDowell III (D-Wilmington North). "You've got a bunch of suburbanites who are trying to make their schools as lily white as possible. They haven't been able to get the schools to do anything about it, so now they're trying us."[116]

The opposition was intense, especially from the local paper, which regularly editorialized against the bill.[117] But the bill passed easily. The vote in the State Senate was 18-2; in the House, 36-3. The governor, Tom Carper, signed the bill into law as the Neighborhood Schools Act of 2000.

Opposition to the neighborhood schools scheme remained intense; the focus simply shifted to the local school districts. As they devised their Neighborhood School Plan, members of the Christina School District's Neighborhood Schools Committee held a public meeting with state legislators. "My stomach hurts," reported committee member Ruth Kelly. "If I lived in Wilmington, I'd be so upset. This bill is not going to serve city kids. It's going to resegregate the schools. It doesn't make me happy."[118] The Colonial School District struggled with its plan. "Twenty years ago, we went through all of this," said Gary L. Walker, Colonial School Board member. "Separate but equal is not good. A lot of families got really disturbed about it. Emotions got really high. We worked through that. We got a program that seems to be working. Why do we want to put ourselves through all that again?" "I want to know why they want to change it," said Will Pharis, a sixteen-year-old student at Glasgow High. "Kids aren't complaining about it. They should leave things the way they are."[119]

The most organized opposition developed in the Brandywine School District, home district of the law's chief sponsor, Wayne Smith. There, parents, students, and other district residents formed a community group—the Kids in Diverse Schools Coalition (KIDS)—determined to secure approval of a student assignment plan like the one already in place, one that maintained racially and economically diverse schools. "I prefer that my kids be in a school environment that reflects their society," explained KIDS co-founder Lynne Kielhorn. "I want them exposed to diversity of all kinds."[120] The senior class of the district's Concord High School polled its 175 members to determine their position on the Neighborhood Schools Act; only 7 were in favor of the law. "Many of us," said Concord Senior Kate Bradley, "are outraged."[121]

The Brandywine School Board ultimately submitted the question to district residents: do they favor keeping the existing student assignment patterns, or do they favor a "neighborhood schools" plan? Turnout at the special election was large—roughly 50 percent greater than at the last school board election—and by more than a two-to-one margin, the voters favored the existing pattern. The neighborhood schools plan was in fact rejected by a majority of voters at each of the nineteen polling places in the district.[122] "Obviously, I lost in the Brandywine School District," noted a chagrined Wayne Smith. "Good legislators sometimes lose. It is difficult to move the status quo. But I believe those who elect us want to know they have a legislator willing try to move that status quo if that is what people want."[123]

The great tragedy, of course, is that legislators too often do what the people manifestly do *not* want. That has been true very often in the history of race in Delaware, and it true in the case of the Neighborhood Schools Act. Neither before nor after adoption of the Act have the people of Delaware supported it.[124]

And most Delawareans refused to accept it. In the end, three of the four districts submitted plans to the State Board of Education that openly resisted the resegregation that would inevitably follow from adherence to the Neighborhood Schools Act. One district was brought into grudging compliance when its third submitted plan was approved by the board. A second district suffered two rejections and, at this writing, continues to operate without an approved plan. In the third district, the Brandywine School District, a compelling presentation to the board won approval of a plan that effectively maintained the desegregated status quo. "High poverty schools," the board was compelled to conclude, "even high poverty neighborhood schools, are not fair and equitable to the children attending them."

But reform from the bottom up is difficult, especially when so little seems to change at the top. Nearly a century and a half has passed since the onset of Reconstruction, and Delaware still has not been represented by a black senator or congressperson, still has not been led by a black governor or lieutenant governor, still has not seated a black justice to the bench of its Supreme Court. More than half of Wilmington's population is African American, but in 2005, the

National Association of Law Placement reported that more than 92 percent of the associates at Wilmington's big law firms were white; of the partners, more than 99 percent were white. In its examination of large law firms in the forty-one cities in the country with the largest attorney populations, the organization concluded that the firms in Wilmington, Delaware, were the least racially diverse.[125]

Epilogue

This fall, I took my son to see my old high school play football. It was a fun day. The players were much smaller than I expected, and slower, and, standing on the sidelines with their helmets off, seemed much, much younger than the guys I played with. Memory, I suppose, is funny that way. What is certainly a fact, though, is that the team is much more racially diverse than mine was—a third of these kids, maybe even half, were black.

I felt glad about that and glad that my son could see it. Someday—but not yet—I will show him my high school yearbook. And someday—but not yet—I will take him to the place where I teach. They have this in common: nearly every face he would see would be white. I am not quite ready to explain that to him. After all, he just turned six. And to his very great credit, I do not think he would know what I mean.

Notes

1. John A. Munroe, *History of Delaware* 18–53 (University of Delaware Press, 2001).

2. C. A. Weslager, *The Indians of Delaware*, in *Delaware: A History of the First State* 44, ed. H. Clay Reed (Lewis Historical, 1947)

3. *Id.* at 42–51; C. A. Weslager, *The Delaware Indians: A History* 123 (Rutgers University Press, 2003); Munroe, *History of Delaware*, at 15–18.

4. *Id.*

5. Carol E. Hoffecker, *Delaware: A Bicentennial History* 90 (W. W. Norton, 1977).

6. William H. Williams, *Slavery and Freedom in Delaware, 1639–1865* 2–3 (Scholarly Resources, 1996).

7. Patience Essah, *A House Divided: Slavery and Emancipation in Delaware, 1638–1865* (University Press of Virginia, 1996); *Proceedings of the Assembly of the Lower Counties on Delaware 1770–1776, of the Constitutional Convention of 1776, and of the House of Assembly of the Delaware State 1776–1781* 180, 223, ed. Claudia L. Bushman et al. (University of Delaware Press, 1986); Charles N. Lanier Jr., *Labor in Delaware*, in Reed, *Delaware*, at 551.

8. Williams, *Slavery and Freedom*, at 9.

9. *Id.* at 1–2, 41.

10. Williams, *Slavery and Freedom*, at 18–20. See also Ira Berlin, *Many Thousands Gone: The First Two Centuries of Slavery in North America* 110–11 (Belknap, 1998), describing the same demographic shift throughout the Chesapeake region.

11. Robert L. Hayman Jr., *The Smart Culture: Society, Intelligence, and Law* 139–42 (New York University Press, 2000); *The Negro in Delaware: Legal Status*, in Reed, *Delaware*, at 571.

12. See, e.g.,Williams, *Slavery and Freedom*, at 18: "the development of legal and social guidelines for the treatment of blacks was a gradual process shaped by practical considerations and the accepted values of the eighteenth-century Anglo-Saxon world."

13. Thomas J. Scharf, *History of Delaware, 1609–1888* 519 (L. J. Richards, 1888).

14. Williams, *Slavery and Freedom*, at 23.

15. Harold B. Hancock, *The Indenture System in Delaware, 1681–1921*, 16 Delaware History 47, 50 (1974).

16. Munroe, *History of Delaware*, at 60; Essah, *House Divided*, at 69; Williams, *Slavery and Freedom*, at 44.

17. Essah, *House Divided*, at 43–46, 56–59; Williams, *Slavery and Freedom*, at 147, 152.

18. Monte A. Calvert, *The Abolition Society of Delaware, 1801–1807*, 10 Delaware History 295, 299 (1963); Priscilla Thompson, *Harriet Tubman, Thomas Garrett, and the Underground Railroad*, 22 Delaware History 1, 10–11 (1986).

19. *Proceedings of the House of Assembly of the Delaware State 1781–1792*, at 98.

20. *Id.* at 314.

21. Essah, *House Divided*, at 40–41; Bruce Bendler, *Securing One of the Blessings of Liberty: Black Families in Lower New Castle County, 1790–1850*, 25 Delaware History 237 (1993); Harold B. Hancock, *The Status of the Negro in Delaware After the Civil War, 1865–1875*, 13 Delaware History 57 (1968).

22. Essah, *House Divided*, at 7–8, 39; Munroe, *History of Delaware*, at 97; Williams, *Slavery and Freedom*, at 186; Robert Graham Caldwell, *Red Hannah: Delaware's Whipping Post* 122 (University. of Pennsylvania Press, 1947).

23. National Era (Washington, DC), Vol. 1, No. 9, p. 3, March 4, 1847.

24. National Era (Washington, DC), Vol. 7, No. 396, p. 122, Aug. 3, 1854.

25. Hoffecker, *Delaware*, at 95; Williams, *Slavery and Freedom*, at 172–73.

26. Williams, *Slavery and Freedom*, at 238.

27. Scharf, *History of Delaware*, at 1314.

28. *Delaware: A Guide to the First State* 366–68, ed. Jeannette Eckman et al. (Viking, 1938).

29. James A. McGowan, *Station Master on the Underground Railroad: The Life and Letters of Thomas Garrett* 48–65, 168 (Whimsie, 1977); Priscilla Thompson, *Harriet Tubman, Thomas Garrett, and the Underground Railroad*, at 21.

30. Bendler, *Securing One of the Blessings of Liberty*, at 249–50.

31. Williams, *Slavery and Freedom*, at 223–32.

32. Munroe, *History of Delaware*, at 91–94.

33. Charles R. Harris, *From Apathy to Awareness: The Contributions of Willard Hall to Delaware Education* 52 (Dorrance, 1968).

34. *Letter from William Yates, Esq.*, Colored American (New York), Aug. 12, 1837.

35. *A Horrible Picture*, Colored American (New York), March 9, 1839.

36. North Star, Jan. 5, 1849.

37. Williams, *Slavery and Freedom*, at 195; Essah, *House Divided*, at 128.

38. Bushman, *Proceedings of the House of Assembly*, at 338.

39. The state of black suffrage in colonial Delaware remains ambiguous. Compare Maurice A. Hartnett III, *Delaware's Charters and Prior Constitutions*, in *The Delaware Constitution of 1897: The First One Hundred Years* 29, ed. Randy J. Holland et al. (Delaware State Bar Assoc., 1997) ("This somewhat surreptitiously limited the franchise to white male Christians who owned land or other property worth forty pounds") with Munroe, *History of Delaware*, at 49, 83 (noting the possibility that free blacks may have voted in the colonial era). Testifying before a congressional committee in 1867, Caleb S. Layton—Delaware legislator, secretary of state, and judge—indicated that "[t]he time was, I believe, when the colored people did vote in our State; but I think not since June 1792." "I am under the impression and believe that they voted in what was called the three lower counties of Delaware when we were a part and parcel of Penn." *Records of the Judiciary Committee Relating to the*

Investigation of Conditions in Delaware, House of Representatives, 40th Congress, Record Group 233, Legislative branch (National Archives) [hereafter "Investigation of Conditions in Delaware"]. Delaware is not the only state with such ambiguity in its history. Ira Berlin suggests that "the strictures placed on black suffrage [perhaps] best reveal the patchwork nature of colonial regulation of Negro freemen." Ira Berlin, *Slaves Without Masters: The Free Negro in the Antebellum South* 8 (New Press, 1974). Those strictures were in constant flux and were often unclear. See *id.* at 91. Neighboring Pennsylvania, the source of Delaware's early laws, did not explicitly prohibit black suffrage in its early constitutions; the documents appeared to grant the right to all freemen. But in 1836, the Pennsylvania Supreme Court ruled that the franchise was implicitly limited to white men; the constitution of 1838 then made this restriction explicit. Alexander Keyssar, *The Right to Vote: the Contested History of Democracy in the United States* 54–55 (Basic Books, 2000).

40. Richard B. Morris, *The Course of Peonage in a Slave State*, 65 Political Science Quarterly 238, 240–47, 254, 260 (1950).

41. *Id.* at 240.

42. *Id.* at 254.

43. Essah, *House Divided*, at 115; Reed, *Delaware*, at 576; Munroe, *History of Delaware*, at 193; Williams, *Slavery and Freedom*, at 193.

44. Hoffecker, *Delaware*, at 96.

45. Scharf, *History of Delaware*, at 313.

46. Reed, *Delaware*, at 575; Essah, *House Divided*, at 105, 116; Williams, *Slavery and Freedom*, at 194.

47. *Letter from William Yates, Esq.*, Colored American (New York), Aug. 12, 1837.

48. Hoffecker, *Delaware*, at 96; Williams, *Slavery and Freedom*, at 193–94; Reed, *History of Delaware*, at 575.

49. Munroe, *History of Delaware*, at 120; Hartnett, *Delaware's Charters and Prior Constitutions*, at 43.

50. Munroe, *History of Delaware*, at 101.

51. Hoffecker, *Delaware*, at 101.

52. Williams, *Slavery and Freedom*, at 170.

53. National Era (Washington, DC), Vol. 13, No. 665, p. 154, Sept. 29, 1859.

54. Essah, *House Divided*, at 154, 176.

55. Munroe, *History of Delaware*, at 133–34.

56. *Letter of April 29, 1861*, in Charles Callan Tansill, *The Congressional Career of Thomas Francis Bayard, 1869–1885* 12 (Georgetown University Press, 1946).

57. Williams, *Slavery and Freedom*, at 175.

58. *A Colored Minister Fined, Sold, and Bought in the State of Delaware Last Week*, Christian Recorder (Philadelphia), June 25, 1864.

59. Harold C. Livesay, *Delaware Negroes, 1865–1915*, 13 Delaware History 87 (1968).

60. Scharf, *History of Delaware*, at 377, 378–79. A half-century later, incidentally, when the Nineteenth Amendment—enfranchising women—was submitted to the states, Delaware refused to ratify that as well; the state gets high marks for consistency.

61. Cong. Globe, 36th Cong., 1st Sess. 1683 (1860) (statement of Sen. Bayard).

62. Cong. Globe, 38th Cong., 1st Sess. 1158 (1864) (statement of Sen. Saulsbury).

63. Cong. Globe, 40th Cong., 1st Sess. 13 (1867) (statement of Sen. Saulsbury).

64. Cong. Globe, 38th Cong., 1st Sess. 3134 (1864) (statement of Sen. Saulsbury).

65. Cong. Globe, 39th Cong., 1st Sess. 2080–81 (1866) (statement of Rep. Nicholson).

66. Cong. Globe, 40th Cong., 3rd Sess. App. 168 (1869) (statement of Sen. Bayard).

67. Cong. Globe, 40th Cong., 3rd Sess. 1299 (1869) (statement of Sen. Saulsbury); *id.* at 1310 (statement of Sen. Saulsbury).

68. Munroe, *History of Delaware*, at 150.

69. Cong. Globe, 42nd Cong., 2nd Sess. App. 9 (1872) (statement of Sen. Saulsbury).

70. Cong. Globe, 43rd Cong., 1st Sess. 4160 (1874) (statement of Sen. Saulsbury).

71. Cong. Globe, 41st Cong., 2nd Sess. 3803 (1870) (statement of Sen. Bayard).

72. Cong. Globe, 42nd Cong., 2nd Sess. App. 355 (1872) (statement of Sen. Bayard).

73. *Report of the Commissioner of the Freedmen's Bureau, of All Orders Issued by Him or Any Assistant Commissioner*, 39th Cong., 1st Sess., Exec. Doc. No. 70, at 341 (1866) (finding much opposition to black education in Maryland, including the burning of black churches "to prevent schools being opened in them, all showing that negro hate is not by any means confined to the low south").

74. *Reports of the Assistant Commissioners of Freedmen, and a Synopsis of Laws Respecting Persons of Color in the Late Slave States*, 39th Cong., 2nd Sess., S. Exec. Doc. No. 6, at 90 (1867).

75. *Id.* See also Harold B. Hancock, The Status of the Negro in Delaware after the Civil War, 1865–1875, 13 Delaware History 57, 59 (1968); Jacqueline J. Halstead, *The Delaware Association for the Moral Improvement and Education of the Colored People: "Practical Christianity,"* 15 Delaware History 19, 30–31 (1973); Hancock, *supra*, at 65.

76. Scharf, *History of Delaware*, at 538; *Investigation of Conditions in Delaware, supra* note 26.

77. *A Disenfranchised People*, 141 North American Review 600, 602 (1885); Amy H. Hiller, *The Disenfranchisement of Delaware Negroes in the Late Nineteenth Century*, 13 Delaware History 124, 129, 131–37 (1968).

78. *A Disenfranchised People*, at 604.

79. Roger A. Martin, *Delawareans in Congress: The House of Representatives*, Vol. I, 104–6 (Roger A. Martin, 2003); *A Disenfranchised People*, at 603–4; Hiller, *The Disenfranchisement of Delaware Negroes in the Late Nineteenth Century*, at 142.

80. *The Delaware Election*, N.Y. Times, Nov. 12, 1876, at 1.

81. Henry C. Conrad, *History of the State of Delaware: From the Earliest Settlements to the Year 1907* 227 (Henry C. Conrad, 1908).

82. John H. Gauger, *A Delaware Experiment with Reconstruction Nullification*, 21 Delaware History 164, 170–72, 176 (1985).

83. *Milton Circuit, Delaware*, Christian Recorder (Philadelphia), November 4, 1865.

84. Scharf, *History of Delaware*, at 444–46; Halstead, *The Delaware Association for the Moral Improvement and Education of the Colored People: "Practical Christianity,"* at 22–26; *Investigation of Conditions in Delaware.*

85. *Property of Colored Men in Delaware*, Christian Recorder (Philadelphia), Sept. 28, 1867.

86. Halstead, *The Delaware Association*, at 37; *Delaware*, Christian Recorder (Philadelphia), Nov. 9, 1872.

87. Ronald L. Lewis, *Reverend T. G. Steward and the Education of Blacks in Reconstruction Delaware*, 19 Delaware History 156, 163–64 (1981).

88. *Id.*

89. *Delaware*, Christian Recorder (Philadelphia), Apr. 24, 1873.

90. Christian Recorder (Philadelphia), Jan. 27, 1876.

91. Conrad, *History of the State*, at 817; see also Hoffecker, *Delaware: A Bicentennial History*, at 108; Hancock, *The Status of the Negro in Delaware After the Civil War, 1865–1875*, at 63.

92. Henry R. Horsey et al., *The Delaware Constitutional Convention of 1897*, in *The Delaware Constitution of 1897*, at 55, 62–64.

93. *School Notes*, Christian Recorder (Philadelphia), March 16, 1876.

94. Henry R. Horsey et al., *The Delaware Constitutional Convention of 1897*, at 55, 62–64.

95. Munroe, *History of Delaware*, at 153; *A Disenfranchised People*, at 600, 604.

96. Harold Hancock, *Delaware, 1865–1914*, in Reed, *Delaware*, at 185, 187.

97. Carole E. Hoffecker, *The Politics of Exclusion*, at 60, 63–68.

98. See James E. Newton, *Black Americans in Delaware: An Overview*, in *A History of African Americans of Delaware and Maryland's Eastern Shore* 11, 21, ed. Carole C. Marks (Delaware Heritage, 1996); Pauline A. Young, *The Negro in Delaware: Past and Present*, in Reed, *Delaware*, at 581, 597; Munroe, *History of Delaware*, at 211.

99. Joshua W. Martin III, *Minorities in the Delaware Bar*, in *The Delaware Bar in the Twentieth Century* 657, 659, ed. Helen L. Winslow (Delaware State Bar Association, 1994).

100. See Newton, *Black Americans in Delaware: An Overview*, at 21; Caldwell, *Red Hannah: Delaware's Whipping Post*, at 130; Livesay, at 113–14.

101. *Finds Preacher Guilty*, N.Y. Times, Feb. 3, 1904. In the conventional telling of the White lynching, a disgusted group of Delawareans forms their own mob and drives Elwood out of town. This seems to paint, however, an overly sanguine portrait of the state of affairs, according to a recent study by historian Yohuru R. Williams. Yohuru R. Williams, *Permission to Hate: Delaware, Lynching, and the Culture of Violence in America*, 32 J. Black Studies 3 (2001). Williams's study is meant to be corrective, but it may overstate the counter-proposition when it maintains that violence against black Delawareans was common and that there was "an ever-present climate of hate permeating throughout the white community." *Id.* at 6. It remains the case, after all, that the White lynching is exceptional in Delaware's experience. The only significant Klan violence in Delaware, meanwhile, seems to have involved clashes with local Catholics. See J. L. Miller and Lee Williams, *There Have Been Historic Confrontations, But for the Most Part, the Past Is Punctuated with Skirmishes, Not Wars*, News Journal (Wilmington), Feb. 12, 2006, at 12A.

102. *A Letter from a Pastor's Daughter*, Christian Recorder (Philadelphia), May 11, 1882.

103. *Public Schools in Delaware*, Christian Recorder (Philadelphia), Dec. 7, 1882.

104. See Conrad, *History of the State*, at 818; Lyman P. Powell, *The History of Education in Delaware* 170 (Government Printing Office, 1893); Livesay, at 107–8.

105. Young, *The Negro in Delaware: Past and Present*, at 587.

106. Richard Watson Cooper and Hermann Cooper, *Negro School Attendance in Delaware* 8 (University of Delaware Press, 1923).

107. See Hoffecker, *Delaware*, at 110–12; Young, *The Negro in Delaware: Past and Present*, at 581–85, 587; William H. Conner, *Delaware Since 1914*, in Reed, *Delaware*, at 211, 212.

108. Annette Woolard, *Parker v. The University of Delaware: The Desegregation of Higher Education in Delaware*, 22 Delaware History 111, 112–13 (1986).

109. Emma Amuti, *Black Labor in Wilmington: Black Occupational Mobility from 1850 to 1910*, in Marks, *A History of African Americans of Delaware and Maryland's Eastern Shore*, at 173, 182.

110. Young, *Delaware*, at 594–95; see also Hoffecker, *Delaware*, at 116; Livesay, at 99–101.

111. Jacqueline Jones, *Creek Walking: Growing Up in Delaware in the 1950s* 133 (University of Delaware Press, 2001).

112. Annette Woolard-Provine, *Integrating Delaware: The Reddings of Wilmington* 119–20 (2003); Munroe, *History of Delaware*, at 225–26.

113. Jeanne D. Nutter, *Growing Up Black in New Castle County, Delaware*, 12–16, 29–30, 32, 59, 72, 95–96, 116, 122 (Arcadia, 2001).

114. *Our View*, News Journal (Wilmington), June 17, 2001, at 10A.

115. Al Mascitti, *Public Looks the Other Way as Schools Plan Crumbles,* News Journal (Wilmington), Oct. 31, 2002, at 1B.

116. Nancy Charron and Patrick Jackson, *New Goal: Get Pupils off Buses,* News Journal (Wilmington), April 2, 2000, at 1A. As enacted, the law insists that the affected districts "shall develop a Neighborhood School Plan for their districts that assigns every student within the district to the grade-appropriate school closest to the student's residence, without regard to any consideration other than geographic distance and the natural boundaries of neighborhoods." H.B. 300. 140th Gen. Assem. (Delaware 2000).

117. See, e.g., *Our View,* News Journal (Wilmington), Apr. 2, 2000, at 2C ("The impulse driving House Bill 300 and its many sponsors is not education, but some blissful notion that we can recapture a world that has not existed for two decades. It is social engineering of the same type that aligned school districts in northern Delaware to ensure racial equality. We don't oppose neighborhood schools. We oppose legislative efforts that are likely to resegregate the schools and drive the state of Delaware back into the federal courtroom"); *Our View,* News Journal (Wilmington), Apr. 15, 2002, at 10A ("We think the Neighborhood Schools law constitutes harmful social policy and that it violates the Constitution. . . . If fully implemented as passed, the measure would result in the resegregation of the City of Wilmington, a social injustice that caused the initial desegregation suit more than three decades ago"). *Legislative Record,* News Journal (Wilmington), Apr. 5, 2000, at 5B; *Legislative Record,* News Journal (Wilmington), Apr. 7, 2000, at 5B.

118. Michele Besso, *No Answers for Christina District Panel,* News Journal (Wilmington), Apr. 26, 2001, at 3B.

119. Rhonda B. Graham, *Neighborhood Schools = Solution or Illusion?* News Journal (Wilmington), Dec. 18, 2000, at 8A; Dennis Thompson Jr., *Solution or Illusion: In Christiana, Long Rides Bring a Cry for Change,* News Journal (Wilmington), Dec. 17, 2000, at 6A.

120. Stephen Sobek, *School Plans Sparking Fears of Resegregation,* News Journal (Wilmington), Nov. 25, 2001, at 1, 9A.

121. Stephen Sobek, *Coalition Looking to Amend School Law,* News Journal (Wilmington), Nov. 3, 2001, at 1A.

122. The Brandywine vote was 3,834 to 1,762.

123. Wayne A. Smith, *Rebuttal,* News Journal (Wilmington), Oct. 31, 2002, at 15A.

124. See, e.g., Al Mascitti, *Public Looks the Other Way,* at 1B (noting that the legislature "could have built support for their position among the public and applied pressure to local school boards, but that would have required overcoming the ennui parents so clearly demonstrated in recent weeks").

125. *Women and Attorneys of Color Continue to Make Only Small Gains at Large Law Firms,* at www.nalp.org/press/details.php?id=53 (Nov. 5, 2004). See also Munroe, *History of Delaware,* at 226; Woolard, *Parker v. The University of Delaware,* at 120. On the history of the Delaware desegregation litigation, see Leland Ware, Chapter 8 in this work; on Chancellor Seitz and the desegregation of the University of Delaware and Delaware's public schools, see *Interview of Collins J. Seitz,* Chapter 2 in this work; on Judge Schwartz and the inter-district remedy, see *Interview of Murray M. Schwartz* Ch. 11; on the Neighborhood Schools Act and the response of the local school districts, see Michele Fuetsch and Leland Ware, Chapter 21 in this work.

CHAPTER TWO

An Interview with the Honorable Collins Jacques Seitz Conducted by the Honorable A. Leon Higginbotham Jr. and by David V. Stivison

Introduction

Collins Jacques Seitz was born in Wilmington, Delaware, on June 20, 1914. "To say that Collins Seitz's background was economically humble is an understatement," wrote E. Norman Veasey, Chief Justice of the Delaware Supreme Court.

> His father worked for the DuPont Company in Wilmington until he became ill in the late '20s and died in 1929 just as the Great Depression hit. There were no benefits for his mother, the widow, and this was a harsh and bitter fact which partly shaped his approach to life. He felt the need to be sensitive to the underdog and often to revolt from conformity. So he lived a life where the principle of righting wrongs became a passion.[1]

Seitz graduated from the University of Delaware in 1937 and from the University of Virginia Law School in 1940; both schools were racially exclusive. After receiving his law degree, Seitz returned to Delaware and entered private practice. From 1944 to 1948, Seitz served in the U.S. Army, earning a Bronze Star and a Purple Heart with an oak-leaf cluster. He was an associate with the Wilmington law firm Southerland Berl & Potter when his judicial career began in 1946.

In 1946, Chancellor William Watson Harrington appointed Seitz to the recently created position of Vice Chancellor in Delaware's Court of Chancery.[2] In 1951, Governor Bert Carvel appointed Seitz Chancellor. As Vice Chancellor and later as Chancellor, Seitz presided with distinction over the business litigation that tends to dominate the Chancery docket. Delaware Supreme Court Justice William Duffy recalled that Seitz

> presided over some of the most complex corporate cases in our history, including the contest for command of a great circus, *Ringling v. Ringling Bros.–Barnum & Bailey Combined Shows*; the battle for control of the Loew's (MGM) motion picture empire, *Campbell v. Loew's Inc.*; and the longest trial in Delaware corporate history, *Bata v. Hill*, in which the fate of the worldwide Bata Shoe Company was at stake.[3]

These cases were significant, but, as Justice William Brennan noted, "most will regard his discharge of another vital Chancery Court responsibility—the protection of the civil rights of Negroes—as his still greater achievement." Seitz was just thirty-five years old when he heard the legal challenge to the racially exclusive policies of his alma mater, the University of Delaware. At the end of the litigation, and after personally visiting Delaware's racially segregated universities, Seitz became the first judge in the nation to order the desegregation of an undergraduate institution. Justice Brennan observed,

> His consideration of the case—*Parker v. University of Delaware*—was perforce within the "separate but equal" restraints of *Plessy v. Ferguson*; however, with courage rarely displayed by judges in those anxious times, after personally visiting the state's white and colored colleges, and finding the colored one "grossly inferior," he ordered the black plaintiffs admitted to the white university. His courage was noteworthy in that his nomination for promotion to Chancellor was shortly to be acted upon by the State Senate, and there were many of that Chamber who disapproved not only of the *Parker* decision but also of his many public statements which made known with clarity and directness his insistent support of desegregation movements. The State Senate, after some uncertainty, finally approved his nomination as Chancellor.[4]

The trustees of the university—who included among their number Chancellor Harrington—chose not to appeal the order by Vice Chancellor Seitz. As Justice Duffy would recall, "A young judge, driven by his sense of what was right, Collins thus began the process which turned the State around after two hundred years of segregated education."[5]

Two years later, Chancellor Seitz would find that Delaware's racially segregated public schools were separate, but far from equal. The remedy, Seitz again insisted, was not to be found in equalization, but in the end of racial separation. He ordered the desegregation of a public school—in fact, it was both an elementary and a secondary school—the first such order in the nation's history. That order, appealed by the state, was among those before the Supreme Court in the consolidated cases known as *Brown v. Board of Education*, and Chancellor Seitz's decision was the only one affirmed by the Court. "We cannot know," Justice Brennan recalled, "how influential Judge Seitz's views were in bringing the Court to its unanimous result in *Brown*; we can only feel assured that they played a persuasive role."[6]

President Lyndon B. Johnson appointed Seitz to the U.S. Court of Appeals for the Third Circuit in 1966, where he served as chief judge from 1971 to 1984. He assumed senior status—and a reduced caseload—in May 1989. Seitz served with great distinction on that court, but would remain best known for his role in desegregating America's schools; he was, his wife Virginia Seitz recalled, "most proud of that."

Seitz received honorary degrees from the University of Delaware, Villanova University, Catholic University, the Dickinson School of Law, and the Widener University School of Law. His many other honors included the Distinguished Service Award from the Delaware Bar Association, the first St. Thomas More Award from the St. Thomas More Society of the Diocese of Wilmington, and the Edward J. Devitt Distinguished Service to Justice Award of the American Judicature Society.

Collins J. Seitz died on October 16, 1998.

* * *

A. Leon Higginbotham Jr. was born on February 25, 1928, in Trenton, New Jersey. His mother was a maid; his father was a factory worker. Higginbotham attended the racially segregated Ewing Park Grammar School and became the first African American student in forty years to be admitted to the academic track at Trenton's segregated junior high school. He attended Purdue University from 1944 to 1946; stung by the slights and material disadvantages of racial segregation at Purdue, Higginbotham transferred to Antioch College, from which he graduated in 1949. He earned a law degree with high honors from the Yale University Law School in 1952.

After graduation, Higginbotham served as a law clerk to Justice Curtis Bok of the Superior Court of Pennsylvania and as an assistant district attorney in Philadelphia, before becoming a founding partner of the Philadelphia law firm of Norris, Green, Harris and Higginbotham. Higginbotham then returned to the public sector, serving as a special hearing officer for conscientious objectors for the U.S. Justice Department and a commissioner of the Pennsylvania Human Relations Commission. In 1962, President John F. Kennedy appointed Higginbotham to the Federal Trade Commission; he thus became the first African American to hold the position of federal commissioner.

In 1964, President Lyndon Johnson appointed Higginbotham to the U.S. District Court for the Eastern District of Pennsylvania. In 1977, Judge Higginbotham was appointed to the Third Circuit Court of Appeals; he replaced Collins Seitz as Chief Judge in 1989 and served in that capacity until his retirement in 1993. In 1994, he accepted an appointment as the first Public Service Professor of Jurisprudence at the John F. Kennedy School of Government of Harvard University.

Judge Higginbotham wrote at least fifty scholarly articles and two highly regarded books: *In the Matter of Color—Race and American Legal Process: The Colonial Period* (1978) and *Shades of Freedom* (1996). Among his many awards were the Raoul Wallenberg Humanitarian Award in 1994 and the NAACP's Spingarn Medal in 1996. In 1995, Judge Higginbotham received the Presidential Medal of Freedom, the nation's highest civilian award.

A. Leon Higginbotham died on December 14, 1998.

* * *

David V. Stivison was an attorney and historian. Born in Hocking County, Ohio, in 1947, Stivison graduated from Ohio University in 1969 and then from the Harvard Law School. He worked as an attorney at the Corporation for Ohio Appalachian Development before moving to Philadelphia in 1983, where he worked for the law firm of Morgan, Lewis and Bockius for two years and then established his own practice. Stivison wrote more than one hundred articles and book chapters on legal history. He founded the Magna Carta Research Foundation and was the editor of *Magna Carta in America: A Project of the Magna Carta Research Foundation* (1993). The Corporation for Ohio Appalachian Development David V. Stivison Scholarship Fund Appalachian is named in his memory "as a tribute to his pursuit of academic excellence and his commitment to help others achieve to their fullest potential."

David V. Stivison died in 1997.

* * *

JUDGE HIGGINBOTHAM: The *Parker* opinion[7] was issued in August of 1950 and you were the Vice Chancellor, if I recall it, and you had been a judge for four years, around that?

JUDGE SEITZ: Appointed in '46.

JUDGE HIGGINBOTHAM: Now, when you wrote the *Parker* decision what was your term of office, or to phrase it differently, from some things I've read you were going to come up again for consideration. But did the legislature have to approve you, as I understand it?

JUDGE SEITZ: That's a confusing situation to people that are not on the inside.

JUDGE HIGGINBOTHAM: Okay, why don't you tell us what was the confirmation and appointment process from 1946 when you first went on the court?

JUDGE SEITZ: In 1946 the Vice Chancellor was appointed by the Chancellor not subject to Senate confirmation and served at the pleasure of the Chancellor.[8]

JUDGE HIGGINBOTHAM: And who was the Chancellor?

JUDGE SEITZ: William Watson Harrington from Dover, Delaware.

JUDGE HIGGINBOTHAM: Now, let me just dart back. How old were you when you were appointed in '46?

JUDGE SEITZ: Thirty-one.

JUDGE HIGGINBOTHAM: And you were the youngest judicial officer to ever serve in the last 100 years?

JUDGE SEITZ: Right.

JUDGE HIGGINBOTHAM: Do you recall any adverse comments about your being appointed at the age of thirty-one?

JUDGE SEITZ: I remember a lot of comments.

JUDGE HIGGINBOTHAM: But were they adverse?

JUDGE SEITZ: One was, which has never really been publicly revealed. Which the Chancellor told me later that the Bishop of the Episcopal Diocese waited on him and told him he didn't think he could appoint a Catholic. That was the first Catholic state judge in the history of Delaware.

JUDGE HIGGINBOTHAM: You mean you were or Harrington was?

JUDGE SEITZ: I was; Harrington's not Catholic. So, I was, and the Chancellor, who is a dear friend of mine, told me that later on, I was not opposed by the bar for negative reasons. The bar with very few exceptions wanted, strangely enough, a friend of mine who was in the same law firm to be appointed, who had lost his leg in the war and they thought it would be nice if he were appointed Vice Chancellor. And I supported him. Can I tell you what happened one day?

JUDGE HIGGINBOTHAM: Sure.

JUDGE SEITZ: I'm sitting in my offices of Southerland, Berl and Potter,[9] loving what I'm doing and a call comes, the Chancellor would like to see you. I went over to see him and he said, you know that Pearson has left as Vice Chancellor and I have to appoint a successor and I would like to appoint you. In my brashness I said, "Chancellor, I think you should appoint Dan Wolcott," who is the fellow in the firm and a good friend of mine.

And he said—incidentally his family and the Wolcott family both were in Dover (you have to know these little nuances) and did not get along—and he said to me—he always called me "Seitz," never called me by my first name—he said, "Seitz, you can take this appointment or not, but Wolcott's going to appointment over my dead body."

Well, I didn't know all the background at that time. So, he said, he [offers] . . . this litany of grievances. I finally decided that Dan Wolcott wasn't going to get the appointment. So, I said, "under those circumstances I accept the appointment."[10]

I thought it would be [for] four years, because his term was up in four years as Chancellor, and I was serving at his pleasure, and I thought I would go back to Southerland, Berl and Potter and make big money, right? I made $18,000 a year the year I came on the court and the pay then was $6,500 as a Vice Chancellor.

Well, to get back on track, the Delaware legislature passed the constitutional amendment and it finally became effective in 1949. It made the Vice Chancellor a state judge, a constitutional judge, appointed by the governor and confirmed by the senate. But it automatically extended my term for twelve years, sort of grandfathered it in without anything further. So that I ended up with what amounted to a twelve-year term from '46 to . . .

JUDGE HIGGINBOTHAM: '58.

JUDGE SEITZ: Yes. And so in 1950, when I decided *Parker*, I was then a constitutional judge. And as you remember, maybe, from the stories, *Parker* was a great story, because Chancellor Harrington was a trustee of the University of Delaware. And I took my opinion in and said, "Here Chancellor, I've just enjoined you." He had appointed me to the bench.

JUDGE HIGGINBOTHAM: What was his reaction?

JUDGE SEITZ: He said, "I'm not surprised."

JUDGE HIGGINBOTHAM: Was the *Parker* case the first when you were Chancellor, that brought to you a record of great disparity on racial, on the allocations, racial allocation . . .

JUDGE SEITZ: Oh, yes.

JUDGE HIGGINBOTHAM: You did not have anything prior to that which brought this home to you . . .

JUDGE SEITZ: Exactly.

JUDGE HIGGINBOTHAM: . . . like this case did.

JUDGE SEITZ: Yeah, that was incredible disparity there.

JUDGE HIGGINBOTHAM: And your *Parker* opinion is viewed by the majority of legal historians as a remarkably significant opinion, because you could have written the opinion by talking in terms of the pure inadequacy of the facilities.

The University of Delaware had about eighteen fields and five related subjects in the School of Arts and Science. The black college had at most eight, and of those eight, they didn't have courses for many of them, so that it was very, very clear just by looking at the record that the black college was not the equivalent.

But in your remarkable opinion, you talk not merely of that, but you talk in terms of the intangibles. And you are, as I understand it, one of the first state judges to ever comment on the intangibles that were involved. Do you have any recollection about how you put that together? I know you wrote the opinion yourself because you had no law clerk.

JUDGE SEITZ: That's true. Did you ever walk in a room and say, "What a mess"? Of course, I knew about the University of Delaware, but I'd never been to Delaware State College before. I made a physical inspection, and you go through . . .

I remember the library, which I always look for. What a mess. It was an excuse for a library. Here is a college with books piled on the floor, no rhyme or reason.

JUDGE HIGGINBOTHAM: No bookshelves?

JUDGE SEITZ: No, it was incredible. And you go to the classes, the same thing. It was just a completely depressing atmosphere to walk into.

So, we take a walk over the campus, and examine the whole place, and I think it left that, you know, psychological or whatever one got, the impression about the whole place. It made the comparison easier. A lot of people cite that *Parker* opinion for a proposition that, I guess, that's the first undergraduate school where the relief was immediate admission, right?

JUDGE HIGGINBOTHAM: That's right.

JUDGE SEITZ: And I think I said something about that. It was particularly interesting because that was my own university, you know, I was opening up.

JUDGE HIGGINBOTHAM: I wanted to deal with that. Let me just for the record in case anyone reads the opinion . . . you say that, "The difficulty comes principally from the fact that separate facilities invariably have marked degrees of differences arising from the respective sizes of the institutions compared."

And then you go on to say, "Also many intangible factors help to make up an educational institution in its totalities." Then you say, "These intangible factors such as the reputation of the school, prestige of the faculty, the beauty of the campus, etc., are difficult to measure on the scales of justice."[11]

Your case is very different in *Parker*, because in the other cases that came down as part of *Brown*, the case out of Price Edwards County, the panel did find inequalities in the facilities and programs of the segregated schools, but inasmuch as the "local and State authorities are moving with speed" to remedy the inequalities, judicial relief "could accomplish no more."[12] [With] the case out of South Carolina, *Briggs v. Elliot*,[13] [the] three-judge federal courts also recognize the same inequality that you've spotted.

JUDGE SEITZ: Right.

JUDGE HIGGINBOTHAM: The difference is that the [South Carolina] case, written by Chief Judge Parker, instead of ordering the admission of a black student, ordered that the facilities should be brought up to speed.[14] Which meant by definition, that if you were in the eleventh grade and it's three years or four years before the facilities are designed, are built and up . . .

JUDGE SEITZ: If they are.

JUDGE HIGGINBOTHAM: If they are, that a whole generation would lose their right and access to education. Now, why do you think that you went this way, and someone like Parker went the other, when the disparities were just as evident in each case?

JUDGE SEITZ: I think it's sensitivity. I think I commented on that in *Bulah*, didn't I? I mean, something I said, something about "this takes time, maybe things will be better," in effect. I think that's the difference.[15]

The South, of course, was immersed in different numbers, and that may have influenced them in the public school system. I just, that whole concept is embodied in "deliberate speed," that concern about the problem, which can't be ignored, of course. After all, it was ingrained for these people. It wasn't with me.

JUDGE HIGGINBOTHAM: Well, what's fascinating is that your education was no different than Parker's.

JUDGE SEITZ: No, not at all.

JUDGE HIGGINBOTHAM: You went to southern schools, you went to segregated schools.[16] You went to a university that did not admit blacks in college. A university that did not admit blacks in law school, and Parker had had that same kind of experience and these other judges, except for Judge Waring who said it,[17] had that kind of experience.

JUDGE SEITZ: Yeah.

JUDGE HIGGINBOTHAM: And I wonder whether you have any hypothesis as to why most judges weren't as thoughtful in my view or as sensitive as you.

JUDGE SEITZ: Well, I think it has something to do with your background. I was a maverick. You know, I looked at the Fourteenth Amendment and said, "Does it mean what it says?" I mean, that's so naïve, it probably wouldn't be understood, but I would have done in the "separate but equal" doctrine in *Parker* if I felt free to do it. I might tell you, Justice Rehnquist spoke in Wilmington recently, and he spoke about my opinions because they were honoring me. And he said he was the clerk to Justice Jackson during *Brown*.

JUDGE HIGGINBOTHAM: Yeah, when *Belton* came up.

JUDGE SEITZ: Yeah, and he said, you know, it's interesting that he said he had read my opinion in *Belton*, and that I had rightly restrained, because it was the province of the Supreme Court to decide whether "separate but equal" should be overturned.[18] Isn't that interesting?

JUDGE HIGGINBOTHAM: Well, it's interesting he said that, but did not comment on your recognizing that in your view, that *Plessy v. Ferguson* was a suspect decision in terms of its vitality.

JUDGE SEITZ: Well, is that the one supposed to have tried to advise Jackson not to vote out?[19]

JUDGE HIGGINBOTHAM: That's the impression I have.

JUDGE SEITZ: Yeah.

JUDGE HIGGINBOTHAM: And [according to] people I know who clerked on the Court at that time, Justice Rehnquist seemed to be reluctant to grant relief as a law clerk. He felt that the relief that was granted would probably not be granted.

JUDGE SEITZ: That's the consensus.

JUDGE HIGGINBOTHAM: Now, let's talk a little more about *Parker*. Did you ever get any adverse comment after you allowed blacks to enter the University of Delaware?

JUDGE SEITZ: Never did.

JUDGE HIGGINBOTHAM: Any hate letter or correspondence?

JUDGE SEITZ: No, I never did. You know, I don't think that mainstream Delaware appreciated to know the cloud that was there, because it affected so few students. I think probably only maybe ten or twelve applied for admission to the university after my decision the first year. Incidentally, one of the blacks who did apply was Lenny Williams. I don't know whether you ever run across Lenny, right?

JUDGE HIGGINBOTHAM: Yes, yes, yes. He's a lawyer.

JUDGE SEITZ: Yes, as a matter of fact, later on I offered him a law clerk position but he decided he could do better practicing law.[20] But it was such that its [*Parker's*] immediate impact was not felt because of the level. It was college level. I'm sure people had their own views about me, but that did not—[I of course, took flack] in the later cases, but not in *Parker*.

JUDGE HIGGINBOTHAM: So, was *Parker* ever discussed by the, in the legislature or any comments made to your knowledge after *Parker* was . . .

JUDGE SEITZ: Not to my knowledge, but I'm sure that's true because when we come to my appointment as Chancellor in 1951, we come to that great episode, where the senate did not want to confirm me. And where the governor had to send the State Police out to bring the senators back to confirm me at 3:00 o'clock in the morning.

JUDGE HIGGINBOTHAM: And that the clock could stop.

JUDGE SEITZ: All the Republicans opposed me. One of the Republican senators is a friend of mine, came up later on and said, "We didn't oppose you for personal reasons; we were hoping if you weren't appointed, we'd get a Republican appointed."

I said, "That's a great reason to oppose somebody." But finally, and I don't know what deals the governor made, I was confirmed.

JUDGE HIGGINBOTHAM: Who was the governor then?

JUDGE SEITZ: Carvel, Bert Carvel. But it didn't matter to me. I was very calm about the whole thing, because if I didn't get the appointment, I would, you know, go back to practicing law. But that shows you how close things are, right, in life and a lot of other things. Same thing I'll talk about when we get to the appointment to this court, how close I was not to getting it.

But there was a lot of resentment and it's mentioned in Kluger's book, that commencement address I gave at Salesianum High School, which they talked about.[21] I saw one of the Democratic senators after I was confirmed who said to me, "Contrary to the rumors, I didn't oppose you because you're a Catholic, but because of your racial views." One form of bigotry rather than another, right?

JUDGE HIGGINBOTHAM: If you had not been Catholic, if you had been mainstream Protestant and had issued this opinion, do you think that there would have been less opposition to your appointment?

JUDGE SEITZ: Probably so, but at that point in time the Delaware legislature senate was dominated by lower Delaware, which was notoriously anti-Catholic and it definitely . . .

JUDGE HIGGINBOTHAM: Was it predominantly Republican or predominantly Democrat?

JUDGE SEITZ: Well, the Senate was Democratic. I think it was by one vote, happened to be. I've forgotten the total, but it was the lower two counties dominated the state until the reapportionment . . .

JUDGE HIGGINBOTHAM: Well, *Baker v. Carr.*

JUDGE SEITZ: *Baker v. Carr* changed all that. So, at that time they dominated the legislature. I've never asked Governor Carvel, but I suspect he must have made some kind of a deal, you know. I mean, you don't get things done otherwise.

JUDGE HIGGINBOTHAM: Now, do you have any feeling as to whether corporations—because you have this great reputation, this fair, rational, confident, impartial judge, and in the long run corporations would prefer to even lose the cases by a judge whom they felt was fairer and objective in his own mind, than to have someone who is like a pendulum swinging with political tides—was there any movement by the corporate legal community or the state legal community to support you?

JUDGE SEITZ: There was . . . That was definitely true.

You know, most of the corporate lawyers in Delaware—and we had the great ones, including the senior partner in my old firm, Mr. Southerland—they sort of tolerated my racial views. I mean, I wasn't so good in corporate matters. They were willing to overlook my little foibles about racial views, and I was very close to Mr. Southerland for many years. And he was about as conservative as you can imagine, and he later became the Chief Justice of Delaware, and wrote the opinion affirming my opinion in *Bulah* and on separate but equal.[22]

But a tight-knit community, sort of an anomaly. I was here, out here on my own, largely, so to speak, in views of social justice. But I love corporate law. I don't know why. I love like a fish to water.

JUDGE HIGGINBOTHAM: You also dealt with estates, did you not?

JUDGE SEITZ: Oh, yeah, I handed down one trust decision that increased the University of Delaware's endowment by $50 million. They look kindly on me. Some people think that's why they gave me an honorary degree.

JUDGE HIGGINBOTHAM: Well, you deserved an honorary degree for many reasons.

* * *

MR. STIVISON: The final cases that we want to discuss from your period on the Delaware Court . . . involved some of the first civil rights cases brought in the United States for the purposes of desegregating education institutions. Those were *Belton v. Gebhart* and *Parker v. the University of Delaware*. The earlier of the two was *Parker v. University of Delaware*.

JUDGE SEITZ: That's right.

MR. STIVISON: Would you care to give us a brief outline of how that case developed and the result?

JUDGE SEITZ: That case was decided in 1950. Delaware had, well, Delaware was as segregated as any southern state by law. So, that the University of Delaware did not accept blacks through the undergraduate school at all. There was a Delaware State College where blacks attended and so the students, I think at the behest of the NAACP, applied for admission to the university, asked for admission applications to the university, and were denied them.

And then they brought an action in the Court of Chancery for an injunction claiming that the University of Delaware was far superior to Delaware State College, and under the separate but equal doctrine they were entitled to be admitted to the University of Delaware. And as you know, I am a graduate of the University of Delaware.

MR. STIVISON: Yes.

JUDGE SEITZ: So that, and I knew a great many of the people there.

MR. STIVISON: Now at the time this was brought, you were not Chancellor, you were Vice Chancellor.

JUDGE SEITZ: I was Vice Chancellor.

MR. STIVISON: And why did you receive this case rather than the Chancellor?

JUDGE SEITZ: That's because the Chancellor was a trustee of the University of Delaware, and he was disqualified. And incidentally, as you know, he originally appointed me Vice Chancellor.

MR. STIVISON: Yes.

JUDGE SEITZ: So that it was an interesting relationship. At that time the Vice Chancellor was appointed by the Chancellor, not the governor.

MR. STIVISON: And served at his pleasure.

JUDGE SEITZ: Served at his pleasure, which I did when I was originally appointed. But by the time the University of Delaware case up, they had passed the constitutional amendment and gave me a full tenure. So, I became, you know, a constitutional judge at that time and I did not serve at his pleasure. But we still, of course, were intimately associated. But that case was the forerunner, of course, of *Brown*, because the NAACP had also argued that segregated education itself was unconstitutional.

MR. STIVISON: Now, in the case involving the University of Delaware, you visited both facilities, did you not?

JUDGE SEITZ: I did indeed, with Jack Greenberg of the NAACP and Louis Redding—they were the attorneys for the plaintiffs—and Woods, the counsel for the attorney general.

MR. STIVISON: Now, Louis Redding, if I remember correctly, was the only black lawyer in Delaware at that time.

JUDGE SEITZ: That's right.

MR. STIVISON: He had joined the bar in 1929 and even in 1950 he was the only black lawyer in the state.

JUDGE SEITZ: That's correct.[23]

MR. STIVISON: After your review of the facilities and hearing the arguments, what was your final decision in that case?

JUDGE SEITZ: Well, I—it was open and shut. There was no comparison between the facilities at the University of Delaware and Delaware State College. I remember visiting Delaware State College, and they said, "This is our library." I said, "You've got to be kidding; it's a library?" Books on the floor, you know, nothing organized at all.

MR. STIVISON: And they had no paid librarian, is that not correct?

JUDGE SEITZ: No, no, no. It was, well, the comparisons are set forth in the opinion and my opinion, I guess, is not important for the fact that I concluded they were not equal, because that was manifest. What was important that I enjoined the University of Delaware from considering race in processing applications for admission. It's a technical term, but it's a typical equity injunction, so they couldn't rely on race in passing on the application.

MR. STIVISON: And in other states where the same argument had been made and where, in fact, facilities were found to be unequal . . .

JUDGE SEITZ: Right.

MR. STIVISON: It was not uncommon for the court to say, "Well, these facilities are unequal but we will give you time to bring the black facilities up to equal the white facilities." You did not do that?

JUDGE SEITZ: It's not only unusual, no other court had done it before I did—to say, "We're not going to wait for you to see if you can make the facilities equal; you must admit them today if they're qualified." That was why the opinion was important.

MR. STIVISON: Now, did the state in that case argue, did they even contest the fact that the facilities were unequal?

JUDGE SEITZ: Shall we say, half-heartedly.

MR. STIVISON: Half-heartedly?

JUDGE SEITZ: Their big argument was that we should wait till the legislature appropriated money to bring the black college up to the equivalent of the University of Delaware. That was their point, and they had that precedent all around the country for that, but it seemed nonsense to me.

MR. STIVISON: The reasoning that you applied there, which followed *Plessy v. Ferguson*, you did not . . .

JUDGE SEITZ: Exactly, "separate but equal."

MR. STIVISON: You said, we will look at the 1896 decision. It sets up this standard.

JUDGE SEITZ: Right.

MR. STIVISON: These are not equal; therefore they cannot be separate.

JUDGE SEITZ: Right.

MR. STIVISON: Then the next case after that extended the same reasoning down to the high schools and lower schools in the state.

JUDGE SEITZ: Elementary school.

MR. STIVISON: That had a much wider impact on society.

JUDGE SEITZ: Indeed it did.

MR. STIVISON: And that case was *Belton v. Gebhart* and others.

JUDGE SEITZ: *Bulah v. Gebhart.*

MR. STIVISON: And *Bulah v. Gebhart.*

JUDGE SEITZ: That was the elementary and secondary school.[24]

MR. STIVISON: And again, you had Jack Greenberg and Louis Redding in front of you.

JUDGE SEITZ: Exactly.

MR. STIVISON: And was that basically a carbon copy of the first case, with different parties involved, or were there differences there?

JUDGE SEITZ: In many ways it was a carbon copy, because the comparison between what they called "colored schools" and the "white schools"—well, there was no comparison. I visited the schools in those cases, too, and the facilities were patently—though the state argued to the contrary—they were unequal. Once again, the state's principal argument was, "Well, your Honor, if you find them unequal, tell us so, and order the state to bring the separate schools up to par."

And I think in the opinion of everyone in the field, the importance of that was saying, "We're not going to wait; you're going to admit them immediately." And that, of course, is what caused me to be less than the most popular citizen of Delaware.

MR. STIVISON: Now, when these decisions were released, what kind of reaction did you personally receive from that? Were there editorials? Did you receive flatteries?

JUDGE SEITZ: Well, the newspaper was very much in favor of my decision. The Board of Education was very much opposed to my decision, and I got the usual number of letters. I made mention in my opinion about that schoolteacher—I don't know whether you remember this—when I visited the school, when she was teaching dancing or something in the white school, and how impressed I was with what the children were getting.[25] And that teacher came to see me after my opinion.

MR. STIVISON: Uh-huh.

JUDGE SEITZ: And she said, "I just wanted to tell you, if I knew you were going to mention that in your opinion, that you saw me doing that when you came to the school, I never would have done it. I never would have been doing that." In other words, she was bitter about the fact that I was using that to enter an order in part requiring that the black children be admitted to the white school. That's how bitter she was.

MR. STIVISON: Now, these cases became part of the bundle of appeals that were decided in *Brown v. Board of Education* in 1954.

JUDGE SEITZ: Those two, right.

MR. STIVISON: I believe that Thurgood Marshall hailed your decision in *Parker* as the first victory that the civil rights movement had secured.

JUDGE SEITZ: Yes, he's quoted . . . saying that.[26]

MR. STIVISON: Now, when the U.S. Supreme Court decided *Brown v. Board of Education*, they granted the schools the right to desegregate, overturn *Plessy v. Ferguson*, but said you may use "all deliberate speed" in desegregation. That really was a step backward from the approach that you had adopted, was it not?

JUDGE SEITZ: It was, but they, in fairness to them, they had to—they were considering the whole South, and I think that was, that was one way to get the unanimity in the Court.

MR. STIVISON: What was the effect of your two decisions and then *Brown v. Board of Education* in Delaware? When were the Delaware schools actually desegregated?

JUDGE SEITZ: Oh, very, very quickly.

MR. STIVISON: After *Brown.*

JUDGE SETIZ: And that was done in the federal court then, and that's when the busing cases came up, and then of course a great controversy over busing in Delaware.

MR. STIVISON: So, after your decision had been rendered, their effectiveness was put on hold pending the U.S. Supreme Court appeal?

JUDGE SEITZ: No; I denied a stay on the admission of the student to the white schools, even pending the appeal.

MR. STIVISON: So, those schools were desegregated in fact.

JUDGE SEITZ: In fact, right.

Notes

1. E. Norman Veasey, *Collins Jacques Seitz: Paradigm of Principle, Passion, Professionalism and Persuasion,* 40 Vill. L. Rev. 559, 559–60 (1995).

2. The American colonies transplanted from England a dual system of justice featuring courts of law and courts of equity. The former were governed by the relatively rigid rules—and procedural forms—of the common law; the latter were governed by somewhat more flexible principles of fairness. The courts of equity also had available to them a broader range of remedies: legal relief was typically limited to monetary damages, but equitable relief could include injunctions to refrain from an action or orders compelling an action. Over time, most states—and the United States—merged their systems into unified ones, with a single set of procedural rules. Delaware, however, remained an eccentric exception. Even today, its Superior Court is a court of law presided over by judges, its Chancery Court is a court of equity presided over by chancellors, and the jurisdiction and procedures of each are quite distinct. The actions challenging Delaware's racially segregated schools, for example, were brought in the Court of Chancery because the requested relief—orders compelling the state either to desegregate or equalize the schools—was equitable, available only from the court of equity.

3. William Duffy, *Collins J. Seitz,* 132 U. Pa. L. Rev. 1288, 1288–89 (1984) (citations omitted).

4. William J. Brennan Jr., *Collins Jacques Seitz,* 132 U. Pa. L. Rev. 1279, 1279 (1984).

5. Duffy, *Collins J. Seitz,* at 1289.

6. Brennan, *Collins Jacques Seitz,* at 1280.

7. *Parker v. University of Delaware,* 31 Delaware Ch. 381, 75 A.2d 225 (Del. Ch. 1950).

8. The Delaware state constitution provided for a single Chancellor, and Delaware had just one until 1939 when, at the urging of Chancellor W. W. Harrington, the legislature created the office of Vice Chancellor. Under the statute, the Vice Chancellor was to be appointed by and serve at the pleasure of the Chancellor. The first Vice Chancellor was George Burton Pearson Jr.; his successor, appointed by Chancellor Harrington on February 1, 1946, was Collins J. Seitz. In 1949, Delaware amended its constitution to add

a Vice Chancellor, thus converting the statutory position to a constitutional one. The amendment provided that the "present incumbent"—Vice Chancellor Seitz—would enjoy a twelve-year term in the position (the term commencing from his appointment to the statutory post). Two years later, in June 1951, Vice Chancellor Seitz was appointed Chancellor. See William T. Quillen & Michael Hanrahan, *A Short History of the Delaware Court of Chancery—1792–1992*, 18 Del. J. Corp. L. 819, 846–50 (1993).

9. Southerland Berl & Potter was the 1940s iteration of one of Wilmington's most prominent law firms. Its named partners were Clarence A. Southerland, who in 1951 would become the first chief justice of the Delaware Supreme Court, and E. Ennals Berl and Williams S. Potter, each of whom would serve as president of the Delaware State Bar Association. See generally Joseph M. Kwiatkowski et al., *Solo and Small Firm Practice*, in *The Delaware Bar in the Twentieth Century* 93, 100–1, ed. Helen L. Winslow (Delaware State Bar Association, 1994). Since 1968, the firm has been known as Potter Anderson & Corroon.

10. Daniel F. Wolcott was the son of Delaware Chancellor Josiah Wolcott and the grandson of Chancellor James L. Wolcott. In 1949, three years after Collins Seitz was appointed to the Vice Chancellor's position, Wolcott was appointed Associate Judge of the Delaware Superior Court. When Chancellor Harrington retired the following year, Wolcott was named his successor. Wolcott served as Chancellor for six months and then was appointed to the newly created Delaware Supreme Court. He served fourteen years as a justice on the court, and eight years as chief justice. Henry R. Horsey and William Duffy, *The Supreme Court After 1951: The Separate Supreme Court*, in *The Delaware Bar*, at 369, 382–38.

11. *Parker*, 75 A.2d at 231.

12. *Davis v. County School Board of Prince Edward County*, 103 F. Supp 337 (E.D. Va. 1952), p. 341. The three-judge federal court refused to find segregation per se unlawful. Segregation, it first ruled, was not motivated by unreasonable racial animus: "It indisputably appears from the evidence that the separation provision rests neither upon prejudice, nor caprice, nor upon any other measureless foundation. Rather the proof is that it declares one of the ways of life in Virginia. Separation of white and colored 'children' in the public schools of Virginia has for generations been a part of the mores of her people. To have separate schools has been their use and wont." *Id.* at 339. And the effects of segregation were at least as benign as the motives: "Maintenance of the separated systems in Virginia has not been social despotism, the testimony points out, and suggests that whatever its demerits in theory, in practice it has begotten greater opportunities for the Negro. Virginia alone employs as many Negro teachers in her public schools, according to undenied testimony, as are employed in all of the thirty-one non-segregating States. . . ."

"So ingrained and wrought in the texture of their life is the principle of separate schools, that the president of the University of Virginia expressed to the Court his judgment that its involuntary elimination would severely lessen the interest of the people of the State in the public schools, lessen the financial support, and so injure both races. His testimony, corroborated by others, was especially impressive because of his candid and knowledgeable discussion of the problem. A scholar and a former Governor and legislator of the State, we believe him delicately sensible of the customs, the mind, and the temper of both races in Virginia. With the whites comprising more than three-quarters of the entire population of the Commonwealth, the point he makes is a weighty practical factor to be considered in determining whether a reasonable basis has been shown to exist for the continuation of the school segregation.

"In this milieu we cannot say that Virginia's separation of white and colored children in the public schools is without substance in fact or reason. We have found no hurt or harm to either race." *Id.* at 340.

13. *Briggs v. Elliott*, 103 F. Supp 920 (E.D.S.C. 1952).

14. Judge Parker concluded that "plaintiffs are not entitled to a decree enjoining segregation in the schools but that they are entitled to a decree directing defendants promptly to furnish to Negroes within the consolidated district educational facilities and opportunities equal to those furnished white persons." *Id.* at 923. The evidence persuaded Judge Parker that the state was "earnestly and in good faith endeavoring to equalize educational opportunities" "as rapidly as was humanly possible." *Id.* at 922.

15. In the *Bulah* case, Chancellor Seitz wrote, "It is true that in such a situation some courts have merely directed the appropriate State officials to equalize facilities. I do not believe that such is the relief warranted by a finding that the United States Constitution has been violated. It seems to me that when a plaintiff shows to the satisfaction of a court that there is an existing and continuing violation of the 'separate but equal' doctrine, he is entitled to have made available to him the State facilities which have been shown to be superior. To do otherwise is to say to such a plaintiff: 'Yes, your Constitutional rights are being invaded, but be patient, we will see whether in time they are still being violated.' If, as the Supreme Court has said, this right is personal, such a plaintiff is entitled to relief immediately, in the only way it is available, namely, by admission to the school with the superior facilities. To postpone such relief is to deny relief, in whole or in part, and to say that the protective provisions of the Constitution offer no immediate protection."*Belton v. Gebhart*, 32 Del. Ch. 343, 358–59, 87 A.2d 862, 869–70 (1952).

16. Judge Seitz received his bachelor's degree from the University of Delaware and his law degree from the University of Virginia.

17. Judge J. Waties Waring dissented from the original decision of the three-judge panel in the South Carolina case. That panel, led by Judge Parker, found no constitutional violation in the fact of racial segregation. But based on the testimony, Judge Waring insisted, "It was clearly apparent, as it should be to any thoughtful person, irrespective of having such expert testimony, that segregation in education can never produce equality and that it is an evil that must be eradicated. This case presents the matter clearly for adjudication and I am of the opinion that all of the legal guideposts, expert testimony, common sense and reason point unerringly to the conclusion that the system of segregation in education adopted and practiced in the State of South Carolina must go and must go now." *Briggs v. Elliott*, 98 F.Supp. 529, 547–48 (E.D.S.C. 1951) (Waring, J., dissenting). "Segregation," Judge Waring concluded, "is per se inequality." *Id.* at 548.

18. Chancellor Seitz had concluded "from the testimony that in our Delaware society, State-imposed segregation in education itself results in the Negro children, as a class, receiving educational opportunities which are substantially inferior to those available to white children otherwise similarly situated." *Parker*, 87 A.2d at 865. But he also found that "by implication, the Supreme Court of the United States has said a separate but equal test can be applied, at least below the college level. This Court does not believe such an implication is justified under the evidence. Nevertheless, I do not believe a lower court can reject a principle of United States Constitutional law which has been adopted by fair implication by the highest court of the land. I believe the 'separate but equal' doctrine in education should be rejected, but I also believe its rejection must come from that Court." *Id.*

19. After the initial arguments in *Brown*, Justice Jackson asked his two clerks for advisory memoranda on the case. One of the memos, prepared by William H. Rehnquist, concluded that "I realize that it is an unpopular and unhumanitarian position, for which I have been excoriated by 'liberal' colleagues, but I think *Plessy v. Ferguson* was right and should be re-affirmed." During his 1971 confirmation hearings, Rehnquist insisted that the memo was written to reflect Justice Jackson's views. Some evidence supports that

proposition; other evidence makes the contention seem implausible. For a summary of the events, and the competing views of the memorandum, see Richard Kluger, *Simple Justice* 604–9 (Knopf, 1976).

20. Leonard L. Williams was admitted to the Delaware bar in 1959, just the fifth African American admitted to practice in the state. He practiced with Louis Redding for a number of years and became a Municipal Court judge in 1966. Joshua W. Martin III, *Minorities in the Delaware Bar,* in *The Delaware Bar,* at 657, 662.

21. Collins Seitz's nomination to be Chancellor was pending in the Delaware senate in 1951, when the then–Vice Chancellor was invited to give the commencement address at Salesianum High School, a Roman Catholic school for boys in Wilmington. Seitz used the opportunity to lament the failure of "business, governmental, and religious leaders" to address "the most pressing domestic issue today in Delaware, and in fact in the United States": "A person has real moral courage when, being in a position to make decisions or determine policies, he decides that . . . every Catholic school, church and institution should be open to all Catholics—not at some distant future time when public opinion happens to coincide with Catholic moral teaching—but now." Kluger, *Simple Justice,* at 433.

22. *Gebhart v. Belton,* 91 A.2d 137 (Del. Supr. 1952), *aff'g Belton v. Gebhart,* 32 Del. Ch. 343, 87 A.2d 862 (1952).

23. Although there were nearly 1,500 African American attorneys in the nation in 1950, Redding was the only one in Delaware. He would in fact be the only African American attorney in Delaware until 1956. From 1956–59, Delaware admitted to the bar one black attorney per year; it thereafter admitted no black attorneys until 1973. See Martin, *Minorities in the Delaware Bar,* at 661–63.

24. The suit brought on behalf of Ethel Louise Belton challenged her exclusion from the all-white Claymont High School; the suit brought on behalf of Shirley Barbara Bulah challenged her exclusion from the all-white Hockessin School No. 29 (and from the school buses that transported white students to and from their schools). The suits were consolidated for trial purposes and jointly decided.

25. The reference here is uncertain; it may be to Chancellor Seitz's review of the extracurricular activities at Claymont, which included "an organization to tickle the imagination called 'Tumbling Girls.'" *Belton v. Gebhart,* 87 A.2d at 868.

26. After Chancellor Seitz's decision, Marshall announced to the press, "This is the first real victory in our campaign to destroy segregation of American pupils in elementary and high schools." Kluger, *Simple Justice,* at 449.

CHAPTER THREE

Delaware Voices: Collins J. Seitz Jr.

My father thought that the *Parker* decision desegregating the University of Delaware and the *Belton* and *Bulah* decisions were easy decisions. With more than fifty years of hindsight, no one really believes this to be true, but for my father it is completely believable. The *Plessy* separate but equal doctrine was still alive and well in America and in Delaware. My father did what someone applying a practical approach to things would do. He visited the two institutions, one being his alma mater, the University of Delaware (and my alma mater as well), and then he visited Delaware State College and he saw what was plainly apparent—that the State College was vastly inferior to the University of Delaware in every aspect of educational experience.

My father was probably sensitive at the time to the specter of a reviewing court overturning his decisions, so he made extensive factual findings to which a reviewing court would have had to give great deference and could not credibly attack as erroneous. My father was impatient, but he did not always get ahead of things. The time was not right for him to declare unconstitutional the separate but equal doctrine, and he acknowledged he did not have the power to do so. One of the other judges on his court was on the Board of Trustees of the University of Delaware at the time, and elected officials were shackled by the chains of popular opinion and could do nothing about the problem.

I think the beauty of the University of Delaware decision in *Parker* was in the remedy. It is a fine point, but it is a point that my father was always proud to make. He did not order the admission of blacks to the University of Delaware. He enjoined the university from making admission decisions based upon race. It was a fine point, but I think he saw it as an important one—again a first step, not biting off everything at one time.

My father was a bit of a smart aleck. He loved telling the story about how, once he decided the *Parker v. University of Delaware* decision, he took the court order and went next door to his fellow judge's chambers, who was a University trustee, and said to the judge, "Here Judge, I just enjoined you."

Turning to the *Belton* and the *Bulah* decisions, anyone who followed my father's speaking engagements around Delaware at the time should not have been surprised at the result.

In numerous speeches to public bodies, to civic organizations, high school graduations, and radio spots on WDEL, he kept what he called "the Negro problem" in the forefront and questioned how people of good will and principle who lived by the Constitution could tolerate discrimination against African Americans.

My father was a devout Catholic, but like the university of which he was so fond, the Catholic Church was slow to open its doors to African Americans. He was struck by the unequal treatment of blacks by Catholic Church officials; my father realized that they had refused to admit blacks to Catholic schools in Wilmington or hire blacks to work as nurses at Wilmington's Catholic hospital. In a fairly incendiary speech at the time, my father spoke to the Salesianum High School graduating class of 1951. He confronted the problem head on and called on the church to change its policies. In this speech he said the following:

> Let me first illustrate the moral courage point. In my opinion, the most pressing domestic issue today in Delaware and in fact in the United States generally, is the so-called Negro/white problem, more accurately called the American problem. Many of us would become fighting mad were we told that we did not really believe in the great principles of the Declaration of Independence and of the Constitution of the United States. Yet I submit that too many of us talk out of both sides of our mouths at the same time on this important subject. How can we say that we deeply revere the principles of our Declaration and our Constitution and yet refuse to recognize these principles when they are applied to the American Negro in a down-to-earth fashion?
>
> During election campaigns and in Fourth of July speeches, many speakers emphasize that these great principles apply to all Americans, but when you ask many of these same speakers to act or vote so that those great principles apply in fact to Negro Americans, you may be accused of being unfair, idealistic, or even pro-Communist. It does not take any particular moral courage to come out and favor the great principles upon which our country was founded, but it takes real moral courage not only to say that those great principles apply to the Negro, but also to see that he in fact receives their benefit in his daily life.
>
> A person has real moral courage when, being in a position to make decisions or determine policies, he decides that the qualified Negro will be admitted to the school of nursing; that the Negro, like the white, will receive a fair trial no matter what the public feeling may be; that every Catholic school, church, and institution shall be open to all Catholics not at some distant future time when public opinion happens to coincide with Catholic moral teaching, but now. Are these requests of our business, governmental, and religious leaders too much to ask? I think not.

In *Belton* and *Bulah*, there were stark differences between the black and the white schools. My father, as in the *Parker* decision, issued lengthy findings of fact supporting what was apparent: that inequality existed between the schools. I think the most courageous part of the *Bulah* decision also was in the remedy that was imposed. A popular remedy would have been to accept the state's position that the school board should be given an opportunity to equalize the facilities. That was an argument that had been made successfully around the country. Putting aside popular opinion and true to his impatient character, my father held instead,

> It seems that when a plaintiff shows to the satisfaction of a court that there is an existing and continuing violation of the separate-but-equal doctrine, he is entitled to have made available to him the state facilities which have been shown to be superior. To do otherwise is to say to such a plaintiff, "Yes, your constitutional rights are being invaded, but be patient. We will see whether in time they are still being violated." To postpone such relief is to deny relief, in whole or in part, and to say that the protective provisions of the Constitution offer no immediate protection.

Five months after the Supreme Court's decision in *Brown v. Board of Education,* my father traveled to New York City to receive the James J. Hoey award for interracial justice. The award is given annually to a white and an African American Catholic for outstanding contributions to the cause of interracial understanding. In speaking of the need for better relations between blacks and whites, my father acknowledged the complexity of the problem, but consistent with his ever hopeful vision of the future, said the following:

> We must then be dedicated to the task, but of equal importance we must face the realities. In other words, we must move forward in some cases by appeal to reason, and others by insistence upon right, and in still others by temporizing. The problem has many faces and not the least of which is the need to consider the feelings of the Negroes. Not every Negro parent is willing that their child should be a pioneer and we should not condemn that feeling. We should also avoid the assumption that there is always a right and a wrong involved in every interracial problem. . . . [That] approach is the very one we condemn in the unenlightened opponents of interracial justice.
>
> We must be patient but persistent. It is often easy to take more time when we are not the one who is suffering. I therefore accept this honor on behalf of all people of good will. It will be an added incentive to me and, I trust, to all of the workers in this most worthy work. We still go forward spiritually refreshed and firm in the conviction that what we are doing must be done. It must be done because we believe in the fatherhood of God from which it necessarily follows that all men are our brothers and we are all our brothers' keepers.

Much has changed since my father made these observations, but his conclusion applies as much today as it did over fifty years ago. We must continue our forward progress, firm in the conviction that what we are doing must be done.

CHAPTER FOUR

Remembering Louis Redding

Annette Woolard-Provine

My favorite Louis Redding story concerns the way in which he learned about the Supreme Court's decision in *Brown.* It makes a powerful statement about Louis Redding's character and career. On May 17, 1954, Louis Redding was in his car, alone, driving to New York to visit a law library. This was not an unusual circumstance for him. He practiced law in Delaware and Maryland's Eastern Shore, but he often traveled to New York to do legal research. On May 17, Redding was driving along, listening to the radio, when a news break interrupted the music program. A reporter announced that the Supreme Court had ruled on *Brown* and went on to describe the significance of the decision.

Redding attempted to continue driving, but could not. Louis Redding was a man of great dignity who, by upbringing and temperament, rarely showed emotion. Yet the *Brown* announcement so overwhelmed him that he was compelled to pull over to the side of the road and, as he put it, "just let the news wash over him." This moment was the pinnacle of Redding's life's work, an event for which he had made untold sacrifices. Sitting alone in his car, Redding exhaled and whispered in a barely audible voice, "Oh, boy . . . terrific." A few moments later he restarted his car and continued on to New York.

Redding's reaction was controlled. He did not allow himself much of a celebration. This is 1954. He did not have a cell phone or laptop computer. He had no way of communicating with others who might have been celebrating the decision. Redding heard the news the way he practiced law: quietly, and alone. After hearing the news and pausing briefly, he immediately returned to his business, doing his duty.

That duty began in 1929 when Redding was sworn into the Delaware Bar. He was twenty-eight years old and the first black lawyer in Delaware. He remained the only black lawyer for the following twenty-six years. He had not wanted either distinction.

Redding enrolled in Brown University after graduating from Howard High School in Wilmington, intending to become a doctor, as that had been his father's ambition for him. Louis Redding Sr.—"Papa," as his children knew him—was a force to be reckoned with. He was a tough-love parent who had great ambitions for his children. Papa informed his children that they represented their race in a hostile world and would do so with dignity and excellence. With that mandate, Louis Redding was sent off to college to become a doctor, but he quickly discovered that he hated biology. What he admired were the lifestyles of the Rhode Island, New York, and Boston lawyers he met through his all-black college fraternity, Alpha Phi Alpha. These men worked in law firms, some segregated, others integrated. Redding was drawn to their professional camaraderie. He found discussions of their work intellectually intriguing. And Redding admired the money they made, the preppy clothing they wore, and the prestige they enjoyed in their communities. The sophistication and elegance of New England were very different from provincial, conservative, and Jim Crow Wilmington.

Redding decided to pursue a career in law. Papa, however, had other plans. If Louis would not become a physician, he could seek a career in the law, but he would have to return home to practice. He would break through the local bar's color barrier, representing those who had no voice in the Delaware courts. What Papa was actually requesting was a lifetime of sacrifice and his son understood this.

Louis Redding reluctantly acquiesced to his father's wishes. He returned to a town he hated, a segregated city from which he had escaped. It was a place that was even more confining for its small and struggling black community. Redding knew he would be joining a legal community that did not want him. There would be no professional camaraderie in Delaware. He would be isolated, practicing alone; indeed, until the time of the *Brown* case, he worked alone, on every case, with occasional consultations with the NAACP.

Redding did not earn much money. He handled civil and criminal cases for poor blacks and whites, "the scraps of the Delaware Bar" as one colleague termed it. These were often difficult cases. His clients were usually fearful about their rights. They were not well spoken and did not appear before sympathetic judges and juries. Redding knew that he had to prove his worth every time he walked into a courtroom.

Louis Redding lost many of his early cases. He was an enigma in Wilmington. In the black community he was highly respected, but he was not universally beloved. In the white community, when he was thought of at all, it was often as not a very likable person. In the 1960s, the local newspapers had pre-prepared an obituary of Louis Redding. The headline of that obituary read, "Most arrogant man in Delaware dies." Redding knew how he was regarded, and he did not make many efforts to become more popular. He wore expensive, Brooks Brothers suits. He did not smoke, but he went about with imported cigarettes dangling from his lips. His measured diction and Ivy League accent were incongruous on the streets of Wilmington. Redding carried himself with great dignity and reserve. Indeed, many in the black and white communities thought he was arrogant.

Redding had a small circle of local friends and others from college and law school who lived in other localities. They did not regard him as arrogant. He was determined and confident, but he was a humble man among his friends. Those friendships were enough for Redding. His focus was always on his work. If he was not seen as affable, that was the least of his worries.

There were bright spots in his life, perhaps most notably in 1944, when he married, and throughout the 1950s, when his wife bore him three daughters whom he loved, but rarely saw. The pivotal phase in Louis Redding's life was the time he worked on school desegregation cases: *Parker v. University of Delaware,* which was decided in 1950, and *Bulah v. Gebhart* and *Belton v. Gebhart,* the cases that were among the group of cases remembered as *Brown v. Board of Education.* In interviews, Redding implied that these cases simply dropped into his lap. Actually, he initiated these cases. He had actively sought the right plaintiffs and correct strategy for years.

These cases were pivotal to him for a variety of reasons. *Parker* desegregated the University of Delaware, the state's flagship institution. *Bulah* and *Belton* were incorporated into the *Brown* case that went to the Supreme Court. That decision led to the death of Jim Crow in America. It changed the nature of American education and American society. This was a once-in-a-lifetime opportunity. Redding was well aware of this and grateful to have been part of the effort. He was proud of what he achieved. When the school desegregation cases were developed, Redding experienced, for the first time, the professional camaraderie that he craved as a young attorney. He worked on the cases with Jack Greenberg, who was with the NAACP in New York. Redding thoroughly enjoyed the partnership. The desegregation cases were the start of a winning streak. He not only won *Parker* and *Bulah* and *Belton* at the local level, but was the only plaintiffs' attorney in *Brown* who argued in the Supreme Court after having won in the lower courts.

After the school cases, Redding went on to win several other civil rights cases, including *Evans v. Buchanan,* which forced the state of Delaware to comply with *Brown. Burton v. Wilmington Parking Authority* was appealed to the U.S. Supreme Court where Redding won, striking down discrimination in restaurants. *Burton* is featured in many law school casebooks as an example of the application of the "state action" doctrine. At an advanced age, Louis Redding recalled his career with great pride, noting that he never lost a desegregation case.

Redding's involvement and victory in *Brown* changed his life in other ways. The isolation of his law practice ended. A whirlwind of activity included many professional partnerships. He worked with NAACP lawyers from New York. Littleton Mitchell, the president of the local NAACP, became his close friend and confidant. Redding mentored a generation of young black attorneys who were admitted to practice law in Delaware.

He became a prominent public figure, which did not always have positive effects. He received a constant barrage of hate mail and telephone threats. In Milford, Delaware, his automobile was forced off the road, and he was personally threatened. The IRS hauled him into court for nonpayment of federal income taxes during the time of the *Brown* hearings. He was eventually indicted for income tax evasion, but acquitted after a jury trial. Edmund Carpenter, one of the pillars of Delaware's legal establishment, represented him in the tax case. Redding was summoned by the House Un-American Activities Committee to respond to claims that he was a communist.

Redding also received favorable recognition. He won awards and was interviewed by magazine and newspaper reporters at the local and national levels.

He was finally invited to join the American Bar Association and the Delaware Bar Association. These invitations were particularly meaningful to Redding, as these organizations had excluded him on racial grounds.

Redding maintained a heavy workload until he was well into his seventies. He semi-retired in the 1970s, but did not close his practice until the late 1980s. I started to interview him shortly before he closed his practice. He was a man at peace with his achievements, but one who still regretted that he did not practice law in New England or New York, where he could have visited theatres, attended concerts, and moved about in sophisticated circles. He sacrificed that dream for the greater good.

Redding lived most of his life under Delaware's Jim Crow system. He knew firsthand how much segregation injured its victims. He knew the pain of denied opportunities and the stigma of implied inferiority. But segregation had another dimension for Redding. He knew what his abilities were. He knew the value that he, his siblings, and colleagues offered to Delaware. The stupidity of a society that denied itself those gifts pained Redding. Segregation not only denied opportunities to talented African Americans but it also withheld the valuable contributions they could have made to the white majority. In Redding's view, America would improve not only when it treated blacks as equals but also when it allowed itself to benefit from the genius that they offer.

CHAPTER FIVE

Remembering Thurgood Marshall

Juan Williams

In 1990, I was working as a reporter for the *Washington Post*, and I had just completed a magazine article on Justice Thurgood Marshall. A week before the article would appear in the Sunday newspaper, I took a copy to the Supreme Court to share with Justice Marshall. We had sat together over a six-month period doing interviews for the article, and Marshall, I had learned, could be a gruff and cantankerous individual. He was a person who would sometimes refuse a handshake. He once said to me, "You know, it's one shake for them, a thousand for me, and I've got to eat a sandwich." He could be quite stern. I was more than a little leery of challenging him directly.

When I showed him the magazine, he seemed quite taken by the photographs, even before he read the piece. As he was in a good mood, I thought the visit would be an opportunity to broach a difficult subject. What had become of the *Brown* decision? What was its true legacy?

I began by saying to him, "Justice Marshall, if you look at what's taken place since *Brown,* it's obvious from the most recent statistics that the level of segregation in America's public schools remains very high." I said to him that the level of segregation in America's elementary and secondary schools was as high then as had it been in the late 1960s. Furthermore, looking at the decisions issued by the federal courts, one could conclude that the judiciary had grown tired of taking actions to mandate integration in public schools. They seem to be saying that there is so much residential segregation in America that the burden of achieving the goal of racial integration should not be borne by public schools, which are merely educational institutions.

I told Marshall that I had visited Oklahoma City, where one of the desegregation decrees had been withdrawn. While there, I met with black parents who were arguing with lawyers for the NAACP Legal Defense Fund. The parents did not want to continue with busing programs. They said they were sick and tired of having their children put on buses to be shipped here and there. What they preferred were neighborhood schools where they could attend the PTA meetings easily, watch the school teams play, and participate in other activities. They also said that it was not clear to them that integration had benefited black children. They believed that black teachers were far more nurturing, understanding, loving, and less patronizing than white teachers, and more likely to think that a black child has potential and is someone deserving of their love and attention rather than being viewed as a discipline problem.

I told Marshall about an article in a law review, authored by Clarence Thomas (who would succeed Marshall on the High Court). Thomas claimed that Marshall made a mistake in 1954 by making integration the centerpiece of the effort in *Brown v. Board of Education*. The NAACP should have focused on quality education for all children, regardless of their race. Had it done so, Thomas argued, the divisiveness, polarization, and arguments that have subsequently taken place over school integration might have been avoided; the dollars, energy, and national will would have been focused on providing high-quality schools, without distracting arguments about race.

Justice Marshall, who had been listening patiently, looked up at me with one of his piercing stares. I was afraid he would say, "Just get out, will you?" But instead, he looked at me as if he were looking at someone who walked into the middle of a movie and did not understand the plot.

He said, "You have to understand that back in 1954, we were not interested in creating some Norman Rockwell picture of black children, seated next to white children, seated next to Hispanic children, seated next to Asian children." He said the 1950s were a time when the white students had access to the very best schools in the country: the best in terms of faculty, the best in terms of resources. "We wanted to assure that minority children would have access to those schools. It was never about black children sitting next to white children. If the majority population was protecting the interest of their children, they had to extend the same protections to the minority population."

Marshall conceded that there were developments that he could not have foreseen. He mentioned the high rate of immigration and its impact on the minority populations in cities, and the concentration of black and brown people in inner city neighborhoods. He spoke about his surprise at the decline in the number of school-aged white children in the country. He talked about the suburbanization of the white population. He mentioned the setback in the Detroit case, *Milliken v. Bradley,* in which the Supreme Court ruled in the 1970s that suburban districts were not obligated to participate in metropolitan school desegregation plans. Marshall also spoke with some frustration about the sense that the American public was tired of the quest for integration as a means of guaranteeing equal access to quality education for all children. There was a certain sadness to his remarks.

What came to my mind at that point were previous conversations that I had with Justice Marshall when he described experiences that shaped his understanding of segregation. On one such occasion, Marshall told me a story about having graduated from Howard University Law School, which was then headed by Charles Hamilton Houston. While he was dean of the law school, Houston had been working with the NAACP to examine the damage done by segregation. They were looking for ways in which the law could be used to establish the equality rights of African Americans. One of the first steps in that effort was to document the disparities in black and white public schools in the South.

Not long after Marshall graduated from law school, Houston invited him to take a trip to the South to examine the conditions of black schools. In the 1930s Depression, Marshall did not have many paying clients, so he was all too happy to take the trip. The result was two black men traveling through the South in the summer of 1933 in an old car.

They had bags of food, and blankets and pillows in the backseat of the car, because they could not be sure that they would be allowed to patronize the local hotels and restaurants. Sometimes they slept in the car. They had cameras and notepads, taking pictures as they went along. At one point during the trip, they visited a rural county in the Mississippi Delta, not far from the Louisiana state line. After they arrived, Houston drove to a school building for black children and went inside. There was no floor; the roof was just tarpaper pulled over the top of the shack. When it rained the floors would become thick with mud. What students there were only attended school during the months of December, January, and February, when there were no crops to be planted or harvested. There was no blackboard; the teacher used a piece of coal to write lessons on the wall. These were the conditions that Houston was chronicling while he was inside this building.

Thurgood Marshall was waiting outside eating a sandwich. He was approached by a small, eight-year-old boy, who was clearly a truant. The boy stared at him. Marshall, having recently graduated from law school, thought at first that the child had never seen anyone like him, a black man standing next to a car. The child just stared at him in silence. Marshall then thought that perhaps the child was hungry so he offered a portion of his sandwich. The child shook his head and began to look at an orange Marshall had placed on the hood of the car for his dessert. The child kept pointing at the orange, not saying a word.

Marshall did not want to relinquish the orange, but growing somewhat irritated, he handed it to him. The child took the orange and bit it without removing the rind. Reacting to the bitter taste, the youngster abruptly pulled the orange from his mouth, spraying juice and the pulp on his face. Some of the juice stung his eyes. The child, blinking wildly, flung the orange to the ground. Marshall reacted angrily, shouting, "Oh, my God, what have you done? What the hell is wrong with you? You wasted my orange! What's wrong with you, damn it!"

Houston heard the commotion and, fearing that some crazed segregationist was attacking Thurgood, ran out only to see his six-foot-three former law student shouting at the little boy. "Thurgood," Houston said, "what's going on? What's wrong here?"

Marshall responded, "Dean Houston, you don't understand. This kid took my orange. He bit it right through the rind like a crazy person, then he pulled it out of his mouth, smeared it on his face, got some in his eyes and now he's thrown it on the ground, in the mud, and wasted the orange."

Dean Houston looked at Marshall and said, "Thurgood, you know, I signed your law degree, but I don't think you understand what's going on here. We've been traveling around. Some of these families have invited us in for a meal.

Have you noticed that when we have to use the bathroom we have to go out to an outhouse; in the backyard, there are open troughs filled with human waste? Have you noticed your surroundings?" Houston said. "You don't see any factories or any office buildings; that's because the people here are lucky, Thurgood, if they can get the man in the big house to give them a piece of land on which they can be sharecroppers. That's about it for their economic aspirations."

Turning and pointing at the decrepit school, Houston continued, "Thurgood, this is all the people in this community have to offer their children for an education. This is it." And then he said, "You're going to stand here and scream at this little boy because all he can do is wonder about an orange, because he doesn't know anything about peeling an orange, he doesn't know anything about slicing an orange, doesn't know anything about removing the seeds from an orange. Damn it, Thurgood, this kid's never *seen* an orange."

Thurgood Marshall, twenty-five years old at the time, having grown up in Baltimore, could not believe that there was an eight-year-old child in America who had not seen or eaten an orange. It was beyond his imagination that such a child existed. Marshall wrote this to his mother that night:

> Dear Mom,
>
> You know, I went to law school because I wanted to make you proud. I wanted to be "Lawyer Marshall." I wanted to make some money. But today I met a kid who had never seen an orange.
>
> Dean Houston used to say the lawyer who is not a social engineer is nothing but a social parasite and I really didn't understand what he was talking about. But now, having met an eight-year-old who didn't know what an orange is, an eight-year-old who's never been to school, I'm of the opinion that someone should be a voice for that child in American life, that someone has to stand up and talk about children in this situation.

Marshall returned to Baltimore, but he still did not have many clients. He decided to settle a grudge against the University of Maryland's Law School, a law school that he wanted very much to attend after he had graduated from Lincoln University. Maryland did not accept people of color, so he had not bothered to apply. He persuaded a friend, Donald Gaines Murray, to apply to the University of Maryland Law School. After the application was rejected, Marshall suggested that Murray send a letter to the university's president, asking him why someone who was an honors graduate of Amherst College and a lifelong resident of Maryland would be denied admission to the state's law school.

A few weeks later, a handwritten letter arrived from the university's president stating that the University of Maryland did not accept students of color. Marshall had hoped for such a reply. He now had the policy explicitly stated by the university's president that could be used as the foundation for a lawsuit. Marshall did not expect to win. The political structure in the state was segregationist. But he filed the suit, and a judge at the lowest trial court level, Baltimore City Court, heard the case. The university's lawyers argued that the state intended to build a law school for blacks, some day, in Anne Arundel County, but the legislature had not appropriated the necessary funds. They also claimed that it would have been unreasonable to consider integrating the University of Maryland's Law School because it would diminish the quality of education provided there and damage the reputation of the school.

At the trial, Marshall was accompanied by Charles Houston, who served as co-counsel, and his client, Donald Gaines Murray. Marshall argued that, under that 1896 *Plessy v. Ferguson* decision, separate but equal was the law of the land, but if there was no separate and equal facility to educate black law students, the state was obligated to integrate the existing facility. Much to their surprise, at the conclusion of the trial, Judge Eugene O'Dunn ruled that Murray had to be admitted to Maryland's Law School. A stunned Thurgood Marshall turned to his client and said, "What did he say?" He couldn't believe what he had heard.

By the time *Murray* was decided in the mid-1930s, Houston had moved to New York, where he worked full time for the NAACP. Over the next decade, he used the *Murray* case as precedent to challenge segregation in America's graduate and professional schools. Cases were filed in Missouri, Oklahoma, and Texas, challenging segregation in law schools, nursing schools, pharmaceutical schools, and other graduate programs. These cases were won in the U.S. Supreme Court.

In 1950, the Supreme Court ruled that, even if a state created a separate professional school, it could never be equal to a well-established white institution based on such intangible features as alumni networks, faculty, and reputation. These cases all but overturned *Plessy v. Ferguson* while stopping short of actually doing so. At that point, the NAACP lawyers decided to challenge segregation directly at the elementary and secondary levels. Cases were filed in Kansas, South Carolina, Virginia, Delaware, and the District of Columbia. On May 17, 1954, the Supreme Court ruled, unanimously, that in the area of public education segregation was damaging in ways unlikely ever to be undone to both to black and white children and was, therefore, unconstitutional.

During the meeting where I showed Justice Marshall my magazine article, as he patiently explained the theory underlying *Brown*, he didn't mention the little boy attending the dilapidated, one-room school in Mississippi. He didn't mention the University of Maryland's audacity in saying it would not accept people of color, no matter what their qualifications. Instead, Marshall focused on the tremendous amount of positive change that had taken place over the forty-year period from 1954 to the early 1990s. But he recognized that we still have a long way to travel on the road to equality.

It is important to commemorate *Brown*, as it was a singular event, perhaps the most important ruling in the twentieth century. But we must also understand, fifty years later, that we live in an era of tremendous change. America is now a nation in which more than a third of the population consists of people of color. In the twenty-seven most populous cities, 50 percent of the school-aged children are people of color. Economic success requires a high level of education. But the quality of education needed to compete effectively is not available at many inner city schools. This is one reason why confidence in public education is so low. This is why there is such a contentious debate about magnet schools, charter schools, and vouchers. This is why President Bush pushed for passage of the "No Child Left Behind" legislation, which stresses testing and accountability.

There are conditions that threaten to allow deeper divisions in our society, not solely by race but also on the basis of those who can obtain first-class educations and those who have no chance to do so. This is the threat—and the challenge—that we have inherited fifty years after *Brown*. 30 percent of America's black children attend "hypersegregated" schools that are more than 90 percent black. 80 percent of America's white children attend schools that are more than 90 percent white. The problem is not simply a matter of race. It is also a function of poverty and the resulting social instability that make educating young people all the more difficult.

During the 2004 presidential campaign, the Democratic vice presidential candidate, Senator John Edwards, suggested that education has become a commodity that is bought and sold. We can no longer assume that, like Bill Clinton, any child, by dint of virtue, merit, and hard work, can ascend the ladder of upward mobility, attend Georgetown University and Yale Law School, and be elected president. Education is now an expensive commodity that middle- and upper-class parents purchase for their children. Poor families are simply out of luck.

This is the America in which we reside fifty years after *Brown*. It is a nation that Thurgood Marshall, James Nabrit, and Louis Redding could not have envisioned as they stood on the steps of the Supreme Court building in 1954 and posed for the famous photograph of the three of them, smiling and congratulating themselves. They fought a good fight, but now it is our turn.

I have often been asked why I selected *Eyes on the Prize* as the title of a book I wrote some years ago about the civil rights movement. It comes from an old gospel song with these lyrics:

Keep your eyes on the prize.
Hold on ... hold on.
I know the one thing I did right,
Was the day I started to fight ...
Hold on.

The fiftieth anniversary of the *Brown* decision should not be remembered as an exercise in nostalgia. If *Brown* is to have continuing significance, it must serve as an inspiration for the challenges we confront today. They are, in many ways, a continuation of the challenges Thurgood Marshall, Louis Redding, and others faced more than fifty years ago. They had their moment in May of 1954, but the fight did not end there. The 1954 decision was followed by the "all deliberate speed" ruling in 1955 and the era of massive resistance thereafter. We must drop the pretense and hypocrisy that surround the continuing racial divisions in this country. It is our turn to do what's right: to fight the fight, keeping our eyes on the prize.

CHAPTER SIX

The Difference That *Brown* Made

Robert J. Cottrol

What difference did *Brown* make? Historians, legal scholars, attorneys, and jurists would readily agree as to its place as one of a handful of pivotal cases in the life of the nation and in the history of the Supreme Court. It easily takes its place among the milestones of American jurisprudence, ranking alongside the famous *Marbury v. Madison*, the infamous *Dred Scott v. Sandford,* and the still highly contested *Roe v. Wade.* The case has become a constitutional lodestar, a measuring stick for constitutional methodologies and ideologies for the legal profession and the general public. Yet *Brown* was not simply a case about legal process or the court's proper role in the American system of governance. The decision addressed the nation's most enduring problem: race.

More than a half-century after the 1954 decision, it is not difficult to find those who would argue that the opinion authored by Chief Justice Earl Warren heralded a new era in American race relations, that it helped precipitate the downfall of Jim Crow. Others would contend that *Brown* was a fatally flawed decision that was too weak to have effectively made a difference in the lives of Americans of African descent. Some will claim that the changes that have come about are attributable to other causes: the civil rights revolution, the resulting legislation of the 1960s, and structural changes in American society. Still others will assert that there has been relatively little progress; the apparent racial advances have been more illusory than real. Blacks, they would say, remain entrenched at the bottom of the American social hierarchy, perpetual outsiders, perennial victims of discrimination.

To determine the difference that *Brown* made, one should ask, "How have the circumstances of African Americans changed in the last half-century?" The answer would have to be that the changes have been dramatic. The "colored" and "white" signs, once ubiquitous in many parts of the country, have been removed from the bus stations, water fountains, park benches, and restaurants. The last vestiges of Jim Crow law were eradicated by legislation and court decisions more than a generation ago. Black people occupy positions that would have been inconceivable on that Tuesday afternoon in December 1953, when Thurgood Marshall asked the Supreme Court justices why, out of all of the nation's racial and ethnic groups, Negroes were singled out for separate and unequal treatment. Colin Powell, the son of black, West Indian immigrants, recently served as Secretary of State. Condoleezza Rice, a black woman and childhood friend of one of the girls murdered in the 1962 bombing of a Negro church in Birmingham, Alabama, has succeeded Powell.

African American students are routinely admitted to formerly all-white universities. The same is true for black faculty members, although their numbers are still low in most academic disciplines. Afro-Americans can be found in major law firms and in the executive offices of major corporations. Black elected officials are routinely found in state legislatures and the U.S. House of Representatives. The occasional black governor or senator even serves a term or two.

The African Americans who serve in today's racially integrated armed forces are a far cry from the Negro servicemen in the Jim Crow military of World War I and II. Southern white politicians do not dare to espouse the naked racism of their predecessors. These changes reflect profound advances in American racial attitudes. The liberalization of racial beliefs that began before World War I, and provided the critical backdrop for the *Brown* decision, has intensified. The raw racism that prevailed in daily life, popular culture, and academic circles at the beginning of the last century has become an embarrassing relic, defended only by a marginalized few.

Affirmative action programs have increased the number of minority students admitted to universities and black employees hired by companies, even though those programs are now under heavy criticism. It is noteworthy that the critics of such programs couch their objections in the rhetoric of the civil rights movement, claiming that they are seeking color-blind methods to increase the inclusion of those previously excluded.

The change in racial attitudes among white Americans is even more profound than has generally been acknowledged. Social science surveys indicate an acceptance of interracial relations in family life, marriage, and adoption that would have been unthinkable in 1954 when the *Brown* decision was handed down. Even if some portion of the responses to the surveys reflects socially acceptable answers, the fact that such responses have become the "right" answer indicates a significant cultural change.

The rejection of overt bigotry occurs in some unexpected precincts. Private schools in southern communities that were originally established as segregation academies now routinely enroll black students. White fundamentalist churches often have black parishioners. The election of officials such as former congressmen J. C. Watts of Oklahoma and Mike Espy of Mississippi demonstrates that rural whites will vote for African American representatives. The occasional right-wing, anti-government militia will sometimes have black members. The rejection of the raw racism that prevailed during the first half of the twentieth century has taken root in contemporary America. Racism still exists, but it lacks the official support it had in past generations.

Segregation, however, continues. African Americans are more segregated than any racial or ethnic group in the United States, with the exception of Native Americans. At the dawn of the twenty-first century, nearly half of the black population lives in communities that are 90 percent or more black. The poverty rate for black families is roughly three times the white poverty rate. The percentage of African American children raised in female-headed households has risen dramatically. More than 50 percent of all African American children are raised in such families; the percentage of black children born out of wedlock approaches 70 percent. The unemployment rate for black men is double that of white men. The rate is higher when the unemployment rate for young black men is considered.

The list of African Americans' social disadvantages is long. Inner city black communities have staggering crime rates. The homicide rate for young black men between the ages of fifteen and twenty-four is more than ten times the national average. The alienation of black communities from law enforcement officials is strong. These tensions exacerbate the problem of crime and violence that plague many black communities. Public schools remain highly segregated, but this is not caused by the official policies that were at issue in *Brown*. Opponents of segregated education now face problems more intractable and less amenable to judicial remedies than those confronted by Thurgood Marshall and his associates five decades ago.

Inner city schools are segregated because middle-class parents—white and black—have withdrawn their children from those schools. The movement of the middle-class families to suburban communities, coupled with the increased reliance on private schools in cities, has led to a segregation of poor black children every bit as stark as it was when *Brown* was decided. Empirical studies such as the Harvard University Civil Rights Project's *A Multiracial Society with Segregated Schools: Are We Losing the Dream?* indicate that public schools have been resegregating steadily.

Continued segregation in education is accompanied by other problems. Black educational achievement, as measured by standardized test scores, remains far lower than that for whites. This disparity fuels the national debate over affirmative action, particularly in university admissions. Should students from disadvantaged minority groups be given special consideration in university admissions? Or, should university admissions be race-neutral, despite the long history of racial oppression in America?

For many African American children, schools remain separate and unequal. There are indications that decades of discrimination and isolation have produced conditions that have taken on a cultural life of their own. Some observers believe that inner city children have rejected the attitudes and habits necessary for academic success. Excelling at school, doing well in standardized tests, studying hard, and demonstrating an interest in class are practices that are seen as "acting white"; a rejection of one's racial identity. To the extent that these observations are accurate, they bespeak of a frightening internalization of racist norms that imposed a low ceiling on black intellectual capacity.

Which picture is more representative of the current reality of race relations and the status of Americans of African descent at the beginning of the twenty-first century? Is that reality depicted by the increasingly integrated world of the black middle class and a stable, black working class? Or are conditions better represented by the depressed circumstances of the inner city? Should we judge race in America by pointing to highly educated business managers, college professors, military officers, and presidential advisors? Or does the more accurate picture show functionally illiterate junior high school students in ghetto neighborhoods? Should we applaud changes that have occurred, recognizing the progress that we often take for granted?

The black man driving a municipal bus would have been barred from that job sixty years ago because of his race. Thirty years ago, the African American woman who is a tax advisor would have been precluded from such a position because of her race and sex. Should we decry the fact that young black men, most of whom are innocent of any crime, are far more likely to be detained by police officers because of their color? Is the glass half empty or half full? The answers to these questions provide the keys to understanding the impact of *Brown* on race in America.

For those Americans whose ancestors were imported from Africa in chains to what would become the United States, the question of race has always involved two distinguishable, albeit interrelated, questions. The first involved caste; the second concerned inequality. The caste system exacerbated inequality. This was done when the law required black students to attend segregated and under-resourced schools, when social, economic, and legal barriers reserved the best jobs for white men. The American caste system did more than separate and stigmatize the Negro. It sustained inequalities that persist in educational and occupational attainment, residential patterns, wealth accumulation, and other indicia of success and failure.

The caste system created a wide psychological chasm between black and white Americans. Whites and blacks inhabited different communities in a nation that they shared. This was most true in the South, despite the strong cultural affinities between black and white southerners. This sense of being set apart made African Americans strangers in their own land. The differences were constantly reinforced by a rigid system of exclusion that was enforced by a legal mandate.

Brown's importance lay in its setting the law on the path toward rejection of racial exclusion. *Brown* provided a foundation for later decisions and legislative enactments that established a new set of norms. Before *Brown*, American law sanctioned a system of racial inequality. *Brown* began the process of withdrawing the law's sanction from the caste system that had been a part of American life from the beginning. *Brown* was not the only factor, however. The decision was a catalyst for tremendous changes in legal norms. It was able to do so, in part, because of the courage of ordinary men and women.

This courage started with parents like Harry Briggs of South Carolina, Sarah Bulah of Delaware, and Oliver Brown of Kansas, who challenged segregation in their communities. It also took extraordinary courage for Negro parents after *Brown* to risk their children's safety by sending them to hostile school environments that the Supreme Court ruled could no longer be segregated. The 1954 decision was important, but without the courage of those parents, the Warren opinion would have been a dead letter.

Brown was not self-executing. It took the efforts of courageous Americans of all races who struggled in the civil rights movement to make *Brown* the foundation for laws that rejected the caste system. The civil rights struggles of the 1960s that led to the Civil Rights Act of 1964 and the Voting Rights Act of 1965 played a crucial role in dismantling legal support for the American system of race as caste.

The argument that was originally made in the 1840s in the first school desegregation case, *Roberts v. City of Boston*, by Charles Sumner on behalf of Sarah Roberts, the daughter of a black printer, Benjamin Roberts, finally became national law in America. In the second half of the twentieth century, the law accepted the position argued by Charles Sumner in 1848, and by Thurgood Marshall in 1953, that laws cannot single out Americans of African descent for separation and stigmatization. This proposition has had a powerful influence on American life. It accelerated the rejection of racism as an American cultural norm.

Many Americans view the Constitution with a reverence that takes it beyond the simple status of law. The decision in *Brown v. Board of Education* declaring segregation unconstitutional had an effect on American law as well as on the lives of all Americans. When that decision was combined with subsequent decisions and civil rights legislation, it amplified the voices that were saying that discrimination was wrong and un-American. The synergy between the *Brown* decision and the forces arrayed against racism made the Warren opinion a powerful catalyst for removing barriers and changing racial attitudes. *Brown*'s importance in the history of American race relations is assured, but if it is viewed as having a central importance in the fight against caste and racism, it also provides an important lesson in the law's limitations.

Brown had an important role in challenging the caste system and exclusion, but structural inequality has proven to be a more difficult problem. The profound socioeconomic disparities between blacks and whites can be traced to slavery, segregation, and long-term patterns of exclusion. These disparities were sanctioned by law. The extent to which the law can provide remedies in the future for past wrongs is not clear. What is clear is that the terrain would have been much bumpier and the playing field a lot less level without the efforts of those men and women who developed the strategy, argued the case, and changed history in *Brown v. Board of Education.*

CHAPTER SEVEN

A Glass Half Full

Jack Greenberg

Delaware is, for all practical purposes, where I began practicing law more than a half-century ago, although it feels like only yesterday. As I review in my mind what has occurred since then, it all seems to have happened "once upon a time," as if it were a television documentary or a motion picture. I had done a few other things before the University of Delaware case in 1950, but essentially, my legal career began with *Parker v. University of Delaware,* the case that held unconstitutional the exclusion of black students from the University of Delaware. Prior to 1950, the laws in Delaware required African American students who wanted to attend a state-supported college to enroll in the segregated Delaware State College in Dover.

I remember the *Parker* case so well that it is one of the very few cases of which I remember the citation: 75 A. 2d 225. I had been in the Navy during World War II, graduated from Columbia Law School after the war, and then went to work for the NAACP Legal Defense and Educational Fund in 1949. Thurgood Marshall was chief counsel. He ran the organization in an intuitive, free-form manner. By that time, Marshall already was a giant in the legal profession. Among the great cases he had won was *Smith v. Allwright,* which held unconstitutional the white primary system that kept blacks from participating in the elective process. Another case, *Shelley v. Kraemer*, held unenforceable the restrictive covenants by which white property owners could prevent black citizens from occupying homes in their neighborhoods. He then won the cases that held unconstitutional those laws that kept blacks out of graduate and professional schools.

Louis Redding telephoned Thurgood Marshall, asking him for assistance in a case that he proposed bringing to desegregate the University of Delaware. Without any more discussion with me, Thurgood assigned me to the University of Delaware case simply because, at the time, I was married to someone from Delaware. He actually did not have much of a choice. There were only three other lawyers at the Legal Defense Fund beside himself, and there were more cases than any one of us could handle. Constance Baker Motley was on the staff. She came from Connecticut and was handling Connecticut cases, so she was not available to travel to Delaware. Robert Carter and Franklin Williams had their own important cases. That left me.

I called Louis Redding and introduced myself. His personality was quite famous among those who knew him. He was reticent, reserved, circumspect, and very cautious. There were long pauses between sentences, as he was thinking over what he was going to say, making sure it was right. Over the telephone I could sense that he was wondering who I was, calling him up, trying to get involved in a case with him.

When I came down to meet him for the first time, Redding had an office on the second floor of a building in downtown Wilmington, near the du Pont Hotel, where he was not permitted either to stay or dine at that time. He was the only black tenant in that building. Redding approached me in his cautious way, but very soon we became fast friends. Eventually, Lou Redding became one of my dearest, closest friends, but he was not what one would call a "warm and cuddly" guy. Yet there was nowhere in Wilmington that Redding and I could have lunch together. As with the du Pont Hotel, every place was closed to blacks, except the railroad station and the YWCA.

Lou Redding was a remarkable man. From 1929 to 1956, he was the only black lawyer in the state, though Delaware was not unique in that respect. A number of other states had only a single black lawyer. Alabama had Arthur Shores. Louisiana had A. P. Turead, who was later joined by Ernest "Dutch" Morial, the second black lawyer in the state. Morial's son now heads the National Urban League.

Mississippi had one full-time and two part-time black lawyers. Other states had just a few. Even in New York, where one might expect a great many, the number practicing civil rights was very small. There was only one black lawyer at that time in a full-time civil rights practice. Now there are more black law students at Columbia Law School than there were throughout the entire South in those days. Those men were lonely heroes.

Redding had degrees from Brown University and Harvard Law School, as upscale an education as anyone could get. His father was a postman in Wilmington who wanted his son to have the finest possible education and return to Delaware as a lawyer who would represent his people. Redding wore Brooks Brothers suits and classic Brooks Brothers shirts with roll collars and expensive silk ties. He was the very image of a New England WASP lawyer, except Lou was no WASP. His brother, J. Saunders Redding, was a professor of English at Cornell and a well-known scholar. The Redding family produced offspring of the highest distinction.

By 1950, Thurgood Marshall and the Legal Defense Fund had won cases in the Supreme Court that held unconstitutional the laws excluding black students from graduate and professional school. In *Sweatt v. Painter*, the case against the University of Texas Law School, the Court concluded that a black law school hastily established by the state was unequal to the white University of Texas Law School, one of the leading law schools in the country. The Court held that not only was the black law school unequal in measurable terms but it was also inferior because legal education requires interaction among students and the development of relationships that remain important throughout one's professional life. Compared to the black law school, the University of Texas had bigger and better buildings, a larger and more distinguished faculty, more and better extracurricular activities, and bigger and better libraries. More important, the

Court also found that the separation of black and white students created inequality. Despite these findings, the Court refrained from ruling that segregation per se was unconstitutional.

The Texas case was a revelation to me. The dean of the University of Texas Law School was a famous scholar. This was a dean of a law school who just plain lied on the witness stand. He testified that a two-room, black law school, with no library and no faculty other than two law professors from the University of Texas, and only one student, was equal to the University of Texas Law School—one of the best law schools in the country. Racism was so deeply ingrained that either he believed his statements (which I doubt) or, more likely, he was afraid that the legislature would cut his school's appropriation if he told the truth.

In *McLaurin v. Oklahoma Board of Regents*, a case involving the graduate school of education at the University of Oklahoma, the plaintiff had been segregated in the classroom, the library, and the cafeteria. He sat in the front row of the classroom in a seat labeled "For Negroes Only." The Supreme Court held that this arrangement interfered with the student's ability to learn, but refrained from holding that segregation per se was unconstitutional.

No case had decided that an undergraduate college was obligated to admit a black applicant. The Court's reasoning about the consequences of separation in graduate and professional schools, some argued, did not apply to colleges. *Parker v. University of Delaware* was the first case to address segregation at the undergraduate level. The university's defense was roughly comparable to that offered by the University of Texas in *Sweatt*. The lawyers argued that the University of Delaware was not a state school and, consequently, not covered by the Fourteenth Amendment of the Constitution. It was plain, however, that the state had established the university. The state appointed members of the university board of trustees. The state funded it. The state had all kinds of other involvement, but the lawyers claimed that the university was not a state institution. That argument did not get very far with Chancellor Seitz. How could the lawyers put up such a defense? They couldn't possibly believe the things that they were saying.

They also claimed that Delaware State College, which was obviously unequal even to the naked eye, was the equivalent of the university. The evidence made it plain that this was an untenable position. For example, the university had forty-eight professors who had tenure, thirty-three associate professors earning from $3,000 to $6,700 a year (which was a generous academic salary then), whereas the black college had four professors, period. They earned from $2,200 to $4,300 per year. None of them had tenure.

In preparation for the *Parker* case, we visited both schools. The president of the Delaware State College, Maurice Thomasson, was a wonderful man. He was a brave person in many ways. He supported us, but if he had done so publicly, it could have gotten him in trouble with the state authorities, so he aided us surreptitiously. He took us on a nighttime tour of the campus so we could examine the buildings without being seen. I still remember the decrepit state of some of those buildings. One recollection that sticks with me is a partially detached screen on a screen door on the president's home that was flapping in the wind.

Another image I recall is that of the president of the University of Delaware, John A. Perkins, whom we visited in his office and who testified in the case. Quite unlike the dean at Texas, he was candid and forthright. He described things as they were. He did not defend what the University of Delaware was doing at that time, and he said they were doing it only because state law required them to do so.

The judge in the Delaware case was Collins Seitz, who had the ancient title of "Chancellor." I think Delaware may be the only state in the union that still has separate equity courts and chancellors. When I teach civil procedure, I explain the system to my students. Chancellor Seitz did not satisfy himself merely by reading the records about the two schools. He visited them to see for himself, with us following him as he drove downstate at breakneck speeds, apparently immune from speed limits because he was a judge. We followed him, terrified.

The differences between the two schools were many, all encapsulated in the fact that the university was accredited and the college was not. Central to the differences was that both schools were segregated, an issue that the Supreme Court did not decide until *Brown v. Board of Education.* Seitz concluded that the black college was inferior to the university and held that the university no longer could segregate. But within that ruling is a little story that unfolded during the school segregation case that very soon followed.

It took some courage for Chancellor Seitz to rule as he did because he was elected by the state legislature. Many members of the legislature from southern Delaware did not take kindly to his ruling in the *Parker* case. To anger the southern members of the state legislature, which was the body that would have to reelect him, would not have been easy, but he did the right thing. He held that Delaware State College was unequal.

The first black student to graduate from the University of Delaware was Homer Minus, who became a dentist. Leonard Williams graduated not long after. Williams went to law school and eventually became Lou Redding's partner and also a judge. Very soon after the university case was decided, with the background of Collins Seitz facing reelection by a potentially hostile legislature, a black citizen approached Louis Redding. Claymont, Delaware, did not have a black high school. Black students had to travel into Wilmington to attend high school. The black elementary schools were by no measure equal to the white schools, and moreover, there was a school bus for white students. Whites were very happy to go to school on the bus, but there was no busing for blacks and none of the to-do about busing that we heard after the decision of *Brown*. Redding told the black parents that he would not file a case to travel on the white bus, but he would file a case to desegregate the schools.

We then had to decide where to file the case. If we were to file the case in Chancellor Seitz's court, it might have opened some old wounds, so we decided we would not do that. We filed the case in federal court because we did not want to punish Seitz for what he had done so courageously earlier. After we filed the case in federal court, the attorney general moved to remand the case to state court because, he said, the state court could interpret the state statutes in a way that might not require segregation (which was just ludicrous). But in any event, they sent the case to the state court, and we were happy to be there because, by that time, Seitz had been reelected.

The Delaware cases eventually joined four other cases that the Supreme Court decided under the rubric of *Brown v. Board of Education*. To be quite technical about it, there were just three other cases. *Bolling v. Sharpe*, from the District of Columbia, involved the Fifth Amendment, whereas the four state cases involved the Fourteenth. Most people colloquially refer to all five cases as *Brown*. All of the cases were part of a historic development that began just before World War II, stalled for a while because of the war, and then resumed in the form of cases attacking black students' exclusion from graduate and professional schools.

Brown was part of a campaign to bring an end to racial segregation not only in education but in America. But it did not go in a straight line, as a campaign you might imagine would. It reminds me of the war in Iraq, except that it went a lot better.

Someone once said, "You don't fight the plan; you fight the enemy." We pursued a plan, but when developments threw us in another direction, we moved in that direction. We set out to show that black schools were unequal to the white schools, and that was not a problem in Claymont because there was no black school there. We should have had a case in downstate Delaware, because there was no black high school anywhere in southern Delaware. A black student who finished the eighth grade had to travel to Wilmington, or somehow arrange his or her education in some other way, or not attend high school at all. The entire region had black kids with no high school education.

We described the conditions of the black schools in the Delaware cases. The Hockessin school was one of them. It had multiple classes in a single room. It had an inferior library and no playground. But there was an additional factor that we wanted to establish—that segregation was per se unconstitutional. For that we had expert witnesses, including Kenneth and Mamie Clark, black PhDs in psychology, who conducted what were called "projective tests." Children were given black and white dolls and then asked to tell the Clarks what they thought about them. Some of the black children thought that they themselves resembled the white dolls. Others thought the black dolls were bad and the white dolls were good. The Clarks extrapolated from those tests that segregation distorted reality and damaged the black children's self-image.

There was a psychiatrist whom I enlisted to examine the plaintiffs in the case to form an opinion about how segregation affected them. Frederic Wertham operated a clinic in Harlem. It is still there, I understand. I recall him testifying about a point that stuck with me powerfully. He said, "I hold the scientific opinion that if a rosebush produced twelve roses and only one rose grows, it is not a healthy rosebush. It is up to us to find out what is interfering with its growth and with its health and how the fact of segregation creates in the minds of a child an unsolvable emotional dilemma." He went on to testify that segregation interfered with children's ability to learn, a conclusion to which Judge Seitz referred in his opinion.

The outcome of the cases was that Collins Seitz decided that the black schools were inferior to the white schools. He ordered the white schools to admit our plaintiffs, which they did. He also decided that segregation per se interfered with African American children's ability to learn, but he did not base his decision on that finding because, as he wrote in his opinion, the Supreme Court had upheld segregation and, as a lower court judge, he had no power to rule to the contrary. Seitz ruled for us on the grounds of inequality.

We won and our cases had an important impact on the Supreme Court. Delaware was the first state to do the unthinkable. A Delaware court ruled in favor of the plaintiffs, who began attending white schools. It was a major contribution to the decision of the other school cases. All five cases ended in victory for the plaintiffs, and the cases changed America in fundamental ways.

But before that change could take place, something known as "massive resistance" intervened. This began when 101 southern senators and congressmen signed a manifesto denouncing the Supreme Court. The southern states then set up state sovereignty commissions. These were well-funded bodies that were established to persecute people who were seeking desegregation. Southern officials adopted declarations of "interposition" and "nullification." These were declarations that were originally adopted by the southern states on the eve of the Civil War. The meaning of nullification is pretty self-evident, but interposition? I have often wondered what it was and I have looked it up each time because it is very difficult to conceptualize. It means placing yourself between yourself and the national government; that involves a sort of kind of out-of-body experience.

Southern states adopted pupil-placement laws that made it difficult for black children to attend white schools. They adopted laws that required schools to be closed if black students were admitted. In Virginia, some schools were closed for six years. Southern officials filed lawsuits against the NAACP and the NAACP Legal Defense Fund. One case in Alabama put the NAACP out of business for eight years. There were also violence and other forms of intimidation. There were riots. There was the Little Rock case. Later, there was the Meredith case, in which James Meredith finally entered the University of Mississippi in an atmosphere that included gunfire and bombings. Two people were killed during rioting in Oxford. In Delaware there was the Milford case. Attorney General H. Albert Young became a genuine hero when he said he was going to take the little black children by the hand and take them to school right through the mob. He was heroic because, by saying that, he probably ended a promising political career, killing any opportunity he may have had to be elected senator. But he did the right thing.

After years of massive resistance, the country began to actually desegregate its schools. School desegregation has been spotty, however, proceeding forward to a substantial extent until the mid-1980s, but receding in most parts of the country thereafter.

We have also had desegregation in many other institutions. The *Brown* case gave rise to the civil rights movement. "Freedom riders," who were an important part of the civil rights movement, scheduled their first ride to start in Memphis and end in New Orleans on May 17, the anniversary of *Brown*. Martin Luther King held prayer pilgrimages on May 17 every year. The sit-in demonstrators cited *Brown* as their inspiration.

Rosa Parks was an official of the NAACP. She, of course, was steeped in *Brown* because it was an NAACP and NAACP Legal Defense Fund case. The Montgomery bus boycott that she inspired was not heading toward an inevitable victory. The outcome was uncertain when the Legal Defense Fund filed a lawsuit to hold unconstitutional the bus segregation ordinance. We won that case. The City of Montgomery appealed to the Supreme Court, which held the law was unconstitutional, citing *Brown v. Board of Education*, which means that *Brown* resolved the Montgomery bus boycott.

Brown led to the Civil Rights Act of 1964 and the Voting Rights Act of 1965, though there were other forces at work. It was the end of World War II. The Cold War followed. There was an American policy of anti-colonialism, which was a bit hypocritical, given what was going on in this country at the time, but *Brown* was a catalyst and possibly the most important component of all.

As a consequence of all this, there have been immense gains for African Americans in the United States. More black congressmen have been elected. The mayor of virtually every large city is or has been black. The CEOs (and I find this almost incredible) of Time Warner, Merrill Lynch, Citibank, Xerox, and other major corporations are black. There are now 10,000 black law students in the United States.

There have been immense gains, but at the same time, we must recognize that school integration is in retreat. Today, blacks earn about 60 percent of what whites earn. Black unemployment is double that of whites. Black longevity in Harlem, which is emblematic of the rest of the United States, is less than it is in Bangladesh.

Is the glass half empty or half full? I have wondered why we went through the period of immense struggle after the decision in *Brown*. Why was there massive resistance? Why was it so difficult for at least fifteen years to do anything at all to implement the *Brown* decision?

Last summer, I had an epiphany. I saw, for the first time, something that should have been obvious. However, sometimes you cannot comprehend something until you see it in the proper perspective. I traveled to Eastern Europe to consult on the integration of Roma into the public schools in Eastern Europe. I went there because they are under a mandate from the European community, which has adopted a Race Equality Directive requiring Eastern European countries to integrate the Roma into the public schools. If they do not do so, they will not be admitted to the European Union.

I went to some of the first schools that were integrated, and I was just blown away. Integration was working like a dream. Social workers visited every Roma family in town. Teachers received special instruction on how to handle the integration. Tutors were provided for the Roma students who needed to catch up. Joint social, cultural, and athletic activities were arranged involving the Bulgarians and Roma. Roma students worked together. I attended a meeting with about three or four hundred teachers, administrators, students, and parents, both Roma and non-Roma. Everybody praised the program. The president of Bulgaria presented a speech in which he stated that integration was the best thing for Bulgaria.

Years earlier, in contrast, President Dwight Eisenhower responded to *Brown* skeptically, saying, "Well, I guess the law has to be obeyed." In Bulgaria, however, the response was different.

Brown v. Board of Education could not have accomplished any more than it did during those first fifteen years and even thereafter, because we were dealing with segregationist leaders—the Eastmans, the Talmadges, the Russells, and the Strom Thurmonds—who controlled the Senate and much of the American political system. Political leaders at the highest levels of government opposed *Brown*. In contrast, the political issues in Eastern Europe had been resolved.

I realized then that *Brown* was not a case about schools, though we thought so at the time. It was a case that changed the political system in America. *Brown* functioned like an icebreaker, breaking through a frozen sea, enabling others to proceed through the icy waters. I described this to a friend, a Princeton professor, whose specialty is Franz Kafka. He said that Robert Jackson used the same metaphor in comments about the Nuremburg trials: they were like an axe in an icy sea, breaking things up so the world could proceed. My Princeton friend told me that Jackson actually borrowed the metaphor from Kafka, who wrote that a good book is like an axe chopping through an ice-clogged sea. *Brown* was the icebreaker that enabled the America to chart a course toward racial equality.

To invoke another metaphor, we should not be too upset that, more than fifty years later, the glass is still only half full. Before *Brown*, the glass was completely empty. Perhaps in far less than another fifty years, the glass will be full.

PART II

The Experience: Education and Desegregation

CHAPTER EIGHT

Educational Equity and *Brown v. Board of Education*: Fifty Years of School Desegregation in Delaware

Leland Ware

Introduction

More than fifty years ago the Supreme Court issued its historic ruling in *Brown v. Board of Education*. The decision was among the most important Supreme Court rulings in the twentieth century. It altered the direction of constitutional jurisprudence and dramatically transformed race relations in America. The Court's decision declaring segregation unconstitutional inspired the demonstrations and marches of the civil rights movement of the 1950s and '60s. Those efforts ultimately led to the enactment of civil rights laws that eliminated the legal barriers to racial equality.

Sixty years earlier, the Supreme Court held in *Plessy v. Ferguson*[1] that segregation was constitutional as long as the facilities provided for blacks were equal to those reserved for whites. One year later, in 1897, the Delaware Constitution was amended to mandate separate schools for "white and colored children."[2] During the years that followed, African Americans were excluded from all but the lowest-paying, least desirable occupations. They were compelled to attend separate and unequal schools. Restrictive covenants and other discriminatory practices limited their residential options to segregated neighborhoods in which the principal features were substandard and overcrowded housing. African Americans were excluded from restaurants, hotels, and other public accommodations.

Although Delaware officially remained part of the Union during the Civil War, segregated schools were as prevalent there as in any of the former Confederate states. As late as 1950, there were no public high schools for African Americans in Delaware anywhere south of Wilmington. These conditions were successfully challenged by a pioneering African American lawyer in *Parker v. University of Delaware*, which involved segregation at the state's flagship institution, and *Bulah v. Gebhart* and *Belton v. Gebhart*, the two cases that were decided with *Brown*.

Brown was a product of a long-range, carefully orchestrated legal strategy developed in the early 1930s by lawyers associated with the NAACP. They began with cases demanding that facilities provided for African American students be "equalized" to those maintained for whites, while carefully avoiding a direct challenge to the separate but equal principle established by *Plessy*. Over a period of several years the decisions in the equalization cases gradually undermined the legal foundation on which segregation rested. When the time was ripe, a direct challenge was launched. *Brown* represented the successful culmination of that struggle.

Efforts to implement *Brown* in Delaware and elsewhere were met with fierce opposition. In New Castle County, the largest of the state's three counties, school districts remained under federal court supervision until 1996. As of this writing, Delaware's public schools are racially mixed, but there are substantial performance disparities between black and white students. Dropout rates for African American students are higher and educational attainment levels are lower than those of their white counterparts. Conditions for African Americans have improved, but educational equity has not been achieved.

The Pre-*Brown* Era

The NAACP's Legal Campaign

The National Association for the Advancement of Colored People (NAACP) was established in 1909 by an interracial group of activists to combat the rising tide of discrimination and violence against African Americans. Under the leadership of W. E. B. DuBois, James Weldon Johnson, and others, the NAACP quickly established itself as the leading civil rights organization. For the first twenty-five years of its existence, the association engaged in lobbying, public education, and ad hoc litigation to accomplish its goals. In the early 1930s, however, the NAACP decided to shift its focus to a legal attack against segregation. It earmarked a $100,000 grant it received from a philanthropic organization, the Garland Fund, to finance this effort. Walter White, the executive director of the NAACP, hired Harvard graduate Nathan Margold to undertake a comprehensive study of the segregation laws to determine how they might be successfully challenged in the courts.

A few months later, Margold submitted a document more than two hundred pages long containing a detailed analysis of the segregation laws. Margold concluded that segregation, as practiced, did not comply with *Plessy*'s separate but equal principle because the facilities that were provided for African Americans were always separate, but never equal, to those reserved for whites. One of the many examples concerned the conditions in public schools. In every state in which segregation was practiced, the schools maintained for black students were neglected and their condition deteriorated. The per-pupil expenditures were grossly disproportionate. African American teachers were paid far less than their white counterparts. To remedy these disparities, Margold recommended a series of taxpayer suits against the jurisdictions that practiced segregation.[3]

After receiving Margold's report, the NAACP hired the dean of Howard University's law school, Charles H. Houston, as its first full-time counsel to lead a litigation program. Houston was a brilliant, Harvard-trained visionary. In the early 1930s he transformed Howard Law School from a marginal facility to a fully accredited institution that became the laboratory for civil rights litigation. Houston also inspired a generation of African American law students who went on to lead the civil rights litigation revolution during the 1940s and '50s.[4]

Houston agreed with Margold's analysis, but disagreed with his strategy. Houston was concerned that a direct challenge to *Plessy* in the 1930s might result in a Supreme Court decision reaffirming the separate but equal principle. Houston suggested an indirect approach that became known as the "equalization strategy."[5] Under this approach, the NAACP would file cases arguing that the states practicing segregation were in violation of the Fourteenth Amendment based on the inferior facilities maintained for blacks. Houston also recommended that the litigation focus on graduate and professional schools where the states were most vulnerable. Most states established primary and secondary schools and land-grant colleges for black students, but none provided graduate or professional training opportunities.

Houston believed that if the equality aspect of the separate but equal doctrine were enforced, states that maintained dual systems would be compelled to provide educational facilities for black students that were physically and otherwise equal to those maintained for whites. Southern states could not support the economic burdens of such a system. Under the pressure of litigation, segregation would eventually collapse.[6]

The Graduate School Cases

Houston and Thurgood Marshall, who had been one of Houston's students at Howard, handled the first "equalization" case, *Pearson v. Murray*.[7] The plaintiff Donald Gaines Murray's application for admission to the University of Maryland's law school was denied solely on the basis of his race. A suit challenging the university's decision was filed in a Maryland state court in Baltimore. When the case went to trial, Houston and Marshall forced school officials to admit that the facilities for black students at Princess Anne Academy were not equal to those at the university's main campus.

Maryland, like other southern states, had established a scholarship fund that black students could apply to the costs of attending graduate schools in other states. The state argued that the scholarships satisfied its obligation to provide equal educational opportunities for African American students. During their examinations of state officials, Houston and Marshall proved that the funds were inadequate to satisfy the expenses of the many black students desiring graduate training. At the conclusion of the trial, the judge issued a ruling from the bench ordering the University of Maryland to admit Murray to the law school's entering class the following semester.

The NAACP's next case involved a challenge to the University of Missouri. Lloyd Gaines, a 1935 graduate of Lincoln University in Missouri, applied for admission to the University of Missouri's law school. After his application was denied, Houston and a Missouri lawyer, Sidney Redmond, filed suit against the university in state court. They relied on the Maryland victory and argued that Missouri was obligated to offer legal training to black students as it had for whites.

The Missouri courts ruled against Gaines. The state Supreme Court held that the out-of-state scholarships available to African American students satisfied Missouri's constitutional obligations under *Plessy. Gaines* was appealed, and the NAACP secured its first Supreme Court victory in a school desegregation case. Writing for the majority, Chief Justice Charles Evans Hughes found that the right to equal protection was a "personal one" that could not be satisfied with out-of-state scholarships. The Court held that Missouri had a constitutional obligation to provide legal training to African American students within its borders and that shifting the responsibility to another state could not circumvent that obligation. The Court ordered Gaines's admission to the university.[8]

After *Gaines* the NAACP focused its efforts on teacher salary cases to eliminate racial disparities in compensation.[9] With the entry of the United States into World War II in 1941, the NAACP's attention was diverted to other matters, including defending the rights of African Americans in the military. After the conclusion of the war, however, the focus returned to education, fueled by an unprecedented demand for higher education. Thousands of returning soldiers, including African Americans, enrolled in colleges and universities, armed with GI benefits that subsidized tuition costs.

The Final Phase of the Equalization Strategy

In 1946, the NAACP filed a suit on behalf of Ada Louise Sipuel against the University of Oklahoma, challenging its policy of excluding African Americans. Thurgood Marshall, who had succeeded Houston at the NAACP, argued that Oklahoma was obligated to provide legal training to African American students. After losing at the trial court level, the NAACP lawyers appealed to the U.S. Supreme Court. The Supreme Court held that Oklahoma was obligated to provide legal instruction to black students.[10] State officials responded by renting three rooms in a building across the street from the state capital, hiring a couple of professors, and labeling this arrangement the "Negro" law school. The Supreme Court declined the NAACP's challenge to the state's actions.[11]

That same year, the NAACP filed a similar case in Texas. The plaintiff, Heman Marion Sweatt, was an African American postal worker who applied for admission to the University of Texas Law School at Austin. After Sweatt's application was denied, the NAACP filed suit on his behalf. While the case was pending, Texas, following Oklahoma's example, established a "Negro" law school in Houston by renting some rooms and hiring lawyers to serve as professors. Based on these arrangements, the trial court ruled against Sweatt. While the appeal was pending, the Texas legislature appropriated $100,000 to build a separate law school for African Americans that was ostensibly intended to be physically equal to the Austin facility.

As *Sweatt v. Painter* worked its way through the lower courts, another case was filed in Oklahoma. The plaintiff in the proceeding, George W. McLaurin, was a sixty-eight-year-old professor at Oklahoma's college for black students who applied to the graduate school of education at the University of Oklahoma. Instead of renting out rooms and hiring a meager staff to serve as the black equivalent, Oklahoma reacted by allowing McLaurin to attend classes with white students, but he was required to sit in an alcove behind a sign that read "colored," to sit at a separate table in the balcony of the library, and to eat at a separate table in the dining room. The trial court ruled against the NAACP.

Sweatt and *McLaurin v. Oklahoma* were appealed to the Supreme Court. In *Sweatt*, the Court assumed that the black law school was physically equal to the white school, but held that this was not enough. Education, the Court found, meant more than bricks and mortar. There were certain intangible features, such as prestige of the school, the reputation of its faculty, and the exchange of ideas critical in educational settings that could not be replicated at a segregated law school. *McLaurin* was a case involving segregation within a school. McLaurin attended the same classes and listened to the same lectures as white students, but on a segregated basis. The Court found that the arrangement stigmatized McLaurin and handicapped his ability to pursue an education. In both cases, the Supreme Court finally recognized the stigmatic and other injuries inflicted by the segregated system, but it stopped short of finding that segregation itself was unlawful.

The *Brown* Era

The Delaware Desegregation Cases

While Marshall and the NAACP were filing cases in other states, the effort to desegregate public schools in Delaware was led by an African American lawyer. Louis L. Redding was born in Wilmington, Delaware, where he attended segregated public schools. After graduating from Wilmington's Howard High School in 1919, Redding enrolled in Brown University, where he graduated with honors in 1923. He subsequently enrolled at Harvard's law school in 1925 and was the only African American in Harvard's 1928 graduating class. In 1929, he was the first African American admitted to the Delaware bar.[12]

Redding worked closely with the NAACP after joining the organization's legal committee in 1932. Redding's case, *Parker v. University of Delaware*, was one of the final cases challenging segregation at colleges and universities. During the 1949–50 academic year, thirty African American students at Delaware State College for Negroes applied for admission to the University of Delaware. A special meeting was held on February 18, 1950, at which the University of Delaware's Board of Trustees denied the applications for admission. Redding subsequently filed suit in the Chancery Court. Jack Greenberg, who had recently joined Thurgood Marshall's staff in New York, assisted Redding. The state's lawyers contended that the University of Delaware was a private institution, rather than a state agency, and therefore not subject to the Fourteenth Amendment. They also claimed that the facilities at Delaware State College were equal to those at the University of Delaware.

Chancellor Collins J. Seitz rejected the first argument and ruled that the university was a state agency subject to the Fourteenth Amendment. After visiting Delaware State's campus and comparing it to the University of Delaware, Seitz held that "the physical facilities of Delaware State College are vastly inferior to those at the University. An examination of the curricula and courses offered, the faculties (their credentials, salaries, teaching loads, tenure) and of the libraries led to the same conclusion, as did the fact that the State College has been recently denied renewal of accreditation by the Middle States Association." Seitz ruled that Delaware was not providing African American students with equal educational opportunities and ordered their admission to the University of Delaware.[13] That ruling was not appealed.

After the decisions in *Sweatt* and *McLaurin*, the NAACP lawyers decided that the time was ripe for a direct challenge to segregation. Meetings were held at which the association's lawyers decided that the equalization strategy would be abandoned; all future cases would assert direct challenges to segregation.

Not long after *Parker*, Redding filed separate suits, *Belton v. Gebhart* and *Bulah v. Gebhart*, challenging segregation in two local school districts. The cases were originally filed in federal district court, but Delaware's attorney general argued that the cases involved state law and should be heard in state court. Redding acquiesced, knowing that Chancellor Seitz, who had ruled in his favor in the University of Delaware proceeding, would hear the cases.

The NAACP developed an innovative legal strategy that included the use of social scientist experts who testified about the harm that segregation inflicted on African American schoolchildren. Applying the new strategy, Redding introduced the testimony of fourteen expert witnesses. A professor from Columbia University, Otto Kleinberg, testified that black students had the same learning abilities as white students. A professor from Ohio State, George A. Kelly, described the fatiguing effects of the two-hour bus rides to the black school in Wilmington. Harvard psychologist Jerome Bruner testified that segregation produced frustration, apathy, and hostility in black schoolchildren. Another expert, Steven Wright, described the advantages of Claymont High School, which was maintained for white students. Kenneth Clark presented the results of doll studies in which black children displayed a preference for white dolls and reacted negatively to black dolls.

The experts also measured the effects of segregation on white students. Their studies indicated that segregation tended to reinforce racial prejudices. In response to questions asking how they felt about black children, some of the white students said they wanted to tie the black children's hands and force them to work. Others thought that black children should work while white students were allowed to play. Under cross-examination, the state's expert, George R. Miller, conceded that his own doctoral dissertation concluded that the unequal educational facilities imposed a disadvantage on black students.[14]

After three days of testimony, Chancellor Seitz visited the schools to compare them. On April 1, 1952, Seitz issued a ruling in the two cases finding that "state-imposed segregation in education itself results in the Negro children, as a class, receiving educational opportunities which are substantially inferior to those available to white children otherwise similarly situated."[15] Despite this finding, Seitz ruled that he was compelled by *Plessy* to hold that state-supported segregation did not violate the Fourteenth Amendment. After reaching that conclusion, Seitz turned his attention to the question of whether the state had complied with *Plessy*'s requirements by providing black students with facilities that were equivalent to those established for whites. After completing a detailed comparison of the schools, Seitz found that the facilities maintained for black students were, in all respects, inferior to those reserved for whites. As the state had failed to comply with *Plessy*'s equivalency requirement, Seitz ordered the immediate admission of black students to the white schools. The state appealed, but the Delaware Supreme Court affirmed the lower court's ruling on August 28, 1952.[16] These were the only cases in which the NAACP prevailed at the trial level.

Brown v. Board of Education: *The Supreme Court Arguments*

Brown v. Board of Education consisted of six consolidated cases from five separate jurisdictions: *Brown v. Topeka Board of Education* arose in Kansas and was handled by Robert Carter, a lawyer on the NAACP's staff in New York; Thurgood Marshall was the lead counsel in *Briggs v. Elliott,* the South Carolina case; Spottswood Robinson and Oliver Hill were Virginia-based lawyers who represented the students in the Virginia case, *Davis v. County School Board of Prince Edward County*; James Nabrit, a Howard Law School professor, was the principal attorney in *Bolling v. Sharpe,* which was filed in the District of Columbia; and Louis Redding and Jack Greenberg represented the plaintiffs in the two Delaware cases, *Belton* and *Bulah.*[17]

On December 9, 1952, at 1:35 P.M., the Supreme Court arguments commenced in the school desegregation cases. Robert Carter presented the opening argument on behalf of the students in Topeka, Kansas. Assistant Attorney General Paul Wilson appeared next for the state. At 3:15 P.M., the arguments began in the South Carolina case. Thurgood Marshall presented the arguments for the Clarendon County schoolchildren. After Marshall finished, John W. Davis, a distinguished Wall Street lawyer and former Solicitor General, responded for South Carolina.[18]

On the afternoon of December 10, 1952, Spottswood Robinson commenced his argument on behalf of the students in *Davis.* After Robinson concluded, the attorney for the school board, Justin Moore, responded. When Moore completed his presentation, J. Lindsey Almond argued on behalf of Prince Edward County. The arguments in the District of Columbia case, *Bolling,* followed; NAACP cooperating attorneys, George E. C. Hayes and James Nabrit, presented them. Milton Korman represented the District of Columbia. The Delaware cases, *Belton* and *Bulah,* were the last to be presented. State Attorney General H. Albert Young argued for Delaware. Jack Greenberg and Louis Redding represented the African American students. The arguments concluded on December 11, 1952, at 3:50 P.M.

Several months later, the Supreme Court issued an order that sent the cases over to the next term for reargument. The Court directed the parties to submit briefs addressing a series of questions concerning Congress's intent regarding public schools when it adopted the Fourteenth Amendment. Additionally, the Court questioned the way in which a desegregation order might be implemented if one were issued.

To research the original intent question, Marshall enlisted John A. Davis, a professor of political science at Lincoln University. Davis obtained the assistance of Horace Mann Bond, who was, at that time, the president of Lincoln University. C. Vann Woodward, who later became one of the leading authorities on the Reconstruction period, and John Hope Franklin, a distinguished black historian, also assisted with the research. William Coleman, a young African American lawyer who had graduated first in his class at Harvard and clerked for Supreme

Court Justice Felix Frankfurter, agreed to coordinate research efforts in the various states.

During the next several months, the lawyers, historians, law professors, and other academics assisting the NAACP lawyers grappled with the research concerning the original intent of the framers of the Fourteenth Amendment. They examined records in state archives. There were many long days and nights of exhaustive work. In the end, the researchers were unable to find any unequivocal evidence that directly addressed the Court's questions. The lawyers eventually settled on an argument that the Fourteenth Amendment prohibited state-sponsored segregation. They would contend that *Plessy* rested on a false premise. Segregation was intended, from the outset, to perpetuate racial subordination. The separate but equal doctrine was a convenient legal fiction used to maintain a racial hierarchy.

The lawyers defending the southern school boards reached a different conclusion, relying on, among other things, evidence of segregated schools in the District of Columbia when the Fourteenth Amendment was ratified. They were encouraged by the Court's decision to order reargument. They believed that the historical record and applicable legal precedent amply supported their position.

On September 8, 1953, an important development occurred. Chief Justice Vinson died and was replaced by Earl Warren, a former California governor. After months of anxious waiting, on December 7, 1953, the three days of reargument commenced.

The proceedings commenced at 1:05 P.M. with the *Briggs* case. Spottswood Robinson argued first, covering the legislative history of the Fourteenth Amendment. After Robinson concluded, Marshall presented his argument. John W. Davis followed Marshall. Davis ended by stating that South Carolina had not come before the court in a "sack cloth and ashes," but was confident that its segregated schools were a permissible exercise of the state's authority.

Virginia's Attorney General, Justin Moore, followed Davis. Before Moore could complete his argument, the court recessed for the day. When the Court reconvened on the following morning, Moore concluded his argument. Lindsay Almond followed. After he finished, Marshall presented his rebuttal. Marshall urged the Court to rely on the reasoning of *McLaurin,* which found that segregation violated the Fourteenth Amendment. In a dramatic conclusion, Marshall issued a challenge to the justices, stating that "the only way that this court can decide this case in opposition to our position . . . is to find that for some reason, Negroes are inferior to all other human beings." U.S. Attorney General Rankin followed Marshall. After Rankin concluded, the arguments proceeded in the Kansas case.

While the cases were pending before the Supreme Court, the Topeka school board voted to desegregate its schools. Robert Carter argued that the Kansas case had not become moot because the state claimed that it retained the authority to operate separate schools in districts that elected to preserve segregation. Assistant Attorney General Paul Wilson followed Carter. James Nabrit's arguments in *Bolling* came next. The second round of arguments ended with Louis Redding and Jack Greenberg's presentation of the Delaware cases. The court recessed on December 9, 1953, at 2:40 P.M.

The decision in the school desegregation cases was announced on May 17, 1954, to a packed courtroom. Chief Justice Earl Warren read the opinion. It was written in a straightforward style that could be understood by lay readers. It began with a recitation of the history of the cases from the trials to the arguments before the Supreme Court. The Court found, as a threshold matter, that the original intent of the framers of the Fourteenth Amendment on the question of segregated schools was not clear. The Court then traced the evolution of the separate but equal doctrine from *Plessy* through *McLaurin*.

After describing the importance of education to a democratic society, the Court framed the issue as whether "segregation of children in public schools solely on the basis of race . . . deprives the children of the minority group of equal educational opportunities." It found that it did, concluding that "[t]o separate [black] children from others of similar age and qualifications generates a feeling of inferiority as to their status in the community that may affect their hearts and minds in ways unlikely ever to be undone." Relying on the foundation developed in *Gaines, Sweatt,* and *McLaurin,* as well as the sociological evidence presented by Dr. Clark and others, the Court held that "[s]eparate educational facilities are inherently unequal."[19]

The Post-*Brown* Era

Delaware During the Era of "Massive Resistance"

The Supreme Court's 1954 decision in *Brown* did not address the remedy. The cases were held over and reargued in 1955 to determine the manner in which the Court's decision should be implemented. In the *Brown II* decision, the Court remanded the cases to the trial courts and ordered that the school boards develop plans and to proceed, with "deliberate speed," under the supervision of the local federal courts.[20] Southern states reacted to *Brown* with extreme hostility. They developed a strategy of "massive resistance."[21] For years, southern states openly defied *Brown* or engaged in tactics that caused extended delays in the desegregation process. Like its southern counterparts, Delaware engaged in delaying tactics.

Before the entry of the *Brown II* decree in 1955, the Milford Special School District took steps to desegregate its schools. At the beginning of the 1954–55 academic year, eleven African American students enrolled in a Milford high school. Local residents became apprehensive after they learned that black students were attending classes. After a series of meetings, parents petitioned the school board to resegregate the school. Meetings were held with state officials, which ultimately led to the resignation of the school board members who had approved the desegregation plan. A new board was installed.

The controversy in Milford was reported in the national press. Bryant Bowles, a segregationist and head of the National Association for the Advancement of White People, traveled from Washington, D.C., to organize protests. An anti-integration rally held at a local airport attracted three to five thousand people. Another rally was held on the same evening. Fearing outbreaks of violence, on September 30, 1954, Milford officials yielded to mounting pressures and removed the black students. In October 1954, Louis Redding responded by filing a civil action in Chancery Court seeking to reinstate the students.[22] The trial court ruled in Redding's favor, and the Milford School Board appealed. When the case reached the Delaware Supreme Court, it reversed the decision, after finding that the school board had failed to submit the desegregation plan to the State Board of Education for approval. Local defiance thus succeeded; the schools in Milford remained segregated for more than a decade.[23]

In 1956, Louis Redding filed a class action, *Evans v. Buchanan,* seeking to desegregate Delaware's public schools. The following year, the federal court ruled that the Delaware State Board of Education was obligated to develop and submit a desegregation plan. In 1962, cases were filed against a school district based on its refusal to admit nine black students who attempted to transfer from the all-black Dunlieth school district. In 1968, the Delaware legislature enacted the Educational Advancement Act, which prohibited school districts with 12,000 or more students from consolidating with other districts. At this time, Wilmington was the only district that had an increasing enrollment of black students. The law would have confined most of northern Delaware's black students to Wilmington schools.[24]

The New Castle County Desegregation Litigation

In 1970, the Educational Advancement Act was challenged in the U.S. District Court in Delaware on the grounds that it violated Delaware's duty to disestablish racially identifiable schools. In 1974, 1975, and 1976, three separate decisions were issued in *Evans v. Buchanan.* The first two rulings addressed the violations of the state's duty to desegregate the schools in New Castle County, and the third decision addressed the remedy.[25]

While *Evans* was pending, the Supreme Court held that suburban school districts could not be required to participate in court-ordered desegregation plans unless it could be proven that their actions contributed to segregation in the jurisdiction in which the case arose. In *Milliken v. Bradley,*[26] the Court found that there could be no remedy requiring busing across district lines without a showing of an interdistrict violation.

Although a new standard had been established in *Milliken,* the district court in Delaware ruled in Redding's favor, holding that there was an interdistrict violation in *Evans.* The court ordered a metropolitan remedy that included suburban school districts. This was one of the few desegregation cases in which such a finding was made. The court ruled that the Educational Advancement Act had a significant role in maintaining the racial identifiability of Wilmington and suburban New Castle County schools.[27] The U.S. Supreme Court ultimately affirmed this ruling.[28]

In 1976, the three-judge panel in *Evans* rejected plans submitted by the parties and ordered that the eleven school districts in New Castle County be desegregated and reorganized into a single district. This resulted in a consolidation of the districts and the introduction of busing to achieve the racial balance within individual schools. Whites in New Castle County were adamantly opposed to busing. Surveys revealed that nearly all of the county's whites were opposed to desegregation, as were most of the elected officials. Citizens groups pressured elected officials to take whatever steps necessary to prevent busing. Despite the controversy, the implementation of the court's decree commenced without incident. However, problems arose in individual schools. In 1990, the federal district court ruled that one of New Castle County's school districts, Red Clay, failed to comply with the 1978 desegregation order.[29]

In the early 1990s, however, the Supreme Court's desegregation jurisprudence took a dramatic shift with the decisions in *Board of Education of Oklahoma City v. Dowell, Freeman v. Pitts,* and *Missouri v. Jenkins.*[30] In *Dowell,* the Supreme Court held that the standard for determining unitary status was whether the school board "had complied in good faith with the [original] desegregation decree" and whether all "vestiges of past discrimination had been eliminated to the extent practicable." In *Freeman v. Pitts,* the Court found that when single-race schools continued to exist because of changes in the racial composition of neighborhoods or other external factors, school districts would not be held responsible unless those factors were caused by actions taken by school officials.[31]

Dowell and *Freeman* effectively abandoned the *Green* standard, which imposed an affirmative duty to eliminate all vestiges of segregation "root and branch."[32] Under the Court's revised formulation, school districts were obligated to eliminate lingering vestiges of segregation only to "the extent practicable." This obligation was affirmed in *Jenkins* where the majority explained that the ultimate test for determining unitary status was not a finding that all vestiges of the formerly segregated system had been eliminated "root and branch," but "whether the [constitutional violator] ha[s] complied in good faith with the desegregation decree since it was entered, and whether the vestiges of past discrimination ha[ve] been eliminated to the extent practicable."[33] The Court also found that factors such as segregated housing patterns, which affected the racial composition of schools, would not figure into the remedial calculus unless they could be directly attributed to the actions of school officials.

Dowell, Freeman, and *Jenkins* created a much lower threshold for finding that a school system has reached unitary status. They essentially required courts to hold that the desegregation obligation had been satisfied, even when schools remained racially identifiable as a result of segregated housing patterns. This has resulted in unitary status findings in school districts across the nation.[34]

In 1996, applying this modified standard, the U.S. Court of Appeals for the Third Circuit affirmed a 1995 trial court ruling that the school districts in New Castle County had achieved unitary status and were to be released from federal court supervision. In *Coalition to Save Our Children v. State Board of Education,*[35] the court rejected the arguments of opponents to the unitary status motion. The opponents contended that schools were racially balanced, but black students were not receiving the same quality of instruction as white students. This disparity, they argued, was reflected in disproportionate levels of disciplinary actions inflicted on black students and the overrepresentation of African American students in "special" education programs. The evidence supporting these claims did not prevent the court from finding that unitary status had been achieved. It measured desegregation mainly in terms of the racial balance within schools. The undisputed evidence of substantial performance disparities and a disproportionate percentage of black students in special education classes and other noncollege track programs were, in the court's view, attributable to "socio-economic" factors external to the schools.[36]

This was a bitter disappointment to those who hoped that *Brown* would mean that black students would have access to educational opportunities on the same basis as white students. There was an undisputed correlation between race, discipline, and academic performance. The educational outcomes for black students were, on average, less favorable than for white students in the same buildings.

More recently, the Delaware state legislature dealt another blow to school desegregation when it enacted the Neighborhood Schools Act in 2000, which allows students to attend schools closest to their residences. As a result of this statute, it is likely that the students residing in Wilmington will attend schools with high African American and Latino enrollments, because these groups comprise 90 percent of the city's students.

Educational Disparities Persist

Empirical evidence indicates that educational equity has not been achieved in Delaware. Today, educational attainment averages for African Americans still lag far behind white averages. African American students score well below the state average on mandatory student achievement examinations that were introduced in 1998.[37] Test results released on July 17, 2003, by the Delaware Department of Education show that nearly 75 percent of the state's black eighth graders did not satisfy the required standard in mathematics. Roughly half of those test-takers received scores that could justify their retention in the eighth grade for two more years. At the tenth-grade level, roughly 57 percent of low-income and Hispanic students did not meet the reading standard. Approximately 75 percent of the students in both groups did not meet the mathematics standard.[38]

These low scores will have an irreparable effect on the academic careers of these individuals. Students who do not obtain passing scores on the examinations cannot be promoted to the next grade level. Those who are able to fulfill all other state and local academic requirements will only be eligible to receive a "Basic" high school diploma, the lowest of the three levels established under Delaware's new accountability regime. As a result of low scores on mandatory tests, African American students are disproportionately represented in programs for students with learning disabilities.

Education is not the only area in which there are stark racial disparities. Delaware's African American residents earn, on average, sixty cents for each dollar earned by the average white family.[39] Blacks are underrepresented in professional and upper level management positions and overrepresented in the lowest paying and least desirable occupations. The rate of homeownership for African Americans is 20 percent lower than the rate of white ownership. Even when family incomes are essentially the same, the level of African American home ownership is significantly lower than that of similarly situated whites. Over the last decade, many localities in the state have become more integrated, yet there are many communities that are becoming far more segregated, especially within the city of Wilmington.[40]

Conclusion

The victory in *Brown* sparked a decade of mass marches and organized demonstrations that led ultimately to the civil rights legislation of the 1960s. These laws struck down the legal barriers to racial equality. *Brown* was a turning point in constitutional law and in American race relations, but its legacy remains clouded and uncertain. After the *Brown* decision, Delaware officials engaged in years of delaying tactics and did not begin to make serious efforts to desegregate the state's public schools until the late 1970s. The school districts in New Castle County were released from federal court supervision in 1996 based largely on a modified and considerably relaxed standard for determining unitary status. Despite this finding, the academic performance gap between black and white students persists. Conditions for African Americans in Delaware have improved considerably since 1954 when *Brown* was decided, but educational equity has not been achieved.

Notes

1. 163 U.S. 537 (1896).

2. Delaware Constitution of 1897, Article 10, Section 2.

3. For detailed examinations of the history and circumstances surrounding the NAACP's legal campaign against school segregation, see Richard Kluger, *Simple Justice* (Knopf, 1975); Mark Tushnet, *Making Civil Rights Law: Thurgood Marshall and the Supreme Court, 1936–1961* (Oxford University Press, 1994); Jack Greenberg, *Crusaders in the Courts: How a Dedicated Band of Lawyers Fought for the Civil Rights Revolution* (Basic Books, 1994); Juan Williams, *Thurgood Marshall: American Revolutionary* (Crown, 1998); James K. Patterson, *Brown v. Board of Education: A Civil Rights Milestone and Its Troubled Legacy* (Oxford University Press, 2001); Carl Rowan, *Dream Makers, Dream Breakers: The World of Justice Thurgood Marshall* (Little, Brown, 1994); Howard Ball, *A Defiant Life: Thurgood Marshall and the Persistence of Racism in America* (Crown, 1998); Michael Davis and Hunter R. Clark, *Thurgood Marshall: Warrior at the Bar, Rebel on the Bench* (Carol, 1992); Roger Goldman, David Gallen, *Thurgood Marshall: Justice for All* (Carroll and Graf, 1992); and Randall W. Bland, *Private Pressure on Public Law: The Legal Career of Justice Thurgood Marshall, 1934–1991*, rev. ed. (Kennikat, 1973).

4. Genna Rae McNeil, *Groundwork: Charles Hamilton Houston and the Struggle for Civil Rights* (University of Pennsylvania Press, 1983); Geraldine R. Segal, *In Any Fight Some Fall* (Mercury, 1975).

5. McNeil, *Groundwork*; see also R. Carter, *In Tribute: Charles Hamilton Houston*, 111 Harv. L. Rev. 2149 (1998).

6. *Id.* See also R. Carter, *A Tribute to Justice Thurgood Marshall*, 105 Harv. L. Rev. 33 (1991).

7. 182 A. 590 (Md. 1936); *Court Orders U. of Md. to Admit Amherst Graduate*, Baltimore Afro-American, June 22, 1935.

8. *Missouri ex rel. Gaines v. Canada*, 305 U.S. 337 (1938); L. Bluford, *The Lloyd Gaines Story*, 32 J. Educ. Sociology 242, 243 (1959); L. Grothaus, *The Inevitable Mr. Gaines*, 26 Arizona and the West 21, 26 (1984).

9. Mark Tushnet, *The NAACP's Legal Strategy Against Segregated Education: 1924–1950* (University of North Carolina Press, 1987).

10. *Sipuel v. Board of Regents*, 332 U.S. 631 (1948).

11. *Fisher v. Hurst*, 333 U.S. 147 (1948); Walter White, *A Man Called White: The Autobiography of Walter White* (Viking, 1948).

12. A. Woolard, *A Family of Firsts: The Reddings of Delaware* (1993) (unpublished PhD dissertation, University of Delaware) (on file with author).

13. 75 A. 2d 225 (Delaware Ch. 1950); L. Redding, *Desegregation in Higher Education in Delaware*, 27 J. Negro Educ. 253 (1958); Greenberg, *Crusaders in the Courts*, at 88–89; John Munroe, *The History of the University of Delaware* 362–64 (University of Delaware Press, 1986).

14. 87 A. 2d 862, 865 (Del. 1952). 91 A. 2d 137 (Del. 1952); *Brown v. Bd. of Educ. of Topeka, Shawnee County, Kan.*, 347 U.S. 483 (1954); *Brown v. Bd. of Educ. of Topeka, Kan.*, 349 U.S. 294 (1955); Kluger, *supra*; Greenberg, *supra*, 135–39.

15. *Belton*, 87 A.2d at 865.

16. 91 A.2d 137.

17. 345 U.S. 972 (1953); Oliver Hill, one of the NAACP's lead attorneys in the Virginia case, discussed the litigation campaign in his autobiography, *The Big Bang: Brown v. Board of Education and Beyond* (Four-G, 2000); 87 A.2d 862, 865 (Delaware 1952); 91 A.2d 137 (Delaware 1952); *Brown v. Bd. of Educ. of Topeka, Shawnee County, Kan.*, 347 U.S. 483 (1954); *Brown v. Bd. of Educ. of Topeka, Kan.*, 349 U.S. 294 (1955). There were dozens of lawyers actively involved in the *Brown* litigation who have not received the recognition they deserve for their important contributions. Most of them are identified in *Simple Justice* and *Crusaders in the Courts.*

18. A transcript of the arguments in *Brown* can be found in *Argument: The Oral Argument Before the Supreme Court in Brown v. Board of Education of Topeka*, ed. Leon Friedman (Chelsea House, 1969). See also, Greenberg, *Crusaders in the Court*, at 168–75, 189–94; Kluger, *Simple Justice*, at 544–81, 667–78; William H. Harbaugh, *Lawyer's Lawyer: The Life of John W. Davis* (Oxford University Press, 1973).

19. 347 U.S. 483.

20. 349 U.S. 294.

21. Constance Baker Motley, *Equal Justice Under Law* (Farrar, Straus and Giroux, 1998).

22. *Steiner v. Simmons*, 11 A.2d 574 (Del. 1955).

23. Ed Kee, *The Brown Decision and Milford, Delaware, 1954–1965*, 27(4) Delaware History (1997–98), 205–43.

24. *Evans v. Buchanan*, 256 F. 2d 688 (3d Cir. 1958). See generally, Irving Morris, *The Role of Delaware Lawyers in the Desegregation of Delaware's Schools: A Memoir*, 9 Widener L. Symp. J. 1 (2002); *Evans v. Buchanan*, 207 F. Supp. 820 (D. Del. 1962); 14 Del. Code Ann. Sec. 1004.

25. *Evans v. Buchanan*, 379 F. Supp. 1218 (D. Del. 1974); *Evans v. Buchanan*, 393 F. Supp. 428 (D. Del. 1975); *Evans v. Buchanan*, 416 F. Supp. 328 (1976).

26. 418 U.S. 717 (1974).

27. *Evans*, 393 F. Supp. 428, 447 (D. Del. 1975).

28. *Buchanan v. Evans*, 423 U.S. 963, *reh'g denied*, 423 U.S. 1080 (1975).

29. *Evans*, 416 F. Supp. at 343–46; Jeffrey A. Raffel, *The Politics of School Desegregation: The Metropolitan Remedy in Delaware* (Temple University Press, 1980); *Coalition to Save Our Children v. Buchanan*, 744 F. Supp. 582 (1990).

30. 498 U.S. 237 (1991); 503 U.S. 467 (1992); 515 U.S. 70 (1994).

31. 498 U.S. at 249–50; *Freeman*, 503 U.S. at 496–97.

32. *Green*, 391 U.S. at 438.

33. *Jenkins*, 515 U.S. at 89 (quoting *Dowell*, 498 U.S. at 249–50).

34. Gary Orfield and Susan E. Eaton, *Dismantling Desegregation: The Quiet Reversal of Brown v. Board of Education* (New Press, 1996).

35. 90 F. 3d 752 (3rd. Cir. 1996).

36. *Coalition* at 777–78.

37. Leland Ware, David Rudder, and T. J. Davis, *The Pace of Progress: The State of People of Color in Delaware* (Wilmington Urban League, 2002).

38. *Racial, Income Test Gaps Persist: Black, Hispanic, Poor Students Lag*, News Journal (Wilmington), July 27, 2003.

39. Ware, Rudder, and Davis, *The Pace of Progress.*

40. *Id.*

CHAPTER NINE

Lost Opportunity: The Failure to Integrate Milford's Public Schools in 1954

Orlando Camp and Ed Kee

The year 1954 was one of monumental events. One of the most significant of these events was the *Brown v. Board Supreme of Education* ruling that declared segregation in public education unconstitutional. Eleven African American tenth graders in Milford, Delaware, would be among the first beneficiaries of the *Brown* decision, as well as the first victims of massive resistance to school desegregation. These young and unknowing pioneers—Kenneth Baynard, Leo Blue, Orlando Camp, Charles Fleming Jr., Eugene Harris, Irene Pettyjohn, Lillian Simmons, Madeline Staten, Annie Ruth Thompson, Edna Turner, and Ronnie Vann—would serve as the focal point of what became a national debate on race and education. The debate endured for decades, but the students were quickly forgotten. Milford, the scene of one of the first attempts to integrate schools after the *Brown* decision, waited fifty years to acknowledge that historic effort and the black students who had the courage to cross the color line. Indeed, more than fifty years later, the nation still struggles with issues of race and education.

Segregation of blacks and whites in Delaware public schools was prescribed by the State Constitution of 1897. However, rulings by a judge in Delaware's Court of Chancery produced the first challenge to Jim Crow laws in Delaware schools fifty years later, and cracks in the facade of Delaware's segregated educational system began to appear by the early 1950s. A small number of black students enrolled in the previously all-white University of Delaware in 1951 after a lawsuit forced the institution to desegregate. In the 1953 decisions of *Bulah v. Gebhart* and *Belton v. Gebhart,* Chancellor Collins Seitz found that white elementary schools in Hockessin and Claymont, in northern Delaware, were superior to black schools in those communities. Seitz ruled that black students in those communities had to be admitted to the white schools because of the "separate but equal" principle established in *Plessy v. Ferguson.* The Delaware cases, *Bulah v. Gebhart* and *Belton v. Gebhart*, were appealed to the U.S. Supreme Court and consolidated with cases from four other jurisdictions. All of these cases were decided together as *Brown v. Board of Education* on May 17, 1954.

In *Brown*, the Supreme Court struck down segregation in public schools because it violated the equal protection requirements of the Fourteenth Amendment. A black reporter recalled that May 17, 1954, was "the day we won; the day we took the white man's law and won a case before an all-white Supreme Court with a Negro lawyer. And we were proud."[1]

Brown's implications were far reaching. No other American institution touched more lives and promised more for the future than the nation's public schools. After the *Brown* decision, thousands of local communities had to wrestle with school desegregation and, in the process, were transformed forever. Milford, Delaware, located in a border state but with a distinctly southern outlook, was one of the first communities that attempted to integrate its schools. This effort was well intentioned, but ultimately unsuccessful. In this process of integration, Milford experienced the hope and the despair that accompany dramatic changes to longstanding traditions.

The Setting: Milford, Delaware

In 1954, Milford was a small town with 5,179 residents, of whom 16.7 percent were African American.[2] Most of Milford's blacks were hard pressed to provide material welfare for themselves and their children. One of the authors, Orlando Camp, an African American, remembered growing up in Milford during the early 1950s. He recalled,

> It was a town where both races coexisted, but coexisted with the unwritten rules of segregation. While there was no history of open confrontation between the races, it was clear that certain lines could not be crossed. Milford was a simple place to grow up. It was a peaceful town. Living in Milford in the 1950s was like living in a mythical America. Whites pretended to get along with blacks, and blacks smiled and pretended to be happy with what whites gave them. We justified this approach by telling ourselves that things could be worse and things were not as bad as in the past. Whites treated blacks with a degree of a paternalistic attitude. This was easy to do because it did not cost the whites anything to be nice to blacks. Whites gave up nothing to be kind to blacks. In fact, they gained some self-satisfaction from trying to help, although in perhaps a superficial way, which helped lessen racial guilt.

The Milford community of 1954 had a more diverse economic base than could be found elsewhere in southern Delaware. Farms, vegetable canneries, poultry-processing plants, and related agribusinesses were joined by several small manufacturers, which provided plentiful employment opportunities. The workforce was highly educated. As a result, Milford was perceived to be more prosperous and more progressive than surrounding communities.

For blacks, however, Milford was not a progressive community. Jim Crow laws had a very strong presence in Milford and the rest of Delaware. Milford's public school system, restaurants, and theaters were segregated. The Schine Theatre, located on Walnut Street, the main street of Milford, advertised its balcony as the nicest facility in southern Delaware for colored patrons. Although public transportation was not segregated, housing and job opportunities for blacks were restricted by custom and design. Blacks were limited to the lowest paying, least desirable occupations. Throughout the early 1950s, classified ads in the *Wilmington Morning News* asked for "Colored Woman" or "Colored Man" for domestic positions.[3] Blacks were expected to perform this type of work.

The tradition of segregation was firmly entrenched in Milford by the time John Glenn arrived in 1937. Having just graduated from the University of Pennsylvania, Glenn accepted a position with the Caulk Company as a chemist. Glenn, who is white, grew up and attended integrated public schools in Philadelphia during the 1920s and 1930s. Recalling his first impression of Milford, Glenn remembered that he was shocked. Particularly surprising to Glenn was the low standard of living experienced by most blacks and the tradition of segregation.[4]

Milford High School Integrates

To most of Milford's residents, September 8, 1954, seemed no different from any other opening day for public schools in recent years. A feeling of excitement, anxiety, and anticipation, which always marked the first day back from summer vacation, was in the air as students poured off school buses and out of cars in front of the brick building that housed all twelve grades. However, unbeknownst to most of the students, parents, and even some teachers, the upcoming year would be like no other. For the first time, black students would be enrolled in the previously all-white Milford High School on Lakeview Avenue. The admission of eleven black children to the tenth grade in the fall of 1954 would change Milford forever, and leave lasting memories of a year described some forty years later as "tense times."[5]

Milford was perceived as a prosperous, stable, and even progressive community by the standards of southern Delaware. By October 1, however, Milford would experience mass demonstrations, threats of violence, bomb threats, school boycotts, cross burnings, school closings, national media attention, the en masse resignation of the school board, the formation of a new board, and the abandonment of integration efforts. By the end of the 1954–55 school year, Milford would have struggled through lawsuits, court appeals, and the most divisive and bitter school board election in Delaware history. Ten years would pass before someone with moderate views about race would be elected to the Milford School Board. The sentiment among many of the teachers employed by the Milford school system has been that events surrounding the desegregation, rather than desegregation itself, impaired the quality of public education in Milford for years. The events of 1954 were a harbinger of tensions that would divide not only Milford but also the nation throughout the following decades.

To most Milford residents, the events of the 1954–55 school year seemed to come out of the blue, somehow vaguely related to a Supreme Court ruling handed down the previous May. At best, the Supreme Court's decision in *Brown* seemed unnecessary. At worst, it was part of a plot designed by evil forces to ruin the country. How and why the nation's highest court declared school segregation to be unconstitutional was simply not understood by Milford residents. Later, there was little doubt among them that the hand of the U.S. Supreme Court was touching their lives.

When schools opened in the fall of 1954, 687 white students were enrolled in Milford High. What was unusual was that they were joined, for the first time, by eleven blacks who had been admitted to the tenth grade. Elsewhere in Delaware, eighteen black students were admitted to the previously all-white Dover High School. The Dover and Milford attempts at integration were the first in southern Delaware's public schools. In Wilmington, in northern Delaware, public school integration began without incident.[6]

Several days before school opened, Milford's white teachers got a glimpse of how their district would react to *Brown.* Marjorie Summers, a seventh-grade English teacher at the time, remembered, "At our annual faculty meeting, held just before the school year began, for the first time ever, the black teachers from the Banneker School attended."[7] Another elementary school teacher, Thelma Mayhew, remembered that "colored leaders" threatened a lawsuit or some other type of action that forced the Milford District to attempt integration to make Milford a "test school."[8]

In 1954, integration made sense to community and business leader I. G. Burton because Milford was "going to have to do it sooner or later, so why not phase it in?"[9] William V. Sipple Jr., a school board member in 1954, recalled no outside pressure to integrate. "I happened to miss the meeting at which it was decided to integrate, although I supported it fully," he said. Sipple also maintained that the Milford school board simply responded to the *Brown* decision because it "had to, and should do [it]."[10] Orlando Camp remembered having a limited understanding of *Brown,* as a young high school student in 1954:

> In fact, it was not expressed in any legal terms in our community or in our schools as we began to hear rumblings of changes that might come. We heard some lawyer took a case to court and was fighting in the court to get school rules changed. We didn't hear words like integration, or *Brown v. Board.* But we knew something was happening. The rumblings came from our parents and other adults who were not directly talking to us, but talking with each other, with us kids within earshot. With no television and limited radio, instant access to national media events was virtually non-existent. The only contact we had in our house with the outside world was listening on the party line of the local telephone. We did not understand what it all meant, but we knew something was good when we saw our parents' smiles on their faces that perhaps change would be coming.

On August 30, spurred by black pressure, the Milford school board took even more concrete steps to further integration. It made the following decisions:

- Colored students residing in the district where no facilities were provided would be admitted to the Lake Avenue School.
- The date of the committee meeting to study integration and desegregation was to be set at the regular board meeting on September 13, 1954.
- The superintendent, in cooperation with Mr. Kimmel, board president, was to prepare a tentative list of questions for committee members to be approved at the next board meeting.
- Statistical information regarding the opening of school as to enrollment, per-pupil cost, and the like, was to be prepared.

- Mr. Randolph Fisher, president of the NAACP local branch, was to be notified that the Milford Board of Education would review the NAACP petition on September 13.
- A letter to the State Board of Education was to be prepared stating tentative plans for desegregation.[11]

While the school board was taking these actions, Milford's black community, aware of the *Brown* decision, wondered if the all-white Lake Avenue High School would be open to their children. They turned to Reverend Randolph Fisher, a black Methodist pastor and local representative of the NAACP, for guidance. Fisher was aware of two recent cases in the Delaware Chancery Court, *Belton v. Gebhart* and *Bulah v. Gebhart,* in which the court ruled that, if local segregated schools were not equal, then black students were entitled to attend white schools. Mindful of these two Delaware cases and the *Brown* decision, Fisher advised black parents to enroll their children in Milford High School.[12] Otherwise, black students of high school age would have to continue to make the forty-mile round-trip journey to all-black high schools in Georgetown and Dover.

The NAACP petitioned the board to consider black enrollment. According to Dr. William Kimmel, son of board president Dean Kimmel,

> It was a night in August, when there was a knock on the door and a black attorney and another black man, I don't remember their names, came to visit Dad. Right out of the blue. They had an injunction to integrate the Milford Schools. I stayed on the back porch and listened to them in our dining room.
>
> My dad told them this was going to blow the town apart. They eventually came to a deal to admit the kids to tenth grade; they had just graduated from Banneker and had to go to either Jason in Georgetown or Henry in Dover. It all started that night in Dad's dining room at 430 S. Walnut.[13]

Milford was an obvious choice for school integration in southern Delaware because it was the largest downstate community without a black high school. In addition, Milford had a significant and cohesive black community that could be kept informed of civil rights issues by its churches and its NAACP chapter. Yet while the black community sensed change, the white community was largely indifferent. However, the Milford school board, which had jurisdiction over both black and white public schools, knew it would soon be confronted with requests for integration by black residents.

In early September, local papers published a press release from the Milford school administration announcing that the new school term would start on Wednesday, September 8 and that "[w]hite pupils in grades one through twelve will report [as usual] to the Lake Avenue School. Colored pupils in grades one through nine will report to the Benjamin Banneker School." This press release did not mention the possibility of integration. Only a few residents in Milford knew that eleven black students were about to enter the tenth grade of the all-white Lake Avenue High School.

Some advance notice of this change to the broader community might have tempered the subsequent local reaction. *Wilmington Morning News* columnist Bill Frank stressed that the lack of notice was a factor in producing racial tension throughout the town. Frank received numerous stories that the townspeople and the folks in the Milford area first learned what the school board had done when their children came home from school and told them.[14] Board member William Sipple said there simply was not time to inform the community because the decision to partially integrate was made so close to the beginning of the school year.[15]

As one of the first beneficiaries of *Brown,* Orlando Camp recalled his reaction to first hearing that he would attend the all-white Milford High School. "I was happy for many reasons," said Camp. He continued,

> First, I was happy because I didn't have to take that long damn bus ride to Dover or to Georgetown, which were both an hour and a half ride with all the stops. We only lived four blocks from the white school, which only took me fifteen minutes to walk to school. Also, I was pleased to hear I was going to the white school because even though we were kids, we knew that education was the key to success for our futures. We also knew from talking to our black teachers, that the educational opportunities would be better at the white school simply because the materials, funding, and support were greater than we experienced at Benjamin Banneker. Many of our books were mimeographed from twenty-year-old textbooks; some of the books were underlined and marked by previous students. But our teachers were clever enough to point out that our textbooks may have incorrect or dated information, and they would teach from their knowledge and history of certain events or subjects. Even though the teachers had obstacles to overcome with a scarcity of materials, the teachers at Banneker were not only instructive but also inventive and innovative in bringing the knowledge to us.
>
> I woke up early on Wednesday, September 8th, to get ready to go school. The NAACP had made arrangements for us to be picked up and carried to school in cars owned by local black parents. I don't know this for sure, but apparently that strategy was to avoid any possible incident or trouble if we had attempted to walk to school, which was more than a mile for many of the black children. Nine students were assigned to ride in cars; two who came in from the rural areas were assigned to still-segregated buses. Melvin Staten, father of Madeline Staten, one of the eleven black students, drove his car with several students. Charlie Fleming and Kenneth Baynard rode in from the country on the bus, still a segregated school bus, driven by Amos Bell.
>
> We pulled up in front of the white school, and there were perhaps ten people milling about outside the school. They were not necessarily spectators, but just adults dropping off their children. We went into the principal's office for a brief meeting. He made a brief speech to welcome us, lay out ground rules for behavior along with school policies and procedures. Each of us were then taken to separate homerooms to begin our new school experience. We were assigned to separate homerooms; there were no more than two blacks to each homeroom. I'm sure the school broke us up so that each student would have a chance to blend in with their white classmates, rather than keeping us as one large group of black students. In talking to some of my classmates, this was devastating because it isolated us. It made us feel that we were alone. There was no sense of friendship with our white classmates. This is not necessarily negative; neither side, black or white, had any prior experience in sitting side by side with a common objective, that is, to learn.
>
> The teachers introduced themselves as many of the students remembered, in a courteous fashion, but not friendly. I think it's understandable that they were not sure how to handle this historical situation for the first time, since there had been no special training or meetings about integration. This was well before the days of sensitivity training. If they were seen to be too friendly to the colored kids, the white

community could judge the teachers as "nigger lovers." No doubt, some teachers were unsympathetic to school integration, and yet some teachers understood it and supported it.

Fifty years after those September days of 1954, three interesting perspectives, two white and one black, surfaced about the integration of the Milford High School football team at the Delaware *Brown* symposia in Milford and Dover. Orlando Camp and Ronnie Vann were the first blacks to play on the team. Ed Steiner, a white player, remembered the following:

> Some black kid scored a touchdown during a scrimmage. It was a nice run, and typically when someone scored a touchdown, we really hollered and whooped it up. With this black kid doing it, we didn't quite know how to react. It was something new for us so we politely applauded, generating far less noise and enthusiasm than would have been customary.

Marvin Schellhouse, a senior on the team, also recalled that "during the scrimmage, this black guy faked us out and ran through us for the touchdown. One of my white teammates ran up to me and said, 'Why'd you let that nigger score a touchdown?'" Schellhouse replied, "I didn't let him do anything; he was good." Marvin had always wondered, "What happened to that guy that scored a touchdown?" As he recounted his experience watching the black athlete score the touchdown, he realized that his memory was of Orlando Camp.

It was a pleasant coincidence for Steiner, Schellhouse, and Camp to meet again fifty years later at events that illuminated Milford's story of integration and its relation to the *Brown* decision. Camp was impressed with the honesty of Schellhouse's recollections of his touchdown. He commented,

> I'm not sure of how many defensive backs would have admitted a touchdown being scored on them. I think this tells us a little bit about Marvin's character. Although I remember the incident and not the individuals, I've grown to admire Marvin as a real stand-up guy.
>
> Ed Steiner's and the team's reaction to my touchdown was understandable in 1954. I remember the football team making me feel comfortable, but I also knew that I was going to be challenged by the competitive nature of a good high school football team. There was no sign of racism from any of my teammates. I felt a little like a celebrity because of the news media, standing along the sidelines, watching practice and, more accurately, watching me and Ronnie Vann to see how my white teammates were going to react to us being on the team. I was determined to make a competitive contribution to the team. I knew Milford had a winning record and I knew that any mistakes that Ronnie or I made would be highlighted by the media, and even worse, my new teammates.[16]

In an attempt to conduct school in a normal manner, the new black students were assimilated into school activities during the first and second week of September. However, these students were not always given choices of what activities to participate in. Edna Turner recalled that she "was not asked, but told," as part of her gym class that she was going to play hockey for the school team. "Can you imagine being told that you are going to play field hockey even though you have no experience or desire to play," she said, "This was not a necessarily a bad thing, but just the way it was done."

Kenny Baynard joined the band. As a member of a family of musicians, he played saxophone, piano, and drums. Baynard recalled that he and the other black students

> were excited about our assimilation into the all-white student community because we knew we could compete with them if just given a fair chance. We felt that the white students were fair, but not necessarily friendly. We understood that this was new for them too, and we did not expect more than we received, which was acceptance.

He also remembered one teacher showing him notes with racial slurs that white students were passing to one another during class. The teacher wanted to show him what was going on, but never confronted the students who wrote the notes.

The adults, more than the students, had problems with race, change, and acceptance. Edna Turner bitterly remembered her history teacher telling the class that they should just ship blacks back to their own country. She recalled feeling so very alone. Turner went to the back of the class and sat by herself. "I was not introduced to my classmates," she said, "There was not one friendly teacher. I took my lunch alone, and there was not one friendly face in the cafeteria." Years later, she asked a white co-worker, who was a student with her, why none of the white students would even say hello. Her co-worker's response revealed that they were afraid. White students feared that something could happen to their families if they showed any signs of empathy to the black students.

Understandably, the black tenth graders had varied experiences and reactions to their first year at Milford High School. Eugene "Mouse" Harris was bewildered by some of it. He remembered thinking, "If you didn't want us here, why did you suggest us coming? You don't have to like me, just respect me."

On the other hand, Charlie Fleming Jr., who rode the bus from Houston, Delaware, never carried a chip on his shoulder. He believed that all people were basically the same even if they had different beliefs. Meanwhile, Ronnie Vann believed that one should never back down from a challenge. "This made me stronger as a young man," he said. "I was also disappointed that I was not among the first African Americans to graduate from Milford. I really wanted to be among the first; that should have been us." Orlando Camp summed up their experience: "We were just eleven country kids with no outward signs of hostility or animosity, no chips on our shoulders, and we weren't strutting into school," he recalled, "We were not trying to be Black Panthers, and we were not grabbing for the microphone. We were just trying to get an education."

For many of the black students, their first assignments were a nightmare. They were given Algebra II homework assignments, but they did not have an Algebra I course at the all-black school. They knew they had to catch up. Several white students tried to help by showing the black students examples in the text, but the black students needed more than a few practice examples. They needed to start from the beginning. Orlando Camp remembered,

> We would all gather during lunch break to share our frustrations, anxieties, and work on homework assignments. Several black students asked teachers for extra help, and they were told perhaps you could meet with your family members or community leaders because there was no time to provide extra tutoring. This was another example of the lack of planning and preparation by the school board and administration and faculty. They knew that Banneker was an old school with limited teaching materials and the students would be behind their white peers through no fault of their own. It leads me to believe that the white school establishment intentionally, because of the pressures of Fisher and Redding, attempted the integration of Milford High School with the anticipation of failure. I think there was a feeling among some of the white educators that they wanted to prove that the Negro student was inferior to white students.
>
> All in all, the first day went okay. I really don't remember the questions my mom and grandmom asked, but I'm sure it went something like this: "What do you think; how'd it go?" I probably got something in a closing statement from them like "Hang in there; a good education is something they can't take from you, so don't give up." I'm sure all eleven of us got similar speeches.

The first days of integration were so peaceful that Milford High School's principal, Alex Glasmire, expressed his pleasure at a faculty meeting. In addition, some of the white students expressed their contentment with integration to the local newspapers. One fifteen-year-old-boy said, "I didn't think much about the Negro kids one way or the other." Another commented, "Seemed like they belonged in the school after a couple of days. Nobody minded them. One was a darned good football player—the kids really whooped it up for him when he scored a touchdown at a training game."[17]

Reaction to Change

In retrospect, both white and black students agree that they did not realize the significance of Milford's attempt at integration in 1954. Camp had these reflections:

> We were just ninth graders going into the tenth grade, not realizing that this would be looked back on that Milford had a historical opportunity. I also remember the black community was very supportive. They reinforced the importance of education with pats on the back, kind encouragement, and support, which gave me the courage to keep on, but I really didn't understand what we were accomplishing.

Later, the situation turned ugly. The fear of white and black students dancing together especially brought white suspicions to the surface. I. G. Burton, a white business leader in Milford, recalled,

> There were no problems. But a school dance, scheduled for Friday or Saturday, was the spark that began the whole thing. The dance was the catalyst. I remember that so distinctly. People were really mad about that, afraid of black boys dancing with white girls. There was a strong flow of conversation in this town.[18]

Prior to the dance, rumors spread throughout Milford claiming that a black boy asked a white girl for a date, that a second black student flashed a knife during a quarrel in the boys' washroom, and that a black girl used vulgar language with a teacher. By the end of the second week of school, some of the rumors grew wilder. Not only did the black boy ask for a date but he also made a lewd proposal. Many whites feared African Americans would overrun the high school dance.

Whether these rumors were based on fact or pure fiction has been a subject of debate for fifty years. Ed Steiner, a white eleventh grader at the time, remembered that one of his classmates ran him off the road to tell him that a black boy asked his sister to dance with him at the dance. On the other hand, a filmed interview of two white high school students in 1954 documents their memories of it all being a rumor. One of the boys said, "Some rumors got around about a colored boy making a date for the dance with a girl at school, which wasn't true, it's all rumors."[19] Camp recalled,

> This didn't matter to me, because my mother told me, "Don't even think about going to the dance," which I had no intention of doing anyhow. I have tried to determine if this rumor is true or not, and after extensive interviews with both black and white classmates and teachers, after fifty years, I still don't know. It's hard for me to believe that a black boy in the second week of school integration, after a lifetime of segregation, would work up the nerve to ask a white girl to the dance. What may have happened, a black boy may have said, "I will see you at the dance," and it was taken out of context. That's as far as I'm willing to go, but it was enough to be the catalyst to set the town emotionally on fire.

The rumors and fears led to a mass meeting of whites on Friday, September 17 at the Milford American Legion Hall. There were 1,500 attendees, of whom 800 to 900 signed a petition expressing dissatisfaction over the admittance of Negro students in Milford's public schools. This meeting was the first public objection to integration in Milford. The local newspaper, the *Milford Chronicle*, was suspicious about the events at the Legion Hall. One article stated, "On the surface it appeared that the meeting . . . was spontaneous in origin. It seems to us, however, that somewhere in the background there must have been some person, or persons directing the meeting. A large percentage of those present were not residents of Milford."[20]

Other local newspapers, however, reported that Milford area residents made up the majority of participants in the rally. The *Wilmington Morning News* wrote that delegations from "Cedar Neck, Slaughter Neck, Milford Neck, and Milford all had their say on the issue."[21] Cars were parked along the road for a mile each way from the Legion Hall. Word about the meeting circulated through the town the day before the meeting. People were told that "if you wanted to speak your piece about integration, then come to the meeting." Approximately twenty-five to thirty-five people spoke, all advocating segregation. This meeting was the first opposition in Delaware to school integration since the *Brown* decision.

The petition from the Friday evening protest meeting was delivered to school authorities at 8 A.M. on Monday, September 20. The previous night, the Milford school board and Mayor Edward C. Evans met to discuss mounting tensions. They decided to close all of the district's schools for one day, so that a public meeting could be held in Milford High School's auditorium on Monday morning to discuss integration. In addition, they canceled the school dance because of fears that interracial dancing would precipitate violence.[22]

After the public meeting, the board met all afternoon, took a break, and reconvened that evening. The Monday evening board meeting was closed to the public, but was disrupted by segregationists, shouting and pounding on the windows with sticks. Eventually, the School Board decided to inform two of the protest leaders, Paris Kirby and Donald Postles, that it would present the issue to Governor J. Caleb Boggs and the State Board of Education. The board wanted the governor to answer two fundamental questions: (1) Did the Milford School Board have the authority to admit black students? and (2) Was the board liable if the order to admit black students was rescinded? The board decided on a contingency plan that authorized the Superintendent of Schools to close school if violence erupted, so as to ensure the safety of the students. It also asked Reverend Fisher to encourage parents of the eleven black tenth graders to keep their children home until the following Monday. Fisher agreed, "but only to give the opponents of integration the opportunity to understand that they must respect the decision of the Board."

> Finally, at 11 P.M. that Monday evening, Superintendent Cobbs delivered a news release to the local radio station announcing that Milford schools would reopen in the morning. He insisted that integration continued to be the board's policy and that the black students had agreed to take that week off from school to provide a cooling-off period. The announcement provoked vicious telephone threats to Cobbs and members of the School Board. The board immediately responded to these threats by authorizing Dr. Cobbs to release the following statement: The members of the Milford Board of Education, since they made their announcement of the 11 o'clock news broadcast, have received numerous calls threatening violence in case any Negro children attend the Milford Schools today. In the interest of the safety of all children, the Milford Board of Education has announced Milford schools will be closed until further notice.[23]

Tuesday morning, Principal Glasmire hung a sign on the front door of the high school, "Closed Until Further Notice."[24] The *Wilmington Morning News* headline, "School Shut Indefinitely at Milford,"[25] stunned the community. That day, the Milford A&P store was "like a morgue." Tensions were so thick that they could be "cut with a knife." As one resident recalled, the school, and all it stood for, was being lost, and she couldn't believe or understand it.[26]

At that dramatic Monday night Board meeting, Harry Mayhew resigned from the board. On Tuesday, September 21, he explained to the press that, although he felt his efforts had been "sincere and conscientious," his continued service was no longer in "the best interests of the Milford Board of Education." However, a better explanation for his resignation was that Mayhew was a candidate for state representative from the tenth representative district, and many saw his resignation as a blatant overture for the segregationist vote. In November, Mayhew defeated Republican incumbent, Clarence L. Hudson, by a two-to-one margin. The three remaining members of the board advised the school superintendent that if they resigned, he should turn to the State Board of Education for guidance.

On Thursday, the Milford school board was scheduled to meet with the State Board of Education to discuss school integration. The previous afternoon, at the request of Governor Boggs, Milford school board members met with Delaware Attorney General H. Albert Young in Dover. Young declared that the Milford

School District did not break any federal or state laws by admitting the black students. He also stated that the board would violate the law if it refused to admit the black students. Steeled by the Attorney General's opinion, the Milford board agreed to resign if the State Board of Education refused to support integration in Milford. Headlines in Friday's *Wilmington Morning News* reported, "Milford to Reopen School with Negroes or Else Board Will Quit."[27]

Participants in Thursday's meeting with the State Board of Education reflected a diversity never before seen in Delaware. In addition to Governor Boggs, the attendees included Howard E. Lynch, attorney for the Milford board; William V. Sipple and Ida S. Phillips, members of the Milford board; J. Orphum Small, president of the State Board of Education; Dr. George R. Miller, superintendent of the State Department of Public Instruction and secretary of the State Board; Russell M. Bradley, president of the Lincoln PTA Association; Elbert F. Williams, a representative of the citizens group opposed to integration; James L. Davis of Milford, a former senator of Delaware; three white citizens of Milford—Brown P. Thawley, Paris C. Kirby, and Dr. Cobbs; and three blacks: Louis L. Redding, attorney for the eleven Negro students; the Reverend Fisher; and Wagner Jackson, head of the NAACP in Delaware.

After a long day of discussion and debate, the State Board of Education reached a decision at midnight. Classes in Milford would resume under the supervision of Dr. Miller and the State Board of Education with the eleven black students enrolled. However, the State Board of Education did not formally approve the Milford board's plan for integration, "asserting it would withhold action on that phase pending the obtaining of an adjudication of the situation." The Milford board felt abandoned because they "were left hanging in the wind." In a subsequent informal meeting with board members and school officials in Milford, Governor Boggs muttered, "Nothing can be done." As one observer noted, Governor Boggs and State Superintendent Miller "were like a lost ball in the tall grass."[28]

In its Thursday night decision, the State Board of Education, which had issued directives throughout the summer obligating local boards to submit integration plans for approval, criticized the Milford board for its failure to submit the integration plan for approval prior to implementation. Although this criticism was fair, later events indicate that a timely submission would not have changed the reaction. The Milford board submitted its plan to the State Board of Education on September 10, after classes had begun. The plan itself was the correct legal action, despite the advice of Attorney General Young, who stated that Delaware could take its time to implement desegregation.

In essence, the State Board of Education approved desegregation in Milford, but reprimanded the Milford board for failing to follow the required procedure. Instead of taking a stand, the state board abandoned the local board when it most needed support. The three remaining Milford school board members resigned immediately, as promised, charging that "they had not received the full backing from the State Board." Milford's attorney, Howard Lynch, reported,

> Since the State Board has not seen fit to approve or disapprove their [Milford Board of Education's] action, they do not wish to continue in their position. They feel

> that they are too close to the situation to accept the responsibility of opening the Milford School Monday with Negroes attending without the full backing of the State Board.[29]

After the decision to open school on September 27, with the black students enrolled, Governor Boggs published a plea urging for "calmness and reason." He reminded Delaware citizens that "law and order will be preserved under the law and the American way." Boggs then insisted that "no disorders, threats, or violence would take place."[30] Boggs took no stance on the merits of the issue, but his statement emphasizing law and order probably forestalled violence. With Dr. Miller directing Milford's public schools on behalf of the State Board, a certain irony existed. His PhD dissertation at New York University, completed in 1947, was "Adolescent Negro Education in Delaware: A Study of the Negro Secondary School."[31]

By Friday, September 24, Milford High School had been closed for five days. The State Board of Education intended to reopen the school with the eleven black students on Monday, September 27. Asked about potential trouble with the reopening, Colonel Harry Shew, Superintendent of the Delaware State Police said, "We'll be ready for anything."[32] The presence of the State Police, along with Boggs's plea for order, kept a lid on serious outbreaks of violence. However, threats and demonstrations continued throughout Milford.

On Monday, September 27, Milford High School reopened under the direction of the State Board of Education with only 456 of 1,562 white students present. At Lincoln High School, only 36 students out of 140 attended school. A boycott of school was on. Ten of the eleven black tenth graders returned to class, with eight arriving by car and two by bus. More than twenty state policemen were present and, with a handful of town police, tightened their cordon between the black students and the large crowd. The police action was met with "dead silence," but no incidents occurred.[33] Orlando Camp's mother told him that he would travel to school in a state police car because school authorities lacked confidence in the local police. It was difficult for the local police to participate in the integration because they were members of the local community who wished to remain neutral. The State Police showed up at Camp's home at 7:30 A.M., knocked on the door, and said very few words. Camp recalled that he "came out and got into the back of the police car." Sitting in the back of a police car was not a good feeling for him. In his experience, any time a black male was in the back of a state police car, good things were not likely to happen.

When the police car pulled up to the front of the school, the crowd numbered nearly one thousand people. Camp was struck with the gravity of his situation:

> Although I felt a little like a celebrity getting out of the police car with the reporters taking my pictures, with flash bulbs popping, microphones thrust in our face, at the same time I was walking what I considered to be a gauntlet of white hate. I don't remember seeing a friendly face in the group.

The boycott was working. Beginning at 7:30 A.M., crowds lined the sidewalks in front of Milford High School. Although there was no violence, tension from the crowds penetrated the classrooms. In one third-grade class in which only five children showed up, a handful of students held hands whenever they went into the halls. This simple gesture made them feel more secure in the face of threatening conditions. One elementary school teacher was ready to bolt out the back doors if the crowd came in the front door. Outside, the figure of the black civil rights lawyer, Louis Redding, could be seen moving from one group of white onlookers to the next. Members of the crowd justified their support for segregation by making such comments as these:

- "The Bible gives authority for segregation."
- "If God intended us to be all one, He would have made us one race. He intended, however, that there should be different races and they should stay apart."
- "The Milford Board of Education put this over on us."
- "The people's wishes ought to be respected. Majority should rule all the time."
- "We just don't want our children to go to school with Negroes."
- "The U.S. Supreme Court hasn't handed down an order; all that it has given out is an opinion."[34]

The Arrival of a Demagogue

Over the previous weekend, some prominent Milford business leaders had contacted Bryant Bowles, who led the National Association for the Advancement of White People, to counteract the Negroes' representation by the National Association for the Advancement of Colored People. As one white resident remembered fifty years later, "All we did is to level the playing field; your blacks had Redding and the NAACP, so it was only fair to call in help for us. So we wanted to match that with Bowles and the NAAWP."

On Sunday morning, September 26, the day before Milford High School reopened, residents of southern Delaware received an unusual invitation from the sky. Four small airplanes, equipped with loudspeaker systems, flew across lower Kent and most of Sussex Counties, inviting all to a meeting that afternoon to discuss "keeping segregation as it always has been in Delaware."[35] This meeting was to be held at the Harrington Airport, a few miles west of Milford. It was sponsored by an organization new to Delaware, the National Association for the Advancement of White People (NAAWP). This meeting would mark the arrival of NAAWP's founder, thirty-four-year-old Bryant Bowles, in Delaware.

A crowd of 2,000 to 5,000 people turned out at the airport to hear Bowles and several other speakers. Every speaker advocated a white boycott of Milford's public schools on the next day. Bowles told the crowd, "You certainly have the right to protect your child by keeping it at home if you are afraid there is going to be violence stirred up by the opposition. I would bar the door before it leaves and not after." Bowles held up his three-year old daughter, Denise and cried out, "Do you think I'll ever let my little girl go to school with Negroes? I certainly will not."

William H. Macklin, seventy-four years old, identified himself as the mayor of Cedar Neck, and told the applauding crowd, "If we keep our children home from school maybe somebody'll do something about this situation. Anyone who joins forces with the other race is a traitor to his own race."[36]

That night, a second rally attracted 1,000 people at Lincoln crossroads on Rt. 113 near Milford. At that meeting, Bowles announced that the Reverend Manean Warrington, of Selbyville, had been appointed president of the Delaware chapter of the NAAWP. Warrington told the crowd, "We are not going to let the Supreme Court jam this thing down our throats. No matter if it means bloodshed, we will see it through. I speak to you as a Christian father." Realizing that it was an election year, Bowles told the crowd,

> We need your help. Part of the funds will be used to contact every candidate for public office in the state this election, and ask them to sign a segregation pledge. We will then make reprints of the pledges that are signed, and circulate them so you can vote for the man who is for segregation.

Then Bowles touched on the deepest fear of many whites by stating, "The Negro will never be satisfied until he moves into the front bedroom of the white man's home, and when he tries that a lot of gunpowder will burn." A female speaker articulated this fear as well, stating that the whole crisis boils down to the fact that blacks "were after our girls, that's all. It isn't the schools so much; it's what they're leading up to." Another speaker held up a signed statement from a white female student in Milford's tenth grade that a black student had asked her to go to the movies.[37]

As these remarks were being made, two hundred yards away, in the tall grass at the edge of the field, lay Orlando Camp, Ronnie Vann, Charlie Fleming, and Gordon Camp, listening with great anticipation and curiosity to what Bryant Bowles and the hundreds of white segregationists, curiosity-seekers, and uninformed rednecks were discussing at their gathering. They had caught a ride down to Lincoln with Bobby Hicks, who parked his 1950 Ford about a mile away. The boys walked toward the bonfires and torches glowing in the distance. They could not understand what Bryant Bowles was saying; all they could hear was the crowd yelling with great enthusiasm and intensity. Charlie Fleming recalled, with a chuckle, "We didn't stay too long because soon our naiveté turned to fear, and common sense ruled that it was time to get the hell out of there before we were discovered. God knows what would have happened then!"[38]

After seeing the rally from afar, the black youths knew that white parents had been transformed from spectators to protestors. The boys' anxieties turned to fear because they now knew that the white adult population did not want them to attend white schools in Milford. They could not understand why white parents did not want them to get an education. They had been too naïve to realize that this boycott of desegregation was more about race than education. Now the black youths knew differently.

NAAWP membership forms were distributed in front of the school on Monday. Dues were five dollars per year. Bowles claimed two dollars went for the association's national publication, and three dollars stayed with the local organization. The forms read as follows:

> I am a member of the white race, above the age of 18, and a citizen of the United States. I have never, nor do I intend to ever become a member of any organization that advocates the over throwing of the government of the United States of American through violence. It is understood and agreed that after becoming a member of this organization I reserve the right to vote as I please, worship as I please, or live as I please, but I do believe in the separation of the races of mankind.[39]

When Bryant Bowles arrived in Milford, many saw him as a savior. Bowles was probably invited to Milford by one or more of the local residents, who were opposed to integration. One possible contact person was Douglas Morgan, owner of the farm machinery store near Lincoln. Other possibilities include Brown Thawley of Milford or Franklin Melvin of the neighboring town of Harrington.[40] But it is also possible that newspaper accounts of the first day of protests attracted Bryant Bowles to Milford.

Bowles combined a certain charisma with the willingness to tell "the people what they wanted to hear." Lionel Shockley, a farmer from Cedar Neck, whose father was an active Bowles supporter, recalled that "Bowles was a con man" who exploited racial tension for personal profit.[41] At his NAAWP rallies, a peach basket was passed to conservative, tight-fisted farmers and other working-class people, who found a way to drop five-, ten-, and even fifty-dollar bills into the basket. Bowles bragged to *Life Magazine* that he raised $3,510 in one week.[42]

Milford's black community had no contact with Bowles or his allies. Kenny Baynard, one of the eleven black students, who lived on the outskirts of Milford, remembered that Bowles lived in a rented or donated house in nearby Houston, Delaware. Baynard almost bumped into Bowles when coming out of the local grocery store. Bryant Bowles held the door open for him as he left the store. Kenny recognized him from the photographs in the newspaper. From Baynard's point of view, Bowles simply hated black people. Baynard thought of him as an opportunist who capitalized on the fear spreading through Milford's white community.[43]

Tension in a Small Town

If one American institution is sacred, it is public education because it is seen as a cornerstone of our democracy and way of life. Yet the Milford school system seemed to be in danger of total collapse as the boycott continued during the last days of September 1954. The telephone was the primary weapon of segregationists, as they began what some called a "reign of terror." Anonymous calls urging parents to keep their children home were made in the morning, as children got ready for school. If white families persisted in sending their children, the messages threatened, "You'll be sorry," or "something might happen to you." Playing on a parent's worst fears, the callers also said, "Your kid will get hurt," and "if you don't get your kid out of school, you won't have any kid to get out of school." In some families, one parent would take the children to school, only to have the other parent remove them later during the day.

White children faced insults, threats, and obscenities from adults and other children as they walked to school. Some white children phoned others with such disturbing messages as, "My daddy says I might get killed if I go to school. Why does your daddy make you go?" Caravans of cars sped through Milford, flaunting signs such as "Keep them out" taped to their doors. Despite this threatening atmosphere, none of the students sustained any injuries. The closest brush with physical injury occurred when an eight-year old boy was crossing a street after school to attend a Cub Scout meeting. A parked car suddenly accelerated toward the boy, stopping short of hitting him. The child collapsed in the street and had to be carried away.

Most children did not fall victim to threats arising from the school boycotts. When dropped off at school, one little boy looked back at his father with a sense of fear, as if asking, "What do I do now?" His dad waved him on, and he entered school without incident. One teenaged girl reported that she was "scared at first," but no one ever said anything to her or bothered her. Yet the danger was real, and many parents kept their children at home. Although some of these parents did not support the segregationists, their actions strengthened Bowles's boycott.

A much smaller group of parents acknowledged that there was some risk, but committed to education and to obeying the Supreme Court's decree, they walked or drove their children to school. The anguish that all of Milford's parents experienced in making these decisions is still a painful memory.

Segregationists also targeted businessowners who defied the boycott. Bowles urged his followers to buy only from "our friends." Shopkeepers were told that failure to sign the petition against integration would be remembered and understood by their customers. One farmer and future school board member bragged, "We ran Hume's Hardware out of town. We just didn't do any business with them at all. We went up to Frederica to buy what we needed." Bowles did his best to increase the impact of this boycott on local businesses. During a second NAAWP rally held at the Harrington Airport, Bowles turned up the heat by decrying Delaware businessmen who stood for "race mixing." He bragged about how he interrogated a Milford haberdasher on his views of race before purchasing a suit. Stirred by Bowles, some farmers stopped doing business with a Milford fertilizer company whose management and owners supported integration. Others stopped buying fuel from the husband of a Milford school board member.

However, very few Milford businesses were forced to close by the segregationists. Although one firm's delivery truck was followed around town by a car with a sign that read, "DON'T BUY FROM NIGGER LOVER," the firm suffered no loss of business. In another case, a merchant listened to a female customer harangue him about leaving his child in school. After doing so, she left with "a substantial purchase."[44]

At the Harrington rally, Bowles lied to the crowd by telling them that he was accepting an invitation to attend the NAACP's New York state conference in Peekskill, New York. He accepted the invitation knowing that, on the date of the Peekskill meeting, he would have to appear in court in Dover, Delaware, to answer charges of disrupting public education. Bowles informed the crowd that, although he accepted the NAACP invitation, he declined its offer of lodging. "Even in Peekskill, I am going to call a spade a spade, even a black spade a black spade," Bowles said, "But I'm going to pick my own hotel to stay in." With this comment,

Bowles generally implied that no self-respecting white man would ever stay at a hotel with blacks. Bowles had no respect for the NAACP, and he therefore charged the organization with exploiting blacks in the school fight over integration. Bowles told the crowd in Harrington that there was no need for an organization to "advance" the Negroes. "If they need to be advanced, the road is open to the jungles of Africa," he said. Incredibly, Bowles then stated that his group was not "against Negroes, but those people who are trying to shove the Negro down our throats." He concluded, "We're going to boot them out of the United States if we can."

The behavior of segregationists stiffened the resistance of some whites to the school boycott. Tired of finding his wife in tears from phoned threats to their children, one father snorted, "I'll drive the kids to school, and this telephone stuff can work both ways." He called his friends every morning, reminding them why they should send their children to school. In another case, an NAAWP member phoned a prominent Milford professional and implied that, if his son remained in school, something might happen to him. The father burst out yelling, "You're the only person I know in that infernal organization. So I'll just make you personally responsible for the safety of my boy. If anything happens to him, I'm coming straight to take it out of your hide." Nothing happened to his son, and he was not called again.

Throughout the last days of September, the boycott continued to limit school attendance, and tensions increased. A cross was burned in a field across from Milford High School. Another cross was burned near the Banneker School. Despite the fact that no attempts at integration were made elsewhere in Sussex County, the school boycott was spreading to other towns in southern Delaware. On Monday, September 27, only 3 of 106 students showed up for class in Gumboro. In Millsboro, the figure was only 38 of 644, in Ellendale 18 of 131, and in Lincoln only 12 of 140. By Wednesday, all public schools in those districts were closed for lack of attendance. The boycott in Milford had escalated into a systematic effort to prevent integration in all Sussex County public schools.

In contrast, twenty miles to the north of Milford, in the state capital of Dover, integration was progressing relatively smoothly. Dover High School enrolled eighteen black ninth graders in its college preparatory program without incident. Dover officials had informed the community about integration before the start of the school year. They held a public meeting and kept people informed through the local newspaper, the *Delaware State News.* Moreover, when the crisis in Milford erupted, Dover police, town authorities, and the school board held another public meeting, urging residents to remain calm.[45]

Finding a Resolution to a Crisis

By late September, Milford students were getting used to seeing state police cars encounter a crowd of protesters at their school every day. A settlement of the crisis seemed less and less likely with each passing day. Earlier, there had been some optimism that the town could resolve the dispute over desegregation. With the continuing mass meetings, cross burnings, car caravans, rumors, and the virulent telephone calls, however, hope that "this thing will blow over" soon passed. One resident said, "We've reached the point where it begins to look like only a miracle can save the entire situation."

On Thursday, September 30, a meeting at the governor's office in Dover led to a strategy to break the logjam. Milford had been without a school board since September 23 because of the resignations. The first step decided at the Dover meeting was to establish a school board with the authority to make decisions. Two members of the original board, Dr. Kimmel and William Sipple, agreed to serve once again. Technically, they were never off the Milford school board because the state board never accepted the en masse resignations. The two men were empowered to appoint Edmund Steiner, a wool mill operator, and Wright Ward, a poultry farmer, to the Milford board. Sipple then resigned. Steiner, Ward, and Kimmel appointed David Greene, a poultry processor, to take Sipple's place. Kimmel then resigned, leaving Steiner, Ward, and Greene on the board. These three men then appointed George Robbins, a local farmer. When Ward resigned for health reasons, the three remaining members—Steiner, Greene, and Robbins—appointed George Adams, a dispatcher for Burris Foods, a local trucking company and poultry processor. A new Milford school board was finally in place. The arrangement of board members met the statutory requirement of two representatives from each county. In addition, none of the four members belonged to the NAAWP.

The board reconvened later that day in Milford and came to a decision regarding the Negro students. Standing in front of the school, the new board president, Edmund F. Steiner, read and distributed the following statement:

> In a special meeting of the newly created Milford Board of Education, consisting of Edmund F. Steiner, George A. Robbins, George F. Adams, and David B. Greene, held in the Board of Education Office in the Lakeview School on September 30, 1954, at 2 P.M., Edmund F. Steiner was elected President of the New Milford Board of Education.
>
> The Milford Board of Education believes they should be free to act in this emergency and not be bound by previous activities of the former Milford Board of Education. The Board of Education, therefore, has requested the State Board of Education to support them in their action.
>
> The Milford Board of Education then went into executive session to solve the current issue in order that your children can return to school. As a result of their deliberations, the Milford Board of Education decided, in the interest of the welfare of the children and the community as a whole, to remove the eleven Negro students from the enrollment records of the Milford School, effective 3:10 P.M., September 30, 1954. The school assignment and necessary transportation of these children for their future education is the responsibility of the State Board of Education.
>
> The Milford Board of Education appeals to all the constituents of the Milford Special School District to send their children to school, tomorrow morning, October 1, 1954.

In response to a reporter's question, Steiner strongly denied that local officials made any deal with Bowles. In his typical braggadocio fashion, Bowles had earlier claimed to reporters that he had an understanding with Governor Boggs that blacks would be removed from Milford's public schools. Steiner insisted that this comment was a "complete falsehood" and stated that the governor did not know what action the Milford school board was going to take. Governor Boggs also firmly denied any communications or commitments to Bowles. Apparently, the governor assisted in finding a way to reconstitute the board, but gave it latitude to act independently. However, there is little question that, while the board would act on its own, certain issues and solutions were discussed with Governor Boggs. Nonetheless, the board's decision was primarily "taken for the safety of the eleven Negroes." Edwina Green, widow of board member David Green, remembered that her husband said, "It was the bomb threats that made them close the schools."[46]

Steiner went on to say, "This fellow Bowles is not one of us, but an outsider. His speech last night was defamatory and creates a disturbance. One of these days the people will wake up." When Steiner finished speaking to the press, a photographer asked him to pose in front of the school. A woman passing by yelled, "Don't take his picture; he won't be on the board long enough to get his picture in the paper."[47]

The Milford City Council held two special meetings on September 30 because Mayor Edward Evans was concerned about violence. After the 3:00 P.M. meeting, the Council directed the mayor to contact Reverend Fisher to "determine if the Negro students would attempt to enter school the following morning." Fisher told the mayor that he needed until 9:00 P.M., at which time he would call the mayor with his answer. The mayor then scheduled a 9:00 P.M. City Council meeting. When Fisher subsequently called the mayor, he reported that the black tenth graders would not be attending the Milford schools. As instructed by the school board, they would go to the school the next day, on Friday, October 1, to pick up their belongings at 9:00 A.M. and return home.[48]

Claiming victory, Bowles and his supporters urged parents to send their children to school. The NAACP had a different reaction. Wagner Jackson, president of the Delaware chapter of the NAACP, regretted the "ignominious surrender of duly constituted authorities to a lawless mob." Jackson went on to say that his group was "sickened" and that the responsibility was shared by officials and other persons of "influence and good will who failed to stand up and be counted against the forces of evil." Jackson indicated that the NAACP refused to accept mob rule. The NAACP had already started planning its next move and had been in communication with Thurgood Marshall at the NAACP in New York City.[49]

Milford's experiment with integration was abandoned, much to the joy of segregationists. In less than a month, this quiet town had seen its public schools briefly integrated, closed, boycotted, and then resegregated once again. During those few weeks of September 1954, a clash between tradition and change was won by tradition. Robert McFann wrote in the *Wilmington Morning News* that the crisis reflected "deep cross-currents which are working below the surface, cross-currents which cut across political, economic, and even religious lines. Cross-currents that touch basic human emotions—that evoke in many instances the ugly, deep-rooted prejudices, race hatreds, and religious bias."[50]

There was little question that Bowles struck a responsive chord with a large number of whites in the Milford area. In the *Wilmington Morning News*, another observer wrote the following:

> There is one flat conclusion . . . People in [Kent and Sussex] counties are overwhelmingly against integration—and school boards, caught between this feeling and the order of the Supreme Court, fervently wished for an indefinite time before

> submitting any kind of plan. One man indicated he would move to another state rather than send his child to school with Negro children. He also struck out at those at a higher income levels, "you take the people with money. They might be all for it. They don't say, but sure if they're for it and noble about it what do they do? They send their kids to a private school where you don't find any colored children."[51]

Although black leadership initiated integration in Milford, members of the black community were not involved after whites began to boycott desegregation. One black resident recalled that the black community watched and waited while the problem was worked out. While the threat of violence was directed toward pro-integrationist whites, the black community of Milford witnessed overt expressions of hatred and racism, knowing they were about them.

What about the eleven black students at Milford High School? How did the events of 1954 affect them? Orlando Camp remembered,

> The fear of the white community threatened our freedoms. We lost a lot of freedom in 1954. Milford lost an opportunity to be a leader in the nation and in Delaware. But I was determined that this was not going to define who I was. I always believed that you have to pick yourself up, don't feel society owes you anything, and you are responsible for your success in life, regardless of what obstacles come your way.

In contrast, Kenneth Baynard recalled,

> The only way this integration has affected me is that prejudice and stupidity I cannot tolerate. I have to walk away from it. If you cannot renew your mind, you've got a real problem. I'm not going to live with this mess. So I've learned over the years to just let it go.

Edna Turner remembered her feelings on the day she was removed from Milford High:

> I loved Jason [a black school]. The teachers were interested in you learning and to not be afraid to ask a question. I can't tell you how happy I was to be out. When they kicked me out of school, they did me a favor.

Gordon Camp, Orlando's younger brother, looked back at the events of 1954 from the perspective of a ninth grader, watching his older brother. Gordon remembered,

> I was so enthused when Orlando first started there. They put Milford on the map. And I was thinking about two brothers excelling in academics and in sports. When it ended, it was such a disappointment. I still feel Milford lost a lot of potential intelligent individuals that could have contributed to this society. It was just lost. *Brown* opened the door a crack. A few made it through the keyhole, but they never really got their foot in.[52]

Integration would be delayed for years in Milford and in many other communities in southern Delaware. The events of 1954 were far from finished after the expulsion of the eleven black students from Milford High. Segregationists had won that battle, but the legal and moral war, pitting tradition against change, was just beginning.

With the black students now officially expelled, attendance on Friday, October 1, was just over 80 percent, somewhat below typical attendance in normal circumstances, but well above the boycott levels of 30 percent. By the following Monday, school attendance was back to normal. Milford's black tenth grade students enrolled in the segregated schools of Jason High in Georgetown or Henry High in Dover. Black leaders accepted the state's offer to provide bus transportation, but made the point that these were only temporary arrangements, so that the black students' education would not be interrupted. Guaranteeing further legal action, integrationists promised that, once a court order to integrate Milford's public schools was issued, the black students would return to them.[53]

One of the black students, Edna Turner, received a letter from Louis Redding, which explained the legal maneuvering that ensued after the eleven black students were expelled from Milford High. He called on Edna to persevere and encouraged her to remain patient. "Understand that frequently court cases take a long time," he wrote, "Meanwhile, please do your level best at the Jason Comprehensive High School until we can get a final ruling from the courts."[54]

For Milford's white students, the events of September 1954 faded with time, and the school experience returned to the patterns of previous years. For teachers and administrators, however, the events of September would have a permanent impact. Many teachers, appalled at Milford's negative reaction to this very limited attempt at integration, decided to seek employment elsewhere. As a result, there was significant turnover in faculty over the next two years. Superintendent Cobbs announced his resignation in March 1955, effective at the end of the school year. A heated school board election would be held in may 1955 to fill all four school board seats. This election generated the largest turnout ever seen for a school board election in Milford.

Despite the segregationists' initial victory, uncertainty concerning the future of racial integration continued in Milford. While Bowles and the NAAWP claimed victory, they also warned their followers that the fight had just begun. The NAACP, under Louis Redding's legal guidance, filed an application for an injunction on behalf of the eleven black students in the Delaware Court of Chancery, on Saturday, October 2, 1954. The Supreme Court had already ruled that segregation in American public schools was unconstitutional, but they had not yet created specific guidelines for implementation; these guidelines would be issued by the Supreme Court in 1955.

Although Milford's school district was segregated again, the stories of September's failed attempt caused concern throughout southern Delaware. Truth was replaced by fiction as rumors of bloodshed, race riots, murder, guns, and knives were told and retold all over this part of the state. One man commented that, during the crisis, every store that carried guns in Sussex County had sold out. Although this comment was probably inaccurate, there were more guns around Milford than ten years earlier because people wanted to protect themselves from a perceived threat to their very homes. It was rumored that a regularly scheduled target practice was taking place in one Sussex County town.[55]

Fearful of the damage already done in Milford and aware of the continued tension, Milford businessman I. G. Burton blamed much of the community's problem on state government inaction. On October 4, 1954, he wrote Governor Boggs a letter that read,

> The events of the past few weeks in Milford have been appalling to the citizens of this town. Grave errors have been made by all branches of our governing body. I hope something can and will be done to clarify the situation. On a subject as basic as integration I am at a loss to understand why there has not been a firm and uniform policy established by the State Board of Education and by the executive branch of our government. For the State Board of Education to promulgate a policy of local action is a refusal to be realistic about a basic problem in human relations. I cannot believe the president and board of directors of General Motors would allow the plant managers in their various operations to set basic policy for G.M. nor do I believe it right to expect a local school board to set policy on integration. I believe we have a right to expect a uniform and consistent policy and program in any basic State issue.
>
> In the early 1920s I toured Sussex County with George S. Williams on a campaign of consolidation for our school system. I recall a great amount of opposition to the program from our people. But as it was explained to them, the majority began to understand the benefits that would accrue from consolidation. Information before action backed by a consistent and uniform state program made consolidation an established and valuable asset to us.
>
> I realize we are facing a difficult problem which has been made more difficult by recent action. I cannot understand why those in authority did not realize the depth of feeling in lower Kent and Sussex Counties in time to make a move for peaceful integration under the laws of our country. I am sure our people want to live as law abiding citizens.
>
> I propose the following:
>
> 1. A firm and uniform policy at the State level.
> 2. An immediate educational program through local groups to acquaint our people with the program as it will be placed into action.
> 3. A firm stand by the executive branch of our government in the execution of a uniform policy.
>
> I know these are trying days for you. I hope and pray that feelings will subside and that justice will be done. Time is important and as each day passes we have less of it allotted to us.[56]

Although Burton was a Republican and a strong supporter of Governor Boggs, the governor's October 6 response did nothing to address Burton's concerns. Boggs's letter shows a governor who was more concerned with straddling the fence than making a commitment to a statewide school integration program.[57]

Burton and other town leaders were very concerned that serious violence would result from an expected Delaware Court of Chancery ruling, demanding school integration in Milford. In Burton's office, at his Chevrolet dealership, businessmen, clergy, and doctors met in early October 1954 to develop a strategy for heading off violence. The men developed several strategies at the meeting, including an immediate response to the anticipated Chancery Court decision that was expected to be handed down on Tuesday, October 12.[58] Some members of the committee proposed that a letter be sent to 100 leading citizens, pointing out the following:

> Next Tuesday may be a very crucial day for every man, woman and child in the Milford area. We hope the court will allow time to resolve our differences and set our program in agreement with a uniform state or national policy. However, if the court decides to return the 11 Negro students to the Lake Avenue School we ask all of our fellow citizens to cooperate fully with our school board. Let them handle the situation. They need our backing and cooperation. Let us not forget—the future of our community is at stake.[59]

Although attendees at the meeting decided not to send this letter, they persuaded Theodore Townsend, editor of the *Milford Chronicle*, to run a boxed plea from the mayor on the front page of the October 8 issue with the headline, "Again We Urge Calmness and Clear Thinking."[60]

Meanwhile, Bowles was beginning to lose his credibility. On the same day that integration in Milford public schools ended, newspaper articles disclosed Bowles's police record.[61] Bowles had a history of writing bogus checks in Baltimore and Harford County, Maryland, and in Tampa. Delaware State Police said that they had investigated Bowles in light of the many speeches he had made and the significant number of contributions he had accepted. They reasoned that "the people of Delaware deserve to know his background."

Like most demagogues, Bowles fought back. The NAACP's suit to reinstate integration in Milford touched off more Bowles-inspired rallies, demonstrations, and cross burnings. Bowles attacked Attorney General Young and *Wilmington Morning News* columnist Bill Frank with anti-Semitic remarks that focused on their Russian Jewish heritage. Picking up on the much-repeated theme that integration was inspired by foreigners, communists, Jews, and Catholics, Bowles implied that Young and Frank were part of a plot to mix the races in public school. He addressed the Attorney General by his birth name, Hyman Yanowitz, rather than by the family name that he had used since 1926; Young had already informed Delaware voters of his name change and Jewish heritage during his successful election campaign in 1950.

Finally, Governor Boggs and Attorney General Young had enough of Bowles's resistance. On Sunday, October 10, Bowles was arrested on charges of criminal incitement of "organized mob rule and mass hysteria calculated to disrupt the education of our children" in Kent and Sussex Counties. Bowles, however, was released within four hours after posting $3,000 bail in each county. He attended a rally in Harrington on Sunday night, just two days prior to the Delaware Court of Chancery hearing on the fate of school integration. Bowles bragged, "Some people have had the honor of being arrested by privates, some by corporals, some even by captains. But I have had the honor of being arrested by the Governor."[62]

On Monday, at a large rally attended by political candidates for local office at Morgan's garage in Lincoln, Bowles advocated a "segregation pledge." It is unclear which candidates signed the pledge, although Republicans subsequently pointed their fingers at some of the Democrats running for office. A number of Democrats denied signing the pledge, but admitted that they supported segregation.[63]

As the date of the Court of Chancery hearing approached, Milford's new school board attempted to defuse the tension. On October 4, 1954, it sent a letter home with each student, advising parents that a suit had been filed to reinstate the "colored students." The letter also stated that if the court decided to demand integration, the board would appeal such a decision to the Delaware Supreme Court. The board concluded by requesting "all of the people living in the school district to have patience and await final decision of the highest courts."[64]

Judge William Marvel, Vice Chancellor, conducted the Court of Chancery preliminary hearing on October 12. Bowles refused to attend this hearing because he "didn't see any sign saying, 'restricted to white people.'" When Louis Redding filed the civil action, he also filed a request for a temporary restraining order that would have allowed the black students to attend the Milford School immediately.

Judge Marvel rejected that request. Attorney General Young argued, "Here are eleven children who were attending school without incident. Why were they taken out? Mob rule." Young declared, "The Supreme Court has spoken . . . and now it becomes a matter not of what we feel or think but of compliance with law and order and decrees of courts."[65]

Judge Marvel ruled that because the black students had already been enrolled in Milford's all-white high school, it was unnecessary to wait for instructions from the U.S. Supreme Court for the implementation of the *Brown* ruling. In addition, because their legal right to attend the Milford High School was "clear and convincing," Marvel wrote, "Any inconvenience or distress to the defendants must give way before the much greater injury, which would be inflicted on plaintiffs by denial of their personal and present rights." The Milford school board claimed that denial would not cause the plaintiffs irreparable harm. Judge Marvel rebutted this argument, citing the Supreme Court's position in *Brown* that there was an immediate need for equal protection under law for students in their formative school years. Marvel concluded that the eleven black students had "a clear and legal right" to attend Milford High School.[66]

As promised, the new Milford school board then appealed the Chancery Court's decision to the Delaware Supreme Court. The Supreme Court agreed to delay implementation of the decision until it could decide whether the Chancery Court's injunction was properly issued. The State Supreme Court scheduled its hearing for December 13.

In February 1955, the Delaware Supreme Court handed down a ruling that was unsatisfying to both sides of the integration debate. It ruled that *Brown v. Board of Education* nullified Delaware's segregation laws, but it did not require immediate integration. With *Brown* still undecided, the Delaware Supreme Court took a cautious approach. It insisted that no action be taken to reintegrate Milford until the U.S. Supreme Court handed down a second *Brown* decision with specific guidelines for integration. In short, the Delaware Supreme Court ruled that the original Milford board of education had acted properly, but prematurely. State regulations required local school boards to submit plans for integration to the state board prior to implementation. By acting unilaterally, in violation of regulations, the Milford board "had exceeded its authority." As a consequence, the Delaware Supreme Court ruled that the admission of black students to Milford High School was "contrary to law."[67]

In retrospect, the Delaware Supreme Court's action was partly fueled by the desire to avoid making an unpopular legal decision that could lead to violence. With its ruling, public school integration was delayed indefinitely. Paul Dolan, a political science professor at the University of Delaware, accurately concluded in 1956,

> The initial effort toward peaceful integration failed. The end of segregation is not now in sight in Delaware, and probably nothing concrete will be accomplished in the movement toward universal integration until the United States Supreme Court takes definite, implementry action against segregation in the public schools of the Nation.[68]

Conclusion

On Monday, October 4, the eleven black students enrolled in the all-black William Jason High School in Georgetown. Integration had failed. For Orlando Camp, this change was dramatic. Living only four blocks from the white school, he now had a one and a half-hour bus ride to a segregated school. It took that long in part because of the many stops the bus made to pick up students throughout the county. Camp recalled,

> I asked my mother would she co-sign for me to buy a car at the local Chevrolet dealership, which was, believe it or not, owned by I. G. Burton, who played a major role in supporting integration. My mother and I walked over to I. G. Burton's dealership. My mother and I walked around the car lot where I saw a cool '52 Chevy Bel Aire, black, that I fell in love with. I said, "Mom, this is the car for me." The car cost $1,200. Mr. Burton came out and said to my mother words to the effect, "How do you plan to pay for this car?" I spoke up, "I work part-time at the Steiner's Woolen Mill." My mother said, "I work for the Coopersmith Store and the Aber's family." Mr. Burton asked my mother if she was willing to sign for "this boy," which she was. Mr. Burton asked again, "Who do you work for again?" Burton called Mr. Ed Steiner, Sr. to confirm Orlando's employment.

Establishing credit was all about reputation, character, and work ethic. As long as a person had a job, Burton never asked for a Social Security number or a credit application. It was based upon word of mouth. Burton, true to his character, gave a young boy, white or black, a chance. Camp happily remembered,

> When I drove my new car off the lot with my Mom smiling with pride in the passenger seat, I was as happy as a sixteen-year-old kid could be. From then on, I had to take Mom and my grandmothers anywhere they wanted to go. I think they created trips just to get me to take them to the grocery store or wherever just to ride in the car. I think I washed that car three or four times a week. The experience reinforced my work ethic that if I wanted to have the quality things in life that I would have to work for them. The fact that my mother supported me reassured me that she had confidence in my ability and commitment to meet my obligations. I was grateful for her belief in me, and I was determined to not let her down. I think my mother felt my unspoken frustration with not being able to go to the white local school, so she helped find a way to make the transition from Milford High School to Jason High School easier.

> Whether you are on the side that believes that Milford did all they could to make integration successful, or whether you're on the side that believes that Milford missed a historical opportunity, I was determined that these twenty-four days were not going to define me, nor what I wanted to accomplish in life.

Milford and the State of Delaware missed an important opportunity to lead the way for school integration in lower Delaware. This chance for integration could have provided an example for southern states. Because of Milford's steadfast traditions and racism, and the confusion surrounding events in Milford that fall of 1954, the failure is, in some ways, understandable. Nevertheless, it was indeed a failure.

The state of Delaware failed eleven black students—an ominous beginning to the following fifteen years of school integration struggles across the nation. Those fifteen years were a time of "massive resistance" in the South. The September 1954 events in Milford were a precursor for the widely publicized 1957 violence in Little Rock, Arkansas, where hundreds of heavily armed federal troops were dispatched to restore order. Even after public school integration was finally implemented in the 1960s, the significance of 1954 was not lost in Milford's African American community. As one black octogenarian recalled forty years after 1954, "Integration was everything. It meant we had a chance."[69]

Notes

1. Liva Baker, *With All Deliberate Speed*, American Heritage 42 (1973), 42.
2. Census of the Population: 1950, *Characteristics of the Population: Delaware*, Vol. II, part 8. Washington, D.C., 1952.
3. Wilmington Morning News, Aug. 28, 1951, at 44.
4. Interview with John Glenn, Jan. 13, 1996.
5. Interview with I. G. Burton, March 1, 1994.
6. Delaware State News, September 28, 1954, at 1.
7. Interview with Marjorie Summers, Mar. 1, 1994.
8. Interview with Thelma Mayhew, Mar. 1, 1994.
9. Interview with I. G. Burton, March 1, 1994.
10. Interview with William V. Sipple Jr., Dec. 28, 1994.
11. Milford Board of Education Minutes, Aug. 30, 1954.
12. Selwyn James, *The Town That Surrendered to Hate*, 104 Redbook 70 (April 1955).
13. Interview with William Kimmel, Dec. 20, 1995.
14. Milford Chronicle, Sept. 3, 1954, at 1; Delaware State News, Sept. 3, 1954, at 1; *Frankly Speaking*, Wilmington Morning News, Sept. 23, 1954.
15. Interview with William V. Sipple Jr., Dec. 29, 1994.
16. Information presented at Delaware State Archives Black History Month Event, Feb. 9, 2004, and Social Studies Symposium, Milford High School, Feb. 23, 2004.
17. Information Presented at Reunion Picnic, Kee's Creek Farm, July 25, 2004; James, *The Town That Surrendered to Hate*, at 70.
18. Interview with I. G. Burton, March 1, 1994.
19. James, *The Town That Surrendered to Hate*, at 70; Archives Presentation, Feb. 9, 2004; WHYY-12 Newscast of *Brown v. Board* Symposium at the University of Delaware, Apr. 23, 2004.

20. Milford Chronicle, Sept. 24, 1954, at 4.

21. Wilmington Morning News, Sept. 18, 1954, at 1.

22. Wilmington Morning News, Sept. 21, 1954, at 1.

23. Milford Board of Education, Minutes, Sept. 20, 1954; Wilmington Morning News, Sept. 21, 1954, at 1.

24. *Under Protest*, Time, Oct. 4, 1954, at 49.

25. Wilmington Morning News, Sept. 22, 1954, at 1.

26. Interview with Marjorie Summers, Mar. 1, 1994.

27. Wilmington Morning News, Sept. 23, 1954, at 1, 4.

28. Wilmington Morning News, Nov. 5, 1954, at 1; interview with I. G. Burton, Mar. 1, 1994.

29. Delaware State News, Sept. 24, 1954, at 1

30. Delaware State News, Sept. 27, 1954, at 1.

31. George R. Miller, "Adolescent Negro Education in Delaware: A Study of the Negro Secondary School," PhD dissertation, New York University, 1947.

32. Wilmington Morning News, Sept. 25, 1954, at 1.

33. Wilmington Morning News, Sept. 28, 1954, 1, 4.

34. Interview with Thelma Mayhew, Mar. 1, 1994; Wilmington Morning News, Sept. 28, 1954, at 6.

35. Interview with Charles Harding, July 25, 2004; James, *The Town That Surrendered to Hate,* at 71.

36. Wilmington Morning News, Sept. 27, 1954, at 1.

37. Delaware State News, Sept. 28, 1954, at 1; Wilmington Morning News, Sept. 28, 1954, at 1.

38. Interview with Charles Fleming Jr., Oct. 10, 2004.

39. Wilmington Morning News, Sept. 28, 1954, at 6.

40. Interview with I. G. Burton, Mar. 1, 1994.

41. Interview with Lionel Shockley, Dec. 22, 1995.

42. *An Outsider Stirs Up Small Town Trouble*, 37 Life, 15, 46 (October 11, 1954).

43. Interview with Kenneth Baynard, July 8, 2004.

44. Presbyterian Life, Oct. 30, 1954, at 8; interview with John E. Burris, July 15, 1995; interview with Joseph O. Penuel, Apr. 20, 1995; interview with Lionel Shockley, Dec. 22, 1995.

45. N.Y. Times, Oct. 18, 1954; Presbyterian Life, 36; Wilmington Morning News, Sept. 29, 1954, at 1.

46. Interview with Edwina Green, Mar. 1, 1994.

47. Wilmington Morning News, Oct. 1, 1954, at 1; Delaware State News, Oct. 1, 1954, at 1.

48. Milford City Council Minutes, Sept. 30, 1954.

49. Wilmington Morning News, Oct. 1, 1954, at 1.

50. Robert McFann, *Hope for Early End to Milford Case Dwindles*, Wilmington Morning News, Sept. 30, 1954.

51. Thomas B. Malone, *Integration or Insurrection*, Wilmington Morning News, Aug. 31, 1955, at 1.

52. Interview with Hayes Fountain, July 25, 1994; interviews with former students, July 25, 2004.

53. N.Y. Times, Oct. 18, 1954; Malone, *Integration or Insurrection.*

54. Correspondence of Louis Redding to Edna Mae Turner, Nov. 2, 1954, part of the Milford School District Archives.

55. Malone, *Integration or Insurrection.*

56. Correspondence of I. G. Burton to Governor Caleb Boggs, Oct. 4, 1954.

57. *Id.*
58. Interview with I. G. Burton, Mar. 1, 1994.
59. Personal collection of I. G. Burton.
60. Milford Chronicle, Oct. 8, 1954, at 1.
61. Wilmington Morning News, Oct. 1, 1954, at 1.
62. N.Y. Times, Oct. 12, 1954, at 20; Time Magazine, Oct. 25, 1954, at 43.
63. Milford Chronicle, Oct. 15, 1954, at 1.
64. Milford Board of Education Minutes, Oct. 4, 1954.
65. *Day of the Demagogues*, Time Magazine, Oct. 25, 1954, at 43.
66. Delaware Court of Chancery, *Simmons, et al. v. Steiner, et al.*, Oct. 14, 1954.
67. Delaware Court of Chancery, *Simmons, et al. v. Steiner, et al.*, Oct. 14, 1954; Delaware Supreme Court, *Steiner, et al. v. Simmons, et al.*, Feb. 8, 1955; Wolters, 200.
68. Paul Dolan, *Government and Administration of Delaware* 144 (Crowell, 1956).
69. Interview with Hayes Fountain, July 25, 1994.

CHAPTER TEN

Delaware Voices: Littleton Mitchell

Littleton Mitchell was raised in Milford, Delaware, where he attended a segregated elementary school. He met his wife, the late Jane Mitchell, at Howard High School in Wilmington, which they both attended. At the time, Howard was the only high school for black students in Delaware. Mitchell boarded with a family in Wilmington during the week and hitchhiked home to Milford on the weekends. Mitchell served as an officer in the military during World War II. After his discharge, Mitchell graduated from West Chester University. Starting in 1948, Mitchell worked, until his retirement, at the Governor Bacon Health Center in Delaware City.

Mitchell is best known for his leadership as president of Delaware's NAACP during the height of the civil rights movement. During those tumultuous years, Mitchell worked with the U.S. Department of Health and Human Services in an effort that resulted in the elimination of segregation in Delaware's hospitals; he led a series of demonstrations that resulted in the desegregation of hotels in Delaware; and he organized efforts that ended segregation in theaters in Wilmington and at a local golf course. Mitchell also forced a cemetery to allow blacks to purchase burial lots and participated in litigation that resulted in a court striking down a discriminatory innkeepers' law. Mitchell's efforts also compelled the integration of Delaware's volunteer firefighter companies.

Mitchell's criminal justice activities included preventing a local police department from targeting a black minister with false rape charges and obtaining the release of ten black youths held at a southern Delaware jail who were arrested, without cause, as they walked home from a school dance. He prevented the return of a sixteen-year-old black female to Alabama accompanied only by two white male officers; because of his efforts, officials were required to include a female officer in the transfer. Mitchell forced a reluctant police department, after a long period of inaction, to file charges against two white youths who had assaulted a six-year-old black female. He also worked with the ACLU to ensure equal treatment for inmates incarcerated in Delaware prisons.

Mitchell's work to eliminate employment discrimination included protesting a telephone company's policy of refusing to hire blacks in any capacity and forcing the Delaware State Police to hire black officers. Mitchell also worked to eliminate the abuse of African American and Mexican migrant workers. He helped force the closure of migrant labor camps that maintained substandard living conditions, removed a teenager from a migrant camp where he was being held against his will and a Mexican family from a dilapidated and unsanitary labor camp, and secured free transportation for migrant workers to medical clinics in Wilmington.

Mitchell has devoted his career to advocating racial equality. His work contributed to Delaware's transformation from a rigidly segregated community to a state whose laws prohibit discrimination. Mitchell served on the Brown v. Board of Education *50th Anniversary Commission established by Congress in 2001 to encourage the commemoration of the fiftieth anniversary of the Supreme Court decision.*

Brown's Unfulfilled Promise

There are not many people who were educated under the "separate but equal" system. I would like to paint a picture of what it was like. I'm from Milford, Delaware, which was very separate and unequal when I attended school there. We had a school for whites that was located in a beautiful neighborhood with paved walks and adequate lighting. The school was housed in several buildings; it included grades one to twelve. On the other hand, we had a black school with just five rooms. It was located at the edge of the town. It was not a location that many residents frequented. The school was surrounded on two sides by cornfields. In the back, there was a pasture with cows and horses. The front of the school faced pens used by a slaughterhouse to hold cows. Frequently, the cows got out of their pens, and it seemed that the only place they wanted to feed was on our school lawn. Of course, they left their smelly residue there, which was never cleaned.

Milford's white school had manicured lawns. At the black school, grass grew almost up to our hips and was very seldom cut. As far as the playgrounds were concerned, one school had several sliding boards, a number of swing sets, a basketball court, and a baseball diamond. At the black school, there was a field of grass and one pole with six chains attached to it. It was called a "Giant Stride." You could grab a chain, run around, and swing out to circle the pole. That was on the boy's side of our school. The boys and girls were separated in school. On the girl's side, there was nothing except fields.

The white school had about five maintenance workers; our school had one janitor to take care of the five rooms. The only time our furniture was replaced was when the other school purchased new furniture. Their old furniture was sent to our school. We also had to use their old textbooks. I never had a new textbook until I entered college, where I had to pay for it. Students at the white school would use pencils until they were worn down. Someone would wrap them in strings, put them in nice little boxes, and ship them to our school. This was all part of the "separate but equal" system.

It is important to understand that, in Delaware, the eighth grade was the end of a black student's educational career if he or she could not afford to enroll in the private high school at Delaware State, the segregated college for blacks in Dover, or travel to Wilmington to attend Howard High School. In my class in Milford, there were thirteen of us who graduated. Three of us were able to attend high school and beyond. Many of those who remained in Milford ended up as alcoholics, drug addicts, and prison inmates.

At Howard High School in Wilmington, conditions were not much better. Howard was located adjacent to a large tannery. We didn't have air conditioning. On hot summer days, the windows were open, and the wind blew noxious fumes from the factory into our school rooms. It was almost unbearable. In the sports arena, conditions were almost as bad. We could not compete with any of the high schools in Delaware. To compete in sports, we had to play against teams from the black high schools in Maryland, Washington, D.C., and Virginia, though we sometimes competed with integrated schools from Pennsylvania. The one place where there was athletic democracy was the racially integrated Penn Relays, an annual track event that is held in Philadelphia.

Jason High School was constructed as a black school in Georgetown, Delaware, because the students were scattered over such a large area, there were students who rode the bus eighty miles to attend a school that was approximately sixteen miles from their homes. The late Louis L. Redding, Esquire, wanted to be certain that he knew exactly how far these children were riding to school, so he got in his car and followed the bus. He wanted to determine the exact distance they were traveling. It turned out to be eighty miles.

Louis L. Redding was a civil rights lawyer who argued the Delaware cases that were among the five consolidated cases remembered collectively as *Brown v. Board of Education*. In 1963 Redding made a speech in which he observed, "The principal bearing we have in this state today is lethargy, the apathy, the indifference of the Negroes who would be benefited in taking advantage of the opportunity that is legally theirs. If this can be overcome, I think Delaware will be completely integrated." Those words are as true today as they were in 1963.

I was appointed to serve on the national commission for the celebration of *Brown v. Board of Education*. We convened one meeting at the University of Kansas where we received some very disturbing information. We were told that only 500 colleges and universities would convene programs commemorating the *Brown* decision. The 500 colleges and universities were evidently the only institutions that considered this historic event worthy of celebration.

The *Brown* commission visited more than a few predominantly white colleges and some historically black colleges. We wanted to learn what students knew about the 1954 decision. At the predominantly white colleges, we found a total of fifteen white students who knew anything about the *Brown* decision. At the historically black colleges we found only one student who knew anything about *Brown*. One college held a *Brown v. Board of Education* celebration where one of the lawyers who argued *Brown* in the Supreme Court, Professor Jack Greenberg, was the keynote speaker. It was held in an auditorium that could seat 600 people. When Professor Greenberg spoke, we counted thirty-five people in the audience, which included only two faculty members from the college and two students.

In contrast, during our visits to private elementary schools we were surprised to find that students were learning not only about the *Brown* decision but also about the Tuskegee Airmen and the 701st tank battalion, a black World War II unit that received a Medal of Honor from President Bill Clinton just a few years ago.

There were many disappointments. Most frustrating was the fact that, in 1990, southern school systems were 50 percent integrated and that figure has since dropped to 30 percent. What this signals is that *Brown v. Board of Education* provided the legal precedent for equal educational opportunity, but that goal has not been achieved. As a result, the members of the national *Brown* commission are urging the public to understand the significance of the decision and the impact that it has had on our nation. *Brown* was not limited to the educational systems of our country. It has had a domino effect that extended to every segment of our society. Academic and legal scholars consider *Brown v. Board of Education* one of the most important decisions that the Supreme Court has ever rendered.

From our travel and observations, the members of the national *Brown* commission have concluded that our educational system is experiencing significant difficulties. It may be in need of total restructuring. What can be done? The commission has not offered solutions, nor does it intend to. This is not our responsibility, but as citizens, we can offer suggestions. Individuals across the country should obtain information concerning their school systems, information about how they function. Residents of school districts should identify those who are responsible for school administration and get to know them. They should become informed about school policies, which will allow them to speak with authority about what is going on.

We should all get involved in the affairs of schools and, most important, encourage young African Americans to enter the teaching profession, especially males. We should promote an increase in teacher salaries. Teachers prepare our future leaders. Every child deserves the best instruction available. We should remove administrators who are not implementing the *Brown* decision. There are a few of them still around, and they are masquerading old attitudes under all kinds of new disguises. We need open-minded judges who believe in the equal opportunity that the Supreme Court unanimously directed in *Brown*, and we need to change the administration in Washington.

My final suggestion is the easiest. Every person should look in a mirror and ask, "What can I do; what haven't I done to assist the educational system that I'm complaining about?" Our educational system needs all of us. When the schools completely resegregate, it will be too late. The education ball is in our court. The question is, What are we going to do with it?

CHAPTER ELEVEN

An Interview with the Honorable Murray M. Schwartz

Judge Murray M. Schwartz presided over the New Castle County school desegregation litigation from the late 1970s through the early 1990s. Judge Schwartz was born in 1931. He attended public schools in Ephrata, Pennsylvania, and graduated from the Wharton School in 1952 and from the University of Pennsylvania School of Law in 1955. He earned a Master of Laws in Judicial Process from the University of Virginia in 1981.

Judge Schwartz clerked for U.S. District Court Judge J. Caleb Wright upon his graduation from law school and was clerking for him in 1956 when Louis Redding filed a federal class action suit to desegregate the Clayton School District in Delaware. In 1969, Judge Schwartz became a part-time Bankruptcy Referee and, in 1973, was nominated to the U.S. District Court for the District of Delaware by Richard Nixon. Judge Schwartz would serve on the court for fifteen years, including five years as Chief Judge.

Judge Schwartz's first brush with widespread public notoriety came in 1977, when he found violations of the Fourteenth Amendment in the conditions at the Delaware state prison in Smyrna (*Anderson v. Redman*, 429 F.Supp. 1105 (D. Del. 1977)). The following year, he issued his momentous order in the Delaware school desegregation case. Judge Schwartz assumed senior status in 1989, but retained the desegregation cases until 1991.

The Saint Thomas More Society of Delaware awarded Judge Schwartz its Saint Thomas Award for his "strong and pervasive sense of justice" and "outstanding service to the community." In 2004, the Delaware State Bar Association awarded Judge Schwartz its First State Distinguished Service Award, presented to a member of the Delaware bar "who has maintained the integrity and honored recognition of the legal profession in community affairs and unceasingly advances the ideals of citizen participation and community accomplishment."

Judge Schwartz sat for the following interview on November 16, 2004.

PROF. HAYMAN: Judge Schwartz, thank you very much for agreeing to talk with us.

JUDGE SCHWARTZ: You're welcome.

PROF. HAYMAN: Judge Schwartz, I'd like talk to you a little bit at the beginning about your early involvement with the Delaware desegregation case. Could you tell us first about the work of the three-judge panel?

JUDGE SCHWARTZ: Yes. The three-judge district court found a constitutional violation and it also provided a remedy, which was one large district comprised of the desegregation area.[1] The suburban defendants and the State Board of Education appealed that remedy Order to the Supreme Court. The Supreme Court noted that it didn't have a constitutional violation before it, it simply had a remedy for a constitutional violation, and as a consequence it felt, properly so, that one judge should be handling the remedy stage.[2] So it sent it to the Third Circuit Court of Appeals, and then the Third Circuit Court of Appeals considered that remedy of the three-judge court.[3]

PROF. HAYMAN: How did you then become the judge who would be in charge of implementing that remedy?

JUDGE SCHWARTZ: Judge Wright, Caleb Wright, brought me to Delaware. I was his first law clerk. Incidentally, I took his place on the bench. He was, as I said, one of the three judges on the three-judge panel. The others were Judge Layton and Judge Gibbons. Judge Gibbons was a Third Circuit judge, so it was clear he would not handle it, and I was confident that Judge Layton would not take it, so that left only Judge Wright.

PROF. HAYMAN: Judge Layton had, in fact, dissented from some of the holdings, hadn't he?

JUDGE SCHWARTZ: Yes, he had. So I went to Judge Wright who, as I said, not only brought me to Delaware, but he was my mentor, and we stayed fairly close friends. When I saw what had happened, I approached Judge Wright because I was concerned. He had come to the bench over the opposition of New Castle County attorneys. He had proven to be a very capable and much admired judge. He was either sixty-six or sixty-seven at that point.

PROF. HAYMAN: And you were somewhat younger?

JUDGE SCHWARTZ: Yes, considerably younger. I went to Judge Wright and told him that I thought it was going to be very ugly. He had done his bit. He had made his contribution, and I was willing to take over the remedy phase, and he acquiesced in that, and that's how I got the case.

PROF. HAYMAN: Did you have some sense then what you were getting into?

JUDGE SCHWARTZ: Yes. It was clear that people had become unhappy, very unhappy, so yes, I had that sense.

I knew that now with eleven districts, one of which was Wilmington that was predominantly black, and then I think it was DeLaWar, which was essentially integrated, and then nine other suburban districts that were predominantly white, that probably each district or most of the districts would have their own counsel, so there was going to be a lot of lawyers in the case, and the state board of course would have its counsel, and it would be very hotly contested.

PROF. HAYMAN: Was Judge Wright relieved when you told him you were willing to take the case?

JUDGE SCHWARTZ: I can't say whether he was relieved or not. You have to know Judge Wright; he's now deceased, unfortunately, so you won't have that privilege. But he was willing to give it up. We didn't know what was going to happen.

PROF. HAYMAN: Did he continue to talk to you about the case after you took it over?

JUDGE SCHWARTZ: Not to the best of my recollection. It was sort of a given that once you take a case, unless you go to someone, to another judge to discuss it, they're not going to readily intrude. And we had a wonderful bench at that time. It was Judge Wright, Judge Stapleton, Judge Latchum, and myself. Latchum was the oldest nonsenior judge, Stapleton was next, and I was the baby.

PROF. HAYMAN: Can we talk a little bit about the January 1978 Order, which I suppose most people will consider the most monumental in the implementation stage of the decree?[4] One of the arguments that is made in the case on behalf of the state was in support of a "reverse volunteerism" plan. Do you recall what that plan was about?

JUDGE SCHWARTZ: Yes. It was interesting.

There were two voluntary plans. One was voluntary transfer, which is self-explanatory. The other plan was "reverse volunteerism." The defendants came up with the idea that each student from the former black district of Wilmington would be assigned a suburban school and then they could volunteer to go back to their own school. That's what the plan was.

PROF. HAYMAN: And the voluntary transfer plan by contrast was you can select out of the district to which you have been assigned.

JUDGE SCHWARTZ: Correct.

PROF. HAYMAN: Now this is after the Supreme Court's *Green* decision[5] expressing skepticism toward these "voluntary" "freedom of choice" plans; did the state seriously press its contention that these "volunteer" plans would satisfy the desegregation mandate?

JUDGE SCHWARTZ: I think you have to look at it as the state wanting to do the least it could do to upset the suburban district parents in terms of having their children bused, so in that sense, yes, they were serious. And because they were serious, it had to be regarded as something out there, not something that would necessarily carry the day, but it was there. You could not ignore anything that was put out there, just cavalierly push it off.

PROF. HAYMAN: Was there a point in your deliberations where you thought perhaps maybe this is enough?

JUDGE SCHWARTZ: No. However, and this was much later, before I issued the remedy opinion you mentioned, I tried to settle the case and the State Board of Education in the suburban districts said essentially, "We will take every Wilmington district child and admit them to whichever district it was going to be," and that's all they put on the table at the time.

PROF. HAYMAN: So to clarify, the Wilmington students would be the only ones who would be moving; they would be the only ones who would attend another school.

JUDGE SCHWARTZ: That's correct. I asked the plaintiffs if they were interested in that remedy, after first pointing out the weaknesses in their position and the weaknesses to the defendants, the weaknesses of their position. I don't want to say I urged it on them, but I certainly was interested in settling the case. The plaintiffs understandably turned it down because it put the entire burden of the remedy on them, yet they were the ones who endured the constitutional violation. So that was an effort to settle the case. It somewhat encompassed not voluntary transfer, but an offshoot of voluntary transfer.

PROF. HAYMAN: Ultimately it seems that it's your concern about that unfairness that influenced your decision to reject the 10-2 plan in favor of the 9-3 plan; is that fair?

JUDGE SCHWARTZ: That's fair.

PROF. HAYMAN: Can you explain a little bit about the 10-2 plan and 9-3 plan?

JUDGE SCHWARTZ: Sure—10-2 provided that all children would spend two consecutive years in the formerly predominantly black districts and ten years in the predominantly former white districts. The 9-3 was the same idea, but it had some additions. Nine-three provided for all children—not white children, not black children, but all children—to spend three consecutive grades in the former predominantly black districts and nine grades in the predominantly white districts.

There was one other very important item in the plan: that it had to have a complete one through twelve grade structure. Now by doing that, it meant that the school authorities could not just send all children to, say, third and fourth grade in the City of Wilmington or, if it's 9-3, just grades four, five, and six into the City of Wilmington.

It might seem, looking at it today, like, "Well, what's the big deal between 10-2 and 9-3?" In terms of the burden being borne by the black children in terms of busing, they would be bused for nine grades instead of ten grades. And the reason for 9-3 and not 8-4, or what have you, was that it was the maximum number of children in terms of school seating capacity in the Wilmington district for this purpose. You could not get four consecutive grades into the Wilmington district.

PROF. HAYMAN: And with a 9-3 plan, and insisting that the plan incorporate all twelve grades, it provides for an opportunity for three consecutive years of education at Wilmington High School which would not have happened with a 10-2 plan.

JUDGE SCHWARTZ: That's correct.

PROF. HAYMAN: The 9-3 plan, as I understand it, was first proposed by a planning committee that had been established by the school districts. Were they the ones who proposed a variety of different 9-3 plans?

JUDGE SCHWARTZ: They did. I think there were five.

What happened is this. The plaintiffs had excellent counsel. All counsel were good, but Paul Diamond had a lot of experience because he handled desegregation, major desegregation in several of the cases that went up to the Supreme Court. I'm not sure if he suggested it or I popped the question from the bench, whether there was room for three grades. I do remember that I looked at the gross numbers. Just by way of example, if there were 80,000 children, if you could say that a quarter of them could fit into the Wilmington schools, that is were there 20,000 seats, and I'm just using that hypothetically, the answer was "yes." But now how it would work out with the various schools was a different story.

So I then suggested that I needed help and asked the suburban districts—again, this is just memory and I could be wrong on some of the details—to supply people who would be on a committee, which we later called the "Planning Committee," to see if 9-3 were feasible. That committee had very, very capable individuals on it. They also were brave. Here they are, the majority is working for the suburban districts who do not want 9-3, yet they came up with this solution that 9-3 was possible, and that took a lot of courage on their part.

PROF. HAYMAN: It's my understanding that they actually met at the courthouse for their planning sessions; is that right?

JUDGE SCHWARTZ: That's correct. The Planning Committee—I don't want to say it was my committee, but it certainly was the committee for the litigation—I gave them their directive and they met in my jury room in the courthouse, which was just down the hall from chambers, so they were isolated and insulated.

Of course, they still had to go home at the end of the day, and to me they were just amazing, because they were so brave, and because this is before the time when computers were really around or in vogue, so they had to fit these numbers in different schools built for different children, and they came up with five ways of doing it.

PROF. HAYMAN: You, of course, reacted quite favorably to their plans and ultimately approved a 9-3 plan.

JUDGE SCHWARTZ: That's correct.

PROF. HAYMAN: I want to talk a little bit about some of the ancillary relief in that case and it included a rather interesting list of services. I'm going to read just some of them to you if you don't mind: "in-service training," "remedial educational services" for the students, a "multicultural curriculum," a "human relations program," as well as programs to guard against bias in tracking and discipline,[6] which, as we know, would emerge as problems. Where did you derive your inspiration for those programs?

JUDGE SCHWARTZ: I'd like to take the credit, but it was the plaintiffs who proposed it—again, the team headed by Paul Diamond. I don't even know or don't remember if I tweaked it at all, but the credit belongs to plaintiff's counsel.

And that's true in a lot of litigation. A lot or most of the good ideas come from counsel.

PROF. HAYMAN: When you saw those proposals, though, just to take an example, the proposal for a multicultural curriculum, what appealed to you about that idea or any of these other ideas? What made you think this is something we really need to have as a part of the plan?

JUDGE SCHWARTZ: We were talking about or facing two distinct cultures—the white culture and the black culture—and they really didn't know much about each other and there were a lot of racial stereotypes, probably going both ways, but the whites probably held more unfavorable racial stereotypes than the blacks did. Those problems, incidentally, still haven't been solved.

So that was the reason for actually all of this ancillary relief. The teachers weren't prepared for it. The teachers in the suburbs didn't have many black children; they had some. And in Wilmington they didn't have that many white children, so it was all going to be new.

PROF. HAYMAN: Is that notion—that we are in some senses two people who, because of segregation, haven't really gotten to know each other—is that a notion that you carried into the case do you suppose, or is that something you think that you really learned in the process of the litigation?

JUDGE SCHWARTZ: I knew it. I mean, you can't close your eyes to what was happening and you couldn't close your eyes to different value systems, and I just knew it. It was not a case of, "okay, why are you asking for this?" I knew why they were asking.

PROF. HAYMAN: Those programs and services, of course, are going to cost money, and that takes us to the part of the case where you decide where that money is going to come from. Part of that involved the fixing of an assessment rate and the portion of this opinion where you fix the local assessment rate seems remarkably apologetic. It's as if you feel really bad that you have to do that. Is that the way you felt when you were doing that part of the opinion?

JUDGE SCHWARTZ: I never realized that it was apologetic. I was annoyed.

PROF. HAYMAN: With the legislature?

JUDGE SCHWARTZ: Well, with the state generally, because there was going to be, as far as everyone knew at the time, one district—that was no secret, as soon as these other plans got out of the way—and we had 9-3 on the table. So you had eleven school districts, Wilmington and the ten suburbs, with different tax rates and different pay scales, not only for teachers, but for everybody, and they had to become one. So I was rather confounded that the legislature refused to act.

Now I understood the political realities. I can't say I was sympathetic with them. But they would not act, and so I set a tax rate that I felt would be enough money. It was a maximum the district could ask for. They could choose less but, let's face it, we all know that they would never choose less than they could get, and I just set the rate. I was annoyed, not angry, but I couldn't understand how a responsible legislature could just wash their hands of the whole thing.

PROF. HAYMAN: I have to say that the frustration does pretty clearly come through in parts of the opinion, I thought particularly in the parts of the opinion where you assess costs, and you seem not the least bit apologetic about assessing costs to the state. The General Assembly had been remarkably quiet, hadn't it, up to this point?

JUDGE SCHWARTZ: Yes. Well, they were quiet, but they did pass one House resolution. I think it asked President Carter to remove me from the case.[7] I don't remember exactly what it was.

PROF. HAYMAN: You weren't particularly concerned about that.

JUDGE SCHWARTZ: No, no.

To the best of my recollection, plaintiff's counsel at that time received no compensation and were doing all of this gratis because they cared. I don't know what their source of funds was. I'm sure there were some advocacy groups that were funding part of it. And I had no sympathy for the state because it was battling as hard as it could battle, and that was its privilege, but then it had to expect to pay, and it was not like it was battling where it could be a sure winner or even have a 50/50 chance. The violation had been established and a remedy was coming. It was just a case of what.

I think you can get a picture of the state's viewed remedy simply by the discussion we've already had. Start with voluntary transfer, then reverse volunteerism, which puts no burden on the whites, and then there's a lot in between, then 10-2 and eventually 9-3, and the majority of the burden still was on the black population, but it couldn't be avoided.

Sympathy, I don't think, should ever play a part in a judge's decision, and neither should annoyance and frustration, but that does not prevent you from looking at the facts and saying: "They've got to pay. They know what they were doing. They have to pay."

PROF. HAYMAN: Your decision in this case was affirmed by the Third Circuit.[8] The state then petitioned and the suburban school districts petitioned the Supreme Court for a writ of certiorari. Can you briefly explain your understanding of what happened then at the Supreme Court?

JUDGE SCHWARTZ: Well, no one really knows what happened at the Supreme Court, but you can look at some objective facts and say it was peculiar.

First, the remedy was in place. Children were being bused. But there was no action by the Supreme Court for—I don't want to say an unprecedented—but for an unusually long time, seventeen or eighteen months.[9]

Second, when the Court did act, it denied certiorari, even though the dissent accompanying the denial of certiorari made clear there were four votes for certiorari, which is all that was needed.

One can only speculate as to why it took roughly seventeen or eighteen months for the Court to rule on the petition for certiorari. But it's an objective fact that Justice Marshall had been lead counsel in *Brown*, and had therefore previously appeared in the litigation involving the Hockessin and Claymont school districts, both of which had been extinguished and made part of the single district created by the remedy order. Justice Marshall had not participated in the Supreme Court decisions in the constitutional violation phase of the litigation;[10] he did participate in the denial of certiorari on the remedy order. The time-honored mantra is that each judge or Justice individually decides whether recusal is necessary. That time-honored mantra might have been the subject of some time-consuming discourse among the Justices during the remedy phase, because of Justice Marshall's prior recusal during the violation phase. Again, I have to stress that what I have said is pure speculation on my part, because only the participants know why there was such a long delay before ruling on the certiorari petition.

Unlike the unexplained delay in acting on the certiorari petition, the Court told us why it would decline to issue the writ even though there were four votes for certiorari. The four dissenting justices wanted a full Court, and Justice Stevens had recused. There is a constant caution that nothing should be read into a denial of certiorari. On the other hand, one can be certain that with Justice Marshall participating, if certiorari had been granted, there would have been a 4-4 tie on the Court, with the result that the Third Circuit's unanimous decision upholding the remedy order would have controlled.

The dissent to the denial of certiorari was written by then Justice Rehnquist, and he had some language to the effect that the remedy was more draconian than any remedy ever approved by the Court in a school desegregation case.[11] He clearly was unhappy. Two others joined him, Justices Stewart and Powell. Near the end of the opinion there was a brief paragraph stating that Chief Justice Burger would have joined in the granting of certiorari if he had a full court.[12]

PROF. HAYMAN: Let's talk a little bit about the legislative response. The General Assembly does eventually get around to acting and they do establish a tax rate. You subsequently receive a writ of mandamus from the Third Circuit when, after your initial review of that tax rate, you still find it deficient.[13] As you revisit that dispute now and the Third Circuit's decision, did the Third Circuit get it right? Were you insufficiently deferential to the legislature?

JUDGE SCHWARTZ: The Third Circuit was absolutely correct. I should have been reversed on the tax rate issue. The jargon used was "not sufficiently deferential to the State legislature," and that certainly was correct. That's what happened.

What I overlooked was that even though it wouldn't be enough money and could impair the desegregation effort, the fact of the matter is all children, black and white children, were being treated equally. They all would be in an educational system that conceivably did not have enough money. I might add, just as an aside, that within a few weeks after the buses rolled, the teachers went out on a six-week strike, and of course for the most part that was about money, and the district had less money to play with. But I was wrong. No getting around it.

One other thing is worth noting. When the General Assembly finally adopted a tax rate, now it was something not to be feared. They were heroes. There was a tax rate and they're making it a lower tax rate and they're acting responsibly for their constituents. And the same thing happened with the four districts. It was something that was wanted and so they acted. It was politically safe to do so.

PROF. HAYMAN: The General Assembly, when it finally decided to act, also developed a four-district plan for desegregation rather than a single district model. As you did with the tax rate on remand from the Third Circuit, when you analyzed their four-district plan, you ultimately determined that it was constitutional.[14] It seemed that there was insufficient evidence of a discriminatory intent on behalf of the General Assembly, and it was your view that it would not impair the desegregation effort. I'm curious. How close were those questions at the time?

JUDGE SCHWARTZ: To me, not close at all.

The fact of the matter is that, prior to the remedy order going into effect, there had been eleven districts, and so there were different administrative systems set up in each district, obviously more accountable and/or at least reachable by the parents. There was enormous dissatisfaction with what was considered to be an unwieldy district and so dividing it into four districts was fine. Somewhere, and I don't remember where, there had at some point been something said about four districts, but I just don't remember what it was.

Now when the legislature acted, however, it inadvertently left a gigantic hole. With one district, you could look to the State Board of Education and to the single district to enforce the decree that was covering twelve grades in one district. But when you had four districts, there could have been disagreements among the districts about which grades come in the city of Wilmington, and I will tell you at the time it was grades four through six that many school officials wanted to concentrate in Wilmington. Of course they couldn't do everything they wanted because of the required one through twelve–grade structure, but they could try to put more four through six in Wilmington than any other grades.

There was no focused responsibility, no clear accountability. So I approved the four districts, but conditioned it upon responsibility, if my recollection is correct, being placed at the State Board for enforcement of the decree. That got rid of all these potential problems that would have occurred, and you had one group you could look to and you didn't have to get involved in all the fights about which grades, which children, the whole thing.

PROF. HAYMAN: It was your sense then that the General Assembly was acting in good faith in the creation of the four-district plan?

JUDGE SCHWARTZ: I think it was, and, I must say, it rather quickly approved the placement of responsibility for enforcing the decree.

PROF. HAYMAN: Did you get the sense at some point in the process that the General Assembly was setting you up as the foil, that they were pretty clear what role they wanted you to be perceived as playing?

JUDGE SCHWARTZ: There's a book out by Celia Cohen[15] and she happens to mention this very point. I don't remember the language. But the attitude of the legislature was, "Let Schwartz do it." I think that's her language. And that was true. They did not want to act. If they acted, they probably were out of office at the next election.

PROF. HAYMAN: But if they reacted to what you had done . . .

JUDGE SCHWARTZ: Yes, that was safe. So that's the way I view it. And I don't know if anyone would quarrel with that.

PROF. HAYMAN: Did you sense it at the time?

JUDGE SCHWARTZ: I wasn't thinking in those terms. I was just looking at the fact that there's a problem here, it has to be solved, and perhaps I'm not the one who should really be doing it, but no one else is doing it, and so I must do it.

PROF. HAYMAN: I want to talk a little bit about the reaction to the opinions. Can you summarize your sense of some of the negative reaction to the opinions?

JUDGE SCHWARTZ: There was disappointment. I'm now talking primarily about the white parents. They were angry, they were frightened, and they felt helpless, if you want to consider from the white parents' point of view. They had lost control of their child's education and who their child went to school with. So I think that pretty well sums it up.

Now I have to say that you can't paint with too broad a brush. There were some white parents who approved, but they were in a distinct minority.

I don't know as much about the black parents. I do know that some felt there was a sense of unfairness in that their children had to be bused for nine years while the white children only had to be bused for three years. I can understand how they felt if they didn't understand the constraints of the seating capacity in the schools in Wilmington. Otherwise I'm sure many were in favor of what was happening at the time. And you also had the necessity of facing the realization that they were losing their power base in the school district in Wilmington. So that, too, played a part. Otherwise I really can't comment too much about it, how the black parents felt. I am confident that many approved.

PROF. HAYMAN: Some of the negative reaction to the opinion was quite personal. Was there a time that you were ever frightened for your own health and safety or that of your family?

JUDGE SCHWARTZ: I wouldn't say frightened. I would say concerned and vigilant.

We took some steps at the house. We had windows, of course, in the front of the house. I was agonizingly aware that there were still a lot of people around who had worked with powder. I'm talking now in the '70s. I was concerned about a fire bomb being thrown through the window on the first floor. In fact, the Marshal Service refused a request for barrier glass, but they offered to put as many marshals as needed twenty-four hours a day out at our house. Well, we have a woods across from us and a woods behind us, not big woods but still a woods, and my wife and I discussed whether we wanted our girls to grow up in a siege mentality and we decided we didn't. So we turned them down.

Right before the buses rolled—probably that weekend—I no longer could control the situation. My recollection is the county police and State Police got into the act, and also the Marshal Service.

PROF. HAYMAN: You rather regularly received threats; is that right?

JUDGE SCHWARTZ: Yes. I will tell you just a couple of stories, where documentation might still be available someplace.

Two days after the buses rolled, which was right after Labor Day in '78, I received a phone call from Frank Grant who was an FBI agent at the time. He asked if he could come down, something he wanted to discuss with me. So he came down and he solemnly placed a tape recorder or, I don't know, maybe an answering machine for the phone, on my desk and he started playing it, and the call had come in to Senator Biden's office. Now I have no idea why it was Senator Biden's office. I doubt that Senator Biden ever knew about it. It was a death threat, and it sounded like the guy apparently had too much to drink.

So Frank started playing it. He says, "You recognize the voice?"

"No."

"Well, what do you think about it?"

And I said, "Well, what else is new?"

Frank just looked at me. And that was that.

Other threats came directly. Usually my kids would leap to the phone. And I had not gone to an unlisted number at that point on the theory that it was better to let people vent. That's better than having them store it up.

But I was up on the second floor one day, and apparently I must have been the closest to the phone, so I picked it up and this guy started with the usual threats.

As he went on and on, he said, "Well, I'm coming over with my boys," whatever that meant, and I guess I must have lost my cool a little bit and I said, "Well, come on over. I'll be waiting."

And I went downstairs and told my wife Sara Lu, and she looks at me and she says, "Well, what are you gonna do if they come?"

It was a good question. I didn't know.

They did not show up. But that gives you some idea of the type of atmosphere.

PROF. HAYMAN: Did you ever take to wearing any protective gear?

JUDGE SCHWARTZ: I did, reluctantly. The Marshal's Office supplied a bullet-proof vest and a bullet-proof liner for a raincoat. I wore them as little as possible. The State Police supplied another bullet-proof vest, but it was one you could wear under your dress shirt. I didn't like any of them and so they were used very, very rarely.

PROF. HAYMAN: Your colleagues on the bench were undoubtedly aware of what was happening. Were they generally supportive?

JUDGE SCHWARTZ: Yes. Yes. They knew what was happening to a fair degree. We had a very unusual, very powerful bench at that point, but the answer is yes.

PROF. HAYMAN: Did they ever express to you their gratitude that you were the one who had taken the case and endured the pains?

JUDGE SCHWARTZ: Honestly, there's no reason they should have. It comes with the territory.

PROF. HAYMAN: How about local political leaders?

JUDGE SCHWARTZ: I don't want to paint with a broad brush, but I do not remember any local political leader getting involved unless it was on the negative side.

PROF. HAYMAN: Do you recall being specifically pleased or disappointed with the reaction of anyone in particular?

JUDGE SCHWARTZ: Yes, but, if you don't mind, I would prefer not to talk about it.

PROF. HAYMAN: That would clearly be a case of disappointment, I guess.

JUDGE SCHWARTZ: Right. Understandable, but disappointment.

Now, there was a group that apparently was meeting I think on Mondays, and I don't really know who was in that group, but I suspect there were several political leaders and other knowledgeable people, and they were meeting for the express purpose of trying to make sure that desegregation proceeded peacefully. But I don't know much about them. They never communicated with me. They just went about doing their thing.

And they must have been successful because the day the buses rolled, according to the press, 1,500 media types descended upon Wilmington, ready to write about the violence, and they all left within three days empty-handed. So something was done right. I'm not sure if it was working with the police. Whatever this group was doing, they were doing a good job.

PROF. HAYMAN: You mentioned the press. What is your sense of the press's reaction? Did you think they were fair? Were they supportive?

JUDGE SCHWARTZ: The press was very supportive. The editorial board was supportive. The reporters were supportive. Yes, they were.

PROF. HAYMAN: If you were asked to characterize the overall reaction to the opinion and subsequent opinions at the time, how would you describe it?

JUDGE SCHWARTZ: Well, overall, I almost have to separate it out into whites and blacks. Overall I would say by a vast majority the whites were unhappy. The black parents, from what I could tell, some approved, some were disappointed, but I don't believe they objected as vociferously as the whites did.

PROF. HAYMAN: Did parents ever communicate to you directly their appreciation at the time, their appreciation about what you were doing? Did you get direct positive affirmation from parents?

JUDGE SCHWARTZ: There were some.

PROF. HAYMAN: Did they write you? Did they call you?

JUDGE SCHWARTZ: I think it was primarily acquaintances who might have said something. I don't remember if any wrote or not. I don't think so. You have to recognize at the time it was a period of some turmoil. But no, the parents just did their thing. Those that approved, if they knew me, would tell me.

PROF. HAYMAN: When you talk to people today, what is your sense? Is it your sense that the retrospective view of that era is more favorable now, that people now appreciate what happened more than they did at the time?

JUDGE SCHWARTZ: Oh, absolutely. I have many people come up now to me, say "what a wonderful, courageous"—whatever word you want to use—"thing you did." But there is still a huge silent group who disapproves. Now I don't think they're as large as those who now approve and decided it was the right thing.

You can use by way of example Brandywine Hundred. When the Neighborhood School Act was passed,[16] the Brandywine District, one of the four created by the legislature, was not anxious to embrace it, and did not as you know. I have to think that those people recognize the value of diversity and they wanted to keep it. So I don't know if you lump those in with those who now approve or not, but I think in a sense you have to.

PROF. HAYMAN: I want to read to you something you wrote about the Red Clay School District in 1991. You described that school district as "a polarized community at odds with itself, primarily because of a lack of commitment to eradication of the vestiges of de jure segregation."[17] In light of what we just talked about with the difference in the reactions of the school districts to the neighborhood schools plan as well as with our national experience, would you say that's a fair description not only of Red Clay but also of New Castle County, and maybe Delaware, and maybe the nation?

JUDGE SCHWARTZ: Insofar as resegregation is occurring, and it's undeniable that it's occurred, yes. I don't think it's thought of in terms of vestiges of de jure segregation and going back to it. At least openly it's not thought of that way. But yes, it's what's happening.

PROF. HAYMAN: Do you think most people imagine—and now I'm the one painting with a very broad brush—do you think they imagine that segregation, de jure segregation, really is a thing of the past, that we've advanced beyond it, and that any segregation we're seeing today is not, in fact, resegregation, or a revival of segregation, or a vestige of de jure segregation, but simply "choice"?

JUDGE SCHWARTZ: I don't think they think about it. And indeed one can say that they won't have to think about it because of what has occurred in the Supreme Court.

PROF. HAYMAN: I suppose you could argue that they don't have to think about it in Delaware, too, now that the decree has been terminated.

JUDGE SCHWARTZ: Well, that's correct. The Delaware legislature has created the path for resegregation. They don't have to think about it. The decree's not there.

And, incidentally, I cannot criticize Judge Robinson for dissolving the decree.[18] In the early '90s there were three Supreme Court cases that lowered the bar for finding unitary status,[19] which is just a code word for "there's been enough" to satisfy legal requirements. I feel she was under an obligation to dissolve the decree. She had no choice, to my way of thinking.

PROF. HAYMAN: The *Dowell* case says, as I recall, that you can terminate a decree if the vestiges of segregation have been eliminated to the extent practicable, and then virtually invites that conclusion in identifying the factors.[20] In her opinion, Judge Robinson finds that the vestiges of segregation have been eliminated to the extent practicable. It's your view that this was a result that was virtually compelled by the Supreme Court's opinions?

JUDGE SCHWARTZ: Yes. I don't think any decree could survive now if it made its way to the Supreme Court.

PROF. HAYMAN: If we've eliminated the vestiges of segregation to the extent practicable, who or what is responsible for resegregation or for continuing segregation?

JUDGE SCHWARTZ: I don't know. You could point to a lot of things. Here I'd point to the Neighborhood Schools Act and the Delaware legislature. I think what happened was, and I could be wrong, they expected gigantic changes after Judge Robinson terminated the remedy decree. It didn't happen. So the legislature took things into its own hands. And for the most part it was politically popular. And it is appealing. But I think in the long term, the people—both in Delaware and in the nation—will regret it.

PROF. HAYMAN: Why do you think that is?

JUDGE SCHWARTZ: Because of what they will have lost.

In one of the Michigan affirmative action cases,[21] Justice O'Connor noted the improvement in minority population grades and test scores. It goes without saying that those scores improved over time when desegregation was at its zenith. Regrettably, a byproduct of resegregation—with all the inequalities that entails—will more probably than not be a slowdown in academic improvement, if not a deterioration. A likely corollary is that the achievement gap between majority and minority public school students will widen.

At the same time, numerous Fortune 500 companies and the military filed briefs in the Supreme Court supporting the goal of diversity, at least in higher education. One can conclude, without going into the reasons, that big business and the military view diversity as essential not only to their own interests but also to the national interest in raising our educational level.

I went through Justice O'Connor's opinion, and you see a list of the benefits of diversity in education laid out there. I'm paraphrasing a bit, but here's the list. Enhanced racial diversity promotes cross-racial understanding; helps break down racial stereotypes; enables students to better understand students of different races; promotes favorable learning outcomes; better prepares students for an increasingly diverse workforce and society; provides the skills needed in an increasingly global marketplace by exposing students to diverse people, cultures, ideas, and viewpoints; and provides the military with the highly qualified, racially diverse officer corps that is essential to national security.

While Justice O'Connor was talking about higher education here, it seems to me that these benefits are equally discernible in primary and secondary schools, the only difference being that they start to accrue even earlier.

PROF. HAYMAN: Do you think most people perceive those benefits? Do you think that resegregation is a conscious rejection of the benefits of diversity?

JUDGE SCHWARTZ: Well, resegregation for the most part has come about as an expression of the will of the white majority. In that sense, the white population is content with what it perceives as the advantages of segregation, and the unarticulated premise is that those advantages are more important than the benefits of diversity.

But in roughly thirty years, the white population is likely to be the minority race in the United States, and the shift in population dynamics may well bring an attendant shift in political power. As the implications of these shifts become more apparent, I suspect the white population will realize that it requires the benefits of diversity in its own self-interest. And the only way to achieve those benefits will be through the elimination of segregation.

PROF. HAYMAN: And certainly some white people perceive and desire the benefits of racial diversity.

JUDGE SCHWARTZ: Yes. Look at what is happening locally, in the Brandywine School District. It opted to avoid the resegregation caused by the Delaware Neighborhood School Act.[22] It preferred to retain diversity in its schools, recognizing that children are influenced by the values and attitudes of their parents. The result is that the white parents' children presently attending school in the Brandywine district—and after them, their grandchildren—will be far better prepared to function in a diverse society, perhaps one in which they will be a minority. In one sense, it is no different than the minority children in the Brandywine district partaking of the benefits of diversity so as to better "get along" and compete in a white-dominated society.

PROF. HAYMAN: For those, then, who do regret the resegregation of schools, what is the solution? Is there any possibility in your mind of remedy through the courts, or is it now clear to you that the remedy has to be found in the political process?

JUDGE SCHWARTZ: Political process, perhaps as a function of the changing demographics. As for the courts, I just don't think that the present Supreme Court would be prepared to uphold any renewed efforts to promote desegregation. I could be wrong. But just looking at our history, I don't think so.

PROF. HAYMAN: I want to ask you about something that a writer once suggested about you. He suggested that desegregation has been your "particular burden to bear for the rest of your life." Is that a fair assessment?

JUDGE SCHWARTZ: No, not really.

PROF. HAYMAN: Why not?

JUDGE SCHWARTZ: This may sound strange, but I didn't then and I don't now consider it a burden. A district court judge's job is to decide cases while always striving for the correct legal result. In this sense, desegregation was just another case, though a very challenging one. At the same time, far from being a burden, I feel fortunate in having had the case.

Notes

1. In *Evans v. Buchanan*, 379 F.Supp. 1218 (D. Del. 1974), a three-judge court consisting of Judges Gibbons, Layton, and Wright held that the schools in Wilmington were still unconstitutionally segregated; it requested the State Board of Education to propose alternative remedies limited to the Wilmington schools, and incorporating other schools in New Castle County. Following the Supreme Court's decision in *Milliken v. Bradley*, 418 U.S. 717 (1974), which prohibited interdistrict remedies for segregation absent proof of an interdistrict violation, the three-judge court revisited the case to determine the propriety of interdistrict remedies. The court, per Judge Wright, found sufficient proof of interdistrict segregation in the New Castle County schools to warrant consideration of an interdistrict remedy, and thus renewed its order for alternative proposals. *Evans v. Buchanan*, 393 F. Supp. 428 (D. Delaware 1975). Judge Layton dissented. The following year, the three-judge court determined that an interdistrict remedy was appropriate and ordered the consolidation of the Wilmington city and surrounding suburban schools to effectuate desegregation. *Evans v. Buchanan*, 416 F. Supp 328 (D. Del. 1976). Judge Layton again dissented in part.

2. *Evans v. Buchanan*, 416 F. Supp 328 (D. Del. 1976); *appeal dismissed by Delaware State Board of Education v. Evans*, 429 U.S. 973 (1976).

3. *Evans v. Buchanan*, 416 F. Supp 328 (D. Del. 1976), *aff'd as modified by Evans v. Buchanan*, 555 F.2d 373 (3rd Cir. 1977); *cert. denied by Newark School District v. Evans*, 434 U.S. 880 (1977); *reh'g denied by Newark School Dist. v. Evans*, 434 U.S. 944 (1977).

4. *Evans v. Buchanan*, 447 F. Supp. 982 (D. Del. 1978).

5. *Green v. New Kent County School Board*, 391 U.S. 430 (1968).

6. Eds. note: *Evans v. Buchanan*, 447 F. Supp. 982, 1015–17 (D. Del. 1978).

7. A resolution calling on President Carter to remove Judge Schwartz from the court was passed in November 1997. *See* Jeffrey A. Raffel, *The Politics of School Desegregation: The Metropolitan Remedy in Delaware* 161 (Temple University Press, 1980).

8. *Evans v. Buchanan*, 447 F. Supp. 982 (D. Del. 1978); *aff'd by Evans v. Buchanan*, 582 F.2d 750 (3rd Cir. 1978).

9. The Third Circuit issued its decision affirming Judge Schwartz's order on July 24, 1978; the petitions for certiorari were filed that October. The opinion denying certiorari was issued by the Supreme Court on April 28, 1980. *Delaware State Bd. of Ed. v. Evans*, 446 U.S. 923 (1980).

10. Justice Marshall did not participate in the decision dismissing for lack of jurisdiction the original appeal from the three-judge court's determination of an interdistrict violation. *Evans v. Buchanan*, 416 F. Supp 328 (D. Del. 1976); *appeal dismissed by Delaware State Board of Education v. Evans*, 429 U.S. 973 (1976); neither Justice Marshall nor Justice Stevens participated in the decision denying certiorari to the subsequent Third Circuit decision. *Evans v. Buchanan*, 416 F. Supp 328 (D. Del. 1976), *aff'd as modified by Evans v. Buchanan*, 555 F.2d 373 (3rd Cir. 1977); *cert. denied by Newark School District v. Evans*, 434 U.S. 880 (1977); *reh'g denied by Newark School Dist. v. Evans*, 434 U.S. 944 (1977).

11. The Wilmington schools litigation, Justice Rehnquist wrote, "has now culminated in the a countywide remedy more Draconian than any ever approved by this Court." *Delaware State Bd. of Ed. v. Evans*, 446 U.S. 923 (1980) (Rehnquist, J., dissenting), *denying cert. to Evans v. Buchanan*, 582 F.2d 750 (3rd Cir. 1978). Justice Rehnquist insisted that the desegregation remedy fashioned by Judge Schwartz was "far more comprehensive and disruptive than that which the established violations warranted" and resulted in the "total substitution of judicial for popular control of local education." *Id.* at 927. "This Court," he concluded, "does a disservice to local government and the people of Delaware, and very likely in the long run to the Equal Protection Clause of the Fourteenth Amendment, by once again declining to review a case of such fundamental importance." *Id.* at 928.

12. "The Chief Justice agrees these cases merit review here but only when a full Court is available to consider the important issues presented by the petitions for certiorari." *Delaware State Bd. of Ed. v. Evans*, 446 U.S. 923, 928 (1980) (Rehnquist, J., dissenting), *denying cert. to Evans v. Buchanan*, 582 F.2d 750 (3rd Cir. 1978).

13. *Evans v. Buchanan*, 582 F.2d 750 (3rd Cir. 1970); *rev'g* 455 F. Supp. 692 (D. Del. 1978).

14. *Evans v. Buchanan*, 512 F. Supp. 839 (D. Del. 1981).

15. Celia Cohen, *Only in Delaware: Politics and Politicians in the First State* (Grapevine, 2002).

16. Neighborhood Schools Act of 2000, codified at Del. Code Ann. tit. 14, § 223.

17. *Coalition to Save Our Children v. State Bd. of Ed.*, 757 F. Supp. 328, 358 (D. Del. 1991).

18. *Coalition to Save Our Children v. State Bd. of Ed.*, 901 F. Supp. 784 (D. Del. 1991), *aff'd* 90 F.3d 752 (3rd Cir. 1996).

19. *Board of Education v. Dowell*, 498 U.S. 237 (1991); *Freeman v. Pitts*, 503 U.S. 467 (1992); *Missouri v. Jenkins*, 515 U.S. 70 (1995).

20. *Board of Education v. Dowell*, 498 U.S. 237, 250 (1991).

21. *Grutter v. Bollinger*, 539 U.S. 306 (2003).

22. For a summary of these events, see Jeffrey A. Raffel, *After the Court Order: The Changing Faces of School Desegregation in the Wilmington Metropolitan Area*, 9 Widener L. Symp. J. 81, 109–10 (2002).

CHAPTER TWELVE

The Resegregation Decisions and the New Federalism

Roger L. Goldman

Introduction

Looking back at more than fifty years of Supreme Court cases since *Brown v. Bd. of Educ.* was decided in 1954, one observes three distinct time periods in the Court's approach to remedying segregation in the public schools:

1. The period from *Brown II*'s "all deliberate speed" decision in 1955,[1] during which the Court proceeded cautiously, one case at a time, in striking down obstructionist efforts by local school boards to avoid desegregation,[2] but upholding state plans that facially did not assign pupils on the basis of race,[3] until the 1968 case of *Green v. County Sch. Bd.*[4]
2. The era of *Green*, during which the Court was committed to eliminating segregation "root and branch" by placing an affirmative duty on school boards to come up with a plan that works to end segregation,[5] through the *Keyes* decision in 1973,[6] which was the first case to apply the affirmative duty of *Green* in the context of the North.
3. The retreat from a commitment to rooting out segregation, beginning with the 1974 case of *Milliken v. Bradley*[7] and culminating in three cases in the 1990s, referred to as the "resegregation decisions."

In short, for twenty years, the Court used its power to strike down segregated systems, while for the next thirty years, but especially since 1991, it has tolerated segregation, so that the promise of *Brown* has been broken for many schools districts in the United States today. Summarizing the consequences of the resegregation decisions, one critic wrote they "effectively closed the doors of federal courts to black parents whose children were consigned to 'separate and unequal' schools."[8]

The reason for the Court's change of direction was the appointment of a majority of Justices in the 1970s and after who disagreed with the Court of the late 1960s on the meaning of equal protection under the Constitution. The Justices who unanimously decided *Green* in 1968 included Earl Warren, William Brennan, William Douglas, Arthur Goldberg, and Thurgood Marshall, all of whom were dedicated to ending segregated schools. In contrast, the Justices appointed by Presidents Nixon, Reagan, and George H. W. Bush were much more concerned with the "New Federalism"[9]—respecting state and local sovereignty at the expense of individual rights and limiting the power of both federal courts and Congress. These justices included William Rehnquist, Antonin Scalia, Sandra Day O'Connor, and Anthony Kennedy. Of course, the greatest difference on the issue was between Thurgood Marshall, who argued *Brown*, and the Justice who replaced him on the Court, Clarence Thomas.

The concern of Justices like Marshall and Brennan was to use the majestic phrases of the Constitution—"equal protection," "due process"—to protect the poor and the powerless from legislative and executive excesses. The New Federalist Justices were more concerned with expanding the control of those branches of state government by returning to what they claimed was the original intent of the framers of the Constitution and the amendments. To Justice Brennan, this elusive effort to ascertain original intent was an improper methodology for constitutional interpretation. Criticizing Justice Scalia's originalist opinion in *Michael H. v. Gerald D.*, which rejected a due process challenge to a state statute denying a father's parental rights over his illegitimate child, Justice Brennan wrote as follows:

> The document that [Justice Scalia] construes is unfamiliar to me. It is not the living charter that I have taken to be our Constitution; it is instead a stagnant, archaic hidebound document steeped in the prejudices and superstitions of a time long past. *This* Constitution does not recognize that times change. I cannot accept an interpretive method that does such violence to the charter that I am bound by oath to uphold.[10]

Justices differ on the weight they give to precedent; that is, earlier Supreme Court decisions interpreting the Constitution. Some believe that such decisions are entitled to great weight and should be overturned rarely. Others believe that, because only the Supreme Court can reverse its prior decisions, it should be willing to do so if earlier Courts misinterpreted the Constitution. None of the recent decisions known as the "resegregation" decisions has explicitly overruled a prior decision, but it is clear that, especially since 1991, the Supreme Court is not following the path of the *Green* Court in 1968, which charged school boards "with the affirmative duty to take whatever steps might be necessary to convert to a unitary system in which racial discrimination would be eliminated root and branch."[11]

The Early Years: 1954–1968

It was strongly felt by the members of the Supreme Court that both *Brown I*—the 1954 decision striking down laws mandating segregated schools—and *Brown II*—the 1955 decision setting forth the standards for implementing the remedy for violation of *Brown I*—should be decided unanimously. After years of separate but equal laws, found to be constitutional by the Supreme Court in the *Plessy* decision of 1896,[12] a decision to hold segregated schools unconstitutional was bound to engender outrage in the southern and border states. Thus, the Court felt that a unanimous *Brown I* decision was important; indeed, that solidarity among the Justices was even more apparent in the 1958 case of *Cooper v. Aaron*, in which they took the unusual step of each signing the opinion that unanimously affirmed *Brown*. And it was the desire for unanimity that caused the *Brown II* Court to come up with the intentionally ambiguous phrase "with all deliberate speed." Some of the Justices believed that the South needed time to adjust to the decision, whereas others wanted immediate relief, fearing that local school boards and federal district courts would focus on "deliberate" rather than "speed," which indeed was what occurred in the years immediately after *Brown II*.

During this period, outright resistance to *Brown* was common.[13] In *Cooper v. Aaron*,[14] the resistance of Governor Faubus and the Arkansas Legislature to school desegregation efforts caused a constitutional crisis, which ended with President Eisenhower's sending federal troops to ensure compliance with a desegregation plan in Little Rock's Central High School. In *Griffin v. County Sch. Bd.*,[15] the public schools in Prince Edward County, Virginia, were closed, and private academies were opened, funded by the state, for whites only. Although the Court invalidated these overt challenges to *Brown*, it permitted less obvious devices to maintain segregation by approving pupil placement laws that did not mention race on the face of the statute, but had the effect of continuing the dual school system.[16] By 1968, the impatience of the Justices with the slow progress of actual desegregation, and the strength of the civil rights movement, which brought to the attention of the entire nation the South's massive resistance to *Brown*, caused the Court to alter its approach.

The Middle Years: 1968–1973

In the 1968 case, *Green v. County Sch. Bd.*,[17] Justice William Brennan, writing for a unanimous Court, placed an affirmative duty on school boards to achieve desegregation plans that worked to dismantle dual schools. In the companion case to *Green*, *Monroe v. Bd. of Commissioners*,[18] the Court rejected a free transfer plan that the school board argued was necessary to prevent white flight. And a year later, in a per curiam opinion, *Alexander v. Holmes County Bd. of Educ.*,[19] the Court summarily reversed a Fifth Circuit order permitting delay of desegregation for one year in several Mississippi school districts. The Court, citing *Green*, stated that "all deliberate speed" could no longer justify the delay in desegregating the schools and that school districts must terminate dual school systems "at once and . . . operate now and hereafter only unitary schools." The focus changed from purifying the process of student assignment to getting results.

Warren Burger replaced Earl Warren as Chief Justice in 1969 and authored the first of the urban desegregation cases, *Swann v. Charlotte-Mecklenburg Bd. of Educ.* in 1971.[20] Although the context was still a southern school district with a history of separate but equal laws, this case approved remedies that would be necessary to achieve integration in an urban setting, including busing. Although it was unnecessary to address the issue of what would happen should the system achieve unitary status, Burger's opinion stated that judicial intervention would be unnecessary, unless the later segregation was caused by the state.

The third important case of this era, *Keyes v. Sch. District*,[21] was the first to reach the Court involving a school system that was not segregated by law but rather by actions of school officials. In *Keyes*, the district court had found that the school board had deliberately engaged in segregation in one part of the city and ordered the desegregation of those schools, but had refused to include other segregated schools in this order because there had been no showing that the board had a policy of segregation with respect to those schools. The Supreme Court held that, where a school board has engaged in substantial segregative acts in one part of the district, it was likely those actions applied to the entire district. In such circumstances, the burden shifted to the board to prove that this was not the case. The Court also found that, once proof of intentional segregation has been made in the northern context, the same remedies that applied in the southern and border states were appropriate. There was a strong dissent in *Keyes*, by Justice William Rehnquist, who had taken his seat on the Court one year earlier. Rehnquist argued that *Green* had misread *Brown*: all that case required was that the state or local school boards merely had to end its formal segregationist policies—it did not have the further duty to achieve actual desegregation of the schools. Rehnquist would eventually persuade a majority of the Court to agree with his *Keyes* dissent.

Milliken v. Bradley *and the Resegregation Decisions of 1991–1995*

Whereas Chief Justice Earl Warren was a strong supporter of ending segregated schools, his two successors as Chief Justice, Warren Burger and William Rehnquist, led the Court in the opposite direction. In *Milliken v. Bradley* in 1974, Chief Justice Burger got four others justices to join him in reversing a decision by the district court in Detroit that applied the remedies Burger had approved just three years earlier in his *Swann* opinion. Unlike the Charlotte and Denver cases, which involved a single school district, *Milliken* was the first interdistrict case to reach the Court: the city schools were largely black and the surrounding suburban schools were largely white. Although the City of Detroit, the State Board of Education, and the State of Michigan were all found to have engaged in unconstitutional segregation, there was no direct proof that the suburban districts had caused the segregation in the schools within the City of Detroit. The district court had held that the Constitution was violated because the state controlled the local school districts and an interdistrict remedy would be proper. The Supreme Court reversed, holding that the remedy could not cross school district lines. Foreshadowing the New Federalism decisions of the 1990s, the Court indicated that a major reason for its reluctance to permit the remedy was that it would make federal judges super-superintendents of the public schools, thereby diminishing the role of local school board officials.

Burger's opinion prompted an impassioned—and prescient—dissent from Thurgood Marshall:

> Our Nation, I fear, will be ill served by the Court's refusal to remedy separate and unequal education, for unless our children begin to learn together, there is little hope that our people will ever learn to live together. . . . In the short run, it may seem

> to be the easier course to allow our great metropolitan areas to be divided up each into two cities—one white, the other black—but it is a course, I predict, our people will ultimately regret.

Milliken was a closely divided 5-4 decision, with Justice Harry Blackmun, who had been appointed to the Court just three years earlier, joining Burger in the majority. Based on Blackmun's actions in desegregation cases in later years, it is likely that the older Justice Blackmun would not have voted the way he had as a junior Justice in *Milliken*. A switch in that one vote would have had a major impact on the development of the law in the northern school context. The result of *Milliken* was to protect suburban school districts from desegregation orders, unless the plaintiffs could meet the difficult burden of proving that the actions of the suburban districts caused segregation in the city, or vice versa. Between 1971 and 1996, "more than ten million white families have moved from big cities to the suburbs, or have enrolled their children in private schools."[22] *Milliken* ensured that integrative remedies could not cross school district lines.[23]

Without an interdistrict integrative remedy, the Court, in *Milliken II* in 1977,[24] approved intradistict remedies, such as smaller class sizes. Thus, the only way a court could order an interdistrict remedy was if there was proof that official acts in one district caused segregation in the other. Like *Milliken I*, the *Milliken II* Court instructed the lower federal courts to consider the interests of state and local governments in managing their own affairs.

The Decisions

The first time the Court was faced with the question of how long a desegregation decree was to remain in effect was the 1976 case, *Pasadena Bd. of Educ. v. Spangler*.[25] After an order to desegregate the schools, all schools were racially balanced in 1970, but by 1974, five of the thirty-two schools became racially imbalanced as a result of demographic shifts. The district court ordered annual pupil reassignment so that no school would have an imbalance. The Supreme Court reversed, with Justice William Rehnquist holding that the district court had abused its discretion by requiring pupil reassignment each year, because in later years, the resegregation was not shown to have been caused by the school board. Thus, *Pasadena* held that, once unitary status has been achieved, later resegregation caused by private acts was not remediable by federal courts. The difficult question, however, was how to determine whether unitary status had been achieved—under *Green*, that would occur only when segregation had been removed "root and branch." But three cases in the 1990s made it clear that *Green* would no longer be the standard.

The case that most clearly indicated that the Court was no longer committed to the "root and branch" standard of Green is the 1991 case of *Board of Educ. of Oklahoma City v. Dowell*,[26] involving a school system that was segregated by law at the time of *Brown*. After the school district was sued in 1961, the district court issued an order in 1963 to desegregate schools, but by 1972, the neighborhood school plan adopted by the district did nothing to desegregate the schools. The district court ordered a city-wide busing plan, which resulted in substantial integration. In 1977, the school district successfully sought to be released from district court supervision, and the board continued the busing plan. In 1984, the school district reverted to the neighborhood school plan for children in K–4, but allowed any child to transfer from a school in which she was in the majority to a school in which she would be in the minority. That plan was challenged on the grounds that it would have resulted in many one-race schools. The Tenth Circuit disapproved of the neighborhood school plan and ordered the school district to develop a new plan, but the Supreme Court reversed. The majority of the Court noted that federal court supervision of school districts was intended to be temporary and, in the interests of local control, should only be kept in place where there was intentional segregative conduct by local officials. So long as there was good faith compliance with the original decree and if the vestiges of past discrimination had been eliminated to the extent practicable, the board could be released from the decree. Given the past de jure segregation of the schools, the dissenters believed that the relevant question was whether the past discrimination was the cause of the currently racially separate schools. Moreover, the dissenters believed that the length of time that a district court's decree might have to remain in place was not a relevant consideration.

The next resegregation case was *Freeman v. Pitts*,[27] involving DeKalb County, Georgia, a suburb of Atlanta. The case involved the question whether desegregation of some, but not all, aspects of a school system permitted a district court to end supervision of those parts of the system that were desegregated. *Green* had identified six areas of a school district that needed to be desegregated: student assignment, faculty, staff, transportation, extracurricular activities, and facilities. In DeKalb County, the school district had satisfied the court order with respect to student assignment and physical facilities, but not with teacher and principal assignments, resource allocation, and some aspects of the educational programs. The Court of Appeals held that, until all parts of a system were desegregated, the system had not achieved unitary status. The Supreme Court disagreed and held that district courts could end supervision over the school district in stages, because that would achieve the purpose of returning the schools to state and local control as soon as practicable. The Court also found that segregated schools that persist as a result of segregated housing patterns would not prevent a unitary status finding unless these conditions could be attributed to actions of school officials.

The third and final resegregation case was *Missouri v. Jenkins* involving the Kansas City, Missouri, school district.[29] Missouri law mandated separate but equal education at the time of *Brown*. The federal district court had entered many orders designed to create magnet schools that would attract suburban white students into the largely black city schools by such means as modernizing the schools, improving educational programs, and giving salary increases to attract qualified teachers. The district court required that funding continue until minority standardized test scores rose to meet national norms. The Supreme Court disagreed with the district court with respect to the student transfers from the suburban communities because, as in *Milliken I*, there was no proof of an interdistrict violation. Similarly, the Court disapproved the remedy of increasing teachers' salaries because it was not tied closely enough to remedying "previous legally mandated segregation."[30] The Court also found that there was no proof that intentional segregation had caused minority students to score lower on standardized tests. The Court held that white flight and poor academic performance of minority children were caused by external, private factors—de facto causes—not by intentional actions of governmental officials—de jure segregation—and the Constitution is only violated when there is governmental action.

The Decisions in Context

The Court's thirty-year retreat from the promise of *Brown* and *Green* is consistent with its general approach to cases arising under the Bill of Rights and the Fourteenth Amendment's equal protection clause. In place of the Warren Court's emphasis on individual rights and liberties, the Burger and Rehnquist Courts stressed the countervailing interests of a respect for states' rights and local control. One of the best ways to ensure local autonomy is to limit the power of federal courts to exercise control over state and local governmental bodies, as the Court did from *Milliken I* in 1974 through *Jenkins II* in 1995, when it ceded control of public schools to local officials even though schools in urban districts remained segregated as a result of racially segregated housing patterns.

The assumption underlying the resegregation decisions is that schools have been desegregated to the extent that it is possible to do so. Any segregation that continues is caused by housing patterns, which reflect what the Supreme Court characterized as the "private choices" of individual families. This is a debatable premise as black and Latino families do not have the range of housing choices that are available to whites with comparable incomes and credit histories. Studies regularly produced by the U.S. Department of Housing and Urban Development and other organizations demonstrate that their choices are constrained by discriminatory practices that perpetuate segregated neighborhoods.

Given the Court's resegregation jurisprudence, which will inevitably lead to racially separate schools—low-income blacks in the cities, whites and a few middle-class blacks in the suburbs, resulting in segregated, high-poverty schools in urban communities—are there other possible constitutional challenges available other than school desegregation lawsuits?

One effort that failed was the claim that public school financing systems based on the local property tax ensures that poorer school districts have less to spend on a per-pupil basis than schools in wealthier school districts. However, in the 1973 case of *San Antonio Independent Sch. Dist. v. Rodriguez*,[31] the Court held that this was not the type of discrimination that is of constitutional significance as it was economic rather than racial. (An earlier Supreme Court case held that discrimination against the poor is not the same thing as discrimination on the basis of race under the equal protection clause.[32]) *Rodriguez* also rejected the claim that students in the poor districts were being denied their fundamental right to education; the Court held that education is not a fundamental right under the Constitution. A state does not have a constitutional obligation to provide free public education.[33]

The *Rodriguez* case in 1973 was an early example of the "New Federalism." It illustrates how the Supreme Court's concern about the limitations of federal authority influenced its decision about whether there was a constitutional violation in the first place: it is clear from the opinion that the Court was doubtful that federal courts could devise a remedy for the violation because school financing is such a complex issue, is traditionally left to the states, and is best left in the hands of local government. (It was surely no accident that the opinion was assigned to Justice Powell, former board chair of the Richmond, Virginia, school district.) Similarly, *Milliken I* was another example of how concern for the effect of intrusive federal court remedies on local governmental entities influenced the substantive decision: the Court held that, for there to be an interdistrict remedy, plaintiffs must prove that suburban districts have discriminated against city students, a very difficult task as these are independent entities with no formalities. And a major factor in the Court's decision was that, if district lines could be breached, federal judges would be forced to combine school districts and thus exercise control over the new district.

It has often been said that the best solution to school integration is not the transfer of students among districts but the promotion of integrated housing. But given the reality that suburban housing prices prevent low-income minority residents of hypersegregated inner cities from moving to the suburban communities, the only way to achieve integrated housing is to locate affordable housing in the suburbs, which usually means subsidized, multifamily housing. Is it constitutional for a community to enact zoning ordinances that limit housing to single-family housing on one-acre lots, even if the impact is to exclude large numbers of racial minorities? In *Arlington Heights v. Metropolitan Housing Corp.*,[34] a developer of low- and moderate-income housing sought to rezone property in the suburbs from single to multifamily, claiming that the zoning had a racial impact. The Supreme Court held that, even though there was a racial impact, the Constitution was not violated because there was no proof that the zoning ordinance was enacted with the intent to exclude minorities; adverse impact was not enough. Proof of discriminatory intent is quite difficult in such cases as officials rarely express racial animus as the motive for their actions.[35]

The results of *Milliken, Rodriguez*, and *Arlington Heights* are devastating for poor minority children. *Milliken* ensures that suburban schools districts will remain largely nonminority and the city school districts will be largely minority. *Rodriguez* ensures that the poor school districts, often composed of minority families, will not have the resources to provide quality education. And *Arlington Heights* ensures that housing integration in many residential suburban communities will be kept to a minimum.

With the virtual ending of desegregation decrees, the increased segregation in urban communities will have serious consequences for minority students, majority students, and society in general. The largest student transfer in the nation between a city and its suburbs took place in St. Louis, Missouri. As many as 13,000 black city students annually attended majority white county schools over a nineteen-year period. That plan was the result of the voluntary settlement of a desegregation case, in which more than twenty suburban school districts agreed to accept students from the city. The settlement avoided a trial, which could have resulted in the creation of a single metropolitan-wide school district. One of the major benefits of the plan was the increase of students who graduated from county high schools and went on to college.[36] In 1999, the parties agreed to end district court supervision: one reason for the 1999 agreement was the Court's decision in the third resegregation case, *Missouri v. Jenkins II*, which "inspired a widespread belief that a majority of the Supreme Court would no longer support desegregation plans similar to those in St. Louis."[37] With the end of the court-supervised plan after the 1999 settlement, and the withdrawal of some of the county districts from the plan because the state is no longer required to pay the transportation costs, the result will be increased minority enrollment in segregated city schools with high levels of poverty and lower graduation rates. The higher the dropout rate, the more likely prison populations will increase;[38] because many states deny ex-felons the right to vote, the number of citizens without this fundamental right will grow.[39]

The Anticipated Approach to School Desegregation by the Roberts Court

There is no reason to assume that President George W. Bush, who promised to appoint Justices with views similar to Justices Scalia and Thomas, will in any way change the Court's approach to desegregation. His appointments—John Roberts to replace Chief Justice Rehnquist and Judge Samuel Alito to replace Justice O'Connor—appear to be "New Federalists" who share the same views concerning the role of the Supreme Court in this area: states and local school boards should have the primary role in education and federal district courts should relinquish control. Indeed, while a lawyer in the Reagan White House, John Roberts opposed busing decrees approved by the Supreme Court, although during his confirmation hearings, he noted that these policies were not necessarily his views, as he was merely representing the views of his client at the time, the president. While on the U.S. Court of Appeals for the District of Columbia, his views of the extent of congressional power under the commerce clause suggest that he will join those on the Court who want to continue to limit those powers.[40] Similarly, it is likely that both Justices will join those Justices who have limited Congress's power to enforce the civil rights amendments.

Another area of constitutional law that is likely to have an impact on the future of public school desegregation concerns vouchers that can be used in private and parochial schools. The Rehnquist Court upheld the use of vouchers in Cleveland, holding that vouchers for parochial schools do not violate the establishment clause of the First Amendment.[41] Should Congress and the states use vouchers in a large-scale manner, funding for public schools will be eroded by the infusion of public funds into private and parochial schools. There is no reason to believe that these schools would be any more integrated than public schools to the extent they are located within cities with large minority populations. Further, these schools will not be obligated to accept everyone who applies and could select only the most talented minority students, leaving behind the most disadvantaged.

Conclusion

The bleak picture of increasingly segregated school districts is, accordingly, not likely to change with the arrival of the new Justices. For the foreseeable future, the prognosis is that the Court will continue its retreat from its earlier promise to end segregation "root and branch." And without the prodding of the Court, it is very unlikely that the president or Congress will take the lead in making sure our nation, in the words of Justice Brennan, does not have black schools or white schools, "but just schools."[42]

Notes

1. *Brown v. Bd. of Educ.*, 349 U.S. 294 (1955) (*Brown II*).

2. Examples of defiance to *Brown* include *Cooper v. Aaron*, 358 U.S. 1 (1958), involving the Little Rock school board's request to the federal court to delay implementation of the desegregation plan because of the opposition of the governor and state legislature; and *Griffin v. Sch. Bd.*, 377 U.S. 218 (1964), in which public schools were closed in Prince Edward County, Virginia, and private academies were opened for white children only.

3. For example, in *Shuttlesworth v. Birmingham Bd. of Educ.*, 358 U.S. 101 (1958), the Court in a per curiam opinion upheld a facial challenge to the Alabama School Placement Law of 1955. That law permitted assignment of students on such factors as the qualification of the pupil for certain types of teaching, the physical effect on the student of being placed in certain schools, the possibility of breaches of the peace, etc. The effect of such laws was to keep the schools segregated.

4. *Green v. County Sch. Bd.*, 391 U.S. 430 (1968).

5. In rejecting the school board's "freedom of choice plan," which was not, in fact, bringing an end to segregation, the Court in *Green* focused on the results, not the process, and shifted the burden to school boards to explain why they chose a method that was less effective in bringing about desegregation. In *Swann v. Charlotte-Mecklenburg Bd. of Educ.*, 402 U.S. 1 (1971), the Court set forth the kinds of remedies that would be appropriate to bring about desegregation, including the use of racial balance in the schools as a starting point; disapproval of one-race schools, unless the school board met its burden to explain why such schools were necessary; gerrymandering of attendance zones to bring about desegregation; and busing of students.

6. *Keyes v. Sch. Dist.*, 413 U.S. 189 (1973).

7. *Milliken v. Bradley*, 418 U.S. 717 (1974). Two cases during this time period, decided in 1979, involving standards for assessing what actions constitute segregation, did make it easier for plaintiffs to prove a school district was in violation of *Brown I. Columbus Bd. of Educ. v. Penick*, 443 U.S. 449 (1979) and *Dayton Bd. of Educ. v. Brinkman*, 443 U.S. 526 (1979).

8. Peter Irons, *Jim Crow's Children, The Broken Promise of the Brown Decision* 289 (Viking Penguin, 2002).

9. "New Federalism" seeks to devolve to the states power that had accrued to the federal government since the New Deal. It is reflected in Supreme Court decisions curtailing the reach of Congress's power to regulate interstate commerce: *U.S. v. Lopez*, 514 U.S. 549 (1995)(Congress cannot make it a crime for an individual to possess a firearm in a school zone); protecting state sovereignty under the Tenth Amendment; *Printz v. U.S.*, 521 U.S. 898 (1997) (Congress cannot force state and local law enforcement officers to conduct background checks on persons wishing to purchase handguns); in decisions limiting the power of Congress to enforce the Fourteenth Amendment, *Kimel v. Florida Bd. of Regents*, 528 U.S. 62 (2000) (Congress does not have the power to protect state employees from age discrimination); and in cases restricting the ability of citizens to sue the state in both state and federal court for violation of federal law, *Seminole Tribe of Florida v. Florida*, 517 U.S. 44 (1996) (the Eleventh Amendment bars suit by individuals for violations of federal

statutes against the state in federal court) and *Alden v. Maine*, 527 U.S. 706 (1999) (sovereign immunity bars suit under federal statute against state in state court).

10. 491 U.S. 110, 141 (1989).

11. *Green v. County Sch. Bd.*, 391 U.S. 430, 437–38 (1968).

12. *Plessy v. Ferguson*, 163 U.S. 537 (1896).

13. Michael J. Klarman, *From Jim Crow to Civil Rights: The Supreme Court and the Struggle for Racial Equality* (Oxford University Press, 2004).

14. 358 U.S. 1 (1958).

15. 377 U.S. 218 (1964).

16. *Shuttlesworth v. Birmingham Bd. of Educ.*, 358 U.S. 101 (1958). For a discussion of the strategy of passive resistance by the governors of Mississippi, Florida, and North Carolina, see Anders Walker, *Ghost of Jim Crow: Law, Culture, and the Subversion of Civil Rights, 1954–1965*, PhD dissertation, Yale University, 2003.

17. 391 U.S. 430 (1968). Two years earlier, Judge John Minor Wisdom of the Fifth Circuit had invalidated pupil placement and freedom of choice plans in seven consolidated cases from Alabama and Louisiana, *U.S. v. Jefferson County Bd. of Educ.*, 372 F.2d 836 (5th Cir. 1966), *modified and aff'd en banc*, 380 F.2d 385 (1967), *cert. denied*, 389 U.S. 840 (1967). For the influence of the civil rights movement on Judge Wisdom's decision, see James T. Patterson, *Brown v. Bd. of Education: A Civil Rights Milestone and Its Troubled Legacy* 145 (Oxford University Press, 2001).

18. 391 U.S. 450 (1968).

19. 396 U.S. 430 (1969). The Court issued a similar per curiam decision overturning a Fifth Circuit decision permitting delay of integration in several states in *Carter v. West Feliciana Parish Sch. Bd.*, 396 U.S. 290 (1970).

20. *Swann v. Charlotte-Mecklenburg Bd. of Educ.*, 402 U.S. 1 (1971).

21. 413 U.S. 189 (1973).

22. Irons, *Jim Crow's Children*, at 289.

23. Justice Stewart, concurring in *Milliken I*, 418 U.S. at 755, stated that "[w]ere it to be shown, for example, that state officials had contributed to the separation of the races . . . by purposeful, racially discriminatory use of state housing or zoning laws, then a decree calling for transfer of pupils across district lines or for restructuring of district lines might well be appropriate."

24. *Milliken v. Bradley*, 433 U.S. 267 (1977).

25. 427 U.S. 424 (1976).

26. 498 U.S. 237 (1991).

27. 503 U.S. 467 (1982).

29. 515 U.S. 70 (1995).

30. *Id.* at 100. The first time the Kansas City case had reached the Supreme Court, it reversed the district court's decision to order a tax increase to help pay for desegregation remedies, *Missouri v. Jenkins*, 495 U.S. 33 (1990).

31. *San Antonio Independent Sch. Dist. v. Rodriguez*, 411 U.S. 1 (1973).

32. *James v. Valtierra*, 402 U.S. 137 (1971).

33. The *Rodriguez* Court stressed that, because some education was being provided, this was not a case where there was a total denial of any education. In a subsequent case, in which children of illegal aliens were denied any education, the Court distinguished *Rodriguez* and held that, if the state is providing a free public education to others, it could not discriminate against children of illegal aliens, *Plyler v. Doe*, 457 U.S. 202 (1982).

34. *Arlington Heights v. Metropolitan Housing Corp.*, 429 U.S. 252 (1977).

35. Some U.S. Courts of Appeals have held that Title VIII of the 1964 Civil Rights Act (Fair Housing Act), 42 U.S.C. § 3601, is violated where a policy has an adverse racial impact, even if there is no proof the policy was intended to discriminate. *United States v. City of Black Jack*, 508 F.2d 1179, 1184 (8th Cir. 1975), *cert. denied*, 422 U.S. 1042 (1975)); *Gamble v. City of Escondido*, 104 F.3d 300, 304–5 (9th Cir. 1997).

36. "The graduation rate of city transfer students was on average two to three times as high as the graduation rates in the city schools, particularly in those schools where the graduation rates of all students is high. More significant . . . is the anecdotal evidence from African American city students confirming the advantages that individual students gained from participating in an integrated school where the norm was to graduate and attend college." Gerald W. Heaney and Susan Uchitelle, *Unending Struggle: The Long Road to an Equal Education in St. Louis* 150 (Reedy Press, 2004).

37. *Id.* at 200.

38. A black man born between 1965 and 1969 had the following chances of being incarcerated in 1999, depending on his education level: less than high school, 58.9 percent; high school graduate or GED, 18.4 percent; some college, 4.9 percent. Becky Pettit and Bruce Western, *Mass Imprisonment and the Life Course: Race and Class Inequality in U.S. Incarceration*, 69 American Sociological Review 162, Table 4 (2004).

39. "1.4 million African American men, or 13 percent of the black adult male population, are disenfranchised, reflecting a rate of disenfranchisement that is seven times the national average. More than one-third (36 percent) of the total disenfranchised population are black men." Human Rights Watch, Sentencing Project, *Losing the Vote: The Impact of Felony Disenfranchisement Laws in the United States* 2 (1998), http://www.SentencingProject.org/pdfs/9080.

40. In his dissent from the denial of an en banc rehearing of a case involving the federal Endangered Species Act, *Rancho Viejo, LLC v. Norton*, 334 F.3d 1158, 1160 (D.C. Cir. 2003), he indicated that the panel's opinion, upholding the act under the commerce clause, 323 F.3d 1062, *cert. denied*, 540 U.S. 1218, *reh'g denied*, 541 U.S. 1006 (2004), was inconsistent with Supreme Court precedent and could not justify Congress's protection of "a hapless toad that, for reasons of its own, lives its entire life in California."

41. *Zelman v. Simmons-Harris*, 536 U.S. 639 (2002).

42. *Green*, at 441. Although many state courts, pursuant to state constitutional provisions that are much more explicit than the U.S. Constitution in requiring the provision of an adequate public school education, have required that educational spending in poor districts be increased, those state provisions will not solve the problem of segregated schools. The best that can be hoped for in these state court efforts is that, even though the schoolchildren will be separated on the basis of race, at least the funding for the schools will be more equal.

After high school, I attended the University of Delaware. I went there primarily because I had a guidance counselor at Wilmington High School who suggested that I should not enroll because she did not think I would succeed. My response to that was, "Just tell them that I'm coming." I applied, was accepted, and participated in a lot of advocacy work the entire time that I was there. Our accomplishments at the university significantly benefited the black student community. We were able to establish a minority affairs board, a Black Culture Center, a black Homecoming King and Queen, and a black studies program. I was also on the Charter Line of Omega Psi Phi Fraternity Inc., which was the first black Greek letter organization at the University of Delaware.

I graduated from the university and went on to work as the executive director of what was then called the Parent Educational Resource Center. This center was set up by the Wilmington Home School Community Council to work toward the peaceful implementation of the school desegregation orders. That was my first job after college, and I held the position from 1974 to 1981.

I became an advocate for students during that time, representing kids who faced suspension and expulsion hearings. We attempted to eliminate the disturbances and problems that existed within the schools. There wasn't a lot a resistance to the orders of the court at the time, but several schools were experiencing a lot of trouble. We had some problems with a couple of schools starting in 1977 with the voluntary desegregation plan. We would go and work with the kids inside the schools, kids who were both white and black, ironing out problems that existed. In 1978 when the full order was implemented, several more schools were experiencing a lot of problems. We went out there and worked all of the problems out. It was at this time in my life when I really became a strong advocate for children.

The 1978 court order required that a "9-3" student assignment plan be implemented. All students would attend formerly predominantly "white" suburban school districts for a maximum on nine years and would spend at least three years in the formerly "black" school districts. The order also forced the district to attempt to overcome the effects of segregation by addressing and improving the training of teachers, the school's discipline program, its faculty assignments, its curriculum offerings, and its counseling services.

In 1981, the board of education appealed to the court to split the super district at the time into four smaller districts. The original plaintiffs at the time were not available, so we formed the Coalition to Save Our Children. We were determined to fight that proposed change, but we lost.

After we formed the Coalition to Save Our Children, I changed jobs and became the executive director of the Hilltop Lutheran Neighborhood Center. I continued my advocacy work, and I continued to work with the Coalition to Save Our Children as a volunteer. I was its treasurer from 1981 to 1988 and the chairperson from 1988 until the court order was lifted. During that period of time, we took the Red Clay School District into federal court twice because it had failed to comply with the court order. For the first time in the history of the litigation, Red Clay and the State Board of Education were ordered to address the substantive problems, such as student test scores, matriculation rates into college, staff racial composition, and several others that were in the order, all having to do with performance in education, discipline, suspensions, and expulsions. It had to assess its progress on an annual basis and work toward eliminating any disparities between the races. That was a reported case, and the school district had to report on the substantive progress of its students until the order was lifted. In 1993 and 1994, the four districts and the state board filed for a declaration of unitary status, and we fought that all the way through the Third Circuit, but lost 2-1.

Looking back on my tenure as chairperson, I'm unable to identify anything that I would have done differently. If anything at all, I may have worked a little harder in the pursuit of a settlement, as opposed to fighting the case in court. We did, however, finally get an agreement, but Judge Robinson sabotaged it. She issued an opinion in which she stated that the settlement agreement was "ill conceived" and ordered us to prepare for trial.

The state of the public education system in Wilmington is much worse today than it was when the desegregation litigation commenced in the 1970s. When Christina School District passed its new student assignment plan, which was, in my view, a resegregation plan in 2004, I was in attendance at the meeting. I said the board was a bunch of new millennium segregationists. On the one hand the board wanted to celebrate the fiftieth anniversary of the *Brown v. Board of Education* decision, and on the other it was about to totally resegregate the district's elementary schools. Its position was, in effect, no different from that of George Wallace, the Alabama governor who stood in the schoolhouse doors shouting, "Segregation tomorrow, segregation forever!" And you know what, the *News Journal* never printed one word of my speech. The reason the paper didn't print it was because there was no longer a coalition; I was just a community center director, so, so what! What I had to say as a community leader didn't matter, and that had to change.

In 2000 the legislature passed a neighborhood schools law. From July through December of 2000, when we were talking about proposals with the neighborhood school committee, I said repeatedly that the next stage of litigation, if I had anything to do with it, would be about green and not black and white. What I meant was that it needed to be about money and resources as opposed to busing kids. That was my view then, and that is my view now. My full intention is to be a part of some degree of advocacy that goes forward to provide more resources to the newly resegregated schools, which are found in three of the four districts. My advocacy efforts would be much stronger and carry more weight as a city councilman as opposed to being just a community advocate. As a councilman, I would be more credible in the eyes of the Office of Education, the courts, and the local governments. Elected officials carry political weight when they are proponents of a particular issue. A community center director just doesn't have that kind of influence.

In 2004, people around the country were celebrating the fiftieth anniversary of the *Brown v. Board of Education* decision, but I wasn't in a celebratory mood. We were successful to the extent that we eliminated schools that black children can't go to. That's great. But the fact is that the achievement gap is spreading wider and wider, and there is a need to look at the situation as a whole. Are black children better off now than they were in 1978? The answer to the question is no!

Even though I was young, and I was a maverick, I was one of three community leaders at the time who opposed the implementation of the court order. Research was conducted, and we went out and visited other jurisdictions. After reviewing other situations, anyone could tell what was going to happen within our jurisdiction. The outcome was crystal clear.

Well, what happened? Our jurisdiction experienced an extraordinary increase in the number of suspensions of black and Hispanic kids. There was also a huge increase in the placement of black and Hispanic children in special education tracks. There was an extraordinary decline in the number of minority faculty members and administrators, and there was nothing that would suggest that there had been a substantial increase in overall performance. We had seen the events occur in other jurisdictions, and sure enough, we met the same fate. What we saw in other areas was exactly what happened here.

The other bad part of this resegregation effort is that the City of Wilmington has absolutely no responsibility for the education of its own children. To make matters worse, most of the city's elected officials and other politicians like having no responsibility. They can brush it off and say that "it is someone else's problem." No other city on the east coast of the United States and probably in the country throws their hands up in the air when it comes to the education of its own children. Something needs to be done for the sake of our children. That's why I do the things that I do, and that's why I decided to run for office. I intend to address these important education issues as an elected official. You just cannot let this go and allow folks to do what they want to do at the cost of the education of our children.

Let's talk about the Delaware General Assembly. The General Assembly said that we need to increase and will increase funding for all-day kindergarten by 2008. In my view, it is too little and too late. We need the funding now! If you can't fund everyone or if everyone doesn't want it, you need to allocate funds for the schools and the districts that need it the most. There are kids who desperately need the funding, kids who have already been recognized as being at risk through the child-find programs. Testing identifies which children need additional support and assistance. Often the great majority of those in need reside in low-income, disenfranchised communities. We could at least begin the process to assist those kids now.

The current president of the Christina school board cut a deal to vote on and pass a measure that would add an additional $200 of spending per pupil in the district, for those schools where the majority of children qualify for free and reduced lunch. Two hundred dollars pays for crayons and pencils. The literature is crystal clear, and it suggests that we need an additional two to four thousand dollars per child, not a mere two hundred. Some suggest that we need an additional four to seven thousand dollars more per child! We need to focus on educating these kids. We need to give them a chance. And that's what I am going to be shooting for. I am going to ask the school officials to do it, and then I am going to ask the state board to do it. After all of them refuse, which I think that they will, I am going to get outside third parties to compel them to do it.

Today, more than fifty years after the *Brown* decision, there is no school that a black child cannot attend. But here is today's problem: once you go into the schools, the classrooms are segregated! The school is segregated within its own walls. It's a problem statewide from Georgetown to Claymont. It's universal in the state of Delaware. Most students in the college-prep, honors, advanced placement, and academic levels are of backgrounds of higher income and are usually white, whereas most students in the general and special education levels are of lower income and are primarily black and Latino. These children need a voice. Someone needs to address these issues so they have a chance to succeed and can look toward a higher education.

But there are problems even with higher education. The few times that I have been back to the University of Delaware, I've been somewhat disappointed. The fact is that there has not been any substantive progress in terms of advancing the causes of minority students, with the exception of the engineering program. There has been no substantive increase in the number of black and minority students graduating from the institution.

To its credit, the University of Delaware does provide us with funding for our Early Head Start program. The Head Start program is an excellent initiative here in Delaware. I work with the staff here to increase the number of children receiving early education, which is really important because it prepares them for the next step. We also work with several agencies in the local community to improve the lives of children and parents. We have a professional relationship, and an important one, with the University of Delaware.

Overall, I view the last thirty years with a sense of profound disappointment. Our fight for educational equality has been long and it is far from over. But we will keep pushing until we achieve our goal of equal educational opportunities.

PART III

The Legacies: Desegregation and Resegregation

CHAPTER FOURTEEN

Legacies of *Brown v. Board of Education*

James T. Patterson

When Ralph Ellison heard about the *Brown v. Board of Education* decision in May 1954, he wrote a friend, "What a wonderful world of possibilities for the children."

Other African American leaders were equally excited. Harlem's *Amsterdam News* editorialized, "The Supreme Court decision is the greatest victory for the Negro people since the Emancipation Proclamation." Thurgood Marshall, chief litigator for black defendants in the case, recalled, "I was so happy, I was numb." At the time, Marshall estimated that state-supported school segregation would be wiped out, nationwide, within five years.

I was so taken with Ellison's comment about the "wonderful world of possibilities for the children" that I wanted to use it as the title or subtitle for my book on the case. My publisher, however, demanded a title that would tell readers clearly what was in the book. Therefore, it has the wonderfully catchy and imaginative title of *Brown v. Board of Education: A Civil Rights Milestone and Its Troubled Legacy.*

Still, it is Ellison's high hopes—and those of many other African Americans in 1954—to which I return again and again in my book on the *Brown* case, and on which I want to reflect here. To what extent may we say, more than fifty years later, that the high hopes of Ellison, Marshall, and others have been realized?

Now, there are any number of legacies that can be examined, but let me focus on three questions:

1. How great an impact did the decision have on advancing the powerful civil rights movement that mushroomed in the early 1960s?
2. Has the *Brown* decision—and desegregation of schools—made a significant difference in the academic and lifetime achievement of black students?
3. What can we say has been the legacy of *Brown* on American race relations generally?

When the civil rights movement gained force in the 1960s, the answer to the first question—whether the *Brown* decision greatly advanced it—seemed obvious: the impact on the movement was huge. Americans had only to look at the chronology of events following *Brown*, which suggested that the ruling was the first strong link in a chain of causation leading to the great acceleration of the civil rights movement in the 1960s. Only one and a half years after *Brown*, for instance, came the memorable boycott of buses in Montgomery, Alabama. Three years later, in 1957, President Eisenhower had to send in federal troops to maintain token desegregation of Central High School in Little Rock. These events would not have happened, of course, without *Brown*. And then in the 1960s, the movement swelled, ultimately forcing Congress to pass the historic Civil Rights Act of 1964 and the Voting Rights Act of 1965.

There are also events in this chain that seem to link directly to the *Brown* decision. For instance, Martin Luther King Jr. staged a Prayer Pilgrimage to Washington in 1957 on May 17, the third anniversary of *Brown*. The first group of 1961 Freedom Riders, organized by CORE, also announced that they intended to reach their final destination, New Orleans, on May 17.

In hindsight, however, we may be justified in wondering—as many scholars have done in recent years—how vital the *Brown* ruling was as a stimulant to the civil rights activism that took off only in the 1960s. In the first place, the decision, although supported at the time by a small majority of northern whites, did not transform these whites into forceful champions of desegregation. Until the 1960s—when militant civil rights activism dramatically altered northern opinion—most Americans, including liberals such as Eleanor Roosevelt, counseled for incremental, cautious change. Leaders of the legal profession were also cautious. In the summer of 1957, thirty-eight of forty-six state chief justices declared that the Supreme Court ought to exercise more restraint.

It also seems fair to say that the *Brown* decision did not inspire many black people to take to the streets in the late 1950s. Indeed, we look mostly in vain today for evidence of widespread direct action protest against southern white resistance to school desegregation in the late 1950s. Except in Montgomery, civil rights activism of all sorts was relatively quiescent in the late 1950s: in fact, in 1955, 1957, and 1959 there were fewer civil rights demonstrations in the United States than there had been in 1943, 1946, 1947, and 1948.

Now, I do not mean here to make the foolish claim that *Brown* made no difference to the civil rights movement or to the desegregation of schools. On the contrary, we can see modest progress, following *Brown*, against school segregation in a few areas of the border states. Moreover, the Court used *Brown* as its constitutional basis for decisions in the late 1950s that struck down segregation in some other public facilities—municipal golf courses, beaches, and, of course, the buses in Montgomery. The decision has continued to be important as a matter of constitutional law. More generally, *Brown* encouraged the Warren Court to advance the rise of so-called public interest litigation, thereby stimulating a widespread rights consciousness that was later to become a major force in the United States. And we can agree finally that the courageous *Brown* decision had important symbolic value to African Americans throughout the nation: after all, the law was at last on their side.

Still, historical evidence does not enable us to measure with assured accuracy the importance of that symbolism in advancing the civil rights movement.

More generally, I agree with scholars such as Michael Klarman, who has argued that Marshall and his fellow lawyers clung for too long to their faith in litigation (which was understandable, given their exciting triumph in 1954). In so doing they may have discouraged strategies of direct action—strategies that were required to move the nation. The *Brown* decision was necessary for the rise of the civil rights movement, but without the direct action protest it was not sufficient.

Now the nearly fifteen-year success of white opposition to *Brown*, which left nearly 99 percent of southern black public school students in all-black schools in 1964 (ten years after *Brown*) and later, has also led many scholars to lament what they regard as the timidity of the Court in 1954. Chief Justice Earl Warren and his fellow Justices, they point out, failed to denounce racism or de facto segregation; they did not rule against segregation or racial discrimination (including state laws banning racial intermarriage) outside of public schools; even in 1955 (*Brown II*), they set no timetable for compliance with their decision; and they supplied only vague criteria for helping lower court judges determine what might be compliance.

These criticisms, although understandable in hindsight, mainly reflect widespread gloom about progress in civil rights since the 1960s. Failing fully to appreciate the circumstances facing the Justices in the highly racist Jim Crow world of 1954, these criticisms tend to forget that declaring the unconstitutionality of state-mandated racial segregation in schools was at that time a bold, radical, and historic step that elected officials had refused to take.

Still, it is a fact that *Brown* was not enforced for many years. It is also a fact that many larger socioeconomic and educational forces—forces existing largely independently of the decision—were very important stimulants, more important perhaps than *Brown,* of the civil rights movement. These forces—many of them advancing liberal ideas that led to *Brown* itself—included massive South-to-North and rural-to-urban migrations of blacks, rising economic and educational levels of whites as well as blacks, struggles against colonialism in black Africa, and the Cold War. How could America claim to be the leader of the so-called Free World if it denied basic rights to its African American population? Some of these forces, notably the Cold War, influenced a few Supreme Court Justices in 1954 and became increasingly strong by the 1960s.

These forces were as important as *Brown* in promoting change in race relations, for they predisposed the Justices at least to seriously consider knocking down segregation in the public schools. As Philip Elman, a liberal Justice Department official, later observed, "In *Brown* nothing the lawyers said made a difference. Thurgood Marshall could have stood up and recited 'Mary had a little lamb,' and the result would have been exactly the same." Jack Greenberg, a top associate of Thurgood Marshall, offered a similar judgment years later. "There was a current of history," he said, "and the Court became part of it."

These reservations concerning the impact of *Brown* on the civil rights movement when in 1996 I signed the contract for my book, which was published in 2001 as the first in a new Oxford University Press series entitled Pivotal Moments in American History. To sum up, the case was indeed important, especially as a constitutional precedent against state-mandated segregation. *Brown* also inspired many later court strategies by civil rights lawyers and stimulated many other movements for rights, including feminism and affirmative action. But whether the case was "pivotal" for the civil rights movement is open to debate.

Now, let me turn to my second question: to what extent has desegregation of the schools—once *Brown* was finally implemented (mostly after 1968)—promoted academic achievement among blacks?

In 1954, Thurgood Marshall and most other foes of segregation did not think very deeply about that question. It was self-evident to them that the existence of the Jim Crow system in schools meant ill-supported education for blacks. Inevitably, they thought, desegregation would result in better schooling for black children. But there already existed a few voices that had expressed doubts about large hopes concerning the future educational benefits of school desegregation. America's most prominent black intellectual, W. E. B. Du Bois, had articulated these doubts in a controversial essay published in 1935. "A Negro school," he wrote, "where children are treated like human beings, trained by teachers of their own race, who know what it means to be black . . . is infinitely better than making our boys and girls doormats to be spit and trampled upon and lied to by ignorant social climbers, whose sole claim to superiority is ability to kick 'niggers' when they are down."

Since the 1960s, of course, many other African Americans have echoed such doubts about school desegregation. Derrick Bell, the well-known liberal law professor, wrote in 1994, "The insistence on integrating every public school that is black perpetuates the racially demeaning and unproven assumption that blacks must have a majority white presence in order to either teach or learn effectively."

Perhaps the most striking example of thinking along these lines came from Supreme Court Justice Clarence Thomas in the case of *Missouri v. Jenkins* in 1995. Thomas strongly rejected a central psychological theory underlying *Brown*—that black children develop feelings of inferiority and experience low academic motivation in racially segregated schools. Thomas countered, "The theory that black students suffer an unspecified psychological harm from segregation that retards their mental and educational development . . . not only relies upon questionable social science research rather than constitutional principle, but it also rests on an assumption of black inferiority."

As the statements of Bell and Thomas indicate, views such as these cut across the ideological spectrum. In part, they reflect the understandable pessimism by black people that has accompanied the resistance by white people to desegregation of schools. The statements also expose profound discouragement among Americans about the so-called white–black test score gap. The scores of blacks on key academic achievement and aptitude tests had increased slowly but encouragingly between the early 1970s, when desegregation at last advanced in the South, and the late 1980s, thereby narrowing the black–white gap. But the gap still remains huge. Alarm about low academic performance by black students in tests such as these has accelerated not only white flight but also the phenomenon of so-called bright flight—of some black as well as white parents. Even Thurgood Marshall sent his young children in the early

1960s to mostly white private schools in New York City. When criticized by integrationists, he replied, "I think my children should have the best education that I can afford."

For all these reasons, research into the sources of these gaps and action to narrow them are imperative if racial desegregation of the schools is to move ahead in the future. Meredith Phillips and Christopher Jencks, careful students of test score gaps, have concluded that fighting the gaps "would do more to move America toward racial equality than any politically possible alternative." Another scholarly assessment (by Alan Krieger and Diane Whitmore) modified the famous remark by Du Bois in 1903—"the problem of the 20th century is the problem of the color line"—to this statement in 2002: "The problem of the twenty-first century might be the color line in academic achievement."

Let me conclude briefly with reflections about my third question: the broader impact of *Brown* and of desegregated schools on race relations generally since 1954. First, let me repeat the obvious: because truly nonsegregated schools have always been difficult to find since *Brown*, it is hard to prove that the decision has contributed greatly to the promotion of better race relations generally. One measure of such relations is presumably the extent to which whites have come around, over time, to accepting desegregation of the schools. By this measure, it is easy to argue that *Brown* has not worked wonders. For one thing, until the late 1960s, resistance to such desegregation was total in the Deep South. Thereafter, especially in the 1970s, total southern resistance to school segregation was finally checked, thereby enabling a considerably greater mixing of blacks and whites in schools. This process continued, though much more slowly, in the 1980s. But already existing de facto segregation in other parts of the country persisted, and in many places, white flight to the suburbs has increased segregation.

Moreover, in the last ten to fifteen years, a process of resegregation has been advancing in the South as well as the North. Data from the Harvard Civil Rights Project reveal that the percentage of black students who attend "majority-white" schools in the South has declined from a peak of 43 percent in 1988 to around 30 percent in 2003. This is roughly the percentage that existed in the early 1970s, once the courts had finally enforced the desegregation process. Percentages of blacks in such schools are even lower in most other parts of the nation. It is fair to say that school integration, having finally overcome massive resistance, now struggles in a climate of passive indifference.

Many people, blacks included, have therefore grown despondent. Linda Brown-Thompson, whose father was the "Brown" of *Brown v. Board*, reflected in 1994, "Sometimes I wonder if we really did the children and the nation a favor by taking this case to the Supreme Court. I knew it was the right thing for my father and mother to do then. But after nearly forty years we find the Court's ruling unfulfilled." Elizabeth Eckford, one of the "Little Rock Nine" who challenged segregation in Little Rock in 1957, also had doubts. "There was a time when I thought integration was one of the most desired things," she said in 1997. "I appreciate blackness [now] more than I did then."

But to single out unhappy survivors such as Eckford is to tarnish another, brighter picture. The other eight black students among the Little Rock Nine, for instance, proclaimed themselves glad, in retrospect, that they had challenged segregation. All went on to colleges or universities. Other black adults, too, have looked back positively on their experiences in nonsegregated schools, insisting that these experiences were beneficial in many ways—proving to them, for instance, that whites are not necessarily smarter and offering them exposure to the all-important social and economic "networks" of a larger multicultural world than predominantly black schools could normally have provided. As Orlando Patterson, who has written thoughtfully about such issues, concluded in 1997, integrated schools often (though not always) do promote better racial understanding among whites, and they give to blacks what he calls "informal education—that is, greater savvy about the ways and networks of the majority population."

For these reasons, greater racial integration of schools remains a worthy goal. To tolerate further resegregation in public education is to risk the greater resegregation of society at large and therefore to heighten racial isolation and denial of equal opportunity. As the sociologist Christopher Jencks put it, "The more you let society pull itself apart, the less commitment the haves have to the have-nots." Or as Marshall said in his much-cited dissent in *Milliken v. Bradley* (1974), "Unless our children begin to learn together, there is little hope that our people will learn to live together."

I close this essay with a final thought concerning strategies for the promotion of racial justice: lawyers and courts must normally have large popular backing and sustained political support if they hope to promote progress, at least in the short run. The Supreme Court did not receive this support, of course, in the late 1950s from the government or from the white American public. Backing from white Americans since the 1950s, moreover, has been scattered and weak. For these reasons Ellison's dream of a "wonderful world for the children" has not been realized. Instead, the decision has had what the subtitle of my book calls a "troubled legacy."

As Jack Greenberg, a top attorney with Marshall, described this legacy in 1994, "Altogether school desegregation has been a story of conspicuous achievements, flawed by marked failures, the causes of which lie beyond the capacity of lawyers to correct. Lawyers can do right, they can do good, but they have their limits. The rest of the job is up to society."

CHAPTER THIRTEEN

Delaware Voices: Jea Street

Jea Street is a community activist who was deeply involved in efforts to desegregate schools in New Castle County, Delaware. A native of Wilmington, Street attended public schools and graduated from the University of Delaware in 1974. From 1974 to 1981, he was employed as the executive director of the Parent Educational Resource Center. This organization was established by the Wilmington Home School Community Council to work toward the peaceful implementation of school desegregation orders. In 1981, Street and other community activists founded the Coalition to Save Our Children. This group replaced the original plaintiffs in the New Castle County school desegregation litigation. In March 1981, Street was appointed executive director of Lutheran Hilltop Community Center, where he is still employed. Street was an officer in the Coalition to Save Our Children and served as its chair from 1988 until the unitary status order was entered in 1996. He was recently elected to serve on the New Castle County Council.

I am a native of Wilmington. I attended the city's public schools and have been involved with the community all my life. I was born and raised in the Baptist Church. I represent the third generation of my family to come out of that church. My family was always involved in advocacy and the civil rights struggle. My mother and two uncles in particular were very active and involved with the NAACP and its pursuit of equality, justice, and civil rights. I grew up with that atmosphere in my house.

In the 1960s I was a student at Wilmington High. This was the period of the civil rights struggle and an era of loss, illustrated by the assassination of Dr. Martin Luther King Jr. During that time, Wilmington High was basically divided equally among white and black students. There was some serious racial division in our communities and at the school. When Dr. King was assassinated, riots broke out at the school. The schools were closed and the police came in with riot gear. That was one of the saddest days that I have ever seen.

Part of that experience compelled me to get involved with and commit myself to social services and the community. While I was in high school, we tried to change things. We started a high school fraternity, focusing on community service projects and giving back to the community. High school fraternities at the time were unheard of, but we had success and contributed a great deal to our community. I graduated from Wilmington High School in 1970.

CHAPTER FIFTEEN

Haunted by *Brown*

Robert Justin Lipkin

Brown v. Board of Education occupies a hallowed place in the canon of contemporary constitutional law. Not only is *Brown* considered an exemplar of American democracy but it is at the same time thought to be virtually beyond criticism.[1] Indeed, some commentators insist that rejecting *Brown* disqualifies any scholar or theory from being taken seriously.[2] With this in mind, I cautiously reassess *Brown* by considering various alternative strategies for eliminating American apartheid, what these strategies imply for American constitutionalism, and the brand of democracy this constitutionalism creates.

The Conventional Depiction of *Brown*

Brown v. Board of Education, according to one conventional and compelling depiction, exemplifies the American genius for vindicating individual rights under our constitutional scheme. It is a story of how the Supreme Court slew Jim Crow segregation, the last vestige of slavery in the United States, and by doing so placed the nation firmly on the road toward racial justice.

Here is how the conventional depiction goes: in 1954, challenged by a small cadre of dedicated Americans and wearying of a system of segregated public education, the Supreme Court, seeing no possibility of congressional remediation, boldly intervened.[3] A unanimous Court shocked the nation by striking down laws requiring segregated schools. *Brown*, in this view, stands for the propositions that all Americans are equal before the law and that legal equality precludes government-sanctioned segregation throughout American society. In reversing more than a half-century of segregation, the Supreme Court, by a courageous, revolutionary act, emerges as the champion of freedom and justice for all. Three cheers for the Supreme Court!

The conventional depiction regards *Brown*, at least symbolically, as representing the zenith of this nation's struggle to overcome its racist legacy and to realize the simple truth that racism hurts. It hurts its victims and its perpetrators, as well as those who stand by and tolerate its perpetual harm. Any decent person should internalize what has come to represent *Brown*'s meaning, to wit: America's noblest ideals simply cannot tolerate racial apartheid. And perhaps more important is the realization that racial subordination is irrational, unethical, and unjust. The *Brown* decision has helped educate generations of schoolchildren, from every racial background, and has imparted to them America's need to acknowledge and reject its shameful racist legacy.

This conventional depiction of *Brown* resonates in my memory of growing up in Brooklyn. One afternoon, while walking home from the schoolyard, I spied a fresh stack of the *Brooklyn Eagle* placed prominently on the candy store's newsstand, its pages shouting, "High Court Bars Segregated Schools." That image took hold as a foundational element in my then-fledgling political consciousness.[4] I knew something good had just occurred and that this good would open the floodgates to a greater good. It vindicated my inchoate conviction that mine was a fundamentally decent nation where good would ultimately triumph over evil. As I grew up, *Brown* remained the symbol of what was great about America. For me, America's greatness lay not in its attainment of perfection, whatever that would be like, but rather in its capacity for change, its commitment to remediating wrongs, and, perhaps most important and most relevant today, its penchant for expanding the idea of who counts as a full and equal citizen. *Brown* clearly exemplified this capacity for change as well as the imperative to expand the American community by seeking out for inclusion those marginalized and oppressed people.[5]

Before I entered the legal academy, it was inconceivable for me even to consider the possibility that *Brown* had any defects at all, let alone that its specter someday might haunt the struggle for racial justice. When my constitutional law professor began challenging *Brown*'s reasoning in class, as constitutional law professors do, I thought to myself, "How unlucky to have a professional obligation to criticize the reasoning in *Brown*." As a former philosophy professor myself, I could certainly understand finding flaws in Plato's dialogues or in Kant's critiques, but trying to trip up the reasoning in *Brown,* even for the purpose of motivating law students, seemed to be a fool's errand, a thankless task that I, at least, would never be caught doing. The prospect that *Brown* was incorrectly decided or that it represented a wrong turn on the road to freedom was simply beyond my ken.

Indeed, even now writing these words is difficult, because *Brown* was never merely a Court decision for me, nor was it only a change in politics and society, nor was the principle it expresses just an essential element in any satisfactory account of justice. *Brown* was all of these things, to be sure, but also much more. For me, *Brown* represented the expression of a fundamental attitude toward myself and others, especially toward others brutalized by the operations of the very country I believed offered the promise of genuine equality for everyone. Consequently, critically assessing *Brown* challenges both how I think of my own identity as an American citizen and my idea of how evil should be overcome within a democracy. In a deeply ineffable sense, my challenging *Brown* puts me at war with myself.

One pervasive, and not implausible, response to my reassessment will be that it is completely unrealistic to suggest that desegregation of American schools could have come about in any way other than by seeking judicial intervention. According to this response, it is nothing short of utopian to consider alternatives to *Brown*.[6]

However, utopian reasoning should not always be denigrated.[7] Disciplined and sensitively deployed utopian imagining, or what I would prefer to call "ideal theorizing," sometimes helps us achieve a deeper understanding of the obstacles to change as well as more promising routes toward change. Consequently, I wish to explore alternatives to *Brown*, not for the purpose of denigrating the decision, but rather to fulfill its commitment to change. In a democratic republic, neither racial traditions nor morally correct judicial decisions should be considered sacrosanct or ineliminable. Exploring alternatives to *Brown* tends to honor *Brown*'s own remarkable rejection of the idea of "sacrosanct" and ineliminable traditions in American democracy.

Before embarking on my criticism of *Brown*, I need to make clear my admiration for the men and women who were the central players in the unfolding judicial strategy that led up to *Brown*.[8] My criticism of *Brown* and even my challenging the strategy to seek remedial action through the courts should not be taken in any way as denigrating their efforts. The torturous, heartbreaking, yet supremely heroic road taken by these patriotic Americans represents a spell-binding story of how the "abused and scorned" secured rights denied them for so long and in the process how they helped bring us all closer to the promise of America's birth.[9] Their story is a valiant exercise in the nobility of the human spirit. Historians, in my view, cannot capture the empowering humanity that drove this quest any more than they can convincingly depict the thirst for justice that was its ultimate motivation. We cannot even *imagine* the torment these heroic individuals endured or the tears they shed, nor should we even try.[10] What we should do is to realize the Herculean effort it took to bring us to the point in history we are at now, one that is overall better than the days before *Brown v. Board of Education*, and we should cultivate and nurture the gratitude that the actors in this drama deserve.

A Framework for Assessing Constitutional Decisions

Before exploring alternatives to *Brown*, it is necessary to indicate roughly what objections this seminal decision faces. Three perspectives exist for assessing *Brown* as well as any other Supreme Court decision. We can evaluate a judicial decision's interpretive soundness, its institutional appropriateness, and its moral content, if it has any. A complete evaluation of *Brown v. Board of Education* would examine its reasoning from each of these perspectives. From the interpretive perspective, it can be argued that *Brown* fails because no single interpretive rationale, even after fifty years of failed attempts, has reached a consensus among jurists and constitutional theorists.[11] Most, if not all, interpretive accounts, deploying conventional interpretive factors, appear successful, if at all, only by assuming the legitimacy of *Brown* in one of the interpretive premises. This preaching to the converted fails to provide an impartial explanation and justification of *Brown*'s reasoning. If no conventional interpretive factors explain and justify the result in *Brown*, its legitimacy becomes suspect unless one characterizes it as a species of revolutionary adjudication. And revolutionary adjudication is sound only if the Court, not Congress, is the legitimate institution to make the final decision concerning constitutional meaning.[12]

This institutional point entails that *Brown*, like many so-called landmark decisions, is problematic because fundamental changes in constitutional meaning should be brought about by the people or their representatives, not the courts. From the institutional perspective, as I argue later, *Brown*'s constitutional jurisprudence has come into conflict with the elected branches' attempts to more fully fashion remedies for the effects of segregation, however minimal, through affirmative action.

From the moral perspective, it is difficult to appreciate how anyone could think that race justifiably damns a group of people from fully enjoying the benefits of full citizenship in a democratic society. That said, *Brown* contains an invidious paternalism that is morally undesirable, indeed to put it bluntly, morally offensive. [13] The opinion in *Brown* ties African American children's capacity to learn to the presence of whites in the same class or school. This invidious paternalism, in my view, is tied to the paternalism of slavery that rationalizes white supremacy on the ground that it is in the slave's best interest. It entirely obscures the fact that many African Americans succeeded in unequal, segregated schools. Imagine how well they might have performed in equal segregated schools. That the decision in *Brown* might be part of a broader attempt to eradicate racial segregation is irrelevant to the question of whether the kind of stigma on which *Brown* is grounded is paternalistic.[14] Additionally, a complete examination of the reasoning in *Brown* would show that, the more narrowly *Brown* is interpreted, the less morally attractive the decision is. By contrast, the more broadly interpreted the decision is, the greater its moral attractiveness, but then its legitimacy as constitutional law is brought into question.

A complete evaluation of *Brown* would include a discussion of each of the three perspectives as well as the interrelationships between and among them. Here I restrict myself to the institutional perspective, leaving a discussion of the other perspectives to another occasion.[15]

The Institutional Dimension: Which Governmental Branch Should Eliminate Segregation?

The conventional depiction sees *Brown* as the final guardian of individual rights. In *Brown*, the Court champions the interests of African Americans against legislatures that either fail to prevent a violation of their rights or, worse still, actively create and defend laws denying these rights. Is this depiction accurate? Were there any alternatives to judicial redress of the rights of African Americans?

Underlying these questions is a challenge to the alleged propriety of judicial supremacy, which places the courts as the authoritative institutional basis of constitutional review. Judicial supremacy is a necessary element of the Court's role in *Brown*.[16] Yet judicial supremacy itself has been harmful to African Americans. For all the *Brown* decisions there are the *Dred Scott* and *Plessy* rulings, and of course, for all of us, there is *Bush v. Gore*. Taking the effective interpretation in critical cases away from the political branches and the people leaves the American Constitution in the hands of judges who simply lack any special qualifications for ascertaining constitutional meaning. If constitutional meaning is tied to rationality, ethics, and justice—and it must be if it is worthy of our support at all—the effective authority to alter constitutional meaning must rest with the electorate and the political branches representing it. If the political branches or the people interpret the Constitution incorrectly, remediation through political action is always possible. By contrast, once the Court speaks, it silences the voice of the people, absent years of waiting for a reconstituted Court to reverse the earlier decision. The political process might also take years, but such a process is democratically more authentic in placing ultimate resolution of controversy in the hands of the electorate.[17]

Republicanism, Democracy, and *Brown*

A useful, if oversimplified, framework for addressing the question of judicial supremacy delineates two approaches. One approach, a "republican" (with a small "r") approach, contends that individual rights are potentially placed in jeopardy when the people or their representatives have the final say over constitutional meaning. If the electorate prevails without constraint, how can minority rights be protected? If the people or their representatives decide what is constitutional, the very idea of constitutionalism is negated. The opposing side, the "democratic" approach (with a small "d"), insists that the people or their representatives must have the final say concerning constitutional meaning for there to be self-rule in the first place.[18] The distinction between republicanism and democracy permits us to inquire whether the strategy for extirpating racism in American society should have counted on the judiciary as the lead or instead whether it should have sought legislative redress.

The question of judicial supremacy and its pertinence to *Brown* can be brought out in this manner. Republicans argue that the desegregation of public schools and the elimination of de jure racism would never have occurred or at least would not have occurred in 1954 had the strategy been to seek legislative redress. Only an independent institution can put a brake on transient passions when they are incompatible with the Constitution. Democrats reply that judicial supremacy is counter-majoritarian, replacing the people's voice with the collective voice of nine old and, almost necessarily, out-of-touch individuals. Without some effective form of judicial accountability, democracy is illusory. Unelected, virtually irremovable Justices are unaccountable.[19] Whether there is any way to reconcile these two positions can be seen as the primary question of constitutional law.[20]

Understanding the full meaning of *Brown* requires understanding the controversy between republicans and democrats. The decision in *Brown* did not only address a fundamental moral wrong; it also resurrected and continued to entrench judicial supremacy. Put in other terms, *Brown* tells us that when things go egregiously wrong we can rely on the courts to save us from ourselves. What this re-entrenchment overlooks, however, are the costs of relying on the courts for salvation.[21]

The Costs of *Brown*

The costs of *Brown* are many, including igniting a significant immediate backlash in the South and later in the North and helping the virtual elimination of moderate and liberal factions in the Republican Party.[22] Another permanent cost of *Brown* pertains to the role of the Supreme Court in American democracy. *Brown* revivified a Marshallian conception of judicial review that included judicial supremacy.[23] James Bradley Thayer pointed out that the existence of judicial review distorts constitutional debate among legislatures and among the people simply because everyone knows that the Court has the final say on such matters.[24] Following Thayer, Mark Tushnet points out that judicial review creates a "judicial overhang." The fact that the Supreme Court is always present to overturn legislation often misleads legislators, promotes legislative irresponsibility, and distorts discussion of pending legislation as well as the legislation itself.[25]

Brown depends on judicial supremacy, and judicial supremacy makes *Plessy* possible. Paradoxically, then, *Plessy* is one of the costs of *Brown*. Had a system of judicial supremacy never been in place, a *Plessy*-like legislative decision might have been easier to reverse. Here the political battle would be joined. In 1896, perhaps legislative supremacy would have permitted segregation, but so did the Court decision in *Plessy*. But what about 1937? 1945? 1950? 1954? 1964? Without *Plessy*, *Brown*-like state laws would be easier to pass. The early civil rights movement—through the courts—began in the 1920s. It took more than three decades to achieve *Brown*, which itself is far from the racial Promised Land. Moreover, *Plessy*'s control of this process deprived America of the sort of deliberative debate that occurs politically when change is sought legislatively. Had Jim Crow segregation been established through the elected branches alone, arguably change would have probably come about earlier.[26]

Another cost of *Brown* is the deep resentment directed toward the Court for what was perceived as its intrusion into important constitutional controversies. In *Brown*, this resentment made resistance persistent and effective. Moreover, even when resistance ends, subtle, sometimes duplicitous, reversals occur.[27] Even when reversal does not occur, *judicially* inspired constitutional revolutions do not become entrenched in the individual's consciousness as readily as legislative revolutions. Although today almost everyone agrees or, so they say, that invidious discrimination is unconstitutional, the de facto discrimination that plagues the inner cities is simply *judicially* excluded from the prohibited category.[28] The courts view *intent* as the culprit of American apartheid. Realizing intent as only one of the factors in racial segregation would have been far more likely, though in no way certain, by adopting a legislative strategy. Indeed, ultimately civil rights legislation did come about without requiring intent, a position the Court refuses to endorse.

Affirmative Action as a Cost of *Brown*

One of the greatest costs of *Brown* is its effect on affirmative action as a partial remedy for years of state-enforced segregation. Consider the following hypothetical pertaining to more recent circumstances. Suppose, through enormous political action, including civil disobedience, in the 1950s and 1960s that de jure segregation in public schools was reversed legislatively. In this scenario, is there any doubt that (some form of) affirmative action would now be constitutional?

Plessy-like legislation sets the framework for affirmative action; namely, that racial classifications are constitutionally permissible. Although *Plessy*, as a judicial decision, permits legislation implementing affirmative action, *Brown* arguably does not.[29] And because *Brown* controls these issues, affirmative action is at least arguably unconstitutional. Thus, absent *Brown*, affirmative action legislation in all likelihood would be easier to pass without the Court striking it down.

To be precise, implementing affirmative action legislation would be easier in two situations: (1) in a regime of legislative supremacy absent both *Brown* with *Plessy* and (2) in a regime of judicial supremacy absent *Brown*. Let us consider each situation.

In a regime of legislative supremacy, segregation, desegregation, and affirmative action are all brought about and defended legislatively, if at all. This political approach emphasizes electoral change. Here, the charge of utopianism has its greatest sting. How can one seriously suggest organizing African Americans to vote *Plessy* educational systems out of existence, when property tax, poll tax, and other forms of intimation were used to deny African Americans access to electoral change? However, this complaint becomes less obvious if one looks at the civil rights movements of the 1950s and 1960s; political action of just the sort suggested here won the day. The Civil Rights Act of 1964 and the Voting Rights Act of 1965 were arguably more causally efficacious in ending Jim Crow segregation generally throughout the South than *Brown* or any of the Supreme Court decisions pertaining to public schools. In addition, these acts are not susceptible to the charge of counter-majoritarianism, a charge made not only by constitutional theorists but also by ordinary folks.[30] Just listen to conservative talk show callers excoriate judges in the Terri Schiavo case (as well as in *Roe* and *Lawrence*) or liberal Americans castigating the Court for its decision in *Bush v. Gore*.

What might have happened if the NAACP or other civil rights groups had chosen the legislative route rather than the judicial one? A number of factors suggest that desegregation might have come about legislatively without dragging along the counter-majoritarian charge associated with judicial review.[31] First, desegregation is the morally correct position. It was difficult, even in 1954, to take seriously the proposition that African Americans should not be full members of the American community. And though anyone in the United States has the right to associate or not associate with whomever he or she pleases as long as there is mutual consent, this right does not extend to the public sphere where reasons for nonassociation must be rational. No one could argue that an inclination not to associate with African Americans is any more rational than an inclination not to associate with people having red hair or partially detached ear lobes. At least those supporting *Brown* cannot consider it rational. And most Americans agree strongly with this moral commitment. Second, although not necessarily in 1954, the political synergy behind desegregation was increasing after World War II. Third, legislative revisions of social traditions tend to become more entrenched than judicial transformations. The Civil Rights Acts of 1964 and 1965 are a greater foundation to integration than the *Brown* decision.[32] Citizens might continue to argue about integration, but sooner than later integration as a legislative principle would find the only sort of repose available in a democracy. Fourth, a legislative approach obviates the need to work around precedents. Without *Plessy*, *Brown*-like legislation might be easier to achieve. And without *Brown*, a *Bakke*-like law would be easier to pass.[33]

What might have occurred in a regime of judicial supremacy absent *Brown*? Because white majorities passed affirmative action laws in the 1970s, in this regime, it is likely that they would not be struck down or modified by the Court. There would be no judicial controversy over whether strict scrutiny or a less severe level of review is appropriate for "benign" classifications.[34] In a regime of judicial supremacy, the current Court's crabbed interpretation of equal protection, based on an implausible but possible interpretation of *Brown*, would be absent, and the Court would no longer have this weapon to use against affirmative action. Wouldn't any appellate attorney prefer arguing for affirmative action with *Plessy* as precedent, not *Brown*, or without either?

From this perspective, *Brown* can be blamed for the failure to implement broad, democratically based affirmative action programs.[35] The Court reads *Brown* formalistically, requiring all racial classifications to be subject to the highest level of judicial review. A more plausible interpretation ties racial classifications to the negative effects—subordination—of segregation on the self-image of African American children. Following this approach targets only invidious racial classifications designed to subordinate African Americans through humility and oppression. However, the Court somehow has managed to reject this interpretation or corrupt its importance. Had *Brown* never been decided, both federal and state affirmative action laws would be clearly constitutional or at least not unconstitutional simply because they include racial classifications. Thus, the Court's interpretation of equal protection in *Brown* is an obvious impediment to implementing affirmative action. This constitutes an important example of how *Brown* has become part of the problem, not the solution.[36]

It must be pointed out that the idea of invalidating legislation merely because it contains a racial classification, absent evidence of subordination, is absurd on its face. Racial classifications themselves hurt only if their purpose or effect is to subordinate or to defend a general system of subordination. Discrimination against whites, absent a proven retaliatory motive, is simply not invidious discrimination at all. For example, suppose empirical evidence demonstrated clearly that African Americans were not as susceptible to the ill effects of weight gain as whites. Suppose further that weight gain was an even greater public health problem than it is today. In this hypothetical, Congress or a state legislature passes a law allocating more funds to combat weight gain for whites than for African Americans. Finally, suppose African Americans were treated fairly in other areas of health care. Would such a law obviously violate equal protection? Despite the modern Court's insistence that racial classifications must always be strictly scrutinized, it is not obvious that this makes any sense at all. In this example, why isn't this hypothetical law supremely rational? If it is, what if the positions of whites and African Americans were reversed? Would a law allocating more funds to African Americans violate the equal protection of whites if the law generally provided whites with the appropriate health care?[37] It is extraordinarily difficult to see why.

The Enforcement of *Plessy*

Leaving the issue of *Brown*'s effect on affirmative action, perhaps the issue of American apartheid should have been confronted more directly. Suppose the NAACP Legal Defense Fund had followed through on its initial strategy to enforce *Plessy v. Ferguson.* Derrick Bell proposes this approach on the supposition that, because implementation of *Plessy* was impracticable, the states would have no alternative but to integrate public schools. I want to explore a different version of this approach. Suppose the states could afford to enforce *Plessy*. Would this strategy have been desirable? The answer to this question depends, of course, on just what the question asks. If the question asks whether a system of truly equal but segregated schools satisfies the principles of *ideal* justice, the answer is resoundingly "no." However, that may not be the proper question. Instead, the question might be as follows: Would such schools satisfy the minimal conditions of *transitional* justice? Would the quest for racial justice have been enhanced by sending African Americans to equal, but segregated schools as a stage in the quest for justice?

Given the resources and will for equalizing support for all schools, African American children would have become anything their talents allowed them to become.[38] What would be the likely results? It is not improbable to suppose that, in these circumstances, there would be a dramatic increase in the number of African American lawyers, physicians, accountants, and so forth.[39] This would satisfy the need in African American communities for professionals and other skilled workers. Moreover, there would be a spillover effect. Because well-qualified professionals are often scarce in white communities, African Americans would have opportunities to fill the needs of these communities too. Integration would occur incrementally by the operations of market forces.

These professionals would be living examples to young African Americans that their schools were equal to white schools and therefore they could become anything that whites could become. Similarly, a large cadre of well-educated African Americans would make it much more difficult for white children to insist that white adults and African American adults are fundamentally different, and as a result, a well-educated class of African Americans would acquire economic and electoral power to petition the legislature to eliminate *Plessy*-based education systems. In other words, a properly implemented system of "separate but equal" would itself have planted the seeds of its own demise, not through the courts but through the legislature and the market.

Similarly, a properly implemented *Plessy* would contribute to, not detract from, the esteem of African American children. It would have enabled young African Americans to experience greater educational success. African American children would then be in a position to say to white children, "See, Our schools are just as good as yours, and therefore we are just as good as you." No doubt, state-mandated public segregation was a central feature of a comprehensive system of subordination. However, this caste system could have been attacked by first providing African American children with the education they so desperately needed. Recall W. E. B. Dubois's important insight: "Negro children need neither segregated schools nor mixed schools. What they need is education."[40] Properly educating African Americans, even in segregated schools, might have been the door to escaping American apartheid, and by walking through it, educated African Americans would have the weapons necessary for dismantling it.

Would such a solution be ideal? Of course not. Consider again Dubois's words: "Other things being equal, the mixed school is the broader, more natural basis for education of all youth. It gives wider contacts; it inspires greater self-confidence; and suppresses the inferiority complex. But other things seldom are equal, and in that case, Sympathy, Knowledge, and Truth, outweigh all that the mixed school can offer."[41] This emphasizes the cost for African Americans of integrating schools. Integrating public schools has been a de facto disaster. So-called "integrated" public schools provide a woefully inadequate education for all public school children, but especially inner city students. Because many inner city schools serve predominantly African American students, these students are denied an adequate education under integration.

Progressives, who so tirelessly fought for integration, understandably see only its institutional virtues and none of its costs. Among these costs include the stigma of attending school with the majority race. Small numbers of African Americans attending integrated schools would have a greater battle with self-esteem given an indifferent or hostile majority population in the school.[42] Integration can be more stigmatizing than segregation because it brings African American children face to face with "naked race-hatred and a curriculum blind to their needs."[43] Reactions to these features of integration can be self-destructive to African American youth. Why, even today, some African American children in integrated schools denigrate doing their homework because doing so means they are "acting white." It is the presence of whites in integrated schools that causes this undesirable collateral effect, and it is this collateral effect that impedes the education of African American children. This problem must be taken seriously.

By contrast, the moral force of *Brown* blinds us to the institutional virtues of alternatives. I do not pretend that the virtues of these alternatives would necessarily outweigh the virtues of *Brown*. My more modest point is that we should consider the benefits of these alternatives to *Brown*, not merely their costs. Considering both benefits and burdens of *Brown* might help us in future battles select the most effective vehicle of constitutional and social change.

Constitutional Review without Judicial Supremacy but with Judicial Review: An Interbranch Possibility

Why not consider a conception of constitutional review that eschews judicial *supremacy* altogether? Alternatives to judicial supremacy exist, even ones that include judicial review. Suppose American constitutionalism included a congressional override. That is to say, suppose the judiciary existed as it does today—reviewing state and federal statutes—but with one qualification. In this hypothetical, Congress can override decisions of the Supreme Court. The notion of a congressional override has a distinguished lineage. Chief Justice Marshall himself embraced this mechanism at least in some circumstances. Judge Robert Bork has also come out in favor of a congressional override. Suppose it was available in the 1950s. Would Congress have upheld the decision in *Brown*? Two possible answers present themselves.

First, if Congress had the override in its legislative arsenal, would it have used it to override *Brown*? It all depends on the precise nature and operation of the override. Would a simple majority suffice or would a super-majority be required? If a super-majority is required, what is its number? Must the president sign a congressional override for it to be law? These are important questions that must be confronted for this alternative to be practicable. For now, however, let us put them aside, and simply hypothesize the existence of a congressional override, however vaguely defined.

In the 1950s, it is not clear how many members of Congress would have been courageous enough to vote to uphold *Brown*. Suppose Congress used its override to overrule *Brown*. This would mean that segregated public schools would continue to exist in many parts of the nation. But what would follow the override? Whenever judicial or legislative decisions are made, they represent a target for the losing side. If eliminating segregation failed due to a congressional override, the people could mobilize as they did in the early 1960s in every state of the Union to vote the rascals out of office. The use of the override in the case of *Brown* would have been the motivational spark for electing to Congress candidates who would reverse the congressional override, assuming that was possible. After all, what a good target a congressional override of a unanimous Supreme Court decision would have made. Imagine newspaper, radio, and television sound-bites bellowing, "Restore the decision of a valiant Court against a racist Congress."[44]

Second, suppose Congress upheld the decision in *Brown*. Would the members of Congress be unseated for upholding *Brown*? Again the losers would target Congress, striving to unseat members who voted to support *Brown*. I think it very unlikely that political forces could have mobilized in 1954 to reverse a unanimous Supreme Court decision in this case. Consider the factors relevant to the improbability of such an override. The United States had just fought a war against racism, a war in which African Americans distinguished themselves as heroic warriors defending America.[45] Moreover, the fact that the world was watching would have placed enormous pressure on Congress to uphold *Brown*.[46] The pressure to support the congressional defense of *Brown* would be overwhelming. Again imagine newspaper, radio, and television advertisements insisting, "Justice requires supporting the courageous Congress's defense of the High Court."

In the unlikely circumstances that Congress reversed itself concerning segregation, the battle would at least be focused on the ultimate creators of constitutional meaning, namely, the people. Given the ultimate immorality of racism, shorn of the question of whether segregation is constitutional, I believe that the legislative victory of racial justice would ultimately be realized. It is a belief that we must all share. Isn't it?

Conclusion

American society has not come close to realizing *Brown*'s promise or the promise of racial justice generally.[47] Desegregation of American public schools has been agonizingly slow and only minimally successful. Although it true that, as a society, we have eliminated de jure segregation, more subtle forms of racism persist. Assessing progress toward racial justice is difficult because "[w]hat appears to be progress . . . is, in fact, a cyclical process. Barriers are lowered in one era only to reveal a new set of often more sophisticated but no less effective policies that maintain blacks in a subordinate status."[48] Whether this process ultimately will lead to the racial Promised Land—where personal and political decisions never appeal to race as a form of subordination—is difficult to say. One thing is for sure: contemporary American society has miles to go before the process of eliminating American apartheid succeeds. Would alternatives to *Brown* have been quicker or more effective? We will never know.[49]

Nevertheless, exploring alternatives to *Brown* that do not rely on judicial supremacy promises important benefits. American democracy, as it is practiced today, has failed to explain the compatibility between democracy and a system of virtually unaccountable judges. Either democracy is compatible with judicial supremacy or it is not. If it is compatible, we need an effective theory explaining how this is possible. If it is not compatible, we need to begin the process of seeking alternatives to our present judicial practice. Recognizing that *Brown*, both as a cause and an effect of judicial supremacy, is problematic must be taken seriously if ours is to continue as a republic we can keep.

Notes

1. One should inquire, however, whether anything can be an exemplar of American democracy and at the same time be beyond criticism. According to some conceptions of democracy, this would be oxymoronic. The most plausible idea of self-government conceptually lies somewhere on a spectrum from direct majoritarianism to full-blown republicanism. Without attempting to provide anything resembling a complete definition, my conception of self-government may be characterized as "republican democracy." Republican democracy, as I conceive it, includes constraints on the transient preferences of current majorities and a commitment to deliberating over the common good. Much too simply put, these constraints and the process of deliberation arguably are the republican elements in this conception; the final word on constitutional interpretation resting with the people themselves is the democratic element. That said, I use the contrast between republicanism and democracy to help appreciate the significance of and relationship between and among these conceptions of self rule, *Brown*, and judicial supremacy.

2. Jack M. Balkin, *What Brown Teaches Us About Constitutional Theory*, 90 U. Va. L. Rev. 1537 (2004). This unstated requirement on scholarship and theory makes for strange bedfellows. Both Robert Bork and Ronald Dworkin, sharing little else in politics or constitutional theory, are committed to an eerily similar rationalization of the decision in *Brown*. Robert Justin Lipkin, *Constitutional Revolutions: Pragmatism and the Role of Judicial Review in American Constitutionalism* 336, n. 40 (Duke University Press, 2000).

3. One remarkable consequence of this intervention is the modification of this country's system of federalism, a system that distributes power between the federal and state governments.

4. As did another experience occurring later that summer. During my family's first trip to Florida, we stopped for refreshments at a Dairy Queen in Georgia. My older sister approached the water fountain marked "Colored" and was about to drink when an angry white employee redirected her to the fountain marked "Whites." My sister was fourteen

at the time, and no activist, so she refrained from drinking from the "Colored" fountain. Nonetheless, she could not bring herself to drink from the "Whites" fountain and thus refrained from drinking at that Dairy Queen at all. An eight-year-old neighbor, accompanying us on our vacation, spied the "Colored" water fountain and shouted gleefully and in earnest, "Look, colored water." In retrospect, the starkness of Gunnar Myrdal's "two Americas" has no greater reality than through the conduct and words of children. Gunnar Myrdal, *American Dilemma* (Harper, 1944).

5. In my view, the process of including outcasts in the community of full and equal citizens is a salient feature of both the proper conception of the moral community and the most attractive conception of the constitutional community. For a discussion of the former see Robert Justin Lipkin, *The Theory of Reciprocal Altruism*, 30 Phil. Stud. (Ireland) 108 (1983–84) (describing two foundational principles of ethics: (1) the principle of inclusion and (2) the principle of expansion). For a discussion of the latter, see Kenneth Karst, *Belonging to America* 80 (Yale University Press, 1989) (crediting the civil rights movement as "re-defining our national community"). Currently, the nation is in the process of debating the possibility of expanding the community even further to include gays and lesbians. In constitutional law, *Lawrence* has begun this expansion by including same-sex couples in the class of people whose intimate relations should be protected. It is too soon to tell how far this expansion will go. The next stage of expansion might be to include gays and lesbians in the class of people eligible to marry. However, *Lawrence* left this question unanswered. See Robert Justin Lipkin, *The Harm of Same-Sex Marriage: Real or Imagined*? 3 Widener Law Review (2004–5).

6. I think this is a mistake now and was probably a mistake also at the time *Brown* was decided. Consider Derrick Bell's thoughtful reflection: "Contending with [the resistance to *Brown*] made it unlikely that any of those trying to implement *Brown*, including myself, would stop to consider that we might be on the wrong road." Derrick Bell, *Silent Covenants: Brown v. Board of Education and the Unfulfilled Hopes for Racial Reform* 19 (Oxford University Press, 2004).

7. Gordon Wood forcefully rebuts the general denigration of the U(topian) word: "The republican revolution was the greatest utopian movement in American history. The revolutionaries aimed at nothing less than a reconstitution of American society. They hoped to destroy the bonds holding together the older monarchial society—kinship, patriarchy, and patronage—and to put in their place new social bonds of love, respect, and consent. They sought to construct a society and governments based on virtue and disinterested public leadership and to set in motion a moral movement that would eventually be felt around the globe." Gordon S. Wood, *The Radicalism of the American Revolution* 229 (Vintage, 1992). If the American rejection of traditional political society was utopian but successful, then reassessing *Brown* seems all the more reasonable.

8. The battle toward ending segregation was fought on many fronts. I have concentrated on the story of the *legal* process leading up to *Brown* and have taken my inspiration from Robert J. Cottrol, Raymond T. Diamond, and Leland B. Ware, *Brown v. Board of Education: Class, Culture, and the Constitution* (University Press of Kansas, 2003); Richard Kluger, *Simple Justice* (Knopf, 2004); Michael Klarman, *From Jim Crow to Civil Rights;* and Mark V. Tushnet, *The NAACP's Legal Strategy Against Segregated Education, 1925–1950* (University of North Carolina Press, 2005).

9. Martin Luther King Jr. more eloquently expresses this sentiment: "Abused and scorned though we may be, our destiny is tied up with the destiny of America. . . . For more than two centuries our foreparents labored in this country without wages; they made cotton king; and they built the homes of their masters in the midst of brutal injustice and shameful humiliation—and yet out of a bottomless vitality they continued to thrive and

develop. If the inexpressible cruelties of slavery could not stop us, the opposition we now face will surely fail. We will win our freedom because the sacred heritage of our nation and the eternal will of God are embodied in our echoing demands." Martin Luther King Jr., *Letter from Birmingham City Jail*, reprinted in *A Testament of Hope: The Essential Writings and Speeches of Martin Luther King Jr.* 301, ed. James M. Washington (Harper, 1986).

10. Images can help us relive this sorrowful period in American history. For example, in the recent HBO film *Something the Lord Made*, Vivian Thomas, who later became a pioneer in heart surgery, and one of his acquaintances are walking down a sidewalk and repeatedly stand to the side whenever white people approach. I cannot imagine what Thomas and his acquaintance felt, though their reaction seemed rather perfunctory, making their oppression even more insidious.

11. In *What Brown v. Board of Education Should Have Said*, ed. Jack M. Balkin (New York University Press, 2001), a group of distinguished constitutional theorists give remarkably different answers to this question. This reflective dissensus, of course, does not mean that no interpretively sound account of equal protection exists that demonstrates why the result in *Brown* is correct. But after so many years and so many impressive, though failed, attempts, one should not be condemned for being skeptical of ever formulating an intersubjectively plausible explanation of the reasoning in *Brown*. To say that the failure to arrive at a consensus over the correct methodology for explaining and justifying what *Brown* should have said is "the greatest testament to" its soundness and therefore is a "strength not a weakness" misinterprets the nature of the failure. It is not that all the conventional interpretive methodologies explain and justify *Brown*; rather the failure is that none do or, to put it differently, interpretative methodology is irrelevant to the decision in *Brown*. Moreover, the controversy is not only over which methodology generates *Brown* but what *Brown* should have *said*. What is the appropriate scope of *Brown*? Was it merely about schools or all governmental institutions, or something even broader? To say "*Brown* was not merely a case about schools" but "the culmination of a decades-long attack against an elaborate system of racial subordination" might be true. But then why didn't it say so? An institution that must conceal its actual judgment about whether blacks should be full and equal citizens in the American republic should be suspect at least.

12. For an attempt to demonstrate the explanatory and justificatory plausibility of *Brown* as an example of revolutionary adjudication, see Robert Justin Lipkin, *Constitutional Revolutions*.

13. It is invidiously paternalistic by suggesting that, given the appropriate educational materials, African American children cannot succeed on their own. In a similar vein regarding the societal (white) role in blocking African Americans from seeking education (and other) benefits, Henry Louis Gates Jr. writes, "It's important to talk about life chances—about the constricted set of opportunities that poverty brings. But to treat black people as if they're helpless rag dolls swept up and buffeted by vast social trends—as if they had no say in the shaping of their lives—is a supreme act of condescension." *Breaking the Silence*, Op-Ed, N.Y. Times, Aug. 1, 2004.

14. Using social stigma generally as a reason for eliminating racial apartheid is not invidiously paternalistic because it says that racial subordination hurts and prevents the subordinated from realizing themselves as full and equal citizens. However, no one has succeeded without circularity in demonstrating that *Brown* really is about social stigma generally. And even if one could succeed, it would be only by ignoring *Brown*'s text. Compare *Brown*'s text with Justice Harlan's dissent in *Plessy*. Where in *Brown* do we see anything comparable to "[I]n view of the constitution, in the eye of the law, there is in this country no superior, dominant, ruling class of citizens. There is no caste here. Our constitution is color-blind, and neither knows nor tolerates classes among citizens"? Where does Chief

Justice Warren excoriate *Plessy* as "pernicious" as Justice Harlan excoriates *Dred Scott*? Comparing the actual words of both opinions makes it difficult to see how the text of each case equally rejects racial apartheid.

15. This article is part of a larger, ongoing project examining the relationship among judicial supremacy, American constitutionalism, and self-government.

16. Mark Tushnet, *Taking the Constitution away from the Court* (Princeton University Press, 1999); Larry Kramer, *We the Court*, 115 Harv. L. Rev. 4 (2001); Gerald Rosenberg, *The Hollow Hope: Can the Courts Bring About Social Change?* (University of Chicago Press, 1991); Klarman, *From Jim Crow to Civil Rights*.

17. Its authenticity is in its direct involvement of the electorate. This does not mean that only majoritarianism is authentic. Constraints on present majorities can also be democratically authentic, but only when the electorate has an effective say over their operation.

18. I elide the notions of "the people" and "their representatives," not because these are conceptually indistinct terms, but rather because this is not the occasion to explain their differences adequately.

19. When the Supreme Court has the final say over constitutional meaning, the people have little or no say in interpreting the Constitution. If congressional representatives had the final word, then the people could replace their representatives should the latter embrace an errant constitutional interpretation. As Lincoln put this point, "[I]f the policy of the Government upon vital questions affecting the whole people is to be irrevocably fixed by decisions of the Supreme Court, the instant they are made in ordinary litigation between parties in personal actions the people will have ceased to be their own rulers, having to that extent practically resigned the government into the hands of that eminent tribunal." Abraham Lincoln, *First Inaugural Address*, reprinted in *A Compilation of the Messages and Papers of the Presidents, 1789–1897*, ed. James D. Richardson, Vol. 6, 5, 9 (Joint Committee on Printing, 1897). Only by retaining effective control over the Court can American democracy flourish.

20. See Frank Michelman, *Brennan and Democracy* (Princeton University Press, 1999).

21. Also overlooked is the role of the executive even in a regime of judicial review. For example, it has recently been argued that Roosevelt's Justice Department set the standard of conduct on race for the Truman and Eisenhower presidencies. Kevin J. McMahon, *Reconsidering Roosevelt on Race: How the Presidency Paved the Road to Brown* 201 (University of Chicago Press, 2004).

22. Mark Tushnet, *Democracy Versus Judicial Review: Is It Time to Amend the Constitution?* (Dissent, 2005).

23. The party line in constitutional scholarship—one that in my view misreads case law from *Marbury* on—is that judicial supremacy did not arrive until *Cooper v. Aaron*, 358 U.S. 1 (1978).

24. James B. Thayer, *The Origin and Scope of the American Doctrine of Constitutional Law*, 7 Harv. L. Rev. 129, 136 (1893).

25. Tushnet, *Taking the Constitution away from the Court*, at 57–65.

26. No doubt, legislative delegitimatization of Jim Crow in the South during the period from 1920 to 1954 would have been impossible or next to impossible. But using this as a reason for choosing a judicial strategy to abolish racial apartheid over a legislative one is plausible only if one already assumes that the courts institutionally are better than legislatures at bringing about authentic change. Without that assumption, the same prelegislative tactics that drove the nonviolent activism of the civil rights movement, might have been far more effective—though undoubtedly far more dangerous—than pursuing a judicial strategy. Moreover, the voting rights of southern blacks were not actualized until the Voting Rights Act of 1965. *Brown* was ineffective in securing these rights without legislative intervention.

27. In fact, some commentators argue that the decisions in *Board of Educ. of Oklahoma City Pub. Sch. v. Dowell*, 498 U.S. 237 (1991) and *Freeman v. Pitts*, 503 U.S. 467 (1992) have begun to return our constitutional conception of racial policy back toward *Plessy*. Robert L. Hayman Jr. and Nancy Levit, *The Constitutional Ghetto*, Wisc. L. J. (1993), at 632. I do not suggest that legislative decisions are not reversible or even that they are less readily reversible than judicial decisions. The question of which institutions are more likely to reverse fundamentally important political and moral decisions, the legislature or judiciary, is one that political science must answer.

28. In this regard, *Brown* seems to make questions of race irrelevant to the problems African Americans face. If *Brown* has brought about equality, there is no need to contemplate more radical transformation in race relations. Louis Michael Seidman, *Brown and Miranda*, 80 Calif. L. Rev. 673, 714.

29. So sayeth the Court, not I.

30. Jack Balkin rejects the counter-majoritarianism complaint. According to Balkin, the Supreme Court acts in concert with national majorities against regional majorities. Balkin, *What Brown v. Board of Education Should Have Said*, at 2–3. Others contend that judicial review occurs in part because the elected branches want it to occur, making judicial supremacy at best infrequent and at worst a myth. This latter claim cries out for an examination that cannot be conducted now.

31. Societal changes typically involve direct political action, legislation, and litigation. Arguably, only litigation was a realistic strategy in the 1950s. See Balkin, *What Brown v. Board of Education Should Have Said*, at 15.

32. See Rosenberg, *The Hollow Hope*, and Klarman, *From Jim Crow to Civil Rights*. Notwithstanding these sobering denials of *Brown*'s causal efficacy, many people refuse to be shaken in their confidence that the Civil Rights Acts of 1964 and 1965 would have ever been passed if not for the momentum—even if largely symbolic—begun by *Brown*.

33. Put another way, "judicial review simply puts legislated programs of affirmative action at risk." Mark Tushnet, *Taking the Constitution away from the Court*.

34. Unless, of course, absent *Brown*, the Court resurrected *Korematsu*, which was the first case to articulate strict scrutiny for racial classifications. Oddly, though Thurgood Marshall discussed *Korematsu* in his brief for *Brown*, the *Brown* opinion makes absolutely no mention of *Korematsu*'s analytic framework, which might have made the reasoning in *Brown* from the interpretive perspective more plausible.

35. When *Brown* was decided, its principle was progressive; a generation later this same principle was used to bankrupt any strong implementation of affirmative action. At least one interpretation of the principle in *Brown*, a progressive principle in itself, becomes used to block broader advances in racial justice. This phenomenon of "ideological drift" should startle anyone interested in conceptual and moral change. J. M. Balkin, *Ideological Drift and the Struggle over Meaning*, 25 Conn. L. Rev. 869, 871 (1993) (stating, "Ideological drift in law means that legal ideas and symbols will change their political valence as they are used over and over again in new contexts. This description envisions an idea or symbol changing its political significance over time while its content is held constant"). Perhaps an even greater cost is the Court's perverse use of *Brown* to virtually eviscerate *Brown's* imperative to institute and maintain integrated schools. *Parents Involved in Community Schools v. Seattle School Dist. No.* 1, 551 U.S. ___, 127 S.Ct. 2738 (2007). No better example exists of how judicial decisions, even great judicial decisions, are placed at risk by a system of judicial supremacy.

36. A more attractive interpretation of *Brown*, in my view, ties discrimination to subordination.

37. This is not an entirely fanciful hypothetical. *Black People Suffer Fewer Effects of Weight Gain, Studies Suggest*, Sunday News Journal, June 27, 2004 (reporting a study suggesting that overweight African Americans do not suffer the ill effects of weight gain to the same degree as whites).

38. By contrast, *Brown* seems to stand for the principle that even if schools for African Americans were in all respects better than white schools, and "even if their performance was superior to that of white students and superior to what could be achieved in an integrated school, still their educational opportunity would be unequal [inferior] to that afforded to whites." Louis Michael Seidman, *Brown and Miranda,* at 709. Such a view surely reflects a perspective replete with condescension and paternalism.

39. If true, it could be argued that integration prevented the natural development of African American children because they were in daily contact with their oppressors—white teachers and white students.

40. W. E. B. Dubois, *Does the Negro Need Separate Schools*? 4 J. Negro Educ. 328 (1935). Dubois was convinced that only by operating their own institutions would black Americans make the progress they would have made but for the racial hierarchy in American society. Dubois's view weighs in favor of paying African Americans reparations for the lost opportunities that white American stole from them.

41. *Id.*

42. The presence of sympathetic teachers in segregated schools for African American children suggests that integration, in effect, may not be a panacea. The experience of some members of the Delaware Milford Eleven is directly relevant here. Consider the words of Turner Sharp: "I loved Jason [the high school for Milford's African American children]. The teachers were interested in you learning—and to not be afraid to ask a question. I can't tell you how happy I was to be out [of the Milford High School]. When they say they kicked me out of the school, they did me a favor." Sunday News Journal, July 11, 2004, at A7, col. 3, 11.

43. Bell, *Silent Covenants*, at 112.

44. Given today's "sound-bite" political culture, mobilization now would be even easier and more effective than at earlier times in our history.

45. One captivating example is the record of African American pilots in World War II, who flew more than 15,000 sorties and destroyed more than 1,000 German aircrafts. For their valor, these pilots received hundreds of medals, including 150 Distinguished Flying Crosses.

46. Mary L. Dudziak, *Cold War Civil Rights: Race and the Image of American Democracy* 110 (Princeton University Press, 2000).

47. School segregation is rampant, and racism, at least in its extreme form, is on the rise. Regarding the latter, it is briskly sobering to learn that on May 15, 2004, white supremacists demonstrating in Topeka, Kansas, near the site of the Monroe School, presently a national museum, carried signs reading "White Students Are Victims of Brown" and "Integration Is State-Sponsored Terrorism." Photograph in 34 Southern Poverty Law Center Report (June 2004). When will such madness end?

48. Derrick Bell, *Race, Racism, and American Law* 27 (Aspen, 2000).

49. Some suggest that *Brown* is responsible for some of the difficulty in educating young African Americans. Again as Henry Louis Gates Jr. writes, "[I]n too many black neighborhoods today, academic achievement has actually come to be stigmatized. 'We are just not the same people anymore,' says the mayor of Memphis, Dr. Willie W. Herenton. 'We are worse off than we were before Brown v. Board,' says Dr. James Comer, a child psychiatrist at Yale.' And a large part of the reason for this is that we have abandoned our own black traditional core values, values that sustained us through slavery and Jim Crow segregation.'" Gates, *Breaking the Silence.*

CHAPTER SIXTEEN

The Centrality of *Brown*

Paul Finkelman

Introduction

In 1954 *Brown v. Board of Education* seemed like a revolution in law and justice. Just a few weeks after the term ended, Justice Stanley Reed of Kentucky, who had been the last holdout on the Court to endorse Chief Justice Earl Warren's opinion, said that *Brown* was the most important case in his fifteen years on the bench "and that if it was not the most important decision in the history of the Court, it was very close."[1] *Time* magazine declared that, except for *Dred Scott v. Sandford*, no other decision in the Court's history "was more important."[2] It was obvious how different those two cases were. Dred Scott is universally acknowledged as a "wrong" decision—many scholars and commentators consider it the worst decision in Supreme Court history. Even at the time it was decided many in the nation considered it morally wrong and constitutionally illegitimate.[3] *Brown*, on the other hand, was seen in much of the nation as a great moral victory. As the *Cincinnati Enquirer* noted shortly after *Brown*, the Court had acted as "the conscience of the American nation."[4] African Americans were, of course, particularly pleased with the decision in *Brown*. Upon hearing the result, Thurgood Marshall, who had successfully argued the case before the Supreme Court, recalled, "I was so happy I was numb."[5] Nearly a half-century after the decision, Professor Jack Balkin of Yale Law School correctly observed that *Brown* "is the single most honored opinion in the Supreme Court's corpus."[6] Harvard's Morton Horwitz, one of the nation's leading legal historians, concluded that *Brown* is "perhaps the most important judgment ever handed down by an American Supreme Court."[7]

It is somewhat ironic, then, that on the fiftieth anniversary of *Brown*, many scholars and some civil rights activists regarded the decision as a failure. Harvard Law School professor Charles Ogletree, although acknowledging that he has personally benefited from the "blessings and good fortune" of growing up in the wake of *Brown*, nevertheless reached the "sad conclusion . . . that fifty years after *Brown*

A version of this chapter previously appeared in the *Harvard Law Review*, 118 Harv. L. Rev. 973 (2005). Reprinted by permission of the author.

there is little left to celebrate."[8] Derrick Bell, the great civil rights activist, teacher, and scholar, suggested that the decision perhaps did more harm than good. He saw *Brown* as "unassertive" in its "finally failed implementation," and he wondered about the importance of a decision that "accomplished so little."[9] Indeed, Bell suggested that perhaps the Court should not have overturned the "separate but equal" doctrine set out in *Plessy v. Ferguson*, but rather should have enforced the "equal" prong of this test and required that southern—and northern—states give blacks equal education.[10]

The Inevitability of *Brown*

Michael Klarman, a law professor at the University of Virginia, echoes this pessimism in his prize-winning book, *From Jim Crow to Civil Rights*.[11] Klarman's particular critique has several prongs. First, he argues that *Brown* "[wa]s not an example of the Court's resistance to majoritarian sentiment, but rather of its conversion of an emerging national consensus into a constitutional command" (p. 310). Second, and relatedly, he argues that this consensus would have crystallized even in the absence of *Brown* (pp. 442, 468). Third, he claims that, although desegregation was inevitable, *Brown* nonetheless did contribute to the advancement of civil rights—but only by radicalizing southern politics and fomenting widespread violence, thereby speeding up the pace of reform (pp. 442, 452, 466). Klarman sees little value in *Brown* as a legal decision or as a moral basis for legal change, but rather sees its main value in the reaction it caused in the South. This chapter challenges these arguments.

Before turning to that critique, I first note three key reasons why we should not see *Brown* as a failure. First, the decision was not designed to create integrated schools across the nation. Critics of *Brown*, who argue that it failed to created a fully integrated school system, forget that this was not the goal of the decision and it was not the goal of the NAACP, which litigated the case. The goal of the NAACP in bringing the case, and of the Court in deciding it, was more modest. The goal was to abolish formally segregated schools: to get rid of the dual school system, which was almost entirely a southern phenomenon, and replace it with unitary schools. At a formal level, this goal has been accomplished; we no longer have separate schools. Most segregation today is due to housing patterns, employment patterns, and private decision making by white parents who have chosen to remove their children from the public schools. This outcome is not ideal, and it is dangerous to the health of our schools and our society, but it is unreasonable to blame this outcome on *Brown*. The Court could not undo years of economic and social discrimination or alter existing housing patterns in urban centers. Nor could the Court compel white parents to send their children to public, integrated, schools. But the Court could, and did, declare that the mandatory separation of the races was fundamentally wrong. That declaration was no small accomplishment; it was in fact a giant step toward real racial equality in America.

Second, it is important to see how much has changed because of *Brown*. In his opinion, Chief Justice Warren carefully distinguished between school segregation and other forms of segregation. He narrowly limited the case to schools, but the

Brown decision obviously had broader implications. Within a few years, the Court struck down all state-sponsored segregation. Only thirteen years after *Brown*, the Court abolished the last formal aspect of race discrimination, striking down Virginia's anti-miscegenation law in *Loving v. Virginia*.[12] Meanwhile, in the Civil Rights Act of 1964 and the Fair Housing Act of 1968, Congress prohibited almost all forms of private discrimination, and it revolutionized the protection of black political rights in the Voting Rights Act of 1965. It would be too much to argue that *Brown* was the sole cause of all of these changes. Many brave civil rights workers risked their safety—and some of them lost their lives—to achieve these goals. But it is hard to imagine that these changes could have occurred, or occurred so quickly, without *Brown*. Certainly, if the Court had reaffirmed *Plessy* in 1954, as Derrick Bell has suggested the Court should have done, it would be impossible to imagine the vast changes in civil rights of the next decade and a half coming so quickly and with relatively little violence. A reaffirmation of *Plessy*, even with a demand for strict enforcement to the "equal" aspect of the doctrine, would have also reaffirmed that blacks were in fact not equal. In *Brown*, Chief Justice Warren got it exactly right: "We conclude that, in the field of public education, the doctrine of 'separate but equal' has no place. Separate educational facilities are inherently unequal."[13]

Third, *Brown* was a cultural watershed. For the first time in our history, the Supreme Court spoke with authority on the wrongfulness of segregation. Not since the passage of the Civil Rights Act of 1875 had any branch of the federal government denounced discrimination so clearly and so emphatically. For decades many Americans had known that segregation was fundamentally wrong, even if they were unwilling to take a stand against it. In *Brown* the Court did precisely what Klarman argues a Court cannot do: it showed leadership—heroic leadership—and pointed the way to a new social order. For blacks this was a revolution. It is no wonder that Thurgood Marshall was "numb" after the decision.

Was Brown *the Product of Social Forces?*

Klarman devotes more than a third of his book to analyzing the decision-making process that led to the case. But although he attempts to situate *Brown* within his theory that judges reflect popular social opinion, his own research undermines that very position.

Relying on notes taken at Supreme Court conferences by Justices Burton, Clark, Douglas, and Jackson (p. 543, n. 6), Klarman demonstrates how members of the Court struggled with the case in the 1952 term, when *Brown* was first argued. He shows that the Justices expected there to be hostility to the decision, including violence, evasion, and outright defiance. Justice Hugo Black predicted that South Carolina would shut down its school system (p. 294). Justice Black was correct in predicting this tactic, but it would be some counties in Virginia, rather than South Carolina, that would follow this route. After a careful analysis of the notes of the Justices from the conferences, Klarman concludes that in 1952 there were four Justices ready to strike down segregation (Black, Douglas, Burton, and Minton), two opposed to striking down segregation (Vinson and Reed), and three (Frankfurter, Jackson, and Clark) who were ambivalent (p. 278).[14]

The position of these last three Justices illustrates the problem segregation and the *Brown* litigation posed for many Americans. These Justices knew that segregation was morally wrong, but Klarman notes that they were unconvinced about the constitutionality of striking down the separate but equal doctrine (pp. 295–97). These Justices were surely capable of finding a constitutional hook to reach that result, as in fact they ultimately did. What the Justices lacked in 1952, it seems, was the leadership to take them where the majority of them knew they ought to go. They also needed someone to steel their nerves to go there. In what is the best part of his book, Klarman offers a wonderful analysis of each Justice's background and ideology to explain why some in 1952 were ready and willing to take a difficult step toward a needed revolution in race relations, whereas others were not. For example, Justice Black, the fearless Alabaman, knew the dangers of striking down segregation better than anyone on the Court, but unlike Justices Frankfurter, Jackson, and Clark, he was ready from the beginning to accept those risks. Klarman offers a cogent argument about the history of the Court since the New Deal to conclude that it "is not surprising" that the Justices "would be uneasy about invalidating segregation" (p. 307). All their lives they had been critical of judicial activism. They had grown up hating *Lochner* and the judicial activism of the Court from the 1880s to the 1930s (pp. 307–8), and now they were contemplating a very activist decision that would overthrow the settled law of at least eighteen states.

Klarman effectively demonstrates that the *Brown* decision was not a foregone conclusion. Change the personnel, as he notes, and the case goes the other way. "Had there been five Stanley Reeds, *Plessy* would probably have been reaffirmed" (p. 308). Five Stanley Reeds is not so farfetched. In 1941, President Roosevelt put the arch-segregationist James F. Byrnes of South Carolina on the Bench. Fortunately, Byrnes resigned fifteen month later to go back to politics. From 1950 to 1955 he was the segregationist governor of South Carolina who denounced *Brown* and opposed all integration. Had Vinson not died and James Byrnes remained on the Bench, the Court might have had one Reed, one Vinson, and one James Byrnes. Had those three conservatives persuaded two of the fence sitters, perhaps Frankfurter and Clark, to join them, *Brown* might have been decided in 1953 with a very different outcome. Alternatively, even if the Court did not support a reaffirmation of *Plessy*, there would have been at best a 6-3 decision for integration. Klarman's own history of the discussion within the Court, plus the realization that *Brown* might have been 6-2 instead of 9-0, undermines one of Klarman's major arguments about *Brown* and more generally about how the Court works. He claims that the Court mirrors public opinion and that the Justices are neither heroes nor villains. But a small change in personnel and suddenly, the outcome is different. Moreover, it is clear that the ultimate decision in *Brown* did not fully mirror public opinion. Klarman shows how World War II and some tentative civil rights advances in the 1940s set the stage for *Brown*,[15] but argues that because of these few civil rights advanced, *Brown* simply reflected the age in which it was decided. But Klarman also asserts that when the Court decided *Brown* "about half of all Americans agreed with that ruling" (p. 443). This of course means that about half of all Americans *did not* agree with the outcome.

The internal conflict in the Court shows that *Brown* was not simply a reflection of the times. *Brown* forced a number of the Justices, especially Frankfurter, to reject some of their long-held jurisprudential views. The case also forced some of the Justices, like Reed, to reconsider their personal prejudices and deeply held beliefs about proper social relations.

Brown was without question an "activist" opinion, along the lines of those that struck down progressive legislation earlier in the century and New Deal legislation from 1933 to 1937. Here the Court was interfering with state legislative and social experimentation in just the way that the *Lochner* Court had. Justices such as Frankfurter had spent much of their careers fighting this kind of jurisprudence. Now they were being asked to implement it. Thus, the Justices had to overcome a good deal of public opinion and, more important, a great deal of legal culture and their own personal jurisprudential values to reach the conclusion that they did. In other words, they had to bestir themselves to make a hard choice. One might call this heroic; certainly, it is to be commended and praised. Rarely has the Court so unequivocally done the right thing.

The foregoing analysis of the jurisprudential issues surrounding *Brown* leads to Klarman's main critique of *Brown*: that it was the wrong case and the wrong decision because it led to violence and radicalization in the South and because it did not accomplish its goal.

Did Brown *Prompt Southern Radicalization and Violence?*

Klarman argues that *Brown* intensified Southern radicalism[16] and led to massive violence. He claims that this violence did speed up the pace of civil rights reform, but only because the violence led to federal intervention to protect civil rights. Because he believes such reforms were inevitable (because *Brown* was a product of its time), Klarman argues progress could have been achieved more peacefully in the absence of *Brown*. This is both logical and historical inconsistency with this argument. *If* the Court's decision was a product of its times, then there should not have been violent opposition to it. Since there was such opposition (although, as I argue below, it was not particularly violent), then *Brown* surely was not a product of its time and thus an end to separate schools was not inevitable.

Klarman's claim that *Brown* led to increase southern radicalism is curious. He argues that after *Brown* the South "abandoned the tried-and-true evasive techniques that for decades had successfully nullified the constitutional rights of blacks, in favor of outright defiance" (p. 462). Thus, the South "declared war on the Court" and "nullified *Brown*" (p. 462). Whether this defiance was so bad, in the long run, is open to question. *Brown* was a radical, indeed revolutionary, decision. It struck at the core of segregation and racism. Thus, we should not be surprised that *Brown* resulted in southern resistance. Klarman argues that *Brown* "radicalized politics" and "fomented violence" (pp. 465–66). Klarman also argues that the response to *Brown* "increased the chances that once civil rights demonstrators appeared on the streets, they would be greeted with violence rather than with gradualist concessions" (p. 468). This claim, along with the assertion that *Brown* was a failure, is the center of Klarman's argument that school desegregation was an exceedingly dangerous approach for the NAACP to take and that other litigation efforts, such as those aimed at voting rights, might have produced more peaceful (albeit slower) solutions.

It is not clear, however, how much of the violence was caused by *Brown* or even by school desegregation orders. The closest thing to a truly violent response to school desegregation occurred in Little Rock. But no one was killed in Little Rock, and there was not really much violence. Troops were called out, the city was "occupied," and desegregation took place. The resistance to school desegregation was massive, of course, and continues in some ways to this day, at least on the social level. Little Rock was, in the end, a dispute about power—the power of the courts, the power of the president, and the power of the governor of Arkansas. Governor Orval Faubus and his segregationist allies overplayed their hand, ultimately compelling President Eisenhower to use the power of the national government to enforce court orders. But the violence was quite limited and stands in dramatic contrast to the violence in other parts of the South against the civil rights movement and against calls for integration that did not involve the public elementary and secondary schools. The integration of the University of Mississippi led to violence, riots, and death.[17] "Ole Miss" as a symbol of segregation led to much more violence than Little Rock. But this violence was not a result of *Brown*, and it did not involve the traditional public elementary and secondary schools, which were at issue in *Brown*. The freedom rides did not lead to any deaths, but scores of civil rights workers were savagely beaten by mobs as the police looked on or even helped the mobs. The freedom riders were not fighting for school desegregation, but were trying to desegregate public transportation. Southern white terrorists bombed the house of Martin Luther King Jr. because of the Montgomery bus strike, not school integration.

Klarman claims that *Brown* caused all this violence because it radicalized southern politics. He argues that "[i]n the absence of post-*Brown* political fanaticism . . . one can imagine freedom riders arriving in Birmingham and Montgomery without police commissioners inviting Klansmen to beat them, and one can imagine blacks demonstrating for voting rights in Selma without law enforcement officers brutalizing them" (p. 442). Quite frankly, it is impossible to "imagine" the world as Klarman does. Klarman believes that *Brown* led to violence, but in fact it rarely did. There were some instances of mobs preventing integration—Little Rock is the most obvious example—and even the occasional bombing of a school.[18] However, the violence over school desegregation paled in comparison to the lethal bombings triggered by demands for public accommodations desegregation and the murders of voting rights activists. Klarman argues that *Brown* "created concrete occasions in which violent opposition to school desegregation was likely" (p. 441), but he does not discuss this violence because there was almost none to discuss. In fact, the opposition to *Brown* was for the most part quite nonviolent; although *Brown* predated some racial violence, as mentioned above, it is curious that virtually all the violence of the civil rights period (roughly 1950 to 1967) occurred outside the context of public school desegregation orders. In response to court-ordered integration, the strategy—developed by people such as Lewis Powell, the future Supreme Court Justice—was to delay, defy, massively resist, and evade the law. But this strategy was not a "radicalization," and it was not violent. The southern states were prepared to fight a long-running battle against school desegregation in the district courts and in school boards. Some counties in Virginia closed their public schools rather than integrate. But this was not a battle in the streets, and it did not involve violence.

Klarman's claim is that *Brown* created an inflamed atmosphere that led to widespread violence. That such violence occurred is indisputable. But for *Brown* to have been the spark, one would think that the very instances of its implementation would have been among those that involved violence. Significantly, most of the civil rights violence—the police attacks on marches at the Edmund Pettis Bridge, the bombing of the Birmingham schools, the murders in Philadelphia, Mississippi, occurred a number of years after *Brown*, and had nothing to do with school desegregation.

Believing that *Brown* was the spark for violence, Klarman then makes the case that voting rights would have been a more direct and peaceful tool for achieving civil rights. He claims that the Supreme Court's decision in *Smith v. Allwright* (1944),[19] which abolished the white primary, "launched a revolution in politics in the urban South" (p. 454). If so, it was one of the quietest revolutions in history. Even Klarman concedes that in 1952, nearly a decade after *Smith*, "[e]ighty percent of southern blacks were still disfranchised" (p. 451). By 1960 there was only a minuscule number of black elected officials in the former Confederacy, even in the urban South. Some southern cities had a few black policemen, and there were a handful of black elected officials in the Upper South, such as in Delaware.[20] Oliver Hill, one of the lawyers who would later argue *Brown*, won a Richmond, Virginia, city council seat for one term in 1948, but was defeated in 1950. Blacks were otherwise shut out of political power in that state until after the Voting Rights Act of 1965.[21]

Klarman is correct that *Smith v. Allwright* led to an increase (although hardly a numerically impressive one) of black voters in the South, but it is not clear how effective it was in changing southern politics, except in a very few places, such as Atlanta. *Smith* came out of Texas, but the decision had almost no effect on electoral politics in Texas. After *Smith* a few blacks served as precinct judges in black precincts, but not until Hattie Mae White won a seat on the Houston School Board in 1958 was there a black elected officeholder in the state. Significantly, White's election to an at-large seat took place at the time blacks were seeking integration under *Brown*. This fact seems to undermine Klarman's contention that *Brown* made things worse for blacks in the South. In this election, voters in Houston, including white voters, were willing to support a black candidate campaigning for school integration. However, the overall impact of *Smith* was minimal in the state. Indeed, despite *Smith*, no blacks won election to the Texas state legislature in the twentieth century until 1966.[22]

Klarman claims that voting rights litigation would have brought about peaceful reform, but it is impossible to imagine how a *Brown*-like decision on voting rights would have led to less violence in the South. The most violent responses to the civil rights movement came when there were attempts to gain political rights. Klarman argues that the South was more willing to accept an integrated electorate than integrated public schools. Thus, he suggests that the NAACP might have been better off moving on voting rights instead of schools. But the history of civil rights suggests that Southern whites were enormously hostile to black voters, especially in the Deep South, where blacks were most concentrated.

In 1951, three years before *Brown*, Klansmen, perhaps working with the local sheriff, assassinated Harry T. Moore, the leader of the NAACP in Florida.[23] During his twenty years as a schoolteacher, Moore became active in registering black voters throughout the state. After he was fired from his teaching position in 1946 because of his activism, he continued to work for voter registration. The tragedy of Moore's murder suggests that any attempts to undermine segregation and the white southern power structure would have been met by a radical response. In addition to Moore's killing, there were several other voting-related murders in the South in the period before the decision in *Brown* that could have radicalized the region. Klarman details some violent incidents in passing, noting the murders, bombings, and savage beatings of blacks in Georgia, Louisiana, Mississippi, and Florida (p. 250).

These pre-*Brown* murders and beatings undermine Klarman's Pollyanna-ish understanding of southern race relations between World War II and *Brown*. These incidents also undermine his arguments that school desegregation struck a particular nerve in the South that led to radicalization and that *Brown* provoked more backlash than "earlier racial changes" (p. 392). If public school integration was more incendiary than other types of racial reform, it would not have been the case that voting rights agitation—and not school integration—provoked the greatest levels of violence. Murdering people who were involved in voter registration was a far more radical response than a few Virginia counties' closing of their schools to avoid integration. No one was murdered trying to register black children in the public schools; people were murdered trying to register black voters.

After *Brown*, the most violent responses to civil rights continued to be focused not on schools, but on voting and the integration of transportation and public accommodations. Attempts to register voters provoked a number of murders, including those of Michael Schwerner, Andrew Goodman, and James Chaney in Philadelphia, Mississippi. The Selma-to-Birmingham march led to the sickening attacks by the Alabama state police on marchers at the Edmund Pettus Bridge. That march focused on voter registration, not school integration. On that march the Klan murdered a white volunteer from Detroit, Viola Liuzzo, a mother of five children who came south to work for racial justice. In 1964, Klansmen murdered Lemuel Penn outside of Athens, Georgia, because they incorrectly believed he had come from out of town to test the new Civil Rights Act. The motivation for this murder had nothing to do with school integration.

Klarman argues that voting rights would have been a more productive route for ending segregation because voting would have led to a shift in political power. He asserts that *Smith v. Allwright* "had more dramatic short-term consequences for black voter registration than *Brown* had for school desegregation" (p. 454) and also argues that "southern whites were far less committed to preserving black disenfranchisement than they were to maintaining school segregation" (p. 200).[24] Yet Klarman later notes that in 1952 only 20 percent of Southern blacks could vote (p. 451) and that "southern whites would not permit most blacks to vote until Congress forced them to" (p. 452). This is hardly impressive evidence that *Smith v. Allwright* had a "dramatic short-term consequence." Klarman observes that enfranchisement happened "only after *Brown* had elicited and exposed the most brutal aspects of Jim Crow, to the horror of national television audiences" (p. 452). Here Klarman is partially right, but also deeply wrong. He is absolutely correct that the violence perpetrated on civil rights demonstrators changed "national opinion" (p. 452) and led to the Civil Rights Act of 1964 and the Voting Rights Act of 1965. But the bulk of this televised violence[25] was not connected to *Brown* or public school desegregation. The most dramatic violence—in Alabama, Mississippi, Louisiana, and Georgia—came in response to voter registration drives and attempts to integrate public transportation and public accommodations.[26] In parts of Louisiana, for example, "[s]hootings and arson soon became commonplace" in the early 1960s when blacks tried to register to vote. The violence perpetrated against advocates of black voting precisely illustrates why a fight for voting rights was even more problematic and more dangerous than a fight for school integration.

Furthermore, voting rights might have been even harder to secure than school desegregation. The states required children to attend school. Thus, once assignments to integrated schools were made, the students had a legal right to attend them and the parents had a legal obligation to bring their children to school. If whites boycotted the schools, blacks would still have access to the newly integrated public schools, and often to the better facilities of the previously all white school. By contrast, there is no legal obligation to vote. Voting requires an act of will. But voters are reluctant to act if they fear violence or murder committed by white terrorist organizations like the Ku Klux Klan or retribution exacted by their white employers. Cumbersome registration procedures also inhibited voting by African Americans and other minorities. Today, black children in the South attend schools that are no longer formally segregated. But large numbers of black adults—far more than whites—are not registered to vote. To this day there are persistent allegations of intimidation by the police and other public officials of black voters in some southern states.[27]

Klarman claims that "[b]y the early 1960s, most southern whites could probably have tolerated desegregated transportation and black suffrage, had *Brown* not converted all racial challenges, in their minds, into fundamental assaults on Jim Crow" (p. 442). This assertion is implausible given the violence that was occurring before *Brown* and given that most of the violence after *Brown* was not focused on school segregation issues. It is unlikely that southern whites could have perceived demands for integrated transportation or the right to vote as anything but "fundamental assaults on Jim Crow," even in the absence of *Brown*. It is hard to understand why Klarman can imagine that demands for integrated transportation, or the right to vote, were not "fundamental assaults on Jim Crow." Klarman seems to be arguing that southern blacks should have quietly asked for piecemeal changes—bus integration, perhaps access to a lunch counter here and there, perhaps being allowed to vote in some places. He further imagines that the white South was willing to accept such incremental, piecemeal changes, but he believes that this opportunity for such gradualist chipping away at segregation was destroyed by *Brown*, which radicalized the South because it threatened all forms of segregation.

Klarman's speculations about what might have been are undermined by the reality of what actually did happen. *Brown* did not lead to any significant violence in the South. But the assaults on other pillars of segregation—transportation, public facilities, public accommodations, employment, and the voting booth—all resulted in strong and often violent resistance. Thus, Klarman's claim that *Brown* "provoked greater white resistance than did earlier racial changes" (p. 392) seems wrong or at least misleading. *Brown* led to political resistance and legal subterfuge, such as school-assignment laws designed to prevent integration. But *Brown* did not lead to very much violent resistance.[28]

The two most dramatic murders of southern civil rights leaders—Medgar Evers in 1963 and Reverend Martin Luther King Jr. in 1968—had nothing to do with school integration. Both men led movements that threatened the economic and political power structures of the South. King in particular had never been at the forefront of the school issue. He was concerned about segregation and economic justice on a broad scale, and most of his energies were directed at issues beyond schools. His fame came from the bus boycott and the Selma campaign, which were about transportation and voting, respectively. It was the challenge to segregation across the board, and not just to schools, that led to much of the violence in the South. To put it bluntly, no one died trying to register a child in an elementary school; people did die trying to register black voters.

What Brown *Accomplished*

Reading Klarman, one would think that *Brown*'s primary accomplishment was to fan the flames of southern violence. This portrayal does a tremendous disservice to a decision that changed the face of America. A full picture of what *Brown* accomplished can only be understood by looking at what America, especially the South, looked like on the eve of *Brown*. It would be too much to argue that *Brown* singlehandedly destroyed segregation. Other forces contributed to integration as well, including the broader civil rights movement, the brave acts and martyrdom of many activists, and the actions taken by the federal government—particularly President Eisenhower's use of federal troops at Little Rock, President Kennedy's intervention at the University of Mississippi, and President Johnson's forceful support of civil rights. With the Civil Rights Act of 1964 and then the Voting Rights Act of 1965, Congress also played a critical role in bringing an end to segregation. It is unlikely that those laws would have been passed without the activism in the South and the horrible violence perpetrated against civil rights demonstrators by southern vigilantes and southern law enforcement officers as well as the murders and assassinations by white terrorists. The fire hoses in Birmingham, the billy clubs at the Edmund Pettus Bridge—both seen throughout the nation on television—and the murders in Philadelphia, Mississippi, shocked Northerners, both in and out of Congress, into realizing that the South would never voluntarily accept racial equality.[29] It could only come about by legislation and its enforcement.

Although all of these events, actions, and laws were critical, it is impossible to imagine that the civil rights revolution would have succeeded so quickly in sweeping away de jure segregation without *Brown*—and not, as Klarman asserts, because *Brown* ushered in the violence that prompted the revolution. Rather, it is because *Brown* fundamentally undermined all segregation laws, even though Chief Justice Warren limited it to schools. The logic of *Brown* led to a further attack on segregation in public accommodations and to demands for equal voting rights. Furthermore, *Brown* gave civil rights activists courage by signaling that one branch of the national government was unanimously in favor of their cause. Without *Brown*, civil rights demonstrators might have been afraid to openly challenge segregation. With *Brown*, they dared to struggle, because they knew they had a powerful ally in Washington.

In *Brown*, Chief Justice Warren and his colleagues sent a strong moral message—a heroic message—that the Court would no longer tolerate segregation. That message logically led to decisions protecting civil rights workers and striking down various forms of segregation. The Civil Rights Act of 1964 and the Voting Rights Act of 1965 were the logical outcome of *Brown*. To put it another way, had the Court ducked the issue of separate but equal in *Brown* or had the Court simply demanded equalization of facilities, as Derrick Bell argued on the fiftieth anniversary of *Brown*, there would have been no institution providing the moral authority to lead to an end to segregation. However equal, blacks would have remained separate and distinctly second class. The moral authority of *Brown* mattered as such, and mattered a great deal. It is no wonder Thurgood Marshall pinched himself with delight after the decision. However limited its scope or slow the timetable for its implementation, he immediately understood that the decision would bring an end to legalized segregation soon—and it did.

To understand the importance of *Brown*—to see why *Brown* was such a great success—we must recall the state of American race relations in the years before *Brown*. Despite the modest racial advances that followed World War II, *Brown* in fact came down during an era of widespread racial discrimination and oppression. In the early 1950s, the United States was a profoundly segregated country. The majority of blacks, just under 70 percent, lived in the South, where segregation was deeply entrenched in the law and culture of the society. Blacks in the North did not face the day-to-day de jure segregation of the South, and some northern states banned discrimination and segregation. Nevertheless, many northern blacks lived in a society in which informal and de facto segregation affected their lives in myriad ways. In 1947 the President's Committee on Civil Rights reported that "New York State, in particular, has an impressive variety of civil rights laws on its statute books"[30] and that a "few other states and cities have followed suit, especially in the fair employment practice field." However, many, perhaps most, privately owned businesses ignored such laws and rarely had to defend their actions in the courts. Blacks reported that, despite laws that prohibited discrimination and explicit segregation, it was "difficult to find a meal or a hotel room in the downtown areas of most northern cities." Enforcement of such laws was lax, and businesses "discouraged [blacks] from patronizing places by letting them wait indefinitely for service, charging higher prices, giving poor service, and publicly embarrassing them in various ways."[31] Although illegal, "whites only" signs could still be found in some places in the North. But generally such signs were unnecessary, as some businesses simply refused to serve or accommodate blacks.

Throughout the North, de facto segregation was common in housing, which led to separation of the races in many public schools. In some parts of the North, especially southern Illinois and Indiana, schools were segregated by local officials, despite state laws prohibiting such practices. Northern public colleges and universities were integrated, but blacks were often treated as second-class students.[32]

However bad conditions for blacks were in the North, it was the South where segregation was most virulent and oppressive, and of course that is where seven out of ten blacks lived. On the eve of *Brown*, Southern blacks faced discrimination and segregation at every turn in their lives. If born in a hospital, southern blacks entered the world in a separate hospital; they would be buried in a segregated cemetery.[33] It was "generally illegal for Negroes to attend the same schools as whites; attend theaters patronized by whites; visit parks where whites relax; eat, sleep, or meet in hotels, restaurants, or public halls frequented by whites."[34] This list was "only a partial enumeration" of the "highly refined" system of statutorily mandated discrimination that "cut[] across the daily lives of southern citizens from the cradle to the grave." It was a system that "brand[ed] the Negro with the mark of inferiority and assert[ed] that he [was] not fit to associate with white people."[35]

Virtually all public and private educational institutions in the South, from nursery school to college, were segregated. The only exceptions were a few small, private, historically black colleges that occasionally had a white student or two[36] and a few state graduate and professional schools that were integrated in the late 1940s and early 1950s as a result of lawsuits based on the failure of southern states to provide similar educational opportunities for blacks.[37] In the Upper South, a very small number of state colleges and universities had begun to accept some black undergraduates in programs such as architecture and engineering, in which state-funded historically black colleges did not provide training.

Klarman vastly exaggerates the pace of integration of graduate and professional schools in the South, claiming that in the years before *Brown* "most southern states had peacefully desegregated graduate and professional schools under lower court orders. . . . Even in the Deep South, four of Louisiana's seven public universities had desegregated" (p. 393). He makes this point to bolster his argument that *Brown* retarded racial progress in the South. But in fact, there had been very little progress. Most graduate and professional programs in the South were still segregated in 1954, and those that were integrated had for the most part only a few blacks in their programs. For example, Horace Ward applied to the University of Georgia Law School in 1950, only to be rejected. After a protracted legal battle, a federal judge finally dismissed Ward's suit in 1957; Ward ended up attending Northwestern University Law School. The University of Alabama did not accept its first black graduate student until 1956. Klarman himself describes the refusal of the University of Florida Law School to admit Virgil Hawkins during a nine-year litigation odyssey that ended in 1958 when Hawkins entered Boston University's graduate school (pp. 256–58). No blacks were in the graduate or professional programs at the University of Mississippi or South Carolina during this period.[38] Even where graduate programs accepted blacks, they did so under the rubric of "separate but equal." Thus, the University of Virginia accepted a black law student only because there was no law school at the state's only public institution of higher education for blacks, Virginia State College. For the same reason, the state schools accepted some black undergraduates before *Brown*. Black applicants would only be granted admission to the University of Virginia or Virginia Polytechnic Institute if the programs they sought were unavailable at Virginia State College. "For the most part segregation in higher education persisted" in Virginia in the years before *Brown*.[39]

In 1948, in response to the emerging graduate and professional school cases, the governors of fourteen segregating states entered into a "regional compact" to provide segregated graduate and professional education for Southern blacks. Their plan was to provide segregated graduate education somewhere in the South for all fields, by spreading out the programs across the South. The regional compact was never implemented in any serious way, and even if it had been, it would probably have done little for black education in the South. In reality, most southern states ignored the education of their black citizens as much as they could. Louisiana, for example, created some twenty "trades schools" between 1934 and 1948 for whites, but did not provide any such schools for blacks. Klarman claims there was a "quiet revolution" in the South, as some two thousand blacks entered previously white universities in southern and border states by 1955 (p. 393). However, Klarman offers no evidence on where these students attended college. Only Delaware had opened its state university to a substantial number of blacks. Moreover, he does not indicate how many of these students entered previously all-white schools as a result of *Brown*. This "revolution" was so quiet in Louisiana and other parts of the Deep South—those places with the highest percentages of black residents—that it was barely heard at all. There was in fact no revolution in these places until *Brown* and its progeny forced revolutionary change.[40]

At the primary and secondary levels, the disparity in public expenditures guaranteed that blacks would have inferior educational facilities. Except where litigation forced equalization of salaries, principals, supervisors, and teachers in white schools were paid almost without exception more than those in black schools. Classes for blacks had more children than classes for whites, schools for blacks were open fewer days, and the facilities were vastly inferior. One of the four cases that was consolidated as part of the *Brown* litigation was *Briggs v. Elliot*, which came from Clarendon County, South Carolina. The situation in that county illustrates the reality of segregated public education in the pre-*Brown* South, and illustrates why the NAACP and black parents decided to fight segregation in the public schools—where their children were being deprived of the tools necessary to compete in the economies of postwar America. In the 1949–50 school year, the county spent $179 per pupil for white children and $43 per pupil for black children. The county had sixty-one school buildings, which were worth $194,575, for its 6,531 black students. The 2,375 white students went to twelve different schools, worth a total of $673,850. The schools for blacks were dilapidated at best; some were "plain falling-down shanties." They lacked modern heating or indoor plumbing. In this very rural county, the school system refused to provide a bus for black children, although it provided school buses for whites. Indeed, it was the refusal to provide a bus that led to the *Briggs* suit that eventually became part of the *Brown* litigation.[41]

The deplorable educational conditions across the South ultimately led the NAACP to target schools in its quest to end all segregation. Black leaders fully understood that poor schools crippled blacks in all other areas of society. Without a decent education, blacks were doomed, generation after generation, to face poverty and a lack of political and social power. Even while he argues that the schools were the wrong place to attack segregation, Klarman seems to understand why in fact they were the right place. He notes that "Jim Crow was so ruthless and pervasive that internally generated change was difficult to accomplish" (p. 444). Indeed, without school desegregation, blacks would have remained undereducated and therefore crippled in an economy that increasingly required some education for success. Klarman also claims that southern blacks in the early 1950s were more intent on fighting for voting rights than for integrated schools (p. 465). But given the requirements of literacy tests and poll taxes, it is hard to imagine how poor, undereducated blacks might have been able to vote, short of a massive federal intervention that was inconceivable in the 1950s. Given the long record of white violence and lynchings directed at blacks who tried to vote and at persons of both races who tried to register blacks to vote, it is not surprising that the NAACP did not initiate its attack on segregation at the ballot box. The murders of black and white activists involved in voter registration from the 1940s through 1965 illustrate the wisdom of this decision and the weakness of Klarman's argument.

Segregation also profoundly affected criminal justice in the South. On the eve of *Brown*, "some two-score southern cities" had at least a few black police officers.[42] Klarman trumpets this fact as the kind of success that meant race relations were changing. This conclusion in turn leads him to argue that *Brown* retarded these changes. But in reality, the few black policemen in some southern cities had almost no effect on the structure of the criminal justice system or the nature of race relations in the South. Most southern cities and towns did not in fact have any black policemen. Moreover, most southern blacks, after all, did not live in those cities with a few black policemen, and the number of black policemen was too small to affect very much. Most southern blacks still lived in rural areas and small towns, where policing was segregated and often oppressive. Moreover, there were no blacks on the state police forces, or highway patrols, in the deep South.[43] Police brutality toward blacks was the norm, and only the most egregious cases ever reached the federal courts, where some relief might be found.

If arrested, even by a black policeman, African Americans went to segregated jails and when convicted were sent to segregated prisons. In Florida and Georgia, it was illegal for any law enforcement officer to handcuff or chain blacks and whites together. Other southern states had similar laws and rules. Segregated facilities meant that black prisoners would face worse conditions than their white counterparts. No matter how bad jail and prison conditions were for whites, they would always be worse for blacks. Furthermore, the use of chain gangs gave public officials an incentive to prosecute all black lawbreakers vigorously, because convicts represented laborers who built and maintained roads and other public facilities.[44]

In court blacks were invariably represented by white attorneys, if they had representation at all. Because of the segregated educational system, very few blacks were able to attend law school. Even after *Sweatt v. Painter*, which integrated the University of Texas School of Law, most of the southern state law schools either remained segregated or had only a token number of black students. Although some white attorneys represented their clients with zeal and passion worthy of the fictional Atticus Finch,[45] others were dilatory or worse. In the age before *Gideon v. Wainwright*, poor defendants were not guaranteed a lawyer in noncapital cases, and thus many blacks faced the court system without any formal legal advice or help. They faced white judges and all-white juries. In the Deep South, prison often meant laboring on a chain gang or in a rural work camp, where life was truly Hobbesian: brutal and short.[46]

Virtually all other facilities were equally segregated. Southern states segregated homes for the aged, orphanages, and institutions for juvenile delinquents. Industrial schools were segregated where they existed. Louisiana had three industrial schools: one each for young white males, white females, and black males. Louisiana did not offer black female youthful offenders the option of learning a skill or trade in preparation for their rehabilitation.[47] In most southern states, African Americans with a hearing problem, a mental illness, or tuberculosis went to special institutions for blacks only. Ironically, even state schools for the blind were segregated in the South, even though presumably most of the students could not actually see each other. Louisiana required not merely that buildings to house and educate black and white blind children be separate, but that they be "on separate ground[s]." Although all of these institutions were in theory "separate but equal," in practice they were never equal. No matter how bad conditions might have been for whites, they were invariably worse for blacks.[48]

As the South became increasingly industrialized, segregation led to further economic marginalization for blacks. South Carolina provided $100 fines and up to thirty days imprisonment at hard labor for textile manufacturers or their officials who failed to follow elaborate rules for racial separation.[49] The law set out in great detail that no company engaged in textile or cotton manufacturing—the most important industry in the state—could allow members of

> different races to labor and work together within the same room, or to use the same doors of entrance and exit at the same time, or to use and occupy the same pay windows or doors for paying off its operatives and laborers at the same time, or to use the same stairway and windows at the same time, or to use at any time the same lavatories, toilets, drinking water buckets, pails, cups, dippers or glasses,

Other states had similar rules. In Oklahoma, Tennessee, and Texas, mines were required to have separate shower facilities and clothing lockers. These laws did more than just humiliate blacks and remind them of their inferior legal status. The laws also prevented them from advancing in their jobs or even getting jobs. Separate facilities for blacks meant that factory owners would have to invest more money in their mills, mines, and factories. It often made greater economic sense simply to hire only whites, leaving blacks outside of the growing industrial job market.[50]

Everywhere in the South, public accommodations were segregated by law—separate, but almost never actually equal. Southern states required separate drinking fountains, restrooms, motels, hotels, elevators, bars, restaurants, and lunch counters for blacks. Trains had separate cars for blacks, and buses reserved the last few rows for blacks, always keeping them, symbolically and literally, at the back of the bus. Taxis served whites or blacks, not both. Waiting rooms at bus stations, train stations, and airports were separate as well. At theaters blacks sat in separate sections at the back or in the balcony. Practice on these issues always varied. Although many states mandated separate waiting rooms at train and bus stations, Florida found yet one more way to segregate and humiliate blacks: by requiring that railroads also provide separate ticket windows for black travelers.[51]

Segregation pervaded social and recreational life as well. Louisiana required separate ticket windows and entrances at circuses and tent shows. A subsequent law required that these ticket offices be at least twenty-five feet apart. North Carolina banned interracial meetings of fraternal orders, and many cities and states followed Birmingham's segregation of "any room, hall, theatre, picture house, auditorium, yard, court, ball park, public park, or other indoor or outdoor place." Texas specifically prohibited interracial boxing, whereas most cities and towns segregated seating at baseball fields. Local ordinances or customs made it illegal for blacks and whites to compete against each other in sporting events or unlikely that they would do so. Some states made certain that such competition would not happen. Georgia specifically segregated billiard rooms and poolrooms. Missouri, South Carolina, and Oklahoma segregated public parks and playgrounds. In Louisiana it was illegal for blacks and whites to reside in the same dwelling, and the existence of "partitions, or separate entrances" would not be a defense to a charge under this law. Oklahoma provided for "segregation of the white and colored races as to the exercise of rights of fishing, boating and bathing" as well as "to the exercises [*sic*] of recreational rights" at parks, playgrounds, and pools. The state authorized the public service commission "to require telephone companies . . . to maintain separate booths for white and colored patrons."[52]

Even the sacred was not protected from Jim Crow. In what today would be seen as a clear violation of First Amendment protections of religious free exercise, Tennessee required that houses of worship be segregated. Texas and North Carolina segregated their public libraries by statute, although other states did not, presumably because no one in the state legislatures had ever imagined that blacks would be using public libraries. Nevertheless, when blacks tried to use them, they were either refused access or forced into segregated facilities. Georgia never seemed to tire of finding things to segregate and thus in its 1937–38 legislative session provided that the names of white and black taxpayers be entered separately in the tax digest. Similarly, Florida stored textbooks from black and white schools in different buildings.[53]

Such laws seem almost comical, as though the state legislatures constantly searched to find something new to segregate. As Judge William H. Hastie of the Third Circuit concluded, "The catalog of whimsies was long."[54] These "whimsies," codified by law, reminded blacks over and over again that in the American South, and much of the North, they could never expect equal treatment, even in houses of worship.

Beyond the statutes, the "whimsies" manifested themselves in customs and extralegal forms of segregation. In his classic study of American race relations, *An American Dilemma*, the economist Gunnar Myrdal observed the following in the 1940s:

> Every Southern state and most Border states have structures of state laws and municipal regulations which prohibit Negroes from using the same schools, libraries, parks, playgrounds, railroad cars, railroad stations, sections of streetcars and buses, hotels, restaurants and other facilities as do the whites. In the South there are, in addition, a number of sanctions other than the law for enforcing institutional segregation as well as etiquette. Officials frequently take it upon themselves to force Negroes into a certain action when they have no authority to do so.[55]

On the eve of *Brown*, the situation for blacks in the United States, North or South, was ugly and grim. Starting with a series of decisions around 1950, the Court began to chip away at segregation.[56] *Brown* accelerated this trend, and by the end of the decade the Court had applied the logic of *Brown* to virtually all aspects of legally mandated segregation. Finally, with the passage of the 1964 Civil Rights Act, virtually all private acts of discrimination came under attack. Before then, segregation was painful and pervasive. In 1963, just a year before the Civil Rights Act was passed, Reverend Martin Luther King Jr., in his famous "Letter from Birmingham Jail," described the nature of segregation, as he explained why blacks could no longer wait for equality:

> [W]hen you suddenly find your tongue twisted and your speech stammering as you seek to explain to your six-year-old daughter why she can't go to the public amusement park that has just been advertised on television, and see tears welling up in her eyes when she is told that Funtown is closed to colored children . . . when you have to concoct an answer for a five-year-old son who is asking: "Daddy, why do white people treat colored people so mean?"; when you take a cross-country drive and find it necessary to sleep night after night in the uncomfortable corners of your automobile because no motel will accept you; when you are humiliated day in and day out by nagging signs reading "white" and "colored"; when your first name becomes "nigger," your middle name becomes "boy" (however old you are) and your last name becomes "John," and your wife and mother are never given the respected title "Mrs."; when you are harried by day and haunted by night by the fact that you are a Negro, living constantly at tiptoe stance, never quite knowing what to expect next, and are plagued with inner fears and outer resentments; when you are forever fighting a degenerating sense of "nobodiness"—then you will understand why we find it difficult to wait.[57]

Conclusion: The Centrality of *Brown*

Brown set into motion the forces that eliminated segregation. For that reason, *Brown* remains the greatest decision of the last century and the centerpiece of justice in America. Klarman and the other critics of *Brown* are right that it did not accomplish all it might have. It did not lead to a full social revolution. Schools in America are segregated because our economy remains segregated. But rarely has any society seen such a great social change at such a small cost in human life and misery. Klarman is also correct that *Brown* radicalized southern politics. Why should we expect anything else? *Brown* was a frontal assault that threatened the entire social, political, and economic structure of the South. Yet it did not simply radicalize southern politics. It radicalized all American politics by pushing the nation to a rights-centered jurisprudence. That was its great accomplishment and legacy.

Klarman argues that *Brown* set back southern reform because of the backlash against the opinion (pp. 464–65). He believes that an assault on voting discrimination would have been more readily accepted in the South, even though no one died trying to achieve school integration and the Klan and other Southern terrorists murdered people to prevent voter registration. Blatant and pervasive voter discrimination only ended when Congress and the Johnson administration used federal registrars, the FBI, and federal marshals to enforce the Voting Rights Act. Federal intervention came about only because *Brown* changed the moral climate. And *Brown* could change the moral climate precisely because it was not about political power or economic power. It did not threaten those who had power. Rather, *Brown* put a human face to the horror and tragedy of segregation. It was a case about a seven-year-old girl who wanted to attend the elementary school closest to her home. Virtually all Americans could understand this.

Klarman is right that the Supreme Court cannot, by a simple decision, change society. Nor could a decree about schools alter housing patterns or economic status. Equal schooling remains an unachieved goal. The irony of *Brown* is that it led to the destruction of segregation virtually everywhere in our country except the schools. But having done so was no small accomplishment. Indeed, *Brown* led to a revolution in our social order, and it moved the nation along the path toward what should have always been a matter of simple justice.

Notes

1. Richard Kluger, *Simple Justice* 709 (Knopf, 1976) (quoting John Fassett, one of Justice Reed's clerks, who may have been paraphrasing the Justice's statement) (internal quotation marks omitted).
2. Time, May 24, 1954, at 21, quoted in *id.* at 709.
3. Paul Finkelman, *Dred Scott v. Sandford: A Brief History with Documents* 4–6 (Bedford, 1997).
4. Kluger, *Simple Justice*, at 710 (quoting an unspecified Cincinnati Enquirer editorial) (internal quotation marks omitted).
5. *Id.* at 714 (internal quotation marks omitted).
6. Jack M. Balkin, *Brown v. Board of Education: A Critical Introduction*, in *What Brown v. Board of Education Should Have Said: The Nation's Top Legal Experts Rewrite America's Landmark Civil Rights Decision*, ed. Jack M. Balkin, 3, 4 (New York University Press, 2001).
7. Morton J. Horwitz, *The Warren Court and the Pursuit of Justice* 15 (Hill and Wang, 1998).
8. Charles J. Ogletree Jr., *All Deliberate Speed: Reflections on the First Half Century of Brown v. Board of Education* xi (W. W. Norton, 2004).

9. See Derrick A. Bell, *Dissenting*, in *What Brown v. Board of Education Should Have Said*, at 185, 199 ("By dismissing *Plessy* without dismantling it, the Court seems to predict if not underwrite eventual failure").

10. Derrick Bell, *Silent Covenants: Brown v. Board of Education and the Unfulfilled Hopes for Racial Reform* 196 (Oxford University Press, 2004). One important exception to this trend, Robert J. Cottrol et al., *Brown v. Board of Education: Caste, Culture, and the Constitution* (University Press of Kansas, 2003), is a solid, careful, and elegantly written book that is clearly the best short history of the case. It is ideal for teaching not only about the case but also about the history of segregation. See also Robert J. Cottrol, *Justice Advanced: Comments on William Nelson's Brown v. Board of Education and the Jurisprudence of Legal Realism*, 48 St. Louis U. L. J. 839 (2004) (discussing the role of legal realism in *Brown* and concluding that the Court's decision was a response to profound changes in thinking about race); Jack Greenberg, *Brown v. Board of Education: An Axe in the Frozen Sea of Racism*, 48 St. Louis U. L. J. 869 (2004) (arguing that *Brown* made the United States more receptive to racial change).

11. Michael Klarman, *From Jim Crow to Civil Rights* (Oxford University Press, 2004).

12. 388 U.S. 1 (1967). For a history of this case, see Peter Wallenstein, *Tell the Court I Love My Wife: Race, Marriage, and Law—An American History* (Macmillan, 2002).

13. *Brown v. Board of Education*, 347 U.S. 483, 495 (1954).

14. Had James F. Byrnes remained on the Court, Sherman Minton would not have had a seat. With Justice Byrnes on the Court, there would have been three votes for upholding segregation, three for striking it down, and three that were uncertain. It is not hard to imagine two of the uncertain Justices joining Justices Vinson, Reed, and Byrnes, if not in support of segregation, then in support of *stare decisis*.

15. One of the more noted and symbolic advances was the integration of major league baseball. See, generally, Arnold Rampersad, *Jackie Robinson: A Biography* (Ballantine, 1997); Paul Finkelman, *Baseball and the Rule of Law Revisited*, 25 T. Jefferson L. Rev. 17 (2002).

16. Klarman asserts that "Court decisions . . . reflected social attitudes and practices more than they created them" (p. 443). But Klarman argues that *Brown* led to a radicalization of southern politics and that an assault on some other aspect of segregation might not have had the same effect. This argument is internally inconsistent. If the decision reflected popular opinion, then there should not have been an extreme backlash. The paradox is solved, of course, by understanding that *Brown* was a radical departure from some public opinion and that it did not in fact reflect the opinions of most southern whites. This fact certainly undermines Klarman's thesis that the Court reflected public opinion. Surely, the Southerners on the Court—Justices Black, Clark, and Reed—emphatically did not reflect the opinions of where they came from. At least these three Justices were "heroic" in their willingness to face the wrath of family and friends to achieve the right, just, and moral result.

17. William Doyle, *An American Insurrection: The Battle of Oxford, Mississippi, 1962* (Doubleday, 2001).

18. The few instances of desegregation-spurred violence that Klarman mentions involved assaults on particular desegregation advocates or their property (pp. 353, 411). Most of the incidents he recounts, however, were not the product of desegregation orders and were not targeted in particular at desegregation advocates.

19. 321 U.S. 649 (1944).

20. To Secure These Rights: The Report of the President's Committee on Civil Rights 19–21 (1947); see e-mail from Ellen Rendle, Curator of Maps and Photographs, Historical Society of Delaware, to Ronald Whittington, Special Assistant to the Dean, College of Human Services, Education, and Public Policy, University of Delaware, and Leland Ware,

Louis L. Redding Professor of Law and Public Policy, University of Delaware (Oct. 28, 2004, 15:35 EST) (on file with the Harvard Law School Library).

21. Peter Wallenstein, *Blue Laws and Black Codes: Conflict, Courts, and Change in Twentieth-Century Virginia* 103–4, 201 (University of Virginia Press, 2004).

22. Rupert N. Richardson et al., *Texas: The Lone Star State* 392 (9th ed.) (Prentice Hall, 2005); *id.* at 408. This was the year that Barbara Jordan won a seat in the Texas Senate and two black men were elected to the Texas House of Representatives.

23. Ben Green, *Before His Time: The Untold Story of Harry T. Moore, America's First Civil Rights Martyr* 9–10, 60–61 (University Press of Florida, 1999).

24. Michael R. Belknap, *Federal Law and Southern Order: Racial Violence and Constitutional Conflict in the Post-Brown South* 144–48, 160–61, 186–91 (University of Georgia Press, 1987). Klarman bases his conclusion on an opinion poll in the late 1940s that "showed a clear southern majority in favor of abolishing poll taxes" (p. 200). But this analysis is flawed for three reasons. First, almost all poor Southerners, white and black, opposed the poll tax. In much of the South, adults too poor to pay the tax made up a large percentage of the population. Opposition by only a small number of better-off whites was thus enough to create a majority against the tax. Second, as the first point implies, the poll tax disfranchised large numbers of whites; thus, opposition to it was not necessarily a valid reflection of support for black voting. Third, literacy tests, intimidation, and simply the difficulty of registering and voting were sufficient to suppress the black vote.

25. A possible exception was minor rioting in Little Rock in 1957—well before the push for the 1964 and 1965 Acts. *See* Belknap, *Federal Law and Southern Order*, at 44–51.

26. See, generally, Adam Fairclough, *Race and Democracy: The Civil Rights Struggle in Louisiana, 1915–1972* (University of Georgia Press, 1995); Belknap, *Federal Law and Southern Order.*

27. See Jennifer C. Day and Avalaura L. Gaither, *U.S. Census Bureau, Voting and Registration in the Election of November 1998*, at 4 tbl.B, 5 tbl.C (2000), available at http://www.census.gov/prod/2000pubs/p20–523.pdf; see, e.g., Don Van Natta Jr., *Democrats Tell of Problems at the Polls Across Florida*, N.Y. Times, Nov. 10, 2000, at A26.

28. The violence that did occur was relatively isolated. *See* Belknap, *Federal Law and Southern Order*, at 29–30.

29. See *id.* at 128–58, 183–84; Carl M. Brauer, *John F. Kennedy and the Second Reconstruction* 234 (Columbia University Press, 1977).

30. Campbell Gibson and Kay Jung, *Historical Census Statistics on Population Totals by Race, 1790 to 1990, and by Hispanic Origin, 1970 to 1990, for the United States, Regions, Divisions, and States* tbl.A-9 (Population Div., U.S. Census Bureau, Working Paper Series No. 56, 2002), http://www.census.gov/population/www/documentation/twps0056.html (the exact amount is 69.9 percent); To Secure These Rights, at 18, 78.

31. To Secure These Rights, at 78.

32. See Gunnar Myrdal, *An American Dilemma: The Negro Problem and Modern Democracy* 601–2 (Harper, 1944); Davison M. Douglas, *Jim Crow Moves North: The Battle over Northern School Segregation, 1865–1954* (Cambridge University Press, 2005); Davison M. Douglas, *The Limits of Law in Accomplishing Racial Change: School Segregation in the Pre-Brown North*, 44 UCLA L. Rev. 677, 709 (1997).

33. Pauli Murray found that only two states, Mississippi and South Carolina, specifically provided for segregation in public hospitals. Pauli Murray, *States' Laws on Race and Color* 17 (Women's Division of Christian Services, 1951). This finding illustrates the gap that sometimes existed between statutes and practice. Everywhere in the South, private and public hospitals were segregated. This separation was accomplished by local ordinance, administrative practice, interpretation of statutes, and custom. Furthermore, because no

federal laws or southern state laws prohibited private discrimination, nonpublic hospitals segregated patients or refused to treat blacks without any need for legislation. In many places cemeteries were segregated by local ordinance, custom, or the decision of the owner of the cemetery. North Carolina had a statute requiring this kind of segregation. See *id.* at 329–30.

34. To Secure These Rights, at 79.

35. *Id.*

36. J. Clay Smith Jr., *Emancipation: The Making of the Black Lawyer: 1844–1944* (University of Pennsylvania Press, 1993), 54–56 (discussing whites at Howard Law School and another black law school).

37. One school was integrated somewhat ahead of this trend: the University of Maryland Law School was integrated in 1935 as a result of litigation brought in state court by the NAACP. Maryland's highest court upheld the ruling in 1936, after Donald Gaines Murray had already enrolled in the University of Maryland Law School. *Pearson v. Murray*, 182 A. 590, 594 (Md. 1936). This case was the only civil rights victory of this kind won in a southern state court. For an excellent discussion of this litigation, see Kluger, *Simple Justice*, at 186–94. The U.S. Supreme Court also played a role in the integration of a few graduate institutions. See *McLaurin v. Okla. State Regents for Higher Educ.*, 339 U.S. 637, 642 (1950) (requiring equal treatment of African American students at the University of Oklahoma Graduate School of Education); *Sweatt v. Painter*, 339 U.S. 629, 636 (1950) (integrating the University of Texas Law School); *Sipuel v. Bd. of Regents of the Univ. of Okla.*, 332 U.S. 631, 632–33 (1948) (integrating the University of Oklahoma Law School). Although the NAACP challenged the states on the provision of "equal" education when they failed to integrate, none of these cases challenged segregation per se.

38. See Peter Wallenstein, *Black Southerners and Non-Black Universities: Desegregating Higher Education, 1935–1967*, 19 Hist. Higher Educ. Ann. 121, 127 (1999); Robert A. Pratt, *We Shall Not Be Moved: The Desegregation of the University of Georgia* 11, 52–61 (University of Georgia Press, 2002); *see Lucy v. Adams*, 350 U.S. 1, 1–2 (1955) (overturning *Lucy v. Adams*, 228 F.2d 620 (5th Cir. 1955), and ordering the University of Alabama to admit Autherine Lucy and Polly Anne Myers to its graduate school); Wallenstein at 107–8, 132–33; Peter Wallenstein, *Higher Education and Civil Rights: South Carolina, 1860s–1960s*, 23 Hist. Higher Educ. Ann. 1 (2004).

39. Wallenstein, a 108.

40. See Murray, *States' Laws on Race and Color*, at 666; *id.* at 666–75 (noting that the compact was probably constitutionally void in light of *Sweatt v. Painter*, 339 U.S. 629 (1950)); *id.* at 177–79; Gibson and Jung, *Historical Census Statistics on Population Totals by Race, 1790 to 1990*, app. A.

41. *See* To Secure These Rights, at 63–64; Kluger, *Simple Justice*, at 8; *Briggs v. Elliott*, 98 F. Supp. 529 (1951) (E.D.S.C. 1951), *vacated and remanded*, 342 U.S. 350, *aff'd on reh'g*, 103 F. Supp. 920 (E.D.S.C. 1952), *rev'd sub nom. Brown v. Bd. of Educ.*, 347 U.S. 483 (1954); *see* Kluger, *Simple Justice*, at 13–26.

42. To Secure These Rights, at 19–20.

43. See, generally, W. Marvin Dulaney, *Black Police in America* (Indiana University Press, 1996).

44. See Murray, *States' Laws on Race and Color*, at 31–32 (Alabama); *id.* at 45 (Arkansas); *id.* at 84–85 (Florida); *id.* at 114–15 (Georgia); *id.* at 238, 247 (Mississippi); *id.* at 480 (Virginia); *id.* at 85, 114–15; *id.* at 32, 45; *see* Tessa M. Gorman, *Back on the Chain Gang: Why the Eighth Amendment and the History of Slavery Proscribe the Resurgence of Chain Gangs*, 85 Cal. L. Rev. 441 (1997).

45. Harper Lee, *To Kill a Mockingbird* (Lippincott, 1960).

46. The failure of white Alabama lawyers to offer any sort of meaningful defense for their clients in the Scottsboro case is detailed in *Powell v. Alabama*, 287 U.S. 45, 53–59 (1932). See also David J. Bodenhamer, *Fair Trial: Rights of the Accused in American History* 92–94 (Oxford University Press, 1992); Dan T. Carter, *Scottsboro: A Tragedy of the American South* 19–48 (rev. ed.) (Louisiana State University Press, 1979).

47. *See* Murray, *States' Laws on Race and Color*, at 71 (Delaware). Delaware's law appears to be the only statutory regulation of institutions for the aged, probably because very few states had homes for aged blacks. On orphanages, see *id.* (Delaware); *id.* at 343 (North Carolina); *id.* at 370 (Oklahoma); *id.* at 439 (Tennessee); *id.* at 445 (Texas). On juvenile institutions, see *id.* at 23 (Alabama); *id.* at 40 (Arkansas); *id.* at 79 (Florida); *id.* at 91 (Georgia); *id.* at 176–77 (Louisiana); *id.* at 239 (Mississippi); *id.* at 338 (North Carolina); *id.* at 369 (Oklahoma); *id.* at 409 (South Carolina); *id.* at 430 (Tennessee); *id.* at 464–65 (Virginia).

48. *Id.* at 176–77. On institutions for people with hearing problems, etc., see *id.* at 23, 29–30 (Alabama); *id.* at 42–43 (Arkansas); *id.* at 72 (Delaware); *id.* at 75 (District of Columbia); *id.* at 79 (Florida); *id.* at 90 (Georgia); *id.* at 175–76, 188 (Louisiana); *id.* at 239 (Mississippi); *id.* at 338–39 (North Carolina); *id.* at 369–71 (Oklahoma); *id.* at 409 (South Carolina); *id.* at 430, 437 (Tennessee); *id.* at 445, 448 (Texas); *id.* at 463–64, 476 (Virginia). On state schools for the blind, see *id.* at 23 (Alabama); *id.* at 175 (Louisiana); *id.* at 239 (Mississippi); *id.* at 338 (North Carolina); *id.* at 369 (Oklahoma); *id.* at 429 (Tennessee); *id.* at 445 (Texas); *id.* at 463–64 (Virginia).

49. *Id.* at 414–15; see also C. Vann Woodward, *The Strange Career of Jim Crow* 83 (Oxford University Press, 1955).

50. Murray, *States' Laws on Race and Color*, at 414; *id.* at 372 (Oklahoma); *id.* at 437 (Tennessee); *id.* at 452 (Texas).

51. To Secure These Rights, at 76–77; Murray, *States' Laws on Race and Color*, at 32–34 (Alabama); *id.* at 115–17 (Georgia); *id.* at 191–95 (Louisiana); *id.* at 374–76 (Oklahoma); *id.* at 619–20 (Mobile ordinance); *id.* at 628 (Atlanta ordinance). The Georgia statute allowed taxis to carry people of both races "under such conditions of separation of the races as the [Georgia Public Service] Commission may prescribe," but it is impossible to imagine how that rule might have operated. Other states segregated all commercial vehicles, which would have included taxis. *Id.* at 117.

52. *Id.* at 87–88. Id. at 89, 171, 188, 253–54, 339, 370, 372, 417–18, 443, 615.

53. William H. Hastie, *Toward an Equalitarian Legal Order, 1930–1950*, 407 Annals Am. Acad. Pol. & Soc. Sci. 18, 20 (1973); Murray, *States' Laws on Race and Color*, at 342 (North Carolina); *id.* at 450 (Texas); John Hope Franklin, *Race and History: Selected Essays, 1938–1988*, at 277–91 (Louisiana University Press, 1989); Murray, *States' Laws on Race and Color*, at 82, 115.

54. Hastie, *Toward an Equalitarian Legal Order*, at 20.

55. Myrdal, *An American Dilemma*, at 628.

56. See *Henderson v. United States*, 339 U.S. 816, 824 (1950) (striking down segregation on interstate trains); *McLaurin v. Okla. State Bd. of Regents for Higher Educ.*, 339 U.S. 637, 640–42 (1950) (holding that the state may not force an African American graduate student to sit apart in the cafeteria, library, and classrooms after it has admitted him to the graduate school); *Sweatt v. Painter*, 339 U.S. 629, 636 (1950) (ordering the admission of an African American to the University of Texas Law School); *Shelley v. Kraemer*, 334 U.S. 1, 20 (1948) (holding that courts could not enforce racially restrictive covenants).

57. *Letter from Martin Luther King Jr. to Fellow Clergymen* (Apr. 16, 1963), in Martin Luther King Jr., *Why We Can't Wait* 77, 83–84 (1964).

CHAPTER SEVENTEEN

Brown, Social Movements, and Social Change

Jack M. Balkin

I want to offer five key lessons about social movements and courts—five lessons about how social movements achieve their goals and, in the process, change the practical meaning of the U.S. Constitution. My central example will be *Brown v. Board of Education* and the struggle for black civil rights, but I will also discuss a few other cases, including *Lawrence v. Texas*,[1] the 2003 decision that was a great victory for the gay rights movement.

The first lesson is that the Supreme Court is not counter-majoritarian; it is nationalist. We are all familiar with the expression "judicial activism" and the charge that courts are basically anti-democratic institutions that are always vetoing what majorities want. But that stereotype is wrong, or at the very least it is misleading. Political scientists tell us that the Supreme Court is an integral part of the national political coalition. It never strays too far from the views of national majorities, and in particular from the views of national elites. Very often federal courts and the Supreme Court ratify the views of national majorities and impose those views on regional majorities in states. That is why the Supreme Court is less anti-majoritarian than nationalist.

Studies have confirmed this phenomenon repeatedly.[2] For a few recent examples, consider several decisions from 2003 by the Rehnquist Court, which most people believed was a very conservative Court. The Supreme Court struck down state sodomy laws in *Lawrence v. Texas*, it upheld the application of the Family and Medical Leave Act to state governments in *Hibbs v. Department of Social Services*,[3] and it upheld the use of race-conscious affirmative action to promote diversity in *Grutter v. Bollinger*.[4] How did this happen? Did the members of the Supreme Court suddenly have a brain transplant? Of course not. Although the Supreme Court may contain many conservative Justices, the Supreme Court as an institution does not stray too far from the political center—wherever that center happens to be—and from the views of national elites. One of the most interesting features of the *Grutter* case was that amicus briefs from a group of Fortune 500 corporations and from members of the U.S. military argued that the nation could not do without race-conscious affirmative action.[5] You cannot get much more establishment than the Fortune 500 and the U.S. military.

This feature of Supreme Court decision making puts the Supreme Court's 1954 decision in *Brown v. Board of Education* in a different light. The Supreme Court was not really swimming against the tide in the way most people imagine. In 1954, only seventeen states required segregation of public schools. Four other states had a local option, including Kansas, which is why the Topeka schools were segregated. The remaining twenty-seven states (there were only forty-eight at the time) had already abolished de jure segregation.[6]

Moreover, the 1940s and early 1950s had seen an important transformation in popular attitudes about race relations. People became increasingly optimistic about the possibility of real change. World War II in particular had been a watershed event. The United States had sacrificed many thousands of lives to fight a racist regime in Nazi Germany. Increasingly, people believed, it made little sense for America to condone racial apartheid at home.

American politics had changed too. The Democratic party was no longer solely the party of slaveocracy and Jim Crow. Franklin Roosevelt welcomed blacks into the New Deal coalition. Harry Truman, one of the great champions of civil rights, created the U.S. Commission on Civil Rights in 1947, which produced a famous report, "To Secure These Rights," that formed a blueprint for future civil rights legislation. In February 1948 he delivered the first presidential message on civil rights to Congress, and he proposed a permanent civil rights division in the Justice Department, anti-lynching legislation, abolition of the poll tax, and prohibition of segregation in interstate transportation, which would have effectively overturned the result in *Plessy v. Ferguson.*[7] The same year Truman issued two executive orders desegregating the Armed Forces and creating a Fair Employment Board to govern the U.S. Civil Service.[8] Truman then ran for president in 1948 on a party platform that supported black civil rights. The Dixiecrats bolted the party, but Truman won the election anyway. Two years later, in 1950, Truman's Justice Department asked the Supreme Court to overrule *Plessy v. Ferguson* in *Sweatt v. Painter*.[9] But the Court wasn't as bold as Harry Truman. The Justices waited until four years later to do so.

By 1954, then, the Supreme Court was responding to a long-term change in national attitudes about race spurred on by World War II. Foreign policy elites believed that Jim Crow was an embarrassment and was harming American interests in the Cold War; they pressured the Supreme Court to overrule *Plessy*.

Although the Supreme Court follows the views of national majorities, it is important to understand that national majorities do not necessarily want the same things that social movements want. For example, the State Department and other foreign policy elites simply wanted a declaration that Jim Crow was unconstitutional. They did not want wholesale social change, much less massive social redistribution from whites to blacks. And certainly the vast majority of white America did not want that either. Not surprisingly, then, in the years immediately after *Brown* was decided, the Supreme Court was relatively silent on the issue of school desegregation. Its most important intervention during this period was to reassert federal supremacy in *Cooper v. Aaron*.[10] The fight for racial equality turned to the lower courts, with only limited success. In fact, only after the passage of the Civil Rights Act of 1964, the landslide election of 1964, and the Voting Rights Act of 1965 was there any significant desegregation in the South.[11] Desegregation took place only after public support had been mobilized and national coalitions got behind the idea. By 1964, all three branches of the federal government were more or less united in pushing a civil rights agenda, and so civil rights made progress.

Now compare the story of *Brown* with the story of *Lawrence v. Texas*, which struck down state laws banning same-sex sodomy. Like *Brown*, *Lawrence* may seem anti-majoritarian at first, but it also reflects and confirms a significant long-term change in social attitudes in the United States. In 1960 every state banned same-sex sodomy. By 1986, when the Supreme Court upheld Georgia's anti-sodomy law by a 5–4 vote in *Bowers v. Hardwick*,[12] only twenty-five states banned the practice, and it had been decriminalized in twenty-five others. The trend was clear, and the Supreme Court almost overturned these laws in 1986, but Justice Powell changed his mind at the last minute. By 2003, when *Lawrence* was decided, only thirteen states still decriminalized same-sex sodomy, and in none of those states were the laws against sodomy seriously enforced.[13] To be sure, having sodomy laws on the books had important collateral consequences for gays and lesbians in issues like employment, adoption, and so on, but the criminal provisions were hardly used at all. In the meantime, gays and lesbians had become familiar and increasingly accepted in movies, television, and popular culture.

Thus, in 2003, the Supreme Court was hardly swimming against the tide, even less so than it had been in 1954. After all, massive resistance followed the *Brown* decision. But there has been no massive resistance in the thirteen states that maintained sodomy laws before *Lawrence*. Gays have not been thrown into prison in order to defy the Supreme Court. Instead, the debate has moved on, in a very short period of time, to the question of same-sex marriage. Think about that: only a year after the decision in *Lawrence* was handed down, Americans became embroiled in a heated controversy over whether people who recently were branded outlaws for even forming intimate relationships should be permitted to solemnize those relationships in civil unions or marriages. This demonstrates as well as anything that the Supreme Court was confirming a big change in national social attitudes that had already occurred and that it was getting recalcitrant states in line with that change.

Here is the second lesson: courts tend to protect minorities just about as much as majorities want them to. This follows fairly directly from Lesson One. Given that the Supreme Court tends to respond to the values and interests of national political coalitions and national elites, the Court will protect minority interests to the extent that doing so is congruent with the values, interests, and self-conception of majorities. Conversely, to the extent that minorities demand more—for example, a significant redistribution of resources—the Supreme Court will probably offer little additional help, because doing so would be going against the wishes of the dominant political coalition.

I noted earlier that during the 1960s all three branches of government had coalesced on a national civil rights policy. This was the period when Congress passed new civil rights laws and the Supreme Court imposed new national policies concerning civil rights, criminal procedure reform, and school prayer on state governments, and particularly the South. In fact, one way of understanding what happened in the 1960s is that all three branches of government ganged up on the South and imposed national values, and particularly the values of national elites, on southern state and local governments.[14] The Civil Rights Act and the Voting Rights Act are part of this change. So too is the Warren Court's revolution in criminal procedure: it was motivated by an increasing national concern with the mistreatment of blacks by the criminal process in the South.

However, after the 1968 election, a gradual retrenchment began.[15] Richard Nixon appointed four conservatives to the Supreme Court, and the Supreme Court, following changes in national public opinion, began to impose limits on how far courts would advance the goals of the Second Reconstruction. The retrenchment that followed the 1968 election is the other side of my point that the Supreme Court protects minorities just about as much as majorities want them protected. The national political coalition wanted the changes of the 1960s slowed down, and so they were slowed down.

People often argue that the job of the Supreme Court is to protect "discrete and insular minorities"[16] from those deficiencies and defects in the political process that fail to take the interests of minorities into account. The idea is that the Supreme Court's basic function is to protect minority groups who are spurned in society, who are politically powerless, and who have no one else to stand up for them.

It is a nice idea, but it is largely a myth. That is not the way it really works in practice. In general, minorities do not get much protection from the courts until they have shown that they have political muscle or that they are otherwise a force to be reckoned with. Minority groups that do not even appear on the radar screen of political concern are pretty much ignored by courts, and their claims are often routinely dismissed. The best way to obtain protection from the courts is to make a fuss in the political process. In constitutional law, as elsewhere, it is usually the squeaky wheel that gets the grease.

During the first half of the twentieth century, many blacks left the stagnation of southern rural life and moved North to large cities, a phenomenon that is sometimes called the Great Migration. Blacks migrated to the North in the hope of better jobs and a freer life, but one of the important side effects of the Great Migration is that blacks moved from a region in the country where they could not vote to a region where they could. Traditionally blacks had been loyal Republican voters, because the Republicans were the party of Lincoln, but as disenfranchisement swept the South in the early twentieth century and the Republicans realized that they could do little to stop it, the Republican party gradually wrote off the black vote. That gave the emerging liberal, urban wing of the Democratic Party a chance to contest the Republicans for black votes in the North and the border states. The Great Migration accelerated this trend, transforming the two major political parties in the process.

Thus, as a result of the Great Migration, a funny thing happens in American politics in the middle of the twentieth century. Roughly between 1930 and 1960, blacks become swing voters whose support can make the difference in close elections. You may have heard of soccer moms and NASCAR dads. They are groups of key voters who may vote for either party; as a result, both major political parties try to court them. Between 1930 and 1960, blacks were somewhat like soccer moms and NASCAR dads. Both parties had an interest in appealing to them, although the parties were constrained by American racial attitudes, particularly in the South. Roosevelt saw an opportunity to make blacks part of the New Deal coalition. Harry Truman owed his 1948 victory to an increase in African American support for the Democrats, and thus it was no accident that Truman was a great champion of black civil rights.

As the votes of black people began to matter, the two major political parties began competing with each other to appeal to blacks; each party developed a liberal wing that was strongly pro-civil rights. These changes in the agenda of the two major political parties, in turn, affected the sorts of people who were appointed to the courts, and particularly the Supreme Court. That is one reason why the Supreme Court eventually featured a coalition of Justices liberal on black civil rights who were appointed by presidents from both political parties. Increased black political power played a central role in changing conditions for blacks and led to Truman's executive orders and the judicial decisions of the Warren Court. Thus, blacks were protected as discrete and insular minorities not because they were completely powerless but because their political power had slowly increased from the 1930s onward.

This brings me to my third lesson: social movements change constitutional law, but not as they intend. This lesson follows from the previous two. Because the Supreme Court tends, over the long run, to converge toward the views of national majorities, social movements for political change tend to succeed only when they gain political muscle, can credibly threaten to make trouble for majorities, or otherwise become important to majorities. In particular, social movements tend to succeed best when they are able to call upon the interests, the values, or the self-conception of majorities. Let me distinguish these three elements.

The first element is the appeal to interests. National political elites and State Department officials were embarrassed by Jim Crow and believed that it undermined American foreign policy in the Cold War.[17] That gave them and civil rights leaders a common interest in desegregation, although for different reasons.

The second element is the appeal to shared values. Social movements succeed when they successfully appeal to widely held values of the American people and convince them that their movement is asking for the application of values that Americans believe they have always treasured. The civil rights movement was able to summon the idea of equality guaranteed by the Declaration of Independence and the idea that the United States is a country that believes in liberty, equality, and equal citizenship. Martin Luther King Jr.'s famous "I Have A Dream" speech brilliantly connected the interests of the civil rights movement to the values of freedom and liberty and to the ideals of the Founders.

The third element is the appeal to the majority's self-conception. Majorities, like everyone else, like to think well of themselves. They are susceptible to persuasion when they are shamed or embarrassed by their own practices or by the practices of others. When Sheriff Bull Connor turned the fire hoses and dogs on little children protesting in Birmingham, and when Alabama state troopers began beating protesters at the Edmund Pettus Bridge in Selma, national audiences were horrified. They were embarrassed and ashamed because of what these acts said about America. They wanted to believe that they lived in a country where such incidents did not happen. Violence against civil rights protesters threatened their view of Americans as decent people who loved equality and liberty. This helped shift public opinion in favor of the Civil Rights Act of 1964 and the Voting Rights Act of 1965.[18]

Nevertheless, those who live by majorities also die by majorities. As I noted, the 1968 election began a long, slow retrenchment against the civil rights movement that led to the end of our Second Reconstruction. Every successful social movement—and many unsuccessful ones—leads to counter-mobilizations. These mobilizations and counter-mobilizations contend for the hearts and minds of the public. When the interests and values of majorities and social movements no longer coincide, progress becomes much more difficult. And because courts tend to move toward the center of gravity of public opinion, courts start to become less helpful to minority interests soon thereafter. That is roughly what happened during the 1970s and 1980s.

This brings me to my fourth lesson: all roads lead to reform.

The first three lessons explained that social movements succeed by appealing to the interests, values, and self-conception of national majorities. But institutional settings for social movement activism are equally important. At the risk of oversimplifying, there are three basic institutional avenues for social movement politics: (1) litigation—seeking redress in the courts; (2) legislation—seeking redress in Congress or state legislatures; and (3) direct action—trying to change people's minds through street protests, boycotts, sit-ins, and other types of demonstrations.

The fight for civil rights for African Americans involved all three of these approaches. The civil rights movement, especially after 1960, focused on direct action. The NAACP's litigation campaign appealed to the courts. The push for the 1964 Civil Rights Act and the 1965 Voting Rights Act sought legislative reform.

When we celebrate *Brown v. Board of Education* today, we also celebrate the long campaign by the NAACP to challenge segregation in the courts. Until the beginning of the direct action phase of the civil rights movement, the strategy of the NAACP relied heavily on litigation. The reason is that, until around 1960, there were really few other viable alternatives for pushing change at the national level.

Between 1875 and 1957, there was not a single civil rights bill passed in the U.S. Congress. An important reason was the power of southern Democrats, who wielded the combined powers of the filibuster and the seniority system. Ironically, they maintained their power to block change in part because blacks were largely disenfranchised in the states they represented. With southern congressmen and senators blocking all federal civil rights bills, legislative solutions were not possible. Harry Truman was able to push for reforms through executive orders, but these had only limited reach outside the internal operations of the federal government.

The other possible avenue for change was direct action. However, it was not possible to have a successful direct action movement in the South before the mid-1950s. The reason is quite simple: if you think there was violence directed against the civil rights movement in the 1960s, just imagine the amount of violence that would have been delivered against any attempt at a civil rights movement in the Deep South in the '20s, '30s, and '40s.[19] Lynchings were still quite common, and they were employed ruthlessly to stamp out all forms of dissent. With legislation and direct action unavailable until the middle of the 1950s, that left only one path of reform for the social movement—litigation. And that is exactly the strategy that the NAACP employed. It brought a series of carefully orchestrated cases to try to chip away at the constitutional and legal foundations of Jim Crow.

The lesson to draw from this is not that litigation is the best way for a social movement to pursue change. The NAACP chose litigation out of necessity—there was simply no other avenue that was likely to be as effective. Rather, the lesson one should draw is that things go best for a social movement when it can pursue all three avenues of relief at once. That is the sense in which "all roads lead to reform"—it is not that any road will get you there equally well, but that it is necessary to take all the roads simultaneously if you want to get where you are going. As we have seen, courts are more likely to recognize social movement claims when these claims are winning a favorable reception in other arenas as well. When a social movement is working on all three fronts, courts do not have to do everything by themselves, and other institutions—Congress, the executive branch, and the various organs of the administrative state—are working to achieve the same basic objective. An obvious historical example is the period between 1964 and 1968, in which all three branches of the federal government were controlled by liberal Democrats and their party—along with liberal and moderate Republicans—pushed for black civil rights.

This brings me to my fifth and final lesson: striking down criminal laws is easy; managing a welfare state is hard to do.

What do I mean by a welfare state? Governments can govern in lots of different ways. They can make new crimes, they can create civil causes of action, and they can produce administrative regulations. These are all aspects of the regulatory state.

But modern governments do far more than this. They create jobs. They engage in public works projects. They spend and distribute tax revenues. They create or subsidize public goods like health care and education. These are the tasks of a welfare state.

It is relatively easy for courts to supervise the activities of the regulatory state, because it is administratively easy for courts to strike down criminal penalties and civil causes of action and hold that certain administrative regulations are unconstitutional. It is administratively easy in part because these laws normally have to go through the courts to be enforced. By refusing to enforce them, courts can usually ensure that other actors in the political system will comply.

By contrast, imposing constitutional requirements on a government's welfare state activities is far more difficult, especially when courts ask government officials to spend money to pursue goals such as equal educational opportunity, adequate health care or housing, or minimum levels of subsistence. Achieving these goals requires complicated tradeoffs, and it is often difficult to prove when they have been met. Government compliance with court orders may be hard to monitor, and government officials usually have lots of different ways to disclaim responsibility, drag their heels, and resist the courts. Instead of declaring a single law unconstitutional and refusing to enforce it, courts may have to persuade different sets of government actors with different interests and agendas to work together over fairly long periods of time. Finally, achieving equal educational opportunity costs money and may require significant expenditures that cut into the government's budget and drain funds from other projects and services. Government officials may be unwilling or unable to raise additional revenues and may continually plead that they lack the funds necessary to carry out the necessary reforms.

Problems like these arise whenever courts try to make a government's welfare state activities conform to constitutional values. In fact, they are quite similar to the problems courts in other countries have faced in trying to enforce constitutional guarantees of social rights like housing, health, and employment. The history of court-ordered school desegregation in the United States has much in common with the history of the enforcement of the social guarantees that appear in many post–World War II constitutions around the world.

For example, the South African constitution is one of the most progressive in the world. It includes constitutional guarantees of health care, housing, and education. However, when people living in a shanty town petitioned the South African Supreme Court to enforce their rights to adequate housing, the Court realized that there were a limited number of things it could do in the face of a recalcitrant government.[20] The history of that litigation is similar in many ways to the history of litigation in desegregation suits and suits for education equality in the United States. The reason is that courts face the same sorts of obstacles in enforcing constitutional norms where the welfare state is concerned. Often, constitutional courts can do little more than exhort their governments to make reasonable efforts to vindicate these rights, and even then courts must continually worry that their legitimacy will be tarnished if they push too hard and governments evade their directives or, even worse, simply ignore them.

What have we learned about social movements? Social movements succeed when they gain the attention and the support of the national political coalition. Social movements succeed when they appeal to the interests, the values, and the self-conception of majorities. Finally, social movements succeed when they do not rely on one single avenue of relief, but try to use all avenues of relief at once. In particular, they should not just rely on courts if they can help it.

That does not mean that courts are unimportant. It just means that they cannot do the job alone. Usually they need a little help or a little direction from other places in the system. Courts are a little bit like placekickers on a football team. They cannot tackle a speedy running back on their own, but they can slow him down so others can tackle him, or, if the other players tackle him first, the placekicker can pile on.

That is the way we should think about *Brown*. The Supreme Court did its part, but it did not do everything. It could not do everything. Yet it helped in the way that courts can help. We should not view the Supreme Court as an isolated hero responding to injustice when no one else would. Rather, we should view it as one part of a complicated mix of actors who together did something great and brought about a profound change in America. That picture makes the Supreme Court less central in some ways, but no less important.

And that is the picture I want to leave you with. The running back is sprinting down the field. The linebackers tackle him and throw him to the ground, and as the running back lies there moaning and groaning, the judges come along and say, "It's time to do some justice!" and they throw themselves on the pile. That's courts for you—bad at tackling, but good at piling on.

Notes

1. 539 U.S. 558 (2003).

2. The key article is Robert A. Dahl, *Decision-Making in a Democracy: The Supreme Court as a National Policy-Maker*, 6 J. Pub. L. 279 (1957). For a review of the recent political science literature, see Barry Friedman, *Mediated Popular Constitutionalism*, 101 Mich. L. Rev. 2596 (2003), and Terri Jennings Peretti, *In Defense of a Political Court* 80–132 (Princeton University Press, 1999).

3. 538 U.S. 721 (2003).

4. 539 U.S. 306 (2003).

5. *See, e.g.*, Consolidated Brief of Lt. Gen. Julius W. Becton Jr. et al. as Amici Curiae in Support of Respondents, *Grutter v. Bollinger* (No. 02–241), *Gratz v. Bollinger* (No. 02–516)(the Military Brief); Brief of General Motors Corporation as Amicus Curiae in Support of Respondents, *Grutter v. Bollinger* (No. 02–241), *Gratz v. Bollinger* (No. 02–516); Brief for Amici Curiae 65 Leading American Businesses in Support of Respondents, *Grutter v. Bollinger* (No. 02–241), *Gratz v. Bollinger* (No. 02–516); Brief of 3M et al. as Amicus Curiae in Support of Respondents, *Grutter v. Bollinger* (No. 02–241), *Gratz v. Bollinger* (No. 02–516).

6. Michael J. Klarman, *From Jim Crow to Civil Rights: The Supreme Court and the Struggle for Racial Equality* 344–45 (Oxford University Press, 2004); Gerald Rosenberg, *The Hollow Hope: Can Courts Bring About Social Change?* 42 (University of Chicago Press, 1991).

7. 163 U.S. 537 (1896).

8. See President's Commission on Civil Rights: To Secure These Rights (1947); Exec. Order No. 9980, 3 C.F.R. 720 (1948) (establishing a Fair Employment Board within the Civil Service Commission); Exec. Order No. 9981, 3 C.F.R. 722 (1948) (ordering desegregation of U.S. Armed Forces). For accounts of Truman's policies on civil rights, see Michael R. Gardner, *Harry Truman and Civil Rights: Moral Courage and Political Risks* 28–32, 43–48, 58–61, 65–86, 105–21, 152–55, 171–95, 204–5, 213–14 (Southern Illinois University Press, 2002); William C. Berman, *The Politics of Civil Rights in the Truman Administration* 55, 61–64, 67–68, 74–78, 83–85, 116–18, 120–21, 123, 140, 165–68, 185–86, 238–40 (Ohio State University Press, 1970).

9. 339 U.S. 629 (1950). See Klarman, *From Jim Crow to Civil Rights*, at 210; the Justice Department made this request in a trio of cases decided in 1950: *U.S. v. Henderson*, 339 U.S. 816 (1950), *Sweatt v. Painter*, and *McLaurin v. Oklahoma State Regents*, 339 U.S. 637 (1950). Brief for the United States, *Henderson v. United States* 35–49; Memorandum for the United States as Amicus Curiae, *McLaurin v. Oklahoma State Regents*, and *Sweatt v. Painter* 9–14.

10. 358 U.S. 1 (1958).

11. Michael Klarman, *Brown, Racial Change, and the Civil Rights Movement*, 80 Va. L. Rev. 7, 42–46 (1994); Rosenberg, *The Hollow Hope*, at 52. Between 1955, when *Brown II* was decided, and 1964, the Court decided three cases: *Griffin v. Prince Edward County School Board*, 377 U.S. 218 (1964); *Goss v. Board of Education of Knoxville*, 373 U.S. 683 (1963); and *Cooper v. Aaron*. Although in each case the Court reminded the nation that school segregation was unconstitutional, and struck down obvious attempts to circumvent *Brown*, the Court had little effect on the actual desegregation of the public schools until after the 1964 Civil Rights Act.

12. 478 U.S. 186 (1986).

13. *Lawrence v. Texas*, 539 U.S. at 572.

14. Lucas A. Powe Jr., *The Warren Court and American Politics* 490–91, 493–94 (Harvard University Press, 2000).

15. See Jack M. Balkin and Reva Siegel, *The American Civil Rights Tradition: Anticlassification or Antisubordination?* 58 U. Miami L. Rev. 9 (2004).

16. *United States v. Carolene Prods. Corp.*, 304 U.S. 144, 152 n.4 (1938).

17. Mary Dudziak, *Cold War Civil Rights: Race and The Image of American Democracy* 80–81 (Princeton University Press, 2000).

18. Klarman, *Brown, Racial Change, and the Civil Rights Movement*, at 141–49.

19. Klarman, *From Jim Crow to Civil Rights*, at 446. This is not to say that black leaders did not try to protest outside the South or put pressure on Washington politicians. For example, in May 1948, A. Philip Randolph and Rev. Grant Reynolds threatened to begin a civil disobedience campaign if Congress refused to pass legislation outlawing discrimination and segregation in the Armed Forces. Berman, *The Politics of Civil Rights in the Truman Administration*, at 98–99. Truman's executive order No. 9981, desegregating the Armed Forces, was in part an attempt to forestall such a campaign. *Id.* at 117.

20. See, e.g., *Republic of South Africa v. Grootboom*, 2000 (11) BCLR 1169 (CC), at 41, available at http://www.concourt.gov.za/files/grootboom1/grootboom1.pdf; 2000 SACLR Lexis 126 (holding that under the guarantee of the right to housing of Section 26 of South Africa's Constitution, the government had an obligation to "establish a coherent public housing programme directed towards the progressive realisation of the right of access to adequate housing within the State's available means"). In the *Grootboom* case, the South African Constitutional Court did not hold that the government would have to provide a "minimum core" level of housing care, nor did it require that any specific amount be appropriated for housing in the government's budget. It simply stated that "a reasonable part of the national housing budget [must] be devoted to [providing housing to those in desperate need], but the precise allocation is for national government to decide in the first instance." *Id.* at 66.

CHAPTER EIGHTEEN

Race and Sex Segregation in Schools Fifty Years After *Brown*

Nancy Levit

The Rush Toward Segregation

The question has been posed whether a fiftieth anniversary remembrance of *Brown v. Board of Education* would be a celebration or a eulogy. I hope it is the former, and more, I hope it is a call to recognize the extensibility of *Brown*, the reach of *Brown*—its application to government-endorsed segregation on the basis of other identity characteristics, particularly sex and sexual orientation. More than fifty years have passed since *Brown*, and currently, segregation based on race and sex is sweeping our nation's educational systems. Courts are rapidly dismantling desegregation orders, and when those orders end, school districts racially resegregate. At precisely the same time that this end to desegregation is occurring, our governments are beginning to sponsor sex segregation in schools as well. In this chapter, I examine this embrace of segregation as manifested in the trend of official sponsorship of segregation in education based on identity characteristics.

Any student of history is familiar with the timeline in the half-century since *Brown v. Board of Education*: the massive resistance and footdragging through the 1970s, particularly on the part of southern states; the desegregation orders stemming from *Brown*; and the reluctant compliance with those orders by school districts into the 1990s. In the past decade, the judiciary has shivered away from the promise of *Brown*, with a surge of federal district courts declaring the school districts under their supervision to have achieved "unitary status."

Courts have ended, or soon plan to end, desegregation suits in at least three dozen school districts, many in major metropolitan areas, such as Boston, Buffalo, Charlotte, Cleveland, Dallas, Denver, Kansas City, Little Rock, Miami, Norfolk, Oklahoma City, Savannah, San Diego, and Wilmington. Since 1974, when Congress passed anti-busing legislation, it has been the official policy of the U.S. government to have students attend neighborhood schools. State legislatures are joining the effort toward resegregation by passing Neighborhood Schools Acts, which encourage or require students to attend the public schools closest to their homes. A study by the Harvard Civil Rights Project shows that when desegregation orders end and schools retreat from integration efforts, school districts rapidly resegregate.[1] In 2007, the U.S. Supreme Court held unconstitutional policies voluntarily adopted by the Louisville and Seattle school districts to combat segregation by using race as one consideration in school assignments.[2] In the context of race, both the judiciary and the legislature seem to agree with the words of former president Ronald Reagan that desegregation is a "[failed] social experiment that nobody wants."[3]

The parallels between the return to racial segregation and the welcoming of sex segregation seem to be going unnoticed. Across the country, individual public schools and public school districts show increasing interest in single-sex education. In 1994, "only three public schools in the United States offered single-sex educational opportunities"; for the 2008–9 school year, 392 public schools across the country were either completely single-sex or have single-sex classes for some subjects.[4] Single-sex classes, particularly for math or science, are also on the rise. This grouping by sex draws on very weak evidence of biological differences between boys and girls and on administrative concerns of teachers who would like to remove the gonadal distractions of opposite-sex students in a single classroom.[5]

Single-sex education received new support in 2002, when President Bush signed into law the No Child Left Behind Act. The purpose of this act is to "close the achievement gap with accountability, flexibility, and choice, so that no child is left behind." It not only expressly promotes single-sex schools and classes in public schools, as long as comparable opportunities are provided for both sexes, but it also provides $450 million in federal funds for experiments such as single-sex education. In 2006, the U.S. Department of Education amended the regulations implementing Title IX to expand opportunities for single-sex primary and secondary education to meet particular student needs or to offer a "diversity" of educational alternatives.[6] The government now officially sponsors "experiments" in sex segregation, just as it rushes to declare the "experiment" over in the case of racial desegregation orders.[7]

Educators have also begun using identity characteristics other than race and sex to segregate public education. In the fall of 2003, the New York City school system opened Harvey Milk High School, the nation's first public high school for lesbian, gay, bisexual, and transgendered (LGBT) students. The Harvey Milk High School is being defended in part along the same rationale as that advanced in single-sex school cases: because students are choosing to segregate themselves, the Constitution should not be offended. Both single-sex and LGBT schools rely on the force of arguments made in the larger school choice movement: that the fact of "choice" averts constitutional concerns. Stereotypic facets of its curriculum—an "academically rigorous school that will . . . specialize in computer technology, arts and a culinary program"—aside, the school is intended as a safe haven for 170 LGBT New York students who face bullying and physical violence in regular school settings. In fact, LGBT teenagers do suffer extraordinary levels of vicious physical and mental abuse, high dropout rates, depression, and suicide.[8]

Given the unsafe environment for LGBT students in regular public schools, segregated education on the basis of sexual orientation probably has the best remedial justification. But it is of a piece with the separatism on the basis of identity characteristics seen in the race and gender contexts. It shares the same flawed remedial approach: rather than confront the prejudices of discriminatory coeducation nationwide, the response is to cordon off a small enclave, segregate students into it based on one aspect of identity, and make that offering available to a select few.

The segregationist movement stems from a peculiar alliance of conservative forces, who have long believed that separation of the races and sexes is natural and appropriate, and liberal groups who, recently and particularly with respect to gender, see separatism either as a tool of liberation or as the lesser of bad alternatives compared to a flawed coeducational system.

What is striking in both the race and gender contexts is the anti-empiricism of courts and commentators in regard to the phenomenon of segregation itself. In the desegregation context, some activist conservative courts have rushed to end their supervisory jurisdiction over desegregation cases. They rely in part on the doctrinal urgings of the Supreme Court to return school districts to local control and partly on selective and politicized reception of the empirical evidence submitted in the individual cases. In their hurry to declare that districts have attained unitary status, courts ignore available evidence, disparage or diminish the value of social science evidence, and narrowly limit inquiry to ignore how segregation operates and the consequences that flow from it.

Courts have decided very few cases of intentional single-sex or single-race education under the current form of heightened constitutional scrutiny. At present, the single-sex education issue is playing out in the court of public opinion. Yet commentators' evaluation of the social science evidence regarding the successes and failures of sex-exclusive schooling suffers from the same methodological flaws as courts' evaluation of sociological evidence in desegregation cases: reliance on selected studies or pieces of anecdotal information to support pre-existing positions, incomplete attention to the cumulative wealth of evidence, and an unwillingness to correlate the developing body of social science research with the legal or doctrinal tests.

Another similarity in these movements toward separation based on identity characteristics is the language used by their proponents. Supporters of single-sex schools and those who favor ending desegregation both use the language of "choice" and "natural differences." Parents, the argument goes, should be able to have "choices" about their children's education: they should be able to "choose" neighborhood schools or single-sex classrooms. "Natural" gender differences between boys and girls necessitate single-sex schools. People of different races want to be "among others just like themselves." The language is chillingly reminiscent of the Dixiecrat segregationists of the 1940s and 1950s, whose banner stated the platform they supported: "the segregation of the races and the racial integrity of each race; the constitutional right to *choose* one's associates." It also resembles the terminology used by the early to mid-nineteenth-century anatomists, eugenicists, and physical anthropologists of race who believed in the importance of race as a biological construct, a natural ordering of races, the natural superiority of the white race, and the belief that the races were by nature, incompatible.[9]

Anti-empiricism and the Triumph of Apartheid

What is striking in both the race and gender contexts is that courts and commentators both take an unscientific approach to the phenomenon of segregation. Conservative courts have rushed to end their jurisdiction over segregation. These lower courts have accepted the Supreme Court's invitation to return school districts to local control by dissolving desegregation decrees.

What have they left out? What is not factored into the decision to dissolve the decrees? Above all, courts give little consideration to the impact that lifting the decree will have on students. It seems irrelevant that schools might become resegregated once decrees are lifted. Right from the start, the bulk of social science studies concerning the costs and benefits of racially integrated schools are relegated to the sidelines.

In assessing unitary status, most courts do not consider dimensions of educational opportunities, such as academic performance differences, racial tracking, the overrepresentation of minority students in special education and their underrepresentation in gifted and talented programs, racial gaps in test scores, disparities in dropout rates, and differential rates of discipline.

One reason for the anti-empiricism in the desegregation context is that the doctrinal law that has developed there sharply curtails inquiry outside certain limited areas. Cumulatively, *Dowell*, *Freeman*, and *Jenkins*—what Professor Leland Ware has aptly named the "resegregation trilogy"—created "a three-fold shift from an affirmative duty to eliminate all vestiges of segregation to acquiescence to resegregation." The message of *Dowell*, *Freeman*, and *Jenkins* is that it is time to end the experiment of desegregation. The standard for unitary status is now one that "virtually every school district can satisfy."[10]

The *Green* factors of student, staff, and faculty composition, transportation, extracurricular activities, and facilities have become a "checklist" that invites numeric computation "of black to white students and faculty and concrete comparisons of activities and facilities." They have also become an artificial way of limiting inquiry into the principal issue in the desegregation context: whether the vestiges of past segregation remain. *Freeman*'s approval of the incremental withdrawal of judicial supervision confines the district court's later investigation to considerations of whether the school district has complied in the specified areas.[11]

Freeman and *Jenkins* curtailed the remedial authority of courts in another extremely important way. In *Dowell*, the Supreme Court had cautioned the district court on remand to ascertain whether current residential segregation was a result of economics and personal preferences, but seemed to leave open the possibility that residential segregation could be a "vestige of former school segregation." The *Freeman* Court upheld the district court finding that the present racial imbalance in schools was caused not by the school district, but by "independent factors," such as the "private choices" that produce "massive demographic shifts." In *Jenkins,* the Court flatly stated that "external factors" such as "demographic changes . . . do not figure in the remedial calculus." The *Jenkins* Court specifically rejected the district court's reliance on "white flight" as a justification for its interdistrict program of magnet schools and added its own speculation that court-ordered desegregation itself—rather than the lingering effects of de jure segregation—may have caused the white departure to the suburbs. The burden was now on plaintiffs to trace any residential segregation that occurred because of de jure segregation. Unsurprisingly, since *Jenkins,* it is the rare case that considers residential segregation a vestige of prior de jure segregation.[12]

Although changing societal attitudes takes time—perhaps measured in generations—the Supreme Court, lower federal courts, and even commentators have expressed their impatience with the duration of desegregation orders. Indeed, the Supreme Court has issued specific language limiting the anticipated duration of federal court supervisory jurisdiction. In the past decade, the Supreme Court has introduced each of its desegregation opinions by commenting on the duration of the suit, "despite the longevity of the violation and the usual delays in ordering and implementing the remedy."[13] An important indicator of the viability of integration is whether it will last: whether state-sponsored racially divisive attitudes have indeed been altered. Yet courts have made findings of unitary status after districts have been under desegregation orders for very few years, and most courts in unitary status hearings reject arguments regarding the threat of resegregation.

Although plaintiffs now have the burden to demonstrate the vestiges of segregation attributable to defendants, the law artificially constrains the evidence they can introduce. The Supreme Court has issued essentially a "checklist" of factors that define whether a school system has attained unitary status, along with repeated urgings for lower federal courts to dissolve desegregation orders as quickly as possible. Many lower courts have heeded this call. Numerous desegregation decisions, particularly in the last decade, seem to be a product of an activist conservative judiciary that repeatedly expresses impatience with desegregation, looks selectively at empirical evidence about whether desegregation remedies have been effective, and considers resegregation noncontroversial and unrelated to de jure segregation. As Gary Orfield, professor of education and co-director of the Harvard Project on Civil Rights, laments, "Some of the same courts that provided all deliberation and no speed in desegregation have been engaged in an unseemly rush to desegregate."[14]

This anti-empiricism allows apartheid to triumph.

The dismantling of desegregation has paralleled the rocketing to prominence of single-sex schools and classes. The Supreme Court has addressed single-sex educational programs twice—both cases concerned advanced education (military university and nursing graduate school) in the context of an absence of comparable programs for the excluded sex. In *Mississippi University for Women v. Hogan,* the Supreme Court held that a publicly funded women's nursing college could not exclude men from its program. Because Mississippi provided no other single-sex educational opportunity for men, the Court specifically left open whether a state could establish separate but equal public educational institutions. Although the Court touched on the exclusion of women from public spheres, it ultimately viewed that history as unrelated to the school's justification of the single-sex nursing program as "educational affirmative action." The Court in *Hogan* found no specific legislative intent that the single-sex admissions policy act as compensation for any present discrimination and cautioned that classifications cannot be based on "archaic and overbroad generalizations about women."[15]

United States v. Virginia (*VMI*) was not specifically about single-sex elementary or secondary schools. In *VMI*, a female high school student sought admission to the all-male Virginia Military Institute (VMI). The Supreme Court found VMI's male-only admissions policy unconstitutional. It also rejected Virginia's attempt to create a parallel female-only, but mostly ceremonial corps of cadets at Virginia Women's Institute for Leadership, as a "pale shadow" of the educational choices, funding, facilities, alumni influence, and prestige available to men at VMI. In a footnote, the *VMI* majority left open the possibility of a state "evenhandedly" supporting "diverse educational opportunities," observing that "it is the mission of some single-sex schools 'to dissipate, rather than perpetuate, traditional gender classifications.'"[16]

The court's *VMI* opinion was guilty of a serious omission. Conspicuously absent was any reference to *Brown v. Board of Education*. Nowhere in the twenty-three-page *VMI* opinion is *Brown* even mentioned as relevant precedent. The Court was unwilling to contemplate the possibility that sex segregation might send similar messages of inferiority.

In neither *Hogan* nor *VMI* did the Court address whether government-sponsored separatism is inherently unequal. Indeed, neither case directly addressed the message sent by sex exclusivity itself.

The *VMI* opinion did give us the modern constitutional test. When courts assess the empirical evidence about single-sex schools, they will need to evaluate whether segregation is supported by an exceedingly persuasive justification.

And what about that sociological data?

The popular media touting of celebrated single-sex experiments is at odds with the cumulative evidence emerging from studies in the sociology of education. Although some early studies indicated advantages for women in single-sex colleges, those studies from the 1960s flatly "did not control for socio-economic status."[17] Female students in all-girl classes or schools certainly have more opportunities to participate in activities, because there is only one sex in the class or school. Anecdotal and self-reporting studies indicate somewhat higher measures of self-esteem and student satisfaction with the warmth or friendliness of an all-girl environment. Yet the popularly accepted notion that single-sex education is "better for girls" is not supported by more recent studies and those with careful methodological controls.[18]

Although single-sex classes may promote some self-assurance in girls, this does not translate into analytic or academic advantages. The American Association of University Women captured the findings of numerous studies: "Whereas girls perceive the classrooms in many cases to be superior, and may register gains in confidence, these benefits have not translated into measured improvements in achievement."[19] When studies control for student background differences (such as prior academic achievements, test scores, race, socioeconomic status, and educational aspirations), school selectivity, reputation, class sizes, curriculum, and resources, the studies show *no* consistent advantages in *educational quality* in single-sex schools or classes. Indeed, once conflating variables are controlled, performance differences between coeducational schools and single-sex schools entirely disappear.[20]

Consider reports of the success of the Young Women's Leadership School in New York (TYWLS). TYWLS, a small public high school whose budget is supplemented by private grant money, opened in East Harlem in the fall of 1996, with a seventh-grade class of fifty girls. As of this writing, the school has more than four hundred students in grades seven through twelve; these students are predominantly members of racial minorities. Even amid fairly good evidence of some performance differences relative to other schools in New York City, the key question—whether the results are attributable to the sex-exclusive nature of the schooling—is unanswered. Worse, it is unexplored.[21]

If the lessons of earlier single-sex research are any indication, once other variables are controlled, the effects attributable to sex exclusivity will likely disappear. At TYWLS, were the academic successes due to the fact of sex segregation and not the infusion of economic resources (the Harlem school even provides tea and muffins in the morning for its students), the curriculum, class size, academic counselors who meet with each student every single day, the self-selectivity of the students and parents (the very fact of attendance means a parent who, by and large, is more interested in the child's learning), or the Hawthorne effect, resulting from the high expectations? Was it really the presence of boys in the classroom that had been impairing the academic performance of these girls at TYWLS? This level of student and parent engagement calls into question not only whether the results at TWYLS can be extrapolated, but importantly, whether the results are attributable to the selection of girls who will succeed, thereby weeding out those who would not thrive despite an infusion of resources, the commitment of supportive families, and the learning environment of small classes.

Although some researchers have found that single-sex education may have some advantages for minority-race boys, the general consensus is that males do not flourish in single-sex environments. Providing separate classes for boys is either a neutral or negative along dimensions of socialization and academic quality. For both sexes, but particularly for boys, placement in sex-segregated classes is associated with the development of attitudes that favor traditional, even stereotypic views of gender roles.[22]

This concern that segregation based on sex can reinforce gender stereotypes is supported by a study of the experimental California academies. In 1997, as a pilot project California provided $5 million to institute twelve public single-sex academies, equal to each other down to the number of pencils. A study conducted by researchers from the University of Toronto and the University of California at San Diego, and sponsored by both the Ford and Spencer Foundations, evaluated the academies between 1998 and 2000, interviewing more than three hundred students, parents, teachers, and administrators and observing classes. One of the researchers' findings was that administrators viewed the state grant as a means of assisting at-risk students (which, the researchers acknowledge, may conflate other conclusions).

Another important finding was that, although the California administrators insisted on equal resources, assumptions about the different educational needs of boys and girls caused the educators to explicitly reinforce traditional gender stereotypes. As one example, during a unit on frontier exploration, the boys learned survival skills and the girls learned how to quilt and sew. The researchers concluded that overall "[b]oys tended to be taught in a more regimented, traditional, and individualistic fashion, and girls in more nurturing, cooperative and open environments."[23]

When courts do begin to assess the recent empirical evidence about single-sex schools, they will need to evaluate whether segregation is supported by an "exceedingly persuasive justification." One can only hope that that they will look at the wealth of evidence, not just selected anecdotal reports or "studies" without adequate methodological controls. Empirical inquiry needs to be systematic and searching. To comport with principles of scientific method, it should look for cumulative, comprehensive, and converging evidence and employ consistency in exploratory methods. One hopes that courts will carefully evaluate whether the claimed benefits from single-sex classes are attributable to sex segregation or to other variables, such as the experimental nature of the program, religious school influences, better student-teacher ratios, smaller class size, more experienced teachers, novelty, or additional resources.

With respect to both race and sex segregation, news reports provide little systematic information about studies on government-sponsored separatism or research on the benefits of integration. News accounts of improvements made under desegregation orders are almost uniformly tied to reports of requests for the lifting of those orders; they are rarely linked to the racial isolation, achievement gaps, and inequalities in educational opportunities that remain.

An enormous amount of coverage is given to school districts' requests to be "free" from court orders requiring desegregation, to parents' desires for neighborhood schools, and to the failures of busing. Very little interest exists in the contemporary or complete racial picture. Although some reports lament resegregation after the lifting of desegregation orders, many others proclaim the failures of desegregation and counterpoise integration and academic quality. Newspaper articles largely ignore successful integration, choosing to focus instead on perceived failures and on integration programs that have been discarded in favor of neighborhood schools. They tout the benefits of school choice using vague, unsubstantiated theories and state the belief that neighborhood schools will improve education and parental involvement without any supporting research. Articles on single-sex schools and classes usually ignore the issue of state sponsorship of segregation and instead focus on the ability of a school or a parent to choose a single-sex alternative.[24]

Newspaper articles reduce complex and nuanced studies of single-sex education to simplistic and favorable blurbs. They report the latest trial run or episodic result at a single school and make glossy pronouncements about the general state of research. These experiments in single schools or classes are reported simply as successes with no consideration of other variables that might have affected the trial. The danger with such reporting is that most people have little training in statistics; if they had that training, they might apply a discount to reports on an individual study or experience because it is unrepresentative. Work in the field of heuristics demonstrates that "people are overly influenced by single-case information."[25]

Articles in the popular media focus on human interest stories. This feeds the ways people like to receive information. In the "everybody loves a winner" tradition, newspaper and popular press articles report the success stories: satisfying experiences of girls in single-sex classes and women in single-sex colleges. Much of newspaper reporting is event based. Programs that do not work—single-sex schools that close, for example— tend to be nonevents: their demise is not proclaimed; they die quiet deaths. Compare the much-heralded opening of the California all-boys and all-girls academies with the absence of reports on the closing of all but two of them. Newspaper articles written well after the results of the Ford Foundation–sponsored study of the California academies ignore the study's results and offer instead vague political or economic excuses for the closing of the schools. Some newspaper articles fail to mention at all that any of the California pilot schools closed.[26]

It is much harder to say nothing or to publish reports about the null hypothesis. Proof of a negative does not command publication opportunities. Research results showing *no* differences between single-sex and coeducation, for example, reside in file cabinets across the country. The media, although happy to report on numerous variations of men being from Mars and women from Venus, fail to report that men and women are both from Earth.

The Jurisprudence of "Choice" and "Diversity"

Proponents of single-sex and neighborhood schools have made a curious plea for tolerance of segregation as a matter of choice. The proposition is that parents should have the choice of single-sex or coed schools because this choice provides a diversity of educational options. The separatist education movement mistakenly advances an option play concept of choice—parents should have the choice of single-sex or coeducational schools—that masquerades as the constitutional concept of diversity.

The choice and diversity arguments are rarely explored. Sometimes, perhaps often, those who might want integrated schools or better schools will not have the power to make other choices; they will not be able to choose integrated or better schools because those choices are not available. Excellent research documents that choice exacerbates segregation and undermines educational opportunities, particularly for economically disadvantaged students of color.[27]

The diversity argument? It is a slippery one. What precisely is the meaning of diversity in the context of single-sex schools? The diversity argument says that school systems should be free to provide a variety of educational choices, but diversity in this context refers to system-wide diversity. When a school district creates single-sex classes, the students experience no diversity on the basis of gender within the individual school or classroom. They are in either an all-boy or an all-girl environment. Sex separatism does not share the original constitutional diversity rationale of affording students the opportunity to learn with peers with a variety of racial, ethnic, social, or economic backgrounds. Nor is the same-sex educational choice diverse in the sense of larger social experiences, given the pervasiveness of sex segregation in society. In fact, the logic of the diversity argument becomes almost Orwellian in its implicit contradiction. Sameness is diversity. It is painful as an irony for diversity to be used in the service of segregation.

In addition to empirical data that are overlooked, tilted media reporting, and philosophical arguments about choice and diversity, the last point is that we seem to have lost the understanding of what makes government-sponsored segregation based on identity characteristics wrong. Even if the tangible aspects of the educational programs are equal, the intangible message of the separatism was at the heart of *Brown*. Fifty years ago, the Court in *Brown v. Board of Education* said unequivocally that state-sponsored racial segregation stigmatizes: "To separate [grade and high school children] from others of similar age and qualifications solely because of their race generates a feeling of inferiority as to their status in the community that may affect their hearts and minds in a way unlikely ever to be undone."[28] Government sponsorship of segregation says that different races or opposite sexes do not belong in the classroom together. The argument is presented more starkly in single-sex school cases. It is that some sort of contamination will occur through the intermingling of boys and girls. The argument is made with some stealth in the desegregation context, that parents should be able to choose neighborhood schools so that students can attend with other like-minded—read: same-race—students.

Supporters are making a sort of revivified *Plessy* argument that the use of race and gender classifications to segregate does not imply inferiority. But segregation based on identity characteristics cannot be divorced from its historical or social meaning.

Conclusion

Decisions about neighborhood and single-sex schools are being made in the first instance at the grassroots level by school boards, teachers, principals, parents, and legislatures, and this is where we can have an impact. We can advocate for accurate media portrayals of the evidence about the quality of education in race- and sex-segregated environments. We can question whether the media reporting of experiments in separatist schooling corresponds with performance results of more systematic studies. We can engage in debates about choice and diversity and explore whether sameness—the homogeneity of race and sex—really promotes the constitutional concept of the diversity. Within schools, we can target specific academic concerns, such as gender inclusivity in mixed-sex classrooms. Let us first try experiments that are more likely to be successful and less likely to be unconstitutional.

We need to return to the message of *Brown*: that separate educational facilities are inherently unequal. If history offers any lesson, surely it is that government separation of equals will recreate the very inequality that so many have fought so hard to overcome.

Notes

An expanded version of this chapter can be found in the Illinois Law Review, *Embracing Segregation: The Jurisprudence of Choice and Diversity in Race and Sex Separatism in Schools*, 2005 U. Ill. L. Rev. 455.

1. Erica Frankenberg, Chungmei Lee, and Gary Orfield, *A Multiracial Society with Segregated Schools: Are We Losing the Dream?* (Harvard University Press, 2003).

2. *Parents Involved in Community Sch. v. Seattle Sch. Dist. No. 1* (*PICS*), 127 S. Ct. 2738 (2007).

3. Congressional anti-busing legislation, passed in 1974, the Equal Education Opportunities Act, 20 U.S.C. §§ 1701–1758 (1994), declares that it is the official "policy of the United States that . . . the neighborhood is the appropriate basis for determining public school assignments." 20 U.S.C. § 1701(a)(2) (1994). On state laws, see, e.g., Delaware Code Ann. tit. 14, § 223 (2002); for discussion of this law, see Robert L. Hayman Jr., *Neutral Principles and the Resegregation Decisions*, 9 Widener L. Symp. J. 129, 131 (2002). President Reagan and a response in the Charlotte Observer are quoted in Robert L. Hayman Jr. and Nancy Levit, *The Constitutional Ghetto*, 1993 Wis. L. Rev. 627, 723.

4. Gary J. Simson, *Separate but Equal and Single-Sex Schools*, 90 Cornell L. Rev. 443, 447 n.27 (2005); National Association for Single Sex Public Education, http://www.single-sexschools.org/schools-schools.htm (last visited July 15, 2008).

5. *Single-Sex Public Schools in the United States*, available at http://www.singlesex-schools.org/schools.html; Lois K. Solomon, *Trial Run: Schools Split Class by Gender*, South Florida Sun-Sentinel, Sept. 2, 2003, at 1A.

6. 34 C.F.R. § 106.34(b)(1)(i) (2007).

7. Pub. L. No. 107–10, § 501, 115 Stat. 1425 (2002).

8. *NYC To Open Public Gay High School*, Chicago Tribune, July 29, 2003, at 3; Carl Campanile, *School's "Out"—City Is Launching First HS for Gay Teens*, N.Y. Post, July 28, 2003, at 3; the Gay, Lesbian and Straight Education Network conducted a national survey of lesbian, gay, bisexual, and transgender students. It showed that 84 percent of the respondents heard anti-gay remarks at school "frequently or often," 31 percent had "missed at least one entire day of school in the past month because they felt unsafe based on sexual orientation," 84 percent reported being verbally harassed, 31 percent physically harassed, and 21 percent physically assaulted because of their sexual orientation. Gay, Lesbian and Straight Education Network, *The 2001 National School Climate Survey: Lesbian, Gay, Bisexual and Transgender Students and Their Experiences in Schools* 2 (2001), http://www.glsen.org/binary-data/GLSEN ARTICLES/pdf file/1029.pdf.

9. See, e.g., Anne Marie Owens, *Boys' Brains Are from Mars*, National Post, May 10, 2003, at A22 (reporting on a lecture, "The Case for Boys Schools," at a National Association of Independent Schools conference by "Leonard Sax, a pediatrician smitten by the single-sex schools movement, [who] was talking about how boys are hard-wired in so many ways for qualities that are not typically valued by schools or teachers: action, directness and loudness"); *Acting Locally*, News and Observer (Raleigh, NC), Sept. 7, 2002, at A16; Jim Morrill and Henry Eichel, *Strom Thurmond, 1902–2003*, Orlando Sentinel, June 27, 2003, at A1; Robert L. Hayman Jr., *The Smart Culture: Society, Intelligence, and Law* 99–166 (New York University Press, 1998); Robert L. Hayman Jr. and Nancy Levit, "Un-natural Things: Constructions of Race, Gender, and Disability," in *Crossroads, Directions, and a New Critical Race Theory* 158, 162, Francisco Valdes et al., eds. (Temple University Press, 2002).

10. Leland Ware, *Race and Urban Space: Hypersegregated Housing Patterns and the Failure of School Desegregation*, 9 Widener L. Symp. J. 55, 63, 70 (2002).

11. Erwin Chemerinsky, *The Segregation and Resegregation of American Public Education: The Courts' Role*, 81 N.C. L. Rev. 1597, 1618 (2003); Bradley W. Joondeph, Note, *Killing Brown Softly: The Subtle Undermining of Effective Desegregation in Freeman v. Pitt*, 46 Stan. L. Rev. 147, 160 (1993); William L. Christopher, *Ignoring the Soul of Brown: Board of Education v. Dowell*, 70 N.C. L. Rev. 615, 635 (1992).

12. See generally Gary Orfield, *Metropolitan School Desegregation: Impacts on Metropolitan Society*, 80 Minn. L. Rev. 825, 829–30 (1996) (criticizing courts for blaming white flight on desegregation and "using this as a basis for ending desegregation orders. The courts have not considered, however, the possibility that their own limited remedies may have made lasting desegregation impossible"). See also William D. Henderson, *Demography and Desegregation in the Cleveland Public Schools: Toward a Comprehensive Theory of Educational Failure and Success*, 26 N.Y.U. Rev. L. and Soc. Change 457, 474 (2000–2001) (refuting the Supreme Court's conjecture that causation ran from the desegregation order to white flight: "In *Jenkins*, two decades of white outmigration to the suburbs already had left the Kansas City, Missouri school district 65 percent black when the desegregation litigation commenced in 1976. When the creation of the magnet schools was ordered in 1985, after an eight-year period of mandatory student reassignments, the black enrollment had only increased to 68.3 percent").

13. Wendy Parker, *The Supreme Court and Public Law Remedies: A Tale of Two Kansas Cities*, 50 Hastings L. J. 475, 548 (1999).

14. Gary Orfield, "Conservative Activists and the Rush Toward Resegregation," in *Law and School Reform: Six Strategies for Promoting Educational Equity* 39, 54, ed. Jay P. Heubert (Yale University Press, 1999).

15. 458 U.S. 718 (1982).

16. 518 U.S. 515 (1996); *id.*, at 534 n. 7.

17. Beth Willinger, *Single Gender Education and the Constitution*, 40 Loy. L. Rev. 253, 268 (1994)(describing M. Elizabeth Tidball's studies of women "achievers," defined solely by inclusion in *Who's Who of American Women*, and based on women's experiences at the Seven Sisters colleges, noting that these women "came from privileged backgrounds, had tremendous resources, and . . . were going to succeed no matter where they went"); Alexander W. Astin, *What Matters in College? Four Critical Years Revisited* 324 (Jossey-Bass, 1993).

18. Many studies have found no overall satisfaction differences. See, e.g., Daryl G. Smith, *Women's Colleges and Coed Colleges: Is There a Difference for Women?* 61 J. Higher Educ. 181, 184–85, 191–92 (1990). *See also* Mikyong Kim amd Rodolfo Alvarez, *Women-Only Colleges: Some Unanticipated Consequences*, 66 J. Higher Educ. 641, 645 (1995) (using national CIRP student data surveys from students at 34 women's colleges and female students at 274 coeducational schools and finding that students at women's colleges had a more positive social self-confidence but less confidence in their job preparation skills and abilities).

19. Pamela Haag, "Single-Sex Education in Grades K–12: What Does the Research Tell Us?" in American Ass'n Univ. Women Educ. Found., *Separated by Sex: A Critical Look at Single-Sex Education for Girls* 13, 22 (Foundation, 1998).

20. Nancy Levit, *Separating Equals: Educational Research and the Long-Term Consequences of Sex Segregation*, 67 Geo. Wash. L. Rev. 451, 472–505 (1999). See also Valerie E. Lee, "Is Single-Sex Secondary Schooling a Solution to the Problem of Gender Inequity," in *Separated by Sex*, at 41, 43 (offering a meta-analysis of research on private schools and finding that it demonstrates "no consistent pattern of effects for attending either single-sex or coeducational independent schools for either boys or girls"); Herbert W. Marsh, *Effects of*

Attending Single-Sex and Coeducational High Schools on Achievement, Attitudes, Behaviors, and Sex Differences, 81 J. Educ. Psychol. 70, 71 (1989) ("Once preexisting characteristics such as intelligence, prior academic achievement, motivation, and social class are controlled, however, the differences tend to be much smaller or nonsignificant"); Judith L. Stoecker and Ernest T. Pascarella, *Women's Colleges and Women's Career Attainments Revisited*, 62 J. Higher Educ. 394, 403 (1991) ("the career attainments previously linked to attendance at a women's college may be attributable more to differential student recruitment than to the socialization occurring in a distinctive institutional environment").

21. *Girls Only?* Christian Science Monitor, Sept. 5, 1996, at 20; Tanyanika Samuels, *Women's Foundation Reveals Grant Recipients*, Kansas City Star, Dec. 4, 2002; Tomiko Brown-Nagin, *Toward a Pragmatic Understanding of Status-Consciousness: The Case of Deregulated Education*, 50 Duke L. J. 753, 807 (2000); Rosemary C. Salomone, *Same, Different, Equal: Rethinking Single-Sex Schooling* 24 (Yale University Press, 2003).

22. Providence College sociology professor Cornelius Riordan suggests that minority race and sex segregation for economically disadvantaged students—segregation essentially by race and sex and class—may be academically beneficial. *See* Cornelius Riordan, *Girls and Boys in School: Together or Separate?* (Teachers College Press, 1990); Cornelius Riordan, "The Future of Single-Sex Schools," in *Separated by Sex*, at 53, 54; Cornelius Riordan, *Single-Gender Schools: Outcomes for African and Hispanic Americans*, 10 Res. Soc. Educ. and Socialization 177, 192–202 (1994). See, e.g., Valerie E. Lee, *Is Single-Sex Secondary Schooling a Solution to the Problem of Gender Inequity*, at 41, 43; Valerie E. Lee and Marlaine E. Lockheed, *The Effects of Single Sex Schooling on Achievement and Attitudes in Nigeria*, 34 Comp. Educ. Rev. 209, 225 (1990); Paul C. LePore and John Robert Warren, *A Comparison of Single-Sex and Coeducational Catholic Secondary Schooling: Evidence from the National Educational Longitudinal Study of 1988*, 34 Am. Educ. Res. J. 485, 505 (1997). See also Cornelius Riordan, "The Case for Single-Sex Schools," in *Single-Sex Schooling: Proponents Speak* 43, 44, ed. Debra K. Hollinger and Rebecca Adamson (U.S. Department of Education, 1993) (admitting that for males in "single-sex secondary or post-secondary schools" the attitudinal results "are generally null or negative"). See also Herbert W. Marsh and Kenneth J. Rowe, *The Effects of Single-Sex and Mixed-Sex Mathematics Classes Within a Coeducational School: A Reanalysis and Comment*, 40 Austl. J. Educ. 147, 153 (1996); Lesley H. Parker and Leonie J. Rennie, *Teachers' Perceptions of the Implementation of Single-Sex Classes in Coeducational Schools*, 41 Austl. J. Educ. 119, 124–25 (1997); and Margaret L. Signorella et al., *Single-Sex Versus Mixed-Sex Classes and Gender Schemata in Children and Adolescents: A Longitudinal Comparison*, 20 Psychol. Women Q. 599, 599, 606 (1996).

23. Amanda Datnow, *Single-Sex Schooling: Critique of Report Relies on "Disturbing Overgeneralization,"* Educ. Wk., Oct. 17, 2001, at 36, available at 2001 WL 12047039 ("Our study suggests that the way in which educators viewed significant differences between males and females informed their notions about classroom practice with respect to curriculum, pedagogy, and discipline; the structure and practices of the single-gender academies often contributed to the belief that boys and girls are different, to the point of ignoring the commonalties"). See also Jonathan N. Reiter, *California Single-Gender Academies Pilot Program: Separate but Really Equal*, 72 S. Cal. L. Rev. 1401 (1999); and Heather Sokoloff, *Single-Sex Schools Reinforce Gender Stereotypes—Study: Experiment in Public Education Fails*, National Post, May 25, 2001, at A13.

24. See, e.g., Jane Eisner, *Single-Sex Schools Are Valid Choice for Today*, Phila. Inquirer, May 19, 2002, at C1 ("Choice is the fundamental byword in education today, and there's no reason such schools as Girls High can't be among the choices—because of its tradition and in spite of it. For that reason, the Bush administration's shift on single-sex education in public schools is welcome"); Murray Light, *Same-Sex Schools Aren't a Good Idea*, Buff.

News, May 26, 2002, at H5 ("The Education Department said the change gives school districts greater flexibility and gives parents more choices"); Karen Stabiner, *Boys Here, Girls There: Sure, If Equality's the Goal*, Wash. Post, May 12, 2002, at B1 ("Single-sex public schools and classes, as odd as it may sound, are about inclusion; any school district that wants one can have one and everyone can learn from the experience").

25. Julian V. Roberts and Anthony N. Doob, *News Media Influences on Public Views of Sentencing*, 14 Law & Hum. Behav. 451, 453 (1990). See also Daniel Kahneman and Amos Tversky, *On the Reality of Cognitive Illusions*, 103 Psychol. Rev. 582 (1996).

26. See Rob Hotakainen, *Single-Sex Schools Are Separate, but Not Always Equal*, Star Tribune (Minneapolis–St. Paul), June 9, 2002 ("Experiments have been conducted with single-sex schools across the country, with varying results. In California, then-Gov. Pete Wilson started a 12-school pilot program in 1997, but it lacked political support and was terminated when he left office"); Massie Ritsch, *Single-Gender Schools Gaining Favor, Success*, L.A. Times, May 28, 2002 at A1 ("California attracted much attention in the late 1990s for its experiment with separate academies for boys and girls. When the state funding ran out, all but one of the six schools closed. Students at the remaining San Francisco 49ers Academies in East Palo Alto have improved their grades and behavior and are less likely to skip school or drop out, the school reports"); Marc Fisher, *One-Gender Schools Would Offer Flexibility*, Contra Costa Times (Walnut Creek, CA), May 19, 2002 ("In recent years, a few brave schools responded by separating boys and girls. California set up single gender academies, largely to boost girls' performance in math and science"). Indeed, most of the connections drawn between the Ford Foundation's study and the closing of the California pilot schools come from newspaper articles written overseas. *See Boys Will Be Boys—Educating Children Separately*, Economist (London), May 11, 2002.

27. John R. Logan, *Choosing Segregation: Racial Imbalance in American Public Schools, 1990–2000*, Lewis Mumford Center for Comparative Urban and Regional Research, http://mumford1.dyndns.org/cen2000/SchoolPop/SPReport/page1.html.

28. 374 U.S. 483, 495 (1954).

CHAPTER NINETEEN

Pre-white and Post-black: The Aesthetics of Oppression

Patricia J. Williams

One of the most controversial issues facing all schools in today's world is the current debate about economic status as a factor in deciding to whom to extend the remedy of affirmative action. I have always thought that poverty or relative economic disadvantage ought to be one of the factors in a university's commitment to diversity. As with all the other categories of the so-called piggyback claims in the wake of the civil rights movement of the 1960s—age, gender, disability, and the like—I believe that broad definitions of the quest for integration unite and strengthen us in the end. Yet I am also extremely concerned that, in recent debates, economic status is being discussed as a complete substitute for integration by race, and the attempt to ground affirmative action in the history of Jim Crow and its scarring legacy is increasingly pooh-poohed as mere whining. This is a distressing turn of events, particularly because there do not exist the same constitutional grounds for claims of economic disparity as for race.

Obviously, the fate of affirmative action in any form is a freighted issue, with its future to some extent predetermined by the battle over the composition of the courts that looms around us. But given that reality, it is interesting nonetheless to explore the degree to which economic status seems to be a kind of cipher for race, but in complicated ways. I began that exploration by thinking about the neighborhood in which I grew up, which at that time was a white working-class neighborhood in Boston. My family had been there since the early 1900s, in the house where my grandmother raised my mother, and for fifty years or so, we were the only black people in the immediate area.

The rest of the residents were immigrants from all over Europe. They were from Ireland, Germany, Russia, southern Italy, and Portugal. They had a multitude of good reasons for wanting to escape to the United States, and they carried their traumas with them. They prospered in this little neighborhood, a neighborhood of so-called workmen's cottages—small wooden-framed houses that were built by the great New England breweries of that era, such as Haffenreffer and Reingold. In the post-1950s era, sociologists would classify this sort of neighborhood as one marked by upwardly mobile aspirations and ideals. But growing up in the middle of it, I must say that those aspirations did not seem to be a prominent feature of their thinking, at least not in the way that we think of upwardly mobile today, in the sense of looking to the future or desiring more in the way of consumer goods. It was an era when boys still wanted to grow up to be what their fathers had been—policemen, firemen, postal clerks, and factory workers—and girls were raised to get married. Rather, the dynamic felt more like escapism from the past. It was profoundly calibrated toward rebutting the humiliations of what their recent forebearers had experienced when occupying the peasant status in the old country. "Peasant" was an epic equivalent to what in other parts of America might have been phrased as "white trash." They were fighting words.

Now, eventually this self-consciousness emerged as the full-blown anxiety about middle classness that today marks much of American social life, but at that time I remember my neighbors were fully intent upon erasing every last ethnic marker they could. In other words, their sense of visible ethnicity, in the Anglophilic Brahmin Boston of that time, was a more keenly felt marker of low status than economics. All our neighbors were so extremely focused on how they might be seen; they were so worried about how to wrap themselves in the symbolic trappings of America as a means to escape the oppressions of the old world, and so they laughed at each others' accents until they lost the accent. They studied Shirley Temple movies and peroxided their hair, then ironed the curls out of their hair, then pin-curled sausage-shaped spirals back in again. They Anglicized their names. They cringed at the stories about jovial Italian organ grinders that were popular back then as much as my family shuddered at stories about grinning banjo-picking slaves. They hated their noses or their brother's ginger hair or their father's crinkly black mustachios. They looked down on anyone whose large toe exceeded the length of the second, for an elongated second toe was an unquestioned indicator of elegance and royal blood. There were people in my neighborhood who proudly and loudly traced their lineage to disgraceful degrees of royal bastardy, people who looked to Cinderella as allegorical redemption, so much in those days did everyone yearn to "pass."

Luckily everyone in my family is blessed with long, elegant second toes. But that could only do so much, and my sister and I were always "the Negro children" or "the colored kids." Yet I am not sure that any of my recent immigrant neighbors ever fully thought of themselves as truly white until the beginning of that Great Migration of blacks from the rural southern states to the North, that immense migration toward hoped-for freedoms that transformed urban centers into so-called inner cities.

A remarkable change occurred in those years of the early to mid-sixties. I remember the first black family other than ours that came to this neighborhood, a family of former sharecroppers from Mississippi. When they moved in, they were not greeted as just another part of an escaping immigrant wave, another part of the abused peasantry, albeit of home-grown origin. They were not seen as another group of those struggling with accents, the new dark-skinned serfs.

This family had two little boys who took the same route to school as I did, and I can remember walking some distance behind them, observing the adults on my street observe the boys, and it was alarming to watch face after face at house after house peer from behind the busyness of curtains. It made my stomach hurt with fear to see the reactions of these people I had thought of as friends, these people who had come to the neighborhood after my grandparents and so many of whom had been welcomed to the neighborhood with my grandmother's baked goods, these people who had grown up with my mother. Seeing these two little boys, and then the flood of others who followed, the neighbors' faces were transformed into constricted, tight, frowning masks of disapproval. I would like to think that those neighbors saw something of themselves in the black laborers who came to settle in their midst. "They look like farmers," sneered one haughty neighbor who herself was the grandchild of potato farmers. It is the most forgiving interpretation I can attach to the panic that characterized the wholesale exodus that was "white flight" from that neighborhood. "The property values are falling, are falling!" was the alarm that burned its way up and down the streets.

These days, the neighborhood I grew up in is largely black. Boston University is talking about building a biohazards laboratory there so it could explore the infectious potential of the Ebola virus, and charges of environmental racism fill the newspapers. The property values are plummeting in anticipation of such a move. Yet aside from race—if there can be an aside from race—the neighborhood's other demographics are very much as they always were. It is made up of honest, hard-working laborers, police officers, security guards, secretaries, and health workers. The residents are no longer predominantly migrants from Mississippi, but now come from Haiti, the Dominican Islands, the Virgin Islands, and Brazil.

It is very interesting how the quest for economic integration so often dovetails with the question of racial integration. The question of economic diversity became a wholesale displacement of the quest for racial inclusion soon after Ward Connerly's proposition for color-blind standards became popularized in California and in Texas. In response, Texas and a few other states instituted a "10 percent solution." That is, the top 10 percent of any graduating class from any public school—those schools in the poorer districts as well as those in the wealthy districts—would be automatically admitted to that state's college system. This form of economic diversity actually increased the numbers of ethnic and racial minorities, thus clearly revealing the degree to which economic status overlaps with racial disparity.

The City of Boston is attempting to do away with racial integration as a goal in upgrading neighborhood schools, including the schools in the neighborhood where I grew up. It is using a familiar argument: time has passed. Segregation is not the result of state action any more, but just de facto social "choice." Perhaps. Here are some statistics to give that "de facto" status some flesh. Nationally, 88 percent of schools in which the population is 90 percent or more black have most of their students living in poverty. It is hard to do worse than that, but in Boston, 97 percent of those mostly black schools are also schools with a majority of students living in poverty. By way of contrast, in those schools where the population is at least 90 percent white, only 1 percent have a majority of poor students.

Complicating this whole picture is a kind of invisible emotional aesthetic—a set of unspoken taboos that reinforce the free-floating overlap of race and economics into something like a caste system. That intractability is yet further reinforced by the recent burgeoning of the technology of sorting. It is not only police who gather information about us based on race, but all kinds of entities. We live in a world of market clustering, of political polling, of predictions. Now, not just young black men have profiles, but—particularly since the USA Patriot Act—so do whole new categories of suspect human beings from nuns to musicians to Arab Americans. We are categorized as shoppers, as voters, as Internet users. Every last preschooler has a predictive indicator.

So we are sorted and spaced in a way that overlaps to a certain degree with some of the traditional markers that divided us based on what we look like. Such is life, I suppose. But it worries me because I think it builds upon specific histories of perception and perhaps magnifies some of the "differences" we would be better off discarding. Moreover, our new hybridized economic profiles might feel cleaner and more innocent, but again, I think it serves no one to brush aside or bury the racialized root causes of those categorical divides because race is just so tense and makes everybody upset.

But in that reconfiguration, we must remember that economic equality is not constitutionally mandated. We can address our class problems surely, but such action will always be voluntary under the current legal structure of our country. And to the extent we have tried to deal with economic status, I wonder if we have not come face to face with an ugly aspect of resistance in what we call the culture wars; that is, the raised eyebrows and sad complaint that this or that person just doesn't fit in. You know, nothing personal, but they just don't go out for golf or squash. It exposes, I think, our old friend ethnicity, as well as race and economics, as underpinning "culture"—a culture that is rooted in something weighted toward an English notion of Christian middle-class culture.

So let me try this from the other side. Let us look at what we do when we disparage the poor in this country. Let us take that disparagement from its Paris Hilton/*Hee-Haw*/Jerry Springer entertainment function and really look at what we mean if we are serious about the enterprise of economic integration in our schools. When we say "low class," we do not just make it mean economic. We mean a kind of aesthetic as well, and that is a very difficult social force to deal with. We have not begun to deal with the seemingly unconscious—I will generously assume it is unconscious—shaming rituals heaped upon our hardest working and least fortunate.

I think about the densely populated neighborhood where I grew up, soon to be home to a biohazards laboratory that, whatever the scientific safeguards, has already lowered property values just at the whisper of its planned existence. This is a neighborhood of poor good people with no place to flee.

Statistics show that 91 percent of the students in Boston's outer suburbs are white. Few are poor. In Boston's inner city black neighborhoods, the houses are worth much less than those in the suburbs. The tax base is lower. Yet people need jobs, even if only *schlepping* biohazards. The median income of black people is 62 percent of median white income, but the net worth—that is the overall asset wealth—of black people is only 12 percent of the median net worth of white people.

This economic disparity actually affects the definition of who is black and who is white. There is a circularity of economic status and social aesthetics and racial category. After all, historically (that is, before the Civil War), whiteness was not simply determined by skin color, and we have forgotten that. Legal historian Ariela Gross has documented how other evidence of whiteness included ancestry, the famous "one drop" blood rule, the exercise of citizenship and voting rights, self-representation or claimed identity, reputation and acceptance among others, and "white conduct and character," or what Gross calls "the performing of whiteness." According to Gross, a white man's honor resided in the public sphere, in the statesmanlike behavior toward superiors and inferiors, his adherence to the gentlemen's code of conduct, his mastery of slaves, and his exercise of citizenship. In the 1835 South Carolina case of *State v. Cantey*, for example, the judge observed that, despite an ambiguous appearance, "it may be well and proper that a man of worth, honesty, industry and respectability should have the rank of a white man while a vagabond of the same degree of blood should be confined to the inferior caste."

So this is one way of inscribing cultural attributes, manners, as well as economic status into determinants of one's racial status. One must also wonder if this history is not echoed in the chilling belief structures that linger with us today. Let me posit some admittedly glib hypotheticals to make a point. Today, "real blacks" are not just those who are dark skinned or impoverished or politically disenfranchised, but those who supposedly exhibit that malleable cipher for black character, the "culture of pathology." Real whites, meanwhile, remain known by the mobility of their hair and by lips so thin they need collagen implants before the calipers can get a read on them, and adherence to a moral code so pure they need neither abortion nor birth control but just a good clean Petri dish into which to scrape select genetic characteristics for reproduction.

In between these two conceptual extremes (and again I am not being entirely serious here; I apologize) remains the legacy of enslaved whites and uppity blacks who in today's world seem to occupy a limbo of what I call pre-whiteness and post-blackness. Pre-whites include not only downsized poor white factory workers but also those whom the mainstream media always mark as aspirational immigrants, those who do not look yet like real Americans but who, with hard work at two or more jobs and lots of intermarriage, should be white in no time.

A post-black, on the other hand, is that light-skinned ubiquitous pretender to victimhood who malaprops his way through the one professional job that should have been divided among ten better qualified whites and who is known less for the content than the contentiousness of his character. Post-blacks exist in the realm of that utterly paradoxical category of social projection, the, "new black middle class" that includes anyone, from security guards to Oprah Winfrey, deemed not a member of the "black underclass."

In sum, the slipperiness of how we define “real blacks” by that last status—the “underclass” (i.e., something that is not even “low class,” but is actually *beneath* class)—is something that points the way for all our future work. It underscores the extent to which these portrayals still hold such uninformed and unquestioned sway and the degree to which we Americans may find our best work still ahead.

CHAPTER TWENTY

Charter Schools in the Context of *Brown*: Panacea or Faustian Bargaining?

Jeffrey A. Raffel

Charter schools are "semi-autonomous public schools, founded by educators, parents, community groups or private organizations that operate under a written contract with a state, district or other entity."[1] The first state charter school enabling law was passed by Minnesota in 1991, and a decade later there were more than 2,000 charter schools in the nation. Across the nation as of July 2008 there were almost 4,100 charter schools in forty states and the District of Columbia serving more than 1.2 million students.[2]

The growth in the charter school movement has been fueled in part by the support and participation of African Americans. There are several reasons for this commitment. Some African American leaders and parents have concluded that school desegregation has not worked and that black children have borne the brunt of desegregation plans. Others argue that only the poor lack choices; those with resources can escape inadequate public schools by moving to school districts with quality schools or sending their children to private or parochial school. Charters are also attractive to those in our largest cities who see urban schools as failures.

Even though African Americans do provide substantial support to and involvement in charter schools, those schools do evoke concern. Although many charter schools are desegregated, many are not because of their location in the inner city or their theme or educational philosophy. The question of whether charter schools have led to greater school segregation is certainly relevant for considering *Brown*'s legacy. African American advocates of charter schools might well argue that the issue here is not desegregation, but *opportunities* for black students. Their argument would be that charter schools have improved education for African American students. After all, charter schools are designed to achieve the following objectives:

- Create new schools to serve as laboratories for successful teaching strategies
- Free schools from rules so they can meet higher expectations
- Open the system to new school providers
- Let parent choice drive the entire system to improve

Thus, charter schools are viewed as improving the educational achievement of black students, although perhaps by increasing school segregation.[3]

Cottrol, Diamond, and Ware, in *Brown v. Board of Education: Caste, Culture, and the Constitution,* note that in the 1930s and early 1940s the NAACP faced the possibility of what they termed a "Faustian bargain." The *Gaines* decision had led to increased graduate and professional opportunities for blacks in segregated postsecondary institutions. "The NAACP could have accepted segregation in exchange for more resources and expanded opportunities but they chose to press ahead in battle for school desegregation with a frontal assault on *Plessy*."[4] Do we face a Faustian bargain more than fifty years after *Brown* by accepting greater school segregation in exchange for increased educational achievement for African American students through the widespread adoption of charter schools?

This leads to my research question: Have charter schools improved the quality of education and achievement for African American students, and has any progress been at the expense of school desegregation?

Charter Schools in Delaware, a *Brown v. Board of Education* State

Delaware, often called a microcosm of the United States because of its border location, rural/suburban/urban areas, and bellwether status, is a good state in which to examine this research question in greater detail. The fact that Delaware had two cases subject to the *Brown v. Board of Education* decision makes it even more appropriate to see how charter schools have played a role in Delaware's response to *Brown* and its aftermath.

A significant portion of Delaware's African American community has embraced the charter school movement. The Wilmington committee that considered how to respond to the Neighborhood Schools Act, a anti-busing response to the lifting of the federal court order requiring city–suburban busing to achieve school desegregation, recommended two plans, one of which called for Wilmington to become a charter district. Several charter schools have been founded in Wilmington and attract many city students. Even at the University of Delaware there is an interest in charters by African American leaders and future leaders—four analytical papers on charter schools, all written by African American students, were submitted in the last few years.[5] There are indications that city and suburban charter schools have led to a decrease in school desegregation, and questions about the educational effectiveness of charters have been raised, especially as they attract students from the traditional school systems. This chapter explores the research question stated above integrating national data with information from Delaware.

The Current Status of Charter Schools

There has been significant growth in the number of charter schools in Delaware. In Delaware in 1997 less than 1 percent of the state's public school students were in charter schools; by 2001–2 almost 5 percent of the state's public school students attended in charters.

Delaware's eleven charter schools serving 5,000 students place it after Arizona and Michigan as the state with the third-highest percentage of public school students in charters across the United States. Delaware's charter schools illustrate the range of charters across the nation—from the Delaware Military Academy (a junior ROTC school), Kuumba Academy (which emphasizes parental involvement), Thomas Edison Academy (run by a private corporation), Wilmington Charter School (a cooperative effort of six of Delaware's leading science and technology companies: Astra Zeneca, Christiana Health Care, Conectiv, DuPont, Hercules Incorporated, and Verizon), through the Newark Charter School, which is more like an academically focused neighborhood school with a parent board.

There are some indications that charter school growth has slowed, with proponents arguing that the educational establishment has placed obstacles in the path of expansion and opponents suggesting that charter schools have not been as successful as originally proposed. Supply issues may have also slowed charter growth as funding for buildings and the supply of willing educational entrepreneurs are limited. In Massachusetts the state legislature passed a moratorium on initiating charter schools while their benefits and financial aspects could be evaluated. Governor Romney, however, vetoed the act, and an attempt to override the veto in the legislature failed.[6]

Innovation and Educational Practice

Charter schools are categorized by their governance arrangement and not by their educational philosophy or practices. The National Working Commission on Choice in K–12 Education, a group funded by the Bill and Melinda Gates and Annie E. Casey Foundations to make recommendations on how to implement choice while maximizing benefits and minimizing harmful aspects of choice, concluded, "Choice is not an instructional program and its effects are conditional. . . . Choice itself does not cause any outcome, good or bad. Everything depends on what happens next."[7] Another recent review of charters concluded, "We know far less about what happens inside charter school classrooms than we know how charter schools are organized and governed."[8] But what we do know indicates that the great range of types of charters found even in Delaware, nicknamed "the Small Wonder," reflects the national situation—charters can include every type of school, from military academies to science and math high schools. Thus, RAND researchers concluded in their research on California's charters in 2003 that there is "*no single charter school approach and therefore no single charter school effect.*"[9] Variety, however, does not necessarily translate into innovation.

Although charter schools have been advocated as a means to increase innovation in public education, primarily because of the presumed effects of competition and market responsiveness, this is by no means what researchers are finding. A recent study of four states with the most charter schools found that, although charter schools sometimes gave parents in a particular jurisdiction an alternative not available before, few charters are innovating and most are providing traditional or basic education. The study suggests that the major force that was supposed to lead to innovation—competition—actually fosters the use of traditional and proven models in an effort to attract and retain parents and children and avoid risky and costly ideas.[10] Charters may have the *opportunity* to innovate, but it can be argued that innovation is more likely to take place when organization survival is not at stake and not dependent on consumers who are relatively traditional.

If charters have not brought educational innovation, have they at least done a better job of traditional schooling and thereby improved student achievement?

Charter Schools and Student Achievement

We have a great amount of anecdotal information and test score data on student achievement in charter schools, and many of these reports are not positive. In Ohio a reporter in 2003 concluded, "This was the first year charter schools got report cards, which gives them an academic label based on test scores, attendance, and graduation rates. Had they been children, the schools might have gotten a spanking."[11] Nearly 80 percent of the schools failed to show "adequate yearly progress." In 2004, 67 percent of children in the public schools of Texas passed the state assessment tests, but only 42 percent of the charter school students did as well.[12]

Delaware charter schools have yielded positive and negative reports as well. The East Side Charter School in Wilmington has done exceptionally well—all third graders passed the state reading and math tests, despite 88 percent of the students coming from low-income homes. Perhaps the eleven months each year of schooling, small school size (just under 150 students), the full-day kindergarten, and the teachers who work well into the late afternoon are the reasons.[13] The Charter School of Wilmington has two and one-half pages of "Recent Achievements" singled spaced on its Web site, from its "superior performance" on the Delaware Public School Accountability Ratings to winning the Science and Math Excellence in Teaching Award in 1999. But only 8 percent of this high school's students are African American, and few are low income. The results for other city charters, as discussed below, have not been so positive. Reporter Michele Fuetsch notes that four of the nine charter schools in the state open long enough to be rated under the No Child Left Behind legislation did not make adequate progress.[14] Although students at Wilmington Charter School and Newark Charter School topped the state, these seemingly successful charter schools are not serving inner city minority students.

The results of Delaware's most recent science and social studies testing indicated that 88.7 percent of the state's fourth graders met the science standards in 2003 and 68.2 percent met the social studies standards. Charters in which a lower percentage of students met both standards were the Academy of Dover Charter

School, Kuumba Academy Charter School, Marion T. Academy Charter School, and the Thomas A. Edison Charter School. Three of these four under-average charter schools, each serving almost all African American students, were in Wilmington. Their sixth-grade results were equally disappointing. On the other hand, the Newark Charter School's students, drawn from suburban families in an area known for its interest in education, topped the charts in sixth grade in both science and social studies. Again, the scores reflect the types of children who attend these schools. Perhaps a complicated multivariate analysis would report a slight increase in one of these schools over the results "expected" from the usual extremely high relation between parental background and test scores, but it is clear that if there is a charter effect on achievement in Delaware, it is minor at best.[15]

Several national reviews incorporating more scientific evidence have been completed that attempt to take into account the types of students that charter schools are educating by either comparing test scores to those in other schools serving students in nearby neighborhoods, looking at scores over time, or somehow trying to "control" for the initial achievement of the students. The most positive of these studies indicates "that charter schools are keeping pace with conventional schools."[16] A RAND study of charter schools in the states with the most charters—Arizona, Michigan, and Texas—concluded, "In sum, evidence on the academic performance of charter schools is mixed."[17]

Researchers from the Consortium for Policy Research in Education concluded that it is difficult to measure the achievement effects of charter schools because charters differ across states, are relatively new, have unstable enrollments, and use many different standardized tests.[18] A recent review of charter school effects on student achievement bemoans the paucity of research, even in states such as Delaware that have had charters for almost a decade. It concludes, "Thus, irrespective of study quality, the main finding is that charter schools appear to have a negligible (if slightly negative) aggregate net impact on student achievement . . . [although] there also appears to be considerable variations across states." (Arizona's charters had a positive impact; Michigan's were negative; Texas's charters were mixed. it could not explain why some states had success and others did not.)[19]

In the summer of 2004, the effect of charter schools on student achievement received a great deal of national attention. The lead headline in the August 18, 2004, *New York Times* was "Charter Schools Trail in Results, U.S. Data Reveals."[20] The American Federation of Teachers (AFT) released a study using National Assessment of Educational Progress (NAEP) data from the U.S. Department of Education showing that students in charter schools had done worse on the national assessments than students in traditional public schools.[21] The uproar over the report and its coverage led to a full-page ad in the *New York Times* funded by the Center for Education Reform, a major charter school advocate, and signed by leading social scientists, such as Jay P. Greene (Manhattan Institute), Eric A. Hanushek (Stanford), Paul T. Hill (University of Washington and formerly of RAND), Tom Loveless (Brookings), Terry Moe (Stanford), Paul Peterson (Harvard), and Herbert Walberg (University of Illinois, Chicago), criticizing the AFT study for ignoring questions of adequacy of comparison groups and using cross-sectional rather than longitudinal data. Critics of the AFT report, including the director of the National Center for Educational Statistics and the Department of Education, argued that many charter schools served the most disadvantaged students and thus were not fairly compared to traditional public schools serving a more privileged clientele. Indeed, many charters are targeted at dropouts, students from disadvantaged backgrounds, and even those who have been expelled.[22]

Although researchers raised valid methodological points about the AFT report, after this brouhaha even those who accepted the critique found it difficult to argue that charter schools as a whole were more effective than traditional schools. Indeed, in November 2004 a study conducted for the U.S. Department of Education that adjusted for the racial and economic background of the students found that students in charter schools were less likely than those in traditional public schools to meet state standards in the five states studied.[23]

In summary, to the best of our current knowledge, on the average, children who attend charters do not learn any more than they would have if they attended their traditional public school.

Several questions arise from these studies and review article:

- Given the wide range of pedagogical approaches used in charter schools why would we expect a singular effect on student achievement?
- Have charters that are more effective in raising student achievement been in existence longer than those that are not as effective?
- How can we control for parental motivation, which is quite likely to lead to charter school students being more motivated and receiving greater parental support than those remaining in traditional public schools?
- To the extent that charters are more effective, is that the result of the placement of charter schools in areas where students are most in need, and therefore the good results are an effect of what evaluators term "regression to the mean," rather than of more effective education?
- When charters are more effective, is that effectiveness due to the unique characteristics of the charters (e.g. smaller schools, smaller class sizes, more attuned to student interests), or can conventional public schools replicate what the charter schools are doing that is successful?
- And, most important for this work, what are the effects of charters on African American students, especially those who have not done well historically in inner cities? (Studies generally present aggregated and not race-specific results.)

These questions have not been adequately answered, and they suggest that we have a way to go before truly understanding the benefits of charter schools for African American children. However, there is strong evidence that charter schools per se will not be a panacea for black children.

Parental Satisfaction

Although there is no consensus on the effectiveness of charters in increasing student achievement, there is a consensus that parents with children in charter schools are more satisfied with their children's education than those with children in traditional public schools. Gill and colleagues conclude that parents are generally happy with charter schools and report "high levels of satisfaction" with them.[24] The National Working Commission on Choice concludes, "Research consistently shows that parents who choose are more satisfied with schools than parents who do not choose."[25]

A recent Delaware survey manifests this satisfaction. Noble reports that almost all parents surveyed with children in a charter school in Delaware judged their schools as "somewhat" or "very" successful.[26] The *Wilmington News Journal* recently reported on the "Lucky Few" who had been accepted to Newark Charter as well as other charters; 490 applicants applied for 162 openings for the fifth-grade class in the Newark Charter School. As per state law, the "lucky few" allowed to enroll were selected by lottery.[27]

Given the consensus on parental satisfaction with charters, attention has shifted to *why* this satisfaction exists. Schneider and Buckley's work is the most sophisticated in trying to determine why parental satisfaction with charters is higher than satisfaction with conventional schools. They propose four possible reasons:

- Consumer sovereignty: choice results in a better match between the child's needs and the school's program.
- Better "products": charter schools may develop better parent-school relationships or be more attentive to student needs.
- Act of choice itself: people who choose need to justify their choice or feel good about the act of choosing.
- Bias of those parents who make the choice of charters: they are different in their views before they make that choice.

Their study of choice in Washington, D.C., suggests that the higher level of satisfaction with teachers, principals, facilities, and schools that parents with children in charters report is based upon more than their involvement in choosing their child's school.[28]

Thus, evidence exists that charter schools yield African American parental satisfaction but not necessarily increased academic achievement. Given these impacts, what has been the effect of charter schools on school desegregation?

School Desegregation

The initial studies of segregation and charter schools were not consistent. Gill et al. found that California's charter schools were serving similar racial/ethnic populations as the conventional schools, but were more likely to attract blacks and somewhat more likely to be desegregated than other schools in the district.[29] The U.S. Department of Education study found that, although white students accounted for a smaller percentage of the enrollment in charters than in traditional schools, seven of ten charter schools had enrollments similar to that of neighboring school districts.[30] The National Working Commission on Choice concluded, "Much depends on the incentives embodied in state law"; that is, if the state encouraged charters to serve disadvantaged students, more minority students were served.[31]

The most comprehensive and recent study of the extent of segregation of students in charter schools, conducted by associates of Gary Orfield (Frankenburg and Lee), found that charter schools in the sixteen states with at least 5,000 students in charter schools in the 2000–2001 school year were *more segregated* than the public schools. Specifically they reported, "70 percent of all black charter school students attend intensely segregated minority schools compared with 34 percent of black public school students." Interestingly, in these states a majority of charter school students were nonwhite.[32]

Perhaps because Delaware's schools are so desegregated, charters have been a segregating influence. Delaware schools have remained among the most desegregated in the nation. Although dropping somewhat on the top ten list, Delaware's schools are still models of desegregation.[33] In contrast, Delaware's charter schools are not. Wilmington now has six charters, all but two of which serve minority students almost exclusively: East Side Charter: 144 students, no whites; Kuumba Academy, 240 students, no whites; Marion T. Academy, 606 students, 10 whites; Thomas Edison Charter, 776 students, 20 whites. The Delaware Military Academy recently opened with 305 high school students, of whom 22 percent are black. The Charter School of Wilmington has 918 students, including 75 or 8.2 percent African American students. There are twice as many Asians at the school. In suburban New Castle County, the Newark Charter School (grades 5–7) has an enrollment of 621—82.3 percent white and 9.8 percent black—and the MOT Charter, south of the canal, has 594 students, only 6 percent black.

Although African American students in charters that are all black or almost all black (N = 4) now account for less than 10 percent of the black public school students in New Castle County, they account for about 20 percent of the African American students in Wilmington. Audrey Noble, director of the University of Delaware's Education Research and Development Center, has concluded, "The student bodies of Delaware's choice schools appear to be less diverse than the populations of the districts from which they draw. . . . Some Delaware choice schools enroll very high percentages of minority students; others enroll very few."[34]

Thus, both recent national and Delaware data indicate that, although minorities have gained access to charter schools, this access has increased the overall segregation of schools.

Conclusions and Implications

At the beginning of this chapter, I asked whether charter schools presented another Faustian choice: were African Americans who advocated charter schools giving up school desegregation for more educational opportunity and greater student achievement? A review of the available evidence indicates that we have few data that charter schools will help improve the educational achievement of black students. Although they do result in higher levels of parental satisfaction, this comes at the cost of increased segregation. Of course, in many communities one could argue that they do not exact that cost because the demographic, legal, and political forces against desegregation are too great anyway. In Delaware, however, where schools are about as desegregated as anywhere in the nation, some school desegregation has been sacrificed by encouraging charter schools. *Charters have not brought educational equality to African American students.* As the National Working Commission on Choice concludes, "Choice is unlikely to be the panacea for American schools trumpeted by its advocates. It is equally unlikely to be the death of public support for American education, the fear of its detractors."[35]

But we should be warned that, at least as far as we can conclude today, charter schools may not improve the educational achievement of African American students and probably will lead to increased school segregation despite (or because of) their popularity in the black community. As we look to the future of this market-based alternative, the best advice is: Caveat emptor—buyer beware!

Notes

1. Accessed at http://www.ecs.org/ecsmain.asp?page=/html/IssueCollapse.asp on July 14, 2008.

2. Accessed at http://www.edreform.com/index.cfm?fuseAction=document8documentID =1964 on July 14, 2008. This is the Web site for the Center for Education Reform, an organization that advocates for charter schools.

3. Paul T. Hill and Robin J. Lake, *Charter Schools and Accountability in Public Education* (Brookings, 2002). Michael Owens argues that vouchers, a more radical choice strategy than charters, are supported by black parents but opposed by black leaders. Michael Lee Owens, *Why Blacks Support Vouchers*, N.Y. Times, Feb. 26, 2004.

4. Robert J. Cottrol, Raymond T. Diamond, and Leland B. Ware, *Brown v. Board of Education: Caste, Culture, and the Constitution* 107 (University Press of Kansas, 2004).

5. Theopolis Gregory, *Reconsider Charter Schools as an Option for the City*, News Journal (Wilmington), Sept. 17, 2001, at A-13; Bryan G. Nance, "Reengineering as a Model to Manage the Charter School Implementation Process: Charter Schools as Seen Through a Business Process Reengineering Prism" (analytical paper submitted to the faculty of the School of Urban Affairs and Public Policy, University of Delaware, May 1999); Dawn Curry, "Charter Schools Taking a LEADing Role: A Study of Leadership and Management Training Needs in Delaware's Public Charter Schools" (analytical paper submitted to the faculty of the School of Urban Affairs and Public Policy, University of Delaware, May 2001); Marcus A. Henry, "Delaware Charter Schools: A Comparative Analysis and Review" (analytical paper submitted to the faculty of the School of Urban Affairs and Public Policy, University of Delaware, May 2001); Wendell Howell, "A Historical View of School Vouchers and Charter Schools: The Advocates, Outcomes, and Implications" (analytical paper submitted to the faculty of the School of Urban Affairs and Public Policy, University of Delaware, May 2002).

6. Education Commission of the States (ECS), http://www.ecs.org (accessed on January 15, 2004); Howell, "A Historical View of School Vouchers and Charter Schools"; Legislative Analyst's Office, 2004, Assessing California's Charter Schools. Sacramento, CA, Jan. 20. Available from http://www.lao.ca.gov/2004/charter_schools/012004_charter_schools.htm (accessed on April 2, 2004); Darcia Harris Bowman, *Charter School Openings Lowest in Six Years*, Education Week, Feb. 18, 2004; Suzanne Sataline, *Vetoes Freeze on New Charter Schools: Lawmakers Considering an Override*, Boston Globe, June 26, 2004. Several city districts, however, are now considering expanding their commitments to charters including Buffalo and New York City. Catherine Gewertz, *Donors Will Underwrite N.Y.C.*

Charter Schools, Education Week, Nov. 5, 2003; Catherine Gewertz, *Buffalo Board Votes to Court Charter Schools*, Education Week, July 7, 2004.

7. National Working Commission on Choice in K–12 Education, *School Choice: Doing It the Right Way Makes a Difference* (The Brown Center on Educational Policy, Brookings Institution, 2003).

8. Katrina Bulkley and Jennifer Fisler, *A Decade of Charter Schools: From Theory to Practice* (Consortium for Policy Research in Education, University of Pennsylvania, 2003).

9. Cathy Krop, Dan McCaffrey, Melinda Sandler, and Dominic Brewer, *Charter School Operations and Performance: Evidence from California* (RAND, 2003).

10. Ron Zimmer, Richard Buddin, Derrick Chau, Brian Gill, Cassandra Guarino, Laura Hamilton, and Christopher Lubienski, "Charter School Innovation in Theory and Practice: Autonomy, R & D, and Curricular Conformity," in *Taking Account of Charter Schools: What's Happened and What's Next?* ed. Katrina E. Bulkley and Priscilla Wohlstetter, 72–90 (Teachers College Press, 2004).

11. Scott Stephens, *State Gives Charters Poor Marks,* Plain Dealer (Cleveland), Sept. 2, 2003.

12. Terrence Stutz, *Charters Score Below Public Schools,* Dallas Morning News, Oct. 21, 2004.

13. Michele Fuetsch, *Eastside Sets Standard to Be Proud of: Despite Obstacles Every Third-Grader at Small School Passed Math, Reading Tests,* News Journal (Wilmington), July 31, 2003.

14. Michele Fuetsch, *Delaware Schools Reeling: Unforgiving Federal Ratings Fail to Show Actual Progress,* News Journal (Wilmington), Aug. 12, 2003.

15. Audrey Noble, *School Choice Revisited* (presentation to the School Choice in the New Era of Federal Accountability Summit, Rehoboth, DE, Oct. 23, 2003); Michele Fuetsch, *Scores: Social Studies Spending Lags,* News Journal (Wilmington), Feb. 20, 2004, at A1, A8.

16. Zimmer, "Charter School Innovation in Theory and Practice."

17. Brian P. Gill, Michael Timpane, Karen E. Ross, and Dominic J. Brewer, *Rhetoric Versus Reality: What We Know and What We Need to Know About Vouchers and Charter Schools* (RAND, 2001).

18. Bulkley and Fisler, *A Decade of Charter Schools.*

19. Gary Miron and Christopher Nelson, "Student Achievement in Charter Schools: What We Know and Why We Know So Little," in *Taking Account of Charter Schools: What's Happened and What's Next?* ed. Katrina E. Bulkley and Priscilla Wohlstetter, 161–75 (Teachers College Press, 2002).

20. Diana Jean Schemo, *Charter Schools Trail in Results, U.S. Data Reveals,* N.Y. Times, Aug. 17, 2004, at A1.

21. F. Howard Nelson, Bella Rosenberg, and Nancy Van Meter, *Charter School Achievement on the 2003 National Assessment of Educational Achievement* (accessed at http://www.aft.org on September 2, 2004)

22. Debra Viadero, *AFT Charter Study Sparks Heated National Debate,* Education Week, Sept. 1, 2004, at 9.

23. Sam Dillon and Diana Jean Schemo, *Charter Schools Fall Short in Public Schools Matchup,* N.Y. Times, Nov. 23, 2004, at A19. Ted Kolderie, a charter school advocate, argues that the charter school movement should be viewed as a systems change effort, and thus examining student achievement or innovation across the great range of charters misspecifies the appropriate research question. "Studies of this sort are an embarrassment to the research community." Ted Kolderie, "*Chartering*"*: How Are We to Evaluate It?* Education Week, Oct. 8, 2003, at 30. The more appropriate question would focus on what kinds of charter schools have what kinds of effects.

24. Gill et al., *Rhetoric Versus Reality.*

25. National Working Commission on Choice in K–12 Education, *School Choice.*

26. Noble, *School Choice Revisited.*

27. Kathryn Canavan, *Lucky Few: Emotions Run High in the School Admissions Process,* News Journal (Wilmington), Feb. 5, 2004, at CH6–7.

28. Mark Schneider and Jack Buckley, *Making the Grade: Comparing DC Charter Schools to Other DC Public Schools,* 25 Educational Evaluation and Policy Analysis 203–15 (2003).

29. Gill et al., *Rhetoric Versus Reality.*

30. RPP International, *The State of Charter Schools* 2000; *Fourth Year Report.* Washington, DC: Office of Educational Research and Improvement, U.S. Department of Education (January 2000).

31. National Working Commission on Choice, at 22.

32. Erica Frankenburg and Chungmei Lee, *Charter Schools and Race: A Lost Opportunity for Integrated Education* (Harvard University Press, 2003 (available from http://civilrightsproject.harvard.edu/; accessed on July 18, 2003). One of the more illuminating studies analyzed charter school location in Washington, D.C., and found that charters were more likely to locate in areas with higher percentages of minorities but that these areas were also higher income (i.e., they were more likely to target middle-class blacks). Jeffrey R. Henig and Jason A. McDonald, *Location Decisions of Charter Schools: Probing the Market Metaphor,* 83 Social Science Quarterly 962–80 (2002).

33. Gary Orfield and Chungmei Lee, *Brown at 50: King's Dream or Plessy's Nightmare?* The Civil Rights Project, Harvard University (available from http://civilrightsproject.harvard.edu/; accessed on January 29, 2004); http://www.doe.state.de.us/docs/pdf/dedoe-ethnicreport2003.pdf (accessed on January 16, 2005);

34. Noble, *School Choice Revisited.*

35. National Working Commission on Choice, at 4.

CHAPTER TWENTY-ONE

Race, Class, and Resegregation in Delaware: Delaware Schools Fifty Years After *Brown*

Michele Fuetsch and Leland Ware

Introduction

In 1954, the Supreme Court held that segregation in public education was unconstitutional. The 1955 decision in *Brown II* set an indefinite timetable for implementing the decision, stating that desegregation should proceed "with all deliberate speed." After a decade of virtually no progress toward desegregation, the Supreme Court held in 1968 that school districts had an affirmative duty to proceed immediately to eliminate all vestiges of segregation "root and branch." In the 1990s, this standard was lowered to a duty to eliminate the remnants of segregation to "the extent practicable." The questions, after more than fifty years of school desegregation efforts, are whether either standard has been satisfied and, if not, does the failure mean that *Brown* was a flawed decision.

Brown inspired the civil rights movement of the 1950s and '60s. It led directly to the elimination of an elaborate network of laws and customs that enforced discrimination and segregation. A generation of African Americans has benefited from unprecedented educational, employment, and entrepreneurial opportunities that were completely foreclosed during the segregation era. The revisionist scholars who criticize *Brown* discount this reality.

Certainly, there have been many difficulties with school desegregation efforts, but these were not caused by the *Brown* decision; the problems stemmed from failed leadership, demographic trends, and the flawed ways in which the decision was implemented. A powerful minority consisting of judges, elected officials, and other community leaders went to great lengths to frustrate not only the Supreme Court's vision but also the aspirations of African Americans and the many whites who supported desegregation. Those efforts delayed, but did not defeat, desegregation.

This chapter examines the current status of school desegregation in Delaware. The first section discusses the implementation and segregative effect of the Neighborhood Schools Act. The second section analyzes data that show continuing performance disparities among Delaware's black, white, and Hispanic students. The data also show that African American students' dropout rates are higher than those of their white counterparts and that blacks are disproportionately categorized as learning disabled. The final section is an assessment of the decades-long effort to achieve educational equity in Delaware. The analysis shows that, although considerable gains have been made by Delaware's African Americans in the decades following *Brown*, vestiges of de jure segregation persist. Furthermore, the burdens of the continuing problems with Delaware's schools are disproportionately borne by the state's most vulnerable population: African American and Latino students residing in inner city communities.

The Neighborhood Schools Act

Delaware was one of the five jurisdictions involved in the original *Brown v. Board of Education* decision in 1954. The Delaware school districts directly involved in *Brown* accepted the African American students without incident, but the Supreme Court's ruling did not desegregate all of the state's schools. In the fall of 1954, eleven African American students quietly enrolled in Milford High School in southern Delaware. Milford residents objected after they learned that the black students were attending classes. Tensions mounted, large anti-integration rallies were organized, and eventually local officials yielded to community sentiment and expelled the black students. A civil action was subsequently filed seeking to reinstate the students.[1] The trial court ordered reinstatement, but when the case reached the Delaware Supreme Court, it avoided the merits and ruled that the school board had failed to submit its desegregation plan to the State Board of Education for approval. The schools in Milford remained segregated for more than a decade.[2]

In 1968, Delaware's legislature enacted the Educational Advancement Act, which prohibited any school district with a population of 12,000 or more students from consolidating with other school districts. This law only affected the Wilmington schools, which by then had an increasingly black student population. In 1970, a group of African American parents reactivated a case pending in the federal district court in Delaware claiming, among other things, that the Educational Advancement Act violated Delaware's duty to disestablish racially identifiable schools. A three-judge panel ruled that the Educational Improvement Act played a significant role in maintaining segregation in Wilmington and suburban New Castle County schools. In 1976 a federal court, in *Evans v. Buchanan*,[3] found that the school districts in New Castle County had violated their obligation to desegregate their schools. The court ordered that the eleven school districts in New Castle County be desegregated and reorganized into a single district.

In 1978 the court modified its earlier ruling and allowed the single district to be divided into four separate districts. The City of Wilmington was divided so that a portion was placed in each of the four new districts. To promote racial balance in individual schools, the court ordered school districts to transport the black students residing in Wilmington to suburban schools and to bus the white suburban students to city schools. All students were required to spend three years in city schools and nine years in suburban schools. After several years of busing to achieve racial balance, in 1996, the Court of Appeals for the Third Circuit affirmed a trial court ruling that the school districts in New Castle County had achieved unitary status and were released from federal court supervision.[4]

From the outset, there were many opponents to the busing program. After the unitary status ruling, busing opponents mounted a successful legislative campaign to end the practice, which culminated with the enactment of the Neighborhood Schools Act (NSA) in 2000. This law requires students to be assigned to schools closest to their homes.[5] State Representative Wayne Smith led the effort that resulted in the bill's enactment after years of battling to end Delaware's court-ordered busing program.[6]

The Neighborhood Schools Act required school districts to realign their busing routes and feeder patterns to allow students to attend schools closest to their homes. It also required school districts to comply with mandatory grade configurations. Under its provisions, elementary schools must consist of grades K–5 or K–6, junior high schools are required to include grades 6 through 8 or 7 through 9, and high schools must include grades 9 or 10 through 12. All of the state's school districts were required to submit plans for implementing the NSA for approval to the State Department of Education by November 15, 2001. If the plans were not approved, the districts were obligated to modify them and to resubmit them for approval. A school district could secure approval for a plan that did not use the designated grade configuration or consistently assign students on the basis of proximity if it could show that the plan was a better means of advancing the goals of the act.

The stated intent of the law was to "establish and implement a plan for neighborhood schools in northern New Castle County that is fair and equitable to all affected children in New Castle County."[7] The bill's principal sponsor, state representative Wayne Smith, claimed that his motive for introducing the bill was to be responsive to public support for neighborhood schools; some of the students in the Christina District spent as much as two and one-half hours traveling to and from their schools. Smith also stated that neighborhood schools facilitated parental involvement and reduced transportation costs.[8]

Many were skeptical of Smith's motives. A columnist for the *Wilmington News Journal* observed, "Like many other anti-integration efforts masquerading as civil rights law, H.B. 300 prohibits the use of race to make decisions. Actually, though, its intention is to prevent race from being used as a factor to force whites to share their suburban educational resources with poor blacks and Latinos from Wilmington."[9]

The editorial pages of the *News Journal* repeatedly criticized the law: "One thing is certain: if the Delaware neighborhood schools law is fully implemented, Wilmington will be left with a concentration of high-poverty schools. That would not only be morally unacceptable, it very likely would be unconstitutional because race and poverty have a high correlation in the city."[10]

Wilmington's African American community was sharply divided about the merits of the law. A Wilmington Neighborhood Schools Committee was appointed to make recommendations to the mayor and city council. The chairman of the committee stated in its report that "the Wilmington Neighborhood

Schools Committee has recently gone on record reflecting a majority view that the Neighborhood Schools Act is potentially unconstitutional and could illegally create racially identifiable high-poverty schools."[11]

Most African Americans opposed the law, but some did support neighborhood schools because they did not like the long bus rides and did not believe that their children were welcomed and treated fairly in suburban schools. Reflecting what some commentators have described as "integration fatigue," some African Americans believed that high-quality instruction in an all-black environment would have been preferable to the mistreatment their children experienced in suburban schools.

These sentiments were largely reflections of frustration and disappointment. They were grounded in emotion, rather than reason, and premised on a nostalgic view of a time when black teachers in segregated schools nurtured their students, stressed academic excellence, and performed well in difficult conditions. However, pre-*Brown* enclaves of academic excellence, such as Washington's Dunbar High School, were rare then and cannot be replicated now. Furthermore, the students and teachers who attended the best of such schools bitterly resented the limitations that segregation and discrimination imposed.

The Neighborhood Schools Act ended a court-ordered program that was established to desegregate schools in New Castle County. This was one of the few localities in which a federal court had approved a metropolitan desegregation plan that included a city and the surrounding suburban communities. In most jurisdictions, court-supervised desegregation programs were limited to intradistrict busing that did not include suburban neighborhoods.[12] The schools in New Castle County, which were racially balanced before passage of the Neighborhood Schools Act, would no longer be after full implementation of the NSA. As high levels of residential segregation persist in Wilmington, the law would effectively resegregate many of the city's schools.

Recognizing the NSA's segregative effect, three of the four New Castle County school districts with Wilmington students resisted implementing the NSA's proximity requirements. One of them, the Brandywine school district, was granted an exemption. The two remaining districts, Christina and Red Clay, submitted original and revised plans, both of which were rejected by the State Board of Education. Red Clay presented a third plan in 2004 after the legislature amended the NSA and made clear that a third plan could be submitted. That plan was subsequently approved by the State Board of Education in 2004.[13] Christina operated without an appoved plan until it was ordered to do so after a group of parents filed suit in a Delaware state court.

The Colonial School District

When the NSA was enacted in 2000, Colonial was already planning to realign its school configurations. The district had appointed a task force to develop attendance zones for its schools, with target enrollments for individual schools based on the enrollment capacity of each school. The task force recommendations became the foundation for Colonial's Neighborhood School Plan; the district submitted this plan for implementing the NSA on August 15, 2001.

There are several densely populated areas in the Colonial district that made it difficult to assign all students to the schools closest to their homes while remaining within the schools' enrollment capacities. Subject to this limitation, attendance zones were based on distances from students' homes.[14] One school, Martin Luther King Elementary School, which had a black student population of 47 percent before the NSA, now has a black student population of 90 percent.[15] After reviewing Colonial's plan, however, the State Board of Education found that it met the NSA's criteria for approval.

Red Clay Consolidated School District

Red Clay employed a choice program for student assignments. The district relied on a computerized ranking system that accommodated changing circumstances and applicant preferences during the assignment process; applicants could identify and rank order as many as three school choices. Delaware's School District Enrollment Choice law requires districts to give first preference to returning students, second preference to students residing within the school's feeder pattern, and third preference to siblings of students already enrolled in the school. Choice applications were accepted between November and early January each school year.

All applications were assigned a random, computer-generated number. If the applicant's first-choice school had a seat available, the student was assigned to that school. If the student's first preference did not have a seat available, the second choice was considered; if a seat was not available at the second choice, the student's third preference was considered. After the analysis began and seats became available, the computer program reevaluated applications against the new openings.

Students who lived in designated areas in the district were assigned to that feeder pattern when they initially registered to attend school. Feeder patterns are specific geographic areas within the Red Clay district developed during New Castle County's desegregation litigation to promote racial balance in schools. A student's residence determined the feeder pattern to which he or she was assigned.

The availability of seats at a school depended on the school's "choice capacity." Choice capacity was determined by subtracting the number of seats reserved for students in its feeder pattern and previously enrolled students. Any remaining seats were assigned to choice students. After choice students were assigned to a school, they could remain there until they completed the highest grade offered at the school. New choice applications were usually required in the years students move from elementary to middle and to high school. At some grade levels, a student's feeder pattern school is the school closest to his or her home; at other grade levels, it might not be the closest school.

Red Clay's choice program also recognized a "preference zone" for one elementary school, Brandywine Springs, consisting of neighborhoods adjacent to the school. This differed from a feeder pattern because it applied to only one school and was determined by the proximity of neighborhoods to the school building. During the evaluation of choice applications, students residing in the preference zone who applied to Brandywine Springs were given an admission preference over all other applicants, except returning students. The preference zone was developed as a compromise among parents who lived near the school and wanted their children assigned to it and parents who lived farther away but wanted their children to attend Brandywine Springs. The choice process for middle and high school students was similar to the one used for elementary students.

Red Clay's Neighborhood Schools Plan

Neighborhood school zones were developed in connection with Red Clay's Neighborhood School Plan. The zones were created by dividing the district's elementary schools into three groups based on their distance from each other. Thereafter, what Red Clay described as the "geometrically nearest area" was determined for each such school. The zones divided the Red Clay's landmass into three sections, each of which contained several elementary schools. Neighborhood school zones were not designated for the middle or high schools.

Red Clay's Neighborhood School Plan did not guarantee students a seat in any particular school. Seats in feeder pattern schools were guaranteed only to students who submitted a choice application. Students who did not submit choice applications would be assigned to schools closest to their homes with space available, after the choice process was concluded and returning students were identified and assigned seats.

The district's plan also used the Neighborhood School Zone when making student assignments. Elementary students who did not submit choice applications would be guaranteed assignments to one of the schools in the zone. As each elementary school within the zone was located in a different feeder pattern, the zone did not guarantee students who did not make a choice assignments to their feeder pattern schools. Zones were not established for middle and high schools. Students at those levels who did not submit choice applications would be assigned to the school closest to their homes with space available after the choice applications were processed.

The district's Neighborhood School Plan retained the preference zone for assignments to Brandywine Springs. It also created a preference zone for a new school that the district planned to construct. The Neighborhood School Plan for middle and high school students was similar to that proposed for elementary schools, except that there were no neighborhood school zones for the higher grade levels. Middle and high school students who did not submit choice applications would have been assigned to the nearest school with available space. The Neighborhood School Plan also retained the district's policy of maintaining racial balance in schools.

Red Clay argued that strict compliance with the NSA would have resulted in 85 percent of its schools being overcrowded or underutilized. In contrast, its own plan served student needs and minimized the hardships that were likely to develop under the Neighborhood Schools Act. The district contended that its plan was necessary to maintain high levels of school utilization without overcrowding and to keep low the number of high-poverty schools. However, the State Board of Education rejected Red Clay's plan because students were not assigned to schools closest to their homes and because the plan was based partially on the racial composition of individual schools. The state board also found that Brandywine Springs' preference zone was not an equitable arrangement.

Red Clay submitted a second plan. The resubmitted plan was, in large measure, the same as the plan previously rejected. This time Red Clay requested a hardship exemption. It also submitted additional information about enrollment capacity and school poverty concentrations to justify its departure from strict proximity assignments. The board rejected Red Clay's second plan because it assigned students to schools relying primarily on considerations other than geographic proximity and natural neighborhood boundaries. The board also found that Red Clay had not shown that neighborhood assignments would impose an undue hardship. The district already had significant numbers of high-poverty schools. Assignments based on proximity might redistribute impoverished students, but it would not increase the level of poverty concentrations in the district.

The NSA was amended in July 2004. It now provides that "no district shall be required to submit or implement any Neighborhood School Plan for grades 6–12, if the district shall, for the 2002–2003 school year, enroll 40 percent or more of its students through the School District Enrollment Choice Program."[16] More than 40 percent of Red Clay's student population for the 2002–3 school year consisted of choice students. As a result, Red Clay was not obligated to submit a Neighborhood School Plan for grades 6–12.

The amendment also authorized the state board to consider a maximum of three NSA plans. Red Clay subsequently submitted a third plan for approval. Red Clay's third plan realigned all of its elementary schools so that each would offer grades K–5. Most, but not all, of the K–5 students would attend the elementary schools closest to their homes. Red Clay also considered enrollment capacities when making student assignments. Most schools under Red Clay's plan would operate at 70 to 80 percent of capacity. The district repealed its racial balance policy. None of the school assignments was made on the basis of race.

Red Clay's plan included a noncontiguous attendance area involving two of its schools. The attendance area assigned to one school, Warner Elementary, is divided by a tract of land assigned to another school, Highlands Elementary. The state board concluded that Highlands and Warner's attendance zones were consistent with existing neighborhood boundaries.

The state board's decision took into account that many of Red Clay's Hispanic students would not attend schools closest to their homes. English is not the primary language for many of them. Special English-language learning programs would be offered at only four of Red Clay's thirteen elementary schools. Most students requiring English-language instruction would attend the closest schools offering such services, rather than schools nearest their homes. The state board found that this was a permissible departure from the NSA's proximity assignments. After concluding that Red Clay's plan met the grade configuration requirements and assigned students on the basis of distance, choice, enrollment capacity, and hardship considerations, the state board approved Red Clay's plan.[17]

Christina School District

The Christina School District contains two large, noncontiguous areas. Approximately 17 percent of its student population resides in the City of Wilmington, whereas approximately 83 percent resides in Newark and the surrounding suburban communities. The two areas are nearly fifteen miles apart. The district's unusual configuration is the result of efforts to achieve racial balance during New Castle County's desegregation litigation. Christina has nearly 20,000 students served by twenty-five schools: thirteen elementary schools serving grades K–1 or K–4, six intermediate schools with grades 5–6, three middle schools containing grades 7–8, and three high schools serving grades 9–12.

Student assignments are based on the "9–3" plan implemented during the desegregation litigation. Students in grades K–4 living in or near Newark attend suburban elementary schools. Students in grades K–1 living in Wilmington attend K–1 elementary schools in the city. Wilmington students in grades 2–3 attend suburban elementary schools. City students in grades 4–6 were assigned to schools in the city. Suburban students in grades 5–6 also attend schools in Wilmington. All students in grades 7–12 attend middle and high school in Newark and the surrounding suburban communities.

Christina submitted a plan to the state board that retained the existing grade configurations at all levels and realigned attendance boundaries in middle schools and high schools. However, the plan replaced a policy that balanced the racial composition of student populations with Student Enrollment Guidelines that required school populations to be within 20 percent of the average socioeconomic status ratio for the grades offered at the school.

Christina acknowledged that its plan did not meet the NSA's mandatory grade configuration and student assignment requirements. It contended that reconfiguring its schools by grade and assigning students solely on the basis of proximity would have created overcrowded suburban schools, significantly underutilized city schools, and resulted in concentrations of high-poverty students in several schools. The state board concluded that the NSA required Christina to submit a plan that satisfied the requirements of the NSA. Because the plan submitted did not satisfy the requirements, the state board rejected it. Christiana was ordered to produce and submit a plan that complied with the NSA's requirements.

In its second submission, Christina presented two plans for approval: the "Committee Plan," which purported to meet the NSA's grade configuration requirements, and the "Preferred Plan," which was its original plan. The Committee Plan assigned students on the basis of proximity and natural neighborhood boundaries, giving consideration to building capacity. The Committee Plan would have established nineteen K–5 elementary schools, fifteen in Newark and its suburbs; five grade 6–8 middle schools, three in Newark and surrounding suburban areas; and three high schools with grades 9–12, all in Newark or other suburban communities.

The Committee Plan would have assigned more than 21 percent of the district's suburban middle school population to city schools fifteen miles farther away from the students' homes than any of the suburban middle schools. All of the city schools would have had high poverty enrollments under the Committee Plan. The plan also relied entirely on the construction of two new schools and the renovation of two others. If the two schools were not constructed and the others not renovated, Christina's schools would not be realigned into the required grade configurations and students would not be assigned to schools closest to their homes.

The state board concluded that neither plan satisfied the NSA and disapproved both proposals. The board rejected the Committee Plan because of the speculative nature of its construction and renovation components, its lack of compliance with the NSA's grade configuration requirements, and the deviations from neighborhood school assignments for a large number of suburban middle school students. Christina operated without a plan until a lawsuit was filed that resulted in an order requiring it to do so.[18]

Brandywine School District

Brandywine School District submitted its compliance plan in November 2001.[19] Brandywine is the smallest of the four New Castle County school districts; its concentrated population and small land area facilitated the assignment of students to schools close to their homes.[20] The Brandywine School Board established the Brandywine Neighborhood Schools Committee to develop compliance plans. The Brandywine School Board solicited the views of its residents with a referendum that asked voters whether they wanted to establish attendance zones that would resegregate schools. It provided the voters with information showing that a plan based entirely on neighborhood boundaries would produce racially segregated, high-poverty schools. "We had to take this out to the community," said school board member Nancy Doorey. "The average man on the street has to own this. Are we standing by our kids or aren't we? This was the avenue for the whole community to coalesce."

Another community leader, Lynne Kielhorn, stated, "Many people who were supporting the Neighborhood Schools Act hadn't thought it through and realized the implications." Keilhorn continued, "We started flooding the newspaper with letters to the editor, distributed flyers door to door, appeared on a local talk show. We supported our position with data showing the negative impacts on students in high-poverty schools. We developed an email list of 200 names. From there our information would fan out to other lists, such as the local YWCA, the local American Association of University Women, and the Metropolitan Wilmington Urban League."

Three plans were presented to voters, one of which was approved by voters in the school district. Under the Brandywine Plan, none of the schools exceeded the standard for high-poverty schools established by researchers, which is 50 percent or more of the students qualifying for free or reduced lunch. The percentage of students receiving free or reduced lunch ranged from 16 to 47 percent.[21] The Brandywine Plan assigned some students to schools that were not the nearest to their homes to avoid the creation of high-poverty schools, but continued to assign all students to schools closest to their homes for a substantial portion of their K–12 education.

The Brandywine School District also developed a "Challenge Index" for the purpose of comparing the impact of various educational plans. The index considered the number of students in the free and reduced lunch program and those with special education requirements, below-standard scores on the Delaware State Testing Program, average grade point averages below "C," and above-average absence or tardy rates. Brandywine determined that students with these attributes required more attention and resources than students without those attributes. Under the Brandywine Plan, the Challenge Index for schools ranged from 60–150.

In an election in which the three plans were submitted to voters for approval, voters overwhelmingly chose the Brandywine Plan. The State Board of Education approved the Brandywine Plan because it avoided the establishment of high-poverty schools and provided for a more fair and equitable educational experience for all students. Based on evidence presented at the hearing on the Brandywine Plan, the state board concluded that the "district established beyond question that high poverty schools, even high poverty neighborhood schools, are not fair and equitable to the children attending them." This conclusion was based on a number of arguments, but primarily on the conclusion that the problem with high-poverty schools is that students usually have less access to effective teachers and other resources. The state board concluded that the "Brandywine plan is more fair and equitable to the district's students because it offers more opportunity for all students, including those living in poverty, to learn to their potential and does so without impairing the education of their more fortunate peers."

Brandywine also addressed NSA's goal of assuring that school assignments reflect the desires of parents and community, as stated in the act's preamble. In a public vote overseen by the Department of Elections, district residents supported the Brandywine Plan by a 70 percent majority. This high level of support was also documented in public hearings and written submissions made to the State Board of Education. The Delaware State Board of Education agreed with Brandywine's arguments and, weighing the multiple goals of the NSA, determined that the Brandywine Plan met the requirements of the act and better accomplished the goals of the act than the Zip Code Plan or any other nearest-school plan. As a result, the state board approved the Brandywine Plan as the Neighborhood Schools Plan for the district. This ruling allowed Brandywine to maintain its system without any changes and was seen as a sharp rebuke to state representative Wayne Smith, the architect of the Neighborhood Schools Act, who resides in the Brandywine School District.

Continuing Educational Disparities

Educational Attainment Levels

African Americans in Delaware have experienced a significant increase in educational attainment levels since 1960, but at the start of the twenty-first century, their attainment at the college level is still considerably lower than that of whites. On the plus side, the proportion of the black population aged twenty-five years and over with less than a ninth-grade education has declined dramatically. The proportion of high school graduates in that group is up sharply, even outpacing whites, and more black adults than ever have earned college degrees. For Delaware

Hispanics, however, average educational attainment levels since 1960 have shown a more fitful pattern. Progress appeared to stall or fall backward in the 1990s, a pattern that could be the result of mushrooming migration from Mexico and Central America. From 1990 to 2000, the Hispanic population aged twenty-five years or older leapt from 7,565 to 18,301.

The educational attainment of African Americans began to increase in the 1960s. In 1960, more than 60 percent of the adult black population had less than nine years of formal education. By 1970, that proportion was down to 41 percent, by 1990 it was down to 11 percent, and in 2000 it was only 6 percent. In 1970, 31 percent of the black population had nine to twelve years of education, but no high school diploma. The largest increase in a single decade—18 percent—in the proportion of high school graduates occurred during the 1970s. Between 1960 and 1990 the proportion of African Americans with a high school diploma increased from 15 percent to 53 percent. By 2000 the proportion of the black population with a high school diploma reached 60 percent, two percentage points above the proportion of whites with high school diplomas. The proportion of the black population with four or more years of college has almost quadrupled since 1960, reaching 11 percent by 1990 and 14 percent in 2000.

The state's Hispanic population 25 years and older has experienced some improvement in its level of educational attainment but not as much as the black population realized during the same period. In 1970, 26 percent of the Hispanic population had nine or fewer years of formal education. By 1990, that proportion had declined to 20 percent. In 2000 the proportion was up again—to 24 percent. Between 1970 and 1990, the proportion of adult Hispanics with nine to twelve years of education but without a high school diploma consistently ranged between 16 and 20 percent. In 2000 that proportion was 18 percent. In 1970, 40 percent of Delaware's adult Hispanics were high school graduates, but that proportion declined to 36 percent by 1980. The proportion rose again, to 44 percent, in 1990, but did not budge during the following decade, remaining at 44 percent in 2000. The proportion of the Hispanic population consisting of college graduates was 16 percent in 1990, and for several decades that college proportion was significantly higher than the proportion of black college graduates. By 2000, however, the proportion of Hispanic college graduates had fallen to 13 percent.

Historically, the proportion of Delaware's adult white population that completed high school and college was consistently higher than the proportions of the black and Hispanic populations reaching those average educational attainment levels. In 1990, for example, 57 percent of the state's white population consisted of high school graduates and 23 percent were college graduates. Only 6 percent of that white population group had less than nine years of education, a proportion that dropped to 4 percent in 2000. In 1990, 13 percent of the white population had between nine and twelve years of schooling but no high school diploma, a proportion that lessened to 11 percent in 2000. Like the state's black population, the white population experienced a dramatic increase in educational attainment during the 1970s. By 1990, 57 percent of the white population had high school diplomas, but that percentage increased only slightly—to 58 percent —in 2000, putting the white proportion two percentage points *behind* the proportion of black adults with high

TABLE 1 EDUCATIONAL ATTAINMENT LEVELS BY RACE

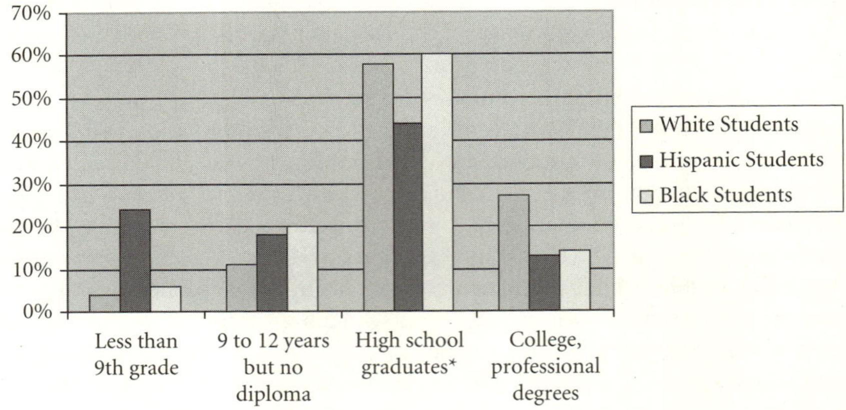

school diplomas. In 1990, however, some 23 percent of the adult white population had college degrees, a proportion that rose to 27 percent in 2000, roughly double that of the African American and Hispanic populations (see Table 1).

Performance Gaps on the Student Testing Program

Delaware's minority students continue to score lower on standardized examinations than white students, despite a campaign launched by the state in the 1990s to upgrade its public schools with an educational accountability system. After hammering out a set of educational standards, educators in the state began in 1996 to develop the Delaware Student Testing Program (DSTP). Similar to the federal No Child Left Behind Act, the centerpiece of the state program is annual student testing. It measures the academic performance of the overall student population, as well as the performance of specific student groups. Framers of the DSTP say it is intended to (1) serve as a measure of progress toward the Delaware educational standards, (2) ensure that students can apply their academic skills to realistic, everyday problems, (3) promote instruction and curriculum improvement by providing timely reports of students' strengths and weaknesses, (4) serve as the main indicator for the statewide accountability system, and (5) assist districts in the identification of students to promote or retain.

In 1997, legislation was enacted to make the DSTP the primary indicator in the educational accountability system. Testing began in the spring of 1998 with reading, writing, and mathematics exams given to students in grades 3, 5, 8, and 10. In the spring of 1999, science and social studies testing were added in grades 8 and 11. In the fall of 1999, students in grades 4 and 6 began taking science and social studies tests. Performance on the reading and math examinations can affect a student's academic coursework and promotion eligibility.

From the start of testing in 1998, there have been racial disparities in the levels of student performance. In the first year, 71.6 percent of the white third graders met the state's reading standard compared with 42.5 percent of the black and 39.8 percent of the Hispanic third graders. In 2005, 90.77 percent of the white third graders met the reading standard, in contrast to only 78.95 percent of the Hispanic and 73.93 percent of the black students. In elementary school math, similar patterns continue. In 1998, 64.32 percent of white fifth graders met the state standard in math compared with only 32.55 percent of Hispanic and 28.64 percent of black students. In 2005, 85.82 percent of white fifth graders met the state standard, in contrast to only 71.56 percent of Hispanic and 61.89 percent of black students (see Table 2).

The academic gains since 1998 for African American and Hispanic students have been impressive, particularly in the elementary grades, where the achievement gap between white and minority student performance is steadily narrowing. However, racial disparities have not disappeared. In every test year from 1998 to 2005, white students have continued to score above the state average on the DSTP third-grade reading test at the same time African American and Hispanic third graders have scored below the average. In addition, in 2005, Hispanic and black students scored below the state average in reading in each of the grades tested: 3, 5, 8, and 10. In the same year, white students tested above the state average in each of those grades (see Table 3).

The achievement gap at the eighth and tenth grade levels, particularly in math, is as wide if not wider in some cases than it was at the first year of testing. As an example, in 1998, when the percentage of white students meeting the state standard in tenth-grade math was compared to the percentage of black students meeting the standard, the achievement gap was 26.6 points. between white and black students. In 2005, the gap between those same groups was some seven points wider, with 62.55 percent of the white students meeting the tenth-grade math standard in contrast to only 28.87 percent of the black students. The 2005 achievement gap in math between white and Hispanic tenth graders did not significantly change from the 24.5-point gap of 1998.

Indeed, in every one of the seven years since testing began, in at least one grade and in at least one subject, the achievement gap has been larger than when the tests were first given. And with eight years now worth of test results, the test

TABLE 2 MATH 2005—PERCENTAGE MEETING STANDARD—Performance Gap

Grade	*White*	*Hispanic*	*2005 Gap*	*1998 Gap*	*Black*	*2005 Gap*	*1998 Gap*
3	87.2	71.54	15.66	29.5	65.47	21.73	34.5
5	85.82	71.56	14.26	31.7	61.89	23.93	35.7
8	66.33	40	26.33	26.8	32.09	34.24	31
10	62.55	39.39	23.16	24.5	28.87	33.68	26.6

TABLE 3 READING 2005—PERCENTAGE MEETING STANDARD—Performance Gap

Grade	White	Hispanic	2005 Gap	1998 Gap	Black	2005 Gap	1998 Gap
3	90.77	78.95	11.82	31.8	73.93	16.84	29.1
5	91.22	79.69	11.53	34.1	75.07	16.15	33.6
8	86.67	66.77	19.9	30.9	66.83	19.84	31.1
10	79.71	53.97	25.74	29.8	50.59	29.12	30.4

scores in reading and math show a clear pattern: the gap has closed significantly in the elementary grades, but has widened at the high school level.

The Impact of the DSTP on Promotion and Graduation

The state DSTP has five categories of student test scores. Each level or category carries with it rewards in terms of promotion or consequences in terms of summer school and, possibly, grade retention. The levels of student scores are as follows:

Level 5 Distinguished

Level 4 Exceeds the standard

Level 3 Meets the standard

Level 2 Below the standard

Level 1 Well below the standard

The DSTP has a significant role in determining the direction of a student's academic career. Beginning with the spring 2002 DSTP, in reading in grades 3, 5, and 8, those who test at Level 1 must attend summer school. Additionally, eighth graders who score at Level 1 in math are also required to attend summer school. These summer school students then take the DSTP again at the end of the summer session in an effort to reach Level 3 or better. Those who do are promoted. Those who do not score at Level 3 are promoted only if other indicators confirm that they are ready to advance to the next grade. Schools are allowed to consider district tests, examinations administered at the end of a course, and classroom projects to determine whether a student is able to meet the standards for that grade level. A district-level Academic Review Committee, consisting of a teacher, an administrator, and a counselor, makes the decisions concerning promotion. The student's teacher from either the previous grade or from summer school presents the student's work to the committee. The Academic Review Committee also consults with families and reviews the indicators along with DSTP scores.

Students in grades 3, 5, and 8 who perform at Level 2 in reading, and students in grade 8 who score at Level 2 in math, are given an "Individual Improvement Plan" that outlines the assistance needed to improve performance. Parents must agree to the improvement plan. Students who are promoted with an improvement plan must take the DSTP again at the end of the next school year and perform satisfactorily. If performance does not meet the state standard, the students are required to attend summer school again. Every special education student is given an "Individual Education Program" that guides instruction and directs the special assistance needed in the classroom and with the DSTP.

Disproportionate Enrollments in Special Education Programs

In 1975, Congress passed the Individuals with Disabilities Education Act, which requires states to provide equal learning opportunities for special education students. Since passage of the federal legislation, though, studies have documented disproportionate—numbers of minority students in special education programs. In 2002, in response to a congressional mandate, the National Research Council (NRC) of the National Academy of Sciences issued a report on minority students in special education programs, which again documented disproportionate representation of those students. More than 14 percent of the nation's African American students are in special education, compared with 11 percent of Hispanics and 12 percent of whites. What is more, disproportionate numbers of black and Hispanic students are placed in certain special education categories, such as "Emotional Disturbance" and "Mental Retardation."[22]

These and other disparities are evident in Delaware's special education population as well. In Delaware in the 2004–5 school year, 17.34 percent of the 38,405 African American students in the public schools were enrolled in special education programs,—a percentage that is three points higher than what the NRC found nationwide for black students. In addition, 12.59 percent of the 10,155 Hispanics in Delaware schools were enrolled in special education, which is also higher than the national average. The percentage of white students in special education, 12.86 percent of 66,949 whites overall, most nearly meets the national percentage of 12 percent found by the NRC.

As of December 2004 in Delaware, 16,723 students between the age of 6 and 21 years were enrolled in special education programs. Analyzing that total racially and ethnically yielded evidence of overrepresentation of minority students. Whites accounted for only 51 percent of the special education group, an underrepresentation given that they constitute 56 percent of the public school population of 119,109 students. Conversely, African Americans comprised 39.8 percent of the special education population versus only 32 percent of the overall student population. Hispanics, meanwhile, made up almost 7.6 percent of the special education students, compared with 8.5 percent of the overall student population (see Table 4).

All special education students are assigned to categories that are nationally uniform, but differ widely from one another in terms of the disabilities they encompass. Placement in the categories for students with visual or hearing impairments, for instance, requires empirical evidence. Placement in other

Table 4 Children with Disabilities Receiving Special Education by Race in 2004

Disabilites	*American Indian*	*Asian*	*Black*	*Hispanic*	*White*	*Total*
Mental Retardation	1	17	1204	153	795	2710
Hearing Impairments	0	8	72	28	144	252
Speech or Language Impairments	2	39	361	111	1115	1628
Visual Impairments	1	1	17	2	21	42
Emotional Disturbance	4	4	403	36	459	906
Orthopedic Impairments	6	14	595	93	1326	2034
Other Health Impairments	0	0	0	0	0	0
Specific Learning Disabilities	23	41	3870	841	4417	9192
Deaf-Blindness	0	1	10	4	27	42
Multiple Disabilities	0	0	0	0	0	0
Autism	1	10	121	9	298	439
Traumatic Brain Injury	0	0	8	2	8	18
Total: (Sum of all the above)	**38**	**135**	**6661**	**1279**	**8610**	**16723**

categories allows for much greater subjectivity on the part of school personnel responsible for deciding which students are assigned to special education and which are placed in such categories as "Mental Retardation" and "Emotional Disturbance." These two categories, referred to by the NRC 2002 report as the "judgmental" categories, are the same ones in which inordinate numbers of black and Hispanic children continue to be found.

In Delaware, 44 percent of the 906 students in the "Emotional Disturbance" category in 2004–5 were black, in contrast to the 39.8 percent of black students overall receiving special education services. Only 3.9 percent of the students in this category were Hispanic and 50.6 percent white, in both cases an underrepresentation. In the "Mental Retardation" category, 55 percent of the students were black, another overrepresentation of African American students. In the same category, 7 percent of the students were Hispanic, which correlates with the approximately 8 percent of Hispanic students receiving special education. However, only 36.6 percent of the students in the "Mental Retardation" category were white, whereas white students comprise 51 percent of the total special education students (see Table 5).

"Among the most frequent reasons for referral to special education are reading difficulties and behavior problems," according to the NRC report.[23] Implementing interventions appropriate for the general education classroom to improve reading instruction and classroom management, the report said, can reduce the number of students who fail at reading and are later identified as having behavior problems.

Dropout Rate Comparisons, 1979 to 2004

The dropout rate for African American and Hispanic students in Delaware has been consistently higher than that of whites and constantly higher than the state's overall dropout rate. In addition, the pattern has remained constant even though Delaware, in the 2001–2 academic year, in order to comply with a federal mandate to count dropouts more accurately, changed how it tracks them. In fact, results obtained with that new tracking method indicate that dropout rates for all students may have been higher than noted previously. In the decades before the federally ordered change, the state's overall dropout rate for students in grades 9

TABLE 5 STUDENTS IN THE "EMOTIONAL DISTURBANCE" CATEGORY BY RACE

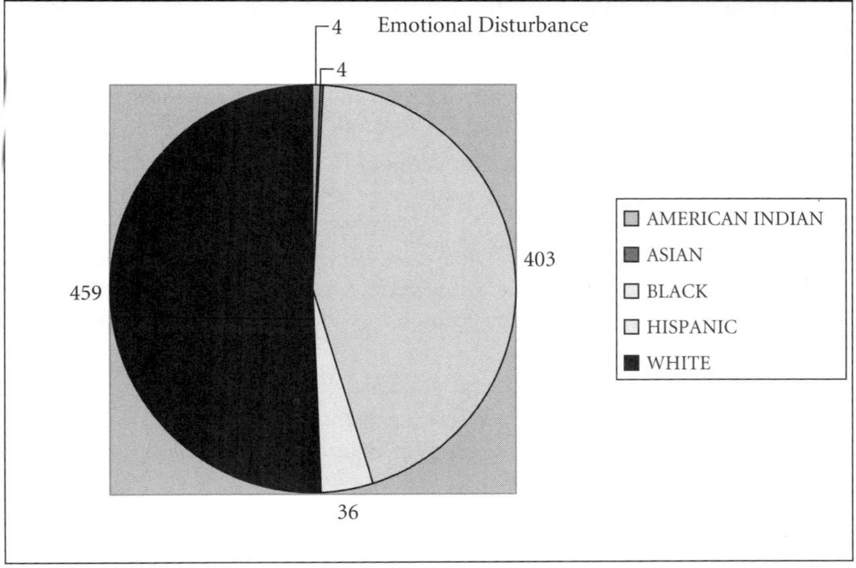

to 12 fell from 7.9 percent in the 1979–80 academic year to 4.2 percent in 2000–01. The lowest dropout rate within those years, 4 percent, was reported in the 1991–92 academic year. The highest rate, 8.1 percent, was in 1981–82. With the implementation of the improved federally imposed data-gathering method, the state's overall dropout rate was 6.2 percent the first year, up 2 percentage points from the previous year.

When the dropout rate is broken down into ethnic and racial categories, white students have the lowest dropout rates, regardless of the year or the data collection method in use; these dropout rates have been consistently lower than the state's overall average dropout rate. For instance, in the school year 1979–80, the white dropout rate was 7.0 percent compared with an overall state rate of 7.9 percent. By 1989–90, the dropout rate for white students had declined to 5.3 percent against a state average of 6.6 percent. The lowest dropout rate for white students, 3 percent, was reported in the 1991–92 academic year, and the highest rate, 8.1 percent, was in the 1981–82 academic year. In 2001–2, however, employing the prescribed federal data-collection method for the first time, the white dropout rate was up, to 4.5 percent but still well below the overall state average rate of 6.2 percent. In 2003–4 the rate for white students rose to 4.9 percent against an average overall state dropout rate of 6 percent.

For African American students, in the 1979–80 academic year, the dropout rate was 12.1 percent, the highest of the past quarter-century; this rate was more than four percentage points higher than the state overall rate of 7.9 percent. In subsequent decades, the rate for black students steadily declined, hitting a low of 5.2 percent in the 1998–99 school year and coming closer to the overall state dropout rate of 4.1 percent. But in the first academic year (2001–2) of the new collection method, the black dropout rate was 8.9 percent against a state overall rate of 6.2 percent. In the 2003–4 academic year, the black rate was 7.4 percent compared with a state overall rate of 6 percent.

Hispanic students have historically had higher dropout rates than either black or white students and, for most of the 1980s, suffered double-digit dropout rates, hitting a high of 22 percent in the 1981–82 academic year. The lowest dropout rate for Hispanics, 5.1 percent, occurred in 1992–93. In only two academic years, 1992–93 and 1993–94, was the Hispanic dropout rate marginally below that of black students. Never has the Hispanic dropout rate been below that of white students nor the state overall dropout rate. Just as with white and African American students, the dropout rates for Hispanic students have been higher since the adoption of the federally mandated data-collection method. The Hispanic rate is again in the double digits, at 12.1 percent for the 2003–4 academic year, more than double the state overall dropout rate of 6 percent and almost triple the white dropout rate of 4.9 percent.

In addition to higher dropout rates, the federal data-collection changes in Delaware are producing larger differentials in white and minority dropout rates. Before the changes occurred in the 2000–2001 academic year, there was a 1.8 percentage point differential between black and white dropout rates. In 2003–4, the differential was 2.5 percentage points. Between Hispanic and white students, the point differential was 3.9 in 2000–2001 but increased to a startling 7.2 points in 2003–4.

Dropouts and Student Enrollment 2003–4 (Grade by Race)

The bulk of Delaware dropouts each year are ninth and tenth graders. Of the 2,103 dropouts reported in the 2003–4 academic year, 37.2 percent were ninth graders, and 26.5 percent were tenth graders. African Americans and Hispanics had the highest ninth- and tenth-grade dropout rates that year: 8 percent for black students in both the ninth and tenth grades and, for Hispanics, 14.4 percent in the ninth and 13.3 percent in the tenth grade. For white students, the rate was 5.8 percent in the ninth grade and 5 percent in the tenth. The racial disparities in rates in these lower high school years suggest that, even among the dropout population, blacks and Hispanics have lower levels of educational attainment and skill development than whites.

Overall, in the 2003–4 academic year, black students accounted for 35.6 percent of all dropouts, although they made up less than 30 percent of the 34,785 students in public high schools that year. In the same year, Hispanics accounted for 11 percent of all dropouts, although they constituted less than 6 percent of high school enrollment. Whites, meanwhile, accounted for only 53.4 percent of the dropouts while accounting for nearly 65 percent of the state's high school enrollment (see Table 6).

Dropout and Percent of All Dropouts, 2003–4 (Gender by Race)

Gender comparisons show that 58 percent of all dropouts in the 2003–4 academic year were male and 42 percent female, a differential of 16 percentage points. Hispanic males had the highest dropout rate, 13.3 percent, followed by 10.8 percent for Hispanic females. At a dropout rate of 5.5 percent for African American females and 9.2 percent for African American males, both those groups had higher dropout rates than either white gender.

Dropout Rate and Percent of All Dropouts, 2003–4 (County by Race)

As the most populous of Delaware's three counties, urban New Castle produces the greatest number of dropouts each year: 1,253 in the academic year 2003–4

Table 6 Dropout Rate and Percent of All Dropouts, 2003–4 (Grade by Race)

	Annual Dropout Rate				**Percent of All Dropouts**			
Grade	*Black*	*Hispanic*	*White/ Other*	*All*	*Black*	*Hispanic*	*White/ Other*	*All*
Grade 9	8%	14.4%	5.8%	7.1%	13.5%	5.1%	18.6%	37.2%
Grade 10	8%	13.3%	5%	6.3%	9.7%	3.2%	13.6%	26.5%
Grade 11	7.5%	9.6%	4.7%	5.7%	7.8%	1.7%	11.5%	20.9%
Grade 12	5.1%	7.5%	4%	4.5%	4.7%	1.1%	9.7%	15.5%
Total	**7.4%**	**12.1%**	**4.9%**	**6%**	**35.6%**	**11%**	**53.4%**	**100%**

compared with 435 for Kent and 415 for Sussex. That means that the New Castle County school districts produced 59.6 percent of the state's dropouts that year, nearly triple the percentage produced by the two, mostly rural counties. Dropout rates for each county, however, were similar: 6.1 percent in New Castle and Sussex counties and 5.7 percent in Kent County. In addition, from county to county, the racial dropout patterns were also similar. Hispanics had higher dropout rates than black or white students, although the Hispanic rate in New Castle, 12.7 percent, was roughly 2 percentage points higher than the rates in the rural counties. Dropout rates for black students were nearly identical in all three counties: 7.4 percent in New Castle and 7.3 percent in both Kent and Sussex (see Table 7).

Race, Class, and Resegregation

The history of public education in the Delaware is one in which opportunities for African Americans have been separate and unequal. Delaware was one of the five jurisdictions involved in the original *Brown* decision in 1954, and it was the only jurisdiction in which the trial court ruled in the plaintiffs' favor. Although considerable gains have been made by Delaware's African Americans in the decades following *Brown*, vestiges of de jure segregation persist. Before the late 1970s, most African American in Delaware attended public schools that were still segregated, decades after the *Brown* decision. From the 1970s through the mid 1990s, African American students attending schools in New Castle County experienced conditions in which the vestiges of segregation had not been eliminated as desegregation efforts remained under federal court supervision. The school districts were declared "unitary" and released from federal court supervision in 1995, but the data detailed in this chapter demonstrate that substantial race-based performance disparities persist.

African Americans in Delaware have experienced a significant increase in educational attainment levels over the past forty years, but their attainment at the college level is still considerably lower than their white counterparts. Despite the significant academic gains since 1998 for African Americans, particularly in the elementary grades, racial disparities have not disappeared.

Table 7 Dropout Rate and Percent of All Dropouts, 2003–4 (County by Race)

	Annual Dropout Rate				Percent of All Dropouts			
County	*Black*	*Hispanic*	*White/ Other*	*All*	*Black*	*Hispanic*	*White/ Other*	*All*
New Castle	7.4%	12.7%	4.8%	6.1%	23.1%	8.2%	28.3%	59.6%
Kent	7.3%	10.5%	4.9%	5.7%	7.1%	1.3%	12.3%	20.7%
Sussex	7.3%	10.8%	5.5%	6.1%	5.4%	1.5%	12.8%	19.7%
Total	**7.4%**	**12.1%**	**4.9%**	**6%**	**35.6%**	**11%**	**53.4%**	**100%**

By every objective measure, African Americans in Delaware's public schools are not performing at the same level as white students. Since the start of the current testing program in 1998, there have been racial disparities in the levels of student performance. In every year since testing began, the achievement gap has been larger, in at least one grade, than when testing commenced.

There are other problems. Disproportionate numbers of black and Hispanic students are placed in special education categories. In Delaware, 44 percent of students in the "Emotional Disturbance" category in 2004–5 were black. The dropout rate for African American and Hispanic students in Delaware has been consistently higher than that of whites. Hispanic students have had higher dropout rates than either black or white students. The Neighborhood Schools Act of 2000 hinders efforts to achieve racial equity in Delaware's public schools. The 1968 state law that prompted *Evans v. Buchanan* would have confined most of the African American students in northern Delaware to schools in Wilmington. The trial court found and the court of appeals agreed that the 1968 law had a segregative effect on the schools in northern Delaware and violated the state's duty to desegregate its schools. The Neighborhood Schools Act, which requires students to attend schools closest to their homes, will have the same effect.

A substantial portion of Wilmington's population still resides in segregated communities.[24] This was what school districts sought to ameliorate when they developed the feeder patterns and attendance zones that were operating before passage of the Neighborhood Schools Act. The federal court's unitary status ruling was based on the racially balanced enrollments that were in place in 1995 when the decision was issued. That scheme is being dismantled by the Neighborhood Schools Act. With the exception of schools located in the Brandywine district, Wilmington schools still have high levels of poverty and racial isolation.

There is no evidence that the NSA will improve the quality of instruction that students receive. It will not enhance learning environments in individual schools. There is, however, a considerable amount of data concerning academic performance in racially isolated, high-poverty schools.[25] Studies consistently show that students attending such schools do not perform as well as their more affluent and more integrated counterparts in suburban communities. The legislature's assumption, that the racial composition of student enrollments will reflect the residential preferences of individual families, disregarded Delaware's long history of segregation and discrimination in the housing markets. Residential segregation in Wilmington is a vestige of that history.

In many inner city communities, residents experience the extreme form of racial isolation that social scientists describe as "hypersegregation." This term measures segregation along five separate dimensions; evenness, exposure, clustering, centralization, and concentration. Evenness measures the proportion of members of one racial group (in this case African Americans) that would have to change their area of residence to achieve perfect integration. Exposure measures the extent to which African Americans are exposed only to other African Americans in their communities. Clustering measures the extent to which census tracts inhabited by African Americans are contiguous. Centralization measures the extent to which African Americans reside near the center of an urban area. Concentration measures the amount of physical space occupied by African Americans so that as segregation increases, African American families are increasingly concentrated in smaller areas. It is of special significance when a number of dimensions reach high values simultaneously. Hypersegregation exists when a group has high levels of segregation in three or more of the five dimensions of segregation.[26]

A return to neighborhood schools will exacerbate the many disadvantages caused by racial isolation. The physical distances from inner city neighborhoods to other locations can be small, but the psychological distance is often enormous. African American enclaves are discrete and insular communities with their own set of cultural and social norms. This can be seen in the attire, body language, and speech patterns of inner city residents, especially those in the younger generation. The rules of interpersonal interactions are different. Subtle forms of nonverbal communication can easily be misinterpreted by those unfamiliar with their meanings. What may be seen in other contexts as hostile or threatening body language can be a necessary survival tool in communities where danger lurks around every corner. An affect reflecting weakness or fear is not a desirable attribute in such communities. A lack of exposure to diverse learning environments makes it difficult for students from inner city communities to succeed in circumstances where different behaviors are the norm.

A return to neighborhood schools will be detrimental to inner city students. When low-income students attend schools with other poor students, all of the students suffer the adverse effects of concentrated poverty. Poor children are less likely to attend preschool programs and are often unprepared for learning when they first enter school. The parents of such students are usually far less educated than the parents of students in middle-class communities. Impoverished students are disproportionately affected by family instability. Students from single-parent households are concentrated in poor neighborhoods. The incidence of teenaged pregnancies is so high that it is common for young women to become pregnant before finishing high school. Crime rates are higher in neighborhoods where poor students reside.[27] Schools with high concentrations of poor and minority students also experience problems associated with drug and alcohol abuse, crime, and gang activity. Teacher turnover rates are high. High-poverty schools lose, on average, more than one-fifth of their faculty each year. As a recent study explains,

> Concentrated poverty turns out to be powerfully related to both school opportunities and achievement levels. Children in these schools tend to be less healthy, to have weaker preschool experiences, to have only one parent, to move frequently and have unstable educational experiences, to attend classes taught by less experienced or unqualified teachers, to have friends and classmates with lower levels of achievement, to be in schools with fewer demanding pre-collegiate courses and more remedial courses, and to have higher teacher turnover. Many of these schools are also deteriorated and lack key resources. The strong correlation between race and poverty show that a great many black and Latino students attend these schools of concentrated poverty.[28]

Impoverished African Americans are more disadvantaged than poor people who are not black or African Americans who are not poor. They experience "intersectional discrimination," which is more severe than race discrimination by itself, or policies that disadvantage poor families. Conditions in hypersegregated, inner city schools make it extremely difficult for those institutions to maintain a nurturing, stable, and intellectually stimulating environment. The Neighborhood Schools Act will force African American students residing in certain areas in Wilmington to attend hypersegregated, high-poverty schools.

Conclusion

The trend toward resegregation is not limited to Delaware. It is occurring at a time when some scholars are questioning the efficacy of *Brown* itself. *Brown* and the civil rights movement of the 1950s and 1960s resulted in the elimination of laws that enforced segregation. Those in a position to do so took advantage of the many opportunities that were not available to African Americans during the segregation era. For this segment of the African American population, *Brown* succeeded in creating unprecedented avenues for advancement. Those who criticize *Brown* underestimate the Supreme Court's role in effectuating dramatic reforms. They also diminish the extraordinary accomplishments of the civil rights lawyers who crafted and implemented the legal strategy that led to the *Brown* decision.

Contrary to the assertions of *Brown*'s critics, the difficulties with school desegregation were not caused by the Supreme Court's opinions; the problems stemmed from elected officials' obstructionist tactics, the ways in which the decision was implemented, and the persistence of high levels of residential segregation in urban communities. Civil rights advocates hoped that desegregating schools would lead to an extension of the desegregation principle to other areas of civic and social life. That has happened with the notable exception of housing patterns in metropolitan communities.

As researchers have documented, segregated neighborhoods have persisted in communities where there are large concentrations of African American and Latino residents.[29] Whites and more affluent minorities tend to live in suburban communities. The boundaries of school districts are typically drawn along the lines of political subdivisions; cities are in one school district, suburban communities are in others. Schools are financed primarily by local property taxes. Many of the inhabitants of inner city communities are lower-income African American and Latino families. The tax base for a typical city district lacks the financial resources available in more affluent suburban districts.

Given this reality, it is not surprising that racially isolated, high-poverty schools are located in so many inner city communities. Busing programs sought to address this isolation by transporting students from one neighborhood to another to achieve racial balance in schools. This was an imperfect solution, but it ameliorated racial isolation and exposed students to diverse learning environments. This is ending as more and more school districts are being declared "unitary" and returning to neighborhood school assignments.

Despite the many reforms in recent decades, substantive equality has not been fully realized. Approximately one-third of the African American population resides in inner city neighborhoods; they are the nation's most spatially isolated and geographically secluded group. They live in large, contiguous, and densely populated tracts that are packed tightly around an urban core. They endure an extreme form of racial isolation social scientists identify as "hypersegregation" to emphasize its multidimensionality.

In many ways, conditions in inner city neighborhoods are more severe than they were during the segregation era. At that time black neighborhoods were functioning communities where teachers, physicians, and other educated and upwardly mobile individuals resided along with domestics and factory workers. They interacted at schools, in places of worship, and at social events; they patronized black-owned businesses. This interaction lent a degree of stability and cohesion to African American neighborhoods. Affluent and educated minorities do not reside in today's inner city communities. Those who live there now have the lowest incomes, least education, and highest unemployment levels. A return to inner city schools will subject students to impoverished, racially isolated, educational environments. When this happens the educational opportunities for the urban underclass will be as separate and unequal as they were fifty years ago, when *Brown* was decided.

Notes

1. *Steiner v. Simmons*, 11 A. 2d 574 (Del. 1955).

2. Ed Kee, *The Brown Decision and Milford, Delaware, 1954–1965*, 27 Delaware History 205–43 (1997–98).

3. See generally, Irving Morris, *The Role of Delaware Lawyers in the Desegregation of Delaware's Schools: A Memoir*, 9 Widener L. Symp. J. 1 (2002).

4. *Coalition to Save Our Children v. State Board Of Education*, 90 F. 3d 752 (3rd Cir. 1996).

5. 14 Del. Ch. Sec. 220 (2003).

6. Rebecca Winters, *Weighing the Long Ride to Diversity*, Time, May 10, 2004, at 36.

7. H.B. 300, 140th Gen. Assem. (Del. 2000).

8. Jamie A. Scaringi, *Delaware's Tug of War over School Desegregation: Constitutional Case Law v. Legislative and Administrative Action*, 9 Widener Symp. J. 165 (2002).

9. Norman Lockman, *Brandywine Turned School Law on Itself*, News Journal (Wilmington), Nov. 18, 2001.

10. News Journal (Wilmington), June 17, 2001 at A3.

11. Wilmington Neighborhood Schools Committee Report, *They Matter Most: Investing in Wilmington's Children and Delaware's Future* (2001).

12. In *Milliken v. Bradley*, 48 U.S. 717 (1974), the Supreme Court ruled that suburban school districts could not be included in school desegregation plans unless it could be shown that their actions contributed to segregation in city school districts.

13. The official decision and order on Red Clay's application were delayed and formally issued in 2005.

14. Delaware, State Board of Education, "Neighborhood School Plans of Delmar, Seaford, Appoquinimink, Colonial, Christina, Red Clay Consolidated and Brandywine School Districts: Decision," Dover: The Board, [2002], http://www.doe.k12.de.us/sbe/NeighSchoolPlans/b280705v1%204copy.pdf, at 20–23.

15. Dale Mezzacappa and Diane Mastrull, *Rough Road to Integration: Delaware Found a Way to Make Busing Work. That May Be About to Change*, Philadelphia Inquirer, May 19, 2004, at 2.

16. 14 Del. C. § 223.

17. Delaware State Board of Education Decision and Order, June 16, 2005.

18. *Harden v. Christina*, 924 A. 2d 247 (Del. 2007).

19. Brandywine School District, "The Brandywine Plan," Delaware State Board of Education, 15 Nov. 15, 2001, at 2.

20. Delaware, State Board of Education, "Neighborhood School Plans of Delmar, Seaford, Appoquinimink, Colonial, Christina, Red Clay Consolidated and Brandywine School Districts: Decision," Dover: The Board, [2002]. http://www.doe.k12.de.us/sbe/NeighSchoolPlans/b280705v1%204copy.pdf, at 47.

21. Eileen Kugler, *Debunking the Middle-Class Myth: Why Diverse Schools Are Good for All Kids* 14 (Scarecrow Education, 2002).

22. National Research Council, Minority Students in Special and Gifted Education (National Academies Press, 2002).

23. *Id.* at 7.

24. CensusScope http://www.censusscope.org/segregation.html (dissimilarity and exposure).

25. Gary Orfield and Chungmei Lee, *Why Segregation Matters: Poverty and Educational Inequality* (2005), *available at* www.civilrightsproject.ucla.edu/research/deseg/Why Segreg Matters.pdf.

26. Douglas S. Massey and Nancy A. Denton, *American Apartheid: Segregation and the Making of the Underclass* (Harvard University Press, 1993).

27. Jonathan Kozol, *The Shame of the Nation: The Restoration of Apartheid Schooling in America* (Crown, 2005).

28. Gary Orfield and Chungmei Lee, *Brown at 50: King's Dream or Plessy's Nightmare* 21–22 (2004), *available at* http://www.civilrightsproject.harvard.edu/research/reseg04/resegregation04.php.

29. Leland Ware, *The Demographics of Desegregation: Residential Segregation Remains High 40 Years After the Civil Rights Act,* 49 St. Louis L. J. 1155 (2005).

CHAPTER TWENTY-TWO

The Geography of Discrimination: The Seattle and Louisville Cases and the Legacy of *Brown v. Board of Education*

Robert L. Hayman Jr. and Leland Ware

Prologue

In 2007, the Supreme Court of the United States rendered its decision in what might be termed a "third-generation" desegregation case, *Parents Involved in Community Schools v. Seattle School District.*

In the first generation of cases, typified by *Brown v. Board of Education*, the Supreme Court ruled that racially segregated schools were inherently unequal and needed to *de*segregate to comply with the "equal protection" command of the Constitution.

In the second generation of cases, consisting mostly of a trio of cases from the early 1990s, the Court ruled that school districts could stop trying to desegregate—and could permit *re*segregation (or never actually achieve desegregation)—if they made a "good faith" effort at it, for a "reasonable period of time."

And now, in this third generation of cases, the Supreme Court is considering whether school districts should be *permitted* to continue their desegregation efforts, beyond the point that they have to; that is, whether they can attempt to achieve or retain desegregated schools after their "good faith" obligations have been satisfied.

It is a welcome sign of progress, we suppose, that school districts around the country—and we are pleased to put Delaware's Brandywine School District in this category—are now struggling to retain desegrated schools with the same industry and creativity that they once devoted to the cause of segregated schools. But it is a sign of something else—something really depressing—that they had to beg the Supreme Court for permission to keep their schools desegregated and that they did not receive it. The third generation of cases, we fear, will remove the final obstacles to the resegregation of our schools. Separate, it seems, is equal after all.

The *Parents Involved* decision provided a perverse vindication for those, like us, who believed in *Brown*'s litigation strategy: it proved, if there was any doubt, that the courts are a necessary if not sufficient part of any social movement.

Desegregation advocates, after all, had won their "grassroots" victory in the local schools. But the Supreme Court had the final say.

And too, the Supreme Court's decision confirmed *Brown*'s place in the constitutional canon. It was out of fidelity to *Brown*, the plurality claimed, that it was compelled to reject the student-assignment plans.

But of course, in a deeper sense, the *Parents Involved* decision was a betrayal of *Brown*, one at odds with that great case's vision and one that imperils *Brown*'s project. Left unchallenged, it threatens to be the final word on desegregation. And so it cannot remain unchallenged. The first of these "third-generation" cases must not be the last.

Introduction

On the last day of its 2006–7 term, the Supreme Court issued the long-anticipated decision in *Parents Involved in Community Schools v. Seattle School District.*[1] The case involved a challenge to assignment plans developed to ensure that student populations in individual schools broadly reflected the racial demographics of the school districts. The purpose of these plans was to prevent de facto segregation in schools. Parents in the two districts filed civil actions contending that the plans were discriminatory because, in some cases, they prevented white students from enrolling in schools they preferred. When the case reached the Supreme Court, the majority found that the school districts violated the equal protection clause of the Fourteenth Amendment. As a practical matter, the Court's decision means the end of integration for inner city students; too little weight was given to the geography of discrimination.

In 2003, the Supreme Court ruled in *Grutter v. Bollinger*[2] that the equal protection clause did not prohibit the University of Michigan's use of race-conscious admissions criteria to promote student body diversity. In an opinion authored by now-retired Justice Sandra Day O'Connor, the majority in *Grutter* ruled that student body diversity is a "compelling" governmental interest. The Michigan case was decided by a 5–4 majority. After that decision, Chief Justice John Roberts and Associate Justice Samuel Alito were elevated to the Court. Justice Roberts' plurality opinion in the Seattle and Louisville cases distinguished *Grutter* on the questionable ground that it involved "unique" circumstances of higher education. Roberts (joined by three other Justices) rejected student body diversity as a compelling educational interest for the challenged plans. And, because the Seattle district had never engaged in de jure segregation and Jefferson County schools had been declared desegregated a few years earlier, the districts had no compelling interest in remedying racial discrimination. Finally, the plurality rejected the other interests urged by the districts—promoting racial integration, racial diversity, and equal opportunity or avoiding racial isolation. The challenged plans, the plurality insisted, were designed "to achieve pure racial balance," a constitutionally proscribed objective.

Justice Kennedy's concurring opinion disagreed with Roberts on this point. Kennedy stated that a "compelling interest exists in avoiding racial isolation, an interest that a school district, in its discretion and expertise, may choose to pursue." However, Kennedy signed on to the plurality's conclusion that the assignment plans were unconstitutional. This created the 5–4 ruling that race-neutral means should have been thoroughly explored before resorting to a process that considered the race of students. Kennedy's concurring opinion, though supportive of diversity efforts, stated that "individual racial classifications . . . may be considered only if they are a last resort to achieve a compelling interest."

As Justice Breyer's dissenting opinion made clear, the plurality's reasoning is inconsistent with a long line of cases in which race-conscious student assignment plans have been approved by the Court. More important, the plurality disregarded the impact of neighborhood demographics on desegregation efforts. The student-assignment plans in Seattle and Louisville were designed to overcome persistent patterns of segregated neighborhoods. Residential segregation is not unique to those cities. African American families do not have the residential options that are available to similarly situated white families. In a study using 2000 census data, researchers found that thirty-three of the top fifty metropolitan areas were extremely segregated and the remaining seventeen were highly segregated. None of the top fifty was within the range that social scientists would consider integrated. This residential pattern was not, as the plurality assumed, the product of private choices of individual families. Research regularly produced by the U.S. Department of Housing and Urban Development and other organizations consistently show that discriminatory practices abound in the nation's housing markets.

This chapter analyzes the Supreme Court's decision in the Seattle and Louisville cases. It first focuses on Justice Roberts's plurality opinion, Justice Kennedy's concurring opinion, and Justice Breyer's dissent. It amplifies Justice Breyer's review of the obstruction and delays encountered in the years after *Brown* was decided, when school desegregation proceeded at a glacial pace. The next section analyzes the effects of segregated neighborhoods on school desegregation efforts and explains how continuing patterns of residential segregation, caused by overt and unconscious discrimination, perpetuate racial isolation in schools. It also examines Delaware's experience under the "race-neutral" Neighborhood Schools Act in an effort to determine what the plurality's approach in *Parents Involved* might portend for the future of desegregation. The final section assesses the constitutional principles that appear to inform the *Parents Involved* decision and inquires whether the decision is, as the plurality claims, "faithful to *Brown v. Board of Education.*"

The *Parents Involved* Opinion

The Student Assignment Plans

Jefferson County Public Schools operates public schools in metropolitan Louisville, Kentucky. In 1973, a federal court found that the district had maintained a segregated school system and entered a desegregation decree. The county operated under court supervision until 2000, when the District Court found that it had achieved unitary status. In 2001, the school district implemented a voluntary student-assignment plan.

Approximately 34 percent of the district's students were black; 66 percent were white. The plan required all nonmagnet schools to maintain a minimum black enrollment of 15 percent and a maximum black enrollment of 50 percent. The plan was intended to promote student body diversity by requiring that school enrollments approximate the percentage of black and white students in the districts. If students had been assigned based on proximity of schools to students' homes, many of the schools would have been de facto segregated because of the high levels of residential segregation in metropolitan Louisville.

At the elementary school level, there were "resides" schools to which students living in a designated geographic area were assigned. Elementary "resides" schools were grouped into clusters. Kindergartners, first-graders, and students new to the district could submit applications designating first and second choices of schools within their cluster. Students who did not submit applications indicating preferences were assigned to schools in their cluster. Assignments in clusters were based on available space and the requirements of the district's diversity guidelines. If a school reached the limits stated in the guidelines, a student whose race would have exacerbated a school's racial imbalance was not to be assigned to that school. After assignments had been made, students at all grade levels students could apply for transfers to other nonmagnet schools in the district. Transfers were denied when space was not available or when the student's race would have increased the overrepresentation of black or white students in a given school.

The Seattle School District operated ten public high schools. Approximately 41 percent of the district's students were white; the remaining 59 percent were classified as nonwhite. Since the late 1960s, various student assignment plans had been used to promote student body diversity. In 1998, the district adopted an assignment plan that allowed incoming ninth graders to choose any of the district's high schools by indicating their assignment preferences in rank order. As some schools were more popular than others, demand was greater than supply for them. If too many students identified the same school as their first choice, the district used "tiebreakers" to determine which students would be assigned there. First preference was given to students who had a sibling enrolled in the school. The second tiebreaker considered the student's race. If an oversubscribed school was not within 10 percentage points of the district's racial balance formula, the district used a tiebreaker to select students whose race would bring the school into balance. If it was still necessary to select students after using the racial tiebreaker, the next tiebreaker relied on the proximity of the school to the student's residence.

Seattle used the racial tiebreaker to ameliorate the effects of segregated housing patterns. Most of the white students lived in northern Seattle, whereas most of the minority students lived in the southern part of the city. Four of Seattle's high schools were located in northern Seattle, five were in southern areas, and one school was located in the center of Seattle. In the 2000–2001 school year, five of the schools were oversubscribed. Three of the oversubscribed schools were "integration positive" because the school's white enrollment in the previous school year was greater than 51 percent. This meant that more minority students who selected one of those three schools as their first choice received placements there than similarly situated white students.

Justice Roberts's Plurality Opinion

When the government uses racial classifications, there must be a "compelling justification" and the means chosen must be "narrowly tailored" to achieving the policy's goals.[3] Chief Justice John Roberts's plurality opinion concluded that the student assignment plans violated the Fourteenth Amendment because they lacked a compelling justification and the means chosen were not narrowly tailored to achieving the school districts' goals of promoting student body diversity. In *Grutter v. Bollinger*, a case involving the University of Michigan's affirmative action admissions program, the Court held that diversity is a compelling governmental interest, stating, among other things, that "the equal protection clause does not prohibit the Law School's narrowly tailored use of race in admissions decisions to further [its] compelling interest in obtaining the educational benefits that flow from a diverse student body." Relying on Justice Powell's analysis in *Regents of the University of California v. Bakke*,[4] a 1978 decision that upheld an affirmative action program at the University of California, the majority in *Grutter* found that diversity "promotes 'cross-racial understanding,'" helps to break down racial stereotypes, and "enables [students] to better understand persons of different races."

Roberts' plurality opinion argued that the Seattle and Louisville cases were not controlled by *Grutter* because diversity in that case consisted of "a far broader array of qualifications and characteristics of which racial or ethnic origin is but a single though important element." In this case, in contrast, "race [was] not considered as a broader means to achieve exposure to widely diverse people, culture, ideas and viewpoints." Instead, "race for some students, standing alone, was the determinative factor." Roberts also contended that the *Grutter* was different because the Court relied on considerations "unique" to higher education, including academic freedom, which occupy a special place in the Court's constitutional jurisprudence.

Robert rejected the school districts' argument that race-conscious assignment plans were needed to reduce racial concentrations in individual schools and to facilitate black students' access to the most desirable schools. Roberts' response relied on the second prong of the strict scrutiny standard; the student assignment schemes were not narrowly tailored. The design and operation of the plans were directed only at achieving racial balance, an objective that the Court has condemned. Allowing racial balance as a compelling state interest would justify the imposition of proportionality throughout American society. The government, Roberts claimed, must treat citizens as individuals, rather than as components of a racial, religious, sexual, or national class.

Roberts disagreed with the school districts' argument that race-conscious student assignments were necessary to ameliorate the effects of segregated housing patterns. Remedying past discrimination does not justify race-conscious governmental action. Citing Justice Powell's plurality opinion in *Wygant v. Jackson Board of Education*,[5] Roberts stated that past "societal" discrimination, without more evidence of present discrimination, is too amorphous a basis for imposing a racially classified remedy. The school districts did not show how their proffered justifications—promoting racial diversity integration and avoiding racial isolation—were any different from racial quotas that the Court had previously condemned. Integration does not require the kind of proportionality reflected in the school district's assignment plans.

The plurality also found that the school districts did not satisfy the narrow tailoring requirement. They had not explored race-neutral alternatives before resorting to a race-conscious approach. The school districts' plans did not provide for an individualized review of applicants. The assignment schemes treated applicants as members of a particular racial group, rather than as individuals. The districts employed racial classifications in a mechanical process similar to the program struck down in *Gratz v. Bollinger*.[6]

Justice Kennedy's Concurring Opinion

Justice Kennedy provided the fifth vote for the majority ruling that struck down the assignment plans as violations of the equal protection clause of the Fourteenth Amendment. Kennedy agreed with the plurality's conclusion that the student assignment plans were not narrowly tailored, but he disagreed with the plurality's interpretation of strict scrutiny. Kennedy stated, "The nation has a moral and ethical obligation to fulfill [its] historic commitment to creating an integrated society that ensures equal opportunity for all of its children." Student body diversity is a compelling educational goal; school districts have a compelling interest in avoiding racial isolation in schools. Kennedy argued that school officials can consider the racial composition of schools and adopt policies that promote student body diversity. They can devise race-conscious measures that address racial isolation in individual schools. Such measures may include "strategic site selection of new schools; drawing attendance zones with general recognition of the neighborhood's demographics of neighborhood; recruiting students and faculty in a targeted fashion; and tracking enrollments, performance and other statistics by race." However, "individual racial classifications . . . may be considered only if they are a last resort."

Kennedy disagreed with the plurality's position concerning the lack of a compelling governmental interest, but he agreed that the assignment plans were not narrowly tailored. The school districts could not explain how decisions concerning individual students were made. Jefferson County could not explain who made assignment decisions, whether there was any oversight of the decision-making process, the precise circumstances in which assignments were made, or how similarly situated students would be affected by race-conscious assignments. Seattle did not explain why students were classified as "white" and "nonwhite" given the diversity among its ethnic minority students. There were large numbers of African American, Asian American, and Latino students. Under Seattle's plan a school with 50 percent Asian American students and 50 percent white students but no black, native American, or Latino students would have been deemed racially balanced, whereas a school with 30 percent Asian Americans, 25 percent African Americans, 25 percent Latino students, and 20 percent white students would not.

Justice Kennedy cautioned against the widespread use of racial classifications, but he did not rule them out. Kennedy agreed with the plurality's finding that *Grutter* could be distinguished from these cases. The school districts' assignment plans relied on mechanical formulas that did not provide for individualized consideration of applicants. Kennedy also stated that there is a constitutional distinction between de facto and de jure segregation. The rules and remedies are different. De jure segregation justified the use of race-conscious remedies; de facto segregation does not. Kennedy acknowledged that the injury to the victim would be the same whether it was based on de jure or de facto discrimination. However, the "societal discrimination" embodied in de facto segregation does not, in his view, justify the use of racial classifications. Maintaining student body diversity is a compelling governmental interest, but the assignment plans in Seattle and Louisville were not narrowly tailored. Race-neutral assignments that promote diversity should have been explored more thoroughly.

Justice Breyer's Dissent

Justice Breyer argued that not every decision influenced by race is equally objectionable. There is a distinction between governmental actions that seek to exclude racial minorities and those that seek to include such groups. The equal protection clause allows school boards to use race-conscious criteria to achieve race-related goals even when the Constitution does not compel them to do so. In *Swann v. Charlotte-Mecklenburg Board of Education*[7] and in subsequent decisions, the Supreme Court has consistently approved voluntary measures designed to combat segregation in schools. The plurality's opinion reflects an unwarranted departure from those precedents.

Justice Breyer believed that the Seattle and Louisville student-assignment plans satisfied the "compelling interest" prong of the strict scrutiny standard. The elements of this interest, as Breyer described them, are (1) remedying the effects of segregation, including housing patterns, employment practices, and social attitudes; (2) overcoming the adverse educational effects of highly segregated schools; and (3) furthering a school district's legitimate interest in producing educational environments that reflect the pluralistic societies in which students will live and work.

Justice Breyer disagreed with the plurality's interpretation of the distinction between de facto and de jure segregation. The actual distinction focuses on what the Constitution compels and what it allows. Jurisdictions that operated de jure systems were required in many cases to take race-conscious actions to eliminate the vestiges of segregation. Localities with de facto segregation have long been permitted to take race-conscious actions to eliminate the vestiges of segregation. The difference is what a school board is obligated to do under the Constitution and what actions are allowed to eliminate the vestiges of segregation.

Justice Breyer also found that the student-assignment plans in Louisville and Seattle were narrowly tailored. The minority and nonminority enrollment limits were one component of plans that relied primarily on nonracial elements. The racial limits in the assignment plans were less burdensome than other race-conscious restrictions that the Court has approved in prior cases. The student assignment plans were designed to overcome a history of segregation in the school districts. They enhanced student choice while reducing reliance on cross-district busing. Breyer argued that the plurality's interpretation of strict scrutiny was too rigid. The plurality did not identify any assignment plans that achieved a school district's objective of making less use of race-conscious criteria. The plurality would have imposed a narrow tailoring requirement that could never be met; it would have been strict in theory but fatal in fact.

School Desegregation Efforts after Brown

In his dissenting opinion, Justice Breyer explained,

> For much of this nation's history, the races remained divided. It was not long ago that people of different races drank from separate fountains, rode on separate buses, and studied in separate schools. In [the] Court's finest hour, *Brown v. Board of Education* challenged that history and helped to change it. For *Brown* held out a promise. It was a promise embodied in three Amendments designed to make citizens of slaves. It was the promise of true racial equality—not as a matter of fine words on paper, but as a matter of everyday life in the Nation's cities and schools. It was about the nature of the democracy that must work for all Americans. It sought one law, one Nation, one people, not simply as a matter of legal principle but in terms of how we actually live.[8]

It is important to recognize that there has never been a time when America's schools were completely desegregated. Desegregation had, at best, only limited success. Between 1968 and 1980, the number of black children attending majority minority schools fell from 77 to 63 percent nationally in the nation and from 81 to 37 percent in the South. By the year 2000, that figure rose to 72 percent for the nation and 69 percent for the South. Between 1968 and 1980, the number of black children attending schools that were more than 90 percent minority had decreased from 64 to 33 percent in the nation and from 78 to 23 percent in the South. By 2000 that number rose to 37 percent in the nation and 31 percent in the South. Currently, approximately one in six black students attends schools with a 99 to 100 percent minority enrollment.

Justice Roberts's plurality opinion discounts the long history of segregation in America. It does not consider adequately the decades of struggle and resistance to efforts to desegregate schools. It treats segregation as if it were a relic of a distant past with no relevance to current conditions. It disregards the high levels of residential segregation that will drive student enrollments when color-blind student assignments are made. Justice Thomas's concurring opinion went so far as to claim that Justice Breyer's dissenting opinion included arguments that were no different from those made by segregationists who opposed *Brown*. However, it requires an inordinate amount of historical amnesia and tortured logic to even imagine the two are the same. The Seattle and Louisville school boards were trying to keep the schoolhouse door open to diversity. The plurality wants to slam it shut.

The dispute in Seattle and Louisville should be evaluated in the context of the long and troubled history of school desegregation efforts. The South's initial reaction to *Brown* was swift and severe. On March 12, 1956, "The Southern Manifesto" was read into the *Congressional Record*. This document was signed by nineteen senators and seventy-seven members of the House of Representatives. It proclaimed, "The Supreme Court of the United States, with no legal basis for such action, undertook to exercise their naked judicial power and substituted their personal political and social ideas for the established law of the land." It also alleged that "outside agitators are threatening immediate and revolutionary changes in our public school systems. If done, this is certain to destroy the system of public education in some of the states." The document concluded with a pledge to "use all lawful means to bring about a reversal of the [*Brown*] decision which is contrary to the Constitution and to prevent the use of force in its implementation."[9] The "Southern Manifesto" set the stage for the South's response to *Brown*, in which school boards engaged in tactics that ranged from passive resistance to outright defiance.

For years, southern states directly flouted the *Brown* decision or engaged in tactics that caused protracted delays in the desegregation process. One dramatic confrontation took place in Little Rock, Arkansas. In 1954, the Little Rock school board issued a statement indicating its intent to comply with *Brown*. In 1955, a federal court approved a plan that proposed desegregation in stages, to be completed by 1963. In September 1957, nine black students were slated to enroll in Little Rock's Central High School. On September 2, however, Arkansas Governor Orval Faubus sent National Guard troops to Central High to prevent the students from enrolling. The next day, the school board petitioned the federal court for a delay in implementing the plan. The court refused the board's request and ordered it to proceed with desegregation. On September 4, acting on Governor Faubus's order, National Guard troops blocked the African American students at the door of Central High School.

On September 20, a federal court granted the NAACP's request for an injunction to prevent Governor Faubus and the National Guard from interfering with the black students' efforts to enroll in Central High. Three days later, the students entered the school through a side door to avoid a mob of angry whites who had gathered in front of the building. Before the end of that school day, rioting had broken out on the school grounds. Television crews filmed scenes showing dozens of angry white adults crowding around young black students, uttering threats and brandishing signs that protested integration. Events rapidly escalated to a breaking point. On September 25, President Dwight Eisenhower dispatched federal troops to Little Rock. When federal troops arrived in tanks and other military vehicles, the black students were finally allowed to attend classes. The army troops were eventually withdrawn, but federalized National Guardsmen remained throughout the school year.

The federal court's denial of the request to suspend the operation of the school board's desegregation effort eventually reached the Supreme Court. The Supreme Court in *Cooper v. Aaron* reaffirmed *Brown* and strongly condemned the actions of the Arkansas officials. It held that "no state legislature or executive judicial officer can war against the Constitution without violating his undertaking support it. . . . A governor who asserts a power to nullify a federal court order is similarly constrained."[10]

Another highly widely publicized event took place in Mississippi when James Meredith attempted to enroll at the University of Mississippi.[11] When his application was rejected, Meredith requested assistance from NAACP's Legal Defense Fund. The NAACP represented Meredith in a trial that ended in an adverse ruling.

The university claimed that Meredith's application had been denied because he had failed to submit the required "alumni certificates," which were endorsements from university graduates. The ruling was appealed to the U.S. Court of Appeals for the Fifth Circuit. The appellate panel issued a decision reversing the trial court and ordered Meredith's admission. Mississippi Governor Ross Barnett announced his intention to defy the federal court order. On September 20, 1962, Meredith attempted to register for classes at the University of Mississippi. Governor Barnett refused to allow him to enroll. The U.S. Department of Justice and the NAACP filed an application for contempt in the federal proceeding, seeking an order to require school officials to obey the ruling requiring Meredith's admission. School officials agreed to allow Meredith to matriculate, but Governor Barnett filed a civil action in state court seeking to enjoin Meredith's admission. The state court granted Barnett's request for an injunction.

Meredith, accompanied by federal marshals, then attempted on September 26 to enroll in the university, but the state police, accompanied by Mississippi's lieutenant governor, prevented Meredith from registering. Not long afterward, a federal court issued an order holding Governor Barnett in contempt. Attorney General Robert Kennedy engaged in secret negotiations with Governor Barnett in an effort to head off another confrontation. After negotiations failed, President John F. Kennedy ordered federal troops to Oxford. When the federal troops arrived, Meredith was taken to a dormitory on the campus. Hundreds of angry whites gathered on the campus, and during the ensuing rioting, gunshots were exchanged and a reporter was shot and killed. Within a few hours 2,500 armed federal soldiers occupied the university's campus with armored vehicles. On September 30, Meredith was finally able to register for classes as federal troops occupied Oxford. As time went by, the federal troops were gradually withdrawn, and the last soldiers departed when Meredith graduated.

These are just two of the most widely publicized confrontations following the *Brown* decision. There were several others, including Alabama governor George Wallace's stand in the "schoolhouse door" to block integration in that state. More often, however, there occurred endless delays and foot-dragging in hundreds of civil actions that languished for years in the federal courts.

In the late 1960s, a decade and a half after *Brown*, the Supreme Court finally took steps to end the South's massive resistance. In *Griffin v. County School Board of Prince Edward County*,[12] a case in which a school board involved in the original *Brown* cases had closed all of its schools to avoid desegregation, Justice Hugo Black concluded, "There has been entirely too much deliberation and not enough speed in enforcing the constitutional rights which we held in *Brown*." Prince Edward County was ordered to reopen its schools. In *Alexander v. Holmes County Board of Education*,[13] the Court ruled that the "continued operation of segregated schools under a standard allowing 'all deliberate speed' for desegregation is no longer constitutionally permissible . . . the obligation of every school district is to terminate dual school systems at once and operate now and hereafter only unitary schools." In *Green v. County Board of New Kent County*,[14] the Court held that states that maintained segregated schools had an affirmative duty to eradicate all vestiges of the formerly segregated system "root and branch" and that school boards were obligated to bear the burden of proving compliance with the new standard. However, by the time these cases were decided, demographic patterns made school desegregation efforts far more difficult.

The Geography of Discrimination

Segregated Neighborhoods and School Desegregation

Segregated housing patterns hampered efforts to desegregate schools from the outset. Residential segregation is longstanding and deeply entrenched in most metropolitan communities.[15] As continuing patterns of residential segregation perpetuate de facto segregation in schools, it is useful to understand how they developed and why they persist. Practices enforcing segregated neighborhoods were established in the early years of the twentieth century after the Supreme Court endorsed segregation in *Plessy v. Ferguson*[16] in 1896. After World War I, black Southerners began to migrate in large numbers to northern and midwestern cities. They were escaping the constant threat of violence and extreme racial restrictions and seeking expanded employment opportunities that rapidly industrializing cities offered. This was at a time when large numbers of European immigrants were moving to America to exploit opportunities created by a severe labor shortage. European immigrants clustered in ethnic enclaves, but they did not experience the restrictions that African Americans encountered. Municipalities enacted local ordinances that confined African Americans to designated neighborhoods. Because the laws involved state action that discriminated on the basis of race, they were challenged and declared unconstitutional in a 1917 Supreme Court decision, *Buchanan v. Warley*,[17] which held that the laws violated the Fourteenth Amendment.

After *Buchanan*, the real estate industry used private covenants to enforce segregated housing patterns. The covenants were restrictions in deeds that prevented property owners and subsequent purchasers from selling and renting property to members of racial and religious minorities who were the targets of the covenants. The Supreme Court implicitly endorsed the validity of covenants in a 1926 decision, *Corrigan v. Buckley*.[18] The lower courts had ruled that, unlike *Buchanan*, the private covenants did not involve state action so there was no violation of the Constitution. The Supreme Court declined to review the lower courts' ruling, leaving it intact. After *Corrigan*, the use of racially restrictive covenants spread rapidly. In localities across the nation, African Americans and other people of color were confined to discrete residential districts whose most prominent features were substandard housing and overcrowded conditions.

As part of its organized efforts to combat segregation, the NAACP launched a litigation campaign against restrictive covenants in the 1940s. This effort culminated in the 1948 Supreme Court decision in *Shelley v. Kraemer*[19] that restrictive covenants were unenforceable because the use of the courts to enforce racially discriminatory agreements constituted state action that violated the Fourteenth Amendment. *Shelley* was a significant symbolic victory, but it did little to eliminate discrimination and segregation in the real estate markets.

In 1954, when *Brown* was decided, neighborhoods were highly segregated as a result of decades of redlining,[20] restrictive covenants, and other discriminatory practices. At that time, population distributions were in the midst of a dramatic transformation as white families were rapidly relocating to suburban communities.[21] This population shift was made possible by a prosperous, postwar economy and federal subsidy programs, such as Veterans Administration and Federal Housing Authority loans. The suburban communities that became a staple of the American landscape were developed during this period. Black families who were willing and able to purchase suburban homes were prevented from doing so by discriminatory practices, many of which were imposed by the federal government, which required restrictive covenants on government-insured mortgage loans.[22]

Exclusionary zoning also contributed to the perpetuation of segregated neighborhoods, particularly in suburban communities. During the late nineteenth century, land use planners decided that the public's health, safety, and welfare would be promoted by separating commercial and industrial uses from residential areas. By the early twentieth century, land use controls extended the separation principle to residential communities. Single-family and multifamily residential units were separated into different zones,[23] thereby excluding many low- and moderate-income families from areas that were designated as single-family districts. Multifamily zones were often limited to older neighborhoods. Renters and lower income families were locked into urban cores.

Segregation was not limited to southern states. *Keyes v. School District No. 1, Denver Colorado*,[24] decided in 1973, involved a challenge to segregation in a school district where the practice had never been required by state laws. Before and after the 1954 decision in *Brown v. Board of Education,* segregation was viewed mainly as a southern phenomenon. However, in many northern communities schools were segregated as a consequence of residential segregation. This became known as "de facto" segregation to distinguish it from de jure segregation in which racial separation was enforced by laws. Segregated neighborhoods outside the South were maintained through racially restrictive covenants, redlining, and other practices that barred African Americans from white neighborhoods.

In 1969, a group of African American parents filed a civil action claiming that the Denver School Board maintained racially and ethnically segregated schools. After a trial, the District Court found that actions including the construction of a new elementary school in the middle of Denver's black community, the manipulation of attendance zones, the use of "optional zones," and the excessive use of mobile classroom units constituted a deliberate policy of racial segregation. The remedy, however, was limited. The trial court ruled that a finding of intentional segregation in some sections of Denver did not mean that there was segregation throughout the school district. The Supreme Court reversed the trial court's ruling. It ruled that proof of intentional segregation in a substantial portion of a school district was sufficient to support a finding of segregation throughout the system. When such a finding is made, school authorities had an obligation to desegregate all of their schools. This was first time that the Court ruled on school segregation in a jurisdiction that had never operated under laws mandating racial separation. *Keys* paved the way for suits in northern cities where schools were de facto segregated. These efforts would encounter obstacles that were even more formidable than the South's massive resistance.

In *Milliken v. Bradley*,[25] a case involving schools in Detroit, the plaintiffs attempted to address residential segregation by including the suburban school districts surrounding Detroit in a metropolitan desegregation plan. As a consequence of segregated housing patterns and "white flight" to suburban communities, the schools in Detroit were rapidly shifting to predominantly black populations; enrollments in suburban districts were nearly all white. The plaintiffs in *Milliken* argued that racial balance could not be achieved without including the suburban districts in the desegregation plan. In 1974, the Supreme Court held that suburban school districts could not be required to participate in court-ordered desegregation plans unless it could be proven that their actions contributed to segregation in the jurisdiction in which the case arose. There could be no remedy requiring busing across district lines without a showing of an interdistrict violation. In most jurisdictions, the Court's ruling in *Milliken* frustrated desegregation efforts, as it insulated suburban districts from the desegregation process.

After *Milliken*, court-supervised school desegregation proceeded slowly for several years. To ameliorate the effect of segregated neighborhoods, school districts relied heavily on busing and other strategies to desegregate schools. In the early 1990s, however, the Supreme Court's desegregation jurisprudence changed direction with the decisions in *Board of Education of Oklahoma City v. Dowell*,[26] *Freeman v. Pitts*,[27] and *Missouri v. Jenkins*.[28] In *Dowell*, the Supreme Court held that the standard for determining unitary status was whether the school board "had complied in good faith with the [original] desegregation decree" and whether all "vestiges of past discrimination had been eliminated to the extent practicable." In *Freeman v. Pitts*, a case involving a school district near Atlanta, the Court found that when single-race schools continue to exist because of changes in the racial composition of neighborhoods school districts would not be held responsible unless those factors were caused by actions taken by school officials.

Dowell and *Freeman* modified the *Green* standard, which imposed an affirmative duty to eliminate *all* vestiges of segregation "root and branch." Under the Court's revised standard, school districts were obligated to eliminate lingering vestiges of segregation only to "the extent practicable." This standard was affirmed in *Jenkins*, in which the majority explained that the test for determining unitary status was not a finding that all vestiges of the formerly segregated system had been eliminated "root and branch," but whether the school district had complied in good faith with the original desegregation decree and whether the vestiges of past discrimination had been eliminated to the "extent practicable." The Court also found that segregated housing patterns, which affected the racial composition of schools, would not prevent a unitary status determination unless they could be directly attributed to the actions of school officials.

Under *Green*, school districts were required to completely eradicate all remnants of the segregated system. After these rulings, they need only show good faith compliance with the original desegregation decree and the elimination of most, but not necessarily all, of any lingering vestiges. The new standard requires courts to hold that the desegregation obligation has been satisfied even when student populations in individual schools remain predominantly black or white as a result of segregated neighborhoods. This is what happened in *Meredith v. Jefferson County School Board of Education*, and it is why the Jefferson County school board continued to make race-conscious student assignments after it was declared unitary. Assignments based on residential proximity would have resulted in de facto segregation.

Continuing Patterns of Residential Segregation and Unconscious Discrimination

The flawed assumption underlying Roberts's plurality opinion in *Parents Involved* is that the locations in which families reside reflect private housing choices.[29] Therefore, to the extent schools and neighborhoods remain predominantly black or white, they merely reflect the preferences of residents. This is not an accurate premise. African American families do not enjoy the range of residential options that are available to white families with similar incomes and credit histories.[30] Despite the provisions of the 1968 Fair Housing Act outlawing discrimination in housing transactions, racial bias abounds in the nation's housing markets. Reports regularly produced by the U.S. Department of Housing and Urban Development (HUD) and other organizations document the discriminatory practices of housing providers.[31] A HUD report based on data derived from a series of matched-pair tests conducted over several months found that African American homebuyers and renters encountered widespread discrimination in U.S. housing markets. White home buyers were consistently favored over blacks in 17 percent of tests. White home buyers were more likely to be able to inspect available homes and to be shown homes in more predominantly white neighborhoods than comparable blacks. Whites also received more information and assistance with financing as well as more encouragement than comparable black home buyers.[32]

Research analyzing the 2000 census shows that high levels of residential segregation persist. Social scientists measure segregation levels using an "Index of Dissimilarity." The index indicates the degree to which racial groups are evenly distributed among census tracts in a given location. Evenness is defined by examining the racial composition of the city as a whole. Thus, if a city has a 20 percent black population and an 80 percent white population, an even distribution would reflect these percentages in each census tract. The index ranges from 0 to 100, reflecting the percentage of one group that would have to move to achieve an even distribution of the racial groups in the area. A value of 60 or above is considered highly segregated. Values of 40 to 50 are considered moderate levels of segregation. Values of 30 or less are considered low.[33] The data show that thirty-three of the top fifty metropolitan areas are highly segregated and that the remaining seventeen are segregated; none was within the range that social scientists would consider integrated.[34] At a time when America is becoming more racially and ethnically diverse, many metropolitan communities are more segregated than they were when *Brown* was decided. If school officials are not allowed to make conscious efforts to diversify student enrollments, schools in metropolitan communities will be almost all white or all black and Latino.

Many of the discriminatory practices are overt and intentional, but much of what drives continuing patterns of residential segregation is caused by unconscious stereotypes. Researchers have consistently documented that whites will desert a neighborhood when it reaches a "tipping point" and becomes "too black." This flight is fueled largely by the perceptions of many whites that the presence of African Americans in a neighborhood causes property values to decline.[35] These perceptions are fueled by unconscious discrimination. Throughout the last two decades, a substantial body of empirical and theoretical work in cognitive psychology has confirmed that the causes of discriminatory actions often operate at an unconscious level without the perpetrator's awareness of the source. In the seminal article, *The Id, the Ego and Equal Protection Reckoning with Unconscious Racism*, Professor Charles Lawrence explained that unconscious bias heavily influences the ways in which whites perceive African Americans.[36] Unconscious discrimination takes place at a subconscious level; the actor is unaware of the forces that influence his or her conduct.

In the years following the publication of *The Id, the Ego and Equal Protection*, legal scholars have produced a large body of research and commentary building on Lawrence's work. In *The Content of Our Categories*,[37] Professor Linda Krieger explained that much of the discrimination that occurs now is not the result of conscious animus. Relying on the work of behavioral psychologists, Krieger explained that decision making relies on "categorization," which is a fundamental part of the process of human cognition. Categorization, grouping like objects together, simplifies the task of processing and retaining information. It allows individuals to identify objects, infer the existence of unobservable traits, and attribute causation to specific events. Categorization operates at an unconscious level. Individuals perceive, categorize, and evaluate information differently depending on the ways in which information is presented and the context in which it is received. The danger of categorization is that it can cause judgment errors that bias decision making. Stereotyping is a form of categorization.

Stereotyping involves, among other things, the creation of a mental image of a "typical" member of a particular category. Individuals are perceived as undifferentiated members of a group, lacking any significant differences from other individuals within the group. Common traits are assigned to the entire group. When a particular behavior by a group member is observed, the viewer evaluates the behavior through the lens of the stereotype. This causes the observer to conclude whether the conduct has empirically confirmed his or her stereotyped belief about the group. Stereotypes can be so deeply internalized that they persist even in the face of information that directly contradicts them. Professor John Calmore explained that "aversive racism is a significant, but unacknowledged, factor in accounting for the almost rigidly persistent features of both housing discrimination and residential segregation."[38]

Some commentators have claimed that continuing residential segregation reflects the preferences of African Americans.[39] Polling data document that most white Americans hold this view. In a recently published study, however, Kryson and Farley found that African Americans prefer mixed communities in which the racial balance is 50 percent white and 50 percent black (a mix that is "too black" for most whites). But unlike the overt and unconscious bias that drives many white home buyers, African Americans' preference for a 50/50 mix stems in part from fears of isolation and white hostility in predominantly white neighborhoods.[40] Discussing upscale, all-black suburban communities outside Washington, D.C., Professor Sheryll Cashin described the "integration exhaustion" that many middle-class blacks experience. This refers to the desire of many affluent African Americans to live in well-appointed homes surrounded by people who have similar educational and income levels, in locations where the potential for unpleasant racial encounters is minimized.[41] This is not a constraint for white home buyers. Voluntary segregation by African Americans is a myth. Most African Americans prefer racially mixed neighborhoods, and many of those who select majority minority communities are influenced by fears of isolation and mistreatment.

Schools and neighborhoods are inextricably intertwined. Segregated neighborhoods cannot be dismissed as a product of "societal" discrimination that is too "amorphous" to justify a race-conscious response. They are a lingering vestige of public policies and private practices that enforced segregation. School officials should be allowed to devise student assignments that ameliorate the effects of segregated neighborhoods. If this is not allowed, students who live in the inner city neighborhoods will remain as isolated as their forebears were in the pre-*Brown* era. If school assignments are based solely on proximity, de facto segregation in neighborhoods will be replicated in school enrollments. By preventing schools districts from considering race in student assignments, the Supreme Court has assured that de facto segregation will increase.

The Delaware Experience

What does the *Parents Involved* decision portend for the future of desegregation? Here, as elsewhere, the Delaware experience provides a helpful case study.

In Delaware, the Neighborhood Schools Act prohibits covered school districts from considering race in student assignments. It requires, in other words, precisely the sort of "race-neutral" assignment plans championed by the *Parents Involved* plurality. Delaware's experience, then, should provide useful clues to the likely impact of the plurality's ruling, should it prevail. Unfortunately, the experience suggests that, under such a rule, the future for desegregation may be bleak.

The effort to end court-supervised desegregation in New Castle County achieved its first and most important victory in 1995, when District Court judge Sue Robinson determined—following the lax standards set in the 1990s "resegregation decisions" of the Supreme Court—that the school board had "eliminated the vestiges of segregation to the extent practicable." Judge Robinson's decision was upheld on appeal (by a 2–1 decision), and the desegregation decree was terminated.

Chief among the "vestiges of segregation" that a school district is charged with eliminating is the segregation of the student body: "racial identifiability," Judge Robinson observed, is "the one clear 'vestige' of a dual system." The New Castle County schools had long been "racially identifiable." They were segregated by a state constitutional mandate and, a generation after *Brown*, remained racially distinct.

But in 1995, Judge Robinson concluded that the four subject school districts featured "among the most racially balanced schools in the United States."

To reach this conclusion, Judge Robinson relied on the testimony of three experts—two for the defendant school board and one for the plaintiff parents. Following the conventions established in the social sciences and accepted by the courts, the experts described the degree of segregation in a given school as a function of two variables: the percentage of minority students in the school and the percentage of minority students (generally, of comparable grade level) in the district as a whole. If the individual schools within a district had minority populations that roughly mirrored the minority populations of the district as a whole—and thus did not vary greatly from one school to the next—then the schools of the district might be described as "racially balanced."

The experts determined which schools had minority populations within ten percentage points—plus or minus—of the minority population of their respective districts. The experts also determined which schools had minority populations that fell within a 20-percentage-point variance; that standard, they noted, had been most commonly employed in desegregation cases since the mid-1980s.

Under either standard, nearly all the schools covered by the desegregation decree manifested acceptable levels of desegregation. In the Brandywine School District, every school fell within the 10 percent variance range and had been within that range since 1981, the onset of interdistrict desegregation. In the Christina School District, every school fell within the 10 percent variance range; two of fourteen elementary schools had been outside the range, but recent zone adjustments brought each school back within the variance. In the Colonial School District, every school fell within the 10 percent variance range; two of ten elementary schools had briefly fallen outside the range, but had been within the variance since 1988. Finally, in the Red Clay School District, every school fell within the 10 percent variance range; three elementary schools, two of five middle schools, and two of four high schools had periods outside the range, but all were within the variance at the time of the litigation. The experts determined that, throughout the history of the interdistrict desegregation, only two schools—one elementary school and one high school, each located in the Red Clay School District—had ever exceeded the 20 percent standard.

The data seemed to be a testament to the efficacy of the court-ordered desegregation plan, which, perhaps ironically, sealed the plan's doom. "Based upon an examination of the 4 districts in all of their facets," Judge Robinson wrote, "the court concludes that the defendants have complied in good faith with the desegregation decrees issued in this litigation, that the defendants are unlikely to return to the segregative practices of their predecessors, and that the vestiges of past discrimination have been eliminated to the extent practicable." "It is time," she concluded, "for the federal court to end its supervision of the public school system of Northern New Castle County."[42]

A three-judge panel of the Court of Appeals upheld the decision the following year. Judge Lee Sarokin dissented from the decision to terminate the decree, but did not dispute Judge Robinson's finding—upheld by the majority of the panel—that the schools were no longer segregated with regard to student assignments.[43] Within four years, the Delaware legislature had enacted its Neighborhood

Schools Act, prohibiting the consideration of race in student assignments in the four districts formerly covered by the desegregation decree.

Since 2000, then, the four covered districts have been prohibited from taking race-conscious steps to maintain desegregated schools and prevent resegregation. The districts, in other words, have operated under the principles championed by Chief Justice Roberts in his *Parents Involved* plurality: the school districts are color blind and indifferent to the racial composition of their schools.

So what has happened to the racial composition of the schools? The expected answer might be "not much." At the time of this writing, just seven years have passed since the act was adopted. Moreover, the school districts have struggled to develop student-assignment plans that complied with the act: Red Clay submitted three plans before receiving approval from the State Board of Education in 2004; at this writing, the Christina School District still does not have an approved plan; and the Brandywine plan, approved in 2001, is widely viewed as defying the spirit, if not the letter, of the Neighborhood Schools Act. In short, it seems a bit early to expect much change in the demographics of the schools.

To determine the extent of demographic change, we reviewed the State Board of Education's official published data for the school year beginning in fall 2006, using the same definitions ("minority" includes African American and Hispanic students) and the same methodology (we used "grade group" comparisons, comparing, for example, the minority population of an elementary school with the minority elementary school population of the districts as a whole) used by the experts and relied upon by Judge Robinson in the 1995 litigation.[44]

In the Brandywine School District, where all the schools fell within a 10 percent variance in 1995, five of eleven elementary schools now fall outside the variance, as do two of the district's three middle schools. One elementary school and one middle school fall outside a 20 percent variance. Minority populations in the elementary schools range from a low of 23.2 percent (95 of 410 students) to a high of 67.5 percent (218 of 323 students).

In the Christina School District, where all the schools fell within a 10 percent variance in 1995, thirteen of eighteen elementary schools now fall outside the variance, as does one of the district's three high schools. Seven of the elementary schools fall outside a 20 percent variance. Minority populations in the elementary schools range from a low of 21.4 percent (101 of 472 students) to a high of 82.1 percent (256 of 312 students).

In the Colonial School District, where all the schools fell within a 10 percent variance in 1995, four of eight elementary schools now fall outside the variance. Two of those elementary schools fall outside a 20 percent variance. Minority populations in the elementary schools range from a low of 31.6 percent (350 of 1107 students) to a high of 77.1 percent (367 of 476).

In the Red Clay School District, where all the schools fell within a 10 percent variance in 1995, all thirteen elementary schools now fall outside the variance, as do four of the district's five middle schools. Eight elementary schools and three middle schools fall outside a 20 percent variance. Minority populations in the elementary schools range from a low of 7.7 percent (60 of 774 students) to a high of 98.5 percent (460 of 467 students).

Six charter schools in the area enroll 3,107 elementary students, 1,940 of whom (62.4 percent) are minorities. The minority populations of the area's six charter elementary schools are, in ascending order, 10.9 percent (73 of 673), 16.5 percent (107 of 647), 97.1 percent (816 of 840), 99.4 percent (499 of 502), and 100 percent (202 of 202 and 243 of 243).

To summarize, all the elementary schools in the four districts fell within the 10 percent variance in 1995. Just over a decade later, forty-one of fifty-six elementary schools fall outside the 10 percent variance; twenty-four of fifty-six schools fall outside a 20 percent variance. All the middle and high schools in the four districts fell within the 10 percent variance in 1995. Now, six of fourteen middle schools and one of the ten high schools fall outside the variance; four of the fourteen middle schools fall outside a 20 percent variance. In total, forty-eight of the area's eighty schools, nearly two-thirds, now fall outside a 10 percent variance; twenty-eight of the eighty—more than a third—fall outside a 20 percent variance.

Our assessment reveals, then, that absent court supervision, and operating under the shadow of the "color-blind" Neighborhood Schools Act, the schools of the four districts have resegregated, rapidly and dramatically.

Parents Involved and the Legacy of *Brown*

If the position staked out in the plurality opinion in *Parents Involved* carries the day, the likely result is a return to racially segregated schools. That real-world consequence, we believe, is more than enough to condemn the opinion. But we object not only to the likely impact of the approach but also to the Court's manifest attitude: the four Justices who comprise the plurality display a stunning indifference to the harms of segregation and a shocking disdain for the desegregation project.

The Court's opinion in *Parents Involved* amounts to a double betrayal of *Brown*: it exalts an empty formalism—"race neutrality"—that is manifestly at odds with *Brown*'s commitment to real equality, and it ignores the harms of segregation that animated the desegregation effort.

Race Neutrality

The a priori premise for the *Parents Involved* Court is that school districts must "stop assigning students on a racial basis." The outcome of the dispute follows with syllogistic simplicity: the school districts here are using race in student assignments; the school districts here must stop it.

But the premise is highly contestable. Indeed, it is our view that the premise is nothing more than a particularized version of a certain ideological predisposition, one that favors "private markets" and "natural" hierarchies. "Race neutrality," that is to say, is a decidedly non-neutral principle.

Free Markets and Private Choices

Concurring in *Parents Involved*, Justice Thomas claims that much contemporary segregation results not from the past segregative acts of the state, but rather from "innocent private decisions, including voluntary housing choices." As a result of such private choices, he concludes, "Schools will fall in and out of (racial) balance in the natural course."

The empirical component of these claims is certainly worth challenging: as we explain elsewhere in this chapter, it is by no means clear that "private choices" are unaffected by the history of de jure segregation, even if the two seem remote in time. Of more immediate concern, however, is the normative component of this claim: that such private choices are sacrosanct and cannot be overridden by the state. The doctrinal foundations of this normative claim are now clear: "private choices" are not themselves sufficiently related to state action, and the segregative effects of those choices are not sufficiently harmful to warrant race-conscious remedies. But what principle compels these rules? Why cannot the people, through their elected school boards, choose instead to establish and maintain racially integrated schools? What is it that commits us, that is to say, to a racial laissez-faire?

Part of the answer, we believe, is to be found in the preference for free markets, a preference that is in turn rooted in (largely latent) assumptions about the efficiency of the markets. Compulsory desegregation (or integration), it seems, is inefficient to the extent that it might be employed either to compensate for or control market behavior that is (and must remain) beyond governmental regulation. Thus, desegregation cannot and should not be used as a tool either to frustrate "private choices" or to alter the landscape created by "natural" demographic changes. Although government may control school admissions, the argument goes, it is the market, not government, that should control the various anterior decisions, including the choice of school district, choice of neighborhood, and ultimately, the choice of school. School segregation, then, is the work of the marketplace, and the marketplace is efficient.

The difficulty with this claim is that it is entirely unsubstantiated. The claim simply relies on an assumption that private markets are efficient. But that assumption is not universally true, and there are compelling reasons to believe that it is not true in the racial segregation context. The embrace of that assumption—without critical assessment and in the face of competing claims—in fact reflects a certain bias: in part, an ideological bias, but also, in part, a segregative bias.

The bias in favor of private market ordering that underlies much of modern law and economics (at least in its "Chicago school" version) is generally traced to the Coase theorem. Ronald Coase offered his theorem as a corrective to what he viewed as the interventionist bias of welfare economists, who were forever justifying market interventions by reference to the "social costs" of private transactions. Such costs, or "externalities," were to be charged—through governmental regulation—to the parties; the result was to "internalize" the "externalities" of a transaction and convert the "social costs" into private ones.

Coase maintained that the regulatory effort was often based on two faulty assumptions: first, that a discrete wrongdoer "caused" the harm, and second, that governmental regulation was needed to minimize the social costs of the harmful action. Regarding the first, Coase insisted on the reciprocal nature of the problem:

> If we are to discuss the problem in terms of causation, both parties cause the damage. If we are to attain an optimum allocation of resources, it is therefore desirable that both parties should take the harmful effect (the nuisance) into account in deciding

> on their course of action. It is one of the beauties of a smoothly operating pricing system that, as has already been explained, the fall in the value of production due to the harmful effect would be a cost for both parties.

And, if left to their own devices, the parties would minimize the costs. Undermining the second assumption, Coase offered his famous theorem: in the absence of transaction costs, the parties themselves would bargain their way to the efficient reallocation of rights. Laws and regulations were of no consequence where the parties could, without cost, bargain them away: "If such market transactions are costless, such a rearrangement of rights will always take place if it would lead to an increase in the value of production."

The key, Coase insists, lies in recognizing the costs of the proposed intervention: the loss of utility suffered by the object of regulation. "The belief that it is desirable that the business which causes harmful effects should be forced to compensate those who suffer damages . . . is undoubtedly the result of not comparing the total product obtainable with alternative social arrangements." The result, in Coase's view, was that "economists, and policy-makers generally, have tended to over-estimate the advantages which come from governmental regulation."[45]

The same logic seems to inform the *Parents Involved* decision. On this reading, desegregation may be understood as an attempt to internalize the social costs of segregative behavior. That behavior may not in itself have been inefficient; employing his own efficiency model, Judge Richard Posner has suggested that compulsory segregation may well be "wealth maximizing." But there are costs to this behavior that transcend the immediate parties (i.e., the segregators and the segregated), and at least some of these costs—in, for example, the political capital of the United States in the Cold War effort—may in fact have partly inspired the Court's initial effort to end segregation. Desegregation effectively charged the costs of discriminatory behavior to those who wanted to engage in it: they could continue to provide inferior educations to black Americans, but only if they were willing either to send their own children to the same poor schools or to pay the costs of private education. The resegregation opinions emerged as a Coasean corrective to the assumption that this intervention was efficient: forcing these costs on pro-segregation white Americans is inefficient and wrong.[46]

There is, of course, a superficial implausibility to this reading: governmental control of the resource at issue precludes a strict laissez-faire approach, and one is compelled to choose between either formal segregation or formal desegregation. The Court is not about to announce its preference for the former. In other words, it cannot now say that formal racial segregation is efficient and that *Brown* was therefore wrong to order its demise. But it can—and has—communicated the same basic message through two related devices. First, the distinction between de jure and de facto segregation allows the Court to resurrect the once discredited distinction between formal desegregation and actual integration: in the current iteration of the old "Parker doctrine," formal desegregation (i.e., an end to segregation laws) is required by the Fourteenth Amendment, but actual integration—what the Court pejoratively refers to as "racial balancing"—is not. Second, separating issues of school segregation from issues of residential segregation allows the Court to charge racial imbalances in the schools to private markets beyond a school district's control. The schools cannot be held accountable either for "private choices" or for "natural" demographic changes. The combined effect of these devices is to allow the Court to maintain, on the one hand, that *Brown* was correct in holding segregation unlawful and to insist, on the other hand, that the actual attempt to compel the integration of schools is inefficient and wrong.

Ultimately, a Coasean analysis might well support the proposition that judicially enforced integration is inefficient. But it just as well might *not* support that proposition, and that is the critical point. The *assumption* of inefficiency belies the claim to neutrality, and that assumption may be flawed for at least four reasons.

First, any efficiency analysis would have to account for the social costs of segregation. These include, among other things, a political underinvestment in—and underutilization of—human capital and a depressed faith in the fairness and justice of American institutions,[47] including our system of education. These are not, admittedly, easy costs to quantify, but it seems implausible to contend that they are insubstantial.

Second, the analysis must consider the transaction costs. The precise scope and implications of the Coase theorem remain very much contested, but this much at least is widely accepted: the Coase theorem undermines the efficiency rationale for governmental regulation in those bargaining situations—and only in those bargaining situations—unencumbered by transaction costs. But as Coase himself acknowledged, in the somewhat more realistic situation where bargaining is not costless, the initial allocation of rights is significant and quite often determinative. In those situations, the private market does not guarantee efficiency.[48]

Surely, significant transaction costs attend the "bargaining" situation in the school segregation context. Consider just the immediate costs of the efforts to organize and effect a changed bargain: the massive social and political change envisioned by desegregation would require a vast mobilization of legal resources and, given the hostility to race-specific laws, may in fact require constitutional change. The costs of effectuating such changes would be overwhelming—and perhaps prohibitive.[49]

Third, the assumption is tenable only if parties are in a bargaining situation. But given the racial disparities in material resources—and the obvious fact that desegregation cannot proceed unilaterally (i.e., by just one race)—the situation is perhaps more likened to a cartel. Two of the attendant difficulties would then be the unwillingness of the majority to bargain and the inability of the minority to move the parties into a bargaining situation. The problem may ultimately be conceived of as an informational one: the majority's unwillingness to even consider integration is the unfortunate product of imperfect information. But that problem simply becomes another cost of, and barrier to, bargaining, one that may be insurmountable without state intervention.[50] Indeed, one way to understand the original desegregation decisions might be as an attempt to cure the imperfection in information by compelling the parties to learn with—and from—one another.

Fourth, the assumption of efficiency assumes constant preferences by the parties. But a growing literature on the endogeneity of preferences exposes the ways in which preferences are shaped by laws and institutions. One irony of the resegregation cases is that they ignore the extent to which *Brown* and its progeny succeeded in curing the informational deficit and thereby reshaping attitudes. Today, majorities of both white Americans and black Americans express a preference for integration, both of their neighborhoods and their schools. To be sure, they may differ considerably in the degree of integration they would prefer—white Americans are much less willing than black Americans to place their children in schools where they would be in a racial minority—but the point is that preferences have evolved, and quite likely have evolved in part due to *Brown*. So significant is the change, in fact, that a growing number of theorists are challenging the view that the persistence of segregation can be explained by white aversion to integration. Game theoretical models are increasingly offered as alternatives, models that accept as genuine the voiced willingness of white Americans to integrate and explain segregation largely by reference to strategic economic behavior. Law, it bears noting, is critical in shaping this behavior by structuring economic incentives both real and perceived: this understanding, to take just one example, is at the heart of those efforts to promote "desegregative attractiveness" that were nullified by the Court in one of the recent resegregation cases, *Missouri v. Jenkins*. In this sense, the *Parents Involved* decision is not so much ironic as it is simply tragic: it perpetuates the economic incentives and the interracial ignorance and stereotypes that create the cycle of segregation.[51]

In summary, the Coase theorem may well have supplied a useful corrective to the assumption that governmental intervention is efficient. But that observation affords no license for an uncritical embrace of the contrary assumption: assuming, without sustained analysis, that judicially enforced desegregation is inefficient is simply to indulge an anti-interventionist bias. And that, of course, is hardly neutral.

Color Blindness and Real Equality

On a surface reading of the *Parents Involved* plurality, the Court is enforcing nothing more—and nothing less—than the state's obligation to be officially indifferent to matters of race. And perhaps that is all there really is to it: the "color-blind" principle might be one of first order. But what is the source of this mandate?

There are, to begin with, two clearly competing visions of equality, of which color blindness—or race neutrality—is just one. The color-blind principle might fairly be described as a principle of formal equality. The state, in this vision, is committed to a position of absolute and abstract symmetry in its engagements with race. Thus, what the state does for one race—or to one race—it must do for all races, regardless of the context, and if the state chooses to ignore matters of race altogether, again, regardless of the context, well, then, this is the very best kind of racial equality of all. In this view, the problem with state-sponsored segregation is that it was overtly race conscious. The solution to the problem is simply to elide all official references to race; to treat race, in other words, as if it does not exist.

But there is an alternative vision of equality, one that might be described as a realist vision. The realist vision embraces all aspects of the real-world context that the formalist vision purposefully ignores: whether state actions are consistent with equality can be assessed only in particularized settings, informed by the lessons of human experience. In this view, the problem with state-sponsored segregation can be fully understood only in its larger context, as part of the official effort to perpetuate racial hierarchy through the systematic isolation and exclusion of the disfavored race. The partial solution—and segregation is understood as part of our much larger problem with race, one requiring coordinated and comprehensive solutions—requires an end to that isolation and exclusion, a real-world disruption of the hierarchical plan.

This is not the occasion to debate the relative merits of the competing visions. It is the occasion to inquire whether one vision or another is more consistent with constitutional principles. If, in other words, the *Parents Involved* plurality has indeed embraced the formalist vision, can it fairly claim that the choice is faithful to the Constitution?

We note at the outset that no legal principle independent of *Brown* would seem to compel—or even justify—this choice. Neither constitutional text, nor the "intent of the framers," nor precedent would seem to support a preference for the formalist vision. The text, to begin with, requires the "equal protection of the law." There is nothing in the language to suggest that the equality thereby guaranteed is of the abstract variety, and in fact, the somewhat peculiar syntax suggests less focus on the "law" than on the "protection" it affords. How can the latter be measured but in the real world? An inquiry into the history of the amendment at least plausibly supports this more realist reading: the need for the amendment was established by a thorough inquiry into the real-world circumstances affecting black Americans, and the defenders of the amendment consistently denounced the sophistry of its opponents, proclaiming in contrast their commitment to secure real protection.[52]

A century-plus worth of precedents, meanwhile, generate at most a mixed message. The early opinion in *Strauder v. West Virginia*[53] evidences an awareness that, in a context of racial hierarchy, symmetrical and even identical treatment (all defendants, black and white, were tried before the same all-white juries) can produce a practical inequality. But within a few years, this understanding yields to the almost pathologically abstract assertion of the *Civil Rights Cases* that black Americans must "cease[] to be the special favorite of the law."[54] Curiously, that assertion is made in the course of a decision invalidating a law that was—on its face—formally neutral. The Civil Rights Act of 1875 did no more than prohibit racial discrimination, by any race and against any race. But there was no secret about its intended beneficiaries. Throughout Reconstruction, it was clear—even to the Supreme Court—that the purpose and practical effect of civil rights measures were to promote the status of black Americans.[55] In any event, the temporary triumph of the formalist vision is completed by the decision in *Plessy v. Ferguson*, which finds equality in segregated rail cars without any inquiry at all into the attending circumstances, and imagines that black Americans perceive in compulsory segregation an assertion of white supremacy—and of their own racial inferiority—only because "the colored race chooses to put that construction upon" the law.[56] That proposition, of course, would be expressly repudiated by the Court in *Brown*, which finds it contrary to modern "psychological knowledge."[57] On this score, *Brown* completes a fairly dramatic jurisprudential revolution initiated by the Court a few years earlier in *Sweatt v. Painter*[58] and *McLaurin v.*

Oklahoma.[59] In the real world, it is easy to discern the inequalities—tangible and intangible—both latent and patent in the scheme of racial segregation. As the first Justice Harlan would have put it, "The thin disguise of 'equal' accommodations . . . will not [fool] anyone"[60]—not even the Supreme Court.

Ultimately, it seems, the "neutral" justification for formal equality is simply rhetorical. Formalism is by definition indifferent to non-neutral concerns, and race neutrality is, by definition, neutral. But beyond the rhetoric, race neutrality is not neutral, for at least two reasons.

First, the rule of neutrality expresses a distinct conservative bias, in the most general political sense. The essence of the rule is that the state properly stands apart from matters of race, that there is to be no intervention in racial affairs, and that, most certainly, the state has neither the obligation nor the power to promote racial equality or, in the instant context, racial integration. The rule of color blindness is the racial equivalent of laissez-faire: the best state action is no state action—just leave it alone.

The conservative position on matters of race is not indefensible: there are tenable arguments on behalf of color blindness, even if the arguments against it—and in favor of race consciousness—are ultimately the more persuasive ones. The critical point, however, is that the conservative position is just that—a position, one of two competing political views. And no neutral constitutional principle commands or even commends it. As Justice Holmes put it in another context, "A constitution is not intended to embody a particular economic theory, whether of paternalism and the organic relation of the citizen to the state or of laissez-faire."[61] Whatever the merits of the conservative position, one cannot plausibly claim that it is neutral.

Indeed, there are compelling arguments to be made that the ordinary principles of constitutional adjudication—conformity to text, to the "original meaning," and to precedent—counsel in favor of the progressive view on race, that the Fourteenth Amendment imposes upon the states an affirmative obligation to ensure equality. The record before the Thirty-Ninth Congress was, after all, replete with instances not merely of official and formal acts of discrimination against the freedmen but also of official failures to prevent or remedy "private" acts of oppression, perpetrated under the watch of indifferent state officials or with their acquiescence or active support.[62] Section One of the Fourteenth Amendment thus commands that no state shall deny "the equal protection of the law," and "when this equal protection is withheld, when it is not afforded, it is denied."[63] As a necessary consequence, the clause gives rise to an affirmative duty on the part of the states: they are obliged not merely to refrain from unequal treatment but also to provide "equal protection." "A State denies equal protection whenever it fails to give it. Denying includes inaction as well as action. A State denies protection as effectively by not executing as by not making laws."[64] Thus when the states regularly fail to protect discrete classes of citizens from acts of oppression or discrimination, they fail to provide the "equal protection of the laws." "If a State fails to secure to a certain class of people the equal protection of the laws, it is exactly equivalent to denying such protection. Whether that failure is willful or the result of inability can make no difference."[65]

Certainly, the Supreme Court has understood the equal protection clause to impose an affirmative obligation on the states in the context of school segregation: the states have an affirmative duty to *de*segregate their schools. An alternative had been proposed. Judge John Parker had advocated the laissez-faire approach toward segregation, insisting that under *Brown*, the Constitution "does not require integration. It merely forbids discrimination."[66] But any doubts about the matter were removed in 1968, when the "facile formula"[67] of the "Parker doctrine" was rejected by a unanimous Court. In *Green v. New Kent County School Board*, the Court held that *Brown* charged segregative school districts "with the affirmative duty to take whatever steps might be necessary to convert to a unitary system in which racial discrimination would be eliminated root and branch."[68] To be sure, at least one member of the current Court is displeased with the state of the law produced by the *Green* decision,[69] but with all respect, his displeasure is no substitute for constitutional principle.

There is another bias lurking behind "color blindness." Recalling that Justice Bradley in the *Civil Rights Cases* had insisted, within a generation of the Emancipation Proclamation, that the freedmen must "cease[] to be the special favorites of the law,"[70] Charles Black wrote the following:

> This disconnection of present from past (not, I think, formerly regarded as characteristic of "conservatism") cannot be made to seem successful today, any more than in 1883. American slavery lasted more than two centuries, not too far from twice the time since its abolition. Even abolition was not the end. Quite soon after the Civil War, the national effort to remedy the situation of the newly free was as good as abandoned; in the places where most of them lived they were not even so much as allowed to vote in the only election that counted; per capita public expenditures in public schools for their children ran far below–sometimes by a factor of one to ten–expenditure in white schools. The paradox of "separate but equal," improvised—like the white primary—with a broad knowing wink, not only imprisoned black children in these schools, but also cut off all black people, children and grown-ups, from any kind of equal participation in the common life of the community. The "state action" doctrine sealed all the cracks in the wall.

"When we find," Black continued.

> this very same people today in painful distress—as to work, food, medical care, housing, as to police cruelty, as to the administration of the penalty of death, even as to respect—out of all proportion to their numbers, must it not show a lack of grace, a lack of a sense of humor (and these two lacks often go together) for us to publish a general Act of Oblivion? Against all such proclamations, we should give ear to the deathless words of Yogi Berra: "It ain't over till it's over." Or, to put the point another way, just when was it that the fat lady was heard to sing?[71]

Here is located the second way in which "color blindness" manifests bias: the commitment to race "neutrality," in fact, manifests a distinctive racial bias. Black Americans know well that the fat lady has not yet sung. It is white Americans, by and large, who imagine that they have heard her voice. The glib dismissal of "race" as a significant factor in shaping opportunities thus reflects a distinctly majoritarian perspective. Color blindness, after all, is a luxury afforded only to those for whom race is not a barrier to acceptance or success, and even for them, it is fantasy divorced from the lived experience of "race." Moreover, indifference to race too readily translates into indifference to racial disparities. The result is a failure not only to appreciate diverse perspectives—to assume, in fact, that the white perspective is the "neutral" perspective—but also to recognize the living legacy of racial advantage and disadvantage.[72]

"Freedom of choice," then, may look to be "color blind" and "race neutral," but in fact it can be neither of those, not as long as our choices are constrained by racial realities. And the realities are that white Americans have a greater capacity for choice and that the exercise of their choice—attended or not by any overt racial animus—has the inevitable effect of limiting the choices available to black Americans. "White flight" from integrated public schools, for example, is an exercise of choice, but it is also an exercise of power—one made possible by racial disparities in material resources. And the exercise of that choice—of that power—leaves fewer choices available to black Americans. Black Americans may desire integrated schools, but they cannot freely choose that option unless white Americans make it available.[73] The difficulty is that, on the surface, it can all seem so neutral. The racial disparities in resources, in power, in "choice," can be almost invisible, either because those who have the luxury "choose" to ignore them or because they are such a constant part of the landscape that we are oblivious to their presence.[74] But racial inequality is a reality, and in a context characterized by that reality, "color blindness" and "freedom of choice" cannot be "neutral."

It is our view, then, that no neutral principle of constitutional law independent of *Brown* compels or even justifies the "color-blind" principle embraced by the *Parents Involved* plurality. So what of *Brown* itself? Is it true, as the plurality suggests, that *Brown* requires race neutrality? For the reasons that follow, we think it plainly is not.

"Race Neutrality" and the Legacy of Brown

In the cases that preceded *Brown*, the Court struggled to come to terms with the harm that inhered in racial segregation. In *Plessy v. Ferguson*, of course, the Court saw no harm at all. In *Plessy*, the Court rejected Homer Plessy's challenge to a Louisiana law requiring segregated rail facilities: Louisiana's "equal but separate" law did not violate the equal protection guarantee of the Fourteenth Amendment. Henry Billings Brown of Massachusetts wrote the opinion for the Court. It was filled with legal fictions.

A legal "distinction," such as that between black and white, was not the same as a legal "inequality":

> A statute which implies merely a legal distinction between the white and colored races—a distinction which is founded in the color of the two races, and which must always exist so long as white men are distinguished from the other race by color—has no tendency to destroy the legal equality of the two races.

There was an argument, Brown acknowledged, that the legal distinction tended to connote the inferiority of the distinguished race. But it was an argument Brown rejected:

> We consider the underlying fallacy of the plaintiff's argument to consist in the assumption that the enforced separation of the two races stamps the colored race with a badge of inferiority. If this be so, it is not by reason of anything found in the act, but solely because the colored race chooses to put that construction upon it.

Moreover, the equality that Plessy sought transcended the guarantees of the Constitution; that document ensured only a "legal equality," not a "social" one:

> The object of the amendment was undoubtedly to enforce the absolute equality of the two races before the law, but in the nature of things, it could not have been intended to abolish distinctions based upon color, or to enforce social, as distinguished from political, equality, or a commingling of the two races upon terms unsatisfactory to either.

And, Brown reasoned, it could be no other way—the Constitution was powerless to affect the natural order:

> The argument also assumes that social prejudices may be overcome by legislation, and that equal rights cannot be secured to the negro except by an enforced commingling of the two races. We cannot accept this proposition. If the two races are to meet upon terms of social equality, it must be the result of natural affinities, a mutual appreciation of each other's merits, and a voluntary consent of individuals. Legislation is powerless to eradicate racial instincts, or to abolish distinctions based upon physical differences, and the attempt to do so can only result in accentuating the difficulties of the present situation. If the civil and political rights of both races be equal, one cannot be inferior to the other civilly or politically. If one race be inferior to the other socially, the Constitution of the United States cannot put them upon the same plane.

The only limitation on segregation laws was that they be "reasonable, and extend only to such laws as are enacted in good faith for the promotion of the public good." "In determining the question of reasonableness," Brown explained, the legislature "is at liberty to act with reference to the established usages, customs, and traditions of the people, and with a view to the promotion of their comfort, and the preservation of the public peace and good order." It is an effective measure of the myopia of the opinion that, under this standard, the Louisiana law was upheld.

Justice Harlan got it right in *Plessy*, when he rejected the empty formalism of "separate but equal." Abstract symmetry could not hide the real inequality:

> It was said in argument that the statute of Louisiana does not discriminate against either race, but prescribes a rule applicable alike to white and colored citizens. But this argument does not meet the difficulty. Everyone knows that the statute in question had its origin in the purpose, not so much to exclude white persons

> from railroad cars occupied by blacks, as to exclude colored people from coaches occupied by or assigned to white persons.

The message behind the Louisiana law was unmistakable, and it was these laws and their implicit lessons—not the "racial instincts" championed by the *Plessy* majority—that were the root of racial animosity:

> What can more certainly arouse race hate, what more certainly create and perpetuate a feeling of distrust between these races, than state enactments which, in fact, proceed on the ground that colored citizens are so inferior and degraded that they cannot be allowed to sit in public coaches occupied by white citizens? That, as all will admit, is the real meaning of such legislation as was enacted in Louisiana.

Harlan did not accede to Brown's myopic vision of "reasonableness": there was nothing "good" about the "order" maintained by such laws, and the "comfort" they secured was certainly not universal. In Harlan's more communal vision, there were two perspectives worth considering—black and white: "The destinies of the two races, in this country, are indissolubly linked together, and the interests of both require that the common government of all shall not permit the seeds of race hate to be planted under the sanction of law."

There was, Harlan conceded, a social order in America. But it was not a natural one, and it was not one that the Constitution could tolerate:

> The white race deems itself to be the dominant race in this country. And so it is, in prestige, in achievements, in education, in wealth, and in power. So, I doubt not, it will continue to be for all time, if it remains true to its great heritage, and holds fast to the principles of constitutional liberty. But in view of the Constitution, in the eye of the law, there is in this country no superior, dominant, ruling class of citizens. There is no caste here. Our Constitution is color-blind, and neither knows nor tolerates classes among citizens. In respect of civil rights, all citizens are equal before the law.

Harlan's analysis reached its climax with an assertion that was oxymoronic except as a statement of protest, as a refusal to permit constitutional aspirations to yield to the reality of inequality: "The humblest," Harlan insisted, "is the peer of the most powerful."

Harlan concluded his opinion by pointing out the lingering contradiction of American life:

> We boast of the freedom enjoyed by our people above all other peoples. But it is difficult to reconcile that boast with a state of the law which, practically, puts the brand of servitude and degradation upon a large class of our fellow citizens,—our equals before the law. The thin disguise of "equal" accommodations for passengers in railroad coaches will not mislead any one, nor atone for the wrong this day done.

With the Supreme Court's blessing, racial segregation would remain the norm in America until after World War II. Educational segregation was somewhat more pronounced in the South, where it was mandated by law, but residential segregation was pervasive throughout the country. The NAACP targeted both: it sought a declaration that racial segregation, in schools and in housing, violated the equal protection guarantee of the Fourteenth Amendment.

The problem with residential segregation was that it appeared to be completely beyond the reach of the Fourteenth Amendment. There was some public housing in postwar America, but most housing was privately owned and most residential segregation was, accordingly, the result of private discrimination. After Justice Bradley's opinion in the 1883 *Civil Rights Cases*, such discrimination did not even implicate the Fourteenth Amendment: only through "state action"—through discrimination by public officials, not private individuals—could Americans be deprived of the "equal protection of the laws."

The discrimination in *Shelley v. Kraemer* was, under Bradley's artificial dichotomy, apparently "private": individual homeowners had agreed that they would not sell to "non-Caucasians" and had memorialized their agreements in restrictive covenants in their deeds. But the Supreme Court, in an opinion written by Chief Justice Fred Vinson, ruled that those covenants had been effectuated only through the actions of state judicial officials, and judicial enforcement of the covenants—without which the restrictions would be meaningless—was "state action" for purposes of the Fourteenth Amendment. It was, on the one hand, merely common sense: of course, judges are public officers, and of course their actions are state actions. But it exposed, on the other hand, the deep conceptual problems with Bradley's public-private dichotomy: no action or decision, and certainly no agreement, is purely private, because all are shaped by and implicitly conditioned on the existence, or absence, of legal sanctions. Or, as Bradley himself had put it, the law "is over, under, in and around, every action, that takes place."

But there was another problem in *Shelley:* the state courts were not discriminating; they would enforce all restrictive covenants. The argument was in part that it was the private parties, not the courts, who harbored the racial animus. That did not matter, Vinson insisted, because "the effect" of state action was the denial of constitutional rights.

The argument was also in part the argument of symmetry that had prevailed in *Plessy v. Ferguson:* there was no legal inequality when the state merely makes a distinction, but otherwise treats all parties, black and white, the same. The state courts, the argument went, would enforce all racially restrictive covenants, separately but equally. But Chief Justice Vinson refused to be lured into the conundrum. There was, first of all, no *real* evidence that restrictive covenants were being enforced against white home buyers. Moreover, symmetrical application would not cure the constitutional defect: "Equal protection of the laws is not achieved through indiscriminate imposition of inequalities." This last was conceptually unsatisfying and rhetorically oxymoronic: it is difficult to find discrimination in indiscriminate behavior. Still, at an intuitive level, Vinson had come closer to the truth: there was something quite unequal going on here, and the state was clearly complicit.

Two years later, the Court struck another blow against the formalist conception of equality. Hemann Sweatt had been denied admission to the University of Texas Law School because of his race; under the separate but equal rule, Texas offered to start a new law school for Sweatt and other black Texans. By the time the case of *Sweatt v. Painter* found its way to the Supreme Court, the new "black" school was in fact open and operating.

But it was not enough. "We cannot find," Vinson again wrote for the Court, "substantial equality in the educational opportunities afforded white and Negro law students by the State." The Court examined both "tangible and intangible factors" to reach its conclusion: resources and facilities on the one hand and reputation and "practical" opportunities on the other. It was precisely the sort of realistic inquiry foreclosed by *Plessy*'s formalism, and it was certain to expose the "thin disguise" of most separate but equal schemes.

Four years later, of course, the Supreme Court found in *Brown v. Board of Education* that "separate but equal" public education was not in fact "equal" at all. The assault on formalism implicit in *Shelley* and *Sweatt* nearly demanded this result: *Shelley* had suggested that racial distinctions were, somehow, unequal, even when they were applied across the board, whereas *Sweatt* had demonstrated how this inequality could be manifest in both tangible and intangible ways. *Brown*, in a sense, simply filled in the blanks. And yet, for at least two reasons, the decision was remarkable all the same.

Part of it was the context. These were not restrictive covenants or law schools; these were public schools, primary and secondary, and changes here would be far reaching. And these were not revolutionary times: Rosa Parks refused to give up her seat on a Montgomery bus to a white man in December 1955, a full year and a half after the first *Brown* decision. Whatever the state of legal thought, then, *Brown* was not, in a practical sense, merely conventional at all.

And, for that matter, it was not conventional in purely legal terms. Chief Justice Earl Warren did in *Brown* what Vinson had declined to do in *Sweatt*: he explicitly rejected the "separate but equal" rule of *Plessy*, in part by rejecting *Plessy*'s absurd suggestion that the badge of racial inferiority is self-imposed. Simultaneously, Warren did in *Brown* what Vinson had been unable to do in *Shelley*: he identified the inequality that inhered even in "indiscriminate" racial segregation. Compulsory segregation, Warren concluded, generated a stigma of racial inferiority: this was the inequality, and it inhered in the very fact of segregation, and it was why—whatever the "tangible" differences between the schools—the segregation of public school students was *inherently* unequal.

Moreover, Warren sought to prove it, and his efforts took him outside the insular realm of the law, beyond legal abstraction and vacuous form and into the world of experience. *Plessy* had declared the world of "social equality" off limits to the law, and Jim Crow's defenders were still making the claim at the time of *Brown*. But calling the harm "social" made it no less real. It was common sense, in part—as for Harlan, "everyone knows" the real message of Jim Crow—but evidence from the social sciences also demonstrated its reality a short footnote provided a cursory summary of the evidence establishing the connection between racial segregation and self-concept, and between self-concept and achievement. A brief full of evidence had been submitted to the Court by a coalition of social scientists; to them, Warren's footnote seemed almost perfunctory. But to conventional legal thinkers, this brief acknowledgment of other disciplines—even the suggestion that there was a social world in which equality might be measured—was revolutionary, and for many of them, it was also wrong.

Brown had rejected the formalist conception of equality, and its progeny followed suit. Upholding *Brown* four years later, the Court—in an extraordinary opinion signed by each of the nine Justices—made patent its commitment to the real equality. In *Cooper v. Aaron*, the Court rejected a school board's argument that its good faith efforts excused its inability to desegregate; regardless, the Court responded, the rights of the schoolchildren to attend desegregated schools could not be frustrated by state action, "whether attempted 'ingeniously or ingenuously.'" Nothing less than compliance with the constitutional mandate would satisfy the Court: "Our constitutional ideal of equal justice under law is thus made a living truth."

A decade later, the Supreme Court reached the apex of the Second Reconstruction. On behalf of the NAACP, Thurgood Marshall had argued before the Court in the cases of *Shelley*, *Sweatt*, *Brown*, and *Cooper*; now Marshall was *on* the Court. In the intervening years, school desegregation efforts had been hindered by a wide variety of bureaucratic schemes. The most common, by 1968, was the "freedom of choice" plan.

Under "freedom of choice" plans, students were assigned to the school they last attended, unless they chose to attend a new school. Such plans conformed to the requirements of *Brown* under the interpretation of that case announced by federal judge John Parker in 1955. "Nothing in the Constitution or in the decision of the Supreme Court takes away from the people freedom to choose the schools they intend," Parker had written. "The Constitution, in other words, does not require integration. It merely forbids discrimination." Under the so-called Parker doctrine, the state's obligations were fulfilled once it eliminated its segregative laws. If students subsequently chose not to integrate, then there was simply nothing the state could do.

In *Green v. New Kent County School Board*, the Court—again unanimously—rejected the Parker doctrine. The state was responsible for segregation, and it would be responsible as well for redressing segregation's harms. Equality was not symmetry, and neither was it neutrality: the state was charged "with the affirmative duty to take whatever steps might be necessary" to eliminate segregation "root and branch." "The burden on the school board today," Justice William Brennan wrote, "is to come forward with a plan that promises realistically to work, and promises realistically to work now."

Little was left now of the old legal formalism. "Race" had been reconstructed: racial inferiority and supremacy were products of the culture. Racial discrimination and segregation were neither natural nor purely private; they were both shaped and sanctioned by the state. Equality was now real; it was practical and it was measurable. Inequality was not inevitable, and neither was it tolerable. The Constitution was not powerless; it could, and it did, require that equality be made "a living truth."

The "race neutrality" championed by the *Parents Involved* plurality is simply a rhetorical variation of the old formalism. Like "separate but equal," it is willfully indifferent to the real-world harms of segregation. Like "social equality," it posits a world immunized from the aspirations of law. It is not *Brown*; it is the anti-*Brown*.

Race "neutrality" in fact manifests a pro-segregative bias. The color-blind commitment is rooted in a very distinct account of segregation, one in which the state bears very little or no responsibility. That account is premised on the view either that no distinct harm to black Americans attends segregation, or that the state did not cause—and cannot cure—those harms. But neither view is tenable.

The first view—that there are no distinctive harms from segregation—is reflected in the early critiques of *Brown*. Herbert Wechsler, for example, insisted that the harm of segregation was not inequality, but rather a deprivation of the freedom of association, a harm that would fall equally on pro-segregation whites if they were forced to integrate. For Wechsler, as for the *Parents Involved* Court, compulsory integration was thus just as harmful as segregation.

But no "neutral" assessment of the harms of segregation could plausibly conclude that it was not—and is not—harmful to black Americans in distinctive ways, in ways that far transcend any infringement on associational interests. First, racial segregation inevitably carried connotations of racial superiority and inferiority: it was the intended message, and it was the received message. The *Brown* Court may have overstated the extent to which that message was internalized by black Americans: the studies were and remain more equivocal than the famous footnote 11 would suggest.[75] And the current Court may have abstracted the threat of stigmatic harm to an absurd degree with its somewhat fantastical suggestion that white voters are stigmatized by race-based electoral districting[76]—a claim that, alongside the recent desegregation cases, looks "anomalous, to say the least."[77] But however much these opinions may misconceive the harm of racial exclusion—only slightly in the *Brown* opinion, but quite radically in the redistricting cases—the undeniable truth is that there is a harm. In our context—one characterized by the vertical ordering of race, of white over black—compulsory segregation reinforced the view that black Americans were inferior to white Americans.[78] Black Americans need not acquiesce in that view, psychologically or otherwise, to be harmed by it. In this regard, the *Plessy v. Ferguson* dictum,[79] sadly echoed by Wechsler,[80] that black Americans *choose* to feel stigmatized by segregation is not only malicious and foolish[81] but it is also simply irrelevant. Segregation perpetuated the myth of white racial supremacy among white Americans, and that was immediately harmful to black Americans. As one might expect, *de*segregation has helped destroy that myth. Throughout the second half of the twentieth century, the percentage of white Americans who were willing to blame racial inequalities on the innate inferiority of black Americans steadily declined. On the other hand, it is clear that work remains to be done. One in ten white Americans is still willing to openly declare support for the proposition that black Americans "have less in-born ability."[82]

In addition, racial isolation and exclusion cause social and economic harms in a context of racial hierarchy. By perpetuating the myth of a racial order among white Americans—among, that is to say, America's power holders and decision makers—segregation forecloses opportunities for social and economic advancement. The Supreme Court itself recognized this possibility six years before the

Brown decision, when it ruled that black law students would not receive an equal legal education if they were segregated from their white peers: "The law school, the proving ground for legal learning and practice cannot be effective in isolation from the individuals and institutions with which the law interacts."[83] Modern evidence confirms the hypothesis on a broad social and economic scale. Desegregation, the evidence suggests, partially but significantly restores to black Americans the educational and occupational opportunities lost through generations of segregation.[84]

Finally, segregation increases the likelihood that educational inequities will assume a distinctive racial cast. The disparities in educational opportunities afforded to the children of relatively poor and relatively wealthy parents are well documented, both empirically and anecdotally. So too is the continuing correlation between race and socioeconomic class. Not surprisingly, the underfunded, underresourced schools and school districts tend to be ones with relatively large proportions of minority students.[85] As long as these schools remain racially identifiable, the inequities, while they persist, will be not only ones of class, but of race. The solution, to be sure, is to eliminate the inequities without regard to race. But until the day comes that such a solution is effected, the inequities will produce—through segregation—a set of distinctive racial harms.

The second view that may inform the race-"neutral" account of segregation is that the state is simply not responsible for the harms of segregation, whatever those harms may be. This may be read either as an empirical claim—that the state did not cause the harms—or as a moral proposition: that the state should not be held culpable.

The empirical claim rests on the belief that the passage of time has cured the taint of de jure segregation and that segregation today—and its concomitant harm—is due not to state action but to some ill-defined combination of private factors. But that case is nowhere made. We are told that it is "absurd to assume" that de jure segregation is the cause of current racial separation and racial disparities.[86] But we are given no support for an alternative account. Where is the proof for the claim that modern segregation is due to private decision making and economics or to demographic changes unrelated to state action? What beyond the "typical supposition" would support the view that white flight is caused by "desegregation, not de jure segregation?"[87] Where is the evidence to substantiate the claim that test score disparities are not products of the history of segregation, but rather are due to—in the wondrously vague language of the *Jenkins III* opinion—"external factors?"[88] State-compelled racial segregation existed; it is an historical fact. Schools and neighborhoods remain segregated today, and black Americans continue to be disadvantaged by virtually every social and economic measure. These too are facts. It seems altogether logical to presume a connection between these facts; at the very least, those who would deny the connection would seem to bear the burden of proof. But none is forthcoming.

Ultimately, the empirical claim seems simply to be the expression of an epistemological preference, the preference for individualistic—or naturalistic—accounts of racial discrimination, racial separation, and racial inequality. Justice Brown in *Plessy* warned against the futility of legislating against "racial instincts."[89]

Integration—or "social equality"—cannot follow from judicial edict, but "must be the result of natural affinities . . . and a voluntary consent of individuals."[90] Presumably, no member of the modern Court would explicitly endorse *Plessy*'s belief in natural segregation. Then again, one struggles to find an alternative interpretation of the "natural course" to which Justice Thomas alludes or, for that matter, to otherwise explain the Court's view that the persistence of segregation and inequality is not due to state action.

The first Justice Harlan, of course, saw it all quite differently. For him, the "seeds of race hate" were planted by the state, and it was compulsory segregation that would "create and perpetuate" racial animosity.[91] There was nothing "natural" about any of it. The point is not that he was right and the *Plessy* majority wrong, although certainly that is the case; rather, it is that there are competing visions here, and the preference for the naturalistic account of our racial order is, at least in the absence of supporting evidence, simply the expression of a bias.

And it may be more than an epistemological bias. "Causation" is a notoriously slippery concept, and slippery too is the distinction between the realms of the "public" and the "private." And so, the inquiry whether current racial separation or racial disparities are "caused" by "public" or "private" acts is, to put it charitably, a challenging one; indeed, no less an authority than Justice Scalia has suggested that determinate answers to such inquiries are virtually unattainable.[92] That is why the question of state responsibility is, perhaps, misconceived when it is presented as an empirical one. The question is not whether the state intentionally caused segregative behavior, demographic changes, or racial disparities in educational achievement. Of course it did *not*, entirely. But of course it *did*, in some respects and to some extent. The question is whether, given the nature of the state participation, the severity of the harm, and the necessity and likelihood of redress, it is right and proper to demand or at least permit remedial action by the state. This is not empirical; it is political. It is maybe even moral. And the answers given by the *Parents Involved* Court are simply embarrassing.

And they are not the answers given by *Brown*. It is a testament to the power of *Brown* that the plurality cannot simply dismiss the opinion. On the contrary, both Chief Justice Roberts and Justice Thomas, in his concurring opinion, pledge their allegiance to *Brown*, purport to carry out its mission, and—in a staggering bit of ill will and thick-headedness—even compare the *Parents Involved* dissenters to the defenders of Jim Crow segregation. *Brown*, they insist, vindicated the color-blind vision; the school districts and its defenders acknowledge color; the school districts and their defenders contravene *Brown*. Q.E.D.

But they are wrong. The boldness and the beauty of the opinion in *Brown v. Board of Education* rested principally in its willingness to confront the truth of segregation. Enforced segregation—even if it was enforced equally on everyone—was harmful. It was not harmful in some abstract, theoretical, first-principle violating sort of way, but was harmful in concrete, experiential, people-hurting kinds of ways. And the harms of segregation were inflicted—intentionally and obviously—on black Americans, whose perceived inferiority was both the *causa causans* of Jim Crow and its inevitable effect.

Racial segregation caused black Americans to suffer. It caused them to suffer the harms that inhere in the peculiar form of isolation that follows from a construction of differences as something ab- or subnormal. Because segregation caused suffering, it was bad; because the suffering was visited unequally—and almost exclusively—on black Americans, it was also unconstitutional.

That is the argument made over and over again in the *Brown* briefs and in the oral arguments. It is the argument ultimately accepted by the *Brown* Court, which felt compelled to support its conclusion with a fairly cursory reference to the social science evidence documenting the unequal harms of segregation. And the broader societal harms of segregation—elaborated upon at considerable length in the *amicus* submissions from the United States—stem entirely from this injustice, from "discrimination against minority groups," and its consequent impacts on America's standing in the world.

Segregation was part of a racial caste system. That is why it was harmful. That is why its defenders clung to it so desperately.

It had always been about "caste." That is evident in the record of the Reconstruction Congresses, in Justice Harlan's dissent in *Plessy* ("There is no caste here"), in the cases that preceded and followed *Brown*, in the *Brown* briefs, and in the histories of resistance to desegregation.

But that is not what one finds in the opinion of the Court in *Parents Involved;* it says not one word about caste. It says not one word about the harms of racial segregation. The only harms it recognizes are the harms that inhere in the bare invocation of "race." "Race" consciousness, it advises, is harmful, regardless of its motives, and the proof of that critical fact is to be found in nothing more than a few scattered opinions of fairly recent vintage, mostly concurrences and dissents, which do indeed say that, over and over again (calling to mind Felix Cohen's observations on the Supreme Court's "due process" cases, in which the Court, by Cohen's reckoning, "professes to consider . . . primarily its own former adjudications on the subject, apparently believing, with the Bellman, that what it says three times must be true").

The *Parents Involved* plurality on the Court purports to find support for their position in the *Brown* briefs, in a sentence broadly condemning "differential treatment" based on race. Additionally, the Court says, the oral arguments in *Brown* support their color-blind vision: Robert Carter, after all, had insisted that no state could "use race as a factor" under the Fourteenth Amendment.

But Judge Carter, it evolves, was not pleased by this appropriation of his words. "It's to stand that argument on its head," he responded, "to use race the way they use it now."

It is possible that Judge Carter is wrong. Maybe he really was arguing for color blindness and not against caste. And it possible that Jack Greenberg is wrong too ("The plaintiffs in *Brown* were concerned with the marginalization and subjugation of black people. They said you can't consider race, but that's how race was being used"), and William T. Coleman ("It's dirty pool, to say that the people *Brown* was supposed to protect are the people it's now not going to protect").[93] And, of course, Thurgood Marshall. Maybe, for that matter, Earl Warren was wrong when he wrote in his opinion that the question before the Court was,

"Does *segregation* of children in public schools solely on the basis of race . . . deprive the children *of the minority group* of equal educational opportunities?"[94] (emphasis added). Maybe none of them really knew what *Brown* was about.

But we think that unlikely. It is the *Parents Involved* plurality, of course, that misreads *Brown* and that—wittingly or not—actually subverts that great case's message.

Conclusion

Ironies abound in the situation we find ourselves in, and perhaps they were all crystallized in the closing moments of the oral argument in *Parents Involved*. The lawyer who argued against the school district's desegregation plan—a plan that dared to prevent racial segregation by actually considering race in student assignments—invoked a familiar name in support of his position. "[M]ay this day be the embryonic beginning," he intoned, "of Dr. King's dream, as paraphrased, that all children are now judged by the content of their character and their education, not by the color of their skin."

Paraphrased indeed. By now, it is an old trick to invoke the name of Martin Luther King Jr. to oppose race-conscious efforts to achieve racial equality or inclusion. But that it is commonplace does not make it any less objectionable. Or any less wrong.

Consider, for just a moment, the bare-bones thesis of the lawyer's claim: that Dr. King would have opposed—or the logic of his arguments would have opposed—an effort to maintain racially integrated schools because the effort dared to notice which students were black and which were white. Simply stating the claim likely reveals its absurdity, but if more proof is needed, plenty is available.

The original *Brown* decision, King wrote in 1958, "brought hope to millions of disinherited Negroes who had formerly dared only to dream of freedom." That hope was not rooted in some abstract belief in "color blindness," but in a commitment to racial justice. Thus King invoked the Court's decision in mobilizing the Montgomery bus boycott of 1955:

> My friends, I want it to be known—that we're going to work with grim and bold determination—to gain justices on the buses in this city. And we are not wrong. We are not wrong in what we are doing. If we are wrong—the Supreme Court of this nation is wrong. If we are wrong—God Almighty is wrong. If we are wrong—Jesus of Nazareth was merely a utopian dreamer and never came down to earth. If we are wrong—justice is a lie. And we are determined here in Montgomery—to work and fight until justice runs down like water, and righteousness like a mighty stream.

King's opposition to racial segregation was rooted in his opposition to racial injustice, and his opposition to racial injustice was an opposition not to "race," but to "injustice." Thus, there was no contradiction to be found in King's support for reparations or in the broad philosophical defenses of—and practical plans for—affirmative action in his Bill of Rights for the Disadvantaged. Race was a reality; we had made it such, and there was no denying it. But we could remake it, and that was his struggle.

Put another way, put the way Dr. King was inclined to put it, it was really all about love. King lived in a world dominated by race hate; he wanted to supplant that above all with a world of love. This love—following the Greek notion of *agape*—was not, Dr. King was fond of saying, "emotional bosh." Loving was not the same as liking.

> Like is sentimental, and it is pretty difficult to like someone bombing your home; it is pretty difficult to like someone threatening your children; it is difficult to like congressmen who spend all their time trying to defeat civil rights. But . . . love is greater than like. Love is understanding, redemptive, creative good will for all men. And it is this idea, it is this whole ethic of love which is the idea standing at the basis of the . . . movement.

And this love was real, it was powerful; "Love," he wrote, "is our great instrument and our great weapon, and that alone." And in the pursuit of this world of love, and in the use of love, King saw few limits:

> Though I was initially disappointed at being characterized as an extremist, as I continued to think about the matter I gradually gained a measure of satisfaction from the label. Was not Jesus an extremist for love . . . ? . . . So the question is not whether we will be extremists, but what kind of extremists will we be. Will we be extremists for hate or for love?

And so, King wrote, "We must never let up in our determination to remove every vestige of segregation and discrimination from our nation, but we shall not in the process relinquish our privilege to love."

That is the difference between Jim Crow, on the one hand, and the effort to dismantle it, on the other; it is the difference between the use of "race" to segregate and the use of "race" to desegregate; it is the difference between racial justice and racial injustice; it is the difference between hate and love.

Parents Involved clearly establishes the stakes in the battle over the legacy of *Brown v. Board of Education*. If the plurality opinion prevails, then the desegregation project is over. The attempt to teach our children in genuinely desegregated schools will be sacrificed to a talking point, an empty formalism, a figment of political imagination. We can pretend that there is no "race," but the reality will be written in our schools, plainly, in black and white.

There will be nothing to celebrate if that day arrives. It will be vindication, to be sure, of the "litigation strategy": if *Parents Involved* proves anything, it is that the courts are a necessary—if not sufficient—part of any social movement.[95] But it is bitter solace. Judicially imposed inequality is a painful reality; we knew that already.

For now however, we can celebrate the fact that *Brown* still lives. Its legacy is there to be claimed; its vision still there to be redeemed.

Desegregation is not yet over.

We can still choose equality.

Notes

1. *Parents Involved in Community Schools v. Seattle School Dist. No. 1*, 551 U.S. ___, 127 S.Ct. 2738 (2007).

2. *Grutter v. Bollinger*, 539 U.S. 306 (2003).

3. *United States* v. *Carolene Products Co.*, 304 U.S. 144, 152, n. 4 (1938); *Korematsu v. United States*, 323 U.S 214 (1944); *Loving v. Virginia*, 388 U.S. 1 (1967).

4. *Regents of the University of California v. Bakke*, 438 U.S. 265 (1978).

5. *Wygant v. Jackson Board of Education*, 476 U.S. 267 (1986).

6. *Gratz v. Bollinger*, 539 U.S. 244 (2003).

7. 402 U.S. 1 (1971).

8. *Concerned Parents*, 551 U.S. ___. (Breyer dissenting)

9. 102 Cong. Rec. 4693 (1956).

10. *Cooper v. Aaron*, 358 U.S. 1, 18 (1958).

11. Jack Greenberg, *Crusaders in the Courts: How a Dedicated Band of Lawyers Fought for the Civil Rights Revolution* (Basic Books, 1994); Constance Baker Motley, *Equal Justice Under Law: The Life of a Pioneer for Black Civil Rights and Women's Rights* (Farrar, Straus and Giroux, 1988).

12. *Griffin v. County School Board of Prince Edward County*, 377 U.S. 218 (1964).

13. *Alexander v. Holmes County Board of Education*, 396 U.S. 19 (1969).

14. *Green v. School Board of New Kent County*, 391 U.S. 430 (1968).

15. Douglas Massey and Nancy Denton, *American Apartheid: Segregation and the Making of the Underclass* (Harvard University Press, 1993).

16. *Plessy v. Ferguson*, 163 U.S. 537 (1896).

17. *Buchanan v. Warley*, 245 U.S. 60 (1917).

18. *Corrigan v. Buckley*, 271 U.S. 323 (1926).

19. *Shelley v. Kraemer*, 334 U.S. 1 (1948).

20. "Redlining" is a discriminatory practice institutionalized by a federal government agency, the Home Owners' Loan Corporation, in the 1930s and widely used in the real estate industry. It was used to evaluate the risks associated with loans made in specific neighborhoods. The Home Owners' Loan Corporation's underwriting guidelines established four categories of neighborhood quality. The lowest of these was color-coded red and declared ineligible for government loans. Black neighborhoods were rated in the fourth category. Massey and Denton, *American Apartheid.*

21. *Id.*, at 74–78.

22. Melvin L. Oliver and Thomas M. Shapiro, *Black Wealth/White Wealth: A New Perspective on Racial Inequality* 18 (Routledge, 1995).

23. *Village of Euclid, Ohio v. Ambler Realty Co.*, 272 U.S. 365 (1926), established the power of localities to develop and regulate land use through zoning.

24. *Keyes v. School District No. 1*, 413 U.S. 189 (1973).

25. *Milliken v. Bradley*, 418 U.S. 717 (1974).

26. *Board of Education of Oklahoma City v. Dowell*, 498 U.S. 237 (1991).

27. *Freeman v. Pitts*, 498 U.S. 1081 (1992).

28. *Missouri v. Jenkins*, 515 U.S. 70 (1995).

29. A Gallup poll found that among whites, 82 percent believed that blacks had the same access to housing as whites. Gallup Poll Social Audit, "Black-White Relations in the United States, 2002–2003 Update." A recent CNN poll contains similar findings. Poll: Most Americans see lingering racism—in others, Dec. 12, 2006: www.cnn.com/2006/US/12/12/racism.poll/index.html.

30. Massey and Denton, *American Apartheid.*

31. See generally John Yinger, *Housing Discrimination Study, Incidence of Discrimination and Variations in Discriminatory Behavior* ix, 1 (U.S. Dep't of Housing and Urban Development, 1991); John Yinger, *Closed Doors, Opportunities Lost: The Continuing Costs of Housing Discrimination* 51–52, 121 (Sage, 1995).

32. Discrimination in Metropolitan Housing Markets: National Results from Phase 1 of the Housing Discrimination Study (2000) http://www.huduser.org/publications/hsgfin/phase1.html.

33. Massey and Denton, *American Apartheid.*

34. See http://mumford1.dyndns.org/cen2000/WholePop/WPreport/page2.html.

35. Bruce L. Ackerman, *Integration for Subsidized Housing and the Question of Racial Occupancy Controls,* 26 Stan. L. Rev. 245, 251–54 (1974) (discussing the 25 to 60 percent "tipping point" at which white families have been documented to flee a neighborhood because its growing numbers of black residents will mark it as a "black neighborhood"); Sheryll D. Cashin, *Middle-Class Black Suburbs and the State of Integration: A Post-Integrationist Vision for Metropolitan America,* 86 Cornell L. Rev. 729, 744–45 (2001) (suggesting the tipping point is 40 percent); Margalynne Armstrong, *Race and Property Values in Entrenched Segregation,* 52 U. Miami L. Rev. 1051, 1053–59 (1998) (discussing the longstanding perception of many white realtors, home sellers, and buyers that the presence of African Americans in a neighborhood causes property values to decline); Oliver and Shapiro, *Black Wealth/White Wealth,* at 147–51 (homes of similar design, size, age, and appearance are priced higher in white communities than in black or integrated communities.).

36. Charles R. Lawrence III, *The Id, the Ego, and Equal Protection: Reckoning with Unconscious Racism,* 39 Stan L. Rev. 317, 323 (1987).

37. Linda Hamilton Krieger, *The Content of Our Categories: A Cognitive Bias Approach to Discrimination and Equal Employment Opportunity,* 47 Stan. L. Rev. 1161 (1995).

38. John O. Calmore, *Raceism Lost and Found: The Fair Housing Act at Thirty,* 52 U. Miami L. Rev. 1067, 1089 (1998).

39. Orlando Patterson, *The Ordeal of Integration: Progress and Resentment in America's "Racial" Crisis* (Basic Civitas Books, 1998); Abigail and Stephan Thernstrom, *America in Black and White: One Nation, Indivisible* (Simon and Schuster, 1999).

40. Maria Kryson and Reynolds Farley, *The Residential Preferences of Blacks: Do They Explain Segregation?* 80 Social Sciences 937–80 (2002).

41. Sheryll Cashin, *The Failures of Integration: How Race and Class Are Undermining the American Dream* 134 (Public Schools, 2004).

42. *Coalition to Save Our Children v. State Board of Education of State of Del.,* 901 F.Supp. 784, 823 (D. Del. 1995).

43. *Coalition to Save Our Children v. State Board of Education of State of Del.,* 90 F.3d 752 (3rd Cir. 1996).

44. The 2006 profile data for each school are available at the Delaware State Board of Education Web site, http://profiles.doe.k12.de.us/. The relevant district-wide percentages were calculated from the sums of these and individual school data.

45. Ronald H. Coase, *The Problem of Social Cost,* 3 J. Law and Econ. 1, 1–8, 13–15 (1960). The concept of "social costs" is generally traced to British economist Arthur Pigou; see Arthur C. Pigou, *The Economics of Welfare* pt. II (Macmillan, 1932); a refined analysis of "externalities"—and perhaps that term—is generally credited to Paul Samuelson. See Paul A. Samuelson, *The Pure Theory of Expenditures,* 36 Rev. Econ. Stat. 387 (1954).

46. Richard A. Posner, *Utilitarianism, Economics, and Legal Theory,* 8 J. Legal Studies 103, 133–34 (1979); Derrick Bell, *Brown v. Board of Education and the Interest-Convergence Dilemma,* 93 Harv. L. Rev. 518, 524–33 (1979).

47. Gary S. Becker, *Nobel Lecture: The Economic Way of Looking at Behavior*, 101 J. Pol. Econ. 385, 386 (1993); see generally David A. Strauss, *The Law and Economics of Racial Discrimination in Employment: The Case for Numerical Standards*, 79 Geo. L. J. 1619 (1991).

48. See generally Coase, *The Problem of Social Cost.*

49. Kathleen C. Engel, *Moving Up the Residential Hierarchy: A New Remedy for an Old Injury Arising from Housing Discrimination*, 77 Wash. U. L. Q. 1153, 1158 (1999); William A. Fischel, *Why Judicial Reversal of Apartheid Made a Difference*, 51 Vand. L. Rev. 975, 985–86 (1998).

50. See Susan Rose-Ackerman, *The Political Economy of a Racist Housing Market*, 4 J. Urban Econ. 150, 151 (1997).

51. Martha C. Nussbaum, *Flawed Foundations: The Philosophical Critique of (a Particular Type of) Economics*, 64 U. Chi. L. Rev. 1197 (1997); Howard Schuman et al., *Racial Attitudes in America: Trends and Interpretations*, rev. ed., 144–49, 240–46 (Harvard University Press, 1998); Abraham Bell and Gideon Parchomovsky, *The Integration Game*, 100 Colum. L. Rev. 1965 (2000). For a summary of the evidence of *Brown*'s impact on attitudes, see Robert L. Hayman Jr. and Nancy Levit, *The Constitutional Ghetto*, 1993 Wis. L. Rev. 627, 717–19 (1993).

52. 39th Cong., 1st Sess., House Rep. No. 30, Report of the Joint Committee on Reconstruction (1866). See generally Robert L. Hayman Jr., *The Smart Culture: Society, Intelligence and Law* 338–48 (New York University Press, 1998).

53. 100 U.S. 303 (1879).

54. 109 U.S. 3, 25 (1883).

55. See, *e.g., The Slaughterhouse Cases*, 83 U.S. 36, 71 (1873): "[O]n the most casual examination of the language of these amendments, no one can fail to be impressed with the one pervading purpose found in them all, lying at the foundation of each, and without which none of them would have been even suggested; we mean the freedom of the slave race, the security and firm establishment of that freedom, and the protection of the newly-made freeman and citizen from the oppressions of those who had formerly exercised unlimited dominion over him."

56. 163 U.S. 537, 551 (1896).

57. 349 U.S. at 494.

58. 339 U.S. 629 (1950).

59. 339 U.S. 637 (1950).

60. *Plessy*, 163 U.S. at 562 (Harlan, J., dissenting).

61. *Lochner v. New York*, 198 U.S. 45, 75–76 (1905) (Holmes, J. dissenting).

62. See, e.g., 39th Cong., 1st Sess., Sen. Ex. Doc. 2, Message of the President of the United States Communicating, in Compliance with a Resolution of the Senate of the 12th instant, Information in Relation to the States of the Union Lately in Rebellion, Accompanied by a Report of Carl Schurz on the States of South Carolina, Georgia, Alabama, Mississippi, and Louisiana; also a Report of Lieutenant General Grant, on the Same Subject (Report on the Condition of the South) (1866) (describing orchestrated schemes to establish de facto slavery); 39th Cong., 1st Sess., House Report 30, Report of the Joint Committee on Reconstruction (1866) (testimony on acts of oppression and official failures to respond); 39th Cong., 1st Sess., House Ex. Doc. 70, Letter from the Secretary of War, in Answer to a Resolution of the House of March 8, Transmitting a Report, by the Commissioner of the Freedmen's Bureau, of all Orders Issued by Him or any Assistant Commissioner (1866) (describing acts of violence and oppression and failure of state governments to secure persons and property); 39th Cong., 1st Sess., House Report 101, Memphis Riots and Massacres (1866) (describing complicity or acquiescence of city and county officials in massacre of black Americans).

63. Cong. Globe, 42nd Cong., 1st Sess., 505–6 (statement of Sen. Pratt).

64. *Id.* at 501 (statement of Sen. Frelinghuysen). *Accord id.* at App. 182 (statement of Rep. Mercur) (deny means "to refuse, or to persistently neglect or omit to give" equal protection); *id.* at App. 315 (statement of Rep. Burchard) ("the protection must be extended equally to all citizens. This duty must be performed through the legislative, executive, and judicial departments of its government. If the law-making power neglects to provide the necessary statute, or the judicial authorities wrongfully enforce the law so as to neutralize its beneficial provisions, or the executive allows it to be defied and disregarded, has not the State denied the enjoyment of that right?"); *id.* at App. 80 (statement of Rep. Perry) ("The States, however, are not only forbidden to abridge or deprive those rights by hostile action, but with equal clearness are forbidden to 'deny to any person the equal protection of the laws' . . . [T]he command is that no State shall fail to afford or withhold the equal protection of the laws"); *id.* at 334 (statement of Rep. Hoar) ("it is an effectual denial by a State of the equal protection of the laws when any class of officers charged under the laws with their administration permanently and as a rule refuse to extend that protection); *id.* at 368 (statement of Rep. Sheldon) (clause embraces cases where state "refuses or neglects to discharge" its duty); *id.* at 459 (statement of Rep. Coburn) ("Affirmative action or legislation is not the only method of a denial of protection by a State").

65. *Id.* at App. 251 (statement of Sen. Morton); *accord id.* at 322 (statement of Rep. Stoughton) ("When thousands of murders and outrages have been committed in the southern States and not a single offender brought to justice, when the State courts are notoriously powerless to protect life, person, and property, and when violence and lawlessness are universally prevalent, the denial of the equal protection of the laws is too clear to admit of question or controversy"); *id.* at 375 (statement of Rep. Lowe) ("It is said that the States are not doing the objectionable acts. This argument is more specious than real. Constitutions and laws are made for practical operation and effect. . . . What practical security would this provision give if it could do no more than to abrogate and nullify the overt acts and legislations of a State?"); Cong. Rec. 43rd Cong. 1st Sess. 412 (statement of Rep. Lawrence) ("If a State permits inequality in rights to be created or meted out by citizens or corporations enjoying its protection it denies the equal protection of the laws. What the State permits by its sanction, having the power to prohibit, it does in effect itself").

66. *Briggs v. Elliott*, 132 F. Supp. 776, 777 (E.D.S.C. 1955).

67. *Bowman v. County Sch. Bd. of Charles City County*, 382 F.2d 326, 336 (4th Cir. 1967) (Sobeloff, J., concurring).

68. 391 U.S. 430, 437–38 (1968).

69. *See Freeman v. Pitts*, 503 U.S. at 503–7 (Scalia, J., concurring).

70. 109 U.S. at 25.

71. Charles L. Black Jr., *"And Our Posterity,"* 102 Yale L. J. 1527, 1529–30 (1993).

72. See, e.g., Schuman et al., *Racial Attitudes*, at 275–76 (summarizing the survey evidence establishing "large differences in the perspectives of blacks and whites about the causes of black disadvantage" and noting that black Americans emphasize *present* discrimination as a barrier to equality, while white Americans, to the more limited extent that they perceive discrimination as a barrier, view it more as a part of the past). Leland B. Ware, *Setting the Stage for Brown: The Development and Implementation of the NAACP's School Desegregation Campaign, 1930–1950*, 52 Mercer L. Rev. 631, 673 (2001). As Leland Ware wrote, "A color-blind standard will treat blacks and whites as if they were similarly-situated, but this standard ignores the history of segregation in America and the pervasive vestiges of that system. African-Americans and other people of color do not enjoy the same privileges as whites." *Id.*

73. *See* Paul Gerwirtz, *Choice in the Transition: School Desegregation and the Corrective Ideal*, 86 Colum. L. Rev. 728, 745–46 (1986).

74. As John A. Powell explains, "Whites use their power to prioritize their choices as white in a hierarchical relationship to people of color. Institutions and practices such as the drawing of jurisdictional boundaries are used to reflect this power. Part of the power of white preference is to cast this racialized arrangement as neutral and invisible. To challenge this practice would be to challenge the norm, or the status quo, and so preferences are unquestioned and privileged. Institutions and practices in society are designed to be responsive to white preference and to frustrate African American preference. This invisibility allows preferences to persist and be fortified, not simply in their being exercised by whites, but also because it is difficult for those seeking justice to mount an attack against an invisible enemy. These arrangements are not simply the reflections of white power and choices but also produce white choices and power." *The Tensions Between Integration and School Reform*, 28 Hastings Const. L. Q. 655, 675–76 (2001). See also Richard Thompson Ford, *The Boundaries of Race: Political Geography in Legal Analysis*, 107 Harv. L. Rev. 1841, 1914 (1994) (concluding that "no political system, including the current one, can remain neutral in the face of the social construction of geography; no system can simply reflect or accommodate 'individual choice' as to residence and geographic association; no system is without some systemic bias. Because a truly neutral system is impossible, we must rewrite the laws to favor, rather than to obstruct, racial and class desegregation").

75. *Brown*, 347 U.S. at 494. There is some dispute over the importance of the social science evidence to the outcome in *Brown*: that evidence may or may not have assisted the members of the Court in reaching their decision. Compare Philip Elman and Norman Silber, *The Solicitor General's Office, Justice Frankfurter, and Civil Rights Litigation, 1946–1960: An Oral History*, 100 Harv. L. Rev. 817, 837–38 (1987) (Elman claiming that Kenneth Clark's "doll test" "trivialized the basic truth and opened himself and the NAACP to ridicule") with Randall Kennedy, *A Reply to Philip Elman*, 100 Harv. L. Rev. 1938, 1945–46 (1987) (defending use of the doll tests and noting the Court's apparent acceptance of them). In all likelihood, the evidence simply documented what was already apparent to all, even though no opinion of the Court had yet said as much. The cited sources thus lent an air of authority to a proposition that should not have needed substantiation. See generally Sanjay Moody, *Brown Footnote Eleven in Historical Context: Social Science and the Supreme Court's Quest for Legitimacy*, 54 Stan. L. Rev. 793 (2002), but a proposition that—as at least some members of the Court recognized—was likely to be controversial all the same. See Richard Kluger, *Simple Justice: The History of Brown v. Board of Education and Black America's Struggle for Equality* 591–616 (Knopf, 1975).

76. See *U.S. v. Hays*, 515 U.S. 737, 744 (1995).

77. See *Miller v. Johnson*, 515 U.S. 900, 932 (1995) (Stevens, J., dissenting).

78. John Hart Ely, *If at First You Don't Succeed, Ignore the Question Next Time? Group Harm in Brown v. Board of Education and Loving v. Virginia*, 15 Const. Comment. 215, 222–23 (1998). As Professor John Hart Ely noted, "The psychic injury . . . alleged [in *Brown*] was not only real but also widespread and, indeed, entirely to be expected." *Id.* Accordingly, Professor Ely concluded, "We also can stop looking the other way when someone raises the alleged irrelevance or shortcomings of the sources on which the Court relied. Of course they weren't perfect—I occasionally admit that even about my own work—but it doesn't take an air-tight demonstration [to prove the point]. . . . You will thus be relieved to learn that . . . [the *Brown* court] got it exactly right. You can go back to sleep, and in the morning worry about something else." *Id.*

79. 163 U.S. 537, 551 (1896).

80. Herbert Wechsler, *Toward Neutral Principles of Constitutional Law*, 73 Harv. L. Rev. 1, 33 (1959): "[I]s there not a point in *Plessy* in the statement that 'if enforced separation stamps the colored race with a badge of inferiority' "it is solely because its members choose 'to put that construction upon it?'" *Id.*

81. Charles L. Black Jr., *The Lawfulness of the Segregation Decisions*, 69 Yale L. J. 421, 422 (1960): As Charles Black put it, "The curves of callousness and stupidity intersect at their respective maxima." *Id.* at 422, n. 8.

82. In 1942, less than half of the white respondents in a *Scientific American* survey expressed the view that white and black Americans were equal in intelligence, Schuman et al., *Racial Attitudes*, at 353. By 1977, just 27 percent of the white respondents in a National Opinion Research Center poll voiced a belief in the innate inferiority of black Americans, a proportion that dropped to 20 percent by 1988 and to 10 percent by 1996. *Id.* at 156–57.

83. 339 U.S. 629 635 (1950).

84. See generally Amy Stuart Wells, *The "Consequences" of School Desegregation: The Mismatch Between the Research and the Rationale*, 28 Hastings Const. L. Q. 771 (2001) (summarizing the studies demonstrating aspirational, educational, and occupational benefits to black Americans). Wells noted that findings suggest that desegregation increases white Americans' "openness to hiring, working with, and being friends with people of different races"). *Id.* at 795.

85. See House Comm. on Education and Labor, 101st Cong., 2d Sess., *A Report on Shortchanging Children: The Impact of Fiscal Inequity on the Education of Students at Risk* 19–24, 44 (Comm. Print, 1990) (prepared by William L. Taylor and Diane M. Piche). For a work that examines the human dimensions of the House Report, see Jonathan Kozol, *Savage Inequalities: Children in America's Schools* (Harper, 1991).

86. *Freeman*, 503 at 506 (Scalia, J., concurring).

87. *Jenkins III*, 515 U.S. at 95.

88. *Id.* at 102.

89. 163 U.S. at 551.

90. *Id.*

91. *Plessy*, 163 U.S. at 560 (Harlan, J., dissenting).

92. *Freeman*, 503 U.S. at 501–3 (Scalia, J., concurring).

93. Adam Liptak, *The Same Words, but Differing Views,* N.Y. Times, June 29, 2007, at A24. "'This is," Greenberg suggested, "essentially the rebirth of massive resistance in more acceptable form."

94. Also see Warren's memoirs, which clearly conceive of *Brown* in anti-caste terms. *The Memoirs of Earl Warren* 306 (Doubleday, 1977) ("*Brown* lashed at three centuries of slavery and its remnants based on the white supremacy theory"). Certainly, the opinion was viewed at the time as a rejection of caste. As the *New York Times* editorialized on the Sunday after the decision, "there was no doubt as to the tremendous impact of the decision *to strike at racial intolerance* at its starting point—among children at school." *Equal Protection: Court Bans Segregation,* N.Y. Times, May 23, 1954, at E1 (emphasis added); *see also "All God's Chillun,"* N.Y. Times, May 18, 1954, at 28 ("This nation is often criticized for its treatment of racial minorities, and particularly of the Negro. There have been grounds for this criticism. Little by little, however, in the folk customs and in such decisions as the one rendered yesterday, we move toward a more perfect democracy").

95. See David S. Meyer and Steven A. Boutcher, *Signals and Spillover: Brown v. Board of Education and Other Social Movements*, 5 Perspectives on Politics 81, 90 (2007) (summarizing the impact of *Brown* in inspiring other civil rights movements and noting that "advocates of social change continue to litigate at least partly because their opponents do").

Bibliographical Essay

David K. King

Introduction

For an in-depth history and analysis of part of the history of the Delaware desegregation cases, the reader is referred to the titles recommended by Irving Morris in the first footnote of "The Role of Delaware Lawyers in the Desegregation of Delaware's Public Schools: A Memoir" (9 *Widener L. Symp. J.* 1), the lead article in the publications of the first Louis L. Redding Civil Rights Symposium:

1. Richard Kluger, *Simple Justice: The History of Brown v. Board of Education and Black America's Struggle for Equality*. Alfred A. Knopf, 2004.
2. Jeffrey A. Raffel, *The Politics of School Desegregation: The Metropolitan Remedy in Delaware*. Temple University Press, 1980.
3. Raymond Wolters, *The Burden of Brown: Thirty Years of School Desegregation*. University of Tennessee Press, 1984.
4. Paul R. Dimond, *Beyond Busing: Inside the Challenge to Urban Segregation*. University of Michigan Press, 1985.

For those seeking a concise overall summary, Irving Morris refers the researcher to Carol Hoffecker's *Federal Justice in the First State: A History of the United States District Court for the District of Delaware* (1992), pp. 171–82.

To these titles, one should add other Delaware-specific articles published as part of the Louis L. Redding Civil Rights Symposium: Irving Morris's aforementioned memoir; Jeffrey A. Raffel's "After the Court Order: The Changing Faces of School Desegregation in the Wilmington Metropolitan Area" (pp. 81–120); and Jamie A. Scaringi's "The Delaware Tug-of-War over School Desegregation: Constitutional Case Law v. Legislative & Administrative Actions" (pp. 165–81). Leland Ware, symposium chair and the Louis L. Redding Professor of Law at the University of Delaware, examines the potential abuses inherent in Delaware's newest legislation in "Redlining Learners: Delaware's Neighborhood Schools Act" (20 *Delaware Lawyer* 14). For a broader study of racial and cultural divides in Delaware, one should look to Ware et al.'s *The Pace of Progress, The State of People of Color in Delaware: A Comparative Analysis of Racial Disparities in Income, Employment, Education, Home Ownership, Business Ownership and Involvement with the Criminal Justice*

System (2002), an examination of the economic, educational, and social status of Delaware's African American and Hispanic citizens.

For those interested in learning something of life and education in Jim Crow Delaware, two period articles that appeared in H. Clay Reed's seminal *Delaware: A History of the First State* (1947) are recommended. The first is an unsigned article "The Negro in Delaware: Legal Status" (Chapter 29, pp. 571–80). The second is Pauline A. Young's article entitled "The Negro in Delaware, Past and Present" (Chapter 30, pp. 581–607). Both articles provide an unflinching overview of the injustices perpetrated on the African American citizenry from colonial times into the mid-twentieth century. Bradley Skelcher's *African American Education in Delaware: A History Through Photographs, 1856–1930* (1999) records some of the sacrifices and struggles Delaware's black communities endured in trying to secure an education for their children; it documents many of the early schools with text and photographs. Jeanne Nutter's video *A Separate Place: The Schools P. S. du Pont Built* (2003) focuses on the legacies of segregation and desegregation in Delaware's educational system. Concentrating on the schools financed and built by P. S. du Pont in the 1920s, the film captures the inequities of the educational system, as well as the courage and determination of former teachers and students. Delaware's noted historian John A. Munroe provides a concise history of African Americans in Delaware in a 1957 essay entitled "The Negro in Delaware," now reissued as a chapter (pp. 135–51) in the most recent compilation of his essays, *The Philadelawareans and Other Essays Relating to Delaware* (University of Delaware Press, 2004).

Last, but certainly not least, is Annette Woolard-Provine's *Integrating Delaware: The Reddings of Wilmington* (2003). Expanding and developing her landmark PhD dissertation on the Redding family, Woolard-Provine traces the lives of the individual family members, their place in the context of the development of the black middle class in twentieth-century Wilmington, and their role in contributing to social justice. If you want a sense of the injustice of de jure segregation, the hurdles that it presented to the aspirations and accomplishments of the Delaware citizens who suffered under it, and the eventual overcoming of these obstacles through a determined commitment to social change and mobility, this is probably the one book that should be read.

This bibliography is organized into broad categories as follows:

- Delaware *Brown v. Board of Education* cases and related cases
- Delaware legislation and laws relating to segregation and desegregation in education
- A selective bibliography of books in general
- Delaware-specific books and articles and archives relating to the Delaware *Brown* cases

Delaware Cases and Related Cases

Plessy v. Ferguson, 163 U.S. 537 (1896). State-sponsored segregation was legitimized by this decision that held that separation of the races was permissible under the Fourteenth Amendment as long as the facilities provided for blacks were equal to those reserved for whites. "The most common instance of this [separation of the races] is connected with the establishment of separate schools for white and colored children, which has been held to be a valid exercise of the legislative power" (p. 544). Subsequently the Delaware Constitution of 1897, article 10, §2 mandated that "separate schools for white and colored children shall be maintained."

Missouri ex rel. Gaines v. Canada, 305 U.S. 337 (1938). Missouri denied Gaines admission to the state's all-white law school, arguing that he could attend an out-of-state law school and Missouri would provide him financial aid. The Supreme Court agreed with the NAACP that this was an unequal provision of state education to its black and white citizens and ordered the black student's admission to Missouri's Law School.

McLaurin v. Oklahoma State Regents for Higher Education, 339 U.S. 637 (1950). McLaurin applied to the University of Oklahoma's Graduate School of Education and was rejected because he was black. The three-judge U.S. District Court held that Oklahoma was violating the U.S. Constitution by excluding McLaurin because the state offered no graduate instruction for him at a black school. Legislation was promised that would permit blacks to attend white universities, but before the new law was passed, the university admitted McLaurin, allowing him to attend classes, but not permitting him to sit in the same classroom with white students. A subsequent amendment to the state's laws permitted blacks to attend white graduate and professional programs (where such programs were not available in black schools) but *only on a segregated basis*. McLaurin was not satisfied, however, and persevered. On appeal, the U.S. Supreme Court held that confining McLaurin to segregated seats in the classroom, library, and cafeteria "handicapped [him] in his pursuit of effective graduate instruction. Such restrictions impair and inhibit his ability to study, to engage in discussions and exchange views with other students, and, in general, to learn his profession" (p. 641).

Sweatt v. Painter, 339 U.S. 629 (1950). Herman Sweatt, a black man, and his Legal Defense Fund (LDF) lawyers applied for a court order to admit him to the University of Texas Law School. The Texas court gave the university six months to offer legal instruction "substantially equivalent" to that at the University of Texas. Texas responded by announcing that it would establish a law school for Sweatt in the basement of a building in Austin. Instruction was to have been given by three part-time professors, but without the benefits essential to the law school experience: other students, a library, law reviews, honor societies, moot courts, etc. Texas courts ruled that the schools were equal, and the state moved to upgrade the black law school as a safeguard against further challenge. The LDF lawyers took the case to the Supreme Court, which found that the black law school was inferior in building, library, and faculty, as well as "qualities that are incapable of objective measurement" such as "reputation of the faculty, experience of the administration, position and influence of the alumni, standing in the community, traditions and prestige" (p. 634). The Court's decision required that Sweatt be admitted to the University of Texas Law School.

Parker v. University of Delaware, 75 A.2d 225 (Del. Ch. 1950). African American Delaware residents were denied the opportunity to apply to the University of Delaware because Delaware State College was the "separate but equal" institution they were supposed to attend. In 1950 the college lost its accreditation, making it hard for the state to defend the proposition that an unaccredited school for African Americans was substantially equal to the accredited state university. Vice Chancellor Collins Seitz visited both institutions and determined that they were not equal. He held that the plaintiffs were entitled to a permanent injunction restraining the university from not allowing African Americans to apply or from establishing a policy of denying African Americans admission to the university (pp. 227 and 234). Represented by Louis Redding and Jack Greenberg, this was the first case nationwide that required an *undergraduate school* to admit blacks.

Belton v. Gebhart, 87 A.2d 862 (Del. Ch. 1952), *aff'd*, 91 A.2d 137 (Delaware 1952). The complaint, represented again by Louis Redding and Jack Greenberg, was filed on behalf of African American high school students who sought entry to the all-white and better equipped Claymont High School. It was consolidated for trial purposes with *Bulah et al. v. Gebhart*, another complaint brought forward by Redding and Greenberg, which sought admission for African American children to the local all-white elementary school in Hockessin. The court's decision held that Delaware's racially segregated schools "though separate, were not equal, and injunction would be issued to prevent authorities from refusing admission of Negro children to schools previously restricted to white children" (p. 862).

Bulah v. Gebhart, 87 A.2d 862 (Del. Ch. 1952). See *Belton v. Gebhart* (1952) immediately above.

Gebhart et al. v. Belton et al. (includes Gebhart v. Bulah), 91 A.2d 137 (Delaware 1952). The Delaware Supreme Court reviewed the Chancery Court's "separate but equal" analysis in elementary and high schools and found the separate institutions "substantially unequal" (p. 148). The state argued that improvements being made would eventually equalize the situation, but the Court upheld the injunction requiring immediate admittance to the all-white schools. This case was consolidated on appeal to the U.S. Supreme Court with other desegregation cases as *Brown v. Board of Education*. The Delaware case was distinguished from the other cases on appeal, however, as the only case where the lower courts had decided *in favor of* the plaintiffs.

Brown v. Board of Education of Topeka, Shawnee County, Kansas (*Brown I*), 347 U.S. 483 (1954). "In the field of public education the doctrine of 'separate but equal' has no place. Separate educational facilities [on the basis of race] are inherently unequal" (p. 495). After striking down the "separate but equal" doctrine, declaring segregation unconstitutional, the question of how desegregation was to be achieved was postponed until the court's next term.

Brown v. Board of Education of Topeka, Kansas (*Brown II*), 349 U.S. 294 (1955). Fifty-four weeks after *Brown I*, the Court set no date for desegregation to occur in its first attempt to define how and when school desegregation was to be achieved. Black students were to be admitted to public schools on a racially nondiscriminatory basis "with all deliberate speed" (p. 301) in plans developed in the federal courts. With no timetable established by the Court, states were able to delay the intention of *Brown I.*

Steiner v. Simmons, 111 A.2d 574 (Del. 1955). On appeal from a decision of the Chancery Court that granted a preliminary mandatory injunction against the Milford Special School District for denying African Americans their rights to attend high school, the Delaware Supreme Court found that, although the U.S. Supreme Court had decided that segregated public schools presented a denial of constitutionally guaranteed equality, it had not yet determined the relief to which the plaintiffs were entitled. "The effect of the decision in the Segregation Cases [*Brown v. Bd. of Educ.*] seems to us to be this: The Supreme Court of the United States has determined a right to exist, but has not yet determined the remedy. Until that remedy shall be fixed, the right is not a present enforceable one. States having segregation laws are not required, at the moment, to desegregate their schools. Whether desegregation shall proceed in this interim is a matter for the proper state authorities to determine" (p. 579). In essence, no school district could lawfully desegregate more rapidly than the state board permitted.

Evans v. Buchanan, 152 F. Supp. 886 (D. Del. 1957). Frustrated by Delaware's dilatory efforts in implementing *Brown I* and *II,* this case consolidated six complaints filed on behalf of African American students. Previously reported as *Evans v. Members of the State Bd. of Educ.*, this opinion provided the first occasion in which the litigation was reported as "*Evans v. Buchanan*," the title it was to carry for three decades. The court found "no appreciable steps" had been taken to comply with *Brown I* and *II* and ordered the State Board of Education to submit a plan of desegregation for the fall term of 1957 (pp. 888–89).

Opinion of the Justices of the Supreme Court in Response to Questions Propounded by the Governor upon the Constitutionality of 56 *Laws, Ch.* 292, 246 A.2d 90 (1968). In response to questions posed by Governor Charles L. Terry Jr., the Supreme Court opined that the delegation of power to reorganize school districts given to the State Board of Education by the Educational Advancement Act of 1968 was "not an improper delegation of legislative power . . . for the reason that it fixes the general principles and standards which are to control the Board in its exercise of its discretion" (p. 94).

Green et al. v. County School Board of New Kent County et al., 391 U.S. 430 (1968). The gradual desegregation of dual school systems permitted by *Brown II* was withdrawn by the Supreme Court in this decision. Challenging the "freedom of choice" plans that placed the burden of integration on blacks, the Court ruled that school authorities are charged with an "affirmative duty" to dismantle dual (or segregated) systems "root and branch" and to the greatest extent feasible. The desegregation goal became a unitary school system, a "system without a 'white' school and a 'Negro' school, but just schools" (p. 442). Desegregation must be achieved with respect to facilities, staff, faculty, extracurricular activities, and transportation—the "*Green* factors" subsequently used in constructing desegregation plans.

Alexander v. Holmes County Board of Education, 396 U.S. 19 (1969). The Court unanimously ruled that desegregated school systems be achieved "at once" and "begin immediately to operate as unitary school systems within which no person is to be effectively excluded from any school because of race or color" (p. 20).

Swann v. Charlotte-Mecklenburg Board of Education et al., 402 U.S. 1 (1971). Striking down "racially neutral" student assignment plans that produced segregated schools as a result of existing residential patterns, the Court specified certain measures and tools available to reach the goal of the greatest degree of desegregation feasible, including the busing of students.

Keyes v. Denver School District No. 1, 413 U.S. 189 (1973). School districts were held responsible for policies resulting in racial segregation. Once intentional segregation was found on the part of a school board in the district, the entire district was presumed to be illegally segregated.

Milliken v. Bradley, 418 U.S. 717 (1974). The first key Supreme Court decision to weaken *Brown*, the Court prohibited efforts for interdistrict, city—suburban desegregation remedies unless it could be demonstrated that the suburbs or the state took actions that contributed to a constitutional violation whose scope and nature required interdistrict relief. This decision effectively ended the option of drawing students from heavily white suburbs to integrate racially isolated city districts.

Evans v. Buchanan, 393 F. Supp. 428 (D. Del. 1975), *aff'd*, 423 U.S. 963 (1975). After the passage of the 1968 Reorganization Act, this earlier desegregation lawsuit was reopened to compel state officials to carry out the mandate of the *Brown* ruling. The African American parents who reopened the lawsuit were joined one year later by the Wilmington Board of Education as party plaintiffs. As Delaware had required racial segregation of its schools, the court held, "[T]o the extent that segregation imposed by state law has had inter-district effects, federal courts can fashion appropriate inter-district remedies. In short, this Court, in light of the *Milliken* holding, is authorized to consider desegregation relief embracing more than the Wilmington district upon findings either that school districts in New Castle County are not meaningfully separate and autonomous, or that there have been racially discriminatory acts of the state or of local school districts causing inter-district segregation" (p. 432).

Milliken v. Bradley II, 433 U.S. 267 (1977). In providing a remedy for the Detroit city schools where *Milliken I* made long-term integration impossible, the Court ruled that a court could order a state to pay for educational programs to repair the harm caused by segregation.

Evans v. Buchanan, 447 F. Supp. 982 (D. Del.), *aff'd*, 582 F.2d 750 (3d Cir. 1978), *cert. denied*, 446 U.S. 923. This ruling ordered a plan for desegregation that included pupil assignments and the creation of a single school district to serve the "desegregation area" established by the court. Pupils were to be assigned according to a plan based upon the "mandatory transportation of students." This plan reassigned all students from the geographic area of the predominantly black districts to the geographic area of the predominantly white districts for nine years, and all students from the geographic area of the predominantly white districts to the predominantly black districts for three consecutive years.

Evans v. Buchanan, 582 F.2d 750 (3rd Cir. 1978). *U.S. Court of Appeals for the Third Circuit, Opinion and Judgment on Appeal, and Writ of Mandamus, Concerning*

Desegregation of Wilmington Public Schools, Evans v. Buchanan, July 24, 1978 [cover title]. Wilmington: SANE of Delaware, Inc., [1978]. "This publication is provided as a community service by SANE of Delaware, Inc." It contains a six-page history of *Evans v. Buchanan* compiled by Dorothy R. Marengo; a copy is on file with the compiler.

Opinion of the Justices, 425 A.2d 604 (Del. 1981). Governor Pierre S. du Pont was asked by school authorities to certify the constitutionality of the School District Reorganization Act of 1980 by requesting the opinions of the Justices of the Supreme Court. The Court opined that the act did not constitute impermissible delegation of legislative power to the State Board of Education, nor did the act constitute enactment of an impermissible local or special law creating or changing boundaries of a school district by the General Assembly.

Riddick v. School Board of the City of Norfolk, Virginia, 784 F.2d 521 (4th Cir. 1986). With this decision a federal court allowed a school district, once declared unitary, to dismantle its desegregation plan and return to local government control.

Board of Education of Oklahoma v. Dowell, 498 U.S. 237 (1991). Once the Oklahoma City School District had been found to have achieved unitary status, and it subsequently decided to return to segregated neighborhood schools, the fact that the district had obtained unitary status released it from the obligation to maintain desegregation.

Freeman v. Pitts, 503 U.S. 467 (1992). Even though a school district has not achieved integration in all of the areas outlined in *Green*, the Court ruled that it can be partially released from its desegregation responsibilities.

Missouri v. Jenkins, 515 U.S. 70 (1995). *Milliken II* remedies should be limited in time and extent, defining the rapid restoration of local control as the primary goal in desegregation cases.

Coalition to Save Our Children v. State Board of Education of the State of Delaware. 901 F. Supp. 784 (D. Del. 1995). This case made a determination that the school districts of northern New Castle County have achieved unitary status, complied in good faith with prior orders, and are unlikely to return to the segregation practices of their predecessors. It determined that vestiges of past discrimination have been eliminated to the extent practicable.

Coalition to Save Our Children v. State Board of Education, 90 F.3d 752 (3rd Cir. 1996). This ruling determined that review of the finding that school districts have achieved unitary status is limited to measuring desegregation almost entirely in terms of racial balance. Plaintiffs must prove that performance disparities are vestiges of de jure segregation and not the result of socioeconomic factors (pp. 752–53).

Legislation and Laws

An Act for the Encouragement and Support of Schools in this State, 6 Delaware Laws Ch. 65 (1821). It allowed that schools or sabbath schools instituted for the education of children were entitled to receive an annual sum "for each white scholar" from the treasurer of the county in which the school was established. Specific criteria had to be met and certified before twenty cents per annum per pupil could be paid.

The act also established an amount of money to be paid per pupil to a teacher "for each and every poor white child taught at any incorporated or other regular English school" and for whose tuition the teacher could not in any other way receive compensation. The exclusion of African Americans from schools was de facto.

An Act for the Establishment of Free Schools, 7 Delaware Laws Ch. 99 (1829). Public support for education in Delaware began with the passage of this act. The support, however, flowed only to schools that existed generally for the benefit of white children. Even though white and nonwhite Delaware landowners paid taxes to support these schools, black children were not intended to receive any benefit. Any effort made by the state on behalf of African American children probably did not occur until the late nineteenth century.

Joint Resolution in Opposition to Making Negroes the Equals of White Men, Politically or Socially, 14 Delaware Laws Ch. 612 (1873). In reaction to the "Supplemental Civil Rights Bill" then before the U.S. Congress, the General Assembly declared its "uncompromising opposition" to all measures "intended or calculated to equalize or amalgamate the Negro race with the white race." It proclaimed "unceasing opposition to making Negroes eligible to public offices, to sit on juries, and to their admission into public schools where white children attend, to their admission on terms of equality with white people in churches, public conveyances, places of amusement, or hotels."

Act to Tax Colored Persons for the Support of Their Own Schools, 15 Delaware Laws Ch. 48 (1875). "These taxes shall be set apart as a separate fund for the support and maintenance of colored schools in this state." African American public education in Delaware was recognized by this act. The actual creation of a black school system, however, was not realized until the state ratified its new Constitution in 1897, which created separate educational systems for white and black children.

An Act to Encourage the Education of the Colored People, 16 Del Laws Ch. 362 (1881). This act appropriated $2,400.00 to be paid annually to the Treasurer of the "Delaware Association for the Education of the Colored People." For a school to be eligible for payment, it had to certify it was open a minimum of three months and maintained an average attendance of at least twenty students. The money was to be divided equally among Delaware's three counties.

Delaware Constitution, art. 10 § 2 (1897). It provided that "separate schools for white and colored children shall be maintained." Delaware's constitution was revised the year after the Supreme Court's decision in *Plessy v. Ferguson*, which held that segregation in public facilities was permissible as long as the states complied with a "separate but equal" doctrine.

Public Schools Act, 30 Delaware Laws Ch. 157 (1919). This act repealed Chapter 71 of the Revised Code entitled "Free Schools" and provided a new Chapter 71 entitled "Public Schools." By this act the state included all black schools in a new state system of education and made the black schools no longer dependent upon the meager support provided by black property owners. The act also established uniform tax rates for both white and black citizens, mandatory school attendance for children under fourteen, and a 180-day school year.

Schools Comprising Public School System. Uniform School System; Separate Schools for White Children, Colored Children, Moors, and Indians, 14 Del. C. Ann.

§141 (1953). This section, which outlined Delaware's segregated school system, was "based on all but the last sentence of §2631 of the Code 1935" (Revision Note, p. 522). It provided for two kinds of schools: "those for white children and those for colored children,"as well as the establishment of schools for "children of people called Moors or Indians" (pp. 521–22).

Educational Advancement Act, 56 Delaware Laws Ch. 292 (1968). This act repealed 14 Delaware C. Ann. §141 (1953) in its entirety, and brought to an end Delaware's state-sponsored segregation of its schools. It provided for the creation of a "framework for an effective and orderly reorganization of the existing school districts of this State through the retention of certain existing school districts and the combination of other existing school districts" (§1001, p. 977). The act was codified as 14 Delaware C. Ann. §201 *et seq.* (1968). See: *Opinion of the Justices* . . ., 246 A.2d 90 (1968).

School District Reorganization Act of 1978, 61 Delaware Laws Ch. 210 (1978). This act amended 14 Delaware Code Ann. It provided for the establishment or reorganization of certain school districts, their governance, the use of federal funds by such districts, and for an election to determine the exclusive bargaining representatives of the public school employees of the reorganized districts.

School District Reorganization Act of 1980, 62 Delaware Laws Ch. 351 (1980). This act amended the 1978 Act, thereby altering the mechanism for school district reorganization. See *Opinion of the Justices*, 425 A.2d 604 (Delaware 1981).

Delaware's Neighborhood Schools Act, 72 Delaware Laws Ch. 287 (2000). It requires that students be assigned to attend schools closest to their homes without regard to how this might affect the racial composition of the student populations. This act may result in the resegregation of the schools in New Castle County, as well as reinforcing the economic and racial segregation centered in the urban communities.

Selective Bibliography of Books in General

Balkin, Jack, ed. *What Brown v. Board of Education Should Have Said: The Nation's Top Legal Experts Rewrite America's Landmark Civil Rights Decision.* New York University Press, 2001. It presents a compilation of mock opinions written by constitutional scholars, which provide alternatives to the actual decision.

Bass, Jack. *Unlikely Heroes . . . The Dramatic Story of the Southern Judges of the Fifth Circuit Who Translated the Supreme Court's Brown Decision into a Revolution for Equality.* Simon and Schuster, 1981. "The Four"—Elbert Tuttle, John Brown, John Minor Widom, and Richard Rives—sought to "liberate the South" from its historical racial injustices by implementing the intent of *Brown* in their courtrooms. The former Fifth Circuit covered the southern states where most of the desegregation battles were fought.

Bland, Randall W. *Justice Thurgood Marshall, Crusader for Liberalism: His Judicial Biography (1908–1993).* Academia Press, 2001. It presents not just a biography of Marshall but also an overview of the NAACP and its beginnings, the strategic plan of the Legal Defense and Educational Fund to litigate in the federal courts, the decisions leading up to *Brown*, and bibliographies of books, briefs, cases, and law reviews.

Caldas, Stephen J., and Carl L. Banston III, eds. *The End of Desegregation?* Nova Science Publishers, 2003. The evolution of desegregation after *Brown* has resulted in a resegregation of America's schools. Federal courts have released school districts from judicial oversight, and traditional desegregation methods of busing and rezoning have been largely abandoned. The educational/social theory that black students perform better if they attend integrated schools has also come under attack. This compilation of essays and research provides extensive endnotes and bibliographies to each chapter.

Clotfelter, Charles T. *After Brown: The Rise and Retreat of School Desegregation.* Princeton University Press, 2004. Accompanied by numerous statistical indices and graphs, the text provides a brief narrative of *Brown* and the social forces that shaped it, the changes in interracial contact and segregation that have occurred in the last fifty years, and the connection between school desegregation and residential location. It includes extensive notes to accompany the text, as well as references to court cases and printed resources.

The Continuing Challenge: The Past and the Future of Brown v. Board of Education: A Symposium. Notre Dame Center for Civil Rights by Integrated Education Associates, 1975. It chronicles a perspective on *Brown* on its twentieth anniversary.

Cottrol, Robert J., Raymond T. Diamond, and Leland B. Ware. *Brown v. Board of Education: Caste, Culture, and the Constitution.* University of Kansas Press, 2003. This book presents an overview of *Brown* within legal, cultural, and historical contexts, arguing that "Brown not only changed the national equation of race and caste—it also changed our view of the Court's role in American life." The text features a bibliography of *Brown* that includes briefs and cases, as well as a chronology of relevant cases and events from 1850 to the Supreme Court's 1968 decision in *Green v. School Board of New Kent County.*

Dimond, Paul R. *Beyond Busing: Inside the Challenge to Urban Segregation.* University of Michigan Press, 1985. See pp. 283–339, 347–52, and 388–91, which cover the proceedings in the case of *Evans v. Buchanan* in the years 1971 to 1980, including the trial before the three-judge court, and the proceedings before the U.S. Supreme Court. This analysis is considered more detailed than that of Wolters regarding the renewal of litigation in the 1970s.

Douglas, William O. *The Court Years, 1939–1975: The Autobiography of William O. Douglas.* Random House, 1980. Chapter 5, "Separate but Unequal," addresses his thoughts on *Plessy v. Ferguson, Brown*, and other civil rights cases.

Franklin, John Hope, and Genna Rae McNeil, editors. *African Americans and the Living Constitution.* Smithsonian Institution Press, 1995. This is a compilation of essays by distinguished jurists, historians, and legal scholars that had its genesis in a symposium held in 1988. Darlene Clark Hine spotlights civil rights attorneys in "Black Lawyers and the Twentieth-Century Struggle for Constitutional Change."

Friedman, Leon, editor. *Argument: Argument: The Oral Argument Before the Supreme Court in Brown v. Board of Education of Topeka, 1952–55*. Chelsea House, 1969. This book includes the oral arguments made by Delaware's Louis Redding, Esq., and H. Albert Young, Attorney General.

Greenberg, Jack. *Crusaders in the Courts: How a Dedicated Band of Lawyers Fought for the Civil Rights Revolution*. Twelve Tables Press, 2004. Written by the NAACP attorney who partnered with Louis Redding in Delaware's desegregation cases, this source discusses the Legal Defense Fund's coordinated strategy in its attack on segregation. After winning the NAACP's graduate and professional school cases (*Sweatt* and *McLaurin*), "it was onward—toward an end to all segregation—and downward—to colleges, high schools, and grade schools" (p. 81).

Kluger, Richard. *Simple Justice: The History of Brown v. Board of Education and Black America's Struggle for Equality*. Alfred A. Knopf, 2004. The 1950 University of Delaware case is discussed on pp. 289–90 and 431–34. At pp. 434–51 there is a discussion of the proceedings in 1951–52 in the Delaware cases subsequently appealed to the Supreme Court in *Brown v. Board of Education*, 347 U.S. 483 (1954) (*Brown I*), and 349 U.S. 294 (1955) *(Brown II*); the book addresses the proceedings in 1952 to 1955 in the Delaware cases before the Supreme Court in *Brown I* and *Brown II* at pp. 541–42, 583–84, 652–53, 680–81, 728–29, 732, and 748.

Kurland, Philip B. and Gerhard Casper, eds. *Landmark Briefs and Arguments of the Supreme Court of the United States: Constitutional Law*. Volumes 49 and 49A. University Publications of America, 1975. These volumes present the written records in *Brown I* and *Brown II* as they were presented to the Court in a convenient and accessible format. It includes the oral argument in *Gebhart v. Belton*, December 11, 1952 (pp. 441–79).

Lofgren, Charles A. *The Plessy Case: A Legal-Historical Interpretation*. Oxford University Press, 1987. It provides a scholarly history of this landmark case, which in its "separate but equal" doctrine provided the basis for the eventual victory of *Brown*. This book contains extensive notes and a table of cases.

The Louis L. Redding Civil Rights Symposium. 9 *Widener Law Symposium Journal* No. 1 (2002). The first Louis L. Redding Civil Rights Symposium was convened in October 2001 at the University of Delaware. This publication of the symposium includes Robert L. Hayman Jr.'s "Neutral Principles and the Resegregation Decisions," Barri A. Orlow's "Fifty Years After *Brown v. Board of Education*: Resegregation of America's Public Schools," Wendy Brown Scott's "The Miseducation of White America," Marshalita Sims-Peterson and Melva Ware's "From Risk to Promise: Changing the Education Contract for Poor Children and Children of Color," and Leland Ware's "Race and Urban Space: Hypersegregated Housing Patterns and the Failure of School Desegregation." The symposium's articles that deal specifically with Delaware are included in this bibliography under the heading, "Delaware-Specific Articles."

McNeil, Genna Rae. *Groundwork: Charles Hamilton Houston and the Struggle for Civil Rights*. University of Pennsylvania Press, 1983. It presents a biography of the notable NAACP attorney, which is based on a revision of the author's PhD dissertation. Its foreword was written by Judge A. Leon Higginbotham Jr., and it includes bibliographies of primary and secondary sources, as well as extensive notes to accompany the text.

Mack, Raymond W., ed. *Our Children's Burden: Studies of Desegregation in Nine American Communities*. Random House, 1968. This book includes Herbert R. Barringer's "Integration in Newark, Delaware: Whatever Happened to Jim Crow?"

Marshall, Thurgood. *Thurgood Marshall: His Speeches, Writings, Arguments, Opinions, and Reminiscences*. Edited by Mark V. Tushnet. The Library of Black America. Lawrence Hill Books, 2001. This book includes Marshall's briefs and oral arguments in *Brown v. Board of Education* (1952), *The School Desegregation Arguments* (1952–55), and *Cooper v. Aaron* (1958). It also includes a selection of his other writings as a lawyer and judge, his judicial opinions, and reminiscences.

Orfield, Gary, Susan E. Eaton, and the Harvard Project on School Desegregation. *Dismantling Desegregation: The Quiet Reversal of Brown v. Board of Education*. New Press, 1996. Published on the forty-second anniversary of *Brown*, this title chronicles the continuing trend toward resegregation and the evisceration of the promise *Brown* held. It provides extensive notes to accompany the text.

Patterson, James T. *Brown v. Board of Education: A Civil Rights Milestone and Its Troubled Legacy*. Pivotal Moments in American History. Oxford University Press, 2001. This study is of particular value for its discussion of the grassroots support behind the NAACP's desegregation efforts and for demonstrating the resistance against which *Brown* has been contested in the courts. The text is accompanied by photographs of many of the named parties to cases, attorneys, and demonstrations against integration. Various appendices, a bibliographic essay, and extensive notes are also provided.

Reams, Bernard D. Jr. and Paul E. Wilson, eds. *Segregation and the Fourteenth Amendment in the States: A Survey of State Segregation Laws 1865–1953; Prepared for United States Supreme Court in re: Brown v. Board of Education of Topeka*. William S. Hein and Co., 1975. The materials in this survey were assembled in preparation for the arguments in *Brown II* at the request of the Court. The survey supplied "evidence" from each of the thirty-six states (the members of the Union when the Fourteenth Amendment was proposed and ratified) of "the intent of . . . the legislatures and conventions which ratified the Fourteenth Amendment as to its impact on racial segregation in public education."

Samuels, Albert L. *Is Separate Unequal? Black Colleges and the Challenge to Desegregation*. University Press of Kansas, 2004. The existence of historically black colleges and universities has been challenged by *Brown*'s tenet that separate educational institutions are inherently unequal. Samuels argues that economic inequality is the primary obstacle to full citizenship for black Americans, and funding for historically black colleges and universities should be increased.

Sarat, Austin, ed. *Race, Law, and Culture: Reflections on Brown v. Board of Education*. Oxford University Press, 1997. This is the publication of essays originally presented at "*Brown* at Forty," a conference held at Amherst College in 1994 that was sponsored by the Charles Hamilton Houston Forum on Law and Social Change. The essays are arranged into three sections: *Brown* and its legal contexts, racial discrimination and anti-discrimination law, and reading the "realities" of race.

Silber, Norman I. *With All Deliberate Speed: The Life of Philip Elman, An Oral History Memoir . . . In Mr. Elman's words, Based on Interviews at the Columbia University Oral History Research Office.* University of Michigan Press, 2004. Justice Department attorney Elman promoted the concept of gradual integration as a means of unifying the Supreme Court in *Brown*, a proposal that eventually found expression in the phrase, "with all deliberate speed." *Brown* is discussed in Chapter 12, "The Solicitor General's Office and Civil Rights."

Tushnet, Mark V. *Making Civil Rights Law: Thurgood Marshall and the Supreme Court, 1936–1961.* Oxford University Press, 1994. This book focuses on the determined efforts of Marshall and other NAACP lawyers in their systematic attack on racism embedded in the law. It includes chapters on the education cases of 1939 to 1945, the determination of a course of litigation, segregated universities, making the record in *Brown*, the law in *Brown*, and resistance to *Brown*. It also includes extensive notes to accompany the text and a bibliography.

———. *Making Constitutional Law: Thurgood Marshall and the Supreme Court, 1961–1991.* Oxford University Press, 1997. Focusing on Marshall's career as a federal judge of the Second Circuit and as Justice of the U.S. Supreme Court, the author presents Marshall's thinking on desegregating schools and affirmative action, as well as equal protection theory and the death penalty.

———. *The NAACP's Legal Strategy Against Segregated Education, 1925–1950.* University of North Carolina Press, 1987. It outlines the strategies employed by the NAACP in its campaign against segregated schools, from the inception of the plan to the decision to litigate *Brown v. Board of Education.* It is accompanied by extensive notes and bibliography.

Wilkinson, J. Harvie, III. *From Brown to Bakke: The Supreme Court and School Integration: 1954–1978.* Oxford University Press, 1979. Written by a former southern newspaper editor who was later appointed a U.S. District Court judge, this book interprets the cases and the social and political dynamics that shaped them.

Williams, Juan. *Thurgood Marshall: American Revolutionary.* Times Books, 1998. This book argues that Marshall's struggles in court to secure an end to racial segregation were grounded in his conviction that only integration would allow equal rights under the law to take hold.

Wolters, Raymond. *The Burden of Brown: Thirty Years of School Desegregation.* University of Tennessee Press, 1984. "The Bus Stops Here: New Castle County, Delaware" (Part IV) provides a critical study of the effects of school desegregation in the Wilmington area from *Brown* to the adoption of the four districts in 1981.

Delaware-Specific Books and Articles

Delaware-Specific Books

Bachmann, Peter J. *Report on the Survey of Public Opinions in Delaware Concerning Alternative Schools and Existing Public Schools.* Delaware Department of Public Instruction, August 1978.

Bresnahan, R. B., and H. I. Showell. *Report on Voluntary Student Transfer Program.* Department of Public Instruction, February 1977.

Cohen, Celia. *Only in Delaware: Politics and Politicians in the First State.* Grapevine, 2002. Written by a state political observer, Chapters 4–6 reveal something of Delaware's desegregation cases and the political climate of the time. The disturbance in Milford fomented by Bryant Bowles is presented at pp. 75–81 in terms of the ramifications it held for both political parties.

Conrad, Henry C. *A Glimpse at the Colored Schools of Delaware.* James and Webb, 1883. The article was taken from a paper read before the annual meeting of the State Teachers' Association held at Rehoboth Beach, Delaware, on August 21, 1883.

Cooper, Richard Watson, and Hermann Cooper. *Negro School Attendance in Delaware . . . A Report to the State Board of Education of Delaware.* University of Delaware Press, 1923. In 1919 Delaware revamped the state's education system and included all "Negro schools." Introducing "a new era in the education of the colored youth of the state . . . schools of the colored district no longer depend . . . upon the meager support provided by taxes upon small holdings of Negro property owners, but share, proportionate to the need, in the school revenues of the system." This report calls on African American parents to get their children to school 180 days a year because "sponsors for negro education will everywhere find it difficult to argue higher taxes for better schools for colored youth" if the children do not attend.

Crosby, Muriel. *An Adventure in Human Relations.* Follett, 1965. This firsthand account of the educational and social issues surrounding desegregation in Delaware was written by the administrator of the Three-Year Experimental Project on Schools in Changing Neighborhoods. The program, set up under the joint sponsorship of the Wilmington Board of Public Education and the National Conference of Christians and Jews, sought to improve the schools and upgrade family and community life during the early years of desegregation of the Wilmington's schools.

Essah, Patience. *A House Divided: Slavery and Emancipation in Delaware, 1638–1865.* University Press of Virginia, 1996.

Frank, Bill. *Bill Frank's Delaware.* Middle Atlantic Press, 1987. The cover's subtitle, *Six Decades Through the Eyes of a Working Newspaperman*, aptly describes the book's content as it is gleaned from the columnist's articles. Of particular note is a tribute to Collins J. Seitz on pp. 285–87.

Green, Robert L., and Frances S. Thomas, eds. *Metropolitan Desegregation.* Plenum Press, 1985. It includes Joe T. Darden's "Neighborhood Racial Composition and School Desegregation in New Castle County, Delaware," Margaret A. Parsons's "Parents and Students' Attitude Changes Related to School Desegregation in

New Castle County, Delaware," Julie Schmidt's "School Desegregation in New Castle County, Delaware: Historical Background," and John H. Schwietzer's "School and Individual Achievement Following Desegregation in New Castle County, Delaware."

Green, Robert L., et al. *Metropolitan School Desegregation in New Castle County, Delaware. Fourth Interim Report to the Rockefeller Foundation prepared by the College of Urban Development, Michigan State University Project . . . June, 1981.*

———. *Metropolitan School Desegregation in New Castle County, Delaware: A Longitudinal Case Study. Prepared for presentation at the Rockefeller Foundation National Conference on Education, New York, October 13–14, 1981, by the Urban Affairs Programs, Michigan State University.*

Hancock, Harold Bell. *Delaware During the Civil War: A Political History.* Historical Society of Delaware, 1961. Originally published in installments in *Delaware History*, the chapters include "Campaign and Election of 1860," "The Coming of the War," "A Divided House," "Two Years of Tension," and "The End of the War." It provides an excellent perspective on the divided loyalties that existed in Delaware.

Heinegg, Paul. *Free African Americans of Maryland and Delaware, from the Colonial Period to 1810.* Clearfield, 2000. Although more heavily weighted in favor of Maryland families, this compilation of information from family histories and official records provides a history of free African American communities during the colonial period and into the early years of the nation.

Hoffecker, Carol. *Federal Justice in the First State: A History of the United States District Court for the District of Delaware* Historical Society for the United States District Court for the District of Delaware, 1992. It contains a concise summary of the desegregation litigation in Delaware on pp. 171–82.

Holland, Jerome H. "A Sociological Analysis of the Situational Complex Confronting the State of Delaware Relative to Implementing the Desegregation-Integration of Public Schools." [n.p., 1955]. Typescript is available at the Historical Society of Delaware.

Jones, Jacqueline. *Creek Walking: Growing Up in Delaware in the 1950's.* University of Delaware Press, 2001. Written under a MacArthur Foundation "genius grant," this book provides an interesting blend of personal reminiscence, family history, the history of Christiana, and issues of civil rights.

Keene, William B., et al. *A Plan for the Division of the New Castle County School District into Four School Districts. Proposed for Adoption by the State Board of Education as a Regulation of the Board as Authorized by Provisions of Delaware Code, Title 14 §122 (a) and in Compliance with Laws of Delaware, Vol. 62, Ch. 351 (SB 593—130th General Assembly). Prepared by . . . the Staff of the State Department of Public Instruction. Release of Staff Plan for Public Review or Comment September 18, 1980. Document No. 95–01/80/08/12.* [Dover: 1980].

McGowan, James A. *Station Master on the Underground Railroad: The Life and Letters of Thomas Garrett.* Whimsie Press, 1977. Garrett's letters are among the best source of information about him as he left no records of his activities as a stationmaster on the Underground Railroad. Many of his letters were written to William Still, editor of the *Pennsylvania Freeman*, the first abolitionist newspaper in Pennsylvania. Still was also a member and then secretary of the Pennsylvania Anti-Slavery Society, and author of *The Underground Railroad*.

Madden, K. C., and Howard E. Row. *Analysis of Nineteen Desegregation Proposals Presented to the State Board of Education with Comments and Recommendations. Composed and Analyzed by the Staff of the State Department of Public Instruction*. Approved August 4, 1975. It provides an analysis of the nineteen proposals presented to the State Board of Education in response to an Order of the U.S. District Court that proposals be presented on June 13, 1975.

———. *History of Education in Delaware*. Department of Public Instruction, 1969. It provides a brief history of African American education on pp. 71–75 and the Delaware Educational Advancement Act of 1968 on pp. 77–81.

———. *A Plan for the Desegregation of Schools in the Wilmington, Delaware School District. Prepared for the State Board of Education by Members of the Staff of the State Department of Public Instruction. Approved August 4, 1975*. This is identical to materials submitted to the Federal District Court of Delaware on August 8, 1975.

———. A *Plan for the Reorganization and Desegregation of Designated School Districts in New Castle County, A Four District Reorganization Plan. Prepared for the State Board of Education by Members of the Staff of the State Department of Public Instruction. . . . Approved Edition . . . February 10, 1978*. It contains fifteen pages of tables and charts.

Marks, Carole C., ed. *A History of African Americans of Delaware and Maryland's Eastern Shore*. Delaware Heritage Commission, November 1998. Originally published by the Christian Council of Delaware and Maryland's Eastern Shore and the University of Delaware Black American Studies Department in 1996, the second edition is published as a Delaware Heritage Press Book. It includes James E. Newton's "Black Americans in Delaware: An Overview," Carol Hoffecker and Annette Woolard's "Black Women in Delaware's History," Clara Small's "Abolitionists, Free Blacks, and Runaway Slaves Surviving Slavery on Maryland's Eastern Shore," James E. Newton and Harmon Carey's "Diamonds of Delaware and Maryland's Eastern Shore: Seven Black Men of Distinction," Margaret Andersen's "Discovering the Past/ Considering the Future: Lessons from the Eastern Shore," Judith Y. Gibson's "Mighty Oaks: Five Black Educators," Peter Dalleo's "Growth of Delaware's Antebellum Free African American Community," Emma Amuti's "Black Labor in Wilmington: Black Occupational Mobility from 1850 to 1910," Theodore J. Davis Jr.'s "Socioeconomic Change: A Community in Transition," and Sidney Jacob's "Interview with Littleton Mitchell." It is available at www.udel.edu/BlackHistory.

Miller, George R. Jr. "Adolescent Negro Education in Delaware—A Study of the Negro Secondary School and Community (Exclusive of Wilmington)." EdD diss., New York University, 1943. At the time of the *Bulah* and *Belton* cases in 1950–51, Miller was in charge of Delaware's Department of Public Instruction. His official position was at odds with his dissertation, a copy of which is available at the Historical Society of Delaware. One of Miller's conclusions reads as follows:

> Segregation of the white and Negro for educational purposes offers innumerable opportunities for discriminatory practices. If one could be assured that equal opportunities for education would be realized under a policy of segregation, one would not consider the practice as entirely unfair. But if one considers education as life, and that the schools must somehow reproduce within themselves opportunities for life experiences, segregation offers little opportunity to meet this requirement (p. 178).

Mowrey, Roger C. *Delaware School District Organization and Boundaries.* Delaware State Department of Public Instruction, 1974.

Munroe, John A. *The Philadelawareans, and Other Essays Relating to Delaware.* University of Delaware Press, 2004. It includes "The Negro in Delaware," an essay originally published in 1957 (pp. 135–51).

Nutter, Jeanne E., compiler. *Growing Up Black in New Castle County Delaware.* Acadia Publishing, 2001. Voices of America. It compiles a selection of narratives of African American experiences in early and mid-twentieth-century Delaware.

———. *A Separate Place: The Schools P. S. du Pont Built.* Hagley Museum and Library, 2003. This video recording presents "the ambiguous legacy of segregation and desegregation in African American education . . . the film is based on compelling interviews with teachers and students whose lives span seventy-five years of African American education."

The Pace of Progress, The State of People of Color in Delaware: A Comparative Analysis of Racial Disparities in Income, Employment, Education, Home Ownership, Business Ownership, and Involvement with the Criminal Justice System [2002]. Metropolitan Wilmington Urban League, Summer 2002. It contains articles by Leland Ware, David Rudder, Theodore Davis, and others.

The Politics of Metropolitan School District Reorganization and Desegregation: Intergovernmental Cooperation and Confrontation in Delaware . . . Draft Version. Compiled by Dennis C. Carey. Stamped: E.S.A.A. Title VII Admin. Component. It includes chapters by Carroll W. Biggs on "Communications: Master Key to Peaceful Desegregation," John G. Parres on "The Politics of Developing a Pupil Assignment Plan," Aida Waserstein on "A Thorn on Everyone's Side," Pierre S. du Pont on "The Governor's Perspective: Desegregation in New Castle County," Jane L. Dilley on "Desegregation: A Human Relations Commission Dilemma," Jonathan Chace on "The Role of the Community Relations Service in the Desegregation of New Castle County Schools: A Federal Perspective" (a paper submitted for publication in *The Politics of School Desegregation—Intergovernmental Cooperation and Conflict in Delaware*); Billy E. Ross on "Training: The Key to Successful School Desegregation," Beatrice Ross Coker on "Segregation in New Castle County Schools: A Black Parents Perspective," Robert H. McBride on "The Importance of the Nonpublic Sector in Successful Desegregation," James I. Mason on "The Research and Development Phase of Desegregation in New Castle County," Joseph E. Johnson on "Administrator for the Plaintiff Board of Education: Another Point of View," Loren J. Thompson on "Curriculum Planning for Reorganization and Desegregation," and Robert F. Massaferi on "Development of a Pupil Transportation Plan—The First Year of Desegregation." It is available in the Abigail Covelli Collection, Special Collections, Morris Library, University of Delaware.

Powell, Lyman P[ierson]. *The History of Education in Delaware.* Bureau of Education Circular of Information No. 3, Contributions to American Educational History . . . No. 15. Washington: Government Printing Office, 1893. "Education of the Colored People," presented on pp. 168–71, quotes Henry C. Conrad, actuary of the Negro schools, on the question of "mixed schools" in Delaware:

> I have never found any disposition among the colored people to desire their children educated in the same school building with white children, or to claim "mixed schools," as has so often been asserted. On the contrary, I believe the overwhelming and practically unanimous sentiment among colored people is emphatically in favor of separate and distinct schools for their own children.

Powell, Walter A. *A History of Delaware . . . Part I, General History from the First Discoveries to 1925, Part II, History of Education.* Christopher Publishing House, 1928. Part I includes a history of slavery in Delaware and the state's attitude toward the slavery issue on pp. 239–49; Part II discusses public schools for black children on pp. 418–21 and the State College for Colored Students on pp. 433–34.

Raffel, Jeffrey A. *Analysis of Alternative Desegregation Plans and Reports of Meetings and Conferences, June 13, 1975.* Jeffrey Raffel, staff director of the Delaware Committee on the School Decision, a committee established to help the county deal constructively and peacefully with the court's decision in *Evans v. Buchanan*, here reviews the positive and negative aspects of the alternative desegregation plans. It is available in the Abigail Covelli Collection, Special Collections, Morris Library, University of Delaware.

———. *Compliance with the School Desegregation Order. Community Survey on Desegregation Issues: Report No.* 3. College of Urban Affairs and Public Policy, University of Delaware, October 1977. It provides an analysis of a survey of Wilmington and suburban school parents from mid-March to mid-April 1977, a few months before desegregation was to begin. It is available in the Abigail Covelli Collection, Special Collections, Morris Library, University of Delaware.

———. *The Politics of School Desegregation: The Metropolitan Remedy in Delaware.* Temple University Press, 1980. This book contains a time line of key events in the Wilmington Metropolitan Case, July 1974–78, on pp. 6–14, desegregation plans on pp. 225–29, as well as a glossary of acronyms of the various groups involved in the issues on pp. 271–72.

Redding, J. Saunders. *The Negro.* Washington: Potomac Books, 1967. U.S.A. Survey Series. An abbreviated version of the seminal *They Came in Chains*, the author expands his discussion to include the period from 1954 to 1967 in "The Universal Declaration of Human Rights" on pp. 67–89.

———. *No Day of Triumph.* Harper and Brothers, 1942. Introduction by Richard Wright. This book contains the personal reminiscences, struggles, and revelations of a literary figure, Delawarean, and brother of Louis Redding, plaintiff attorney in the Delaware desegregation cases. Chapter 1 has been republished by the Delaware Heritage Press under the title *Troubled in Mind: J. Saunders Redding's Early Years in Wilmington, Delaware.*

———. *They Came in Chains: Americans from Africa . . .* Edited by Louis Adamic. J. B. Lippincott, 1950. It provides a history of slavery and black indenture in North America, emancipation and subsequent legal disfranchisement, de jure segregation, the establishment of the NAACP and the Urban League, and black military participation in World War II.

Reed, H. Clay, ed. *Delaware: A History of the First State.* Lewis Historical, 1947. It includes an unsigned article entitled "The Negro in Delaware: Legal Status," Pauline A. Young's "The Negro in Delaware Past and Present," and C. A. Weslarger's "Moors and Nanticokes."

Ross, Billy E. *Project Confidence: A Study of the Effects of Desegregation on the New Castle County School District, 1979–1980. Final Report.* College of Education, University of Delaware, July, 1980. The project director presents a study of the perceptions of administrators, teachers, and students relative to the effects of the second year of desegregation (1979–80) on the programs and personnel of the New Castle County School District. It is available in the Abigail Covelli Collection, Special Collections, Morris Library, University of Delaware.

Seitz, Collins J., Sr. "The Honorable Collins Jacques Seitz interview with the Honorable A. Leon Higginbotham Jr., Friday, February 21, 1986." Draft. Transcribed by Craig Williamson and William Elwood, Center for the Study of Civil Rights, Carter G., Woodson Institute for Afro-American and African Studies, University of Virginia. Copy on file with the compiler.

Skelcher, Bradley. *African American Education in Delaware: A History Through Photographs, 1865–1930.* Delaware Heritage Commission, c. 1999. Based on a report written to develop the historic context needed to begin plans for the preservation of African American schools in the state, this resource documents the African American struggle to establish public education in Delaware in the post–Civil War period through the early twentieth century.

———. *Delaware State University.* The College History Series. Arcadia, 2003. It traces the school's history from its establishment in 1891 (in response to the provisions of the Second Merrill Land Grant College Act of 1890) through the 1980s with text and period photographs.

Still, William. *The Underground Rail Road: A Record of Facts, Authentic Narratives, Letters, &c. . . . of the Slaves in Their Efforts for Freedom, as Related by Themselves and Others, or Witnessed by the Author; Together with Sketches of some of the Largest Stockholders, and Most Liberal Aiders and Advisers, of the Road.* Porter and Coasts, 1872. Written at the request of the Pennsylvania Anti-Slavery Society, this period volume tells the stories of former slaves, some of whom escaped from Delaware and many of whom passed through Delaware on their journey to freedom. It is illustrated with numerous engravings and portraits from photographs.

Summary and Correspondence on Evans v. Buchanan from: Private Persons, Officials, Legislative Items. Compiled by Ambrose W. Haggarty, Public

Information Specialist. Delaware Department of Public Instruction, July 1975. It provides an interesting window on the frequently racist concerns expressed by members of the communities affected by busing and is available in the Abigail Covelli Collection, Special Collections, Morris Library, University of Delaware.

Taggart, Robert J. *Private Philanthropy and Public Education: Pierre S. du Pont and the Delaware Schools, 1890–1940.* University of Delaware Press, 1988. It presents an illustrated history of the attempts by Pierre du Pont to modernize education in Delaware, both as a wealthy and influential private citizen and as state tax commissioner. It contains extensive notes to accompany the text and a bibliograph.

Tilly, Charles, et al. *Race and Residence in Wilmington*, Delaware. Teachers College, Columbia University, 1965. It presents a discussion of 1940, 1950, and 1960 census data concerning black migration to Wilmington; characteristics of the Wilmington white and black populations; spatial distribution of white and black populations and changes in that distribution; and characteristics of housing occupied by white and black families.

Ware, Leland. *The Challenge of Louis Redding's Civil Rights Legacy.* Delaware Public Affairs Reports: 2000, No. 1. College of Human Services, Education and Public Policy, University of Delaware, 2000. This publishes Leland Ware's inaugural address as the first Louis L. Redding Professor for the Study of Law and Public Policy, School of Urban Affairs and Public Policy.

Weeks, Stephen B. *History of Public School Education in Delaware.* Government Printing Office, 1917. A publication of the Department of the Interior, Bureau of Education, this history was issued as Bulletin No. 19.

Weslager, C. A. *Delaware's Forgotten Folk: The Story of the Moors and Nanticokes.* University of Pennsylvania Press, 1943. The Moors are a Delaware people descended from Algonkian-speaking Indians who intermarried with early white settlers and African Americans.

Williams, William H. *Slavery and Freedom in Delaware, 1639–1865.* Scholarly Resources, 1996. It intends "to describe and analyze slavery and freedom, and their impact on the lives of the state's whites as well as its African American, within the peculiar context of Delaware's economic, social, and political history" (p. xi).

Winslow, Helen L., et al., eds. *The Delaware Bar in the Twentieth Century.* Delaware State Bar Association, 1994. It includes Joshua W. Martin III's "Minorities in the Delaware Bar in the Twentieth Century."

Woolard, Annette. "A Family of Firsts: The Reddings of Delaware." PhD diss., University of Delaware, 1993. Written under the guidance of Peter Kolchin, one of the foremost scholars on slavery, Woolard's historical study of Delaware's preeminent African American family is available through University Microfilms.

Woolard-Provine, Annette. *Integrating Delaware: The Reddings of Wilmington.* University of Delaware Press, 2003. Based upon numerous interviews with family members, the unpublished autobiography of the patriarch of this distinguished family, Saunders Redding's extensive personal writings, and extensive research, the author expands on her dissertation, providing a fascinating history of the Redding family and the historical context of their lives and accomplishments.

Delaware-Specific Articles

Allen, Antoine J. "The Pace of Progress in Delaware: The Jury Is Still Out." 20 *Delaware Lawyer* 12 (Fall 2003).

Allen, William T. "The Honorable Collins J. Seitz: Greatness in a Corporate Law Judge." 16 *Delaware Lawyer* 5 (Fall 1998).

Carpenter, Edmund N., II. "A Conversation with Judge Collins J. Seitz, Sr." 16 *Delaware Lawyer* 24 (Fall 1998).

Halstead, Jacqueline J. [see also: Jones, Jacqueline]. "The Delaware Association for the Moral Improvement and Education of the Colored People: 'Practical Christianity.'" 15 *Delaware History* 19–40 (April 1972).

Hancock, Harold Bell, ed. "William Yates's Letter of 1837: Slavery, and Colored People in Delaware." 14 *Delaware History* 205 (April 1971).

Hoffecker, Carol. "The Politics of Exclusion: Blacks in Late Nineteenth-Century Wilmington, Delaware." 16 *Delaware History* 62 (April 1974).

Kee, Ed. "The *Brown* Decision and Milford, Delaware, 1954–1965." 27 *Delaware History* 205 (Fall–Winter 1997–98).

———. "Reverend T. G. Steward and the Education of Blacks in Reconstruction Delaware." 19 *Delaware History* 156 (Spring–Summer 1981).

Lewis, Ronald L., ed. "Reverend T. G. Stewart [*sic*] and 'Mixed' Schools in Delaware, 1882." 19 *Delaware History* 53 (Spring–Summer 1980).

Morris, Irving. "In Memoriam: Louis L. Redding." 22 *In Re*: 7 (November 1998).

———. "The Role of Delaware Lawyers in the Desegregation of Delaware's Public Schools: A Memoir." 9 *Widener Law Symposium Journal* 1 (2002).

Raffel, Jeffrey A. "After the Court Order: The Changing Faces of School Desegregation in the Wilmington Metropolitan Area." 9 *Widener Law Symposium Journal* 81 (2002).

Richards, Helen M. "In Chambers." 16 *Delaware Lawyer* 14 (Fall 1998).

Scargini, Jamie A. "The Delaware Tug-of-War over School Desegregation: Constitutional Case Law v. Legislative & Administrative Actions." 9 *Widener Law Symposium Journal* 165 (2002).

Seitz, Collins J. Jr. "Tribute of a Son." 16 *Delaware Lawyer* 18 (Fall 1998).

Sloviter, Dolores K. "Collins J. Seitz, an Unparalleled Colleague." 16 *Delaware Lawyer* 10 (Fall 1998).

Ware, Leland. "*Brown v. Board of Education*." 27 *In Re:* 10 (March 2004).

———. "Louis Redding's Civil Rights Legacy." 4 *Delaware Law Review* 137 (2001).

———. "Redlining Learners: Delaware's Neighborhood Schools Act." 20 *Delaware Lawyer* 14 (Fall 2002).

Williams, Leonard L. "Louis L. Redding." 16 *Delaware Lawyer* 10 (Summer 1998) 3.

Archives

Delaware Public Archives: State Board of Education Photograph Collection, which includes numerous pre-desegregation school photos; Delaware Department of Public Instruction files; Insurance Evaluation Reports of all Delaware schools in 1941, each of which is accompanied by a photograph of the school; papers of Governor Boggs, including State Board of Education folders; tapes of speeches made by Bryant Bowles at Milford; general reference files; and photographs of individuals.

Hagley Museum and Library: Delaware Auxiliary Association; Pierre S. du Pont Papers; photographs of schools.

Historical Society of Delaware: Miscellaneous materials including a letter from Louis Redding to Littleton Mitchell regarding a meeting to plan the strategy for integrating Delaware's schools, as well as materials relating to the African School Society and Delaware Association for the Moral Improvement and Education of Colored People. *Reports of the Actuary of the Delaware Association for the Education of the Colored People*, Wilmington: [n.p.], 1876–84, are also available.

Jewish Historical Society: Papers and memorabilia of H. Albert Young, Esq. Materials include newspaper clippings on desegregation, and note cards for speeches including "1954—A Climactic Year in Delaware Educational History," a paper presented at the Conference on History of Desegregation in Delaware, University of Delaware, June 1976.

Special Collections, Morris Library, University of Delaware:

- Desegregation of Delaware Archives, 1960–1982 (most dates from 1974 to 1976). This collection was compiled by Abigail Covelli in the 1970s when Delaware was in the process of establishing a desegregation plan for its public school system. The archive consists of resource files used by Ms. Covelli, with a concentration on New Castle County and Wilmington City Schools. Included are desegregation proposals, demographic information, advisory literature, workshop information, and studies and reports of the progress and results of desegregation. A finding aid for the Covelli Desegregation of Delaware Archives is available at www.lib.udel.edu/ud/pec/findaids/deseg.htm.
- Robert H. Richards Jr., Delaware Oral History Collection includes interviews with Louis Redding on Delaware in the Depression and African Americans in Delaware; H. Albert Young on his early years, career, and the events surrounding the *Brown v. Board of Education* decision; Pauline Young on being African American, an activist, Peace Corps volunteer, and a member of the NAACP. An online finding aid for the collection is available at www.lib.udel.edu/ud/spec/findaids/deloral.htm.

Special Collections, Legal Information Center, Widener University School of Law: Papers and memorabilia of H. Albert Young. Materials include newspaper clippings on desegregation, testimonials, photographs, election memorabilia, and information regarding the Wilmington firm of which Young was a founding partner.

About the Contributors

Jack M. Balkin is the Knight Professor of Constitutional Law at Yale Law School and the editor of *What Brown v. Board of Education Should Have Said.*

Joseph R. Biden Jr. is the Vice President of the United States. He was formerly a U.S. Senator from Delaware, member and past chair of the Senate Judiciary Committee, and ranking member of the Senate Foreign Relations Committee.

Orlando Camp is the marketing manager for the Delaware Department of Agriculture and one of the "Milford Eleven," eleven black tenth graders involved in the failed attempt to desegregate the Milford, Delaware, high school in 1954.

Robert J. Cottrol is the Harold Paul Green Research Professor of Law at the George Washington University and the co-editor of *Brown v. Board of Education: Caste, Culture, and the Constitution.*

Paul Finkelman is the President William McKinley Distinguished Professor of Law and Public Policy at the Albany Law School and the author of *Slavery and the Founders: Race and Liberty in the Age of Jefferson.*

Michele Fuetsch is a former reporter for the *News Journal* newspaper in Delaware and has written about education issues for the *Los Angeles Times*, the *Record* in Bergen County, New Jersey, and the *Plain Dealer* in Cleveland.

Roger L. Goldman is the Callis Family Professor of Law and former interim dean at St. Louis University School of Law and the author of *Thurgood Marshall: Justice for All.*

Jack Greenberg is the former director-counsel of the NAACP Legal Defense and Education Fund and the author of *Crusaders in the Courts: How a Dedicated Band of Lawyers Fought for the Civil Rights Revolution.*

Nancy Levit is the Edward D. Ellison Professor of Law at the University of Missouri–Kansas City School of Law and the author of *The Gender Line: Men, Women, and the Law.*

Ed Kee is a specialist for the University of Delaware Cooperative Extension and a recipient of a 2005 Ratledge Family Award for Delaware Public Service.

David K. King is reference librarian at the Widener University School of Law.

Robert J. Lipkin is a professor of law at the Widener University School of Law and the author of *Constitutional Revolutions.*

Littleton Mitchell is the former president of the Delaware Chapter of the NAACP, and Delaware's representative on the *Brown v. Board of Education* 50th Anniversary Commission.

James T. Patterson is the Ford Foundation Professor of History emeritus at Brown University, and the author of the Bancroft Prize-winning *Grand Expectations: The United States, 1945–1974*, and of *Brown v. Board of Education: A Civil Rights Milestone and Its Troubled Legacy*.

Jeffrey A. Raffel is the Charles P. Messick Professor of Public Administration and director, Graduate School of Urban Affairs and Public Policy at the University of Delaware and the author of the *Historical Dictionary of School Segregation and Desegregation*.

Collins J. Seitz Jr. is a partner in the Wilmington, Delaware, law firm Connolly Bove Lodge and Hutz LLP, and the 2004 recipient of the Delaware District Court's Caleb R. Layton Distinguished Service Award.

Jea Street is the co-founder and past chair of the Coalition to Save Our Children, the advocacy group that supplanted the original plaintiffs in the Delaware desegregation litigation.

Juan Williams is a senior correspondent for National Public Radio and the author of *Thurgood Marshall: American Revolutionary*.

Patricia J. Williams is the James L. Dohr Professor of Law at Columbia Law School, columnist for the *Nation*, and the author of *The Alchemy of Race and Rights* and *Seeing a Color-Blind Future: The Paradox of Race*.

Annette Woolard-Provine is the author of *Integrating Delaware: The Reddings of Wilmington*.

Index

E

Q

R

S